ANDROID PROGRAMMING
THE BIG NERD RANCH GUIDE

BILL PHILLIPS & BRIAN HARDY

BiG
nerD
ranch

Android Programming: The Big Nerd Ranch Guide

by Bill Phillips and Brian Hardy

Big Nerd Ranch, Inc.
1989 College Ave.
Atlanta, GA 30317
(404) 478-9005
http://www.bignerdranch.com/
book-comments@bignerdranch.com

The 10-gallon hat with propeller logo is a trademark of Big Nerd Ranch, Inc.

Exclusive worldwide distribution of the English edition of this book by

Pearson Technology Group
800 East 96th Street
Indianapolis, IN 46240 USA
http://www.informit.com

ISBN-10 0321804333
ISBN-13 978-0321804334

First edition, second printing, September 2013

Dedication

For Donovan. May he live a life filled with activities and know when to use fragments.

— B.H.

Acknowledgments

We feel a bit sheepish having our names on the cover of this book. The truth is that without an army of collaborators, this book could never have happened. We owe them all a debt of gratitude.

- Chris Stewart and Owen Matthews, who contributed great foundational content for several chapters.

- Our co-instructors, Chris Stewart and Christopher Moore. We thank them for their patience in teaching work-in-progress material, their suggestions and corrections for that material, and their consultation when we were considering sweeping changes.

- Our coworkers Bolot Kerimbaev and Andrew Lunsford. Their feedback was instrumental in our decision to highlight the use of fragments.

- Our technical reviewers, Frank Robles, Jim Steele, Laura Cassell, Mark Dalrymple, and Magnus Dahl, who helped us find and fix flaws.

- Thanks to Aaron Hillegass. Aaron's faith in people is one of the great and terrifying forces of nature. Without it, we would never have had the opportunity to write this book, nor would we ever have completed it. (He also gave us money, which was very friendly of him.)

- Our editor, Susan Loper, has an amazing ability to turn our programmery ramblings and bad jokes into thoughtful, concise prose. And better jokes. Without her help, this would not have been a fun book to read. She taught us everything we know about clear and approachable technical writing.

- Thanks to NASA. Our little book seems small and silly in comparison to exploring the solar system.

- Ellie Volckhausen, who designed our cover.

- Elizabeth Holaday, our copy-editor, who found and smoothed rough spots.

- Chris Loper at IntelligentEnglish.com, who designed and produced the print book and the EPUB and Kindle versions. His DocBook toolchain made life much easier, too.

- The folks at Facebook, who gave us so much fantastic feedback on the course.

Finally, thanks to our students. We wish that we had room to thank every single student who gave us a correction or opinion on the book as it was shaping up. It is your curiosity we have worked to satisfy, your confusions we have worked to clarify. Thank you.

Table of Contents

Learning Android

As a beginning Android programmer, you face a steep learning curve. Learning Android is like moving to a foreign city. Even if you speak the language, it will not feel like home at first. Everyone around you seems to understand things that you are missing. Things you already knew turn out to be dead wrong in this new context.

Android has a culture. That culture speaks Java, but knowing Java is not enough. Getting your head around Android requires learning many new ideas and techniques. It helps to have a guide through unfamiliar territory.

That's where we come in. At Big Nerd Ranch, we believe that to be an Android programmer, you must:

- *write* Android applications

- *understand* what you are writing

This guide will help you do both. We have trained hundreds of professional Android programmers using it. We lead you through writing several Android applications, introducing concepts and techniques as needed. When there are rough spots, when some things are tricky or obscure, you will face it head on, and we will do our best to explain why things are the way they are.

This approach allows you to put what you have learned into practice in a working app right away rather than learning a lot of theory and then having to figure out how to apply it all later.

You will come away with the experience and understanding you need to get going as an Android developer.

Prerequisites

To use this book, you need to be familiar with Java, including classes and objects, interfaces, listeners, packages, inner classes, anonymous inner classes, and generic classes.

If these ideas do not ring a bell, you will be in the weeds by page 2. Start instead with an introductory Java book and return to this book afterward. There are many excellent introductory books available, so you can choose one based on your programming experience and learning style.

If you are comfortable with object-oriented programming concepts, but your Java is a little rusty, you will probably be okay. We will provide some brief reminders about Java specifics (like interfaces and anonymous inner classes). Keep a Java reference handy in case you need more support as you go through the book.

How to Use This Book

This book is not a reference book. Its goal is to get you over the initial hump to where you can get the most out of the reference and recipe books available. It is based on our five-day class at Big Nerd Ranch. As such, it is meant to be worked through from the beginning. Chapters build on each other and skipping around is unproductive.

In our classes, students work through these materials, but they also benefit from the right environment – a dedicated classroom, good food and comfortable board, a group of motivated peers, and an instructor to answer questions.

As a reader, you want your environment to be similar. That means getting a good night's rest and finding a quiet place to work. These things can help, too:

- Start a reading group with your friends or coworkers.

- Arrange to have blocks of focused time to work on chapters.

- Participate in the forum for this book at forums.bignerdranch.com.

- Find someone who knows Android to help you out.

How This Book Is Organized

In this book, you will write eight Android apps. A couple are very simple and take only a chapter to create. Others are more complex. The longest app spans thirteen chapters. All are designed to teach you important concepts and techniques and give you direct experience using them.

GeoQuiz	In your first app, you will explore the fundamentals of Android projects, activities, layouts, and explicit intents.
CriminalIntent	The largest app in the book, CriminalIntent lets you keep a record of your colleagues' lapses around the office. You will learn to use fragments, master-detail interfaces, list-backed interfaces, menus, the camera, implicit intents, and more.
HelloMoon	In this small shrine to the Apollo program, you will learn more about fragments, media playback, resources, and localization.
NerdLauncher	Building this custom launcher will give you insight into the intent system and tasks.
RemoteControl	In this toy app, you will learn to use styles, state list drawables, and other tools to create attractive user interfaces.
PhotoGallery	A Flickr client that downloads and displays photos from Flickr's public feed, this app will take you through services, multithreading, accessing web services, and more.
DragAndDraw	In this simple drawing app, you will learn about handling touch events and creating custom views.
RunTracker	This app lets you track and display on a map your travels around town (or around the world). In it, you will learn how to use location services, SQLite databases, loaders, and maps.

Challenges

Most chapters have a section at the end with exercises for you to work through. This is your opportunity to use what you have learned, explore the documentation, and do some problem-solving on your own.

We strongly recommend that you do the challenges. Going off the beaten path and finding your way will solidify your learning and give you confidence with your own projects.

If you get lost, you can always visit forums.bignerdranch.com for some assistance.

Are you more curious?

There are also sections at the ends of chapters labeled "For the More Curious." These sections offer deeper explanations or additional information about topics presented in the chapter. The information in these sections is not absolutely essential, but we hope you will find it interesting and useful.

Code Style

There are three areas where our choices differ from what you might see elsewhere in the Android community:

We use anonymous inner classes for listeners.

> This is mostly a matter of opinion. We find it makes for cleaner code. It puts the listener's method implementations right where you want to see them. In high performance contexts, anonymous inner classes may cause problems, but for most circumstances they work fine.

After we introduce fragments in Chapter 7, we use them for all user interfaces.

> This is something we feel strongly about. Many Android developers still write activity-based code. We would like to challenge that practice. Once you get comfortable with fragments, they are not that difficult to work with. Fragments have clear advantages over activities that make them worth the effort, including flexibility in building and presenting your user interfaces.

We write apps to be compatible with Gingerbread and Froyo devices.

> The Android platform has changed with the introduction of Ice Cream Sandwich and Jelly Bean and soon Key Lime Pie. However, the truth is that half of devices in use still run Froyo or Gingerbread. (You will learn about the different and deliciously-named Android versions in Chapter 6.)

> Therefore, we intentionally take you through the difficulties involved in writing apps that are backwards-compatible with Froyo or at least Gingerbread. It is easier to learn, teach, and program in Android if you start with the latest platform. But we want you to be able to develop in the real world where Gingerbread phones still make up more than 40% of devices.

Typographical Conventions

To make this book easier to read, certain items appear in certain fonts. Variables, constants, and types appear in a fixed-width font. Class names, interface names, and method names appear in a bold, fixed-width font.

All code and XML listings will be in a fixed-width font. Code or XML that you need to type in is always bold. Code or XML that should be deleted is struck through. For example, in the following method implementation, you are deleting the call to **makeText(…)** and adding the call to **checkAnswer(true)**.

```
@Override
public void onClick(View v) {
    Toast.makeText(QuizActivity.this, R.string.incorrect_toast,
                 Toast.LENGTH_SHORT).show();
    checkAnswer(true);
}
```

Android Versions

This book teaches Android development for all widely-used versions of Android. As of this writing, that is Android 2.2 (Froyo) - Android 4.2 (Jelly Bean). As Android releases new versions, we will keep track of changes at forums.bignerdranch.com and offer notes on using this book with the latest version.

The Necessary Tools

To get started, you will need the ADT (Android Developer Tools) Bundle. This includes:

Eclipse

> an integrated development environment used for Android development. Because Eclipse is also written in Java, you can install it on a PC, a Mac, or a Linux computer. The Eclipse user interface follows the "native look-and-feel" of your machine, so your screen may not look *exactly* like screenshots in this book.

Android Developer Tools

> a plug-in for Eclipse. This book uses ADT (Android Developer Tools) 21.1. You should make sure you have that version or higher.

Android SDK

> the latest version of the Android SDK

Android SDK tools and platform-tools

> tools for debugging and testing your apps

A system image for the Android emulator

> lets you create and test your apps on different virtual devices

Downloading and installing the ADT Bundle

The ADT Bundle is available from Android's developer site as a single zip file.

1. Download the bundle from http://developer.android.com/sdk/index.html.

2. Extract the zip file to where you want Eclipse and the other tools installed.

3. In the extracted files, find and open the `eclipse` directory and launch Eclipse.

If you are running on Windows, and Eclipse will not start, you may need to install the Java Development Kit (JDK6), which you can download from `www.oracle.com`.

If you are still having problems, return to `http://developer.android.com/sdk/index.html` for more information.

Downloading earlier SDK versions

The ADT Bundle provides the SDK and the emulator system image from the latest platform. However, you will need other platforms to test your apps on earlier versions of Android.

You can get components for each platform using the Android SDK Manager. In Eclipse, select Window → Android SDK Manager.

Figure 1 Android SDK Manager

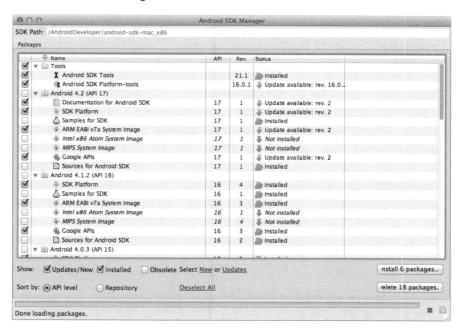

For every version going back to Android 2.2 (Froyo), we recommend selecting and installing:

- the SDK Platform

- an emulator system image

- the Google APIs

Note that downloading these components may take a while.

The Android SDK Manager is also how to get Android's latest releases, like a new platform or an update of the tools.

A hardware device

The emulator is useful for testing apps. However, it is good to have an actual Android device to run apps on as well. The last app in the book will require a hardware device.

1

Your First Android Application

This first chapter is full of new concepts and moving parts required to build an Android application. It is OK if you do not understand everything by the end of this chapter. You will be revisiting these ideas again and in greater detail as you proceed through the book.

The application you are going to create is called GeoQuiz. GeoQuiz tests the user's knowledge of geography. The user presses True or False to answer the question on screen, and GeoQuiz provides instant feedback.

Figure 1.1 shows the result of a user pressing the False button:

Figure 1.1 (It's Istanbul, not Constantinople)

App Basics

Your GeoQuiz application will consist of an *activity* and a *layout*:

- An *activity* is an instance of **Activity**, a class in the Android SDK. An activity is responsible for managing user interaction with a screen of information.

  You write subclasses of **Activity** to implement the functionality that your app requires. A simple application may need only one subclass; a complex application can have many.

  GeoQuiz is a simple app, so it will have a single **Activity** subclass named **QuizActivity**. **QuizActivity** will manage the user interface shown in Figure 1.1.

- A *layout* defines a set of user interface objects and their position on the screen. A layout is made up of definitions written in XML. Each definition is used to create an object that appears on screen, like a button or some text.

  GeoQuiz will include a layout file named activity_quiz.xml. The XML in this file will define the user interface shown in Figure 1.1.

The relationship between **QuizActivity** and activity_quiz.xml is diagrammed in Figure 1.2.

Figure 1.2 **QuizActivity** manages what activity_quiz.xml defines

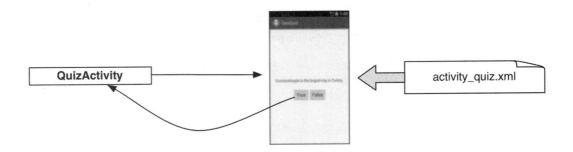

With those ideas in mind, let's build an app.

Creating an Android Project

The first step is to create an Android *project*. An Android *project* contains the files that make up an application. To create a new project, open Eclipse and choose File → New → Android Application Project to open the new application wizard.

In the first dialog, enter GeoQuiz as the application name (Figure 1.3). The project name will automatically update to match the application's. For the package name, enter `com.bignerdranch.android.geoquiz`.

Figure 1.3 Creating a new application

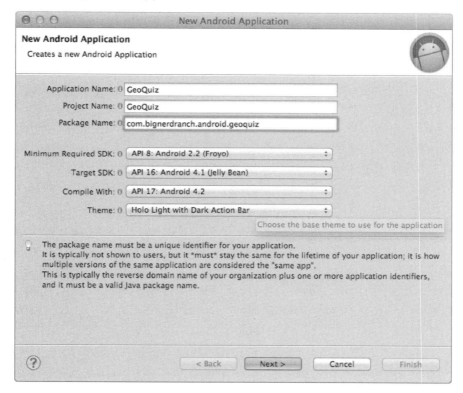

Notice that the package name you entered uses a "reverse DNS" convention in which the domain name of your organization is reversed and suffixed with further identifiers. This convention keeps package names unique and distinguishes applications from each other on a device and on Google Play.

The next four fields configure your application to work with different versions of Android. The default settings are what you need for GeoQuiz, so you can ignore these for now. You will learn about the different versions of Android in Chapter 6.

Android updates its tools several times a year, so your wizard may look slightly different from what we are showing you. This is usually not a problem; the choices to make should stay pretty much the same.

(If your wizard looks very different, then the tools have changed more drastically. Do not panic. Head to this book's forum at `forums.bignerdranch.com`, and we will help you navigate the latest version.)

Click Next.

In the second dialog, uncheck the box to create a custom launcher icon (Figure 1.4). GeoQuiz will use the default launcher icon. Be sure to leave the Create activity box checked.

Figure 1.4 Configuring the project

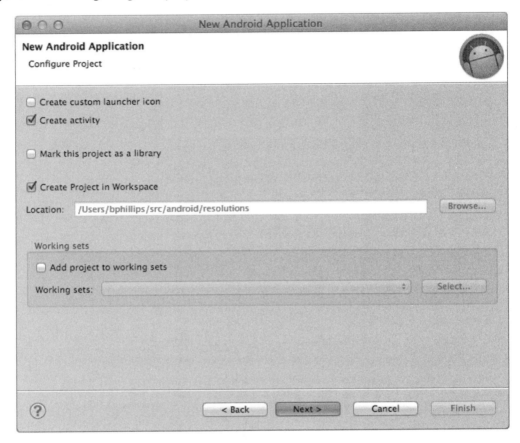

Click Next.

This dialog (Figure 1.5) asks you what kind of activity to create. Choose Blank Activity.

Figure 1.5 Creating a new activity

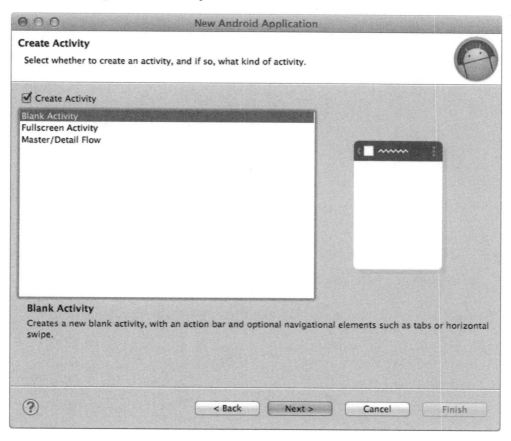

Click Next.

In the final dialog of this wizard, name the activity subclass **QuizActivity** (Figure 1.6). Notice the **Activity** suffix on the class name. This is not required, but it is an excellent convention to follow.

Figure 1.6 Configuring the new activity

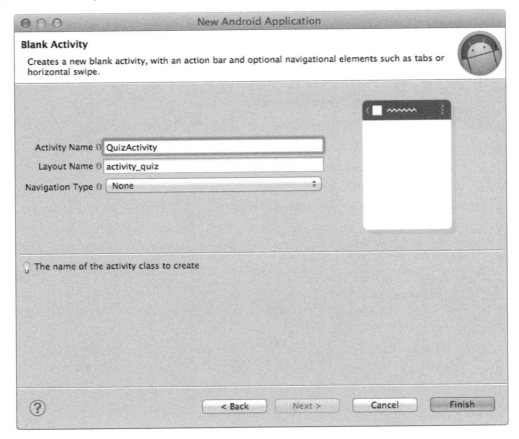

The layout name will automatically update to activity_quiz to reflect the activity's new name. The layout name reverses the order of the activity name, is all lowercase, and has underscores between words. This naming style is recommended for layouts as well as other resources that you will learn about later.

Leave Navigation Type as None and click Finish. Eclipse will create and open your new project.

Navigating in Eclipse

Eclipse opens your project in the *workbench window*, as shown in Figure 1.7. (If you have a brand-new installation, close Eclipse's welcome screen to reveal the workbench window.)

The different panes of the workbench window are called *views*.

The lefthand view is the *package explorer*. From the package explorer, you can manage the files associated with your project.

The middle view is the *editor*. To get you started, Eclipse has opened `activity_quiz.xml` in the editor.

There are also views on the righthand side and the bottom of the workbench. Close any views on the righthand side by clicking the x next to the view's name (Figure 1.7). The views at the bottom are in a *tab group*. Instead of closing these views, minimize the entire tab group using the control at the group's top-right corner.

Figure 1.7 Uncluttering the workbench window

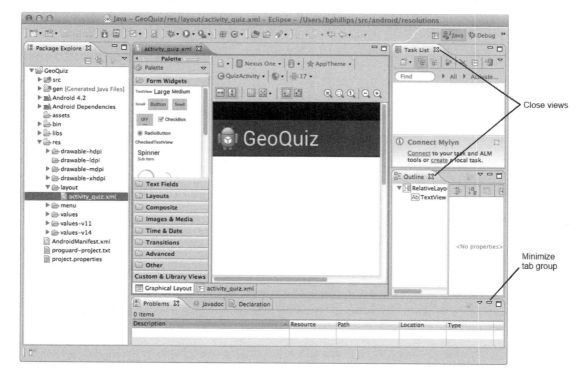

When you minimize a view, it is corralled into a toolbar on the margin of the Eclipse workbench. You can mouse over any of the small icons in these toolbars to see the names of the views and click on any icon to restore that view.

Laying Out the User Interface

By default, Eclipse opened `activity_quiz.xml` in Android's graphical layout tool, which shows you a preview of the layout. The graphical layout tool can be useful, but for now you are going to work in XML to get a better understanding of how layouts work.

To get to the raw XML, select the tab at the bottom of the editor labeled `activity_quiz.xml`.

Currently, `activity_quiz.xml` defines the default activity layout. The defaults change frequently, but the XML will look something like Listing 1.1.

Listing 1.1 Default activity layout (`activity_quiz.xml`)

```
<RelativeLayout xmlns:android="http://schemas.android.com/apk/res/android"
  xmlns:tools="http://schemas.android.com/tools"
  android:layout_width="match_parent"
  android:layout_height="match_parent"
  tools:context=".QuizActivity" >

  <TextView
    android:layout_width="wrap_content"
    android:layout_height="wrap_content"
    android:layout_centerHorizontal="true"
    android:layout_centerVertical="true"
    android:text="@string/hello_world" />

</RelativeLayout>
```

First, notice that `activity_quiz.xml` does not start with a line declaring its version and encoding:

```
<?xml version="1.0" encoding="utf-8"?>
```

As of ADT 21, this line is no longer required in Android layout files. However, you will still see it in many cases.

The default activity layout defines two *widgets*: a **RelativeLayout** and a **TextView**.

Widgets are the building blocks you use to compose a user interface. A widget can show text or graphics, interact with the user, or arrange other widgets on the screen. Buttons, text input controls, and check boxes are all types of widgets.

The Android SDK includes many widgets that you can configure to get the appearance and behavior you want. Every widget is an instance of the **View** class or one of its subclasses (such as **TextView** or **Button**).

Figure 1.8 shows how the **RelativeLayout** and **TextView** defined in Listing 1.1 would appear on screen.

Figure 1.8 Default widgets as seen on screen

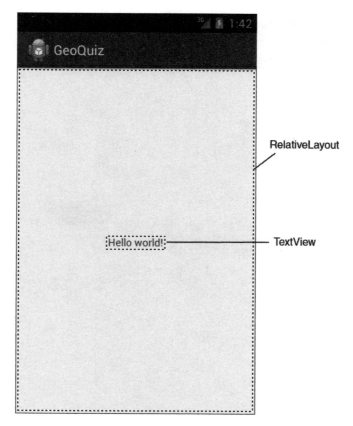

But these are not the widgets you are looking for. The interface for **QuizActivity** requires five widgets:

- a vertical **LinearLayout**

- a **TextView**

- a horizontal **LinearLayout**

- two **Buttons**

Figure 1.9 shows how these widgets compose **QuizActivity**'s interface.

Figure 1.9 Planned widgets as seen on screen

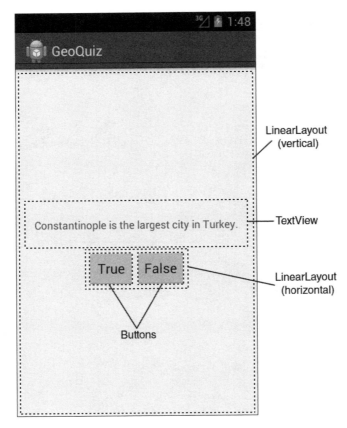

Now you need to define these widgets in `activity_quiz.xml`.

In `activity_quiz.xml`, make the changes shown in Listing 1.2. The XML that you need to delete is struck through, and the XML that you need to add is in a bold font. This is the pattern we will use throughout the book.

Do not worry about understanding what you are typing; you will learn how it works next. However, do be careful. Layout XML is not validated, and typos will cause problems sooner or later.

Depending on your version of the tools, you might get errors on the three lines that start with `android:text`. Ignore these errors for now; you will fix them soon.

Listing 1.2 Defining widgets in XML (`activity_quiz.xml`)

```
<RelativeLayout xmlns:android="http://schemas.android.com/apk/res/android"
    xmlns:tools="http://schemas.android.com/tools"
    android:layout_width="match_parent"
    android:layout_height="match_parent"
    tools:context=".QuizActivity" >

    <TextView
        android:layout_width="wrap_content"
        android:layout_height="wrap_content"
        android:layout_centerHorizontal="true"
        android:layout_centerVertical="true"
        android:text="@string/hello_world" />

</RelativeLayout>

<LinearLayout xmlns:android="http://schemas.android.com/apk/res/android"
    android:layout_width="match_parent"
    android:layout_height="match_parent"
    android:gravity="center"
    android:orientation="vertical" >

    <TextView
        android:layout_width="wrap_content"
        android:layout_height="wrap_content"
        android:padding="24dp"
        android:text="@string/question_text" />

    <LinearLayout
        android:layout_width="wrap_content"
        android:layout_height="wrap_content"
        android:orientation="horizontal" >

        <Button
            android:layout_width="wrap_content"
            android:layout_height="wrap_content"
            android:text="@string/true_button" />

        <Button
            android:layout_width="wrap_content"
            android:layout_height="wrap_content"
            android:text="@string/false_button" />

    </LinearLayout>

</LinearLayout>
```

Compare your XML with the user interface shown in Figure 1.9. Every widget has a corresponding XML element. The name of the element is the type of the widget.

Each element has a set of XML *attributes*. Each *attribute* is an instruction about how the widget should be configured.

To understand how the elements and attributes work, it helps to look at the layout from a hierarchical perspective.

The view hierarchy

Your widgets exist in a hierarchy of **View** objects called the *view hierarchy*. Figure 1.10 shows the view hierarchy that corresponds to the XML in Listing 1.2.

Figure 1.10 Hierarchical layout of widgets and attributes

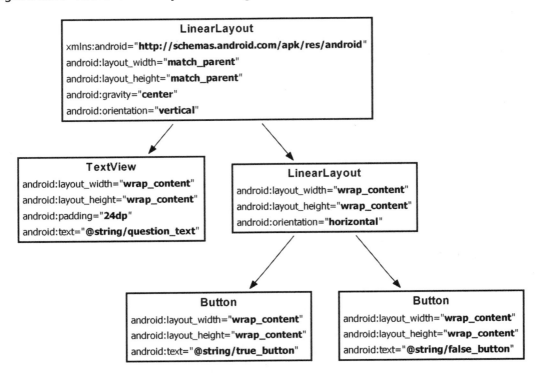

The root element of this layout's view hierarchy is a **LinearLayout**. As the root element, the **LinearLayout** must specify the Android resource XML namespace at http://schemas.android.com/apk/res/android.

LinearLayout inherits from a subclass of **View** named **ViewGroup**. A **ViewGroup** is a widget that contains and arranges other widgets. You use a **LinearLayout** when you want widgets arranged in a single column or row. Other **ViewGroup** subclasses are **FrameLayout**, **TableLayout**, and **RelativeLayout**.

When a widget is contained by a **ViewGroup**, that widget is said to be a *child* of the **ViewGroup**. The root **LinearLayout** has two children: a **TextView** and another **LinearLayout**. The child **LinearLayout** has two **Button** children of its own.

Widget attributes

Let's go over some of the attributes that you have used to configure your widgets:

android:layout_width and android:layout_height

The android:layout_width and android:layout_height attributes are required for almost every type of widget. They are typically set to either match_parent or wrap_content:

match_parent   view will be as big as its parent

wrap_content   view will be as big as its contents require

(You may see fill_parent in some places. This deprecated value is equivalent to match_parent.)

For the root **LinearLayout**, the value of both the height and width attributes is match_parent. The **LinearLayout** is the root element, but it still has a parent – the view that Android provides for your app's view hierarchy to live in.

The other widgets in your layout have their widths and heights set to wrap_content. You can see in Figure 1.9 how this determines their sizes.

The **TextView** is slightly larger than the text it contains due to its android:padding="24dp" attribute. This attribute tells the widget to add the specified amount of space to its contents when determining its size. You are using it to get a little breathing room between the question and the buttons. (Wondering about the dp units? These are density-independent pixels that you will learn about in Chapter 8.)

android:orientation

The android:orientation attribute on the two **LinearLayout** widgets determines whether their children will appear vertically or horizontally. The root **LinearLayout** is vertical; its child **LinearLayout** is horizontal.

The order in which children are defined determines the order in which they appear on screen. In a vertical **LinearLayout**, the first child defined will appear topmost. In a horizontal **LinearLayout**, the first child defined will be leftmost. (Unless the language of the device is a language that runs right-to-left, such as Arabic or Hebrew. In that case, the first child will be rightmost.)

android:text

The **TextView** and **Button** widgets have android:text attributes. This attribute tells the widget what text to display.

Notice that the values of these attributes are not literal strings. They are references to *string resources*.

A *string resource* is a string that lives in a separate XML file called a *strings file*. You can give a widget a hard-coded string, like android:text="True", but it is usually not a good idea. Placing strings into a separate file and then referencing them is better. In Chapter 15, you will see how using string resources makes localization easy.

The string resources you are referencing in activity_quiz.xml do not exist yet. Let's fix that.

Creating string resources

Every project includes a default strings file named `strings.xml`.

In the package explorer, find the `res/values` directory, reveal its contents, and open `strings.xml`. Ignore the graphical interface and select the `strings.xml` tab at the bottom of the editor.

The template has already added a few string resources for you. Remove the unused string named `hello_world` and add the three new strings that your layout requires.

Listing 1.3 Adding string resources (`strings.xml`)

```
<?xml version="1.0" encoding="utf-8"?>
<resources>

    <string name="app_name">GeoQuiz</string>
    <string name="hello_world">Hello, world!</string>
    <string name="question_text">Constantinople is the largest city in Turkey.</string>
    <string name="true_button">True</string>
    <string name="false_button">False</string>
    <string name="menu_settings">Settings</string>

</resources>
```

(Do not delete the `menu_settings` string. Your project came with a menu already prepared. Deleting `menu_settings` will cause cascading errors in other files related to the menu.)

Now whenever you refer to `@string/false_button` in any XML file in the GeoQuiz project, you will get the literal string "False" at runtime.

Save `strings.xml`. If you had errors in `activity_quiz.xml` about the missing string resources, they should now be gone. (If you still have errors, check both files for typos.)

The default strings file is named `strings.xml`, but you can name a strings file anything you want. You can also have multiple strings files in a project. As long as the file is located in `res/values/`, has a `resources` root element, and contains child `string` elements, your strings will be found and used appropriately.

Previewing the layout

Your layout is now complete, and you can preview the layout in the graphical layout tool. First, make sure that your files are saved and error-free. Then return to `activity_quiz.xml` and select the Graphical Layout tab at the bottom of the editor.

Figure 1.11 Preview in graphical layout tool (`activity_quiz.xml`)

From Layout XML to View Objects

How do XML elements in `activity_quiz.xml` become **View** objects? The answer starts in the **QuizActivity** class.

When you created the GeoQuiz project, a subclass of **Activity** named **QuizActivity** was created for you. The class file for **QuizActivity** is in the `src` directory of your project. The `src` directory is where the Java code for your project lives.

In the package explorer, reveal the contents of the `src` directory and then the contents of the `com.bignerdranch.android.geoquiz` package. Open the `QuizActivity.java` file and take a look at its contents (Listing 1.4).

Listing 1.4 Default class file for **QuizActivity** (QuizActivity.java)

```java
package com.bignerdranch.android.geoquiz;

import android.app.Activity;
import android.os.Bundle;
import android.view.Menu;

public class QuizActivity extends Activity {

    @Override
    public void onCreate(Bundle savedInstanceState) {
        super.onCreate(savedInstanceState);
        setContentView(R.layout.activity_quiz);
    }

    @Override
    public boolean onCreateOptionsMenu(Menu menu) {
        getMenuInflater().inflate(R.menu.activity_quiz, menu);
        return true;
    }

}
```

(If you are not seeing all of the import statements, click the ⊕ symbol to the left of the first import statement to reveal the others.)

This file has two **Activity** methods: **onCreate(Bundle)** and **onCreateOptionsMenu(Menu)**.

Ignore **onCreateOptionsMenu(Menu)** for now. You will return to menus in detail in Chapter 16.

The **onCreate(Bundle)** method is called when an instance of the activity subclass is created. When an activity is created, it needs a user interface to manage. To get the activity its user interface, you call the following **Activity** method:

```java
public void setContentView(int layoutResID)
```

This method *inflates* a layout and puts it on screen. When a layout is *inflated*, each widget in the layout file is instantiated as defined by its attributes. You specify which layout to inflate by passing in the layout's resource ID.

Resources and resource IDs

A layout is a *resource*. A *resource* is a piece of your application that is not code – things like image files, audio files, and XML files.

Resources for your project live in a subdirectory of the res directory. In the package explorer, you can see that activity_quiz.xml lives in res/layout/. Your strings file, which contains string resources, lives in res/values/.

To access a resource in code, you use its *resource ID*. The resource ID for your layout is R.layout.activity_quiz.

To see the current resource IDs for GeoQuiz, go to the package explorer and reveal the contents of the gen directory. Find and open R.java. Because this file is generated by the Android build process, you should not change it, as you are subtly warned at the top of the file.

Listing 1.5 Current GeoQuiz resource IDs (R.java)

```
/* AUTO-GENERATED FILE.  DO NOT MODIFY.
...
*/

package com.bignerdranch.android.geoquiz;

public final class R {
    public static final class attr {
    }
    public static final class drawable {
        public static final int ic_launcher=0x7f020000;
    }
    public static final class id {
        public static final int menu_settings=0x7f070003;
    }
    public static final class layout {
        public static final int activity_quiz=0x7f030000;
    }
    public static final class menu {
        public static final int activity_quiz=0x7f060000;
    }
    public static final class string {
        public static final int app_name=0x7f040000;
        public static final int false_button=0x7f040003;
        public static final int menu_settings=0x7f040006;
        public static final int question_text=0x7f040001;
        public static final int true_button=0x7f040002;
    }

    ...
}
```

This is where the R.layout.activity_quiz comes from – it is an integer constant named activity_quiz within the **layout** inner class of **R**.

Your strings also have resource IDs. You have not yet referred to a string in code, but if you did, it would look like this:

```
setTitle(R.string.app_name);
```

Android generated a resource ID for the entire layout and for each string, but it did not generate IDs for the individual widgets in activity_quiz.xml. Not every widget needs a resource ID. In this chapter, you will only interact with the two buttons in code, so only they need resource IDs.

To generate a resource ID for a widget, you include an android:id attribute in the widget's definition. In activity_quiz.xml, add an android:id attribute to each button.

Listing 1.6 Adding IDs to buttons (`activity_quiz.xml`)

```
<LinearLayout xmlns:android="http://schemas.android.com/apk/res/android"
... >

  <TextView
    android:layout_width="wrap_content"
    android:layout_height="wrap_content"
    android:padding="24dp"
    android:text="@string/question_text" />

  <LinearLayout
    android:layout_width="wrap_content"
    android:layout_height="wrap_content"
    android:orientation="horizontal">

    <Button
      android:id="@+id/true_button"
      android:layout_width="wrap_content"
      android:layout_height="wrap_content"
      android:text="@string/true_button" />

    <Button
      android:id="@+id/false_button"
      android:layout_width="wrap_content"
      android:layout_height="wrap_content"
      android:text="@string/false_button" />

  </LinearLayout>

</LinearLayout>
```

Notice that there is a + sign in the values for android:id but not in the values for android:text. This is because you are *creating* the IDs and only *referencing* the strings.

Save activity_quiz.xml. Return to R.java to confirm that you have two new resource IDs in the **R.id** inner class.

Listing 1.7 New resource IDs (R.java)

```
public final class R {
    ...
    public static final class id {
        public static final int false_button=0x7f070001;
        public static final int menu_settings=0x7f070002;
        public static final int true_button=0x7f070000;
    }
...
```

Wiring Up Widgets

Now that the buttons have resource IDs, you can access them in **QuizActivity**. The first step is to add two member variables.

Type the following code into `QuizActivity.java`. (Do not use auto-complete; type it in yourself.) After you save the file, it will report two errors.

Listing 1.8 Adding member variables (`QuizActivity.java`)

```
public class QuizActivity extends Activity {

    private Button mTrueButton;
    private Button mFalseButton;

    @Override
    public void onCreate(Bundle savedInstanceState) {
        super.onCreate(savedInstanceState);
        setContentView(R.layout.activity_quiz);
    }

...
}
```

You will fix the errors in just a second. First, notice the m prefix on the two member (instance) variable names. This prefix is an Android naming convention that we will follow throughout this book.

Now mouse over the error flags to the left of the code. They report the same problem: Button cannot be resolved to a type.

These errors are telling you that you need to import the **android.widget.Button** class into `QuizActivity.java`. You could type the following import statement at the top of the file:

```
import android.widget.Button;
```

Or you can do it the easy way and organize your imports.

Organizing imports

When you organize imports, you ask Eclipse to look at your code and determine what you need from the Java and Android SDKs. It imports what you need and removes any previously imported classes that you are no longer using.

To organize your imports, press:

- Command+Shift+O for Mac

- Ctrl+Shift+O for Windows and Linux

This should get rid of the errors. (If you still have errors, check for typos in your code and XML.)

Now you can wire up your button widgets. This is a two-step process:

- get references to the inflated **View** objects

- set listeners on those objects to respond to user actions

Getting references to widgets

In an activity, you can get a reference to an inflated widget by calling the following **Activity** method:

```
public View findViewById(int id)
```

This method accepts a resource ID of a widget and returns a **View** object.

In QuizActivity.java, use the resource IDs of your buttons to retrieve the inflated objects and assign them to your member variables. Note that you must cast the returned **View** to **Button** before assigning it.

Listing 1.9 Getting references to widgets (QuizActivity.java)

```java
public class QuizActivity extends Activity {

    private Button mTrueButton;
    private Button mFalseButton;

    @Override
    public void onCreate(Bundle savedInstanceState) {
        super.onCreate(savedInstanceState);
        setContentView(R.layout.activity_quiz);

        mTrueButton = (Button)findViewById(R.id.true_button);
        mFalseButton = (Button)findViewById(R.id.false_button);
    }

...
}
```

Setting listeners

Android applications are typically *event-driven*. Unlike command-line programs or scripts, event-driven applications start and then wait for an event, such as the user pressing a button. (Events can also be initiated by the OS or another application, but user-initiated events are the most obvious.)

When your application is waiting for a specific event, we say that it is "listening for" that event. The object that you create to respond to an event is called a *listener*. A *listener* is an object that implements a *listener interface* for that event.

The Android SDK comes with listener interfaces for various events, so you do not have to write your own. In this case, the event you want to listen for is a button "click," so your listener will implement the **View.OnClickListener** interface.

Start with the True button. In QuizActivity.java, add the following code to **onCreate(…)** just after the variable assignment.

Listing 1.10 Set listener for True button (QuizActivity.java)

```
    ...

    @Override
    public void onCreate(Bundle savedInstanceState) {
        super.onCreate(savedInstanceState);
        setContentView(R.layout.activity_quiz);

        mTrueButton = (Button)findViewById(R.id.true_button);
        mTrueButton.setOnClickListener(new View.OnClickListener() {
            @Override
            public void onClick(View v) {
                // Does nothing yet, but soon!
            }
        });

        mFalseButton = (Button)findViewById(R.id.false_button);
    }
}
```

(If you have a View cannot be resolved to a type error, organize your imports using Command+Shift+O or Ctrl+Shift+O to import the **View** class.)

In Listing 1.10, you set a listener to inform you when the **Button** known as mTrueButton has been pressed. The **setOnClickListener(OnClickListener)** method takes a listener as its argument. In particular, it takes an object that implements **OnClickListener**.

Using anonymous inner classes

This listener is implemented as an *anonymous inner class*. The syntax is a little tricky, but it helps to remember that everything within the outermost set of parentheses is passed into **setOnClickListener(OnClickListener)**. Within these parentheses, you create a new, nameless class and pass its entire implementation.

```
    mTrueButton.setOnClickListener(new View.OnClickListener() {
        @Override
        public void onClick(View v) {
            // Does nothing yet, but soon!
        }
    });
```

All of the listeners in this book will be implemented as anonymous inner classes. Doing so puts the implementations of the listener's methods right where you want to see them. And there is no need for the overhead of a named class because the class will be used in one place only.

Because your anonymous class implements **OnClickListener**, it must implement that interface's sole method, **onClick(View)**. You have left the implementation of **onClick(View)** empty for now, and the compiler is okay with that. A listener interface requires you to implement **onClick(View)**, but it makes no rules about *how* to implement it.

(If your knowledge of anonymous inner classes, listeners, or interfaces is rusty, you may want to review some Java before continuing or at least keep a reference nearby.)

Set a similar listener for the False button.

Listing 1.11 Set listener for False button (`QuizActivity.java`)

```
    ...

    mTrueButton.setOnClickListener(new View.OnClickListener() {
        @Override
        public void onClick(View v) {
            // Does nothing yet, but soon!
        }
    });

    mFalseButton = (Button)findViewById(R.id.false_button);
    mFalseButton.setOnClickListener(new View.OnClickListener() {
        @Override
        public void onClick(View v) {
            // Does nothing yet, but soon!
        }
    });
}
```

Making toasts

Now to make the buttons fully-armed and operational. You are going to have a click of each button trigger a pop-up message called a *toast*. A *toast* is a short message that informs the user of something but does not require any input or action. You are going to make toasts that announce whether the user answered correctly or incorrectly (Figure 1.12).

Figure 1.12 A toast providing feedback

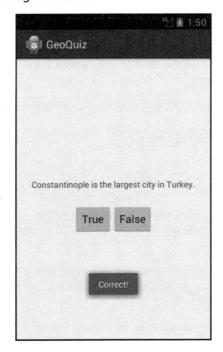

First, return to `strings.xml` and add the string resources that your toasts will display.

Listing 1.12 Adding toast strings (`strings.xml`)

```xml
<?xml version="1.0" encoding="utf-8"?>
<resources>
  <string name="app_name">GeoQuiz</string>
  <string name="question_text">Constantinople is the largest city in Turkey.</string>
  <string name="true_button">True</string>
  <string name="false_button">False</string>
  <string name="correct_toast">Correct!</string>
  <string name="incorrect_toast">Incorrect!</string>
  <string name="menu_settings">Settings</string>
</resources>
```

To create a toast, you call the following method from the **Toast** class:

```
public static Toast makeText(Context context, int resId, int duration)
```

The **Context** parameter is typically an instance of **Activity** (**Activity** is a subclass of **Context**). The second parameter is the resource ID of the string that the toast should display. The **Context** is needed by the **Toast** class to be able to find and use the string's resource ID. The third parameter is usually one of two **Toast** constants that specify how long the toast should be visible.

After you have created a toast, you call **Toast.show()** on it to get it on screen.

In **QuizActivity**, you are going to call **makeText(…)** in each button's listener (Listing 1.13). Instead of typing everything in, try using Eclipse's auto-complete feature to add these calls.

Using auto-complete

Auto-complete can save you a lot of time, so it is good to become familiar with it early.

Start typing the code addition shown in Listing 1.13. When you get to the period after the **Toast** class, a pop-up window will appear with a list of suggested methods and constants from the **Toast** class.

To choose one of the suggestions, press the tab key to focus on the auto-complete pop-up. (If you wanted to ignore auto-complete, you could just keep typing. It will not complete anything for you if you do not press the tab key or click on the pop-up window.)

From the list of suggestions, select **makeText(Context, int, int)**. Auto-complete will add the complete method call for you, including placeholder values for the arguments.

The first placeholder will be highlighted; type in the real value – `QuizActivity.this`. Then press the tab key again to go to the next placeholder, and so on until you have added the code shown in Listing 1.13.

Listing 1.13 Making toasts (`QuizActivity.java`)

```
...
mTrueButton.setOnClickListener(new View.OnClickListener() {
    @Override
    public void onClick(View v) {
        Toast.makeText(QuizActivity.this,
                    R.string.incorrect_toast,
                    Toast.LENGTH_SHORT).show();
    }
});

mFalseButton.setOnClickListener(new View.OnClickListener() {
    @Override
    public void onClick(View v) {
        Toast.makeText(QuizActivity.this,
                    R.string.correct_toast,
                    Toast.LENGTH_SHORT).show();
    }
});
```

In **makeText(…)**, you pass the instance of **QuizActivity** as the **Context** argument. However, you cannot simply pass the variable this as you might expect. At this point in the code, you are defining the anonymous class where this refers to the **View.OnClickListener**.

Because you used auto-complete, you do not have to organize your imports to get the **Toast** class. When you accept an auto-complete suggestion, the necessary classes are imported automatically.

Running on the Emulator

To run an Android application, you need a device – either a hardware device or a *virtual device*. Virtual devices are powered by the Android emulator, which ships with the developer tools.

To create an Android virtual device (AVD), choose Window → Android Virtual Device Manager. When the AVD Manager appears, click the New... button on the righthand side of the window.

In the dialog that appears, you are offered many options for configuring a virtual device. For your first AVD, choose to emulate a Galaxy Nexus device running Google APIs – API Level 17, as shown in Figure 1.13. If you are running on Windows, you will need to change the RAM from 1024 to 512 to get the AVD to behave properly. Then click OK.

Figure 1.13 Creating a new AVD

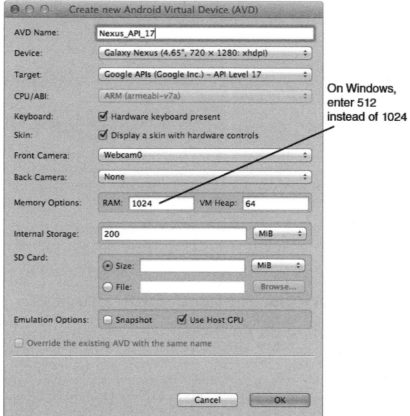

Once you have an AVD, you can run GeoQuiz on it. In the package explorer, right-click the GeoQuiz project folder. From the context menu, choose Run As → Android Application. Eclipse will find the virtual device you created, install the application package on it, and run the app. Eclipse may ask you if you want to auto-monitor with LogCat. Say yes.

Starting up the emulator can take a while, but eventually your GeoQuiz app will launch on the AVD that you created. Press buttons and admire your toasts. (Note that if the app launches and you are not around, you may have to unlock the AVD when you come back. The AVD works like a real device, and it will lock itself after a time.)

If GeoQuiz crashes when launching or when you press a button, LogCat will appear at the bottom of your workbench. Look for exceptions in the log; they will be an eye-catching red color. The Text column will tell you the exception's name and give you the line where the problem occurred.

Figure 1.14 An example **NullPointerException** at line 21

```
Text
at dalvik.system.NativeStart.main(Native Method)
Caused by: java.lang.NullPointerException
at com.bignerdranch.android.geoquiz.QuizActivity.onCreate(QuizActivity.java:21)
at android.app.Activity.performCreate(Activity.java:5008)
at android.app.Instrumentation.callActivityOnCreate(Instrumentation.java:1079)
```

Compare your code with the code in the book to try to find the cause of the problem. Then try running again.

Keep the emulator running; you do not want to wait for it to launch on every run. You can stop the app by pressing the Back button (the arrow that is making a U-turn). Then re-run the app from Eclipse to test changes.

The emulator is useful, but testing on a real device gives more accurate results. In Chapter 2, you will run GeoQuiz on a hardware device. You will also give GeoQuiz more geography questions with which to test the user.

For the More Curious: Android Build Process

By now, you probably have some burning questions about how the Android build process works. You have already seen that Eclipse builds your project automatically as you modify it rather than on command. During the build process, the Android tools take your resources, code, and the AndroidManifest.xml file (which contains meta-data about the application) and turn them into an .apk file. This file is then signed with a debug key, which allows it to run on the emulator. (To distribute your .apk to the masses, you have to sign it with a release key. There is more information about this process in the Android developer documentation at http://developer.android.com/tools/publishing/preparing.html.)

Figure 1.15 Building GeoQuiz

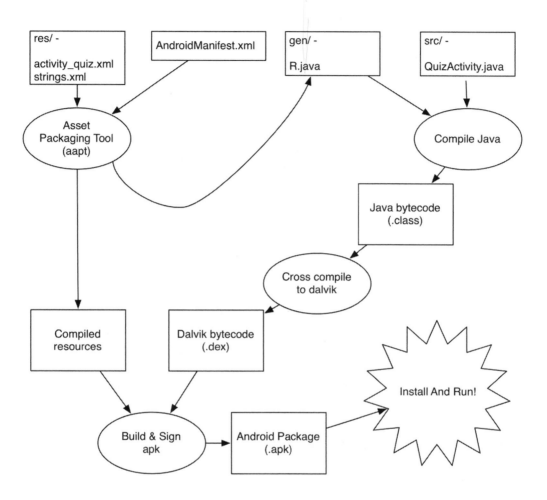

How do the contents of `activity_quiz.xml` turn into **View** objects in an application? As part of the build process, aapt (Android Asset Packaging Tool) compiles layout file resources into a more compact format. These compiled resources are packaged into the `.apk` file. Then, when **setContentView(…)** is called in the **QuizActivity**'s **onCreate(…)** method, the **QuizActivity** uses the **LayoutInflater** class to instantiate each of the **View** objects as defined in the layout file.

Figure 1.16 Inflating `activity_quiz.xml`

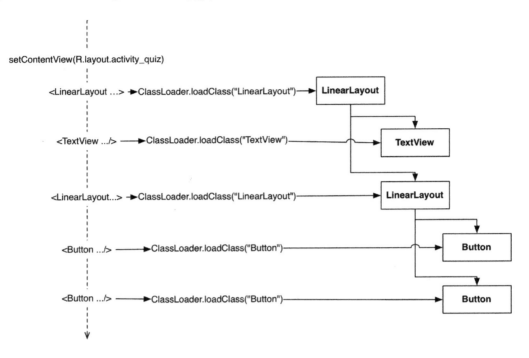

(You can also create your view classes programmatically in the activity instead of defining them in XML. But there are benefits to separating your presentation from the logic of the application. The main one is taking advantage of configuration changes built into the SDK, which we'll talk more about in Chapter 3.)

For more details on how the different XML attributes work and how views display themselves on the screen, see Chapter 8.

Android build tools

All of the builds you have seen so far have been executed from within Eclipse. This build is integrated into the ADT plugin you are using – it invokes standard Android build tools like `aapt`, but the build process itself is managed by Eclipse.

You may, for your own reasons, want to perform builds from outside of Eclipse. The easiest way to do this is to use a command line build tool. The most popular two tools are maven and ant. Ant does less, but it is much easier to use. Start by doing two things:

- Make sure that ant is installed and that you can run it.

- Make sure that both the `tools/` and `platform-tools/` folders in your Android SDK are included in your executable search paths.

Now navigate to your project's directory and run the following command:

```
$ android update project -p .
```

The Eclipse project generator template does not include an appropriate `build.xml` for ant. This first command generates `build.xml` for you. You only need to run it this one time.

Next, build your project. To build and sign a debug `.apk`, run the following command in the same folder:

```
$ ant debug
```

This will actually perform your build. It will create an `.apk` file located in bin/*your-project-name-*debug.apk. Once you have the `.apk` in hand, install it by running this command:

```
$ adb install bin/your-project-name-debug.apk
```

This will install your app on whatever device is connected. It will not run the app, though. For that, you will need to pull up the launcher and launch the app by hand.

2

Android and Model-View-Controller

In this chapter, you are going to upgrade the GeoQuiz app to present more than one question.

Figure 2.1 More questions!

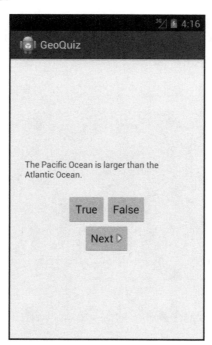

To make this happen, you are going to add a class named **TrueFalse** to the GeoQuiz project. An instance of this class will encapsulate a single true-false question.

Then, you will create an array of **TrueFalse** objects for **QuizActivity** to manage.

Creating a New Class

In the package explorer, right-click the `com.bignerdranch.android.geoquiz` package and select New
→ Class. Name the class **TrueFalse**, leave its superclass as **java.lang.Object**, and click Finish.

Figure 2.2 Creating the **TrueFalse** class

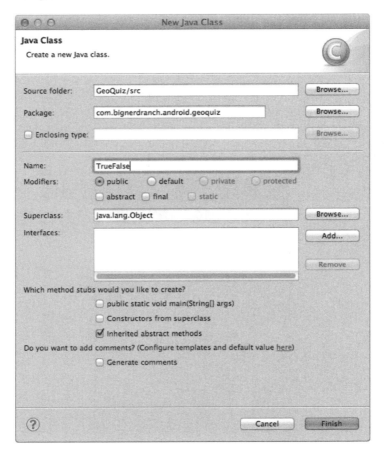

In `TrueFalse.java`, add two member variables and a constructor:

Listing 2.1 Adding to **TrueFalse** class (TrueFalse.java)

```
public class TrueFalse {
    private int mQuestion;

    private boolean mTrueQuestion;

    public TrueFalse(int question, boolean trueQuestion) {
        mQuestion = question;
        mTrueQuestion = trueQuestion;
    }
}
```

Why is mQuestion an int and not a String? The mQuestion variable will hold the resource ID (always an int) of a string resource for the question. You will create the question string resources in a later section. The mTrueQuestion variable indicates whether the statement is true or false.

These variables need getter and setter methods. Rather than typing them in yourself, you can have Eclipse generate the implementations for you.

Generating getters and setters

The first step is to configure Eclipse to recognize the m prefix for member variables and to use is rather than get for boolean variables.

Open Eclipse's preferences (from the Eclipse menu on Mac and from Windows → Preferences on Windows). Under Java preferences, select Code Style.

In the Conventions for variable names: table, select the Fields row (Figure 2.3). Click the Edit button and add m as a prefix for fields. Then add s as a prefix for static fields. (You will not be using the s prefix in the GeoQuiz project, but it will be useful in later projects.)

Make sure the Use 'is' prefix for getters that return boolean is checked. Then click OK.

Figure 2.3 Setting Java code style preferences

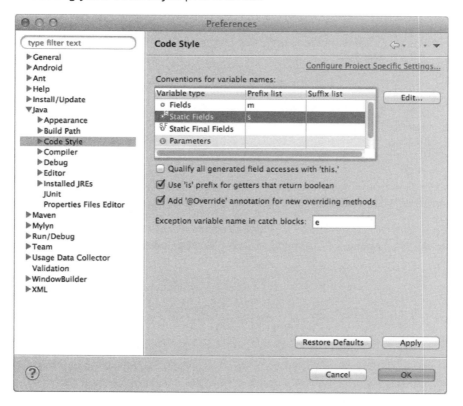

What is the point of setting these prefixes? Now when you ask Eclipse to generate a getter for mQuestion, it will create **getQuestion()** rather than **getMQuestion()** and **isTrueQuestion()** rather than **isMTrueQuestion()**.

Back in TrueFalse.java, right-click after the constructor and select Source → Generate Getters And Setters... Click the Select All button to create a getter and setter for each variable.

Click OK, and Eclipse will generate code for the four methods.

Listing 2.2 Generated getters and setters (TrueFalse.java)

```java
public class TrueFalse {
    private int mQuestion;

    private boolean mTrueQuestion;

    public TrueFalse(int question, boolean trueQuestion) {
        mQuestion = question;
        mTrueQuestion = trueQuestion;
    }

    public int getQuestion() {
        return mQuestion;
    }

    public void setQuestion(int question) {
        mQuestion = question;
    }

    public boolean isTrueQuestion() {
        return mTrueQuestion;
    }

    public void setTrueQuestion(boolean trueQuestion) {
        mTrueQuestion = trueQuestion;
    }

}
```

Your **TrueFalse** class is now complete. In a moment, you will modify **QuizActivity** to work with **TrueFalse**. First, let's take a look at the big picture of how the pieces of GeoQuiz will work together.

You are going to have **QuizActivity** create an array of **TrueFalse** objects. It will then interact with the **TextView** and the three **Button**s to display questions and provide feedback on the user's responses.

Figure 2.4 Object diagram for GeoQuiz

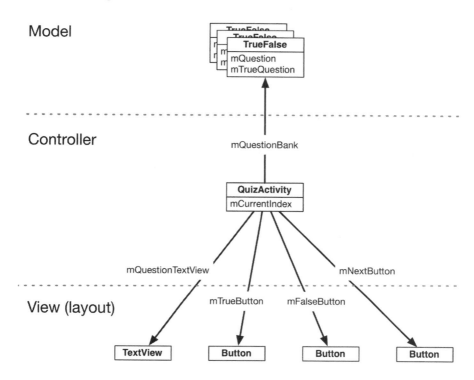

Model-View-Controller and Android

Notice that the objects in Figure 2.4 are separated into three sections labeled Model, Controller, and View. Android applications are designed around an architecture called Model-View-Controller, or MVC for short. MVC states that any object in your application must be a *model object*, a *view object*, or a *controller object*.

- A *model object* holds the application's data and "business logic." Model classes are typically designed to *model* the things your app is concerned with, such as a user, a product in a store, a photo on a server, or a television show. Or a true-false question. Model objects have no knowledge of the user interface; their sole purpose is holding and managing data.

  In Android applications, model classes are generally custom classes you create. All of the model objects in your application compose its *model layer*.

  GeoQuiz's model layer consists of the **TrueFalse** class.

- *View objects* know how to draw themselves on the screen and how to respond to user input, like touches. A simple rule of thumb is that if you can see it on screen, then it is a view.

  Android provides a wealth of configurable view classes. You can also create custom view classes. An application's view objects make up its *view layer*.

  GeoQuiz's view layer consists of the widgets that are inflated from `activity_quiz.xml`.

- *Controller objects* tie the view and model objects together. They contain "application logic." Controllers are designed to respond to various events triggered by view objects and to manage the flow of data to and from model objects and the view layer.

  In Android, a controller is typically a subclass of **Activity**, **Fragment**, or **Service**. (You will learn about fragments in Chapter 7 and services in Chapter 29.)

  GeoQuiz's controller layer, at present, consists solely of **QuizActivity**.

Figure 2.5 shows the flow of control between objects in response to a user event, like a press of a button. Notice that model and view objects do not talk to each other directly; controllers sit squarely in the middle of everything, receiving messages from some objects and dispatching instructions to others.

Figure 2.5 MVC flow with user input

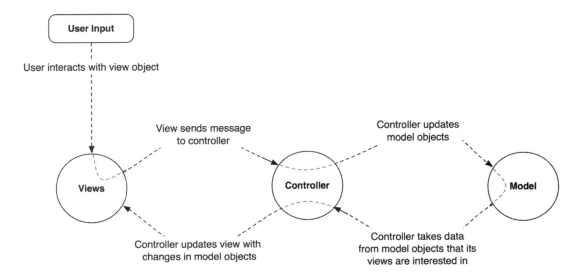

Benefits of MVC

An application can accumulate features until it is too complicated to understand. Separating code into classes helps you design and understand the application as a whole; you can think in terms of classes instead of individual variables and methods.

Similarly, separating classes into model, view, and controller layers helps you design and understand an application; you can think in terms of layers instead of individual classes.

GeoQuiz is not a complicated app, but you can still see the benefits of keeping layers separate here. In a moment, you are going to update GeoQuiz's view layer to include a Next button. When you do that, you will not need to remember a single thing about the **TrueFalse** class you just created.

MVC also makes classes easier to reuse. A class with restricted responsibilities is more reusable than one with its fingers in every pie.

For instance, your model class, **TrueFalse**, knows nothing about the widgets used to display a true-false question. This makes it easy to use **TrueFalse** throughout your app for different purposes. For example, if you wanted to display a list of all the questions at once, you could use the same object that you use here to display just one question at a time.

Updating the View Layer

Now that you have been introduced to MVC, let's update GeoQuiz's view layer to include a Next button.

In Android, objects in the view layer are typically inflated from XML within a layout file. The sole layout in GeoQuiz is defined in `activity_quiz.xml`. This layout needs updating as shown in Figure 2.6. (Note that we are not showing the attributes of unchanged widgets to save space.)

Figure 2.6 New button!

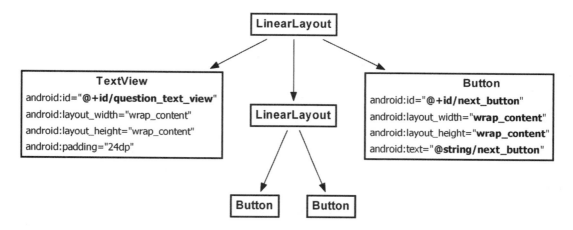

So the changes you need to make to the view layer are

- remove the `android:text` attribute from the **TextView**. You no longer want a hard-coded question to be part of its definition.

- Give the **TextView** an `android:id` attribute. This widget will need a resource ID so that you can set its text in **QuizActivity**'s code.

- Add the new **Button** widget as a child of the root **LinearLayout**.

Return to `activity_quiz.xml` and make it happen.

Listing 2.3 New button... and changes to the text view (`activity_quiz.xml`)

```
<LinearLayout
  ... >

  <TextView
    android:id="@+id/question_text_view"
    android:layout_width="wrap_content"
    android:layout_height="wrap_content"
    android:padding="24dp"
    android:text="@string/question_text"
    />

  <LinearLayout
    ... >

    ...

  </LinearLayout>

  <Button
    android:id="@+id/next_button"
    android:layout_width="wrap_content"
    android:layout_height="wrap_content"
    android:text="@string/next_button" />

</LinearLayout>
```

Save `activity_quiz.xml`, and you may see a familiar error pop up to alert you about a missing string resource.

Return to `res/values/strings.xml`. Remove the question string and add a string for the new button.

Listing 2.4 Updating strings (`strings.xml`)

```
...

  <string name="app_name">GeoQuiz</string>
  <string name="question_text">Constantinople is the largest city in Turkey.</string>
  <string name="true_button">True</string>
  <string name="false_button">False</string>
  <string name="next_button">Next</string>
  <string name="correct_toast">Correct!</string>

  ...
```

While you have `strings.xml` open, go ahead and add the strings for the set of geography questions that will be shown to the user.

Listing 2.5 Adding question strings in advance (`strings.xml`)

```
...
    <string name="incorrect_toast">Incorrect!</string>
    <string name="menu_settings">Settings</string>
    <string name="question_oceans">The Pacific Ocean is larger than
        the Atlantic Ocean.</string>
    <string name="question_mideast">The Suez Canal connects the Red Sea
        and the Indian Ocean.</string>
    <string name="question_africa">The source of the Nile River is in Egypt.</string>
    <string name="question_americas">The Amazon River is the longest river
        in the Americas.</string>
    <string name="question_asia">Lake Baikal is the world\'s oldest and deepest
        freshwater lake.</string>
...
```

Notice that you use the escape sequence \' in the last value to get an apostrophe in your string. You can use all the usual escape sequences in your string resources, such as \n for a new line.

Save your files. Then return to `activity_quiz.xml` and preview your layout changes in the graphical layout tool.

That is all for now for GeoQuiz's view layer. Time to wire everything up in your controller class, **QuizActivity**.

Updating the Controller Layer

In the previous chapter, there was not that much happening in GeoQuiz's one controller, **QuizActivity**. It displayed the layout defined in `activity_quiz.xml`. It set listeners on two buttons and wired them to make toasts.

Now that you have multiple questions to retrieve and display, **QuizActivity** will have to work harder to tie GeoQuiz's model and view layers together.

Open `QuizActivity.java`. Add variables for the **TextView** and the new **Button**. Also, create an array of **TrueFalse** objects and an index for the array.

Listing 2.6 Adding variables and a TrueFalse array (QuizActivity.java)

```
public class QuizActivity extends Activity {
    private Button mTrueButton;
    private Button mFalseButton;
    private Button mNextButton;
    private TextView mQuestionTextView;

    private TrueFalse[] mQuestionBank = new TrueFalse[] {
        new TrueFalse(R.string.question_oceans, true),
        new TrueFalse(R.string.question_mideast, false),
        new TrueFalse(R.string.question_africa, false),
        new TrueFalse(R.string.question_americas, true),
        new TrueFalse(R.string.question_asia, true),
    };

    private int mCurrentIndex = 0;
    ...
```

Here you call the **TrueFalse** constructor several times and create an array of **TrueFalse** objects.

(In a more complex project, this array would be created and stored elsewhere. In later apps, you will see better options for storing model data. For now, we are keeping it simple and just creating the array within your controller.)

You are going to use mQuestionBank, mCurrentIndex, and the accessor methods in **TrueFalse** to get a parade of questions on screen.

First, get a reference for the **TextView** and set its text to the question at the current index.

Listing 2.7 Wiring up the **TextView** (QuizActivity.java)

```
public class QuizActivity extends Activity {

    ...

    @Override
    protected void onCreate(Bundle savedInstanceState) {
        super.onCreate(savedInstanceState);
        setContentView(R.layout.activity_quiz);

        mQuestionTextView = (TextView)findViewById(R.id.question_text_view);
        int question = mQuestionBank[mCurrentIndex].getQuestion();
        mQuestionTextView.setText(question);

        mTrueButton = (Button)findViewById(R.id.true_button);
        ...
    }
}
```

Save your files and check for any errors. Then run GeoQuiz. You should see the first question in the array appear in the **TextView**.

Now let's see about the Next button. First, get a reference to the button. Then set a **View.OnClickListener** on it. This listener will increment the index and update the **TextView**'s text.

Listing 2.8 Wiring up the new button (`QuizActivity.java`)

```java
public class QuizActivity extends Activity {

    ...

    @Override
    protected void onCreate(Bundle savedInstanceState) {
        super.onCreate(savedInstanceState);
        setContentView(R.layout.activity_quiz);

        mQuestionTextView = (TextView)findViewById(R.id.question_text_view);
        int question = mQuestionBank[mCurrentIndex].getQuestion();
        mQuestionTextView.setText(question);

        ...

        mFalseButton.setOnClickListener(new View.OnClickListener() {
            @Override
            public void onClick(View v) {
                Toast.makeText(QuizActivity.this,
                        R.string.correct_toast,
                        Toast.LENGTH_SHORT).show();
            }
        });

        mNextButton = (Button)findViewById(R.id.next_button);
        mNextButton.setOnClickListener(new View.OnClickListener() {
            @Override
            public void onClick(View v) {
                mCurrentIndex = (mCurrentIndex + 1) % mQuestionBank.length;
                int question = mQuestionBank[mCurrentIndex].getQuestion();
                mQuestionTextView.setText(question);
            }
        });
    }
}
```

You now have code in two separate places that updates the `mQuestionTextView` variable. Take a moment to put this code into a private method instead, as shown in Listing 2.9. Then call that method in the `mNextButton`'s listener and at the end of **onCreate(Bundle)** to initially set the text in the activity's view.

Listing 2.9 Encapsulating with **updateQuestion()** (QuizActivity.java)

```
public class QuizActivity extends Activity {

    ...

    private void updateQuestion() {
        int question = mQuestionBank[mCurrentIndex].getQuestion();
        mQuestionTextView.setText(question);
    }

    @Override
    protected void onCreate(Bundle savedInstanceState) {
        ...

        mQuestionTextView = (TextView)findViewById(R.id.question_text_view);
        int question = mQuestionBank[mCurrentIndex].getQuestion();
        mQuestionTextView.setText(question);

        mNextButton.setOnClickListener(new View.OnClickListener() {
            @Override
            public void onClick(View v) {
                mCurrentIndex = (mCurrentIndex + 1) % mQuestionBank.length;
                int question = mQuestionBank[mCurrentIndex].getQuestion();
                mQuestionTextView.setText(question);
                updateQuestion();
            }
        });

        updateQuestion();
    }
}
```

Run GeoQuiz and test your new Next button.

Now that you have the questions behaving appropriately, it is time to turn to the answers. Here again, you will implement a private method to encapsulate code rather than writing similar code in two places.

The method that you are going to add to **QuizActivity** is

```
private void checkAnswer(boolean userPressedTrue)
```

This method will accept a boolean variable that identifies whether the user pressed True or False. Then, it will check the user's answer against the answer in the current **TrueFalse** object. Finally, after determining whether the user answered correctly, it will make a **Toast** that displays the appropriate message to the user.

In QuizActivity.java, add the implementation of **checkAnswer(boolean)** shown in Listing 2.10.

Listing 2.10 Adding **checkAnswer(boolean)** (QuizActivity.java)

```
public class QuizActivity extends Activity {

    ...

    private void updateQuestion() {
        int question = mQuestionBank[mCurrentIndex].getQuestion();
        mQuestionTextView.setText(question);
    }

    private void checkAnswer(boolean userPressedTrue) {
        boolean answerIsTrue = mQuestionBank[mCurrentIndex].isTrueQuestion();

        int messageResId = 0;

        if (userPressedTrue == answerIsTrue) {
            messageResId = R.string.correct_toast;
        } else {
            messageResId = R.string.incorrect_toast;
        }

        Toast.makeText(this, messageResId, Toast.LENGTH_SHORT)
            .show();
    }

    @Override
    protected void onCreate(Bundle savedInstanceState) {
        ...

    }
}
```

Within the button's listeners, call **checkAnswer(boolean)**, as shown in Listing 2.11.

Listing 2.11 Calling **checkAnswer(boolean)** (QuizActivity.java)

```java
public class QuizActivity extends Activity {

    ...

    @Override
    protected void onCreate(Bundle savedInstanceState) {
        ...

        mTrueButton = (Button)findViewById(R.id.true_button);
        mTrueButton.setOnClickListener(new View.OnClickListener() {

            @Override
            public void onClick(View v) {
                Toast.makeText(QuizActivity.this,
                        R.string.incorrect_toast,
                        Toast.LENGTH_SHORT).show();
                checkAnswer(true);
            }
        });

        mFalseButton = (Button)findViewById(R.id.false_button);
        mFalseButton.setOnClickListener(new View.OnClickListener() {
            @Override
            public void onClick(View v) {
                Toast.makeText(QuizActivity.this,
                        R.string.correct_toast,
                        Toast.LENGTH_SHORT).show();
                checkAnswer(false);
            }
        });

        mNextButton = (Button)findViewById(R.id.next_button);
        ...

    }
}
```

GeoQuiz is ready to run again. Let's get it running on a real device.

Running on a Device

In this section, you will set up your system, device, and application to get GeoQuiz running on your hardware device.

Connecting your device

First, plug the device into your system. If you are developing on a Mac, your system should recognize the device right away. On Windows, you may need to install the adb (Android Debug Bridge) driver. If Windows cannot find the adb driver, then download one from your device's manufacturer's website.

You can confirm that your device is recognized by opening the Devices view. The quickest way to the Devices view is to open the DDMS perspective by clicking the DDMS button at the top right corner of the Eclipse workbench. The Devices view should appear on the lefthand side of the workbench. You should see your AVD and your hardware device listed in this view.

To get back to the editor and other views, click the Java button at the top right corner of the workbench.

If you are having trouble getting your device recognized, the first thing to try is resetting adb. In the Devices view, click on the downward pointing arrow at the top-right of the view. This will reveal a menu. The bottom choice is Reset adb. Select this item, and, after a moment, your device may appear in the list.

If resetting adb does not work, you can find more help on the Android developers site. Start at http://developer.android.com/tools/device.html. Or visit this book's forum at forums.bignerdranch.com for more troubleshooting help.

Configuring your device for development

To test apps on your device, you need to set it up to accept applications that are not from Google Play.

- On devices running Android 4.1 or earlier, open the device's Settings and go to Applications. Make sure that Unknown sources is checked.

- On devices running Android 4.2, go to Settings → Security to find the Unknown sources option.

You also need to enable USB debugging on the device.

- On devices running versions of Android earlier than 4.0, go to Settings → Applications → Development and find the option to enable USB debugging.

- On devices running Android 4.0 or 4.1, go to Settings → Developer options instead.

- On Android 4.2, Developer options is not visible by default. To enable it, go to Settings → About Tablet/Phone and press Build Number 7 times. Then you can return to Settings, see Developer options, and enable USB debugging.

As you can see, the options vary considerably across devices. If you are having problems enabling your device, visit http://developer.android.com/tools/device.html for more help.

Run GeoQuiz as before. Eclipse will offer a choice between running on the virtual device or the hardware device plugged into your system. Select the hardware device and continue. GeoQuiz will launch on your device. (If you are not offered a choice and GeoQuiz starts in the emulator, recheck the steps above and make sure your device is plugged in.)

Adding an Icon

GeoQuiz is now up and running, but the user interface would be spiffier if the Next button also displayed a right-pointing arrow icon.

You can find such an arrow in the solutions file for this book (http://www.bignerdranch.com/solutions/AndroidProgramming.zip). The solutions file is a collection of Eclipse projects – one for each chapter.

Download this file and open the 02_MVC/GeoQuiz/res directory. Within this directory, locate the drawable-hdpi, res/drawable-mdpi, and drawable-xhdpi directories.

The suffixes on these directory names refer to the screen pixel density of a device:

mdpi   medium-density screens (~160dpi)

hdpi   high-density screens (~240dpi)

xhdpi   extra-high-density screens (~320dpi)

(There is also a low-density – ldpi – category, but most of the devices with low-density screens are now retired.)

Within each directory, you will find two image files – arrow_right.png and arrow_left.png. These files have been customized for the screen pixel density specified in the directory's name.

In production apps, it is important to provide images for the different screen pixel densities in your projects. Providing different images will reduce artifacts from images being scaled up and down. All of the images in your project will be installed with your app, and the OS will choose the best one for that specific device.

Adding resources to a project

The next step is to add the image files to GeoQuiz's resources.

In the package explorer, reveal the contents of your res directory and find the three subdirectories whose names match those in the solutions file.

Copy the files from each directory in the solutions to the corresponding directory in the package explorer.

Figure 2.7 Arrow icons in GeoQuiz drawable directories

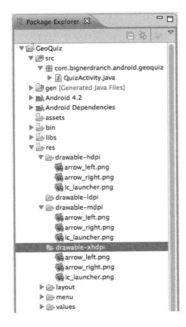

Note that if you drag and drop a file, you will get a prompt like Figure 2.8. Choose to copy the file rather than link to it.

Figure 2.8 Copy. Don't link.

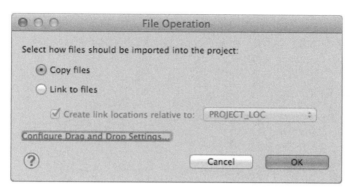

Including images in your app is as simple as that. Any .png, .jpg, or .gif file you add to a res/ drawable folder will be automatically assigned a resource ID. (Note that filenames must be lower-case and not have any spaces.)

After you have copied the files, open gen/R.java and look for your new resource IDs in the **R.drawable** inner class. There are only two new resource IDs: R.drawable.arrow_left and R.drawable.arrow_right.

These resource IDs are not qualified by screen density. So you do not need to determine the device's screen density at runtime. All you have to do is use this resource ID in your code. When the app is run, the OS will determine the appropriate image to display on that particular device.

You will learn more about how Android resource system works starting in Chapter 3. For now, let's put that right arrow to work.

Referencing resources in XML

You use resource IDs to reference resources in code. But you want to configure the Next button to display the arrow in the layout definition. How do you reference a resource from XML?

With a slightly different syntax. Open activity_quiz.xml and add two attributes to the **Button** widget definition.

Listing 2.12 Adding an icon to the Next button (`activity_quiz.xml`)

```
<LinearLayout
    ... >

    ...

    <LinearLayout
        ... >

        ...

    </LinearLayout>

    <Button
        android:id="@+id/next_button"
        android:layout_width="wrap_content"
        android:layout_height="wrap_content"
        android:text="@string/next_question_button"
        android:drawableRight="@drawable/arrow_right"
        android:drawablePadding="4dp"
        />

</LinearLayout>
```

In an XML resource, you refer to another resource by its resource type and name. A reference to a string resource begins with `@string/`. A reference to a drawable resource begins with `@drawable/`.

You will learn more about naming resources and working in the `res` directory structure starting in Chapter 3.

Run GeoQuiz. Admire your button's new appearance. Then test it to make sure it still works as before.

GeoQuiz does, however, have a bug. While GeoQuiz is running, press the Next button to show another question. Then rotate the device. (If you are running on the emulator, press Control+F12/Ctrl+F12 to rotate.)

After you rotate, you will be looking at the first question again. How did this happen and how can you fix it?

The answers to those questions have to do with the activity lifecycle, which is the topic of Chapter 3.

Challenges

Challenges are exercises at the end of the chapter for you to do on your own. Some are easy and provide practice doing the same thing you have done in the chapter. Other challenges are harder and require more problem-solving.

We cannot encourage you enough to take on these challenges. Tackling them cements what you have learned, builds confidence in your skills, and bridges the gap between us teaching you Android programming and you being able to do Android programming on your own.

If you get stuck while working on a challenge, take a break and come back and try again fresh. If that does not help, check out the forum for this book at `forums.bignerdranch.com`. In the forum, you can review questions and solutions that other readers have posted as well as ask questions and post solutions of your own.

To protect the integrity of your current project, we recommend you make a copy in Eclipse and work on challenges in the new copy.

Right-click the project in the package explorer, select Copy, and then right-click again to paste the copied project. You will be prompted to name the new project, and then it will appear in the package explorer ready for work.

Challenge: Add a Listener to the TextView

Your Next button is nice, but you could also make it so that a user could press the `TextView` itself to see the next question.

Hint: You can use the `View.OnClickListener` listener for the `TextView` that you have used with the `Button`s because `TextView` also inherits from `View`.

Challenge: Add a Previous Button

Add a button that the user can press to go back one question. The UI should look something like Figure 2.9.

Figure 2.9 Now with a previous button!

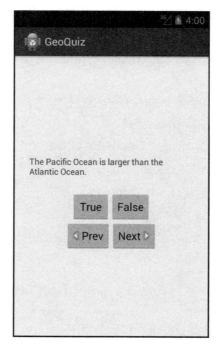

This is a great challenge to do. It requires you to retrace on your own many of the steps in these two chapters.

Challenge: From Button to ImageButton

Perhaps the user interface would look even better if the next and previous buttons showed *only* icons.

Figure 2.10 Icon-only buttons

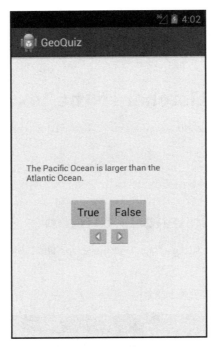

To accomplish this challenge, these two widgets must become **ImageButton**s instead of regular **Button**s.

ImageButton is a widget that inherits from **ImageView**. **Button**, on the other hand, inherits from **TextView**.

Figure 2.11 Inheritance diagram for **ImageButton** and **Button**

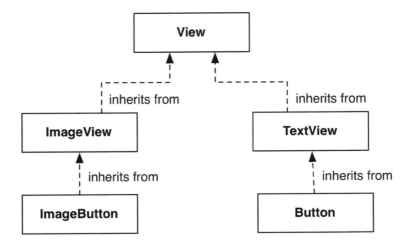

You can replace the text and drawable attributes on the Next button with a single **ImageView** attribute:

```
<Button ImageButton
    android:id="@+id/next_button"
    android:layout_width="wrap_content"
    android:layout_height="wrap_content"
    android:text="@string/next_button"
    android:drawableRight="@drawable/arrow_right"
    android:drawablePadding="4dp"
    android:src="@drawable/arrow_right"
    />
```

Of course, you will need to modify **QuizActivity** to work with **ImageButton**.

After you have changed these buttons to **ImageButton**s, Eclipse will warn you about a missing android:contentDescription attribute. This attribute supports accessibility for low-vision readers. You set the value to a string, and then that string is read aloud when users have the appropriate settings applied.

Finally, add an android:contentDescription attribute to each **ImageButton**.

3

The Activity Lifecycle

Every instance of **Activity** has a lifecycle. During this lifecycle, an activity transitions between three possible states: running, paused, and stopped. For each transition, there is an **Activity** method that notifies the activity of the change in its state. Figure 3.1 shows the activity lifecycle, states, and methods.

Figure 3.1 Activity state diagram

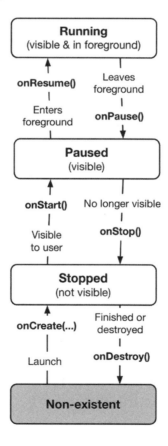

Subclasses of **Activity** can take advantage of the methods named in Figure 3.1 to get work done at critical transitions in the activity's lifecycle.

You are already acquainted with one of these methods – **onCreate(Bundle)**. The OS calls this method after the activity instance is created but before it is put on screen.

Typically, an activity overrides **onCreate(…)** to prepare the specifics of its user interface:

- inflating widgets and putting them on screen (in the call to (**setContentView(int)**))

- getting references to inflated widgets

- setting listeners on widgets to handle user interaction

- connecting to external model data

It is important to understand that you never call **onCreate(…)** or any of the other **Activity** lifecycle methods yourself. You override them in your activity subclasses, and Android calls them at the appropriate time.

Logging the Activity Lifecycle

In this section, you are going to override lifecycle methods to eavesdrop on **QuizActivity**'s lifecycle. Each implementation will simply log a message informing you that the method has been called.

Making log messages

In Android, the **android.util.Log** class sends log messages to a shared system-level log. **Log** has several methods for logging messages . Here is the one that you will use most often in this book:

```
public static int d(String tag, String msg)
```

The **d** stands for "debug" and refers to the level of the log message. (There is more about the **Log** levels in the final section of this chapter.) The first parameter identifies the source of the message, and the second is the contents of the message.

The first string is typically a TAG constant with the class name as its value. This makes it easy to determine the source of a particular message.

In QuizActivity.java, add a TAG constant to **QuizActivity**:

Listing 3.1 Adding TAG constant (QuizActivity.java)

```
public class QuizActivity extends Activity {

    private static final String TAG = "QuizActivity";

    ...

}
```

Next, in **onCreate(…)**, call **Log.d(…)** to log a message.

Listing 3.2 Adding log statement to **onCreate(…)** (QuizActivity.java)

```java
public class QuizActivity extends Activity {

    ...

    @Override
    public void onCreate(Bundle savedInstanceState) {
        super.onCreate(savedInstanceState);
        Log.d(TAG, "onCreate(Bundle) called");
        setContentView(R.layout.activity_quiz);

        ...
```

This code may cause an error regarding the **Log** class. If so, press Command+Shift+O (Ctrl+Shift +O) to organize your imports. Eclipse will then ask you to choose which class to import. Choose **android.util.Log**.

Now override five more methods in **QuizActivity**:

Listing 3.3 Overriding more lifecycle methods (QuizActivity.java)

```java
    } // End of onCreate(Bundle)

    @Override
    public void onStart() {
        super.onStart();
        Log.d(TAG, "onStart() called");
    }

    @Override
    public void onPause() {
        super.onPause();
        Log.d(TAG, "onPause() called");
    }

    @Override
    public void onResume() {
        super.onResume();
        Log.d(TAG, "onResume() called");
    }

    @Override
    public void onStop() {
        super.onStop();
        Log.d(TAG, "onStop() called");
    }

    @Override
    public void onDestroy() {
        super.onDestroy();
        Log.d(TAG, "onDestroy() called");
    }

}
```

Notice that you call the superclass implementations before you log your messages. These superclass calls are required. Calling the superclass implementation before you do anything else is critical in **onCreate(…)**; the order is less important in the other methods.

You may have been wondering about the @Override annotation. This asks the compiler to ensure that the class actually has the method that you are attempting to override. For example, the compiler would be able to alert you to the following misspelled method name:

```
public class QuizActivity extends Activity {

    @Override
    public void onCreat(Bundle savedInstanceState) {
        super.onCreate(savedInstanceState);
        setContentView(R.layout.activity_quiz);
    }

    ...
```

The **Activity** class does not have an **onCreat(Bundle)** method, so the compiler will complain. Then you can fix the typo rather than accidentally implementing **QuizActivity.onCreat(Bundle)**.

Using LogCat

To access to the log while the application is running, you can use LogCat, a log viewer included in the Android SDK tools.

To get to LogCat, select Window → Show View → Other... In the Android folder, find and select LogCat and click OK (Figure 3.2).

Figure 3.2 Finding LogCat

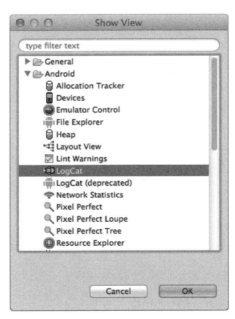

LogCat will open in the right half of your screen and annoyingly shrink your editor. It would be better if LogCat were at the bottom of the workbench window.

To get it there, drag from the tab of the LogCat view to the toolbar at the bottom-right corner of the workbench.

Figure 3.3 Drag from LogCat tab to bottom-right toolbar

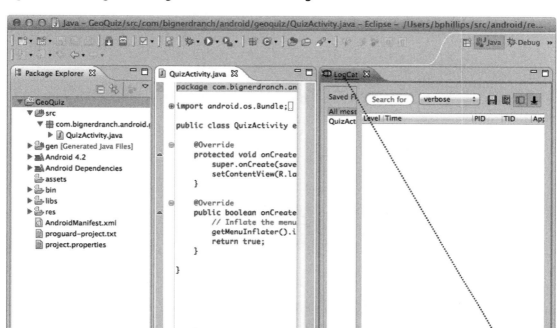

The LogCat view will close, and its icon (a horizontal Andy with Nyan rainbow feet) will appear in the toolbar. Click the icon, and LogCat will reopen at the bottom of the window.

Your Eclipse workbench should now look something like Figure 3.4. You can resize the panes in LogCat by dragging their boundaries. This is true for any of the panes in the Eclipse workbench.

Figure 3.4 Eclipse workbench – now with LogCat

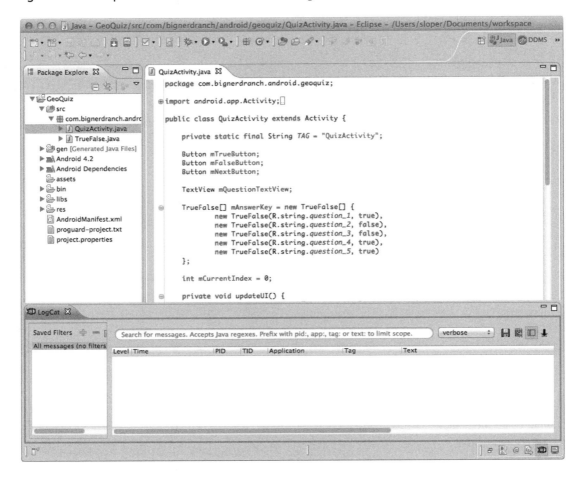

Run GeoQuiz, and messages will start appearing fast and furiously in LogCat. Most of the messages will be system output. Scroll to the bottom of the log to find your messages. In LogCat's Tag column, you will see the TAG constant you created for **QuizActivity**.

(If you do not see any messages in LogCat, LogCat may be monitoring the wrong device. Select Window → Show View → Other... and open the Devices view. Select the device you are currently running on and then return to LogCat.)

To make your messages easier to find, you can filter the output using the TAG constant. In LogCat, click the green + button at the top of the lefthand pane to create a message filter. Name the filter **QuizActivity** and enter **QuizActivity** in the by Log Tag: field (Figure 3.5).

Figure 3.5 Creating a filter in LogCat

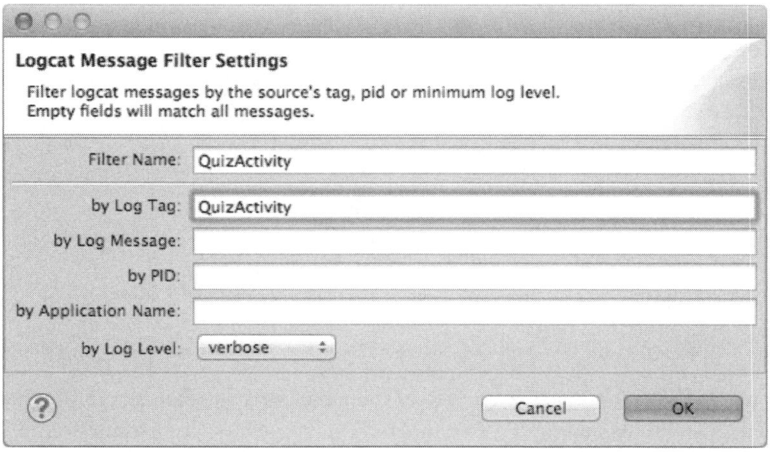

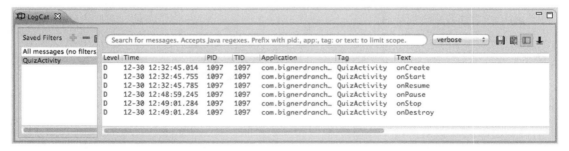

Click OK, and a new tab will open showing only messages tagged **QuizActivity** (Figure 3.6). Three lifecycle methods were called after GeoQuiz was launched and the initial instance of **QuizActivity** was created.

Figure 3.6 Launching GeoQuiz creates, starts, and resumes an activity

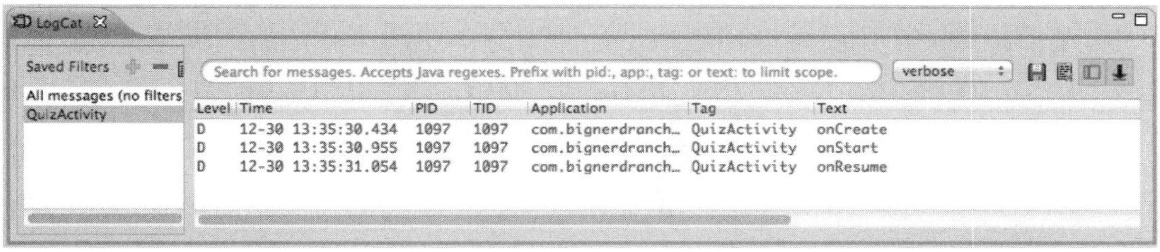

(If you are not seeing the filtered list, select the QuizActivity filter from LogCat's lefthand pane.)

Now let's have some fun. Press the Back button on the device and then check LogCat. Your activity received calls to **onPause()**, **onStop()**, and **onDestroy()**.

Figure 3.7 Pressing the Back button destroys the activity

When you pressed the Back button, you told Android, "I'm done with this activity, and I won't need it anymore." Android then destroyed your activity. This is Android's way of being frugal with your device's limited resources.

Relaunch GeoQuiz. Press the Home button and then check LogCat. Your activity received calls to **onPause()** and **onStop()**, but not **onDestroy()**.

Figure 3.8 Pressing the Home button stops the activity

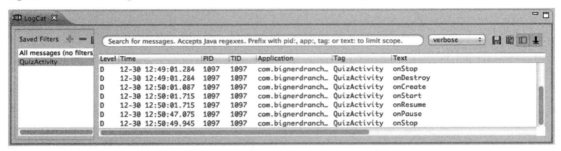

On the device, pull up the task manager. On newer devices, press the Recents button next to the Home button (Figure 3.9). On devices without a Recents button, long-press the Home button.

Figure 3.9 Home, Back, and Recents buttons

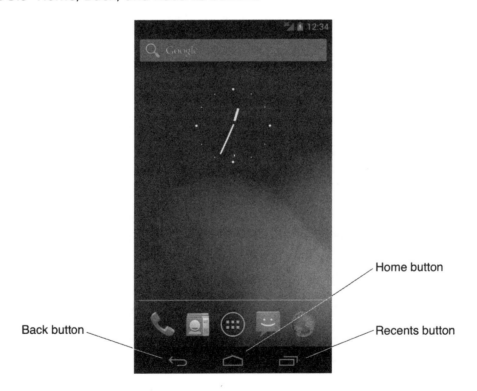

In the task manager, press GeoQuiz and then check LogCat. The activity was started and resumed, but it did not need to be created.

Pressing the Home button tells Android, "I'm going to go look at something else, but I might come back." Android pauses and stops your activity but tries not to destroy it in case you come back.

However, a stopped activity's survival is not guaranteed. When the system needs to reclaim memory, it will destroy stopped activities.

Finally, imagine a small pop-up window that only partially covers the activity. When one of these appears, the activity behind it is paused and cannot be interacted with. The activity will be resumed when the pop-up window is dismissed.

As you continue through the book, you will override the different activity lifecycle methods to do real things for your application. When you do, you will learn more about the uses of each method.

Rotation and the Activity Lifecycle

Let's get back to the bug you found at the end of Chapter 2. Run GeoQuiz, press the Next button to reveal the second question, and then rotate the device. (For the emulator, press Control+F12/Ctrl+F12 to rotate.)

After rotating, GeoQuiz will display the first question again. Check LogCat to see what has happened.

Figure 3.10 **QuizActivity** is dead. Long live **QuizActivity**!

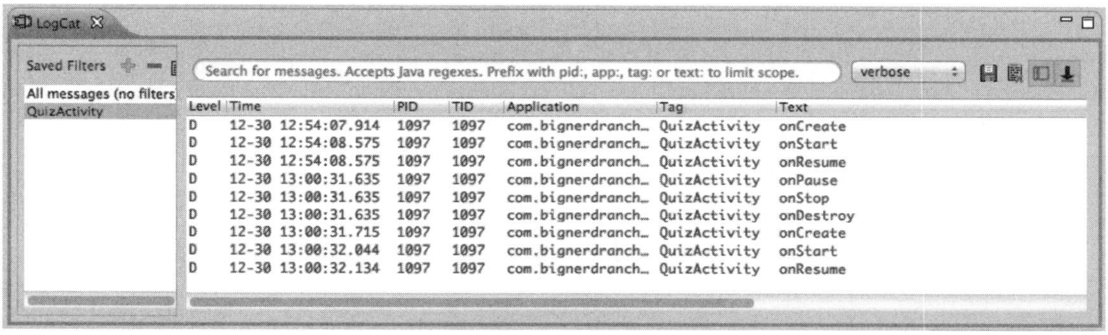

When you rotated the device, the instance of **QuizActivity** that you were looking at was destroyed, and a new one was created. Rotate the device again to witness another round of destruction and rebirth.

This is the source of your bug. Each time a new **QuizActivity** is created, mCurrentIndex is initialized to 0, and the user starts over at the first question. You will fix this bug in a moment. First, let's take a closer look at why this happens.

Device configurations and alternative resources

Rotating the device changes the *device configuration*. The *device configuration* is a set of characteristics that describe the current state of an individual device. The characteristics that make up the configuration include screen orientation, screen density, screen size, keyboard type, dock mode, language, and more.

Typically, applications provide alternative resources to match different device configurations. You saw an example of this when you added multiple arrow icons to your project for different screen densities.

Screen density is a fixed component of the device configuration; it cannot change at runtime. On the other hand, some components, like screen orientation, *can* change at runtime.

When a *runtime configuration change* occurs, there may be resources that are a better match for the new configuration. To see this in action, let's create an alternative resource for Android to find and use when the device's screen orientation changes to landscape.

Creating a landscape layout

First, minimize LogCat. (If you accidentally close LogCat instead, you can always re-open it from Window → Show View...)

Next, in the package explorer, right-click the res directory and create a new folder. Name this folder layout-land.

Figure 3.11 Creating a new folder

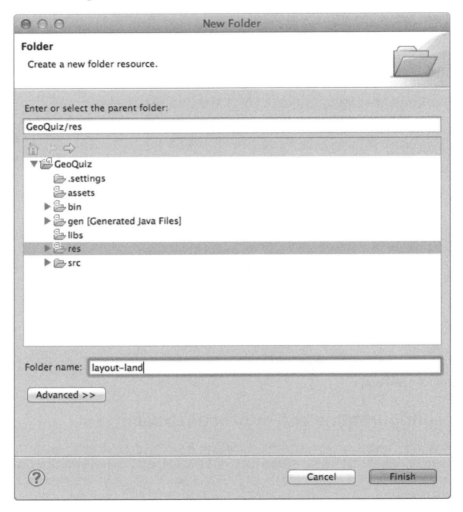

Copy the activity_quiz.xml file from res/layout/ to res/layout-land/. You now have a landscape layout and a default layout. Keep the filename the same. The two layout files must have the same filename so that they can be referenced with the same resource ID.

The -land suffix is another example of a configuration qualifier. Configuration qualifiers on res subdirectories are how Android identifies which resources best match the current device configuration. You can find the list of configuration qualifiers that Android recognizes and the pieces of the device configuration that they refer to at http://developer.android.com/guide/topics/resources/

providing-resources.html. You will also get more practice working with configuration qualifiers in Chapter 15.

When the device is in landscape orientation, Android will find and use resources in the res/layout-land directory. Otherwise, it will stick with the default in res/layout/.

Let's make some changes to the landscape layout so that it is different from the default. Figure 3.12 shows the changes that you are going to make.

Figure 3.12 An alternative landscape layout

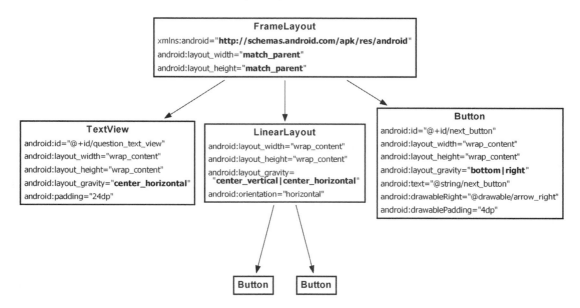

The **FrameLayout** will replace the **LinearLayout**. **FrameLayout** is the simplest **ViewGroup** and does not arrange its children in any particular manner. In this layout, child views will be arranged according to their android:layout_gravity attributes.

The **TextView**, **LinearLayout**, and **Button** need android:layout_gravity attributes. The **Button** children of the **LinearLayout** will stay exactly the same.

Open layout-land/activity_quiz.xml and make the necessary changes using Figure 3.12. You can use Listing 3.4 to check your work.

Listing 3.4 Tweaking the landscape layout (layout-land/activity_quiz.xml)

```xml
<LinearLayout xmlns:android="http://schemas.android.com/apk/res/android"
  android:layout_width="match_parent"
  android:layout_height="match_parent"
  android:gravity="center"
  android:orientation="vertical" >

<FrameLayout xmlns:android="http://schemas.android.com/apk/res/android"
  android:layout_width="match_parent"
  android:layout_height="match_parent" >

  <TextView
    android:id="@+id/question_text_view"
    android:layout_width="wrap_content"
    android:layout_height="wrap_content"
    android:layout_gravity="center_horizontal"
    android:padding="24dp" />

  <LinearLayout
    android:layout_width="wrap_content"
    android:layout_height="wrap_content"
    android:layout_gravity="center_vertical|center_horizontal"
    android:orientation="horizontal" >

    ...

  </LinearLayout>

  <Button
    android:id="@+id/next_button"
    android:layout_width="wrap_content"
    android:layout_height="wrap_content"
    android:layout_gravity="bottom|right"
    android:text="@string/next_button"
    android:drawableRight="@drawable/arrow_right"
    android:drawablePadding="4dp"
    />

</LinearLayout>
</FrameLayout>
```

Run GeoQuiz again. Rotate the device to landscape to see the new layout. Of course, this is not just a new layout; it is a new **QuizActivity** as well.

Figure 3.13 QuizActivity in landscape orientation

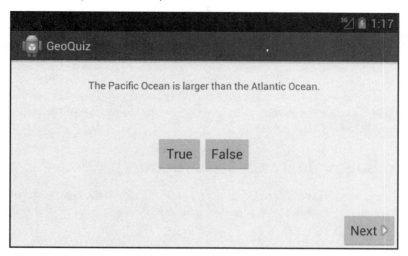

Rotate back to portrait to see the default layout and yet another new **QuizActivity**.

Android does the work of determining the best resource for you, but it has to create a new activity from scratch to do it. For a **QuizActivity** to display a different layout, **setContentView(R.layout.activity_quiz)** must be called again. And this will not happen unless **QuizActivity.onCreate(…)** is called again. Thus, Android destroys the current **QuizActivity** on rotation and starts fresh to ensure that it has the resources that best match the new configuration.

Note that Android destroys the current activity and creates a new one whenever any runtime configuration change occurs. A change in keyboard availability or language could also occur at runtime, but a change in screen orientation is the runtime change that occurs most frequently.

Saving Data Across Rotation

Android does a great job of providing alternative resources at the right time. However, destroying and recreating activities on rotation can cause headaches, too, like GeoQuiz's bug of reverting back to the first question when the device is rotated.

To fix this bug, the post-rotation **QuizActivity** needs to know the old value of mCurrentIndex. You need a way to save this data across a runtime configuration change, like rotation. One way to do this is to override the **Activity** method

```
protected void onSaveInstanceState(Bundle outState)
```

This method is normally called by the system before **onPause()**, **onStop()**, and **onDestroy()**.

The default implementation of **onSaveInstanceState(…)** asks all of the activity's views to save their state as data in the **Bundle** object. A **Bundle** is a structure that maps string keys to values of certain limited types.

You have seen this **Bundle** before. It is passed into **onCreate(Bundle)**

```
@Override
public void onCreate(Bundle savedInstanceState) {
    super.onCreate(savedInstanceState);
    ...
```

When you override **onCreate(…)**, you call **onCreate(…)** on the activity's superclass and pass in the bundle you just received. In the superclass implementation, the saved state of the views is retrieved and used to recreate the activity's view hierarchy.

Overriding onSaveInstanceState(Bundle)

You can override **onSaveInstanceState(…)** to save additional data to the bundle and then read that data back in **onCreate(…)**. This is how you are going to save the value of mCurrentIndex across rotation.

First, in QuizActivity.java, add a constant that will be the key for the key-value pair that will be stored in the bundle.

Listing 3.5 Adding a key for the value (QuizActivity.java)

```
public class QuizActivity extends Activity {

    private static final String TAG = "QuizActivity";
    private static final String KEY_INDEX = "index";

    Button mTrueButton;
    ...
```

Next, override **onSaveInstanceState(…)** to write the value of mCurrentIndex to the bundle with the constant as its key.

Listing 3.6 Overriding **onSaveInstanceState(…)** (QuizActivity.java)

```
        mNextButton.setOnClickListener(new View.OnClickListener() {
            @Override
            public void onClick(View v) {
                mCurrentIndex = (mCurrentIndex + 1) % mQuestionBank.length;
                updateQuestion();
            }
        });

        updateQuestion();
    }

    @Override
    public void onSaveInstanceState(Bundle savedInstanceState) {
        super.onSaveInstanceState(savedInstanceState);
        Log.i(TAG, "onSaveInstanceState");
        savedInstanceState.putInt(KEY_INDEX, mCurrentIndex);
    }
```

Finally, in **onCreate(…)**, check for this value. If it exists, assign it to mCurrentIndex.

Listing 3.7 Checking bundle in **onCreate(…)** (QuizActivity.java)

```
...

if (savedInstanceState != null) {
    mCurrentIndex = savedInstanceState.getInt(KEY_INDEX, 0);
}

updateQuestion();
}
```

Run GeoQuiz and press Next. No matter how many device or user rotations you perform, the newly-minted **QuizActivity** will "remember" what question you were on.

Note that the types that you can save to and restore from a **Bundle** are primitive types and objects that implement the **Serializable** interface. When you are creating custom classes, be sure to implement **Serializable** if you want to save them in **onSaveInstanceState(…)**.

Testing the implementation of **onSaveInstanceState(…)** is a good idea – especially if you are saving and restoring objects. Rotation is easy to test; testing low-memory situations is harder. There is information at the end of this chapter about how to simulate your activity being destroyed by Android to reclaim memory.

The Activity Lifecycle, Revisited

Overriding **onSaveInstanceState(Bundle)** is not just for handling rotation. An activity can also be destroyed if the user navigates away for a while and Android needs to reclaim memory.

Android will never destroy a running activity to reclaim memory – the activity must be in the paused or stopped state to be destroyed. If an activity is paused or stopped, then its **onSaveInstanceState(…)** method has been called.

When **onSaveInstanceState(…)** is called, the data is saved to the **Bundle** object. That **Bundle** object is then stuffed into your activity's *activity record* by the OS

To understand the activity record, let's add a *stashed* state to the activity lifecycle (Figure 3.14).

Figure 3.14 The complete activity lifecycle

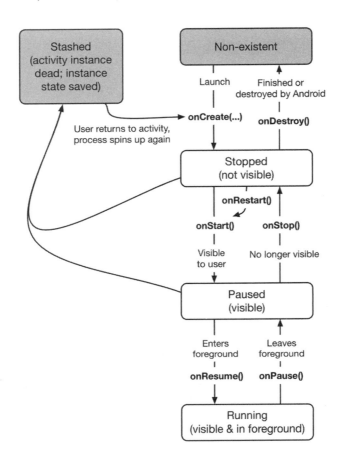

When your activity is stashed, an **Activity** object does not exist, but the activity record object lives on in the OS. The OS can reanimate the activity using the activity record when it needs to.

Note that your activity can pass into the stashed state without **onDestroy()** being called. However, you can always rely on **onPause()** and **onSaveInstanceState(…)** to be called. Typically, you override **onSaveInstanceState(…)** to stash data in your **Bundle** and **onPause()** for anything else that needs to be done.

Under some situations, Android will not only kill your activity but also completely shut down your application's process. This will only happen if the user is not currently looking at your application, but it can (and does) happen. Even in this case, the activity record will live on and enable a quick restart of your activity if the user returns.

So when does the activity record get snuffed? When the user presses the Back button, your activity really gets destroyed, once and for all. At that point, your activity record is discarded. Activity records are also typically discarded on reboot and may also be discarded if they are not used for a long time.

For the More Curious: Testing onSaveInstanceState(Bundle)

If you are overriding **onSaveInstanceState(Bundle)**, you should test that your state is being saved and restored as expected. This is easy to do on the emulator.

Start up a virtual device. Within the list of applications on the device, find the Settings app. This app is included with most system images used on the emulator.

Figure 3.15 Finding the Settings app

Launch Settings and select Development options. Here you will see many possible settings. Turn on the setting labeled Don't keep activities.

Figure 3.16 Don't keep activities selected

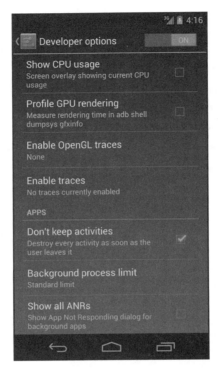

Now run your app and press the Home button. Pressing Home causes the activity to be paused and stopped. Then the stopped activity will be destroyed just as if the Android OS had reclaimed it for its memory. Then you can restore the app to see if your state was saved as you expected.

Pressing the Back button instead of the Home button will always destroy the activity regardless of whether you have this development setting on. Pressing the Back button tells the OS that the user is done with the activity.

To run the same test on a hardware device, you must install Dev Tools on the device. For more information, visit http://developer.android.com/tools/debugging/debugging-devtools.html.

For the More Curious: Logging Levels and Methods

When you use the `android.util.Log` class to send log messages, you control not only the content of a message, but also a *level* that specifies how important the message is. Android supports five log levels, shown in Figure 3.17. Each level has a corresponding method in the `Log` class. Sending output to the log is as simple as calling the corresponding `Log` method.

Figure 3.17 Log levels and methods

Log Level	Method	Notes
ERROR	Log.e(...)	Errors
WARNING	Log.w(...)	Warnings
INFO	Log.i(...)	Informational messages.
DEBUG	Log.d(...)	Debug output; may be filtered out.
VERBOSE	Log.v(...)	For development only!

In addition, each of the logging methods has two signatures: one which takes a *tag* string and a message string and a second that takes those two arguments plus an instance of **Throwable**, which makes it easy to log information about a particular exception that your application might throw. Listing 3.8 shows some sample log method signatures. Use regular Java string concatenation to assemble your message string, or **String.format** if you have fancier needs.

Listing 3.8 Different ways of logging in Android

```
// Log a message at "debug" log level
Log.d(TAG, "Current question index: " + mCurrentIndex);

TrueFalse question;
try {
    question = mQuestionBank[mCurrentIndex];
} catch (ArrayIndexOutOfBoundsException ex) {
    // Log a message at "error" log level, along with an exception stack trace
    Log.e(TAG, "Index was out of bounds", ex);
}
```

4

Debugging Android Apps

In this chapter, you will find out what to do when apps get buggy. You will learn how to use LogCat, Android Lint, and the debugger that comes with Eclipse.

To practice debugging, the first step is to break something. In QuizActivity.java, comment out the code in **onCreate(Bundle)** where you pull out mQuestionTextView.

Listing 4.1 Comment out a crucial line (QuizActivity.java)

```
@Override
protected void onCreate(Bundle savedInstanceState) {
    super.onCreate(savedInstanceState);
    Log.d(TAG, "onCreate() called");
    setContentView(R.layout.activity_quiz);

    mQuestionTextView = (TextView)findViewById(R.id.question_text_view);
    //mQuestionTextView = (TextView)findViewById(R.id.question_text_view);

    mTrueButton = (Button)findViewById(R.id.true_button);
    mTrueButton.setOnClickListener(new View.OnClickListener() {
        ...
    });

    ...
}
```

Run GeoQuiz and see what happens.

Figure 4.1 GeoQuiz is about to E.X.P.L.O.D.E.

Figure 4.1 shows the message that appears when your app crashes and burns. Different versions of Android will have slightly different messages, but they all mean the same thing. Of course, you know what is wrong with your app, but if you did not, it might help to look at your app from a new perspective.

The DDMS Perspective

From the Eclipse menu, select Window → Open Perspective → DDMS.

Figure 4.2 DDMS Perspective

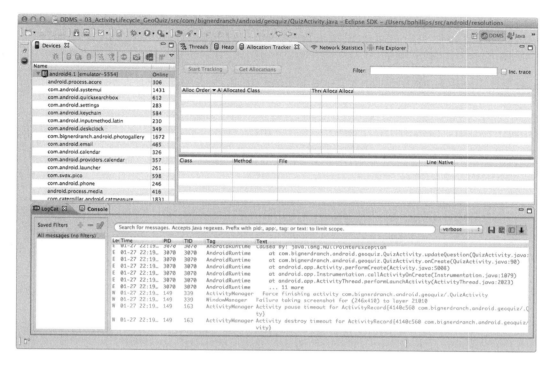

A *perspective* is a pre-defined set of views in Eclipse. You usually want to see different views when you are debugging than when you are editing, so Eclipse puts each set of views together into a perspective.

Perspectives are pre-defined, but they are not set in stone. You can add and remove views from any of them, and Eclipse will remember your choices. If you ever need to start fresh, you can return a perspective to its default state by choosing Window → Reset Perspective...

The default perspective where you have been editing code is called the *Java perspective*. The perspectives that you currently have open are listed near the top-right of the Eclipse workbench, and you can click on those buttons to switch between them.

Figure 4.2 shows the DDMS perspective. DDMS stands for Dalvik Debug Monitor Service. Behind the scenes, DDMS does the footwork for all Android debugging. The DDMS perspective includes LogCat and the Devices view.

The Devices view shows you which devices and virtual devices are connected to your computer. Problems you are having with a specific device can usually be solved in this view.

For example, is your device not showing up as an option when you run an application? Click the downward-pointing triangle at the top-right corner and select Reset adb. Often, rebooting **adb** will find your device. Or is LogCat showing output for the wrong device? No problem – click to select the device you want to see output from, and LogCat will switch to showing output from that device.

Exceptions and Stack Traces

Now back to your app's problem. Expand the LogCat pane so that you can see what has happened. If you scroll up and down in LogCat, you should eventually find an expanse of red. This is a standard `AndroidRuntime` exception report.

Figure 4.3 Exception and stack trace in LogCat

Tag	Text
dalvikvm	Not late-enabling CheckJNI (already on)
ActivityManager	Start proc com.bignerdranch.android.geoquiz for activity com.bignerdranch.android.g
	Activity: pid=3116 uid=10052 gids={1028}
Trace	error opening trace file: No such file or directory (2)
QuizActivity	onCreate() called
AndroidRuntime	Shutting down VM
dalvikvm	threadid=1: thread exiting with uncaught exception (group=0x40a13300)
AndroidRuntime	FATAL EXCEPTION: main
AndroidRuntime	java.lang.RuntimeException: Unable to start activity ComponentInfo{com.bignerdranch
	quiz/com.bignerdranch.android.geoquiz.QuizActivity}: java.lang.NullPointerException
AndroidRuntime	at android.app.ActivityThread.performLaunchActivity(ActivityThread.java:2059)
AndroidRuntime	at android.app.ActivityThread.handleLaunchActivity(ActivityThread.java:2084)
AndroidRuntime	at android.app.ActivityThread.access$600(ActivityThread.java:130)
AndroidRuntime	at android.app.ActivityThread$H.handleMessage(ActivityThread.java:1195)
AndroidRuntime	at android.os.Handler.dispatchMessage(Handler.java:99)
AndroidRuntime	at android.os.Looper.loop(Looper.java:137)
AndroidRuntime	at android.app.ActivityThread.main(ActivityThread.java:4745)
AndroidRuntime	at java.lang.reflect.Method.invokeNative(Native Method)
AndroidRuntime	at java.lang.reflect.Method.invoke(Method.java:511)
AndroidRuntime	at com.android.internal.os.ZygoteInit$MethodAndArgsCaller.run(ZygoteInit.java:7
AndroidRuntime	at com.android.internal.os.ZygoteInit.main(ZygoteInit.java:553)
AndroidRuntime	at dalvik.system.NativeStart.main(Native Method)
AndroidRuntime	Caused by: java.lang.NullPointerException
AndroidRuntime	at com.bignerdranch.android.geoquiz.QuizActivity.updateQuestion(QuizActivity.ja
AndroidRuntime	at com.bignerdranch.android.geoquiz.QuizActivity.onCreate(QuizActivity.java:90)
AndroidRuntime	at android.app.Activity.performCreate(Activity.java:5008)
AndroidRuntime	at android.app.Instrumentation.callActivityOnCreate(Instrumentation.java:1079)
AndroidRuntime	at android.app.ActivityThread.performLaunchActivity(ActivityThread.java:2023)
AndroidRuntime	... 11 more
ActivityManager	Force finishing activity com.bignerdranch.android.geoquiz/.QuizActivity
WindowManager	Failure taking screenshot for (246x410) to layer 21010
Choreographer	Skipped 31 frames! The application may be doing too much work on its main thread.
ActivityManager	Activity pause timeout for ActivityRecord{413bbdc0 com.bignerdranch.android.geoquiz

The report tells you the top-level exception and its stack trace, then the exception that caused that exception and *its* stack trace, and so on and so forth until it finds an exception with no cause.

In most of the code you will write, that last exception with no cause is the interesting one. Here the exception without a cause is a `java.lang.NullPointerException`. The line just below this exception is the first line in its stack trace. This line tells you the class and method where the exception occurred as well as what file and line number the exception occurred on. Double-click this line, and Eclipse will take you to that line in your source code.

The line to which you are taken is the first use of the `mQuestionTextView` variable, inside **updateQuestion()**. The name `NullPointerException` gives you a hint to the problem: this variable was not initialized.

Uncomment the line initializing `mQuestionTextView` to fix the bug.

When you run into runtime exceptions, remember to look for the last exception in LogCat and the first line in its stack trace that refers to code that you have written. That is where the problem occurs, and it is the best place to start looking for answers.

If a crash occurs on a device while it is not plugged in, all is not lost. The device will store the latest lines written to the log. The length and expiration of the stored log depends on the device, but you can usually count on retrieving log results within ten minutes. Just plug in the device, pull up DDMS in Eclipse, and select your device in the Devices view. LogCat will fill itself with the stored log.

Diagnosing misbehaviors

Problems with your apps will not always be crashes. In some cases, they will be misbehaviors. For example, suppose that every time you pressed the Next button, nothing happened. That would be a non-crashing, misbehaving bug.

In QuizActivity.java, make a change to the mNextButton listener to comment out the code that increments mCurrentIndex.

Listing 4.2 Forget a critical line of code (QuizActivity.java)

```
@Override
protected void onCreate(Bundle savedInstanceState) {
    super.onCreate(savedInstanceState);

    ...

    mNextButton = (Button)findViewById(R.id.next_button);
    mNextButton.setOnClickListener(new View.OnClickListener() {
        @Override
        public void onClick(View v) {
            mCurrentIndex = (mCurrentIndex + 1) % mQuestionBank.length;
            //mCurrentIndex = (mCurrentIndex + 1) % mQuestionBank.length;
            updateQuestion();
        }
    });

    ...
}
```

Run GeoQuiz and press the Next button. You should see no effect.

Figure 4.4 Pressing Next does nothing

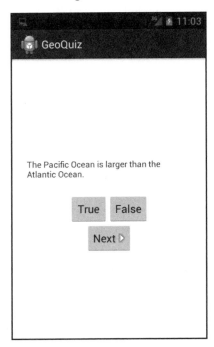

This bug is trickier than the last bug. It is not throwing an exception, so fixing the bug is not a simple matter of making the exception go away. On top of that, this misbehavior could be caused in two different ways: the index might not be changing, or **updateQuestion()** might not be called.

If you had no idea what was causing the problem, you would need to track down the culprit. In the next few sections, you will see two ways to do this: diagnostic logging of a stack trace and using the debugger to set a breakpoint.

Logging stack traces

In **QuizActivity**, add a log statement to **updateQuestion()**.

Listing 4.3 **Exception** for fun and profit (QuizActivity.java)

```
public class QuizActivity extends Activity {
    ...

    public void updateQuestion() {
        Log.d(TAG, "Updating question text for question #" + mCurrentIndex,
            new Exception());
        int question = mQuestionBank[mCurrentIndex].getQuestion();
        mQuestionTextView.setText(question);
    }
}
```

The **Log.d(String, String, Throwable)** version of **Log.d** logs the entire stack trace just like with the AndroidRuntime exception you saw earlier. The stack trace will tell you where the call to **updateQuestion()** was made.

The exception that you pass to **Log.d(…)** does not have to be a thrown exception that you caught. You can create a brand new **Exception()** and pass it to the method without ever throwing it, and you will get a report of where the exception was created.

Run GeoQuiz, press the Next button, and then check the output in LogCat.

Figure 4.5 The results

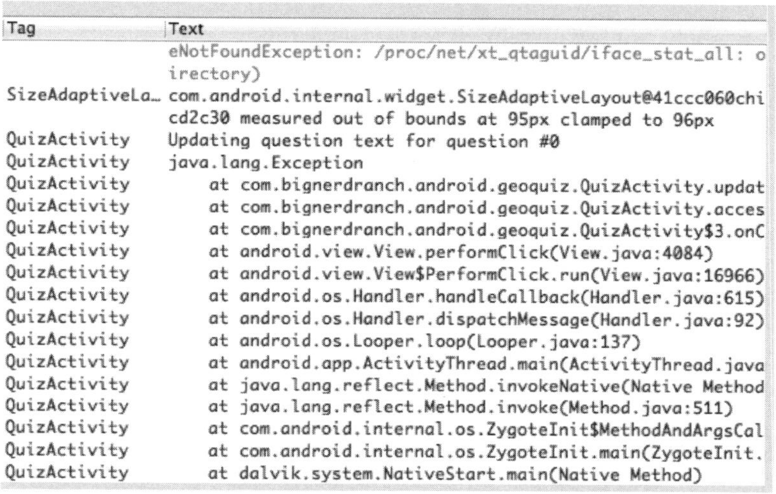

Tag	Text
	eNotFoundException: /proc/net/xt_qtaguid/iface_stat_all: o
	irectory)
SizeAdaptiveLa…	com.android.internal.widget.SizeAdaptiveLayout@41ccc060chi
	cd2c30 measured out of bounds at 95px clamped to 96px
QuizActivity	Updating question text for question #0
QuizActivity	java.lang.Exception
QuizActivity	at com.bignerdranch.android.geoquiz.QuizActivity.updat
QuizActivity	at com.bignerdranch.android.geoquiz.QuizActivity.acces
QuizActivity	at com.bignerdranch.android.geoquiz.QuizActivity$3.onC
QuizActivity	at android.view.View.performClick(View.java:4084)
QuizActivity	at android.view.View$PerformClick.run(View.java:16966)
QuizActivity	at android.os.Handler.handleCallback(Handler.java:615)
QuizActivity	at android.os.Handler.dispatchMessage(Handler.java:92)
QuizActivity	at android.os.Looper.loop(Looper.java:137)
QuizActivity	at android.app.ActivityThread.main(ActivityThread.java
QuizActivity	at java.lang.reflect.Method.invokeNative(Native Method
QuizActivity	at java.lang.reflect.Method.invoke(Method.java:511)
QuizActivity	at com.android.internal.os.ZygoteInit$MethodAndArgsCal
QuizActivity	at com.android.internal.os.ZygoteInit.main(ZygoteInit.
QuizActivity	at dalvik.system.NativeStart.main(Native Method)

The top line in the stack trace is the line where you logged out the **Exception**. Two lines after that you can see where **updateQuestion()** was called from within your **onClick(…)** implementation. Double-click this line, and you will be taken to where you commented out the line to increment your question index. But do not get rid of the bug; you are going to use the debugger to find it again in a moment.

Logging out stack traces is a powerful tool, but it is also a verbose and revealing one. Leave a bunch of these hanging around, and soon LogCat will be an unmanageable mess. Also, a competitor might steal your ideas by reading your stack traces to understand what your code is doing.

On the other hand, sometimes a stack trace showing what your code does is exactly what you need. If you are seeking help with a problem at http://stackoverflow.com or forums.bignerdranch.com, it often helps to include a stack trace. You can copy and paste lines directly from LogCat or save selected output to a text file by clicking the button that looks like a floppy disk at the top-right of the LogCat view.

Before continuing, comment out the TAG constant and delete the log statement in QuizActivity.java.

Listing 4.4 Farewell, old friend (QuizActivity.java)

```java
public class QuizActivity extends Activity {

    ...

    public void updateQuestion() {
        Log.d(TAG, "Updating question text for question #" + mCurrentIndex,
            new Exception());
        int question = mQuestionBank[mCurrentIndex].getQuestion();
        mQuestionTextView.setText(question);
    }
}
```

Commenting out TAG will remove the unused variable warning. You could delete it, but you never know when you will need it again to log messages.

Setting breakpoints

Try using the debugger that comes with Eclipse to track down the same bug. You can set a *breakpoint* on **updateQuestion()** to see whether it was called. A breakpoint will pause execution before this line executes and allow you to examine line-by-line what happens next.

In QuizActivity.java, return to the **updateQuestion()** method. In the first line of this method, double-click the gray bar in the lefthand margin. You should now see a blue circle in the gray bar. This is a breakpoint.

Figure 4.6 A breakpoint

```
private void updateQuestion() {
    int question = mAnswerKey[mCurrentIndex].getQuestion();
    mQuestionTextView.setText(question);
}
```

To engage the debugger and trigger your breakpoint, you need to debug your app instead of running it. To debug your app, right-click on the GeoQuiz project and select Debug As → Android Application. Your device will report that it is waiting for the debugger to attach, and then it will proceed normally.

Once your app is up and running with the debugger attached, your app will pause. Firing up GeoQuiz called **QuizActivity.onCreate(Bundle)**, which called **updateQuestion()**, which hit your breakpoint.

If this is the first time you have used the debugger, you will now see a large rectangle of words about opening the Debug perspective. Open the Debug perspective by clicking Yes.

Figure 4.7 Switch to the Debug perspective

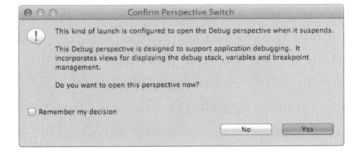

Eclipse will then open the Debug perspective. In the middle of the Debug perspective is an editor view. You can see that this editor has opened QuizActivity.java and highlighted the line with the breakpoint where execution has paused.

Above the editor is the Debug view. This view shows the current stack trace.

Figure 4.8 The Debug view

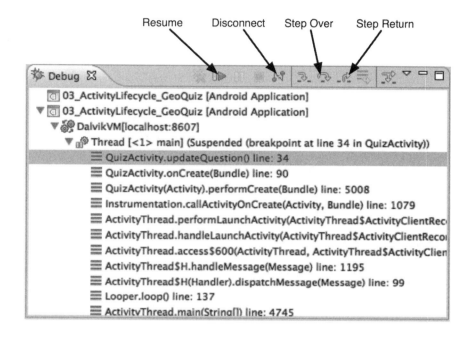

You can use the buttons with the yellow arrows at the top of the view to step through your program. You can see from this stack trace that **updateQuestion()** has been called from inside **onCreate(Bundle)**. You are interested in investigating the Next button behavior, though, so click the Resume button to continue execution. Then press the Next button again to see if your breakpoint is activated (it should be).

Now that you are at an interesting point of execution, you can take a look around. At the top right, find the Variables view. Here you can examine the values of the objects in your program. When you first see this view, you will only see one value: this (the **QuizActivity** itself). Click the disclosure triangle next to this or press the right arrow key to expand it. It should look something like Figure 4.9:

Figure 4.9 A view of your variables

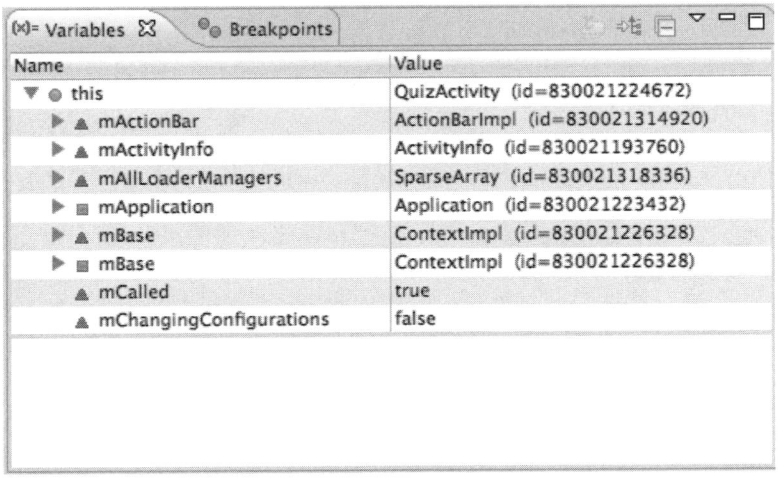

The colorful shapes next to the variable names tell you the variable's visibility:

green circle	public variable
blue triangle	default variable (visible within the same package)
yellow diamond	protected variable
red square	private variable

Your expanded this is a little overwhelming. Your this view includes more than just the instance variables declared in **QuizActivity**. It also includes all the variables declared in its superclass, **Activity**, in **Activity**'s superclass, in its super-superclass, and so on.

You are only interested in one value: mCurrentIndex. Scroll down in the variables view until you see mCurrentIndex. Sure enough, it still has a value of 0.

This code looks perfectly fine. To continue your investigation, you need to step out of this method. Click the button to the right of the Step Over button, whose tooltip reads Step Return. (There is a helper method called **access$1(QuizActivity)** that also gets called, so you will need to click Step Return twice.)

Check the editor view. It has now jumped you over to your mNextButton's **OnClickListener**, right after **updateQuestion()** was called. Pretty nifty.

You will want to fix this implementation, but before you make any changes to code, you need to stop debugging your app. You can do this in two ways: you can either stop the program, or you can simply disconnect the debugger. To stop the program, you choose your program's running process inside the DDMS Devices view and click the red stop sign button to kill the process. Usually it is easier to simply disconnect. To do that, click the Disconnect button labeled above in Figure 4.8. Then switch back to the Java perspective and return your **OnClickListener** to its former glory.

Listing 4.5 Returning to normalcy (`QuizActivity.java`)

```java
@Override
protected void onCreate(Bundle savedInstanceState) {
    super.onCreate(savedInstanceState);
    ...

    mNextButton = (Button)findViewById(R.id.next_button);
    mNextButton.setOnClickListener(new View.OnClickListener() {
        @Override
        public void onClick(View v) {
            //mCurrentIndex = (mCurrentIndex + 1) % mQuestionBank.length;
            mCurrentIndex = (mCurrentIndex + 1) % mQuestionBank.length;
            updateQuestion();
        }
    });

    ...
}
```

You also need to remove your breakpoint. Select the Breakpoints view next to the Variables view. (If you do not see this view, you can open it by selecting Window → Show View → Breakpoints.) From there, you can select the breakpoint and click the dark grey x button at the top of the view.

You have tried out two ways of tracking down a misbehaving line of code: stack trace logging and setting a breakpoint in the debugger. Which is better? Each has its uses, and one or the other will probably end up being your favorite.

Logging out stack traces has the advantage that you can see stack traces from multiple places in one log. The downside is that to learn something new you have to add new log statements, rebuild, deploy, and navigate through your app to see what happened. The debugger is more convenient. If you run your app with the debugger attached (by selecting Debug As → Android Application), then you can set a breakpoint while the application is still running and poke around to find out information about multiple issues.

Using exception breakpoints

If that were not enough decisions to make, you can also use the debugger to catch exceptions. Go back and comment out the line where you assign mQuestionTextView one more time. Then select Run → Add Java Exception Breakpoint... to pull up the exception breakpoint dialog.

Figure 4.10 Setting an exception breakpoint

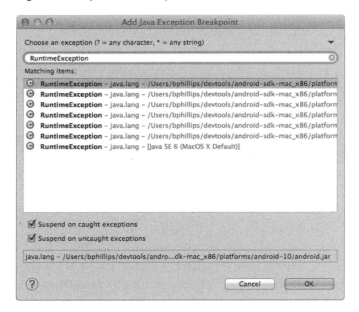

This dialog allows you to set a breakpoint that is triggered when an exception is thrown, wherever it might happen. You can limit it to only uncaught exceptions, or apply it to both caught and uncaught exceptions.

In Android, most exceptions will be caught by the framework, which will then show you the dialog you saw earlier and shut down your process. That means you will usually want to select the Suspend on caught exceptions option for your exception breakpoints.

Next, choose what kind of exception to catch. Type in **RuntimeException** and choose any of the selections that come up. **RuntimeException** is the superclass of **NullPointerException**, **ClassCastException**, and other runtime problems you can run into, so it makes for a nice catch-all.

It will not catch those subclass exception types until you do one more thing, though. Switch to the Debug perspective and look at your Breakpoints view. You should see your shiny new **RuntimeException** breakpoint there. Click on it and check Subclasses of this exception so that your debugger will break on **NullPointerException**, too.

Now debug GeoQuiz. This time, your debugger will jump right to the line where the exception was thrown as soon as it happens. Exquisite.

Now, this is a fairly big hammer. If you leave this breakpoint on while debugging, you can expect it to stop on some framework code, or in other places you do not expect. So you may want to turn it off when you are not using it.

File Explorer

The DDMS perspective offers other power tools for checking out what your application is doing. One particularly handy one is the file explorer. Click the File Explorer view from the tab group on the right.

Figure 4.11 The file explorer

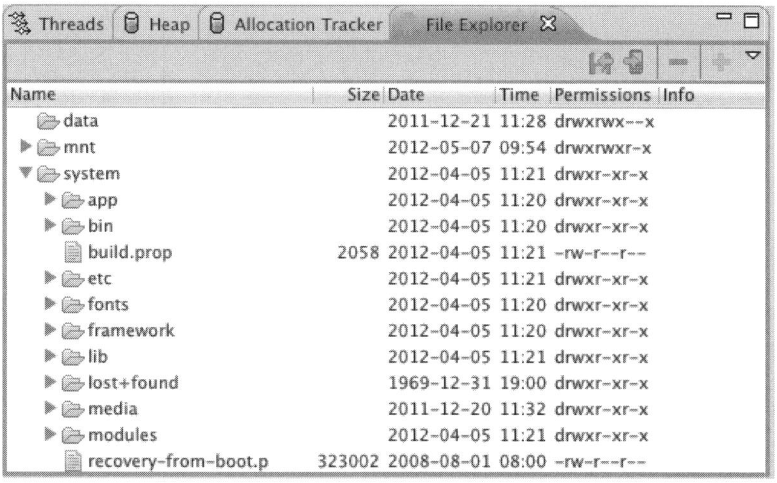

You can use this tool to browse around a device's file system and download and upload files. On a physical device, you will not be able to see inside /data, but on an emulator you can – which means that you can peek into your app's personal storage area. In the latest version of Android, that storage area is in /data/data/[your package name].

Figure 4.12 GeoQuiz's data directory (in an emulator)

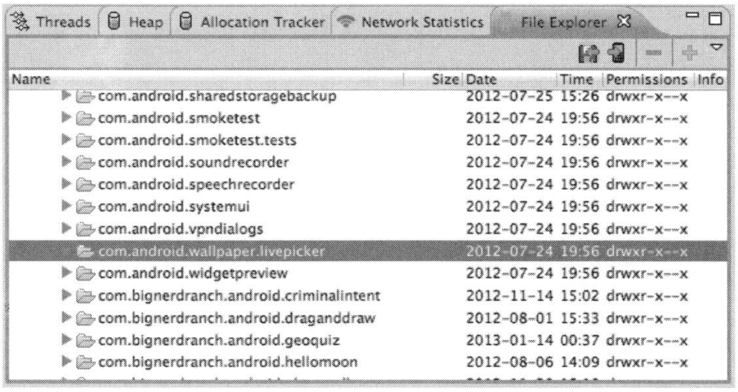

There is nothing to see right now, but in Chapter 17 you will be able to see the files you write to private storage here.

Android-Specific Debugging

Most Android debugging is just like Java debugging. However, you will run into issues with Android-specific parts, such as resources, that the Java compiler knows nothing about.

Using Android Lint

This is where Android Lint comes in. Android Lint is a *static analyzer* for Android code. A static analyzer is a program that examines your code to find defects without running it. Android Lint uses its knowledge of the Android frameworks to look deeper into your code and find problems that the compiler cannot. In most cases, Android Lint's advice is worth taking.

In Chapter 6, you will see Android Lint warn you about compatibility problems. Android Lint can also perform type-checking for objects that are defined in XML. Make the following casting mistake in **QuizActivity**:

Listing 4.6 A simple mix-up (QuizActivity.java)

```
@Override
protected void onCreate(Bundle savedInstanceState) {
    super.onCreate(savedInstanceState);
    Log.d(TAG, "onCreate() called");
    setContentView(R.layout.activity_quiz);

    mQuestionTextView = (TextView)findViewById(R.id.question_text_view);

    mTrueButton = (Button)findViewById(R.id.true_button);
    mTrueButton = (Button)findViewById(R.id.question_text_view);

    ...
}
```

Because you used the wrong resource ID, this code will attempt to cast a **TextView** as a **Button** at runtime. This will cause an improper cast exception. The Java compiler sees no problem with this code, but Android Lint will catch this error before you run your app.

In the package explorer, right-click the GeoQuiz project and select Android Tools → Run Lint: Check for Common Errors to see the Lint Warnings view.

Figure 4.13 Lint warnings

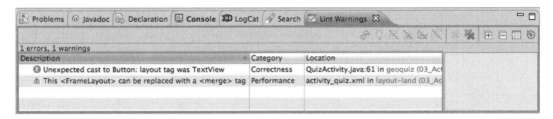

Here you can see Android Lint reporting one error and one warning. You already know about the error: with the wrong resource ID, the cast to **Button** is guaranteed to fail. Go ahead and correct the cast in **onCreate(Bundle)**.

Listing 4.7 Fixing that simple mix-up (`QuizActivity.java`)

```
@Override
protected void onCreate(Bundle savedInstanceState) {
    super.onCreate(savedInstanceState);
    Log.d(TAG, "onCreate() called");
    setContentView(R.layout.activity_quiz);

    mQuestionTextView = (TextView)findViewById(R.id.question_text_view);

    mTrueButton = (Button)findViewById(R.id.question_text_view);
    mTrueButton = (Button)findViewById(R.id.true_button);

    ...
}
```

The warning from Android Lint is less consequential. This warning suggests using a `merge` tag for `layout-land/activity_quiz.xml`. Unfortunately, Android Lint is wrong here. You should not replace **FrameLayout** with a `merge` tag here because you are relying on **FrameLayout** to position your widgets in a specific way.

Issues with the R class

You are familiar with build errors that occur when you reference resources before adding them or delete resources that other files refer to. Usually, resaving the files once the resource is added or the references are removed will cause Eclipse to rebuild without any fuss.

Sometimes, however, these build errors will persist or appear seemingly out of nowhere. If this happens to you, here are some things you can try:

Run Android Lint

Select Window → Run Android Lint. This can often pull the pieces of your project together.

Clean your project

Select Project → Clean. Eclipse will rebuild the project from scratch, which often results in an error-free build.

Recheck the validity of the XML in your resource files

If your `R.java` file was not generated for the last build, you will see errors in your project wherever you reference a resource. Often, this is caused by an XML typo in one of your XML files. Layout XML is not validated, so typos in these files will not be pointedly brought to your attention. Finding the typo and resaving the file should cause `R.java` to regenerate.

Delete your gen directory

If you cannot get Eclipse to generate a new `R.java` file, you can delete the entire gen directory. When Eclipse rebuilds, it will create a new gen directory with a fully-functional **R** class.

If you are still having problems with resources or having different problems, give the error messages and your layout files a fresh look. It is easy to miss mistakes in the heat of the moment. Check out any Android Lint errors and warnings as well. A cool-headed reconsideration of the error messages may turn up a bug or typo.

Finally, if you are stuck or having other issues with Eclipse, check the archives at `http://stackoverflow.com` or visit the forum for this book at `http://forums.bignerdranch.com`.

5

Your Second Activity

In this chapter, you will add a second activity to the GeoQuiz app. An activity controls a screen of information, and this activity will add a second screen that offers users a chance to see the answer to the current question.

Figure 5.1 **CheatActivity** offers the chance to peek at the answer

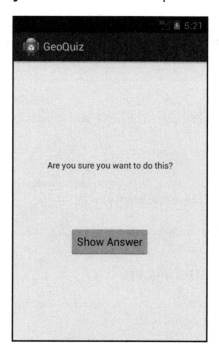

If the user chooses to view the answer and then returns to the **QuizActivity** and answers the question, he or she will get a new message.

Figure 5.2 **QuizActivity** knows if you've been cheating

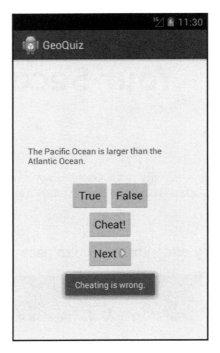

Why is this a good Android programming exercise? You will learn how to

- create a new activity and a new layout without the help of the new application wizard

- start an activity from another activity. *Starting* an activity means asking the OS to create an activity instance and call its **onCreate(Bundle)** method.

- pass data between the parent (starting) activity and the child (started) activity

Setting Up a Second Activity

There is a lot to do in this chapter. You are going to start by creating a new layout for **CheatActivity** and then create the **CheatActivity** class itself.

But first, open strings.xml and add all the strings you will need for this chapter.

Listing 5.1 Adding strings (`strings.xml`)

```xml
<?xml version="1.0" encoding="utf-8"?>
<resources>

  ...
  <string name="question_asia">Lake Baikal is the world\'s oldest and deepest
      freshwater lake.</string>
  <string name="cheat_button">Cheat!</string>
  <string name="warning_text">Are you sure you want to do this?</string>
  <string name="show_answer_button">Show Answer</string>
  <string name="judgment_toast">Cheating is wrong.</string>

</resources>
```

Creating a new layout

The screenshot at the beginning of the chapter shows you what **CheatActivity**'s view should look like.
Figure 5.3 shows the widget definitions.

Figure 5.3 Diagram of layout for **CheatActivity**

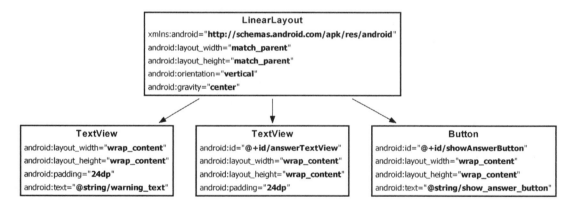

To create the layout file, right-click on the res/layout directory in the package explorer and select
New → Other... Within the Android folder, find and select Android XML Layout File (Figure 5.4). Then
click Next.

Figure 5.4 Creating a new layout file

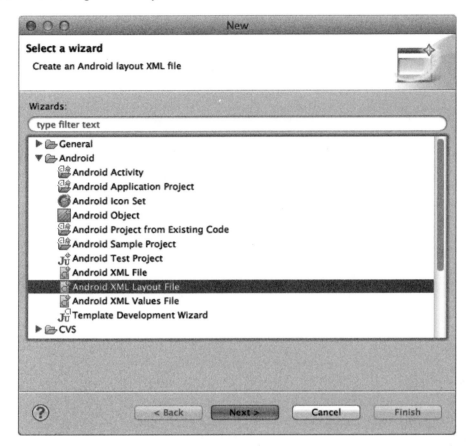

In the dialog that appears, name the layout file `activity_cheat.xml` and select **LinearLayout** as its root element. Then click Finish.

Figure 5.5 Naming and configuring new layout file

When the file opens, navigate to the XML. Notice that this wizard included the line

```
<?xml version="1.0" encoding="utf-8"?>
```

at the top of the file. This line is not required for XML layout files, but it is still added to layout files created from some sources, like this layout wizard.

(By the way, if you are allergic to GUIs, you do not have to use the layout wizard. You can just create a new file named activity_cheat.xml in the res/layout directory and then refresh the res/layout folder so that Eclipse finds it. This is true for most of the Eclipse wizards. Feel free to create XML files and Java class files however you normally would. The new Android application wizard is the only wizard you cannot avoid.)

The layout wizard created the root **LinearLayout** for you. You just need to add an android:gravity attribute and the three children.

Try creating the XML for activity_cheat.xml using Figure 5.3 as a guide. After Chapter 8, we will only show layout diagrams like Figure 5.3 instead of long passages of XML, so it is good to start using them now to create your layout XML. You can check your work against Listing 5.2.

Listing 5.2 Filling out second activity's layout (`activity_cheat.xml`)

```xml
<?xml version="1.0" encoding="utf-8"?>
<LinearLayout xmlns:android="http://schemas.android.com/apk/res/android"
  android:layout_width="match_parent"
  android:layout_height="match_parent"
  android:orientation="vertical"
  android:gravity="center">

  <TextView
    android:layout_width="wrap_content"
    android:layout_height="wrap_content"
    android:padding="24dp"
    android:text="@string/warning_text" />

  <TextView
    android:id="@+id/answerTextView"
    android:layout_width="wrap_content"
    android:layout_height="wrap_content"
    android:padding="24dp" />

  <Button
    android:id="@+id/showAnswerButton"
    android:layout_width="wrap_content"
    android:layout_height="wrap_content"
    android:text="@string/show_answer_button" />

</LinearLayout>
```

Save your file and switch to the graphical layout tool to preview the layout.

You will not be creating a landscape alternative for `activity_cheat.xml`, but there is a way to preview how the default layout will appear in landscape.

In the graphical layout tool, find the button in the toolbar above the preview pane that looks like a device with a green arrow. Click this button to change the orientation of the preview.

Figure 5.6 Previewing `activity_cheat.xml` in landscape

The default layout works well enough in both orientations, so let's move on to creating the activity subclass.

Creating a new activity subclass

In the package explorer, right-click on the `com.bignerdranch.android.geoquiz` package and select New → Class.

In the dialog that appears, name this class **CheatActivity**. In the Superclass: field, type `android.app.Activity` (Figure 5.7).

Figure 5.7 Create **CheatActivity** class

Click Finish, and Eclipse will open CheatActivity.java in the editor.

Add an implementation of **onCreate(…)** that passes the resource ID of the layout defined in activity_cheat.xml to **setContentView(…)**.

Listing 5.3 Overriding **onCreate(…)** (CheatActivity.java)

```java
public class CheatActivity extends Activity {

    @Override
    protected void onCreate(Bundle savedInstanceState) {
        super.onCreate(savedInstanceState);
        setContentView(R.layout.activity_cheat);
    }

}
```

CheatActivity will eventually do more in its **onCreate(…)** method. But, for now, let's move on to the next step: declaring **CheatActivity** in the application's manifest.

Declaring activities in the manifest

The *manifest* is an XML file containing metadata that describes your application to the Android OS. The file is always named AndroidManifest.xml, and it lives in the root directory of your project.

In the package explorer, find and open AndroidManifest.xml in the root directory of the project. Ignore the GUI editor and select the AndroidManifest.xml tab at the bottom of the editor.

Every activity in an application must be declared in the manifest so that the OS can access it.

When you used the new application wizard to create **QuizActivity**, the wizard declared the activity for you. For **CheatActivity**, you have to do it yourself.

In AndroidManifest.xml, add a declaration for **CheatActivity**, as shown in Listing 5.4.

Listing 5.4 Declaring **CheatActivity** in the manifest (AndroidManifest.xml)

```xml
<?xml version="1.0" encoding="utf-8"?>
<manifest xmlns:android="http://schemas.android.com/apk/res/android"
  package="com.bignerdranch.android.geoquiz"
  android:versionCode="1"
  android:versionName="1.0" >

  <uses-sdk
    android:minSdkVersion="8"
    android:targetSdkVersion="17" />

  <application
    android:allowBackup="true"
    android:icon="@drawable/ic_launcher"
    android:label="@string/app_name"
    android:theme="@style/AppTheme" >
    <activity
      android:name="com.bignerdranch.android.geoquiz.QuizActivity"
      android:label="@string/app_name" >
      <intent-filter>
        <action android:name="android.intent.action.MAIN" />
        <category android:name="android.intent.category.LAUNCHER" />
      </intent-filter>
    </activity>
    <activity
      android:name=".CheatActivity"
      android:label="@string/app_name" />
  </application>

</manifest>
```

The android:name attribute is required, and the dot at the start of this attribute's value tells the OS that this activity's class is in the package specified in the package attribute in the manifest element at the top of the file.

There are many interesting things in the manifest, but for now, let's stay focused on getting **CheatActivity** up and running. You will learn about the different parts of the manifest in later chapters.

Adding a Cheat button to QuizActivity

The plan is for the user to press a button in **QuizActivity** to get an instance of **CheatActivity** on screen. So you need new buttons in layout/activity_quiz.xml and layout-land/ activity_quiz.xml.

In the default layout, add the new button as a direct child of the root **LinearLayout**. Its definition should come right before the Next button.

Listing 5.5 Adding a Cheat! button to the default layout (layout/ activity_quiz.xml)

```
    ...
  </LinearLayout>

  <Button
    android:id="@+id/cheat_button"
    android:layout_width="wrap_content"
    android:layout_height="wrap_content"
    android:text="@string/cheat_button" />

  <Button
    android:id="@+id/next_button"
    android:layout_width="wrap_content"
    android:layout_height="wrap_content"
    android:text="@string/next_button" />

</LinearLayout>
```

In the landscape layout, have the new button appear at the bottom and center of the root **FrameLayout**.

Listing 5.6 Adding a Cheat! button to the landscape layout (layout-land/ activity_quiz.xml)

```
    ...
  </LinearLayout>

  <Button
    android:id="@+id/cheat_button"
    android:layout_width="wrap_content"
    android:layout_height="wrap_content"
    android:layout_gravity="bottom|center"
    android:text="@string/cheat_button" />

  <Button
    android:id="@+id/next_button"
    android:layout_width="wrap_content"
    android:layout_height="wrap_content"
    android:layout_gravity="bottom|right"
    android:text="@string/next_button"
    android:drawableRight="@drawable/arrow_right"
    android:drawablePadding="4dp" />

</FrameLayout>
```

Save your layout files and reopen QuizActivity.java. Add a variable, get a reference, and set a **View.onClickListener** stub for the Cheat! button.

Listing 5.7 Wiring up the Cheat! button (QuizActivity.java)

```java
public class QuizActivity extends Activity {

    ...

    private Button mNextButton;
    private Button mCheatButton;

    @Override
    protected void onCreate(Bundle savedInstanceState) {

        ...

        mCheatButton = (Button)findViewById(R.id.cheat_button);
        mCheatButton.setOnClickListener(new View.OnClickListener() {

            @Override
            public void onClick(View v) {
                // Start CheatActivity
            }
        });

        updateQuestion();
    }

    ...

}
```

Now you can get to the business of starting **CheatActivity**.

Starting an Activity

The simplest way one activity can start another is with the **Activity** method

```java
public void startActivity(Intent intent)
```

You might guess that **startActivity(…)** is a class method that you call on the **Activity** subclass that you want to start. But it is not. When an activity calls **startActivity(…)**, this call is sent to the OS.

In particular, it is sent to a part of the OS called the **ActivityManager**. The **ActivityManager** then creates the **Activity** instance and calls its **onCreate(…)** method.

Figure 5.8 Starting an activity

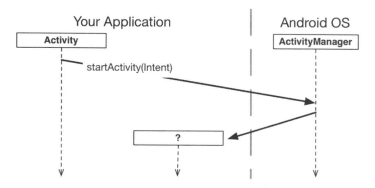

How does the **ActivityManager** know which **Activity** to start? That information is in the **Intent** parameter.

Communicating with intents

An *intent* is an object that a *component* can use to communicate with the OS. The only components you have seen so far are activities, but there are also services, broadcast receivers, and content providers.

Intents are multi-purpose communication tools, and the **Intent** class provides different constructors depending on what you are using the intent to do.

In this case, you are using an intent to tell the **ActivityManager** which activity to start, so you will use this constructor:

```
public Intent(Context packageContext, Class<?> cls)
```

The **Class** object specifies the activity that the **ActivityManager** should start. The **Context** object tells the **ActivityManager** which package the **Class** object can be found in.

Figure 5.9 The intent: telling **ActivityManager** what to do

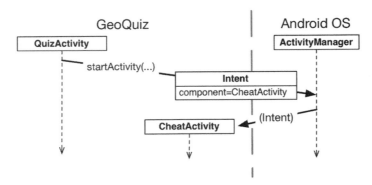

Within mCheatButton's listener, create an **Intent** that includes the **CheatActivity** class. Then pass the intent into **startActivity(Intent)** (Listing 5.8).

Listing 5.8 Starting **CheatActivity** (QuizActivity.java)

```
    ...
    mCheatButton = (Button)findViewById(R.id.cheat_button);
    mCheatButton.setOnClickListener(new View.OnClickListener() {

        @Override
        public void onClick(View v) {
            Intent i = new Intent(QuizActivity.this, CheatActivity.class);
            startActivity(i);
        }
    });

    updateQuestion();
}
```

Before starting the activity, the **ActivityManager** checks the package's manifest for a declaration with the same name as the specified **Class**. If it finds a declaration, it starts the activity, and all is well. If it does not, you get a nasty ActivityNotFoundException. This is why all of your activities must be declared in the manifest.

Explicit and implicit intents

When you create an **Intent** with a **Context** and a **Class** object, you are creating an *explicit intent*. You use explicit intents to start activities within your application.

It may seem strange that two activities within your application must communicate via the **ActivityManager**, which is outside of your application. However, this pattern makes it easy for an activity in one application to work with an activity in another application.

When an activity in your application wants to start an activity in another application, you create an *implicit intent*. You will use implicit intents in Chapter 21.

Run GeoQuiz. Press the Cheat! button, and an instance of your new activity will appear on screen. Now press the Back button. This will destroy the **CheatActivity** and return you to the **QuizActivity**.

Passing Data Between Activities

Now that you have a **QuizActivity** and a **CheatActivity**, you can think about passing data between them. The following diagram shows what data you will pass between the two activities.

Figure 5.10 The conversation between **QuizActivity** and **CheatActivity**

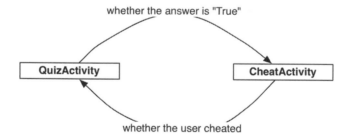

The **QuizActivity** will inform the **CheatActivity** of the answer to the current question when the **CheatActivity** is started.

When the user presses the Back button to return to the **QuizActivity**, the **CheatActivity** will be destroyed. In its last gasp, it will send data to the **QuizActivity** about whether the user cheated.

You will start with passing data from **QuizActivity** to **CheatActivity**.

Using intent extras

To inform the **CheatActivity** of the answer to the current question, you will pass it the value of

    mQuestionBank[mCurrentIndex].isTrueQuestion();

You will send this value as an *extra* on the **Intent** that is passed into **startActivity(Intent)**.

Extras are arbitrary data that the calling activity can include with an intent. The OS forwards the intent to the recipient activity, which can then access the extra and retrieve the data.

Figure 5.11 Intent extras: communicating with other activities

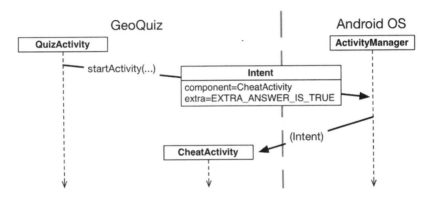

An extra is structured as a key-value pair, like the one you used to save out the value of mCurrentIndex in **QuizActivity.onSaveInstanceState(Bundle)**.

To add an extra to an intent, you use **Intent.putExtra(…)**. In particular, you will be calling

    public Intent putExtra(String name, boolean value)

Intent.putExtra(…) comes in many flavors, but it always has two arguments. The first argument is always a **String** key, and the second argument is the value, whose type will vary.

In CheatActivity.java, add a key for the extra.

Listing 5.9 Add extra constant (CheatActivity.java)

```java
public class CheatActivity extends Activity {

    public static final String EXTRA_ANSWER_IS_TRUE =
        "com.bignerdranch.android.geoquiz.answer_is_true";

    ...
```

An activity may be started from several different places, so you should define keys for extras on the activities that retrieve and use them. Using your package name as a qualifier for your extra, as seen in Listing 5.9, prevents name collisions with extras from other apps.

Next, return to **QuizActivity** and put the extra on the intent.

Listing 5.10 Putting an extra on the intent (QuizActivity.java)

```
    ...
    mCheatButton.setOnClickListener(new View.OnClickListener() {
        @Override
        public void onClick(View v) {
            Intent i = new Intent(QuizActivity.this, CheatActivity.class);
            boolean answerIsTrue = mQuestionBank[mCurrentIndex].isTrueQuestion();
            i.putExtra(CheatActivity.EXTRA_ANSWER_IS_TRUE, answerIsTrue);
            startActivity(i);
        }
    });

    updateQuestion();
}
```

You only need one extra, but you can put multiple extras on an **Intent** if you need to.

To retrieve the value from the extra, you will use

```
public boolean getBooleanExtra(String name, boolean defaultValue)
```

The first argument is the name of the extra. The second argument of **getBooleanExtra(…)** is a default answer if the key is not found.

In **CheatActivity**, retrieve the value from the extra and store it in a member variable.

Listing 5.11 Using an extra (CheatActivity.java)

```
public class CheatActivity extends Activity {

    ...

    private boolean mAnswerIsTrue;

    @Override
    protected void onCreate(Bundle savedInstanceState) {
        super.onCreate(savedInstanceState);
        setContentView(R.layout.activity_cheat);

        mAnswerIsTrue = getIntent().getBooleanExtra(EXTRA_ANSWER_IS_TRUE, false);
    }

}
```

Note that **Activity.getIntent()** returns the **Intent** object that was forwarded in **startActivity(Intent)**.

Finally, in **CheatActivity**, wire up the answer **TextView** and the Show Answer button to use the retrieved value.

Listing 5.12 Enabling cheating (`CheatActivity.java`)

```java
public class CheatActivity extends Activity {

    ...

    private boolean mAnswerIsTrue;

    private TextView mAnswerTextView;
    private Button mShowAnswer;

    @Override
    protected void onCreate(Bundle savedInstanceState) {
        super.onCreate(savedInstanceState);
        setContentView(R.layout.activity_cheat);

        mAnswerIsTrue = getIntent().getBooleanExtra(EXTRA_ANSWER_IS_TRUE, false);

        mAnswerTextView = (TextView)findViewById(R.id.answerTextView);

        mShowAnswer = (Button)findViewById(R.id.showAnswerButton);
        mShowAnswer.setOnClickListener(new View.OnClickListener() {
            @Override
            public void onClick(View v) {
                if (mAnswerIsTrue) {
                    mAnswerTextView.setText(R.string.true_button);
                } else {
                    mAnswerTextView.setText(R.string.false_button);
                }
            }
        });
    }

}
```

This code is pretty straightforward. You set the **TextView**'s text using **TextView.setText(int)**. **TextView.setText(...)** has many variations, and here you use the one that accepts the resource ID of a string resource.

Run GeoQuiz. Press Cheat! to get to **CheatActivity**. Then press Show Answer to reveal the answer to the current question.

Getting a result back from a child activity

At this point, the user can cheat with impunity. Let's fix that by having the **CheatActivity** tell the **QuizActivity** whether the user chose to view the answer.

When you want to hear back from the child activity, you call the following **Activity** method:

```java
public void startActivityForResult(Intent intent, int requestCode)
```

The first parameter is the same intent as before. The second parameter is the *request code*. The *request code* is a user-defined integer that is sent to the child activity and then received back by the parent. It is used when an activity starts more than one type of child activity and needs to tell who is reporting back.

In **QuizActivity**, modify mCheatButton's listener to call **startActivityForResult(Intent, int)**.

Listing 5.13 Calling **startActivityForResult(…)** (QuizActivity.java)

```
...
mCheatButton.setOnClickListener(new View.OnClickListener() {

    @Override
    public void onClick(View v) {
        Intent i = new Intent(QuizActivity.this, CheatActivity.class);
        boolean answerIsTrue = mQuestionBank[mCurrentIndex].isTrueQuestion();
        i.putExtra(CheatActivity.EXTRA_ANSWER_IS_TRUE, answerIsTrue);
        startActivity(i);
        startActivityForResult(i, 0);
    }
});

updateQuestion();
}
```

QuizActivity will only ever start one type of child activity. It does not matter what you send, so here you pass 0 for the required parameter.

Setting a result

There are two methods you can call in the child activity to send data back to the parent:

```
public final void setResult(int resultCode)
public final void setResult(int resultCode, Intent data)
```

Typically, the *result code* is one of two pre-defined constants: Activity.RESULT_OK or Activity.RESULT_CANCELED. (You can use another constant, RESULT_FIRST_USER, as an offset when defining your own result codes.)

Setting result codes is useful when the parent needs to take different action depending on how the child activity finished.

For example, if a child activity had an OK button and a Cancel button, the child activity would set a different result code depending on which button was pressed. Then the parent activity would take different action depending on the result code.

Calling **setResult(…)** is not required of the child activity. If you do not need to distinguish between results or receive arbitrary data on an intent, then you can let the OS send a default result code. A result code is always returned to the parent if the child activity was started with **startActivityForResult(…)**. If **setResult(…)** is not called, then, when the user presses the Back button, the parent will receive Activity.RESULT_CANCELED.

Sending back an intent

In this implementation, you are interested in passing some arbitrary data back to **QuizActivity**. So you are going to create an **Intent**, put an extra on it, and then call **Activity.setResult(int, Intent)** to get that data into **QuizActivity**'s hands.

Earlier, you defined the constant for the extra received by **CheatActivity** within **CheatActivity**. You will do the same for this new extra that **CheatActivity** will send to **QuizActivity**. This is because the incoming and outgoing extras both define the interface for **CheatActivity**. That way, if you want to use **CheatActivity** elsewhere in your app, you are referring to constants defined entirely within **CheatActivity**.

In **CheatActivity**, add a constant for the extra's key and a private method that creates an intent, puts an extra on it, and sets a result. Then call this method in the Show Answer button's listener.

Listing 5.14 Setting a result (CheatActivity.java)

```java
public class CheatActivity extends Activity {

    public static final String EXTRA_ANSWER_IS_TRUE =
        "com.bignerdranch.android.geoquiz.answer_is_true";
    public static final String EXTRA_ANSWER_SHOWN =
        "com.bignerdranch.android.geoquiz.answer_shown";

    ...

    private void setAnswerShownResult(boolean isAnswerShown) {
        Intent data = new Intent();
        data.putExtra(EXTRA_ANSWER_SHOWN, isAnswerShown);
        setResult(RESULT_OK, data);
    }

    @Override
    protected void onCreate(Bundle savedInstanceState) {
        ...

        // Answer will not be shown until the user
        // presses the button
        setAnswerShownResult(false);
        ...
        mShowAnswer.setOnClickListener(new View.OnClickListener() {
            @Override
            public void onClick(View v) {
                if (mAnswerIsTrue) {
                    mAnswerTextView.setText(R.string.true_button);
                } else {
                    mAnswerTextView.setText(R.string.false_button);
                }
                setAnswerShownResult(true);
            }
        });
    }

}
```

When the user presses the Show Answer button, the **CheatActivity** packages up the result code and the intent in the call to **setResult(int, Intent)**.

Then, when the user presses the Back button to return to the **QuizActivity**, the **ActivityManager** calls the following method on the parent activity:

```java
protected void onActivityResult(int requestCode, int resultCode, Intent data)
```

The parameters are the original request code from **QuizActivity** and the result code and intent passed into **setResult(…)**.

Figure 5.12 shows this sequence of interactions.

Figure 5.12 Sequence diagram for GeoQuiz

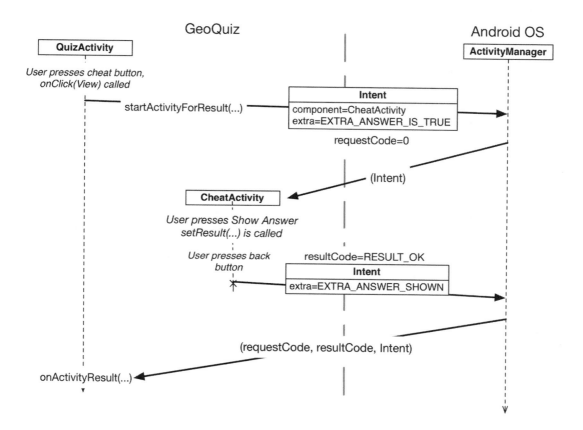

The final step is to override **onActivityResult(int, int, Intent)** in **QuizActivity** to handle the result.

Handling a result

In QuizActivity.java, add a new member variable to hold the value that **CheatActivity** is passing back. Then override **onActivityResult(…)** to retrieve it.

Listing 5.15 Implementing **onActivityResult(...)** (QuizActivity.java)

```java
public class QuizActivity extends Activity {

    ...

    private int mCurrentIndex = 0;

    private boolean mIsCheater;

    ...

    @Override
    protected void onActivityResult(int requestCode, int resultCode, Intent data) {
        if (data == null) {
            return;
        }
        mIsCheater = data.getBooleanExtra(CheatActivity.EXTRA_ANSWER_SHOWN, false);
    }

    ...
}
```

You can see in this implementation of **onActivityResult(...)** that **QuizActivity** has no interest in the request code or the result code. In other cases, you would write conditional code based on those values.

Finally, modify the **checkAnswer(boolean)** method in **QuizActivity** to check whether the user cheated and respond appropriately.

Listing 5.16 Changing toast message based on value of mIsCheater (QuizActivity.java)

```java
private void checkAnswer(boolean userPressedTrue) {
    boolean answerIsTrue = mQuestionBank[mCurrentIndex].isTrueQuestion();

    int messageResId = 0;

    if (mIsCheater) {
        messageResId = R.string.judgment_toast;
    } else {
        if (userPressedTrue == answerIsTrue) {
            messageResId = R.string.correct_toast;
        } else {
            messageResId = R.string.incorrect_toast;
        }
    }

    Toast.makeText(this, messageResId, Toast.LENGTH_SHORT)
        .show();
}

@Override
protected void onCreate(Bundle savedInstanceState) {
    ...

    mNextButton = (Button)findViewById(R.id.next_button);
    mNextButton.setOnClickListener(new View.OnClickListener() {
        @Override
        public void onClick(View v) {
            mCurrentIndex = (mCurrentIndex + 1) % mQuestionBank.length;
            mIsCheater = false;
            updateQuestion();
        }
    });

    ...
}
```

Run GeoQuiz. Cheat and see what happens.

How Android Sees Your Activities

Let's look at what is going on OS-wise as you move between activities. First, when you click on the GeoQuiz app in the launcher, the OS does not start the application; it starts an activity in the application. More specifically, it starts the application's *launcher activity*. For GeoQuiz, **QuizActivity** is the launcher activity.

When the template created the GeoQuiz application and **QuizActivity**, it made **QuizActivity** the launcher activity by default. Launcher activity status is specified in the manifest by the intent-filter element in **QuizActivity**'s declaration (Listing 5.17).

Listing 5.17 **QuizActivity** declared as launcher activity (AndroidManifest.xml)

```xml
<?xml version="1.0" encoding="utf-8"?>
<manifest xmlns:android="http://schemas.android.com/apk/res/android"
  ... >

  ...

  <application
    ... >
    <activity
      android:name="com.bignerdranch.android.geoquiz.QuizActivity"
      android:label="@string/app_name" >
      <intent-filter>
        <action android:name="android.intent.action.MAIN" />
        <category android:name="android.intent.category.LAUNCHER" />
      </intent-filter>
    </activity>
    <activity
      android:name=".CheatActivity"
      android:label="@string/app_name" />
  </application>

</manifest>
```

After the instance of **QuizActivity** is on screen, the user can press the Cheat! button. When this happens, an instance of **CheatActivity** is started – on top of the **QuizActivity**. These activities exist in a stack (Figure 5.13).

Pressing the Back button in **CheatActivity** pops this instance off the stack, and the **QuizActivity** resumes its position at the top.

Figure 5.13 GeoQuiz's back stack

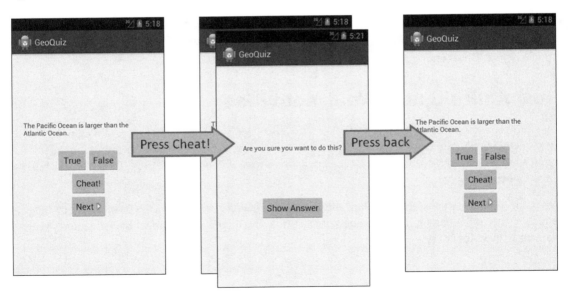

A call to **Activity.finish()** in **CheatActivity** would also pop the **CheatActivity** off the stack.

If you run GeoQuiz from Eclipse and press Back from the **QuizActivity**, the **QuizActivity** will be popped off the stack and you will return to the last screen you were viewing before running GeoQuiz.

Figure 5.14 Looking at Home screen, running from Eclipse

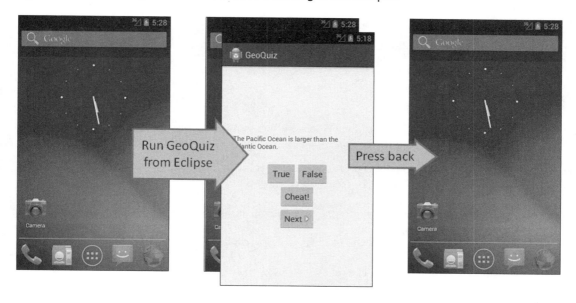

If you started GeoQuiz from the launcher application, pressing Back from **QuizActivity** will return you to the launcher.

Figure 5.15 Running GeoQuiz from launcher

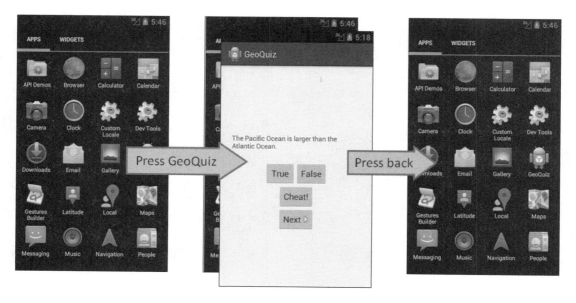

Pressing Back from the launcher will return you to the screen you were looking at before you opened the launcher.

What you are seeing here is that the **ActivityManager** maintains a *back stack* and that this back stack is not just for your application's activities. Activities for all applications share the back stack, which is one reason the **ActivityManager** is involved in starting your activities and lives with the OS and not your application. The stack represents the use of the OS and device as a whole rather than the use of a single application.

(Wondering about the "up" button? We will discuss how to implement and configure this button in Chapter 16.)

Challenge

Cheaters never win. Unless, of course, they persistently circumvent your anti-cheating measures. Which they probably will. Because they are cheaters.

GeoQuiz has a few major loopholes. For this challenge, you will busy yourself with closing them. Here the loopholes are in ascending order, from easiest to hardest to close:

- Users can rotate **CheatActivity** after they cheat to clear out the cheating result.

- Once they get back, users can rotate **QuizActivity** to clear out mIsCheater.

- Users can press Next until the question they cheated on comes back around.

Good luck!

6

Android SDK Versions and Compatibility

Now that you have gotten your feet wet with the GeoQuiz app, let's review some background material about the different versions of Android. The information in this chapter is important to have under your belt as you continue with the book and develop more complex and realistic apps.

Android SDK Versions

Table 6.1 shows the SDK versions, the associated versions of the Android firmware, and the percentages of devices currently running them as of March 2013.

Table 6.1 Android API levels, firmware versions, and % of devices in use

API level	Codename	Device firmware version	% of devices in use
17	Jelly Bean	4.2	1.6
16		4.1	14.9
15	Ice Cream Sandwich (ICS)	4.0.3, 4.0.4	28.6
13	Honeycomb (released for tablets only)	3.2	0.9
12		3.1.x	0.3
10	Gingerbread	2.3.3 - 2.3.7	43.9
9		2.3.2, 2.3.1, 2.3	0.2
8	Froyo	2.2.x	7.5
7	Eclair	2.1.x	1.9

Each "codenamed" release is followed by incremental releases. For instance, Ice Cream Sandwich was initially released as Android 4.0 (API level 14). It was almost immediately replaced with incremental releases culminating in Android 4.0.3 and 4.0.4 (API level 15).

The percentages shown in Table 6.1 will change, of course, but they do reveal an important trend: Android devices running older versions are not immediately upgraded or replaced when a newer version is available. As of March 2013, half of devices are still running Froyo or Gingerbread SDK versions. Android 2.3.7 (the last Gingerbread update) was released in September 2011. In contrast, only 1.6% of devices are running Android 4.2, which was released in November 2012.

(If you are curious, the data in this table is kept current at http://developer.android.com/resources/dashboard/platform-versions.html. You can also find trend data there.)

Why do so many devices still run older versions of Android? Most of it has to do with heavy competition among Android device manufacturers and US carriers. Carriers want features and phones that no other network has. Device manufacturers feel this pressure, too – all of their phones are based on the same OS, but they want to stand out from the competition. The combination of this pressure from the market and the carriers means that there is a bewildering array of devices with proprietary, one-off modifications of Android.

A device with a proprietary version of Android is not able to run a new version of Android released by Google. Instead, it must wait for a compatible proprietary upgrade. That upgrade might not be available until months after Google releases its version, if it is ever available at all. Manufacturers often choose to spend resources on newer devices rather than keeping older ones up-to-date. And sometimes the hardware on an older device is simply not powerful enough to run a newer version of Android.

Compatibility and Android Programming

The delay in upgrades combined with regular new releases makes compatibility an important issue in Android programming. To reach a broad market, Android developers must create apps that perform well on devices running Froyo, Gingerbread, Honeycomb, Ice Cream Sandwich, and Jelly Bean versions of Android, as well as on different device form factors.

Targeting different sizes of devices is easier than you might think. Phone screens are a variety of sizes, but the Android layout system does a good job at adapting. Tablets require more work, but in that case you can use configuration qualifiers to do the job (as you will see in Chapter 22). For Google TV (which also runs Android), though, the differences in UI are large enough that you would usually want a separate app.

Versions are a different story. When releases are incremental, there is little problem with backwards compatibility. However, there has been one especially tectonic shift.

Honeycomb was big

The biggest issue in Android compatibility is navigating the divide between the pre- and post-Honeycomb worlds. The release of Honeycomb was a major shift in Android and introduced a new UI and new architectural components. Honeycomb was just for tablets and Google TV (and not widely adopted), so it was not until Ice Cream Sandwich that these new developments were widely available. Since then, new releases have been more incremental.

Given that more than half of devices still run Gingerbread or older devices, developers cannot make a clean break and forsake that which came before. Eventually older devices will become less prevalent, but this is happening much more slowly than you might imagine.

Thus, Android developers must spend time ensuring backwards compatibility and bridging the gap between Gingerbread (API level 10) and Honeycomb (API level 11) and beyond. Android has provided help for maintaining backwards compatibility. There are also third-party libraries that can help. But maintaining compatibility does complicate learning Android programming.

Often you will have to learn two ways of doing things as well as how to integrate those two ways. At other times, you will learn just one way that seems inordinately complicated because you are addressing at least two sets of requirements.

If you can swing it, we suggest going to sleep for a couple of years. Then you can wake up and learn Android programming once Gingerbread devices no longer make up a meaningful share of the market. If that is not possible, we hope it is at least helpful to understand the reason for some of the complications.

When you created the GeoQuiz project, you set three SDK versions within the new application wizard. (Note that Android uses the terms "SDK version" and "API level" interchangeably.)

Figure 6.1 Remember me?

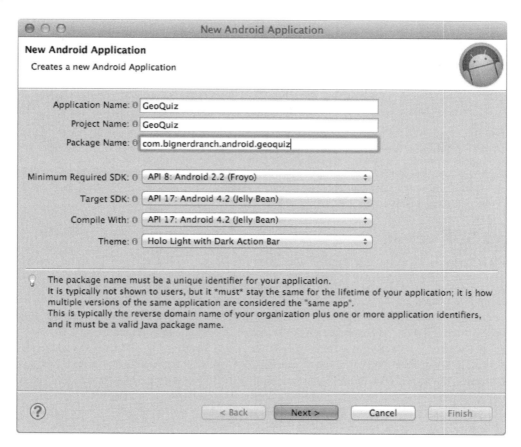

Let's see where each of these settings lives in your project, explain the default choices, and see how to change them.

The minimum required SDK version and the target SDK version are both set in the manifest. From the package explorer, reopen AndroidManifest.xml. Within the uses-sdk element find the values for android:minSdkVersion and android:targetSdkVersion.

Listing 6.1 Finding minSdkVersion in the manifest (AndroidManifest.xml)

```xml
<?xml version="1.0" encoding="utf-8"?>
<manifest xmlns:android="http://schemas.android.com/apk/res/android"
  package="com.bignerdranch.android.geoquiz"
  android:versionCode="1"
  android:versionName="1.0" >

  <uses-sdk
    android:minSdkVersion="8"
    android:targetSdkVersion="17" />

  ...

</manifest>
```

Minimum SDK version

Recall that the manifest is meta-data that the OS uses to interact with your app. The minSdkVersion value is a hard floor below which the OS should refuse to install the app.

By setting this version to API level 8 (Froyo), you give Android permission to install GeoQuiz on devices running Froyo or higher. Android will refuse to install GeoQuiz on a device running, say, Eclair.

Looking again at Table 6.1, you can see why Froyo is a good choice for a minimum SDK version: it allows your app to be installed on 95% of devices in use.

Target SDK version

The targetSdkVersion value tells Android which API level your app was *designed* to run on. Most often this will be the latest Android release.

When would you lower the target SDK? New SDK releases can change how your app appears on a device or even how the OS behaves behind the scenes. If you have already designed an app, you should confirm that it works as expected on new releases. Check the documentation at http://developer.android.com/reference/android/os/Build.VERSION_CODES.html to see where problems might arise. Then you can modify your app to work with the new behavior or lower the target SDK. Lowering the target SDK ensures that your app will still run with the appearance and behavior of the targeted version on which it worked well. Any changes in subsequent releases are ignored.

Build SDK version

The last SDK setting labeled Compile With in Figure 6.1 is the build SDK version. This setting is not found in the manifest. Whereas the minimum and target SDK versions are advertised to the OS, the build SDK version is private information between you and the compiler.

Android's features are exposed through the classes and methods in the SDK. The build SDK version, or *build target*, specifies which version to use when building your own code. When Eclipse is looking to find the classes and methods you refer to in your imports, the build target determines which SDK version it checks against.

The best choice for a build target is the latest API level (currently 17, Jelly Bean). However, you can change the build target of an existing application if you need to. For instance, you might want to update the build target when yet another version of Android is released.

To change the build target, right-click the GeoQuiz project in the package explorer and select
Properties. From the lefthand side of the dialog, select Android and you will see all of your options for
different build targets.

Figure 6.2 Changing the build target

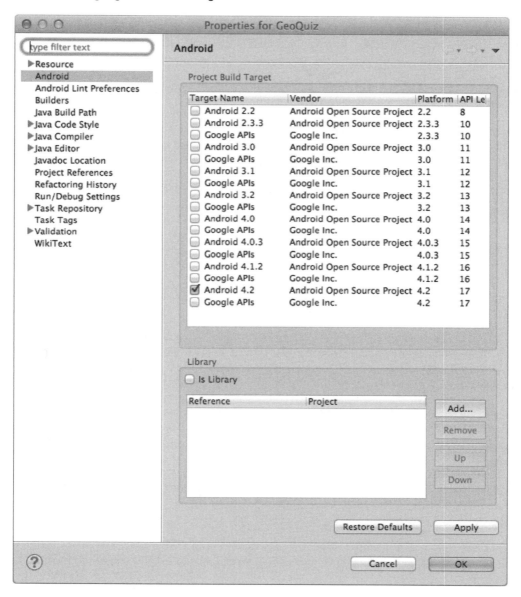

Wondering about the difference between the Google APIs and Android Open Source Project targets?
The Google APIs include the Android APIs plus Google's additions – most importantly the APIs for
using Google Maps.

GeoQuiz's build target is fine as it is, so click Cancel and let's move on.

Adding code from later APIs safely

The difference between GeoQuiz's minimum SDK version and build SDK version leave you with a compatibility gap to manage. For example, in GeoQuiz, what happens if you call code from an SDK version that is later than the minimum SDK of Froyo (API level 8)? When your app is installed and run on a Froyo device, it will crash.

This used to be a testing nightmare. However, thanks to improvements in Android Lint, potential problems caused by calling newer code on older devices can be caught at runtime. If you use code from a higher version than your minimum SDK, Android Lint will report build errors.

Right now, all of GeoQuiz's simple code was introduced in API level 8 or earlier. Let's add some code from API level 11 and see what happens.

Open QuizActivity.java. In **onCreate(Bundle)**, add the following code that creates a subtitle in the action bar that specifies what area of geographic knowledge you are testing.

Listing 6.2 Adding action bar code (QuizActivity.java)

```
protected void onCreate(Bundle savedInstanceState) {
    super.onCreate(savedInstanceState);
    Log.d(TAG, "onCreate() called");
    setContentView(R.layout.activity_quiz);

    ActionBar actionBar = getActionBar();
    actionBar.setSubtitle("Bodies of Water");

    mIsCheater = false;
```

(We are using a literal string here for simplicity's sake. If you really wanted a subtitle or even different subtitles for different groups of quiz questions, then you would add one or more string resources and refer to them here.)

Organize your imports to import the **ActionBar** class. The **ActionBar** class was introduced in API level 11, so this code would crash on a device running a lower version than that. You will see more of **ActionBar** in Chapter 16. Here we will just use it as an example of code that is unfamiliar to Froyo.

After organizing your imports, select GeoQuiz in the package explorer and choose Android Tools → Run Lint: Check for Common Errors. Because your build SDK version is API level 17, the compiler itself has no problem with this code. Android Lint, on the other hand, knows about your minimum SDK version and will complain loudly.

The error messages read something like Class requires API level 11 (current min is 8). Basically, Android Lint will not let you build until you address this compatibility problem.

How do you get rid of these errors? One option is to raise the minimum SDK version to 11. However, raising the minimum SDK version is not really dealing with this compatibility problem as much as ducking it. If your app cannot be installed on Gingerbread and older devices, then you no longer have a compatibility problem.

A better option is to wrap the **ActionBar** code in a conditional statement that checks the device's version of Android.

Listing 6.3 Checking the device's build version first

```
@Override
protected void onCreate(Bundle savedInstanceState) {
    super.onCreate(savedInstanceState);
    Log.d(TAG, "onCreate() called");
    setContentView(R.layout.activity_quiz);

    if (Build.VERSION.SDK_INT >= Build.VERSION_CODES.HONEYCOMB) {
        ActionBar actionBar = getActionBar();
        actionBar.setSubtitle("Bodies of Water");
    }
}
```

The `Build.VERSION.SDK_INT` constant is the device's version of Android. You then compare that version with the constant that stands for Honeycomb. (Version codes are listed at http:// developer.android.com/reference/android/os/Build.VERSION_CODES.html.)

Now your **ActionBar** code will only be called when the app is running on a device with Honeycomb or higher. You have made your code safe for Froyo, and Android Lint *should* be content. However, if you try to run again, you will get the same error.

Suppressing Lint compatibility errors

Unfortunately, Android Lint cannot figure out what you have done here, so you have to suppress the errors explicitly. Add the following annotation before the implementation of **onCreate(Bundle)**. Organize your imports to import `android.annotation.TargetApi`.

Listing 6.4 Giving Android Lint a helpful clue

```
@TargetApi(11)
@Override
protected void onCreate(Bundle savedInstanceState) {
    super.onCreate(savedInstanceState);
    Log.d(TAG, "onCreate() called");
    setContentView(R.layout.activity_quiz);

    if (Build.VERSION.SDK_INT >= Build.VERSION_CODES.HONEYCOMB) {
        ActionBar actionBar = getActionBar();
        actionBar.setSubtitle("Bodies of Water");
    }
}
```

To understand why you need this annotation in addition to the `if` statement, imagine that Android programming is a beach. In the water at this beach, there are sharks – runtime exceptions from using newer methods or classes on older devices. Android Lint is a lifeguard on the beach. It is keeping a lookout, eager to jump in and save you if it looks like a shark is coming near.

The code in Listing 6.4 does two things: it uses shark repellent, and it waves off the lifeguard. The `if` statement is your shark repellent. Wrapped in that `if` statement, the **getActionBar()** method will only be called when it is available, and the sharks will not attack you. The `@TargetApi(11)` annotation is waving off the lifeguard (Android Lint) saying, "Don't worry about these sharks – I've got it under control." Then the lifeguard will refrain from swooping down to pull you out of the water.

So if you wave off the lifeguard with the `@TargetApi` annotation, please make sure you are wearing your `SDK_INT` shark repellent. Otherwise, you will be eaten by runtime exception sharks.

Run GeoQuiz on a Honeycomb or higher device and check out your new subtitle.

Figure 6.3 Action bar with subtitle

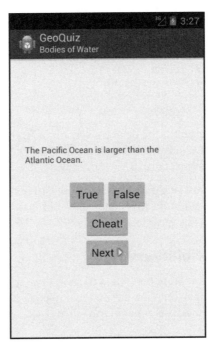

You can also run GeoQuiz on a Froyo or Gingerbread device (virtual or otherwise). It will not have an action bar or a subtitle, but you can confirm that the app still runs safely.

Using the Android Developer Documentation

Android Lint errors will tell you what API level your incompatible code is from. But you can also find out which API level particular classes and methods belong to in Android's developer documentation.

It is good to get comfortable using the developer documentation right away. There is far too much in the Android SDKs to keep in your head, and, with new versions appearing regularly, you will need to learn what is new and how to use it.

The Android developer documentation is an excellent and voluminous source of information. The main page of the documentation is http://developer.android.com/. It is split into three parts: Design, Develop, and Distribute. The Design section of the documentation includes patterns and principles for the UI design of your apps. The Develop section contains documentation and training. The Distribute section shows you how to prepare and publish your apps on Google Play or through open distribution. It is all worth perusing when you get a chance.

The Develop section is further divided into four areas:

Android Training   beginning and advanced developer training modules including
                          downloadable sample code

API Guides   topic-based descriptions of app components, features, and best practices

Reference   searchable, linked documentation of every class, method, interface, attribute constant, etc. in the SDK

Tools   Descriptions and links to developer tools

You do not have to be online to have access to the documentation. If you navigate on your filesystem to where you have downloaded the SDKs, there is a docs directory that contains the complete documentation.

To determine what API level **getActionBar()** belongs to, search for this method using the search bar at the top-right of the browser. The first result will be an API Guide concerning the action bar. However, what you want are results from the reference section. Filter the search results by clicking Reference on the lefthand side.

Select the first result, and you will be sent to the **Activity** class reference page. At the top of this page are links to its different sections. Click the Methods link to see a list of **Activity**'s methods.

Figure 6.4 **Activity** reference page

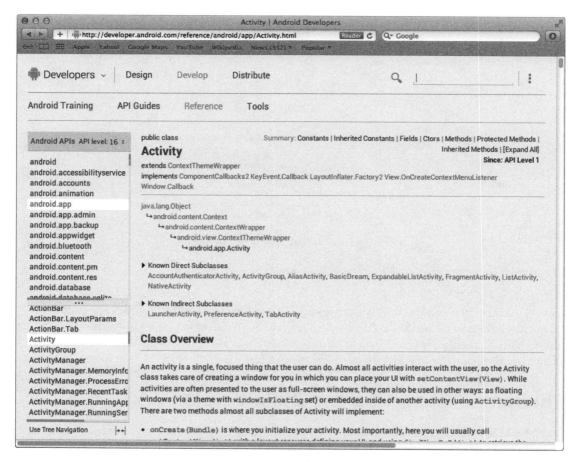

Scroll down, find the **getActionBar()** method, and click on the method name to see a description. To the right of the method signature, you can see that **getActionBar()** was introduced in API level 11.

If you want to see which **Activity** methods are available in, say, API level 8, you can filter the reference by API level. On the lefthand side of the page where the classes are indexed by package, find where it says API level: 17. Click the adjacent control and select 8 from the list. Everything that Android has introduced after API level 8 will be grayed-out.

Figure 6.5 **Activity** methods filtered for API level 8

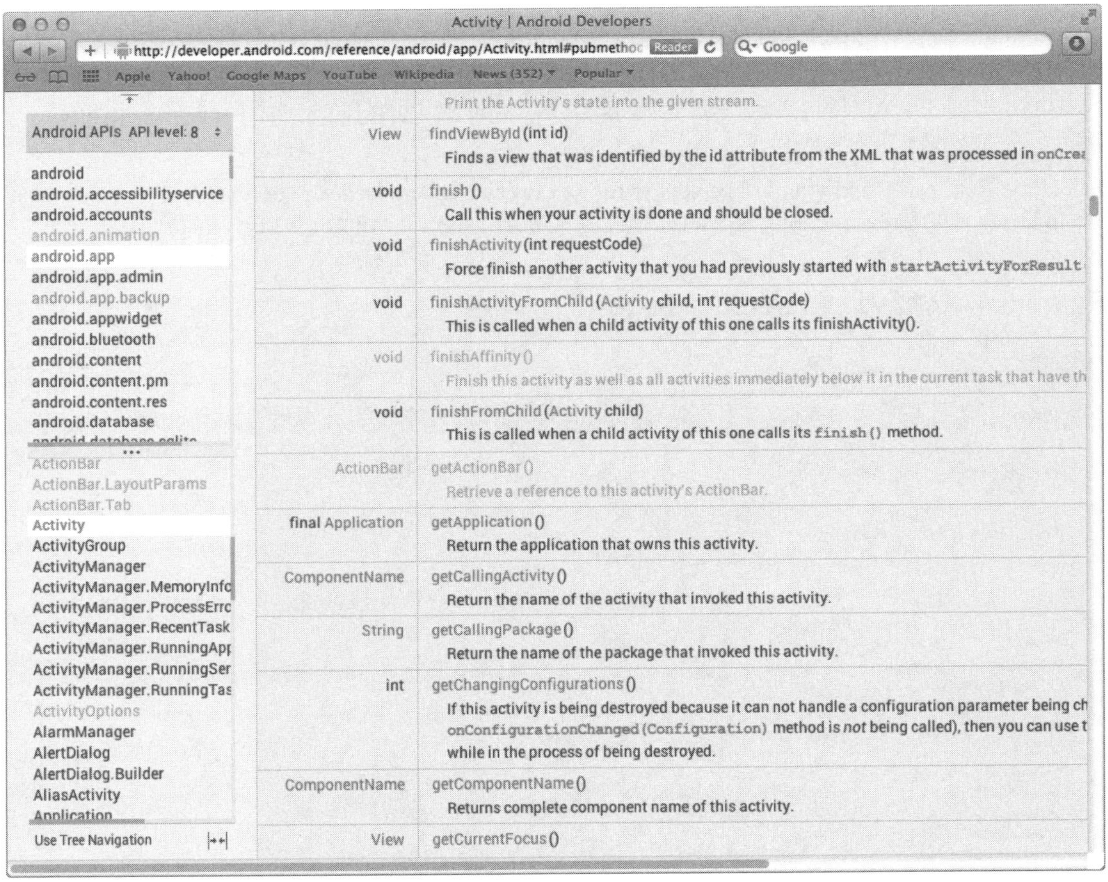

As you continue through this book, be sure to visit the documentation often. You will certainly need the documentation to tackle the challenge exercises, but also consider exploring whenever you get curious about particular classes, methods, or other topics. Android is always updating and improving the documentation, so there is always something new to learn.

Challenge: Reporting the Build Version

Add a **TextView** widget to the GeoQuiz layout that reports the API level that the device is running to the user.

Figure 6.6 Finished challenge

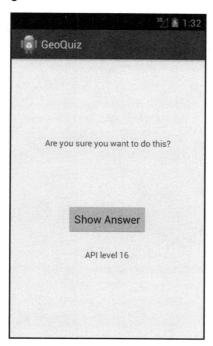

You cannot set this **TextView**'s text in the layout because you will not know the device's build version until runtime. Find the **TextView** method for setting text in the **TextView** reference page in Android's documentation. You are looking for a method that accepts a single argument – a string (or a **CharSequence**).

Use other XML attributes listed in the **TextView** reference to adjust the size or typeface of the text.

7

UI Fragments and the Fragment Manager

In this chapter, you will start building an application named CriminalIntent. CriminalIntent records the details of "office crimes" – things like leaving dirty dishes in the breakroom sink or walking away from an empty shared printer after your documents have printed.

With CriminalIntent, you can make a record of a crime including a title, a date, and a photo. You can also identify a suspect from your contacts and lodge a complaint via email, Twitter, Facebook, or other app. After documenting and reporting a crime, you can proceed with your work free of resentment and ready to focus on the business at hand.

CriminalIntent is a complex app that will take thirteen chapters to complete. It will have a list-detail interface: The main screen will display a list of recorded crimes. Users will be able add new crimes or select an existing crime to view and edit its details.

Figure 7.1 CriminalIntent, a list-detail app

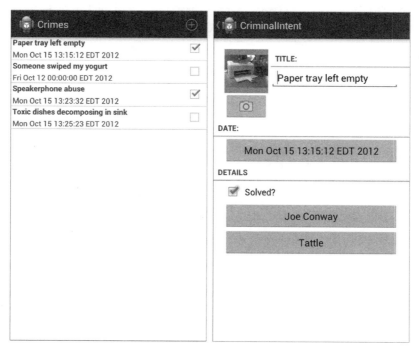

The Need for UI Flexibility

You might imagine that a list-detail application consists of two activities: one managing the list and the other managing the detail view. Clicking a crime in the list would start an instance of the detail activity. Pressing the Back button would destroy the detail activity and return you to the list where you could select another crime.

That would work, but what if you wanted more sophisticated presentation and navigation between screens?

- Imagine that your user is running CriminalIntent on a tablet. Tablets and some larger phones have screens large enough to show the list and detail at the same time – at least in landscape orientation.

Figure 7.2 Ideal list-detail interface for phone and tablet

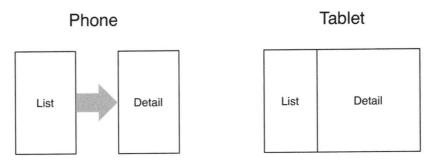

- Imagine the user is viewing a crime on a phone and wants to see the next crime in the list. It would be better if the user could swipe to see the next crime without having to return to the list. Each swipe should update the detail view with information for the next crime.

What these scenarios have in common is UI flexibility: the ability to compose and recompose an activity's view at runtime depending on what the user or the device requires.

Activities were not built to provide this flexibility. An activity's views may change at runtime, but the code to control those views must live inside the activity As a result, activities were tightly coupled to a particular screen used by the user.

Introducing Fragments

You can get around the letter of the law of Android by moving the app's UI management from the activity to one or more *fragments*.

A *fragment* is a controller object that an activity can deputize to perform tasks. Most commonly, the task is managing a user interface. The user interface can be an entire screen or just one part of the screen.

A fragment managing a user interface is known as a *UI fragment*. A UI fragment has a view of its own that is inflated from a layout file. The fragment's view contains the interesting UI elements that the user wants to see and interact with.

The activity's view contains a spot where the fragment's view will be inserted. Or it might have several spots for the views of several fragments.

You can use the fragment(s) associated with the activity to compose and re-compose the screen as your app and users require. The activity's view technically stays the same throughout its lifetime, and no laws of Android are violated.

Let's see how this would work in a list-detail application when displaying the list and detail together. You would compose the activity's view from a list fragment and a detail fragment. The detail view would show the details of the selected list item.

Selecting another item should display a new detail view. This is easy with fragments; the activity will replace the detail fragment with another detail fragment (Figure 7.3). No activities need to die for this major view change to happen.

Figure 7.3 Detail fragment is swapped out

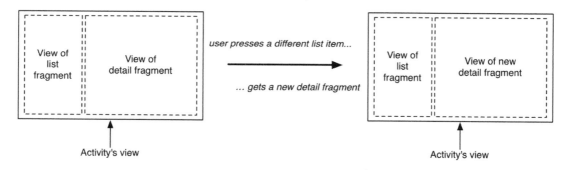

Using UI fragments separates the UI of your app into building blocks, which is useful for more than just list-detail applications. Working with individual blocks, it is easy to build tab interfaces, tack on animated sidebars, and more.

Achieving this UI flexibility comes at a cost: more complexity, more moving parts, and more code. You will reap the benefits of using fragments in Chapter 11 and Chapter 22. The complexity, however, starts now.

Starting CriminalIntent

In this chapter, you are going to start on the detail part of CriminalIntent. Figure 7.4 shows you what CriminalIntent will look like at the end of this chapter.

It may not seem like a very exciting goal to shoot for. Just keep in mind that this chapter is about laying the foundation to do bigger things later.

Figure 7.4 CriminalIntent at the end of this chapter

The screen shown in Figure 7.4 will be managed by a UI fragment named **CrimeFragment**. An instance of **CrimeFragment** will be *hosted* by an activity named **CrimeActivity**.

For now, think of hosting as the activity providing a spot in its view hierarchy where the fragment can place its view (Figure 7.5). A fragment is incapable of getting a view on screen itself. Only when it is placed in an activity's hierarchy will its view appear.

Figure 7.5 **CrimeActivity** hosting a **CrimeFragment**

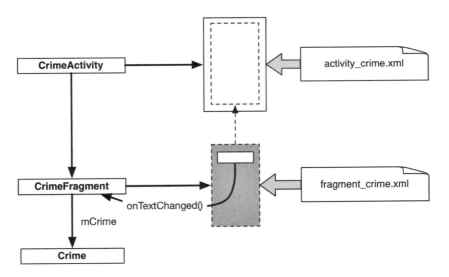

CriminalIntent will be a large project, and one way to keep your head wrapped around a project is with an object diagram. Figure 7.6 gives you the big picture of CriminalIntent. You do not have to memorize these objects and their relationships, but it is good to have an idea of where you are heading before you start.

You can see that **CrimeFragment** will do the sort of work that your activities did in GeoQuiz: create and manage the user interface and interact with the model objects.

Figure 7.6 Object diagram for CriminalIntent (for this chapter)

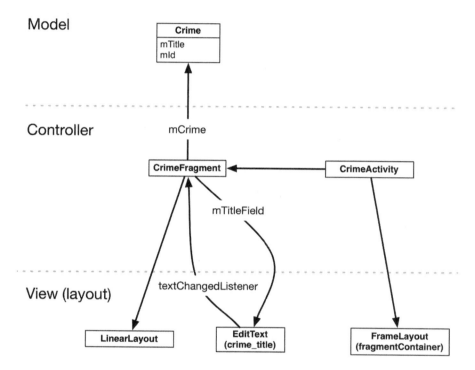

Three of the classes shown in Figure 7.6 are classes that you will write: **Crime**, **CrimeFragment**, and **CrimeActivity**.

An instance of **Crime** will represent a single office crime. In this chapter, a crime will have only a title and an ID. The title is a descriptive name, like "Toxic sink dump" or "Someone stole my yogurt!". The ID will uniquely identify an instance of **Crime**.

For this chapter, you will keep things very simple and use a single instance of **Crime**. **CrimeFragment** will have a member variable (mCrime) to hold this isolated incident.

CrimeActivity's view will consist of a **FrameLayout** that defines the spot where the **CrimeFragment**'s view will appear.

CrimeFragment's view will consist of a **LinearLayout** and an **EditText**. **CrimeFragment** will have a member variable for the **EditText** (mTitleField) and will set a listener on it to update the model layer when the text changes.

Creating a new project

Enough talk; time to build a new app. Create a new Android application (New →
Android Application Project). Name the application CriminalIntent and name the package
com.bignerdranch.android.criminalintent, as shown in Figure 7.7. Build to the latest APIs and
ensure that the app is compatible with devices running Froyo.

Figure 7.7 Creating the CriminalIntent application

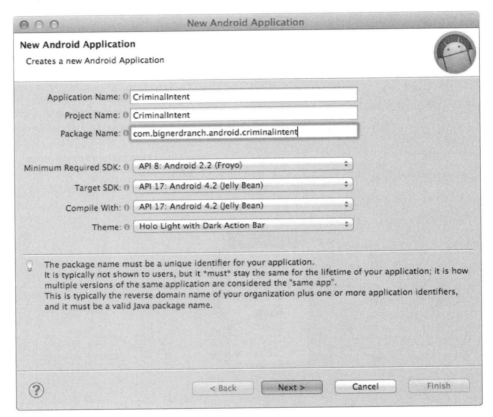

In the next dialog, uncheck the box to create a custom launcher icon and click Next. After that, choose
to create an activity using the blank activity template and click Next.

Finally, name the activity **CrimeActivity** and click Finish (Figure 7.8).

Figure 7.8 Configuring **CrimeActivity**

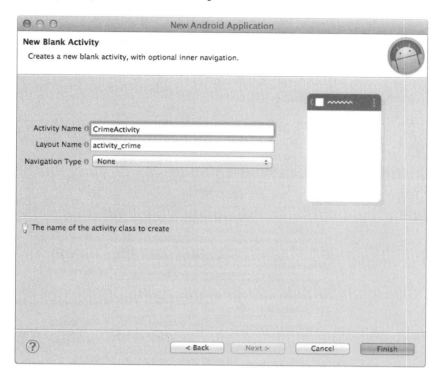

Fragments and the support library

Fragments were introduced in API level 11 along with the first Android tablets and the sudden need for UI flexibility. You have created CriminalIntent with a minimum required SDK of 8, so you must find a way to ensure its compatibility with older versions of Android.

Fortunately, in the case of fragments, ensuring backwards-compatibility is relatively painless: you simply use the fragment-related classes found in Android's *support library*.

The *support library* is already a part of your project. You can find the support library under libs/ android-support-v4.jar where it was added by the template. The support library includes a **Fragment** class (**android.support.v4.app.Fragment**) that you can use on any Android device running API level 4 or higher.

When you use a support library class, it is not just used on older versions where no native class is available; it is also used on newer versions instead of the native class.

Another important support library class is **FragmentActivity** (**android.support.v4.app.FragmentActivity**). Using fragments requires activities that know how to manage fragments. In Honeycomb and later versions of Android, all **Activity** subclasses know how to manage fragments. In earlier versions, **Activity** knows nothing about fragments – and neither will your **Activity** subclass. For compatibility with lower API levels, you subclass **FragmentActivity** instead. **FragmentActivity** is an **Activity** subclass that provides the fragment-managing capabilities of the newer **Activity** class, even on earlier Android versions.

Figure 7.9 Where the different fragment classes live

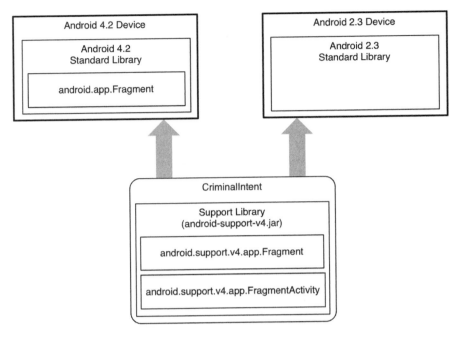

Figure 7.9 shows you the name of each of these classes and where they live. Since the support library (and **android.support.v4.app.Fragment**) lives with your application, it is safe to use no matter where your app is running.

In the package explorer, find and open CrimeActivity.java. Change **CrimeActivity**'s superclass to **FragmentActivity**. While you are there, remove the template's implementation of **onCreateOptionsMenu(Menu)**. (You will be creating an options menu for CriminalIntent from scratch in Chapter 16.)

Listing 7.1 Tweaking template code (CrimeActivity.java)

```
public class CrimeActivity extends Activity FragmentActivity {

    @Override
    public void onCreate(Bundle savedInstanceState) {
        super.onCreate(savedInstanceState);
        setContentView(R.layout.activity_crime);
    }

    @Override
    public boolean onCreateOptionsMenu(Menu menu) {
        getMenuInflater().inflate(R.menu.activity_crime, menu);
        return true;
    }
}
```

Before proceeding further with **CrimeActivity**, let's create the model layer for CriminalIntent by writing the **Crime** class.

Creating the Crime class

In the package explorer, right-click the com.bignerdranch.android.criminalintent package and select New → Class. Name the class **Crime**, leave its superclass as **java.lang.Object**, and click Finish.

In Crime.java, add the following code:

Listing 7.2 Adding to **Crime** class (Crime.java)

```
public class Crime {

    private UUID mId;
    private String mTitle;

    public Crime() {
        // Generate unique identifier
        mId = UUID.randomUUID();
    }
}
```

Next, you want to generate only a getter for the read-only mId and both a getter and setter for mTitle. Right-click after the constructor and select Source → Generate Getters and Setters. To generate only a getter for mId, click the arrow to the left of the variable name to reveal the possible methods and check only the box beside **getId()**, as shown in Figure 7.10.

Figure 7.10 Generate two getters and one setter

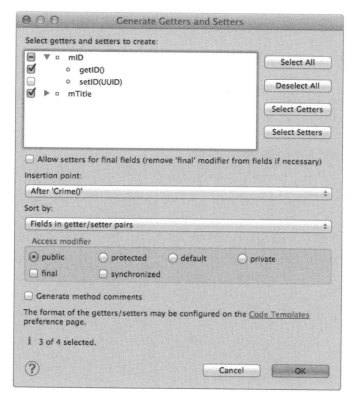

Listing 7.3 Generated getters and setter (`Crime.java`)

```java
public class Crime {
    private UUID mId;

    private String mTitle;

    public Crime() {
        mId = UUID.randomUUID();
    }

    public UUID getId() {
        return mId;
    }

    public String getTitle() {
        return mTitle;
    }

    public void setTitle(String title) {
        mTitle = title;
    }
}
```

That is all you need for the **Crime** class and for CriminalIntent's model layer in this chapter.

At this point, you have created the model layer and an activity that is capable of hosting a fragment in a way that is compatible with Froyo and Gingerbread versions. Now you will get into the details of how the activity performs its duties as host.

Hosting a UI Fragment

To host a UI fragment, an activity must

- define a spot in its layout for the fragment's view

- manage the lifecycle of the fragment instance

The fragment lifecycle

Figure 7.11 shows the fragment lifecycle. It is similar to the activity lifecycle: it has stopped, paused, and running states, and it has methods you can override to get things done at critical points – many of which correspond to activity lifecycle methods.

Figure 7.11 Fragment lifecycle diagram

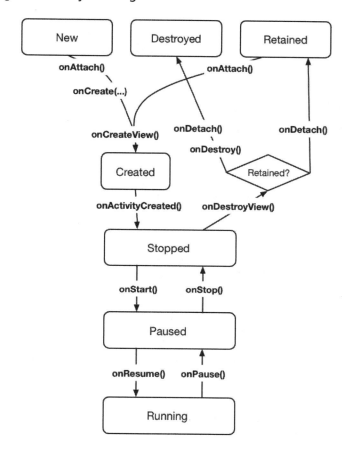

The correspondence is important. Because a fragment works on behalf of an activity, its state should reflect the activity's state. Thus, it needs corresponding lifecycle methods to handle the activity's work.

One critical difference between the fragment lifecycle and the activity lifecycle is that fragment lifecycle methods are called by the hosting activity, not the OS. The OS knows nothing about the fragments that an activity is using to manage things. Fragments are the activity's internal business.

You will see more of the fragment lifecycle methods as you continue building CriminalIntent.

Two approaches to hosting

You have two options when it comes to hosting a UI fragment in an activity:

- add the fragment to activity's *layout*

- add the fragment in the activity's *code*

The first approach is known as using a *layout fragment*. It is simple but inflexible. If you add the fragment to the activity's layout, you hard-wire the fragment and its view to the activity's view and cannot swap out that fragment during the activity's lifetime.

Despite their inflexibility, layout fragments are useful, and you will see more of them in Chapter 13.

The second approach is the more complex way to host, but it is the only way to have control at runtime over your fragments. You determine when the fragment is added to the activity and what happens to it after that. You can remove the fragment, replace it with another, and then add the first fragment back again.

Thus, to achieve real UI flexibility you must add your fragment in code. This is the approach you will use for **CrimeActivity**'s hosting of a **CrimeFragment**. The code details will come later in the chapter. First, you are going to define **CrimeActivity**'s layout.

Defining a container view

You will be adding a UI fragment in the hosting activity's code, but you still need to make a spot for the fragment's view in the activity's view hierarchy. In **CrimeActivity**'s layout, this spot will be the **FrameLayout** shown in Figure 7.12.

Figure 7.12 Fragment-hosting layout for **CrimeActivity**

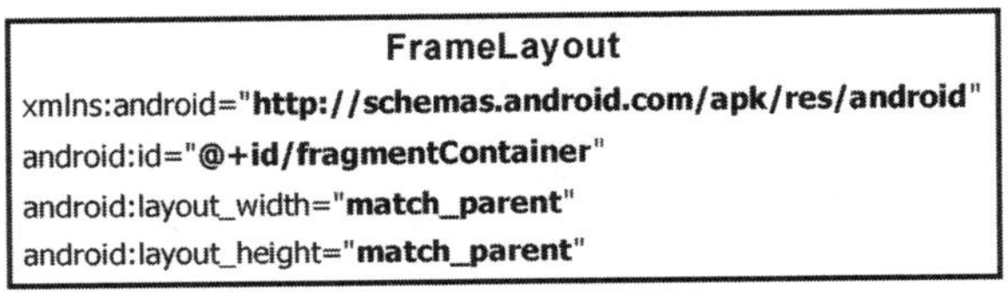

```
                              FrameLayout
        xmlns:android="http://schemas.android.com/apk/res/android"
        android:id="@+id/fragmentContainer"
        android:layout_width="match_parent"
        android:layout_height="match_parent"
```

This **FrameLayout** will be the *container view* for a **CrimeFragment**. Notice that the container view is completely generic; it does not name the **CrimeFragment** class. You can and will use this same layout to host other fragments.

Locate **CrimeActivity**'s layout at res/layout/activity_crime.xml. Open this file and replace the default layout with the **FrameLayout** diagrammed in Figure 7.12. Your XML should match that in Listing 7.4.

Listing 7.4 Create fragment container layout (`activity_crime.xml`)

```xml
<?xml version="1.0" encoding="utf-8"?>
<FrameLayout xmlns:android="http://schemas.android.com/apk/res/android"
    android:id="@+id/fragmentContainer"
    android:layout_width="match_parent"
    android:layout_height="match_parent"
    />
```

Note that, while activity_crime.xml consists solely of a container view for a single fragment, an activity's layout can be more complex and define multiple container views as well as widgets of its own.

You can preview your layout file or run CriminalIntent to check your code. You will only see an empty **FrameLayout** because the **CrimeActivity** is not yet hosting a fragment.

Figure 7.13 An empty **FrameLayout**

Later, you will write code that puts a fragment's view inside this **FrameLayout**. But first you need to create a fragment.

Creating a UI Fragment

The steps to creating a UI fragment are the same as those you followed to create an activity:

- compose an interface by defining widgets in a layout file

- create the class and set its view to be the layout that you defined

- wire up the widgets inflated from the layout in code

Defining CrimeFragment's layout

CrimeFragment's view will display the information contained within an instance of **Crime**. Eventually, the **Crime** class and **CrimeFragment**'s view will include many interesting pieces, but for this chapter, you just need a text field to contain the crime's title.

Figure 7.14 shows the layout for **CrimeFragment**'s view. It consists of a vertical **LinearLayout** that contains an **EditText**. **EditText** is a widget that presents an area where the user can add or edit text.

Figure 7.14 Initial layout for **CrimeFragment**

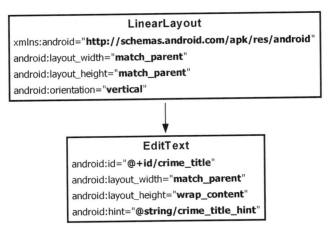

To create a layout file, right-click the res/layout folder in the package explorer and select New →
Android XML File. Make sure that the resource type is Layout and name this file fragment_crime.xml.
Select **LinearLayout** as the root element and click Finish.

When the file opens, navigate to the XML. The wizard has added the **LinearLayout** for you. Using
Figure 7.14 as a guide, make the necessary changes to fragment_crime.xml. You can use Listing 7.5
to check your work.

Listing 7.5 Layout file for fragment's view (fragment_crime.xml)

```
<?xml version="1.0" encoding="utf-8"?>
<LinearLayout xmlns:android="http://schemas.android.com/apk/res/android"
  android:layout_width="match_parent"
  android:layout_height="match_parent"
  android:orientation="vertical"
>
  <EditText android:id="@+id/crime_title"
    android:layout_width="match_parent"
    android:layout_height="wrap_content"
    android:hint="@string/crime_title_hint"
    />
</LinearLayout>
```

Open res/values/strings.xml, add a crime_title_hint string resource and remove the unneeded
hello_world and menu_settings string resources that the template created for you.

Listing 7.6 Adding and deleting strings (res/values/strings.xml)

```
<?xml version="1.0" encoding="utf-8"?>
<resources>
  <string name="app_name">CriminalIntent</string>
  <string name="hello_world">Hello world!</string>
  <string name="menu_settings">Settings</string>
  <string name="title_activity_crime">CrimeActivity</string>
  <string name="crime_title_hint">Enter a title for the crime.</string>
</resources>
```

Save your files. Deleting the menu_settings string caused an error in your project. To fix it, go to the
package explorer and find the file res/menu/activity_crime.xml. This file is a definition of the menu

that the template created, and it references the menu_settings string. You will not be using this menu file for CriminalIntent, so you can simply delete it from the package explorer.

Deleting the menu resource will cause Eclipse to rebuild. Your project should now be error-free. Switch to the graphical layout tool to see a preview of fragment_crime.xml.

Creating the CrimeFragment class

Right-click the com.bignerdranch.android.criminalintent package and select New → Class. Name the class **CrimeFragment** and then click the Browse button to set the superclass. In the window that appears, start typing **Fragment**. The wizard will suggest a few classes. Choose the **android.support.v4.app.Fragment** class, which is the **Fragment** class from the support library. Click OK.

Figure 7.15 Choosing the support library's **Fragment** class

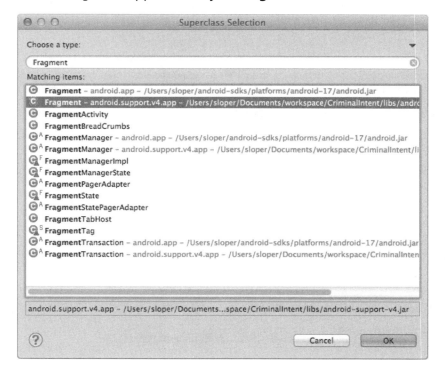

(If you are seeing multiple versions of **android.support.v4.app.Fragment**, make sure to select the one that is part of the CriminalIntent project found in CriminalIntent/libs/.)

Implementing fragment lifecycle methods

CrimeFragment is a controller that interacts with model and view objects. Its job is to present the details of a specific crime and update those details as the user changes them.

In the GeoQuiz app, your activities did most of their controller work in activity lifecycle methods. In CriminalIntent, this work will be done by fragments in fragment lifecycle methods. Many of these methods correspond to the **Activity** methods you already know, such as **onCreate(Bundle)**.

In `CrimeFragment.java`, add a member variable for the **Crime** instance and an implementation of
Fragment.onCreate(Bundle).

Listing 7.7 Overriding **Fragment.onCreate(Bundle)** (`CrimeFragment.java`)

```
public class CrimeFragment extends Fragment {
    private Crime mCrime;

    @Override
    public void onCreate(Bundle savedInstanceState) {
        super.onCreate(savedInstanceState);
        mCrime = new Crime();
    }

}
```

There are a couple of things to notice in this implementation. First, **Fragment.onCreate(Bundle)** is a
public method whereas **Activity.onCreate(Bundle)** is protected. **Fragment.onCreate(…)** and other
Fragment lifecycle methods must be public because they will be called by whatever activity is hosting
the fragment.

Second, similar to an activity, a fragment has a bundle to which it saves and retrieves its state.
You can override **Fragment.onSaveInstanceState(Bundle)** for your own purposes just like with
Activity.onSaveInstanceState(Bundle).

Note what does *not* happen in **Fragment.onCreate(…)**: you do not inflate the fragment's view.
You configure the fragment instance in **Fragment.onCreate(…)**, but you create and configure the
fragment's view in another fragment lifecycle method:

```
public View onCreateView(LayoutInflater inflater, ViewGroup parent,
    Bundle savedInstanceState)
```

This method is where you inflate the layout for the fragment's view and return the inflated **View** to the
hosting activity. The **LayoutInflater** and **ViewGroup** parameters are necessary to inflate the layout.
The **Bundle** will contain data that this method can use to recreate the view from a saved state.

In `CrimeFragment.java`, add an implementation of **onCreateView(…)** that inflates
`fragment_crime.xml`.

Listing 7.8 Overriding **onCreateView(…)** (`CrimeFragment.java`)

```
public class CrimeFragment extends Fragment {
    private Crime mCrime;

    @Override
    public void onCreate(Bundle savedInstanceState) {
        super.onCreate(savedInstanceState);
        mCrime = new Crime();
    }

    @Override
    public View onCreateView(LayoutInflater inflater, ViewGroup parent,
            Bundle savedInstanceState) {
        View v = inflater.inflate(R.layout.fragment_crime, parent, false);
        return v;
    }

}
```

Within **onCreateView(…)**, you explicitly inflate the fragment's view by calling **LayoutInflater.inflate(…)** and passing in the layout resource ID. The second parameter is your view's parent, which is usually needed to configure the widgets properly. The third parameter tells the layout inflater whether to add the inflated view to the view's parent. You pass in false because you will add the view in the activity's code.

Wiring widgets in a fragment

The **onCreateView(…)** method is also the place to wire up the **EditText** to respond to user input. After the view is inflated, get a reference to the **EditText** and add a listener.

Listing 7.9 Wiring up the **EditText** widget (CrimeFragment.java)

```java
public class CrimeFragment extends Fragment {
    private Crime mCrime;
    private EditText mTitleField;

    ...

    @Override
    public View onCreateView(LayoutInflater inflater, ViewGroup parent,
            Bundle savedInstanceState) {
        View v = inflater.inflate(R.layout.fragment_crime, parent, false);

        mTitleField = (EditText)v.findViewById(R.id.crime_title);
        mTitleField.addTextChangedListener(new TextWatcher() {
            public void onTextChanged(
                    CharSequence c, int start, int before, int count) {
                mCrime.setTitle(c.toString());
            }

            public void beforeTextChanged(
                    CharSequence c, int start, int count, int after) {
                // This space intentionally left blank
            }

            public void afterTextChanged(Editable c) {
                // This one too
            }
        });

        return v;
    }
}
```

Getting references in **Fragment.onCreateView(…)** works nearly the same as in **Activity.onCreate(…)**. The only difference is that you call **View.findViewById(int)** on the fragment's view. The **Activity.findViewById(int)** method that you used before is a convenience method that calls **View.findViewById(int)** behind the scenes. The **Fragment** class does not have a corresponding convenience method, so you have to call the real thing.

Setting listeners in a fragment works exactly the same as in an activity. In Listing 7.9, you create an anonymous class that implements the **TextWatcher** listener interface. **TextWatcher** has three methods, but you only care about one: **onTextChanged(…)**.

In **onTextChanged(…)**, you call **toString()** on the **CharSequence** that is the user's input. This method returns a string, which you then use to set the **Crime**'s title.

Your code for **CrimeFragment** is now complete. It would be great if you could run CriminalIntent now and play with the code you have written. But you cannot. Fragments cannot put their views on screen. To realize your efforts, you first have to add a **CrimeFragment** to **CrimeActivity**.

Adding a UI Fragment to the FragmentManager

When the **Fragment** class was introduced in Honeycomb, the **Activity** class was changed to include a piece called the **FragmentManager**. The **FragmentManager** is responsible for managing your fragments and adding their views to the activity's view hierarchy.

The **FragmentManager** handles two things: a list of fragments and a back stack of fragment transactions (which you will learn about shortly).

Figure 7.16 The **FragmentManager**

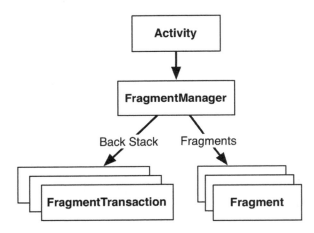

For CriminalIntent, you will only be concerned with the **FragmentManager**'s list of fragments.

To add a fragment to an activity in code, you make explicit calls to the activity's **FragmentManager**. The first step is to get the **FragmentManager** itself. In CrimeActivity.java, add the following code to **onCreate(…)**.

Listing 7.10 Get the **FragmentManager** (CrimeActivity.java)

```java
public class CrimeActivity extends FragmentActivity {
    /** Called when the activity is first created. */
    @Override
    public void onCreate(Bundle savedInstanceState) {
        super.onCreate(savedInstanceState);
        setContentView(R.layout.activity_crime);

        FragmentManager fm = getSupportFragmentManager();
    }
}
```

You call **getSupportFragmentManager()** because you are using the support library and the **FragmentActivity** class. If you were not interested in compatibility with pre-Honeycomb devices, then you would subclass **Activity** and call **getFragmentManager()**.

Fragment transactions

Now that you have the **FragmentManager**, add the following code to give it a fragment to manage. (We will step through this code afterwards. Just get it in for now.)

Listing 7.11 Adding a **CrimeFragment** (CrimeActivity.java)

```
public class CrimeActivity extends FragmentActivity {
    /** Called when the activity is first created. */
    @Override
    public void onCreate(Bundle savedInstanceState) {
        super.onCreate(savedInstanceState);
        setContentView(R.layout.activity_crime);

        FragmentManager fm = getSupportFragmentManager();
        Fragment fragment = fm.findFragmentById(R.id.fragmentContainer);

        if (fragment == null) {
            fragment = new CrimeFragment();
            fm.beginTransaction()
                .add(R.id.fragmentContainer, fragment)
                .commit();
        }
    }
}
```

The best place to start understanding the code that you added in Listing 7.11 is not at the beginning. Instead, find the **add(...)** operation and the code around it. This code creates and commits a *fragment transaction*.

Listing 7.12 A fragment transaction (CrimeActivity.java)

```
        if (fragment == null) {
            fragment = new CrimeFragment();
            fm.beginTransaction()
                .add(R.id.fragmentContainer, fragment)
                .commit();
```

Fragment transactions are used to add, remove, attach, detach, or replace fragments in the fragment list. They are the heart of how you use fragments to compose and recompose screens at runtime. The **FragmentManager** maintains a back stack of fragment transactions that you can navigate.

The **FragmentManager.beginTransaction()** method creates and returns an instance of **FragmentTransaction**. The **FragmentTransaction** class uses a *fluent interface* - methods that configure **FragmentTransaction** return a **FragmentTransaction** instead of void, which allows you to chain them together. So the highlighted code in Listing 7.12 says, "Create a new fragment transaction, include one add operation in it, and then commit it."

The **add(…)** method is the meat of the transaction. It has two parameters: a container view ID and the newly-created **CrimeFragment**. The container view ID should look familiar. It is the resource ID of the **FrameLayout** that you defined in activity_crime.xml. A container view ID serves two purposes:

- It tells the **FragmentManager** where in the activity's view the fragment's view should appear.

- It is used as a unique identifier for a fragment in the **FragmentManager**'s list.

When you need to retrieve the **CrimeFragment** from the **FragmentManager**, you ask for it by container view ID:

Listing 7.13 Existing fragment retrieved by container view ID (CrimeActivity.java)

```
FragmentManager fm = getSupportFragmentManager();
Fragment fragment = fm.findFragmentById(R.id.fragmentContainer);

if (fragment == null) {
    fragment = new CrimeFragment();
    fm.beginTransaction()
        .add(R.id.fragmentContainer, fragment)
        .commit();
}
```

It may seem odd that the **FragmentManager** identifies the **CrimeFragment** using the resource ID of a **FrameLayout**. But identifying a UI fragment by the resource ID of its container view is built into how the **FragmentManager** operates.

Now we can summarize the code you added back in Listing 7.11 from start to finish.

First, you ask the **FragmentManager** for the fragment with a container view ID of R.id.fragmentContainer. If this fragment is already in the list, the **FragmentManager** will return it.

Why would a fragment already be in the list? The call to **CrimeActivity.onCreate(…)** could be in response to **CrimeActivity** being *recreated* after being destroyed on rotation or to reclaim memory. When an activity is destroyed, its **FragmentManager** saves out its list of fragments. When the activity is recreated, the new **FragmentManager** retrieves the list and recreates the listed fragments to make everything as it was before.

On the other hand, if there is no fragment with the given container view ID, then fragment will be null. In this case, you create a new **CrimeFragment** and a new fragment transaction that adds the fragment to the list.

CrimeActivity is now hosting a **CrimeFragment**. Run CriminalIntent to prove it. You should see the view defined in fragment_crime.xml, as shown in Figure 7.17.

Figure 7.17 **CrimeFragment**'s view hosted by **CrimeActivity**

A single widget on screen may not seem like a much of a reward for all the work you have done in this chapter. But what you have done is a lay a solid foundation to do greater things with CriminalIntent in the chapters ahead.

The FragmentManager and the fragment lifecycle

Now that you know about the **FragmentManager**, let's take another look at the fragment lifecycle.

Figure 7.18 The fragment lifecycle, again

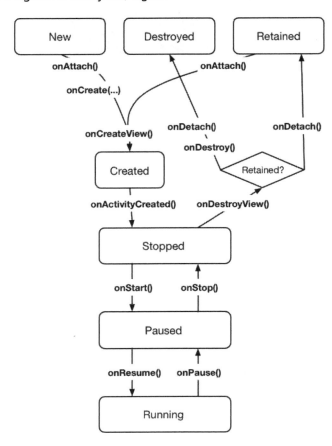

The **FragmentManager** of an activity is responsible for calling the lifecycle methods of the fragments in its list. The **onAttach(Activity)**, **onCreate(Bundle)**, and **onCreateView(…)** methods are called when you add the fragment to the **FragmentManager**.

The **onActivityCreated(…)** method is called after the hosting activity's **onCreate(…)** method has executed. You are adding the **CrimeFragment** in **CrimeActivity.onCreate(…)**, so this method will be called after the fragment has been added.

What happens if you add a fragment while the activity is already stopped, paused, or running? In that case, the **FragmentManager** immediately walks the fragment through whatever steps are necessary to get it caught up to the activity's state. For example, when you add a fragment to an activity that is already running, that fragment gets calls to **onAttach(Activity)**, **onCreate(Bundle)**, **onCreateView(…)**, **onActivityCreated(Bundle)**, **onStart()**, and then **onResume()**.

Once the fragment's state is caught up to the activity's state, the hosting activity's **FragmentManager** will call further lifecycle methods around the same time it receives the corresponding calls from the OS to keep the fragment's state aligned with that of the activity. There is no guarantee about whether the fragment's methods will be called before or after the activity's methods.

When you are using the support library, there is one small difference in the fragment lifecycle: If you add a fragment in **Activity.onCreate(…)**, then **onActivityCreated(…)** is not called immediately after `Activity.onCreate(…)`. Instead, it is called as `Activity.onStart()` is being performed. Why? It is impossible to call `onActivityCreated(…)` at the right time from `FragmentActivity` in pre-Honeycomb SDKs, so it is called as soon as the next lifecycle method occurs. In practice, this usually makes no difference; `onStart()` occurs immediately after `Activity.onCreate(…)` anyway.

The Reason All Our Activities Will Use Fragments

From here on, all of the apps in this book will use fragments – no matter how simple. This may seem like overkill. Many of the examples you will see in following chapters could be written without fragments. The user interfaces could be created and managed from activities, and doing so might even be less code.

However, we believe it is better for you to become comfortable with the pattern you will most likely use in real life.

You might think it would be better to begin a simple app without fragments and add them later, when (or if) necessary. There is an idea in Extreme Programming methodology called YAGNI. YAGNI stands for "You Aren't Gonna Need It," and it urges you not to write code if you think you *might* need it later. Why? Because YAGNI. It is tempting to say "YAGNI" to fragments.

Unfortunately, adding fragments later can be a minefield. Changing an activity to an activity hosting a UI fragment is not difficult, but there are swarms of annoying gotchas. Keeping some interfaces managed by activities and having others managed by fragments only makes things worse because you have to keep track of this meaningless distinction. It is far easier to write your code using fragments from the beginning and not worry about the pain and annoyance of reworking it later, or having to remember which style of controller you are using in each part of your application.

Therefore, when it comes to fragments, we have a different principle: AUF, or "Always Use Fragments." You can kill a lot of brain cells deciding whether to use a fragment or an activity, and it is just not worth it. AUF!

For the More Curious: Developing for Honeycomb, ICS, Jelly Bean, and Beyond

In this chapter, you learned how to use the support library to enable fragments for a project with a minimum SDK less than API level 11. However, if you were developing exclusively for newer SDKs, then you would not need to use the support library. Instead, you could use the native fragment classes in the standard library.

To use standard library fragments, you would make four changes to the project:

- Set the application's build target and minimum SDK to API level 11 or higher.

- Subclass the standard library `Activity` class (`android.app.Activity`) instead of `FragmentActivity`. Activities have support for fragments out of the box on API level 11 or higher.

- Subclass `android.app.Fragment` instead of `android.support.v4.app.Fragment`.

- To get the `FragmentManager`, call `getFragmentManager()` instead of `getSupportFragmentManager()`.

8

Creating User Interfaces with Layouts and Widgets

In this chapter, you will learn more about layouts and widgets while adding a crime's date and status to CriminalIntent.

Upgrading Crime

Open Crime.java and add two new fields. The **Date** field represents the date a crime occurred. The boolean field represents whether the crime has been solved.

Listing 8.1 Adding more fields to **Crime** (Crime.java)

```java
public class Crime {
    private UUID mId;
    private String mTitle;
    private Date mDate;
    private boolean mSolved;

    public Crime() {
        mId = UUID.randomUUID();
        mDate = new Date();
    }

    ...
}
```

Initializing the **Date** variable using the default **Date** constructor sets mDate to the current date. This will be the default date for a crime.

Next, generate getters and setters for your new fields (Source → Generate Getters and Setters...).

Listing 8.2 Generated getters and setters (`Crime.java`)

```
public class Crime {
    ...

    public void setTitle(String title) {
        mTitle = title;
    }

    public Date getDate() {
        return mDate;
    }
    public void setDate(Date date) {
        mDate = date;
    }

    public boolean isSolved() {
        return mSolved;
    }
    public void setSolved(boolean solved) {
        mSolved = solved;
    }
}
```

Your next steps are updating the layout in `fragment_crime.xml` with new widgets and wiring up those widgets in `CrimeFragment.java`.

Updating the Layout

Here is what **CrimeFragment**'s view will look like by the end of this chapter.

Figure 8.1 CriminalIntent, episode 2

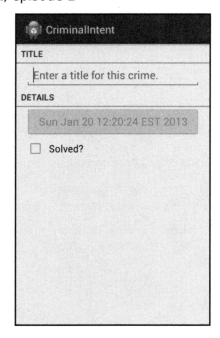

To get this on screen, you are going to add four widgets to **CrimeFragment**'s layout: two **TextView** widgets, a **Button**, and a **CheckBox**.

Open fragment_crime.xml and make the changes shown in Listing 8.3. You may get errors from missing string resources that you will create in a moment.

Listing 8.3 Adding new widgets (fragment_crime.xml)

```xml
<?xml version="1.0" encoding="utf-8"?>
<LinearLayout xmlns:android="http://schemas.android.com/apk/res/android"
  android:layout_width="match_parent"
  android:layout_height="wrap_content"
  android:orientation="vertical"
  >
  <TextView
    android:layout_width="match_parent"
    android:layout_height="wrap_content"
    android:text="@string/crime_title_label"
    style="?android:listSeparatorTextViewStyle"
    />
  <EditText android:id="@+id/crime_title"
    android:layout_width="match_parent"
    android:layout_height="wrap_content"
    android:layout_marginLeft="16dp"
    android:layout_marginRight="16dp"
    android:hint="@string/crime_title_hint"
    />
  <TextView
    android:layout_width="match_parent"
    android:layout_height="wrap_content"
    android:text="@string/crime_details_label"
    style="?android:listSeparatorTextViewStyle"
    />
  <Button android:id="@+id/crime_date"
    android:layout_width="match_parent"
    android:layout_height="wrap_content"
    android:layout_marginLeft="16dp"
    android:layout_marginRight="16dp"
    />
  <CheckBox android:id="@+id/crime_solved"
    android:layout_width="match_parent"
    android:layout_height="wrap_content"
    android:layout_marginLeft="16dp"
    android:layout_marginRight="16dp"
    android:text="@string/crime_solved_label"
    />
</LinearLayout>
```

Notice that you did not give the **Button** an android:text attribute. This button will display the date of the **Crime** being displayed, and its text will be set in code.

Why display the date on a **Button**? You are preparing for the future. For now, a crime's date defaults to the current date and cannot be changed. In Chapter 12, you will wire up the button so that a click presents a **DatePicker** widget from which the user can set the date to something else.

There are some new things in this layout to discuss, such as the style attribute and the margin attributes. But first let's get CriminalIntent up and running with the new widgets.

Return to res/values/strings.xml and add the necessary string resources.

Listing 8.4 Adding string resources (`strings.xml`)

```
<resources>
    <string name="app_name">CriminalIntent</string>
    <string name="title_activity_crime">CrimeActivity</string>
    <string name="crime_title_hint">Enter a title for this crime.</string>
    <string name="crime_title_label">Title</string>
    <string name="crime_details_label">Details</string>
    <string name="crime_solved_label">Solved?</string>
</resources>
```

Save your files and check for typos.

Wiring Widgets

The **CheckBox** needs to display whether a **Crime** has been solved. You also need to update the **Crime**'s mSolved field when a user toggles the **CheckBox**.

For now, all the new **Button** needs to do is display the date in the **Crime**'s mDate field.

In CrimeFragment.java, add two new instance variables.

Listing 8.5 Adding widget instance variables (`CrimeFragment.java`)

```
public class CrimeFragment extends Fragment {
    private Crime mCrime;
    private EditText mTitleField;
    private Button mDateButton;
    private CheckBox mSolvedCheckBox;

    @Override
    public void onCreate(Bundle savedInstanceState) {
    ...
```

Organize your imports to resolve the reference to **CheckBox**.

Next, in **onCreateView(…)**, get a reference to the new button, set its text as the date of the crime, and disable it for now.

Listing 8.6 Setting **Button** text (`CrimeFragment.java`)

```
@Override
public View onCreateView(LayoutInflater inflater, ViewGroup parent,
        Bundle savedInstanceState) {
    View v = inflater.inflate(R.layout.fragment_crime, parent, false);

    ...

    mTitleField.addTextChangedListener(new TextWatcher() {
        ...
    });

    mDateButton = (Button)v.findViewById(R.id.crime_date);
    mDateButton.setText(mCrime.getDate().toString());
    mDateButton.setEnabled(false);

    return v;
}
```

Disabling the button ensures that it will not respond in any way to the user pressing it. It also changes its appearance to advertise its disabled state. In Chapter 12, you will enable the button when you set its listener.

Moving on to the **CheckBox**, get a reference and set a listener that will update the mSolved field of the **Crime**.

Listing 8.7 Listening for CheckBox changes (CrimeFragment.java)

```
...
mDateButton = (Button)v.findViewById(R.id.crime_date);
mDateButton.setText(mCrime.getDate().toString());
mDateButton.setEnabled(false);

mSolvedCheckBox = (CheckBox)v.findViewById(R.id.crime_solved);
mSolvedCheckBox.setOnCheckedChangeListener(new OnCheckedChangeListener() {
    public void onCheckedChanged(CompoundButton buttonView, boolean isChecked) {
        // Set the crime's solved property
        mCrime.setSolved(isChecked);
    }
});

    return v;
}
```

When you import the **OnCheckedChangeListener** interface, Eclipse will offer you a choice between an interface defined in the **CompoundButton** class and one defined in the **RadioGroup** class. Choose the **CompoundButton** interface; **CheckBox** is a subclass of **CompoundButton**.

If you used auto-complete, you may also see an @Override annotation above your **onCheckedChanged(…)** method that Listing 8.7 does not have. You can ignore this difference. @Overrides are not required for methods defined in interfaces.

Run CriminalIntent. Toggle the new **CheckBox** and admire your disabled **Button** that displays the date.

More on XML Layout Attributes

Let's go back over some of the attributes you added in fragment_crime.xml and answer some lingering questions you might have about widgets and attributes.

Styles, themes, and theme attributes

A *style* is an XML resource that contains attributes that describe how a widget should look and behave. For example, the following is a style resource that configures a widget with a larger-than-normal text size.

```
<style name="BigTextStyle">
  <item name="android:textSize">20sp</item>
  <item name="android:layout_margin">3dp</item>
</style>
```

You can create your own styles (and you will in Chapter 24). You add them to a styles file in res/ values/ and refer to them in layouts like this: @style/my_own_style.

Take another look at the **TextView** widgets in `fragment_crime.xml`; each has a `style` attribute that refers to a style created by Android. This particular style makes the **TextView**s look like list separators and comes from the app's *theme*. A *theme* is a collection of styles. Structurally, a theme is itself a style resource whose attributes point to other style resources.

Android provides platform themes that your apps can use. When you created CriminalIntent, the wizard suggested Holo Light with Dark Action Bar as the app's theme and you accepted.

You can apply a style from the app's theme to a widget using a *theme attribute reference*. This is what you are doing in `fragment_crime.xml` when you use the value `?android:listSeparatorTextViewStyle`.

In a theme attribute reference, you tell Android's runtime resource manager, "Go to the app's theme and find the attribute named `listSeparatorTextViewStyle`. This attribute points to another style resource. Put the value of that resource here."

Every Android theme will include an attribute named `listSeparatorTextViewStyle`, but its definition will be different depending on the overall look and feel of the particular theme. Using a theme attribute reference ensures that the **TextView**s will have the correct look and feel for your app.

You will learn more about how styles and themes work in Chapter 24.

Screen pixel densities and dp and sp

In `fragment_crime.xml`, you specify the margin attribute values in terms of `dp` units. You have seen these units in layouts before; now it is time to learn what they are.

Sometimes you need to specify values for view attributes in terms of specific sizes (usually in pixels but sometimes points, millimeters, or inches). You see this most commonly with attributes for text size, margins, and padding. Text size is the pixel height of the text on the device's screen. Margins specify the distances between views, and padding specifies the distance between a view's outside edges and its content.

Android automatically scales images to different screen pixel densities using the `drawable-ldpi`, `drawable-mdpi`, and `drawable-hdpi` directories. But what happens when your images scale, but your margins do not? Or what happens when the user configures a larger-than-default text size?

To solve these problems, Android provides density-independent dimension units that you can use to get the same size on different screen densities. Android translates these units into pixels at runtime, so there is no tricky math for you to do.

Figure 8.2 Dimension units in action on **TextView** (left: MDPI; middle: HDPI; right: HDPI with large text)

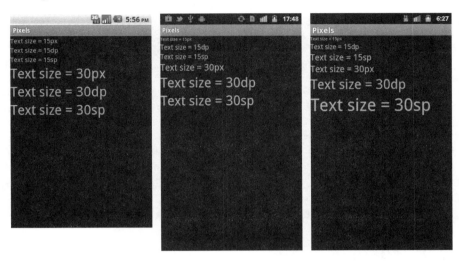

dp (or dip)	Short for *density-independent pixel* and usually pronounced "dip." You typically use this for margins, padding, or anything else for which you would otherwise specify size with a pixel value. When your display is a higher density, density-independent pixels will expand to fill a larger number of screen pixels. One dp is always 1/160th of an inch on a device's screen. You get the same size regardless of screen density.
sp	Short for *scale-independent pixel*. Scale-independent pixels are density-independent pixels that also take into account the user's font size preference. You will almost always use sp to set display text size.
pt, mm, in	These are scaled units like dp that allow you to specify interface sizes in points (1/72 of an inch), millimeters, or inches. However, we do not recommend using them: not all devices are correctly configured for these units to scale correctly.

In practice and in this book, you will use dp and sp almost exclusively. Android will translate these values into pixels at runtime.

Android's design guidelines

Notice that for your margins, you use a 16dp value for the margins in Listing 8.3. This value follows Android's "48dp rhythm" design guideline. You can find all of Android design guidelines at http://developer.android.com/design/index.html.

Modern Android apps should follow these guidelines as closely as possible. The guidelines rely heavily on newer Android SDK functionality that is not always available or easy to achieve on older devices. Some of the recommendations can be followed using the support library, but many require the use of a third-party library, like ActionBarSherlock, which you can read about in Chapter 16.

Layout parameters

By now, you have probably noticed that some attribute names begin with layout_ (android:layout_marginLeft) and others do not (android:text).

Attributes whose names do *not* begin with layout_ are directions to the widget. When it is inflated, the widget calls a method to configure itself based on each of these attributes and their values.

When an attribute's name begins with layout_, that attribute is a direction to that widget's *parent*. These attributes are known as *layout parameters*, and they tell the parent layout how to arrange the child element within the parent.

Even when a layout object like **LinearLayout** is the root element of a layout, it is still a widget with a parent and has layout parameters. When you defined the **LinearLayout** in fragment_crime.xml, you gave it attributes for android:layout_width and android:layout_height. These attributes will be used by the **LinearLayout**'s parent layout when it is inflated. In this case, the **LinearLayout**'s layout parameters will be used by the **FrameLayout** in **CrimeActivity**'s content view.

Margins vs. padding

In fragment_crime.xml, you have given widgets margin and padding attributes. Beginning developers sometimes get confused between these attributes. Now that you understand what a layout parameter is, the difference is easier to explain. Margin attributes are layout parameters. They determine the distance between widgets. Given that a widget can only know about itself, margins must be the responsibility of the widget's parent.

Padding, on the other hand, is not a layout parameter. The android:padding attribute tells the widget how much bigger than its contents it should draw itself. For example, say you wanted the date button to be spectacularly large without changing its text size. You could add the following attribute to the **Button**, save your layout, and run again.

Listing 8.8 Padding in action (fragment_crime.xml)

```
<Button android:id="@+id/crime_date"
  android:layout_width="match_parent"
  android:layout_height="wrap_content"
  android:layout_marginLeft="16dp"
  android:layout_marginRight="16dp"
  android:padding="80dp"
  />
```

Figure 8.3 I like big buttons and I cannot lie...

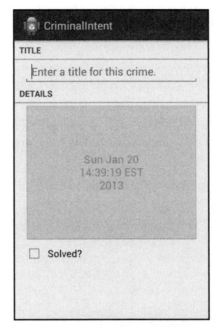

Alas, you should probably remove this attribute before continuing.

Using the Graphical Layout Tool

So far, you have created layouts by typing XML. In this section, you will use the graphical layout tool. In particular, you are going to make an alternative landscape layout for **CrimeFragment**.

Most built-in layout classes, like **LinearLayout**, will automatically stretch and resize themselves and their children on rotation. Sometimes, however, the default resizing does not make the best use of the available space.

Run CriminalIntent and rotate the device to see the **CrimeFragment** layout in landscape orientation.

Figure 8.4 **CrimeFragment** in landscape mode

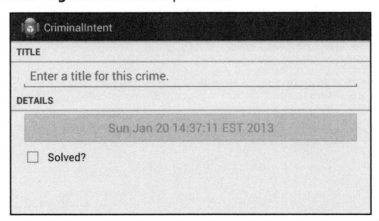

The date button becomes oddly long; it would be better if the landscape layout had the button and check box side by side. To make this happen, create the res/layout-land directory (right-click res/ in the package explorer and select New → Folder). Then copy fragment_crime.xml into res/layout-land/.

To make these changes using the graphical layout tool, first close res/layout/fragment_crime.xml if you have it open in the editor. Then open res/layout-land/fragment_crime.xml and select the Graphical Layout tab.

In the middle of the graphical layout tool is the preview you have already seen. On the lefthand side is the *palette*. This view contains all the widgets you could wish for, organized by category.

Figure 8.5 Views in the graphical layout tool

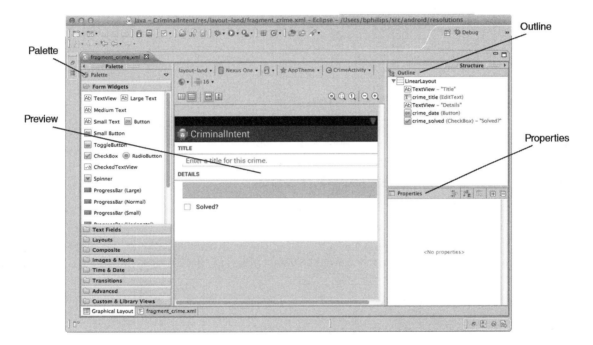

The *outline view* is to the right of the preview. The outline shows how the widgets are organized in the layout.

Beneath the outline view is the *properties view*. In this view, you can view and edit the attributes of the widget selected in the outline.

Now let's consider what changes to make to this layout. Take a look at Figure 8.6.

Figure 8.6 Landscape layout for **CrimeFragment**

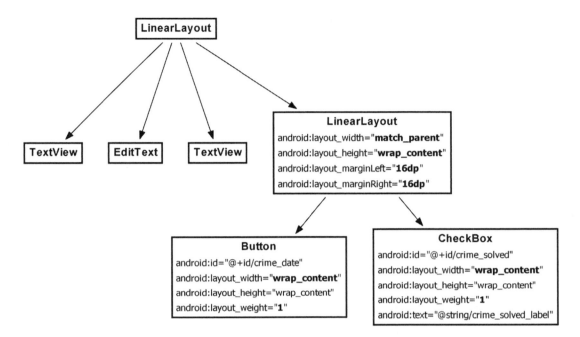

The changes can be broken into four parts:

- add a new **LinearLayout** widget to the layout

- edit the attributes of the **LinearLayout**

- make the **Button** and **CheckBox** widgets children of the **LinearLayout**

- update the layout parameters of the **Button** and **CheckBox**

Adding a new widget

You can add a widget by selecting it in the palette and then dragging to the outline view. Click the Layouts category in the palette. Select LinearLayout (Horizontal) and drag to the outline view. Drop this **LinearLayout** on top of the root **LinearLayout** to add it as a direct child of the root **LinearLayout**.

Figure 8.7 **LinearLayout** added to `fragment_crime.xml`

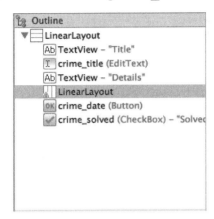

You can add widgets by dragging from the palette to the preview, too. However, layout widgets are often empty or obscured by other views, so it can be hard to see exactly where to drop a widget in the preview to get the hierarchy you want. Dragging to the outline view makes this much easier.

Editing attributes in properties

Select the new **LinearLayout** in the outline view to display its attributes in the properties view. Expand the Layout Parameters category and then the Margins category.

You want the new **LinearLayout**'s margins to match your other widgets. Select the field next to Left and type 16dp. Do the same for the right margin.

Figure 8.8 Margins set in properties view

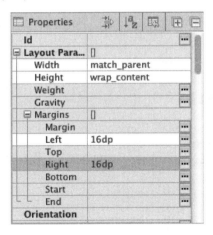

(On some platforms, you will get a pop-up window when attempting to type in these fields. This pop-up is a workaround for a known bug. Unfortunately, the workaround will not allow you to enter a value. So, if this happens, save your file and switch to the XML. Then copy the two margin attributes from the **EditText** to the **LinearLayout**.)

Save your layout file and switch to the XML by selecting the fragment_crime.xml tab at the bottom of the preview. You should see a **LinearLayout** element with the margin attributes you just added.

Reorganizing widgets in the outline view

The next step is to make the **Button** and **CheckBox** children of the new **LinearLayout**. Return to the graphical layout tool, and, in the outline view, select the **Button** and drag it on top of the **LinearLayout**.

The outline should reflect that the **Button** is now a child of the new **LinearLayout**. Do the same for the **CheckBox**.

Figure 8.9 **Button** and **CheckBox** now children of new **LinearLayout**

If widget children are out of order, you can reorder them in the outline view by dragging. You can also delete widgets from the layout in the outline view, but be careful: deleting a widget also deletes its children.

Back in the preview, the **CheckBox** seems to be missing. The **Button** is obscuring it. The **LinearLayout** considered the width (match_parent) of its first child (the **Button**) and gave the first child all of the space leaving nothing for the **CheckBox** (Figure 8.10).

Figure 8.10 The first-defined **Button** child obscures the **CheckBox**

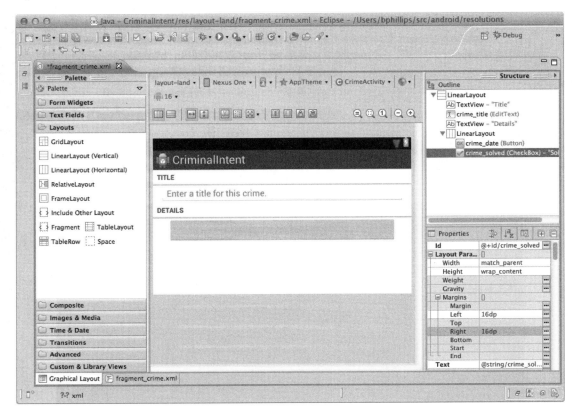

You can introduce some equity in the **LinearLayout**'s parenting by adjusting the layout parameters of its children.

Updating child layout parameters

First, select the date button in the outline. In the properties view, click on the current Width value and change it to wrap_content.

Figure 8.11 Changing **Button**'s width to `wrap_content`

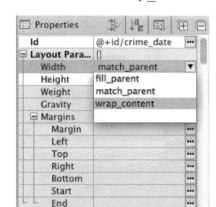

Next, delete both of the button's 16dp margin values. The button will not need these margins now that it is inside the **LinearLayout**.

Finally, find the Weight field in the Layout Parameters section and set its value to 1. This field corresponds to the `android:layout_weight` attribute shown in Figure 8.6.

Select the **CheckBox** in the outline view and make the same attribute changes: Width should be `wrap_content`, Weight should be 1, and the margins should be empty.

Check the preview to confirm that both widgets are now visible. Then save your file and return to the XML to confirm your changes. Listing 8.9 shows the relevant XML.

Listing 8.9 XML for the graphically-created layout (`layout-land/fragment_crime.xml`)

```
...

<TextView
  android:layout_width="match_parent"
  android:layout_height="wrap_content"
  android:text="@string/crime_details_label"
  style="?android:listSeparatorTextViewStyle"
  />
<LinearLayout
  android:layout_width="match_parent"
  android:layout_height="wrap_content"
  android:layout_marginLeft="16dp"
  android:layout_marginRight="16dp" >
    <Button
      android:id="@+id/crime_date"
      android:layout_width="wrap_content"
      android:layout_height="wrap_content"
      android:layout_weight="1" />
    <CheckBox
      android:id="@+id/crime_solved"
      android:layout_width="wrap_content"
      android:layout_height="wrap_content"
      android:layout_weight="1"
      android:text="@string/crime_solved_label" />
  </LinearLayout>
</LinearLayout>
```

How android:layout_weight works

The `android:layout_weight` attribute tells the **LinearLayout** how to distribute its children. You have given both widgets the same value, but that does not necessarily make them the same width on screen. To determine the width of its child views, **LinearLayout** uses a mixture of the `layout_width` and `layout_weight` parameters.

LinearLayout makes two passes to set the width of a view. In the first pass, **LinearLayout** looks at `layout_width` (or `layout_height`, for vertical orientation). The value for `layout_width` for both the **Button** and **CheckBox** is now `wrap_content`, so each view will get only enough space to draw itself (Figure 8.12).

(It is hard to see how layout weights work in the preview because your button's contents are not part of the layout itself. The following figures show what the **LinearLayout** would look like if the button already had its contents.)

Figure 8.12 Pass 1: space given out based on `layout_width`

In the next pass, **LinearLayout** allocates any extra space based on the values for `layout_weight` (Figure 8.13).

Figure 8.13 Pass 2: extra space given out based on 1:1 layout_weight

In your layout, the **Button** and **CheckBox** have the same value for layout_weight, so they split the extra space 50/50. If you set the weight for your **Button** to 2, then it would receive 2/3 of the extra space, leaving 1/3 for the **CheckBox** (Figure 8.14).

Figure 8.14 Extra space divided unevenly based on 2:1 layout_weight

Any floating point number can be a valid weight. Programmers have different conventions for the kinds of weights they use. In fragment_crime.xml, you are using a "cocktail recipe" style weighting. Another common convention is to have weights add up to 1.0 or 100, which would make the weight for the button in the last example 0.66 or 66, respectively.

What if you want the **LinearLayout** to allocate exactly 50% of its width to each view? You simply skip the first pass by setting the layout_width of each widget to 0dp instead of wrap_content. This leaves layout_weight the sole component in the **LinearLayout**'s decision-making (Figure 8.15).

Figure 8.15 When layout_width="0dp", only layout_weight values matter

Summary of graphical layout tool

The graphical layout tool is useful, and Android is improving it with every ADT release. However, it can still be slow and buggy at times. Sometimes, you may want to go back to typing XML. You can switch between making changes in the graphical layout tool and in XML. Just be sure to save the file before switching tabs to be safe.

Feel free to use the graphical layout tool to create layouts in this book. From now on, we will show you a diagram like Figure 8.6 when you need to create a layout. You can decide how to create it – XML, graphical layout tool, or a little of both.

Widget IDs and multiple layouts

The two layouts that you have created for CriminalIntent do not vary significantly, but there may be times when your layouts will. When this is the case, you should ensure that widgets actually exist before you access them in code.

If you have a widget in one layout and not another, use null-checking in the code to determine if the widget is present in the current orientation before calling methods on it:

```
Button landscapeOnlyButton = (Button)v.findViewById(R.id.landscapeOnlyButton);
if (landscapeOnlyButton != null) {
    // Set it up
}
```

Finally, remember that a widget must have the *same* android:id attribute in every layout in which it appears so that your code can find it.

Challenge: Formatting the Date

The **Date** object is more of a timestamp than a conventional date. A timestamp is what you see when you call **toString()** on a **Date**, so that is what you have on your button. While timestamps make for good documentation, it might be nicer if the button just displayed the date as humans think of it – like "Oct 12, 2012." You can do this with an instance of the **android.text.format.DateFormat** class. The place to start is the reference page for this class in the Android documentation.

You can use methods in the **DateFormat** class to get a common format. Or you can prepare your own format string. For a more advanced challenge, create a format string that will display the day of the week as well – for example, "Tuesday, Oct 12, 2012."

9

Displaying Lists with ListFragment

CriminalIntent's model layer currently consists of a single instance of **Crime**. In this chapter, you will update CriminalIntent to work with a list of crimes. The list will display each **Crime**'s title and date and whether the case has been solved.

Figure 9.1 A list of crimes

Figure 9.2 shows the overall plan for CriminalIntent in this chapter.

Figure 9.2 CriminalIntent with a list of crimes

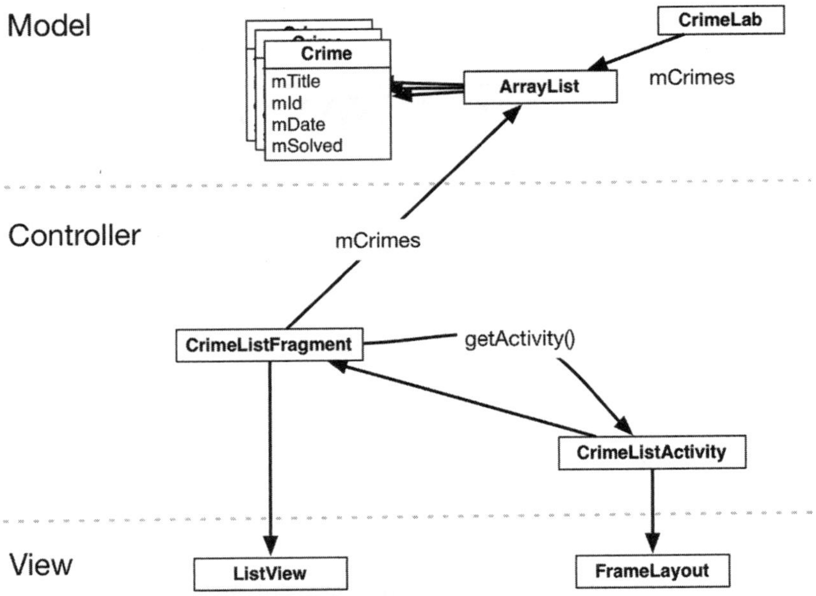

In the model layer, you have a new object, **CrimeLab**, that will be a centralized data stash that stores **Crime** objects.

Displaying a list of crimes requires a new activity and a new fragment in CriminalIntent's controller layer: **CrimeListActivity** and **CrimeListFragment**.

CrimeListFragment will be a subclass of **ListFragment**, which is a subclass of **Fragment** that comes with built-in help for displaying lists. These controllers will interact with each other and **CrimeLab** to access the data in the model layer.

(Where are **CrimeActivity** and **CrimeFragment** in Figure 9.2? They are part of the detail view, so we are not showing them here. In Chapter 10, you will connect the list and the detail parts of CriminalIntent.)

In Figure 9.2, you can also see the view objects associated with **CrimeListActivity** and **CrimeListFragment**. The activity's view will consist of a fragment-containing **FrameLayout**. The fragment's view will consist of a **ListView**. You will learn more about how **ListFragment** and **ListView** interact later in the chapter.

Updating CriminalIntent's Model Layer

The first step is to upgrade CriminalIntent's model layer from a single **Crime** object to an **ArrayList** of **Crime** objects.

ArrayList<E> is a Java class that supports an ordered list of objects of a given type. It provides methods for retrieving, adding, and deleting elements.

Singletons and centralized data storage

You are going to store the array list of crimes in a *singleton*. A *singleton* is a class that allows only one instance of itself to be created.

A singleton exists as long as the application stays in memory, so storing the list in a singleton will keep the crime data available no matter what happens with activities, fragments, and their lifecycles.

To create a singleton, you create a class with a private constructor and a `get()` method that returns the instance. If the instance already exists, then `get()` simply returns the instance. If the instance does not exist yet, then `get()` will call the constructor to create it.

Right-click the `com.bignerdranch.android.criminalintent` package and choose New → Class. Name this class **CrimeLab** and then click Finish.

In `CrimeLab.java`, implement **CrimeLab** as a singleton with a private constructor and a `get(Context)` method.

Listing 9.1 Setting up the singleton (`CrimeLab.java`)

```java
public class CrimeLab {
    private static CrimeLab sCrimeLab;
    private Context mAppContext;

    private CrimeLab(Context appContext) {
        mAppContext = appContext;
    }

    public static CrimeLab get(Context c) {
        if (sCrimeLab == null) {
            sCrimeLab = new CrimeLab(c.getApplicationContext());
        }
        return sCrimeLab;
    }
}
```

Notice the s prefix on the sCrimeLab variable. You are using this Android convention to make it clear that sCrimeLab is a static variable.

The **CrimeLab** constructor requires a **Context** parameter. This is common in Android; having a **Context** parameter allows the singleton to start activities, access project resources, find your application's private storage, and more.

Notice in **get(Context)** that you do not directly pass in the **Context** parameter to the constructor. This **Context** could be an **Activity** or another **Context** object, like **Service**. You cannot be sure that just any **Context** will exist as long as **CrimeLab** needs it, which is for the life of the application.

To ensure that your singleton has a long-term **Context** to work with, you call **getApplicationContext()** and trade the passed-in **Context** for the *application context*. The *application context* is a **Context** that is global to your application. Whenever you have an application-wide singleton, it should always use the application context.

Let's give **CrimeLab** some **Crime** objects to store. In **CrimeLab**'s constructor, create an empty **ArrayList** of **Crime**s. Also add two methods: a **getCrimes()** method that returns the array list and a **getCrime(UUID)** that returns the **Crime** with the given ID (Listing 9.2).

Listing 9.2 Setting up the ArrayList of Crime objects (CrimeLab.java)

```java
public class CrimeLab {
    private ArrayList<Crime> mCrimes;

    private static CrimeLab sCrimeLab;
    private Context mAppContext;

    private CrimeLab(Context appContext) {
        mAppContext = appContext;
        mCrimes = new ArrayList<Crime>();
    }

    public static CrimeLab get(Context c) {
        ...
    }

    public ArrayList<Crime> getCrimes() {
        return mCrimes;
    }

    public Crime getCrime(UUID id) {
        for (Crime c : mCrimes) {
            if (c.getId().equals(id))
                return c;
        }
        return null;
    }
}
```

Eventually, the **ArrayList** will contain user-created **Crime**s that can be saved and reloaded. But for now, populate the array list with 100 boring **Crime** objects (Listing 9.3).

Listing 9.3 Generating crimes (CrimeLab.java)

```java
    private CrimeLab(Context appContext) {
        mAppContext = appContext;
        mCrimes = new ArrayList<Crime>();
        for (int i = 0; i < 100; i++) {
            Crime c = new Crime();
            c.setTitle("Crime #" + i);
            c.setSolved(i % 2 == 0); // Every other one
            mCrimes.add(c);
        }
    }
```

Now you have a fully-loaded model layer and 100 crimes to get on screen.

Creating a ListFragment

Create a new class named **CrimeListFragment**. Click Browse to choose a superclass. Search for and select **ListFragment – android.support.v4.app** and then click Finish to generate **CrimeListFragment**.

ListFragment was introduced in Honeycomb, but it is duplicated in the support library. So compatibility is not a problem as long as you use the support library class, **android.support.v4.app.ListFragment**.

In `CrimeListFragment.java`, override **onCreate(Bundle)** to set the title of the activity that will host this fragment.

Listing 9.4 Adding **onCreate(Bundle)** to the new fragment (CrimeListFragment.java)

```java
public class CrimeListFragment extends ListFragment {

    @Override
    public void onCreate(Bundle savedInstanceState) {
        super.onCreate(savedInstanceState);
        getActivity().setTitle(R.string.crimes_title);
    }

}
```

Notice the **getActivity()** method. This **Fragment** convenience method returns the hosting activity and allows a fragment to handle more of the activity's affairs. Here you use it to call **Activity.setTitle(int)** to change what is displayed on the action bar (or title bar on older devices) to the value of the passed-in string resource.

You are not going to override **onCreateView(…)** or inflate a layout for **CrimeListFragment**. The default implementation of a **ListFragment** inflates a layout that defines a full-screen **ListView**, and you will use this layout for now. In later chapters, you will override **CrimeListFragment.onCreateView(…)** to add more advanced features.

In `strings.xml`, add the string resource for the list activity title.

Listing 9.5 Adding string resource for the new activity title (`strings.xml`)

```xml
    ...

    <string name="crime_solved_label">Solved?</string>
    <string name="crimes_title">Crimes</string>
</resources>
```

CrimeListFragment needs access to the list of crimes stored in **CrimeLab**. In **CrimeListFragment.onCreate(…)**, get the **CrimeLab** singleton and then get the list of crimes.

Listing 9.6 Accessing crimes in **CrimeListFragment** (CrimeListFragment.java)

```java
public class CrimeListFragment extends ListFragment {
    private ArrayList<Crime> mCrimes;

    @Override
    public void onCreate(Bundle savedInstanceState) {
        super.onCreate(savedInstanceState);
        getActivity().setTitle(R.string.crimes_title);
        mCrimes = CrimeLab.get(getActivity()).getCrimes();
    }

}
```

An Abstract Activity for Hosting a Fragment

In a moment, you will create the **CrimeListActivity** class that is designed to host a **CrimeListFragment**. First, let's set up a view for **CrimeListActivity**.

A generic fragment-hosting layout

For **CrimeListActivity**, you can simply reuse the layout defined in `activity_crime.xml` (Listing 9.7). This layout provides a **FrameLayout** as a container view for a fragment, which is then named in the activity's code.

Listing 9.7 `activity_crime.xml` is already generic

```xml
<?xml version="1.0" encoding="utf-8"?>
<FrameLayout xmlns:android="http://schemas.android.com/apk/res/android"
  android:id="@+id/fragmentContainer"
  android:layout_width="match_parent"
  android:layout_height="match_parent"
  />
```

Because `activity_crime.xml` does not name a particular fragment, you can use it for any activity hosting a single fragment. Let's rename it `activity_fragment.xml` to reflect its larger scope.

First, close `activity_crime.xml` in the editor if you have it open. Next, in the package explorer, right-click `res/layout/activity_crime.xml`. (Be sure to right-click `activity_crime.xml` and not `fragment_crime.xml`.)

From the context menu, select Refactor → Rename... Rename this layout `activity_fragment.xml`. When you rename a resource, the references to it are updated automatically.

On older versions of ADT, renaming a resource does not update references. If Eclipse is reporting an error in `CrimeActivity.java`, then you need to manually update the reference in **CrimeActivity**, as shown in Listing 9.8.

Listing 9.8 Update layout file for **CrimeActivity** (CrimeActivity.java)

```java
public class CrimeActivity extends FragmentActivity {
    /** Called when the activity is first created. */
    @Override
    public void onCreate(Bundle savedInstanceState) {
        super.onCreate(savedInstanceState);
        setContentView(R.layout.activity_crime);
        setContentView(R.layout.activity_fragment);
        FragmentManager fm = getSupportFragmentManager();
        Fragment fragment = fm.findFragmentById(R.id.fragmentContainer);

        if (fragment == null) {
            fragment = new CrimeFragment();
            fm.beginTransaction()
                .add(R.id.fragmentContainer, fragment)
                .commit();
        }
    }
}
```

An abstract Activity class

To create the **CrimeListActivity** class, you could reuse **CrimeActivity**'s code. Look back at the code you wrote for **CrimeActivity** (Listing 9.8). It is simple and almost generic. In fact, the only non-generic code is the instantiation of the **CrimeFragment** before it is added to the **FragmentManager**.

Listing 9.9 **CrimeActivity** is almost generic (CrimeActivity.java)

```java
public class CrimeActivity extends FragmentActivity {
    /** Called when the activity is first created. */
    @Override
    public void onCreate(Bundle savedInstanceState) {
        super.onCreate(savedInstanceState);
        setContentView(R.layout.activity_fragment);
        FragmentManager fm = getSupportFragmentManager();
        Fragment fragment = fm.findFragmentById(R.id.fragmentContainer);

        if (fragment == null) {
            fragment = new CrimeFragment();
            fm.beginTransaction()
                .add(R.id.fragmentContainer, fragment)
                .commit();
        }
    }
}
```

Nearly every activity you will create in this book will require the same code. To avoid typing it again and again, you are going to stash it in an abstract class.

Create a new class named **SingleFragmentActivity** in CriminalIntent's package. Make this class a subclass of **FragmentActivity** and check the box marked abstract to make **SingleFragmentActivity** an abstract class (Figure 9.3).

Figure 9.3 Create abstract **SingleFragmentActivity** class

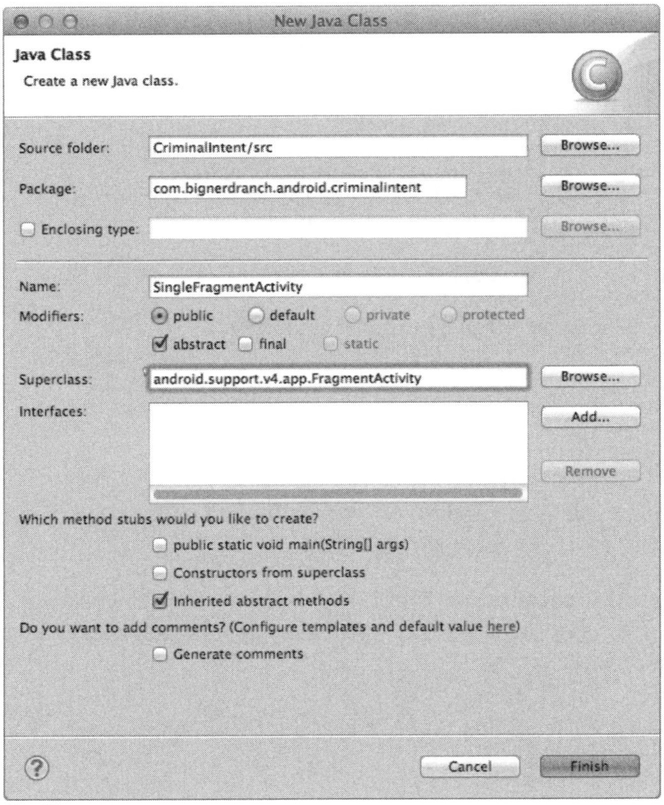

Click Finish and add the following code to SingleFragmentActivity.java. Except for the highlighted portions, it is identical to your old **CrimeActivity** code.

Listing 9.10 Add a generic superclass (SingleFragmentActivity.java)

```java
public abstract class SingleFragmentActivity extends FragmentActivity {
    protected abstract Fragment createFragment();

    @Override
    public void onCreate(Bundle savedInstanceState) {
        super.onCreate(savedInstanceState);
        setContentView(R.layout.activity_fragment);
        FragmentManager fm = getSupportFragmentManager();
        Fragment fragment = fm.findFragmentById(R.id.fragmentContainer);

        if (fragment == null) {
            fragment = createFragment();
            fm.beginTransaction()
                .add(R.id.fragmentContainer, fragment)
                .commit();
        }
    }
}
```

In this code, you set the activity's view to be inflated from `activity_fragment.xml`. Then you look for the fragment in the **FragmentManager** in that container, creating and adding it if it does not exist.

The only difference between the code in Listing 9.10 and the code in **CrimeActivity** is an abstract method named **createFragment()** that you use to instantiate the fragment. Subclasses of **SingleFragmentActivity** will implement this method to return an instance of the fragment that the activity is hosting.

Using an abstract class

Try it out with **CrimeListActivity**. Create a new class named **CrimeListActivity**. You can set its superclass as **SingleFragmentActivity** in the wizard. Just browse to select the superclass, type in **SingleFragmentActivity**, and Eclipse will offer it as a choice. Select it and then click Finish.

Figure 9.4 Selecting **SingleFragmentActivity**

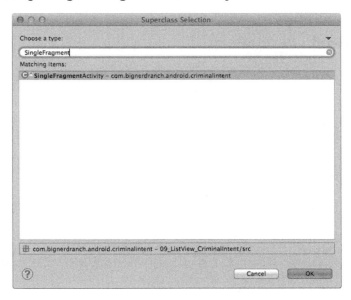

Eclipse will open `CrimeListActivity.java`, and it will already have a stub for **createFragment()**. Have this method return a new instance of **CrimeListFragment**.

Listing 9.11 Implement **CrimeListActivity** (`CrimeListActivity.java`)

```
public class CrimeListActivity extends SingleFragmentActivity {

    @Override
    protected Fragment createFragment() {
        return new CrimeListFragment();
    }

}
```

It would be best if **CrimeActivity** worked the same way. Return to `CrimeActivity.java`. Remove the existing code from **CrimeActivity** and rewrite it as a subclass of **SingleFragmentActivity**, as shown in Listing 9.12.

Listing 9.12 Clean up **CrimeActivity** (CrimeActivity.java)

```
public class CrimeActivity extends FragmentActivity SingleFragmentActivity {
    /** Called when the activity is first created. */
    @Override
    public void onCreate(Bundle savedInstanceState) {
        super.onCreate(savedInstanceState);
        setContentView(R.layout.activity_fragment);
        FragmentManager fm = getSupportFragmentManager();
        Fragment fragment = fm.findFragmentById(R.id.fragmentContainer);

        if (fragment == null) {
            fragment = new CrimeFragment();
            fm.beginTransaction()
                .add(R.id.fragmentContainer, fragment)
                .commit();
        }
    }

    @Override
    protected Fragment createFragment() {
        return new CrimeFragment();
    }
}
```

SingleFragmentActivity will save you a lot of typing and time as you proceed through the book. And now your activity code is nice and tidy.

Declaring CrimeListActivity

Now that you have created **CrimeListActivity**, you must declare it in the manifest. In addition, you want the list of crimes to be the first screen that the user sees when CriminalIntent is launched, so **CrimeListActivity** should be the launcher activity.

In the manifest, declare **CrimeListActivity** and move the launcher intent filter from **CrimeActivity**'s declaration to **CrimeListActivity**'s, as shown in Listing 9.13.

Listing 9.13 Declaring **CrimeListActivity** as the launcher activity
(AndroidManifest.xml)

```
...

<application
  android:allowBackup="true"
  android:icon="@drawable/ic_launcher"
  android:label="@string/app_name"
  android:theme="@style/AppTheme" >
  <activity android:name=".CrimeListActivity">
    <intent-filter>
      <action android:name="android.intent.action.MAIN" />
      <category android:name="android.intent.category.LAUNCHER" />
    </intent-filter>
  </activity>
  <activity android:name=".CrimeActivity"
    android:label="@string/app_name">
    <intent-filter>
      <action android:name="android.intent.action.MAIN" />
      <category android:name="android.intent.category.LAUNCHER" />
    </intent-filter>
  </activity>

</application>

</manifest>
```

CrimeListActivity is now the launcher activity. Run CriminalIntent, and you will see
CrimeListActivity's **FrameLayout** hosting an empty **CrimeListFragment**.

Figure 9.5 Blank **CrimeListActivity** screen

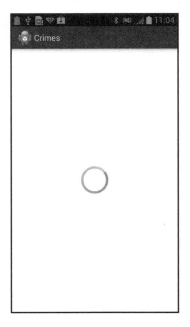

ListFragment shows a progress spinner in its implicit **ListView** when the **ListView** has nothing to display. You have given **CrimeListFragment** access to the array of **Crime**s, but you have not yet done anything to display their data in the **ListView**. You will start work on that next.

ListFragment, ListView, and ArrayAdapter

Instead of a spinner, you want **CrimeListFragment**'s **ListView** to show list items to the user. Each list item should contain data about an instance of **Crime**.

ListView is a subclass of **ViewGroup**, and each list item is displayed as a child **View** object of the **ListView**. Depending on the complexity of what you need the list to display, these child **View** objects can be complex **View** objects or very simple ones.

Your first implementation of providing list items for display will be simple: a list item will only display the title of a **Crime**, and the **View** object will be a simple **TextView**.

Figure 9.6 A **ListView** with child **TextView**s

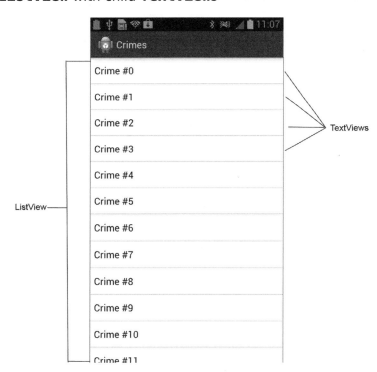

In Figure 9.6, you can see eleven **TextView**s and a hint of a twelfth. If you were able to scroll this screenshot, the **ListView** would show you additional **TextView**s – Crime #12, Crime #13, etc.

So where do these **View** objects come from? Does the **ListView** have them ahead of time? That would be inefficient. A **View** object only needs to exist when it is on screen. Lists can be enormous, and unnecessarily creating and storing view objects for an entire list could cause performance and memory problems.

The wiser course is to create view objects only as they are needed. The **ListView** asks for a view object when it needs to display a certain list item.

Whom does the **ListView** ask? It asks its *adapter*. An *adapter* is a controller object that sits between the **ListView** and the data set containing the data that the **ListView** should display.

The adapter is responsible for

- creating the necessary view object

- populating it with data from the model layer

- returning the view object to the **ListView**

An adapter is an instance of a class that implements the **Adapter** interface. You are going to use an instance of **ArrayAdapter<T>**, which is an adapter that knows how to work with data in an array (or an **ArrayList**) of **T** type objects.

Figure 9.7 shows the pedigree of the **ArrayAdapter<T>** class. Each link in the chain provides another level of specialization.

Figure 9.7 **ArrayAdapter<T>** inherits from **BaseAdapter**, which inherits from **ListAdapter**...

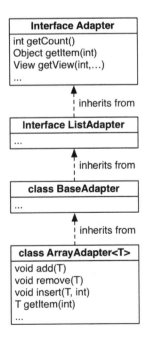

When the **ListView** needs a view object to display, it will have a conversation with its adapter. Figure 9.8 shows an example of a conversation that a **ListView** might initiate with its array adapter.

Figure 9.8 A scintillating **ListView-Adapter** conversation

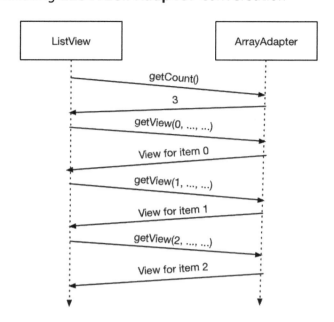

First, the **ListView** asks how many objects are in the array list by calling the adapter's **getCount()** method. (This is important to avoid out of range errors.)

Then the **ListView** calls the adapter's **getView(int, View, ViewGroup)** method. The first argument is the position of the list item that the **ListView** is looking for.

Within its implementation of **getView(…)**, the adapter creates a view object from the correct item in the array list and returns that view object to the **ListView**. The **ListView** then adds the view object to itself as a child view, which gets the new view on screen.

You will learn more about the mechanics of **getView(…)** later in the chapter when you override it to create custom list items.

Creating an ArrayAdapter<T>

Initially, you are going to create a default implementation of **ArrayAdapter<T>** for **CrimeListFragment** using the following constructor:

```
public ArrayAdapter(Context context, int textViewResourceId, T[] objects)
```

In the array adapter's constructor, the first parameter is a **Context** object required to use the resource ID that is the second parameter. The resource ID identifies the layout that the **ArrayAdapter** will use to create the view object. The third parameter is the data set.

In CrimeListFragment.java, create an instance of **ArrayAdapter<T>** and make it the adapter for **CrimeListFragment**'s **ListView** (Listing 9.14).

Listing 9.14 Setting up the **ArrayAdapter** (CrimeListFragment.java)

```
@Override
protected void onCreate(Bundle savedInstanceState) {
    super.onCreate(savedInstanceState);
    getActivity().setTitle(R.string.crimes_title);
    mCrimes = CrimeLab.get(getActivity()).getCrimes();

    ArrayAdapter<Crime> adapter =
        new ArrayAdapter<Crime>(getActivity(),
                                android.R.layout.simple_list_item_1,
                                mCrimes);
    setListAdapter(adapter);
}
```

The **setListAdapter(ListAdapter)** method is a **ListFragment** convenience method that you can use to set the adapter of the implicit **ListView** managed by **CrimeListFragment**.

The layout that you specify in the adapter's constructor (android.R.layout.simple_list_item_1) is a pre-defined layout from the resources provided by the Android SDK. This layout has a **TextView** as its root element.

Listing 9.15 Source code for android.R.layout.simple_list_item_1

```
<TextView xmlns:android="http://schemas.android.com/apk/res/android"
  android:id="@android:id/text1"
  style="?android:attr/listItemFirstLineStyle"
  android:paddingTop="2dip"
  android:paddingBottom="3dip"
  android:layout_width="match_parent"
  android:layout_height="wrap_content" />
```

You could specify a different layout in this constructor as long as its root element is a **TextView**.

Thanks to the default behavior of **ListFragment**, you can run now, and the **ListView** will be instantiated and displayed and will start conversing with its adapter.

Run CriminalIntent. List items will appear instead of a spinner. However, the text that each view is displaying is not particularly helpful to the user.

Figure 9.9 List items showing class names and memory addresses

The default implementation of **ArrayAdapter<T>.getView(…)** relies on **toString()**. It inflates the layout, finds the correct **Crime** object, and then calls **toString()** on the object to populate the **TextView**.

Crime does not currently override **toString()**, so it uses **java.lang.Object**'s implementation, which returns the fully-qualified class name and memory address of the object.

To have the adapter create a more useful view for a **Crime**, open Crime.java and override **toString()** to return the crime's title.

Listing 9.16 Overriding **Crime.toString()** (Crime.java)

```
...

public Crime() {
    mId = UUID.randomUUID();
    mDate = new Date();
}

@Override
public String toString() {
    return mTitle;
}

...
```

Run CriminalIntent again. Scroll through the list to see more crimes.

Figure 9.10 Simple list items showing crime titles

As you scroll, the **ListView** is calling **getView(…)** on the adapter to get the views that it needs to display.

Responding to list item clicks

To respond to the user touching a list item, you override another convenience method of **ListFragment**:

```
public void onListItemClick(ListView l, View v, int position, long id)
```

Whether the user "clicks" with a hardware button, a soft key, or a touch of a finger, the result still goes through **onListItemClick(…)**.

In CrimeListFragment.java, override **onListItemClick(…)** to have the adapter return the **Crime** for the item that was clicked and then log that **Crime**'s title.

Listing 9.17 Overriding onListItemClick(…) to log Crime title (CrimeListFragment.java)

```
public class CrimeListFragment extends ListFragment {

    private static final String TAG = "CrimeListFragment";

    ...

    @Override
    public void onListItemClick(ListView l, View v, int position, long id) {
        Crime c = (Crime)(getListAdapter()).getItem(position);
        Log.d(TAG, c.getTitle() + " was clicked");
    }
}
```

The **getListAdapter()** method is a **ListFragment** convenience method that returns the adapter that is set on the **ListFragment**'s list view. You then call the adapter's **getItem(int)** method using the position parameter of **onListItemClick(…)** and cast the result to a **Crime**.

Run CriminalIntent again. Click a list item and check the log to confirm that the correct **Crime** was retrieved.

Customizing List Items

So far, each of your list items only displays the title of a **Crime** – the result of **Crime.toString()**.

When you want to display more than just a string, you can create custom list items. Implementing custom list items requires two things:

- creating a new layout in XML that defines the view for the list item

- creating a subclass of **ArrayAdapter<T>** that knows how to create, populate, and return the view defined in the new layout

Creating the list item layout

For CriminalIntent, a list item's layout should include the crime's title, its date, and whether the case has been solved (Figure 9.11). This layout calls for two **TextView**s and a **CheckBox**.

Figure 9.11 A handful of custom list items

Crime #3	
Thu Oct 18 10:30:27 EDT 2012	☐
Crime #4	
Thu Oct 18 10:30:27 EDT 2012	☑
Crime #5	
Thu Oct 18 10:30:27 EDT 2012	☐
Crime #6	
Thu Oct 18 10:30:27 EDT 2012	☑

You create a new layout for a list item view the same way you do for the view of an activity or a fragment. In the package explorer, right-click the res/layout directory and choose New → Other... → Android XML File. In the dialog that appears, choose Layout as the resource type, name the file list_item_crime.xml, set the root element to RelativeLayout, and click Finish.

In a **RelativeLayout**, you use certain layout parameters to arrange child views relative to the root layout and to each other. You are going to have the **CheckBox** align itself to the righthand side of the **RelativeLayout**. The two **TextView**s will align themselves relative to the **CheckBox**.

Figure 9.12 shows the widgets for the custom list item layout. The **CheckBox** child must be defined first even though it will appear on the righthand side of the layout. This is because the **TextView**s will use the ID of the **CheckBox** as an attribute value.

For the same reason, the title **TextView** must be defined before the date **TextView**. In a layout file, a widget must be defined before other widgets can use its ID in their definitions.

Figure 9.12 Custom list item layout (`list_item_crime.xml`)

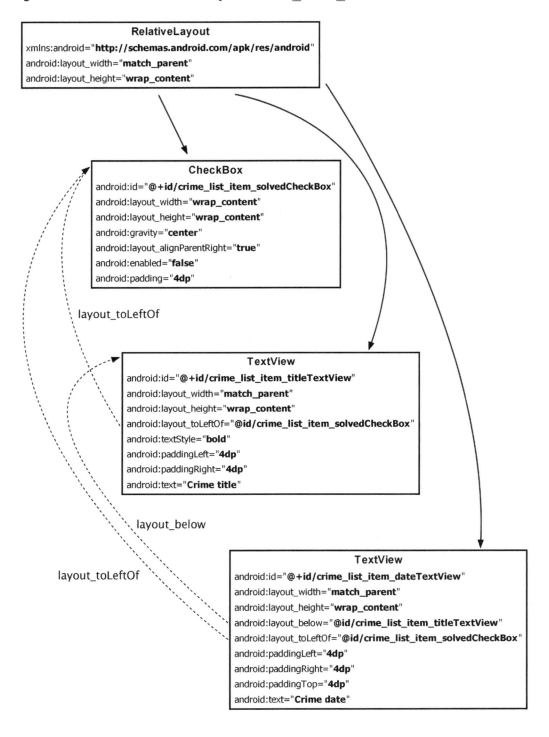

Notice that when you use a widget's ID in another widget's definition, you do not include the +. The + sign is used to create the ID when it first appears in a layout file – typically in an android:id attribute.

Also, notice that you are using literal strings instead of string resources for the android:text attributes. These text attributes are dummy text for developing and testing. The adapter will provide the values that the user will see. Because these particular strings will never be seen by users, there is little benefit to creating string resources.

Your custom list item layout is complete, and you can turn to the next step – creating a custom adapter.

Creating an adapter subclass

Your custom layout is designed to display **Crime**-specific list items. The data for these list items must be obtained using **Crime** accessor methods, so you need a new adapter that knows how to work with **Crime** objects.

In CrimeListFragment.java, create a subclass of **ArrayAdapter** as an inner class of **CrimeListFragment**.

Listing 9.18 Adding custom adapter as inner class (CrimeListFragment.java)

```
public void onListItemClick(ListView l, View v, int position, long id) {
    Crime c = (Crime)(getListAdapter()).getItem(position);
    Log.d(TAG, c.getTitle() + " was clicked");
}

private class CrimeAdapter extends ArrayAdapter<Crime> {

    public CrimeAdapter(ArrayList<Crime> crimes) {
        super(getActivity(), 0, crimes);
    }

}

}
```

The call to the superclass constructor is required to properly hook up your dataset of **Crime**s. You will not be using a pre-defined layout, so you can pass 0 for the layout ID.

The place to create and return a custom list item is the **ArrayAdapter<T>** method:

```
public View getView(int position, View convertView, ViewGroup parent)
```

The convertView parameter is an existing list item that the adapter can reconfigure and return instead of creating a brand new object. Reusing view objects is a performance advantage because you do not constantly create and destroy the same type of object. A **ListView** can only display so many list items at a time, so there is no reason to have a number of unused view objects floating around and using up memory.

In the **CrimeAdapter** class, override **getView(…)** to return a view inflated from your custom layout and populated with the correct **Crime** data (Listing 9.19).

Listing 9.19 Overriding **getView(…)** (CrimeListFragment.java)

```
private class CrimeAdapter extends ArrayAdapter<Crime> {

    public CrimeAdapter(ArrayList<Crime> crimes) {
        super(getActivity(), 0, crimes);
    }

    @Override
    public View getView(int position, View convertView, ViewGroup parent) {
        // If we weren't given a view, inflate one
        if (convertView == null) {
            convertView = getActivity().getLayoutInflater()
                .inflate(R.layout.list_item_crime, null);
        }

        // Configure the view for this Crime
        Crime c = getItem(position);

        TextView titleTextView =
            (TextView)convertView.findViewById(R.id.crime_list_item_titleTextView);
        titleTextView.setText(c.getTitle());
        TextView dateTextView =
            (TextView)convertView.findViewById(R.id.crime_list_item_dateTextView);
        dateTextView.setText(c.getDate().toString());
        CheckBox solvedCheckBox =
            (CheckBox)convertView.findViewById(R.id.crime_list_item_solvedCheckBox);
        solvedCheckBox.setChecked(c.isSolved());

        return convertView;
    }
}
```

In this implementation of **getView(…)**, you first check to see if a recycled view was passed in. If not, you inflate one from the custom layout.

Whether you are working with a new object or a recycled object, you call **Adapter**'s **getItem(int)** method to get the **Crime** for the current position in the list.

After you have the correct **Crime**, you get a reference to each widget in the view object and configure it with the **Crime**'s data. Finally, you return the view object to the **ListView**.

Now you can hook up your custom adapter in **CrimeListFragment**. At the top of CrimeListFragment.java, update the implementations of **onCreate(…)** and **onListItemClick(…)** to use a **CrimeAdapter**, as in Listing 9.20.

Listing 9.20 Using a **CrimeAdapter** (CrimeListFragment.java)

```
        ArrayAdapter<Crime> adapter = new ArrayAdapter<Crime>(this,
            android.R.layout.simple_list_item_1,
            mCrimes);
        CrimeAdapter adapter = new CrimeAdapter(mCrimes);
        setListAdapter(adapter);
    }

    public void onListItemClick(ListView l, View v, int position, long id) {
        Crime c = (Crime)(getListAdapter()).getItem(position);
        Crime c = ((CrimeAdapter)getListAdapter()).getItem(position);
        Log.d(TAG, c.getTitle() + " was clicked");
    }
```

Since you are casting to **CrimeAdapter**, you get the benefits of type-checking. **CrimeAdapter** can only hold **Crime** objects, so you no longer need to cast to **Crime**.

Under ordinary circumstances, you would now be ready to run. However, because you have a **CheckBox** in your list item, there is one more change to make. A **CheckBox** is *focusable* by default. This means that a click on a list item will be interpreted as toggling the **CheckBox** and will not reach your **onListItemClick(…)** method.

This internal quirk of **ListView** means that any focusable widget that appears in a list item layout (like a **CheckBox** or a **Button**) should be made non-focusable to ensure that a click on a list item will work as you expect.

Because your **CheckBox** only reports information and is not tied to any application logic, there is a simple solution. You can update list_item_crime.xml to define the **CheckBox** as not focusable.

Listing 9.21 Making the **CheckBox** non-focusable (list_item_crime.xml)

```
...

<CheckBox android:id="@+id/crime_list_item_solvedCheckBox"
    android:layout_width="wrap_content"
    android:layout_height="match_parent"
    android:gravity="center"
    android:layout_alignParentRight="true"
    android:enabled="false"
    android:focusable="false"
    android:padding="4dp" />

...
```

Run your app and scroll through your custom list items. Click a list item and check the log to confirm that **CrimeAdapter** is returning the correct crimes. If you are able to get the application to run but the layout does not look right, return to list_item_crime.xml and recheck your layout.

Figure 9.13 Now with custom list items!

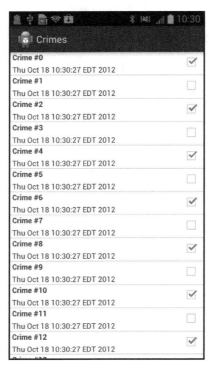

10

Using Fragment Arguments

In this chapter, you will get the list and the detail parts of CriminalIntent working together. When a user clicks on an item in the list of crimes, a new **CrimeActivity** hosting a **CrimeFragment** will appear and display the details for a particular instance of **Crime**.

Figure 10.1 Starting **CrimeActivity** from **CrimeListActivity**

In GeoQuiz, you had one activity (**QuizActivity**) start another activity (**CheatActivity**). In CriminalIntent, you are going to start the **CrimeActivity** from a fragment. In particular, you will have **CrimeListFragment** start an instance of **CrimeActivity**.

Starting an Activity from a Fragment

Starting an activity from a fragment works nearly the same as starting an activity from another activity. You call the **Fragment.startActivity(Intent)** method, which calls the corresponding **Activity** method behind the scenes.

In **CrimeListFragment**'s implementation of **onListItemClick(…)**, replace logging the crime's title with code that starts an instance of **CrimeActivity**. (Ignore the warning about the **Crime** variable being unused; you will be using it again in the next section.)

Listing 10.1 Starting **CrimeActivity** (CrimeListFragment.java)

```
public void onListItemClick(ListView l, View v, int position, long id) {
    // Get the Crime from the adapter
    Crime c = ((CrimeAdapter)getListAdapter()).getItem(position);
    Log.d(TAG, c.getTitle() + " was clicked");

    // Start CrimeActivity
    Intent i = new Intent(getActivity(), CrimeActivity.class);
    startActivity(i);
}
```

Here **CrimeListFragment** creates an explicit intent that names the **CrimeActivity** class. **CrimeListFragment** uses the **getActivity()** method to pass its hosting activity as the **Context** object that the **Intent** constructor requires.

Run CriminalIntent. Click on any list item, and you will see a new **CrimeActivity** hosting a **CrimeFragment**.

Figure 10.2 A blank **CrimeFragment**

The **CrimeFragment** does not yet display the data for a specific **Crime** because you have not told it which **Crime** to display.

Putting an extra

You can tell **CrimeFragment** which **Crime** to display by making the mCrimeId an **Intent** extra. In **onListItemClick(…)**, put the mCrimeId of the selected **Crime** on the intent that starts **CrimeActivity**. This code will have an error because you have not yet created the CrimeFragment.EXTRA_CRIME_ID key. Ignore the error; you will create the key next.

Listing 10.2 Starting **CrimeActivity** with an extra
(CrimeListFragment.java)

```java
public void onListItemClick(ListView l, View v, int position, long id) {
    // Get the Crime from the adapter
    Crime c = ((CrimeAdapter)getListAdapter()).getItem(position);

    // Start CrimeActivity
    Intent i = new Intent(getActivity(), CrimeActivity.class);
    i.putExtra(CrimeFragment.EXTRA_CRIME_ID, c.getId());
    startActivity(i);
}
```

After creating an explicit intent, you call **putExtra(…)** and pass in a string key and the value to pair with it (the mCrimeId). In this case, you are calling **putExtra(String, Serializable)** because **UUID** is a **Serializable** object.

Retrieving an extra

The mCrimeId is now safely stashed in the intent that belongs to **CrimeActivity**. However, it is the **CrimeFragment** class that needs to retrieve and use that data.

There are two ways a fragment can access data in its activity's intent: an easy, direct shortcut and a complex, flexible implementation. First, you are going to try out the shortcut. Then you will implement the complex and flexible solution that involves *fragment arguments*.

In the shortcut, **CrimeFragment** will simply use the **getActivity()** method to access the **CrimeActivity**'s intent directly. Return to **CrimeFragment** and add the key for the extra. Then, in **onCreate(Bundle)**, retrieve the extra from **CrimeActivity**'s intent and use it to fetch the **Crime**.

Listing 10.3 Retrieving the extra and fetching the **Crime** (CrimeFragment.java)

```
public class CrimeFragment extends Fragment {
    public static final String EXTRA_CRIME_ID =
        "com.bignerdranch.android.criminalintent.crime_id";

    private Crime mCrime;

    ...

    public void onCreate(Bundle savedInstanceState) {
        super.onCreate(savedInstanceState);
        mCrime = new Crime();
        UUID crimeId = (UUID)getActivity().getIntent()
            .getSerializableExtra(EXTRA_CRIME_ID);

        mCrime = CrimeLab.get(getActivity()).getCrime(crimeId);
}
```

In Listing 10.3, other than the call to **getActivity()**, the code is the same as if you were retrieving the extra from the activity's code. The **getIntent()** method returns the **Intent** that was used to start **CrimeActivity**. You call **getSerializableExtra(String)** on the **Intent** to pull the **UUID** out into a variable.

After you have retrieved the ID, you use it to fetch the **Crime** from **CrimeLab**. The **CrimeLab.get(…)** method requires a **Context** object, so **CrimeFragment** passes the **CrimeActivity**.

Updating CrimeFragment's view with Crime data

Now that **CrimeFragment** fetches a **Crime**, its view can display that **Crime**'s data. Update **onCreateView(…)** to display the **Crime**'s title and solved status. (The code for displaying the date is already in place.)

Listing 10.4 Updating view objects (`CrimeFragment.java`)

```java
@Override
public View onCreateView(LayoutInflater inflater, ViewGroup parent,
        Bundle savedInstanceState) {
    ...

    mTitleField = (EditText)v.findViewById(R.id.crime_title);
    mTitleField.setText(mCrime.getTitle());
    mTitleField.addTextChangedListener(new TextWatcher() {
        ...
    });

    ...

    mSolvedCheckBox = (CheckBox)v.findViewById(R.id.crime_solved);
    mSolvedCheckBox.setChecked(mCrime.isSolved());
    mSolvedCheckBox.setOnCheckedChangeListener(new OnCheckedChangeListener() {
        ...
    });

    ...

    return v;
}
```

Run CriminalIntent. Select Crime #4 and watch a **CrimeFragment** instance with the correct crime data appear.

Figure 10.3 The crime that you wanted to see

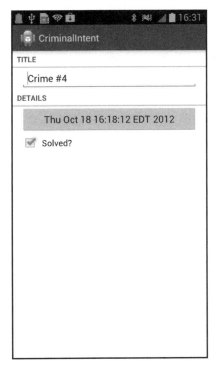

The downside to direct retrieval

Having the fragment access the intent that belongs to the hosting activity makes for simple code. However, it costs you the encapsulation of your fragment. **CrimeFragment** is no longer a reusable building block because it expects that it will always be hosted by an activity whose **Intent** defines an extra named EXTRA_CRIME_ID.

This may be a reasonable expectation on **CrimeFragment**'s part, but it means that **CrimeFragment**, as currently written, cannot be used with just any activity.

A better solution is to stash the mCrimeId someplace that belongs to **CrimeFragment** rather than keeping it in **CrimeActivity**'s personal space. The **CrimeFragment** could then retrieve this data without relying on the presence of a particular extra in the activity's intent. The "someplace" that belongs to a fragment is known as its *arguments* bundle.

Fragment Arguments

Every fragment instance can have a **Bundle** object attached to it. This bundle contains key-value pairs that work just like the intent extras of an **Activity**. Each pair is known as an *argument*.

To create fragment arguments, you first create a **Bundle** object. Next, you use type-specific "put" methods of **Bundle** (similar to those of **Intent**) to add arguments to the bundle.

```
Bundle args = new Bundle();
args.putSerializable(EXTRA_MY_OBJECT, myObject);
args.putInt(EXTRA_MY_INT, myInt);
args.putCharSequence(EXTRA_MY_STRING, myString);
```

Attaching arguments to a fragment

To attach the arguments bundle to a fragment, you call **Fragment.setArguments(Bundle)**. Attaching arguments to a fragment must be done after the fragment is created but before it is added to an activity.

To hit this window, Android programmers follow a convention of adding a static method named **newInstance()** to the **Fragment** class. This method creates the fragment instance and bundles up and sets its arguments.

When the hosting activity needs an instance of that fragment, you have it call the **newInstance()** method rather than calling the constructor directly. The activity can pass in any required parameters to **newInstance(…)** that the fragment needs to create its arguments.

In **CrimeFragment**, write a **newInstance(UUID)** method that accepts a **UUID**, creates an arguments bundle, creates a fragment instance, and then attaches the arguments to the fragment.

Listing 10.5 Writing a **newInstance(UUID)** method (CrimeFragment.java)

```
public static CrimeFragment newInstance(UUID crimeId) {
    Bundle args = new Bundle();
    args.putSerializable(EXTRA_CRIME_ID, crimeId);

    CrimeFragment fragment = new CrimeFragment();
    fragment.setArguments(args);

    return fragment;
}
```

Now **CrimeActivity** should call **CrimeFragment.newInstance(UUID)** when it needs to create a **CrimeFragment**. It will pass in the **UUID** it retrieved from its extra. Return to **CrimeActivity** and in **createFragment()**, retrieve the extra from **CrimeActivity**'s intent and pass it into **CrimeFragment.newInstance(UUID)**.

Listing 10.6 Using **newInstance(UUID)** (CrimeActivity.java)

```
@Override
protected Fragment createFragment() {
    return new CrimeFragment();

    UUID crimeId = (UUID)getIntent()
        .getSerializableExtra(CrimeFragment.EXTRA_CRIME_ID);

    return CrimeFragment.newInstance(crimeId);
}
```

Notice that the need for independence does not go both ways. **CrimeActivity** has to know plenty about **CrimeFragment**, like that it has a **newInstance(UUID)** method. This is fine. Hosting activities should know the specifics of how to host their fragments, but fragments should not have to know specifics about their activity. At least, not if you want to maintain the flexibility of independent fragments.

Retrieving arguments

When a fragment needs to access its arguments, it calls the **Fragment** method **getArguments()** and then one of the type-specific "get" methods of **Bundle**.

Back in **CrimeFragment.onCreate(…)**, replace your shortcut code with retrieving the **UUID** from the fragment arguments.

Listing 10.7 Getting crime ID from the arguments (CrimeFragment.java)

```
@Override
public void onCreate(Bundle savedInstanceState) {
    super.onCreate(savedInstanceState);

    UUID crimeId = (UUID)getActivity().getIntent()
        .getSerializableExtra(EXTRA_CRIME_ID);

    UUID crimeId = (UUID)getArguments().getSerializable(EXTRA_CRIME_ID);

    mCrime = CrimeLab.get(getActivity()).getCrime(crimeId);

}
```

Run CriminalIntent. The app will behave the same, but you should feel all warm and fuzzy inside for maintaining **CrimeFragment**'s independence. You are also well-prepared for the next chapter where you will implement more sophisticated navigation in CriminalIntent.

Reloading the List

There is one more detail to take care of. Run CriminalIntent, click a list item, and then modify that **Crime**'s details. These changes are saved to the model, but when you return to the list, the list view is unchanged.

The list view's adapter needs to be informed that the data set has changed (or may have changed) so that it can refetch the data and reload the list. You can work with the **ActivityManager**'s back stack to reload the list at the right moment.

When **CrimeListFragment** starts an instance of **CrimeActivity**, the **CrimeActivity** is put on top of the stack. This pauses and stops the instance of **CrimeListActivity** that was initially on top.

When the user presses the Back button to return to the list, the **CrimeActivity** is popped off the stack and destroyed. At that point, the **CrimeListActivity** is started and resumed.

Figure 10.4 CriminalIntent's back stack

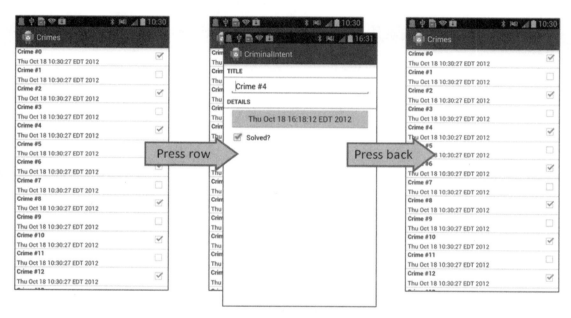

When the **CrimeListActivity** is resumed, it receives a call to **onResume()** from the OS. When **CrimeListActivity** receives this call, its **FragmentManager** calls **onResume()** on the fragments that the activity is currently hosting. In this case, the only fragment is **CrimeListFragment**.

In **CrimeListFragment**, override **onResume()** to reload the list.

Listing 10.8 Reloading the list in **onResume()** (CrimeListFragment.java)

```
@Override
public void onResume() {
    super.onResume();
    ((CrimeAdapter)getListAdapter()).notifyDataSetChanged();
}
```

Why override **onResume()** to update the list view and not **onStart()**? You cannot assume that your activity will be stopped when another activity is in front of it. If the other activity is transparent, your activity may just be paused. If your activity is paused and your update code is in **onStart()**, then the list will not be reloaded. In general, **onResume()** is the safest place to take action to update a fragment's view.

Run CriminalIntent. Select a crime and change its details. When you return to the list, you will immediately see your changes.

You have made progress with CriminalIntent in the last two chapters. Let's take a look at an updated object diagram.

Figure 10.5 Updated object diagram for CriminalIntent

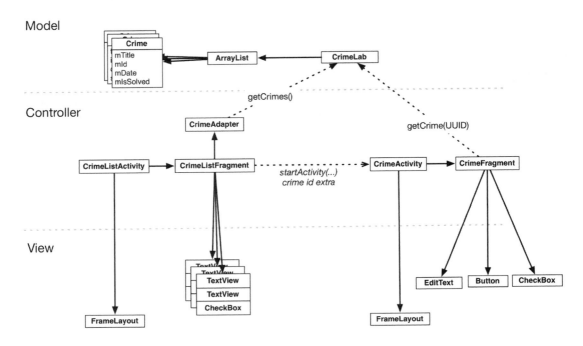

Getting Results with Fragments

In this chapter, you did not need a result back from the started activity. What if you did? Your code would look a lot like it did in GeoQuiz. Instead of using the **Activity**'s **startActivityForResult(…)** method, you would use **Fragment.startActivityForResult(…)**. Instead of overriding **Activity.onActivityResult(…)**, you would override **Fragment.onActivityResult(…)**.

```
public class CrimeListFragment extends ListFragment {
    private static final int REQUEST_CRIME = 1;

    ...

    public void onListItemClick(ListView l, View v, int position, long id) {
        // Get the Crime from the adapter
        Crime c = ((CrimeAdapter)getListAdapter()).getItem(position);
        Log.d(TAG, c.getTitle() + " was clicked");
        // Start CrimeActivity
        Intent i = new Intent(getActivity(), CrimeActivity.class);
        startActivityForResult(i, REQUEST_CRIME);
    }
```

```
    @Override
    public void onActivityResult(int requestCode, int resultCode, Intent data) {
        if (requestCode == REQUEST_CRIME) {
            // Handle result
        }
    }
}
```

Fragment.startActivityForResult(Intent,int) is similar to the **Activity** method with the same name. It includes some additional code to route the result to your fragment from its host activity.

Returning results from a fragment is a bit different. A fragment can receive a result from an activity, but it cannot have its own result. Only activities have results. So while **Fragment** has its own **startActivityForResult(…)** and **onActivityResult(…)** methods, it does not have any **setResult(…)** methods.

Instead, you tell the *host activity* to return a value. Like this:

```
public class CrimeFragment extends Fragment {
    ...

    public void returnResult() {
        getActivity().setResult(Activity.RESULT_OK, null);
    }
}
```

You will get a chance to return an activity result from a fragment in CriminalIntent in Chapter 20.

11

Using ViewPager

In this chapter, you will create a new activity to host **CrimeFragment**. This activity's layout will consist of an instance of **ViewPager**. Adding a **ViewPager** to your UI lets users navigate between list items by swiping across the screen to "page" forward or backward through the crimes.

Figure 11.1 Swiping to page through crimes

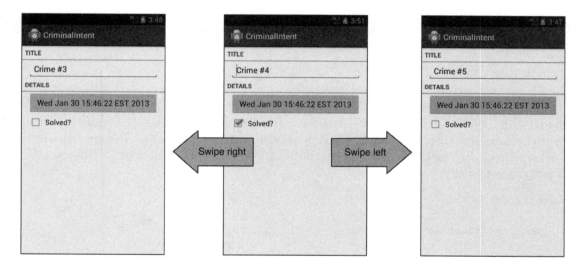

Figure 11.2 shows an updated diagram for CriminalIntent. The new activity will be named **CrimePagerActivity** and will take the place of **CrimeActivity**. Its layout will consist of a **ViewPager**.

Figure 11.2 Layout diagram for **CrimePagerActivity**

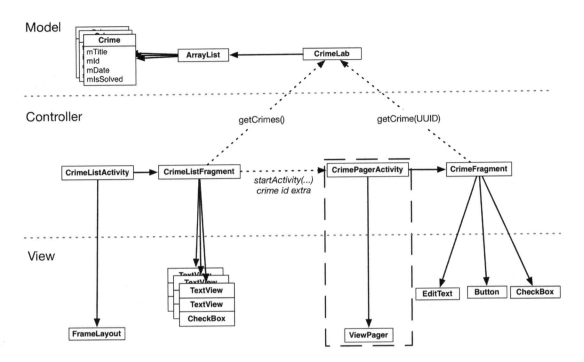

The only new objects you need to create are within the dashed rectangle in the diagram above. Nothing else in CriminalIntent needs to change to implement paging between detail views. In particular, you will not have to touch the **CrimeFragment** class thanks to the work you did in Chapter 10 to ensure **CrimeFragment**'s independence.

Here are the tasks ahead in this chapter:

- create the **CrimePagerActivity** class

- define a view hierarchy that consists of a **ViewPager**

- wire up the **ViewPager** and its adapter in **CrimePagerActivity**

- modify **CrimeListFragment.onListItemClick(…)** to start **CrimePagerActivity** instead of **CrimeActivity**

Creating CrimePagerActivity

CrimePagerActivity will be a subclass of **FragmentActivity**. It will create and manage the **ViewPager**.

Create a new class named **CrimePagerActivity**. Make its superclass **FragmentActivity**. In **onCreate(Bundle)**, simply call through to the superclass – you will create your instance of **ViewPager** in a moment.

Listing 11.1 Set up **ViewPager** (CrimePagerActivity.java)

```java
public class CrimePagerActivity extends FragmentActivity {
    private ViewPager mViewPager;

    @Override
    public void onCreate(Bundle savedInstanceState) {
        super.onCreate(savedInstanceState);
    }
}
```

Laying out views in code

Elsewhere in this book, you have defined view layouts in layout XML files. This is generally a good idea, but there is nothing in Android that requires you to define your layout this way. Your view hierarchy in this chapter will be simple – just a single view. So instead of using an XML file, let's define your hierarchy in code. Since you only have one view here, this is not an involved task.

No magic is necessary to create a view: just call its constructor. Unfortunately, that does not leave you completely free of XML. Resource IDs are still required for some components. **ViewPager** is one of them. The **FragmentManager** requires that any view used as a fragment container must have an ID. **ViewPager** is a fragment container, so you will need to assign an ID to it.

That gives you the following list of things to do:

- create a resource ID for your **ViewPager**

- create an instance of **ViewPager** and assign it to mViewPager.

- configure it by assigning a resource ID to it.

- set your **ViewPager** as the content view of your activity.

Standalone ID resources

Defining a standalone resource ID is not unlike defining a string resource: you create an item element in an XML file in res/values. Create a new Android XML resource file called res/values/ids.xml to store your IDs in, and add an ID called viewPager:

Listing 11.2 Create standalone resource ID (res/values/ids.xml)

```xml
<?xml version="1.0" encoding="utf-8"?>
<resources>

    <item type="id" name="viewPager" />

</resources>
```

With your ID created, you are ready to create and show your **ViewPager**. Instantiate your **ViewPager** and set it as the content view:

Listing 11.3 Create content view programmatically (CrimePagerActivity.java)

```
@Override
public void onCreate(Bundle savedInstanceState) {
    super.onCreate(savedInstanceState);
    mViewPager = new ViewPager(this);
    mViewPager.setId(R.id.viewPager);
    setContentView(mViewPager);
}
```

The **ViewPager** class is from the support library. Unlike **Fragment**, **ViewPager** is only available in the support library; there is not a "standard" **ViewPager** class in a later SDK.

ViewPager and PagerAdapter

A **ViewPager** is like an **AdapterView** (the superclass of **ListView**) in some ways. An **AdapterView** requires an **Adapter** to provide views. A **ViewPager** requires a **PagerAdapter**.

However, the conversation between **ViewPager** and **PagerAdapter** is much more involved than the conversation between **AdapterView** and **Adapter**. Luckily, you can use **FragmentStatePagerAdapter**, a subclass of **PagerAdapter**, to take care of many of the details.

FragmentStatePagerAdapter will boil down the conversation to two simple methods: **getCount()** and **getItem(int)**. When your **getItem(int)** method is called for a position in your array of crimes, you will return a **CrimeFragment** configured to display the crime at that position.

In **CrimePagerActivity**, add the following code to set the **ViewPager**'s pager adapter and implement its **getCount()** and **getItem(int)** methods.

Listing 11.4 Set up pager adapter (CrimePagerActivity.java)

```java
public class CrimePagerActivity extends FragmentActivity {
    private ViewPager mViewPager;
    private ArrayList<Crime> mCrimes;

    @Override
    public void onCreate(Bundle savedInstanceState) {
        super.onCreate(savedInstanceState);
        mViewPager = new ViewPager(this);
        mViewPager.setId(R.id.viewPager);
        setContentView(mViewPager);

        mCrimes = CrimeLab.get(this).getCrimes();

        FragmentManager fm = getSupportFragmentManager();
        mViewPager.setAdapter(new FragmentStatePagerAdapter(fm) {
            @Override
            public int getCount() {
                return mCrimes.size();
            }

            @Override
            public Fragment getItem(int pos) {
                Crime crime = mCrimes.get(pos);
                return CrimeFragment.newInstance(crime.getId());
            }
        });
    }
}
```

Let's go through this code. In the first line, you get your data set from **CrimeLab** – the **ArrayList** of crimes. Next, you get the activity's instance of **FragmentManager**.

Then you set the adapter to be an unnamed instance of **FragmentStatePagerAdapter**. Creating the **FragmentStatePagerAdapter** requires the **FragmentManager**. Remember that **FragmentStatePagerAdapter** is your agent managing the conversation with **ViewPager**. For your agent to do its job with the fragments you return in **getItem(int)**, it needs to be able to add them to your activity. That is why it needs your **FragmentManager**.

(What exactly is your agent doing? The short story is that it is adding the fragments you return to your activity and helping **ViewPager** identify the fragments' views so that they can be placed correctly. More details are in the For the More Curious section at the end of the chapter.)

The pager adapter's two methods are straightforward. The **getCount()** method returns how many items there are in the array list. The **getItem(int)** method is where the magic happens. It fetches the **Crime** instance for the given position in the dataset. It then uses that **Crime**'s ID to create and return a properly configured **CrimeFragment**.

Integrating CrimePagerActivity

Now you can begin the process of decommissioning **CrimeActivity** and putting **CrimePagerActivity** in its place.

First, you want pressing a list item in **CrimeListFragment** to start an instance of **CrimePagerActivity** instead of **CrimeActivity**.

Return to `CrimeListFragment.java` and modify **onListItemClick(...)** to start a **CrimePagerActivity**.

Listing 11.5 Fire it up (`CrimeListFragment.java`)

```
@Override
public void onListItemClick(ListView l, View v, int position, long id) {
    // Get the Crime from the adapter
    Crime c = ((CrimeAdapter)getListAdapter()).getItem(position);
    // Start CrimeActivity
    Intent i = new Intent(getActivity(), CrimeActivity.class);
    // Start CrimePagerActivity with this crime
    Intent i = new Intent(getActivity(), CrimePagerActivity.class);
    i.putExtra(CrimeFragment.EXTRA_CRIME_ID, c.getId());
    startActivity(i);
}
```

You also need to add **CrimePagerActivity** to the manifest so that the OS can start it. While you are in the manifest, remove **CrimeActivity**'s declaration.

Listing 11.6 Add **CrimePagerActivity** to manifest (AndroidManifest.xml)

```
<?xml version="1.0" encoding="utf-8"?>
<manifest ...>
   ...
   <application ...>
      ...
      <activity
        android:name=".CrimeActivity"
        android:label="@string/app_name" >
      </activity>
      <activity android:name=".CrimePagerActivity"
        android:label="@string/app_name">
      </activity>

   </application>

</manifest>
```

Finally, to keep your project tidy, delete `CrimeActivity.java` from the package explorer.

Run CriminalIntent. Press Crime #0 to view its details. Then swipe left and right to browse more crimes. Notice that the paging is smooth and there is no delay in loading. By default, **ViewPager** loads the item currently on screen plus one neighboring page in each direction so that the response to a swipe is immediate. You can tweak how many neighboring pages are loaded by calling **setOffscreenPageLimit(int)**.

But all is not yet perfect with your **ViewPager**. Press Back to return to the list of crimes and press a different item. You will see the first crime displayed again instead of the crime that you asked for.

By default, the **ViewPager** shows the first item in its **PagerAdapter**. You can have it show the crime that was selected by setting the **ViewPager**'s current item to the index of the selected crime.

At the end of **CrimePagerActivity.onCreate(...)**, find the index of the crime to display by looping through and checking each crime's ID. When you find the **Crime** instance whose mId matches the crimeId in the intent extra, set the current item to the index of that **Crime**.

Listing 11.7 Set initial pager item (`CrimePagerActivity.java`)

```java
public class CrimePagerActivity extends FragmentActivity {
    @Override
    public void onCreate(Bundle savedInstanceState) {
        ...

        FragmentManager fm = getSupportFragmentManager();
        mViewPager.setAdapter(new FragmentStatePagerAdapter(fm) {
            ...
        });

        UUID crimeId = (UUID)getIntent()
            .getSerializableExtra(CrimeFragment.EXTRA_CRIME_ID);
        for (int i = 0; i < mCrimes.size(); i++) {
            if (mCrimes.get(i).getId().equals(crimeId)) {
                mViewPager.setCurrentItem(i);
                break;
            }
        }
    }
}
```

Run CriminalIntent. Selecting any list item should display the details of the correct **Crime**.

There is one more feature you can add. You can replace the activity's title that appears on the action bar (or the title bar on older devices) with the title of the current **Crime**. To make this happen, implement the **ViewPager.OnPageChangeListener** interface.

Listing 11.8 Add **OnPageListener** (`CrimePagerActivity.java`)

```java
@Override
public void onCreate(Bundle savedInstanceState) {
    super.onCreate(savedInstanceState);
    mViewPager = new ViewPager(this);
    mViewPager.setId(R.id.viewPager);
    setContentView(mViewPager);

    mCrimes = CrimeLab.get(this).getCrimes();

    FragmentManager fm = getSupportFragmentManager();
    mViewPager.setAdapter(new FragmentStatePagerAdapter(fm) {
        ...
    });

    mViewPager.setOnPageChangeListener(new ViewPager.OnPageChangeListener() {
        public void onPageScrollStateChanged(int state) { }

        public void onPageScrolled(int pos, float posOffset, int posOffsetPixels) { }

        public void onPageSelected(int pos) {
            Crime crime = mCrimes.get(pos);
            if (crime.getTitle() != null) {
                setTitle(crime.getTitle());
            }
        }
    });

    ...
}
```

OnPageChangeListener is how you listen for changes in the page currently being displayed by **ViewPager**. When the page changes, you set **CrimePagerActivity**'s title to the title of the **Crime**.

You are only interested in which page is currently selected, so you only implement **onPageSelected(…)**. The **onPageScrolled(…)** method tells you exactly where your page is going to be, and **onPageScrollStateChanged(…)** tells you whether the page animation is being actively dragged, settling to a steady state, or idling.

Run CriminalIntent to see that each swipe updates the activity's title to the mTitle of the current **Crime**. And that is it. Your **ViewPager** is now fully-armed and operational.

FragmentStatePagerAdapter vs. FragmentPagerAdapter

There is another **PagerAdapter** type that you can use called **FragmentPagerAdapter**. **FragmentPagerAdapter** is used exactly like **FragmentStatePagerAdapter**. It only differs in how it unloads your fragments when they are no longer needed.

Figure 11.3 **FragmentStatePagerAdapter**'s fragment management

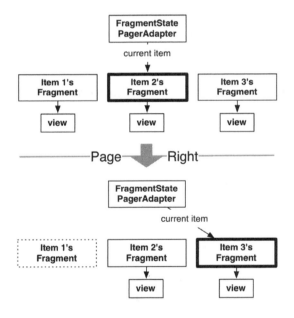

With **FragmentStatePagerAdapter**, your unneeded fragment is destroyed. A transaction is committed to completely remove the fragment from your activity's **FragmentManager**. The "state" in **FragmentStatePagerAdapter** comes from the fact that it will save out your fragment's **Bundle** from **onSaveInstanceState(Bundle)** when it is destroyed. When the user navigates back, the new fragment will be restored using that instance state.

By comparison, **FragmentPagerAdapter** does nothing of the kind. When your fragment is no longer needed, **FragmentPagerAdapter** calls **detach(Fragment)** on the transaction instead of **remove(Fragment)**. This destroys the fragment's view, but leaves the fragment instance alive in the **FragmentManager**. So the fragments created by **FragmentPagerAdapter** are never destroyed.

Figure 11.4 **FragmentPagerAdapter**'s fragment management

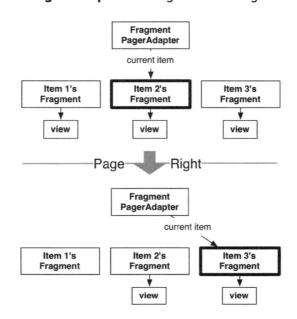

Which kind of adapter you want to use depends on your application. In general, **FragmentStatePagerAdapter** is more frugal with memory. CriminalIntent is displaying what could be a long list of crimes, each of which will eventually include a photo. You do not want to keep all that information in memory, so you use **FragmentStatePagerAdapter**.

On the other hand, if your interface has a small, fixed number of fragments, **FragmentPagerAdapter** is safe and appropriate. The most common example of this scenario is a tabbed interface. Some detail views have enough details to require two screens, so the details are split across multiple tabs. Adding a swipable **ViewPager** to this interface makes the app tactile. Keeping these fragments in memory can make your controller code easier to manage, and because this style of interface usually has only two or three fragments per activity, there is little danger of running low on memory.

For the More Curious: How ViewPager Really Works

The ViewPager and PagerAdapter classes handle many things for you behind the scenes. This section will supply more details about what is going on back there.

Two caveats before we get into this discussion: First, according to the documentation, **ViewPager** is still under development, so these interfaces could change in the future. Second, you do not need to understand the nitty-gritty details in most cases.

But if you need to implement the **PagerAdapter** interface yourself, you will need to know how the **ViewPager**-**PagerAdapter** relationship differs from an ordinary **AdapterView**-**Adapter** relationship.

So why is **ViewPager** not an **AdapterView**? There is an **AdapterView** subclass called **Gallery** that behaves similarly. Why not use that?

Using an **AdapterView** in this case would be a lot of work because you could not use your existing **Fragment**. An **Adapter** expects you to provide a **View** instantly. However, your **FragmentManager** determines when your fragment's view is created, not you. So when **Gallery** comes knocking at your **Adapter**'s door for your fragment's view, you will not be able to create the fragment *and* provide its view immediately.

This is the reason **ViewPager** exists. Instead of an **Adapter**, it uses a class called **PagerAdapter**. **PagerAdapter** is more complicated than **Adapter** because it does more of the work of managing views than **Adapter** does. Here are the basics:

Instead of a **getView(…)** method that returns a view, **PagerAdapter** has the following methods:

```
public Object instantiateItem(ViewGroup container, int position)
public void destroyItem(ViewGroup container, int position, Object object)
public abstract boolean isViewFromObject(View view, Object object)
```

PagerAdapter.instantiateItem(ViewGroup, int) tells the pager adapter to create an item view for a given position and add it to a container **ViewGroup**, and **destroyItem(ViewGroup, int, Object)** tells it to destroy that item. Note that **instantiateItem(ViewGroup, int)** does not say to create the view *right now*. The **PagerAdapter** could create the view at any time after that.

Once the view has been created, **ViewPager** will notice it at some point. To figure out which item's view it is, it calls **isViewFromObject(View, Object)**. The **Object** parameter is an object received from a call to **instantiateItem(ViewGroup, int)**. So if **ViewPager** calls **instantiateItem(ViewGroup, 5)** and receives object A, **isViewFromObject(View, A)** should return true if the **View** passed in is for item 5, and false otherwise.

This is a complicated process for the **ViewPager**, but it is less complicated for the **PagerAdapter**, which only needs to be able to create views, destroy views, and identify which object a view comes from. This loose requirement gives a **PagerAdapter** implementation enough wiggle room to create and add a new fragment inside **instantiateItem(ViewGroup, int)** and return the fragment as the **Object** to keep track of. Then **isViewFromObject(View, Object)** looks like this:

```
@Override
public boolean isViewFromObject(View view, Object object) {
    return ((Fragment)object).getView() == view;
}
```

Implementing all those **PagerAdapter** overrides would be a pain to do every time you needed to use **ViewPager**. Thank goodness for **FragmentPagerAdapter** and **FragmentStatePagerAdapter**.

12

Dialogs

Dialogs demand attention and input from the user. They are useful for presenting a choice or important information. In this chapter, you will add a dialog in which users can change the date of a crime. Pressing the date button in **CrimeFragment** will present this dialog (Figure 12.1).

Figure 12.1 A dialog for picking the date of a crime

The dialog in Figure 12.1 is an instance of **AlertDialog**, a subclass of **Dialog**. **AlertDialog** is the all-purpose **Dialog** subclass that you will use most often.

(There is a **DatePickerDialog** subclass of **AlertDialog** that sounds perfect for what you are doing. However, as of this writing **DatePickerDialog** has some buggy behavior, and using **AlertDialog** is easier than working around these bugs.)

The **AlertDialog** in Figure 12.1 is wrapped in an instance of **DialogFragment**, a subclass of **Fragment**. It is possible to display an **AlertDialog** without a **DialogFragment**, but Android does not recommend it. Having the dialog managed by the **FragmentManager** gives you more options for presenting the dialog.

In addition, a bare **AlertDialog** will vanish if the device is rotated. On the other hand, if the **AlertDialog** is wrapped in a fragment, then the dialog will be recreated and put on screen after rotation.

For CriminalIntent, you are going to create a **DialogFragment** subclass named **DatePickerFragment**. Within **DatePickerFragment**, you will create and configure an instance of **AlertDialog** that displays a **DatePicker** widget. **DatePickerFragment** will be hosted by **CrimePagerActivity**.

Figure 12.2 shows you an overview of these relationships.

Figure 12.2 Object diagram for two fragments hosted by **CrimePagerActivity**

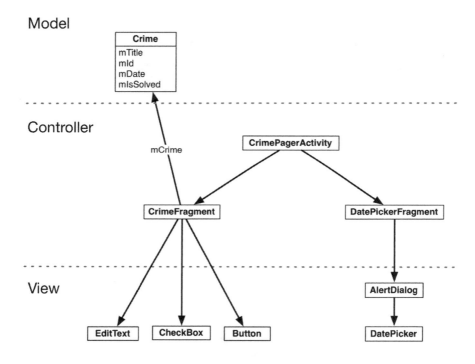

Your first tasks are

- creating the **DatePickerFragment** class

- building an **AlertDialog**

- getting the dialog on screen via the **FragmentManager**

Later in the chapter, you will wire up the **DatePicker** and pass the necessary data between **CrimeFragment** and **DatePickerFragment**.

Before you get started, add the string resource shown in Listing 12.1.

Listing 12.1 Add string for dialog title (`values/strings.xml`)

```
<resources>

    ...
    <string name="crime_solved_label">Solved?</string>
    <string name="crimes_title">Crimes</string>
    <string name="date_picker_title">Date of crime:</string>

</resources>
```

Creating a DialogFragment

Create a new class named **DatePickerFragment** and make its superclass the support library's version of **DialogFragment**: `android.support.v4.app.DialogFragment`.

DialogFragment includes the following method:

> `public Dialog onCreateDialog(Bundle savedInstanceState)`

The **FragmentManager** of the hosting activity calls this method as part of putting the **DialogFragment** on screen.

In `DatePickerFragment.java`, add an implementation of **onCreateDialog(…)** that builds an **AlertDialog** with a title and one OK button. (You will add the **DatePicker** widget later.)

Listing 12.2 Creating a **DialogFragment** (`DatePickerFragment.java`)

```
public class DatePickerFragment extends DialogFragment {
    @Override
    public Dialog onCreateDialog(Bundle savedInstanceState) {
        return new AlertDialog.Builder(getActivity())
            .setTitle(R.string.date_picker_title)
            .setPositiveButton(android.R.string.ok, null)
            .create();
    }
}
```

In this implementation, you use the **AlertDialog.Builder** class that provides a fluent interface for constructing an **AlertDialog** instance.

First, you pass a **Context** into the **AlertDialog.Builder** constructor, which returns an instance of **AlertDialog.Builder**.

Next, you call two **AlertDialog.Builder** methods to configure your dialog:

```
public AlertDialog.Builder setTitle(int titleId)
public AlertDialog.Builder setPositiveButton(int textId,
    DialogInterface.OnClickListener listener)
```

This **setPositiveButton(…)** method accepts a string resource and an object that implements **DialogInterface.OnClickListener**. In Listing 12.2, you pass in an Android constant for OK and null for the listener parameter. You will implement a listener later in the chapter.

(A *positive* button is what the user should press to accept what the dialog presents. There are two other buttons that you can add to an **AlertDialog**: a *negative* button and a *neutral* button. These designations determine the positions of the buttons in the dialog (when there is more than one). On Froyo and

Gingerbread devices, the positive button is left-most. On newer devices, the order is flipped, and the positive button is right-most.)

Finally, you finish building the dialog with a call to **AlertDialog.Builder.create()**, which returns the configured **AlertDialog** instance.

There is more that you can do with **AlertDialog** and **AlertDialog.Builder**, and the details are well-covered in the developer documentation. For now, let's move on to the mechanics of getting your dialog on screen.

Showing a DialogFragment

Like all fragments, instances of **DialogFragment** are managed by the **FragmentManager** of the hosting activity.

To get a **DialogFragment** added to the **FragmentManager** and put on screen, you can call the following methods on the fragment instance:

```
public void show(FragmentManager manager, String tag)
public void show(FragmentTransaction transaction, String tag)
```

The string parameter uniquely identifies the **DialogFragment** in the **FragmentManager**'s list. Whether you use the **FragmentManager** or **FragmentTransaction** version is up to you – if you pass in a **FragmentManager**, a transaction will automatically be created and committed for you. Here, you will pass in a **FragmentManager**.

In **CrimeFragment**, add a constant for the **DatePickerFragment**'s tag. Then, in **onCreateView(…)**, remove the code that disables the date button and set a **View.OnClickListener** that shows a **DatePickerFragment** when the date button is pressed.

Listing 12.3 Show your **DialogFragment** (CrimeFragment.java)

```
public class CrimeFragment extends Fragment {
    public static final String EXTRA_CRIME_ID =
        "com.bignerdranch.android.criminalintent.crime_id";

    private static final String DIALOG_DATE = "date";

    ...

    @Override
    public View onCreateView(LayoutInflater inflater, ViewGroup parent,
            Bundle savedInstanceState) {
        ...

        mDateButton = (Button)v.findViewById(R.id.crime_date);
        mDateButton.setText(mCrime.getDate().toString());
        mDateButton.setEnabled(false);
        mDateButton.setOnClickListener(new View.OnClickListener() {
            public void onClick(View v) {
                FragmentManager fm = getActivity()
                        .getSupportFragmentManager();
                DatePickerFragment dialog = new DatePickerFragment();
                dialog.show(fm, DIALOG_DATE);
            }
        });
```

```
        mSolvedCheckBox = (CheckBox)v.findViewById(R.id.crime_solved);
        ...

        return v;
    }

    ...
}
```

Run CriminalIntent and press the date button to see the dialog. Press the OK button to dismiss the dialog.

Figure 12.3 An **AlertDialog** with a title and a button

Setting a dialog's contents

Next, you are going to add a **DatePicker** widget to your **AlertDialog** using the following **AlertDialog.Builder** method:

```
    public AlertDialog.Builder setView(View view)
```

This method configures the dialog to display the passed-in **View** object between the dialog's title and its button(s).

In the package explorer, create a new layout file named dialog_date.xml and make its root element **DatePicker**. This layout will consist of a single **View** object – a **DatePicker** – that you will inflate and pass into **setView(…)**.

Configure the **DatePicker** as shown in Figure 12.4.

Figure 12.4 **DatePicker** layout (layout/dialog_date.xml)

DatePicker
xmlns:android="**http://schemas.android.com/apk/res/android**"
android:id="**@+id/dialog_date_datePicker**"
android:layout_width="**wrap_content**"
android:layout_height="**wrap_content**"
android:calendarViewShown="**false**"

In **DatePickerFragment.onCreateDialog(…)**, inflate this view and then set it on the dialog.

Listing 12.4 Add **DatePicker** to **AlertDialog** (DatePickerFragment.java)

```
@Override
public Dialog onCreateDialog(Bundle savedInstanceState) {
    View v = getActivity().getLayoutInflater()
        .inflate(R.layout.dialog_date, null);

    return new AlertDialog.Builder(getActivity())
        .setView(v)
        .setTitle(R.string.date_picker_title)
        .setPositiveButton(android.R.string.ok, null)
        .create();
}
```

Run CriminalIntent. Press the date button to confirm that the dialog now presents a **DatePicker**.

Figure 12.5 An **AlertDialog** with a **DatePicker**

You may be wondering why you went to the trouble of defining and inflating a layout when you could have created the **DatePicker** object in code like this:

```
@Override
public Dialog onCreateDialog(Bundle savedInstanceState) {
    DatePicker dp = new  DatePicker(getActivity());

    return new AlertDialog.Builder(getActivity())
        .setView(dp)
        ...
        .create();
}
```

Using a layout makes modifications easy if you change your mind about what the dialog should present. For instance, what if you wanted a **TimePicker** next to the **DatePicker** in this dialog? If you are already inflating a layout, you can simply update the layout file, and the new view will appear.

Your dialog is on screen and looks good. In the next section, you will wire it up to present the **Crime**'s date and allow the user to change it.

Passing Data Between Two Fragments

You have passed data between two activities, and you have passed data between two fragment-based activities. Now you need to pass data between two fragments that are hosted by the same activity – **CrimeFragment** and **DatePickerFragment** (Figure 12.6).

Figure 12.6 Conversation between **CrimeFragment** and **DatePickerFragment**

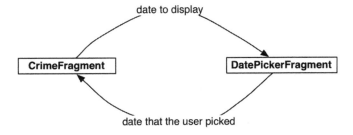

To get the crime's date to **DatePickerFragment**, you are going to write a **newInstance(Date)** method and make the **Date** an argument on the fragment.

To get the new date back to the **CrimeFragment** so that it can update the model layer and its own view, you will package up the date as an extra on an **Intent** and pass this **Intent** in a call to **CrimeFragment.onActivityResult(…)**.

Figure 12.7 Sequence of events between **CrimeFragment** and **DatePickerFragment**

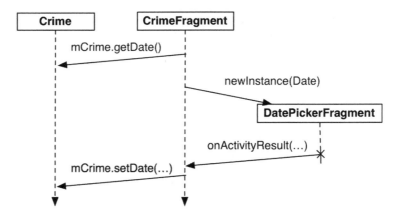

It may seem strange to call **Fragment.onActivityResult(…)** given that the hosting activity receives no call to **Activity.onActivityResult(…)** in this interaction. However, using **onActivityResult(…)** to pass data back from one fragment to another not only works, but it also offers some flexibility in how you present a dialog fragment, as you will see later in the chapter.

Passing data to DatePickerFragment

To get data into your **DatePickerFragment**, you are going to stash the date in **DatePickerFragment**'s arguments bundle, where the **DatePickerFragment** can access it.

Creating and setting fragment arguments is typically done in a **newInstance()** method that replaces the fragment constructor. In DatePickerFragment.java, add a **newInstance(Date)** method.

Listing 12.5 Adding a **newInstance(Date)** method (DatePickerFragment.java)

```
public class DatePickerFragment extends DialogFragment {
    public static final String EXTRA_DATE =
        "com.bignerdranch.android.criminalintent.date";

    private Date mDate;

    public static DatePickerFragment newInstance(Date date) {
        Bundle args = new Bundle();
        args.putSerializable(EXTRA_DATE, date);

        DatePickerFragment fragment = new DatePickerFragment();
        fragment.setArguments(args);

        return fragment;
    }

    ...
}
```

In **CrimeFragment**, remove the call to the **DatePickerFragment** constructor and replace it with a call to **DatePickerFragment.newInstance(Date)**.

Listing 12.6 Add call to **newInstance()** (CrimeFragment.java)

```
@Override
public View onCreateView(LayoutInflater inflater,
        ViewGroup parent, Bundle savedInstanceState) {
    ...

    mDateButton = (Button)v.findViewById(R.id.crime_date);
    mDateButton.setOnClickListener(new View.OnClickListener() {
        public void onClick(View v) {
            FragmentManager fm = getActivity()
                    .getSupportFragmentManager();
            DatePickerFragment dialog = new DatePickerFragment();
            DatePickerFragment dialog = DatePickerFragment
                .newInstance(mCrime.getDate());
            dialog.show(fm, DIALOG_DATE);
        }
    });

    return v;
}
```

DatePickerFragment needs to initialize the **DatePicker** using the information held in the **Date**. However, initializing the **DatePicker** requires integers for the month, day, and year. **Date** is more of a timestamp and cannot provide integers like this directly.

To get the integers you need, you must create a **Calendar** object and use the **Date** to configure the **Calendar**. Then you can retrieve the required information from the **Calendar**.

In **onCreateDialog(…)**, get the **Date** from the arguments and use it and a **Calendar** to initialize the **DatePicker**.

Listing 12.7 Date extraction and **DatePicker** initialization (DatePickerFragment.java)

```
@Override
public Dialog onCreateDialog(Bundle savedInstanceState) {
    mDate = (Date)getArguments().getSerializable(EXTRA_DATE);

    // Create a Calendar to get the year, month, and day
    Calendar calendar = Calendar.getInstance();
    calendar.setTime(mDate);
    int year = calendar.get(Calendar.YEAR);
    int month = calendar.get(Calendar.MONTH);
    int day = calendar.get(Calendar.DAY_OF_MONTH);

    View v = getActivity().getLayoutInflater()
        .inflate(R.layout.dialog_date, null);

    DatePicker datePicker = (DatePicker)v.findViewById(R.id.dialog_date_datePicker);
    datePicker.init(year, month, day, new OnDateChangedListener() {
        public void onDateChanged(DatePicker view, int year, int month, int day) {
            // Translate year, month, day into a Date object using a calendar
            mDate = new GregorianCalendar(year, month, day).getTime();

            // Update argument to preserve selected value on rotation
            getArguments().putSerializable(EXTRA_DATE, mDate);
        }
    });

    ...
}
```

When you initialize the **DatePicker**, you also set an **OnDateChangedListener** on it. When the user changes the date in the **DatePicker**, you update the **Date** to reflect the change. In the next section, you will pass this **Date** back to **CrimeFragment**.

At the end of **onDateChanged(…)**, you write the **Date** back to the fragment's arguments. You do this to preserve the value of mDate in case of rotation. If the device is rotated while the **DatePickerFragment** is on screen, then the **FragmentManager** will destroy the current instance and create a new one. When the new instance is created, the **FragmentManager** will call **onCreateDialog(…)** on it, and the instance will get the saved date from the arguments. It is a simpler way to preserve the value than saving out its state in **onSaveInstanceState(…)**.

(If you have worked more with fragments, you may be wondering why not "retain" **DatePickerFragment** instead? Using a retained fragment is a great tool for handling rotation that you will learn about in Chapter 14. Unfortunately, **DialogFragment** currently has a bug that causes retained instances to misbehave, so retaining **DatePickerFragment** is not a good option.)

Now **CrimeFragment** is successfully telling **DatePickerFragment** what date to show. You can run CriminalIntent and make sure that everything works as before.

Returning data to CrimeFragment

To have **CrimeFragment** receive the date back from **DatePickerFragment**, you need a way to keep track of the relationship between the two fragments.

With activities, you call **startActivityForResult(…)**, and the **ActivityManager** keeps track of the parent-child activity relationship. When the child activity dies, the **ActivityManager** knows which activity should receive the result.

Setting a target fragment

You can create a similar connection by making **CrimeFragment** the *target fragment* of **DatePickerFragment**. To create this relationship, you call the following **Fragment** method:

```
public void setTargetFragment(Fragment fragment, int requestCode)
```

This method accepts the fragment that will be the target and a request code just like the one you send in **startActivityForResult(…)**. The target fragment can use the request code later to tell which fragment is reporting back.

The **FragmentManager** keeps track of the target fragment and request code. You can retrieve them by calling **getTargetFragment()** and **getTargetRequestCode()** on the fragment that has set the target.

In CrimeFragment.java, create a constant for the request code and then make **CrimeFragment** the target fragment of the **DatePickerFragment** instance.

Listing 12.8 Set target fragment (CrimeFragment.java)

```
public class CrimeFragment extends Fragment {
    public static final String EXTRA_CRIME_ID =
        "com.bignerdranch.android.criminalintent.crime_id";

    private static final String DIALOG_DATE = "date";
    private static final int REQUEST_DATE = 0;

    ...

    @Override
    public View onCreateView(LayoutInflater inflater, ViewGroup parent,
            Bundle savedInstanceState) {
        ...

        mDateButton.setOnClickListener(new View.OnClickListener() {
            public void onClick(View v) {
                FragmentManager fm = getActivity()
                        .getSupportFragmentManager();
                DatePickerFragment dialog = DatePickerFragment
                    .newInstance(mCrime.getDate());
                dialog.setTargetFragment(CrimeFragment.this, REQUEST_DATE);
                dialog.show(fm, DIALOG_DATE);
            }
        });

        return v;
    }

    ...
}
```

Sending data to the target fragment

Now that you have a connection between **CrimeFragment** and **DatePickerFragment**, you need to send the date back to **CrimeFragment**. You are going to put the date on an **Intent** as an extra.

What method will you use to send this intent to the target fragment? Oddly enough, you will have **DatePickerFragment** pass it into **CrimeFragment.onActivityResult(int, int, Intent)**.

Activity.onActivityResult(…) is the method that the **ActivityManager** calls on the parent activity after the child activity dies. When dealing with activities, you do not call **Activity.onActivityResult(…)** yourself; that is the **ActivityManager**'s job. After the activity has received the call, the activity's **FragmentManager** then calls **Fragment.onActivityResult(…)** on the appropriate fragment.

When dealing with two fragments hosted by the same activity, you can borrow **Fragment.onActivityResult(…)** and call it directly on the target fragment to pass back data. It has exactly what you need:

- a request code that matches the code passed into setTargetFragment(…) to tell the target who is returning the result

- a result code to determine what action to take

- an **Intent** that can have extra data

In **DatePickerFragment**, create a private method that creates an intent, puts the date on it as an extra, and then calls **CrimeFragment.onActivityResult(…)**. In **onCreateDialog(…)**, replace the null parameter of **setPositiveButton(…)** with an implementation of **DialogInterface.OnClickListener** that calls the private method and passes in a result code.

Listing 12.9 Calling back to your target (DatePickerFragment.java)

```
private void sendResult(int resultCode) {
    if (getTargetFragment() == null)
        return;

    Intent i = new Intent();
    i.putExtra(EXTRA_DATE, mDate);

    getTargetFragment()
        .onActivityResult(getTargetRequestCode(), resultCode, i);
}

@Override
public Dialog onCreateDialog(Bundle savedInstanceState) {
    ...

    return new AlertDialog.Builder(getActivity())
        .setView(v)
        .setTitle(R.string.date_picker_title)
        .setPositiveButton(android.R.string.ok, null)
        .setPositiveButton(
            android.R.string.ok,
            new DialogInterface.OnClickListener() {
                public void onClick(DialogInterface dialog, int which) {
                    sendResult(Activity.RESULT_OK);
                }
            })
        .create();
}
```

In **CrimeFragment**, override **onActivityResult(...)** to retrieve the extra, set the date on the **Crime**, and refresh the text of the date button.

Listing 12.10 Responding to the dialog (CrimeFragment.java)

```
@Override
public void onActivityResult(int requestCode, int resultCode, Intent data) {
    if (resultCode != Activity.RESULT_OK) return;
    if (requestCode == REQUEST_DATE) {
        Date date = (Date)data
            .getSerializableExtra(DatePickerFragment.EXTRA_DATE);
        mCrime.setDate(date);
        mDateButton.setText(mCrime.getDate().toString());
    }
}
```

The code that sets the button's text is identical to code you call in **onCreateView(...)**. To avoid setting the text in two places, encapsulate this code in a private **updateDate()** method and then call it in **onCreateView(...)** and **onActivityResult(...)**.

Listing 12.11 Cleaning up with **updateDate()** (CrimeFragment.java)

```
public class CrimeFragment extends Fragment {

    ...

    private void updateDate() {
        mDateButton.setText(mCrime.getDate().toString());
    }

    @Override
    public View onCreateView(LayoutInflater inflater, ViewGroup parent,
            Bundle savedInstanceState) {
        View v = inflater.inflate(R.layout.fragment_crime, parent, false);
        ...
        mDateButton = (Button)v.findViewById(R.id.crime_date);
        mDateButton.setText(mCrime.getDate().toString());
        updateDate();

    ...

    @Override
    public void onActivityResult(int requestCode, int resultCode, Intent data) {
        if (resultCode != Activity.RESULT_OK) return;
        if (requestCode == REQUEST_DATE) {
            Date date = (Date)data
                .getSerializableExtra(DatePickerFragment.EXTRA_DATE);
            mCrime.setDate(date);
            mDateButton.setText(mCrime.getDate().toString());
            updateDate();
        }
    }
}
```

Now the circle is complete. The dates must flow. He who controls the dates controls time itself. Run CriminalIntent to ensure that you can, in fact, control the dates. Change the date of a **Crime** and confirm that the new date appears in **CrimeFragment**'s view. Then return to the list of crimes and check the **Crime**'s date to ensure that the model layer was updated.

More flexibility in presenting a DialogFragment

Using **onActivityResult(…)** to send data back to a target fragment is especially nice when you are writing an app that needs lots of input from the user and more room to ask for it. And you want this app working well on phones and tablets.

On a phone, you do not have much screen real estate, so you would likely use an activity with a full-screen fragment to ask the user for input. This child activity would be started by a fragment of the parent activity calling **startActivityForResult(…)**. On the death of the child activity, the parent activity would receive a call to **onActivityResult(…)**, which would be forwarded to the fragment that started the child activity.

Figure 12.8 Inter-activity communication on phones

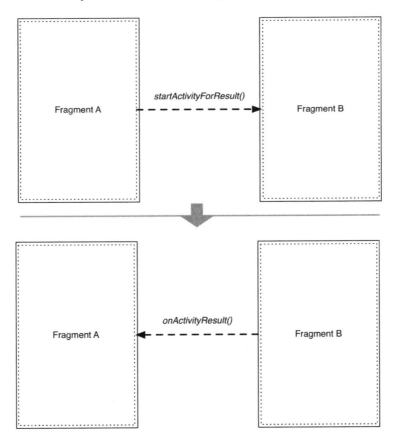

On a tablet, where you have plenty of room, it is often better to present a **DialogFragment** to the user to get the same input. In this case, you set the target fragment and call **show(…)** on the dialog fragment. When dismissed, the dialog fragment calls **onActivityResult(…)** on its target.

Figure 12.9 Inter-fragment communication on tablets

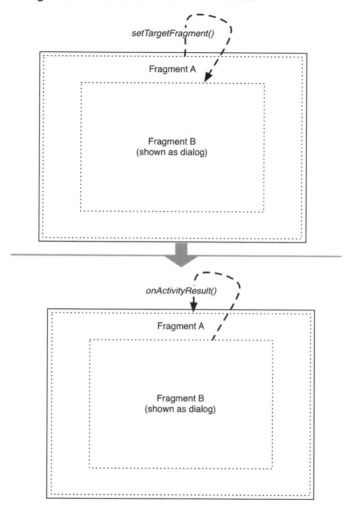

The fragment's **onActivityResult(…)** will always be called, whether the fragment started an activity or showed a dialog. So you can use the same code for different presentations.

When setting things up to use the same code for a full-screen fragment or a dialog fragment, you can override **DialogFragment.onCreateView(…)** instead of **onCreateDialog(…)** to prepare for both presentations.

Challenge: More Dialogs

For an easy challenge, write another dialog fragment named **TimePickerFragment** that allows the user to select what time of day the crime occurred using a **TimePicker** widget. Add another button to **CrimeFragment** that will display a **TimePickerFragment**.

For a harder challenge, stay with a single button interface, but have that button display a dialog that offers the user a choice: change the time or change the date. Then fire up a second dialog when the user makes a selection.

13

Audio Playback Using MediaPlayer

For the next three chapters, you are going to put CriminalIntent on hiatus and build another application. This app will play a historical audio file using the **MediaPlayer** class.

Figure 13.1 Hello, Moon!

MediaPlayer is the Android class for audio and video playback. It can play media from different sources (like a local file or streamed from the Internet) and in many different formats (like WAV, MP3, Ogg Vorbis, MPEG-4, and 3GPP).

Create a new project named HelloMoon. In the first dialog, select Holo Dark for the app's theme.

Figure 13.2 Creating HelloMoon with Holo Dark theme

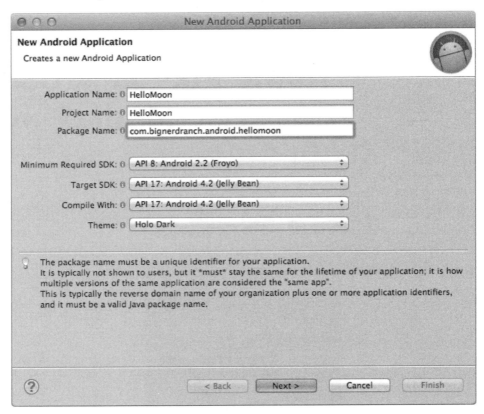

Click Next. This app will not have a custom launcher icon. It will use the blank activity template. Have the template create an activity named **HelloMoonActivity**.

Adding Resources

HelloMoon requires an image file and an audio file that are available in the solutions file for this book (http://www.bignerdranch.com/solutions/AndroidProgramming.zip). Within the solutions, find the following files:

- 13_Audio/HelloMoon/res/drawable-mdpi/armstrong_on_moon.jpg

- 13_Audio/HelloMoon/res/raw/one_small_step.wav

For this simple app, we have created a single armstrong_on_moon.jpg file for screens of medium density (~160 dpi), which Android considers the baseline. Copy armstrong_on_moon.jpg to the drawable-mdpi directory.

The audio file will be placed in the res/raw directory. The raw directory is a catch-all for resources that do not need special handling from Android's build system.

The res/raw directory is not created by default for a project, so you have to add it. (Right-click the res directory and select New → Folder.) Then copy one_small_step.wav to the new directory.

(You can also copy 13_Audio/HelloMoon/res/raw/apollo_17_stroll.mpg into res/raw/. There is information and a challenge at the end of this chapter about playing video that will use this file.)

While you are thinking about resources, open res/values/strings.xml and add the strings that HelloMoon requires:

Listing 13.1 Adding strings (strings.xml)

```xml
<?xml version="1.0" encoding="utf-8"?>
<resources>

  <string name="app_name">HelloMoon</string>
  <string name="hello_world">Hello world!</string>
  <string name="menu_settings">Settings</string>
  <string name="hellomoon_play">Play</string>
  <string name="hellomoon_stop">Stop</string>
  <string name="hellomoon_description">Neil Armstrong stepping
          onto the moon</string>

</resources>
```

(Wondering why HelloMoon uses "Play" and "Stop" strings for buttons instead of icons? You will be localizing this app in Chapter 15. Using icons would make localization less fun.)

Now that you have the necessary resources in place, let's take a look at the overall plan for HelloMoon.

Figure 13.3 Object diagram for HelloMoon

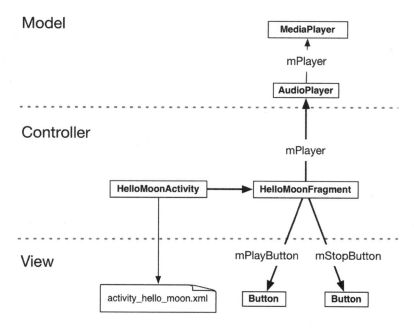

HelloMoon will have one activity, **HelloMoonActivity**, that hosts a **HelloMoonFragment**.

AudioPlayer is a class that you will write to encapsulate the **MediaPlayer**. Encapsulating the **MediaPlayer** is not required; you could have **HelloMoonFragment** interact directly with **MediaPlayer**. But this design helps keep your code nice and separate.

Before you create the **AudioPlayer** class, you are going to set up the rest of the app. By now, you are familiar with these steps:

- define a layout for the fragment

- create the fragment class

- modify the activity and its layout to host the fragment

Defining the layout for HelloMoonFragment

Create a new Android XML layout file named fragment_hello_moon.xml. Make its root element a **TableLayout**.

Use Figure 13.4 to flesh out fragment_hello_moon.xml.

Figure 13.4 Layout diagram for HelloMoon

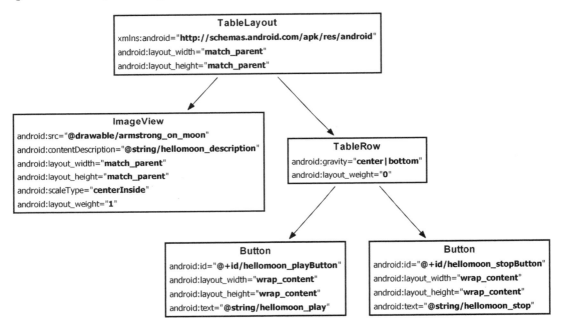

TableLayout works a lot like a **LinearLayout**. Instead of nesting **LinearLayout**s, you can arrange widgets using **TableRow**s. **TableLayout** and **TableRow** can team up to make it easier to arrange views in neat columns. Here, **TableLayout** helps arrange your buttons side by side in equally sized columns.

Why is the **ImageView** not in a **TableRow**? Children of **TableRow** act like "cells" of a table. Your goal here is for the **ImageView** to span the entire screen. If it were the child of a **TableRow**, then **TableLayout** would try to make other cells in its column span the screen, too. As a direct child of the **TableLayout**, it can do what it likes, and leave the **Button**s to act as side-by-side, equal-width columns.

Notice that the **TableRow** widget does not have to declare height and width attributes. It uses the **TableLayout**'s width and height as well as every other attribute of the **TableLayout**. A nested **LinearLayout**, on the other hand, can offer more flexibility in how your widgets will appear.

Preview the layout in the graphical tool. What color background are you seeing? You selected Holo Dark for HelloMoon's theme in the wizard. However, as of this writing, the wizard ignores your theme choice and always assigns a light theme. Let's see how to fix that.

(If you see a dark background, the wizard has been fixed and you will not need to manually reset the app theme as described in the following section.)

Manually resetting the app theme

An application's theme is declared in the application element of the manifest:

```
...
  <application
    android:allowBackup="true"
    android:icon="@drawable/ic_launcher"
    android:label="@string/app_name"
    android:theme="@style/AppTheme" >
    ...
  </application>

</manifest>
```

The android:theme attribute is not required; if a theme is not declared, then the device's default will be used.

You can see that the value given here is a reference to a resource – @style/AppTheme. In the package explorer, find and open res/values/styles.xml. Within the style element named AppBaseTheme, change the parent value to android:Theme.

Listing 13.2 Modifying default styles file (res/values/styles.xml)

```
<style name="AppBaseTheme" parent="android:Theme.Light">
<style name="AppBaseTheme" parent="android:Theme">
```

In the res directory, you also have two qualified values directories and each contain a styles.xml file. The qualifiers on these directories refer to API levels. The values in res/values-v11/styles.xml will be used for API levels 11-13, and the values in res/values-v14/styles.xml will be used for API levels 14 and higher.

Open res/values-v11/styles.xml and change the parent of AppBaseTheme to android:Theme.Holo. This is the theme you want on all devices running API 11 and higher, so the res/values-v14/ directory now gets in the way. Delete it from the HelloMoon project.

Save your files and preview the layout again. Your layout should now have a dark background that blends nicely with your image file.

Creating HelloMoonFragment

Create a new class named **HelloMoonFragment** and make its superclass **android.support.v4.app.Fragment**.

Override **HelloMoonFragment.onCreateView(…)** to inflate the layout you just defined and get references to the buttons.

Listing 13.3 Initial **HelloMoonFragment** setup (HelloMoonFragment.java)

```java
public class HelloMoonFragment extends Fragment {

    private Button mPlayButton;
    private Button mStopButton;

    @Override
    public View onCreateView(LayoutInflater inflater, ViewGroup parent,
            Bundle savedInstanceState) {
        View v = inflater.inflate(R.layout.fragment_hello_moon, parent, false);

        mPlayButton = (Button)v.findViewById(R.id.hellomoon_playButton);
        mStopButton = (Button)v.findViewById(R.id.hellomoon_stopButton);

        return v;
    }
}
```

Using a Layout Fragment

In CriminalIntent, you have been hosting fragments by adding them in the activity's code. In HelloMoon, you are going to use a layout fragment instead. When you use a layout fragment, you specify the fragment class in a fragment element.

Open activity_hello_moon.xml and replace its contents with the fragment element shown in Listing 13.4.

Listing 13.4 Creating a layout fragment (activity_hello_moon.xml)

```xml
<?xml version="1.0" encoding="utf-8"?>
<fragment xmlns:android="http://schemas.android.com/apk/res/android"
  android:id="@+id/helloMoonFragment"
  android:layout_width="match_parent"
  android:layout_height="match_parent"
  android:name="com.bignerdranch.android.hellomoon.HelloMoonFragment">

</fragment>
```

There is only one change that you need to make in **HelloMoonActivity**'s code before you can run the app. Change **HelloMoonActivity**'s superclass to **FragmentActivity**.

Listing 13.5 Make **HelloMoonActivity** a **FragmentActivity** (HelloMoonActivity.java)

```java
public class HelloMoonActivity extends Activity FragmentActivity {
    /** Called when the activity is first created. */
    @Override
    public void onCreate(Bundle savedInstanceState) {
        super.onCreate(savedInstanceState);
        setContentView(R.layout.activity_hello_moon);
    }
}
```

Run HelloMoon. You should see **HelloMoonFragment**'s view hosted by **HelloMoonActivity**.

That is all it takes to host a layout fragment. You named the fragment class in the layout and it was added to the activity and put on screen. Here is what happened behind the scenes. When **HelloMoonActivity** called .setContentView(…) and inflated activity_hello_moon.xml, it found the fragment element. At that point, the **FragmentManager** created an instance of **HelloMoonFragment** and added it to its list. It then called **HelloMoonFragment**'s **onCreateView(...)** and placed the view that this method returns in the spot that the fragment tag was keeping warm.

Figure 13.5 Lifecycle of a layout fragment

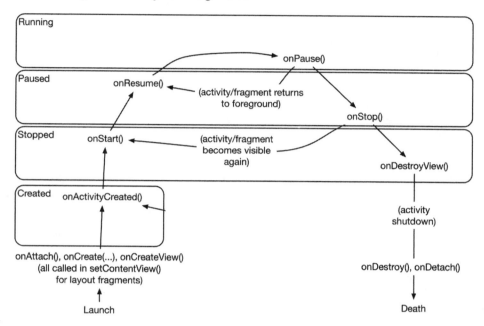

What does this ease cost you? You lose the flexibility and power you get when explicitly working with the **FragmentManager**:

- You can override the fragment's lifecycle methods to respond to events, but you have no control over when these methods are called.

- You cannot commit fragment transactions that remove, replace, or detach a layout fragment. You are stuck with what you have when the activity is created.

- You cannot attach arguments to a layout fragment. Attaching arguments must be done after the fragment is created and before it is added to the **FragmentManager**. With layout fragments, these events all happen out of your reach.

But with a simple app or with a static part of a complex app, using a layout fragment can be a reasonable choice.

Now that your **HelloMoonFragment** is safely hosted, let's turn to the audio portion of our program.

Audio Playback

Create a new class in the com.bignerdranch.android.hellomoon package named **AudioPlayer**. Leave its superclass as **java.lang.Object**.

In AudioPlayer.java, add a member variable to hold an instance of **MediaPlayer** and methods to stop and play this instance.

Listing 13.6 Simple playback code using **MediaPlayer** (AudioPlayer.java)

```java
public class AudioPlayer {

    private MediaPlayer mPlayer;

    public void stop() {
        if (mPlayer != null) {
            mPlayer.release();
            mPlayer = null;
        }
    }

    public void play(Context c) {
        mPlayer = MediaPlayer.create(c, R.raw.one_small_step);
        mPlayer.start();
    }
}
```

In the **play(Context)** method, you call **MediaPlayer.create(Context, int)**. **MediaPlayer** needs the **Context** to make sense of the audio file's resource ID. (There are other **MediaPlayer.create(…)** methods to use if you are getting audio from somewhere else, like the Internet or a local URI.)

In **AudioPlayer.stop()**, you release the **MediaPlayer** and set mPlayer to null. Calling **MediaPlayer.release()** destroys the instance.

Destruction is an aggressive interpretation of "stop," but there is good reason to be aggressive. **MediaPlayer** will hold on to the audio decoder hardware and other system resources until you call **release()**. These resources are shared across all apps. The **MediaPlayer** class includes a **stop()** method. It puts your **MediaPlayer** instance in a stopped state, from which it can eventually be restarted. However, in simple audio playback, it is better citizenship to destroy the instance with **release()** and then recreate it later.

So here is a simple rule: keep exactly one **MediaPlayer** around and keep it around only as long as it is playing something.

To enforce this rule, make a couple of changes to **play(Context)**. Add an initial call to **stop()** and set a listener to call **stop()** when the audio file has finished playing.

Listing 13.7 There can be only one (AudioPlayer.java)

```java
    ...

    public void play(Context c) {
        stop();

        mPlayer = MediaPlayer.create(c, R.raw.one_small_step);

        mPlayer.setOnCompletionListener(new MediaPlayer.OnCompletionListener() {
            public void onCompletion(MediaPlayer mp) {
                stop();
            }
        });

        mPlayer.start();
    }

}
```

Calling **stop()** at the beginning of **play(Context)** prevents the creation of multiple instances of **MediaPlayer** if the user clicks the Play button twice. Calling **stop()** when the file has finished playing releases your hold on the **MediaPlayer** instance as soon as you no longer need it.

You also need to call **AudioPlayer.stop()** in **HelloMoonFragment** to prevent the **MediaPlayer** from continuing playback after the fragment has been destroyed. In **HelloMoonFragment**, override **onDestroy()** to call **AudioPlayer.stop()**.

Listing 13.8 Override **onDestroy()** (HelloMoonFragment.java)

```
...

    @Override
    public void onDestroy() {
        super.onDestroy();
        mPlayer.stop();
    }
}
```

The **MediaPlayer** can continue playing after the **HelloMoonFragment** is destroyed because the **MediaPlayer** works on a different *thread*. We are intentionally ignoring this multi-threading aspect of HelloMoon. You will learn more about managing threads in Chapter 26.

Wiring buttons to play and stop

Return to HelloMoonFragment.java and play some audio. Create an instance of your **AudioPlayer** class and then set listeners on the buttons to play and stop.

Listing 13.9 Hook up Play button (HelloMoonFragment.java)

```
public class HelloMoonFragment extends Fragment {
    private AudioPlayer mPlayer = new AudioPlayer();
    private Button mPlayButton;
    private Button mStopButton;

    @Override
    public View onCreateView(LayoutInflater inflater, ViewGroup parent,
            Bundle savedInstanceState) {
        View v = inflater.inflate(R.layout.fragment_hello_moon, parent, false);

        mPlayButton = (Button)v.findViewById(R.id.hellomoon_playButton);
        mPlayButton.setOnClickListener(new View.OnClickListener() {
            public void onClick(View v) {
                mPlayer.play(getActivity());
            }
        });

        mStopButton = (Button)v.findViewById(R.id.hellomoon_stopButton);
        mStopButton.setOnClickListener(new View.OnClickListener() {
            public void onClick(View v) {
                mPlayer.stop();
            }
        });
        return v;
    }
}
```

Run HelloMoon, press the Play button, and enjoy a piece of history.

You have only scratched the surface of using **MediaPlayer** in this chapter. For information on what else **MediaPlayer** can do, read Android's "MediaPlayer Developer Guide" at http:// developer.android.com/guide/topics/media/mediaplayer.html.

Challenge: Pausing Audio Playback

Give users the option to pause the audio playback. Head to the reference for the **MediaPlayer** class to find the methods you will need to implement pausing.

For the More Curious: Playing Video

When it comes to playing video, you have a couple more options. One way to do it is to use **MediaPlayer**, just like you have been. All you need to do is hook up a place to display the video.

Imagery that updates quickly (like video) is displayed in a **SurfaceView** on Android. Actually, it is displayed on a **Surface**, which the **SurfaceView** hosts. You can get at the **Surface** by obtaining the **SurfaceView**'s **SurfaceHolder**. You will learn about these things in detail in Chapter 19. For now, all you need to know is that you can hook up a **SurfaceHolder** to a **MediaPlayer** by calling **MediaPlayer.setDisplay(SurfaceHolder)**.

Often, it is easier to play video using an instance of the **VideoView** class. **VideoView** does not interface with **MediaPlayer** like **SurfaceView** does. It does interface with **MediaController**, though, which means that it is easy to provide a playback interface.

The only tricky part about using **VideoView** is that it does not accept resource IDs. It only accepts filepaths or **Uri** objects. To create a **Uri** that points to an Android resource, use code like this:

```
Uri resourceUri = Uri.parse("android.resource://" +
    "com.bignerdranch.android.hellomoon/raw/apollo_17_stroll");
```

Create a URI with the android.resource scheme, your package name for the hostname, and the type and name of your resource for the path. This can then be passed to your **VideoView**.

Challenge: Playing Video in HelloMoon

Modify HelloMoon so that it can also play video. If you did not fetch the apollo_17_stroll.mpg file earlier, go back to the solutions file and copy it from this chapter's project into your res/raw directory. Then play it using one of the methods described above.

14

Retained Fragments

Currently, HelloMoon does not handle rotation gracefully. Run HelloMoon, play the audio, and then rotate the device. The audio will stop abruptly.

Here is the problem: On rotation, the **HelloMoonActivity** is destroyed. As this is happening, the **FragmentManager** is responsible for destroying the **HelloMoonFragment**. The **FragmentManager** calls the fragment's waning lifecycle methods: **onPause()**, **onStop()**, and **onDestroy()**. In **HelloMoonFragment.onDestroy()**, you release the **MediaPlayer**, which stops the playback.

Back in Chapter 3, you fixed a rotation-handling issue in GeoQuiz by overriding **Activity.onSaveInstanceState(Bundle)**. You saved out the data and had the new activity read it back in. **Fragment** has an **onSaveInstanceState(Bundle)** method that works the same way. However, saving out the state of the **MediaPlayer** object and restoring it later will still interrupt playback and annoy your users.

Retaining a Fragment

Fortunately, fragments have a feature that you can use to keep the **MediaPlayer** instance alive across a configuration change. Override **HelloMoonFragment.onCreate(...)** and set a property of the fragment.

Listing 14.1 Calling **setRetainInstance(true)** (HelloMoonFragment.java)

```
...
    private Button mPlayButton;
    private Button mStopButton;

    @Override
    public void onCreate(Bundle savedInstanceState) {
        super.onCreate(savedInstanceState);
        setRetainInstance(true);
    }

    @Override
    public View onCreateView(LayoutInflater inflater, ViewGroup parent,
            Bundle savedInstanceState) {
        ...
```

By default, the retainInstance property of a fragment is false. This means it is not *retained*, and it is destroyed and recreated on rotation along with the activity that hosts it. Calling setRetainInstance(true) *retains* the fragment. When a fragment is *retained*, the fragment is not destroyed with the activity. Instead, it is preserved and passed along intact to the new activity.

When you retain a fragment, you can count on all of its instance variables (like mPlayButton, mPlayer, and mStopButton) to keep the same values. When you reach for them, they are simply there.

Run HelloMoon again. Play the audio, rotate the device, and confirm that playback continues unimpeded.

Rotation and Retained Fragments

Let's take a closer look at how retained fragments work. Retained fragments take advantage of the fact that a fragment's view can be destroyed and recreated without having to destroy the fragment itself.

During a configuration change, the **FragmentManager** first destroys the views of the fragments in its list. Fragment views always get destroyed and recreated on a configuration change for the same reasons that activity views are destroyed and recreated: If you have a new configuration, then you might need new resources. Just in case better matching resources are now available, you rebuild the view from scratch.

Next, the **FragmentManager** checks the retainInstance property of each fragment. If it is false, which it is by default, then the **FragmentManager** destroys the fragment instance. The fragment and its view will be recreated by the new **FragmentManager** of the new activity "on the other side."

Figure 14.1 Default rotation with a UI fragment

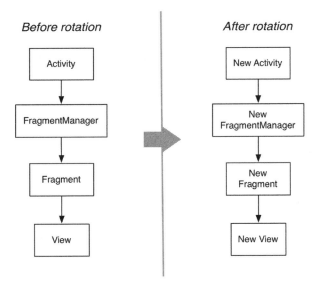

On the other hand, if retainInstance is true, then the fragment's view is destroyed, but the fragment itself is not. When the new activity is created, the new **FragmentManager** finds the retained fragment and recreates its view.

Figure 14.2 Rotation with a retained UI fragment

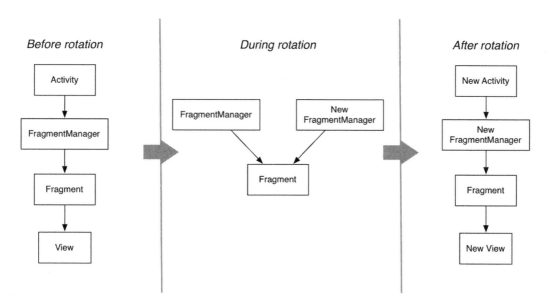

A retained fragment is not destroyed, but it is *detached* from the dying activity. This puts the fragment in a *retained* state. The fragment still exists, but it is not hosted by any activity.

Figure 14.3 Fragment lifecycle

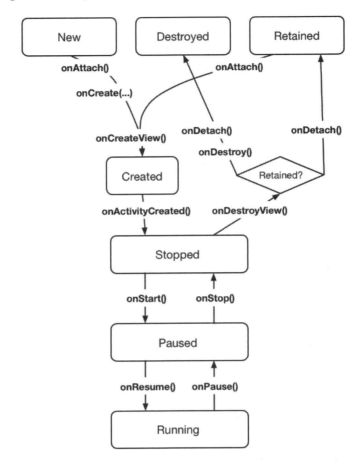

The retained state is only entered into when two conditions are met:

- **setRetainInstance(true)** has been called on the fragment.

- The hosting activity is being destroyed for a configuration change (typically rotation).

A fragment is only in the retained state for an extremely brief interval – the time between being detached from the old activity and being reattached to the new activity that is immediately created.

Retained Fragments: As Nice as All That?

Retained fragments: pretty nifty, right? Yes! They are indeed nifty. They appear to solve all the problems that pop up from activities and fragments being destroyed on rotation. When the device configuration changes, you get the most appropriate resources by creating a brand-new view, and you have an easy way to retain data and objects.

You may wonder why you would not retain every fragment or why fragments are not retained by default. At times, Android seems to discourage retaining fragments with user interfaces. We are not sure why that is the case, but it may end up causing problems in the future if the Android team thinks little of this feature.

Keep in mind, however, that retained fragments are only kept alive when an activity is destroyed for a configuration change. If your activity is destroyed because the OS needs to reclaim memory, then all your retained fragments are destroyed, too.

Rotation Handling and onSaveInstanceState(Bundle)

The **onSaveInstanceState(Bundle)** is another tool you have used to handle rotation. In fact, if your app does not have any problems with rotation, it is because the default behavior of **onSaveInstanceState(…)** is working.

Your CriminalIntent app is a good example. **CrimeFragment** is not retained, but if you make changes to the crime's title or toggle the check box, the new states of these **View** objects are automatically saved out and restored after rotation. This is what **onSaveInstanceState(…)** was designed to do – save out and restore the UI state of your app.

The major difference between overriding **Fragment.onSaveInstanceState(…)** and retaining the fragment is how long the preserved data lasts. If it needs to last long enough to survive configuration changes, then retaining the fragment is much less work. This is especially true when preserving an object; you do not have to worry about whether the object implements **Serializable**.

However, if you need the data to last longer, retaining the fragment is no help. If an activity is destroyed to reclaim memory after the user has been away for a while, then any retained fragments are destroyed just like their unretained brethren.

To make this difference clearer, think back to your GeoQuiz app. The rotation problem you faced was that the question index was being reset to zero on rotation. No matter what question the user was on, rotating the device sent them back to the first question. You saved out the index data and then read it back in to ensure the user would see the right question.

GeoQuiz did not use fragments, but imagine a redesigned GeoQuiz with a **QuizFragment** hosted by **QuizActivity**. Should you override **Fragment.onSaveInstanceState(…)** to save out the index or retain **QuizFragment** and keep the variable alive?

Figure 14.4 shows the three different lifetimes you have to work with: the life of the activity object (and its unretained fragments), the life of a retained fragment, and the life of the activity record.

Figure 14.4 Three lifetimes

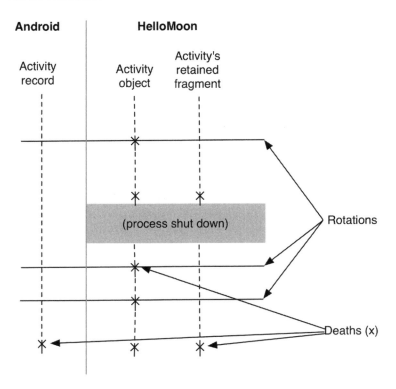

The lifetime of the activity object is too short. That is the source of the rotation problem. The index definitely needs to outlive the activity object.

If you retain **QuizFragment**, then the index will exist for the lifetime of this retained fragment. When GeoQuiz has only five questions, retaining **QuizFragment** is the easier choice and requires less code. You would initialize the index as a member variable and then call **setRetainInstance(true)** in **QuizFragment.onCreate(…)**.

Listing 14.2 Retaining of hypothetical **QuizFragment**

```
public class QuizFragment extends Fragment {

    ...

    private int mCurrentIndex = 0;

    ...

    @Override
    public void onCreate(Bundle savedInstanceState) {
        super.onCreate(savedInstanceState);
        setRetainInstance(true);
    }

    ...
}
```

By tying the index to the lifetime of the retained fragment, it survives the destruction of the activity object and solves the problem of resetting the index on rotation. However, as you can see in Figure 14.4, retaining `QuizFragment` does not preserve the value of the index across a process shut down, which may happen if the user leaves the app for a while and the activity and the retained fragment are destroyed to reclaim memory.

For only five questions, having users start over may be an acceptable choice. But what if GeoQuiz had 100 questions? Users would rightly be irritated at returning to the app and having to start again at the first question. You need the state of the index to survive for the lifetime of the activity record. To make this happen, you would save out the index in `onSaveInstanceState(…)`. Then, if users left the app for a while, they would always be able to pick up where they left off.

Therefore, if you have something in your activity or fragment that should last a long time, then you should tie it to the activity record's lifetime by overriding `onSaveInstanceState(Bundle)` to save its state so that you can restore it later.

For the More Curious: Rotation Before Fragments

Fragments were introduced in Honeycomb and were only available for phones with Ice Cream Sandwich. Rotation problems, on the other hand, have been around since the beginning.

To appreciate the charm of retained fragments, it helps to have an idea of what life was like before they existed. It was like being poked in the eye with a sharp stick:

- You want to retain an object across configuration changes? This requires a method called `onRetainNonConfigurationInstance()`. You override `onRetainNonConfigurationInstance()` to return the object you want to retain. When you want it back later, you call `getLastNonConfigurationInstance()`. Poke.

- You want to retain more than one object in an activity? Too bad. Each activity can only retain one. If you need more than that, you have to find some other way to package those objects up. Poke poke.

- Got an object like `MediaPlayer` that needs to be cleaned up when your activity has kicked the bucket for the last time? You have to detect that `onRetainNonConfigurationInstance()` was not called so that you can do the right thing in `onDestroy()`. Poke. Poke poke poke poke poke.

The `onRetainNonConfigurationInstance()` method is now deprecated, so passing an existing object across rotation is now always done with a retained fragment. If you are comfortable with using fragments, you will find that it is much more pleasant than the old way.

15
Localization

Localization is the process of providing the appropriate resources for your app based on the device's language settings. In this chapter, you are going to *localize* HelloMoon. In particular, you will provide Spanish versions of the audio file and the strings file. When a device's language is set to Spanish, Android will find and use the Spanish resources.

Figure 15.1 ¡Hola, Luna!

Localizing Resources

Language settings are part of the device's configuration, and Android provides configuration qualifiers for different languages. This makes localization simple: you create resource subdirectories with the desired language configuration qualifier and put the alternative resources in them. The Android resource system does the rest.

The language configuration qualifiers are taken from ISO 639-1 codes. For Spanish, the qualifier is -es. In your HelloMoon project, create two new `res` subdirectories: `res/raw-es/` and `res/values-es/`.

The Spanish resources you need are available in the solutions file for this book (http://www.bignerdranch.com/solutions/AndroidProgramming.zip). Within this file, locate

- 15_Localization/HelloMoon/res/raw-es/one_small_step.wav

- 15_Localization/HelloMoon/res/values-es/strings.xml

Copy these files into the corresponding directories that you just created.

That is all you have to do to provide localized resources for your app. To confirm, change your device's settings to Spanish by opening Settings and finding the language settings. Depending on your version of Android, these settings will be labeled Language and input, Language and Keyboard, or something similar.

When you get to a list of language options, choose a setting for Español. The region (España or Estados Unidos) will not matter because you qualified your resource directories with -es, which will match both.

(You can qualify a resource directory with a language-plus-region qualifier that targets resources even more specifically. For instance, the qualifier for Spanish spoken in Spain is -es-rES, where the r denotes a region qualifier and ES is the ISO 3166-1-alpha-2 code for Spain. Note that configuration qualifiers are not case-sensitive, but it is good to follow Android's convention here: use a lowercase language code and an uppercase region code prefixed with a lowercase r.

Run HelloMoon, press Tocar and listen to the Spanish translation of Neil Armstrong's famous words.

Default resources

The configuration qualifier for English is -en. In a fit of localization, you might think to rename your existing raw and values directories raw-en/ and values-en/.

That is not a good idea. These resources are your *default resources*. *Default resources* are resources in unqualified directories. It is important to provide a default resource. If there is no default to fall back on, then your app will crash if Android looks for a resource and cannot find one that matches the device configuration.

For instance, if you had a strings.xml file in values-en/ and in values-es/ but not in values/, then HelloMoon would crash when run on a device set to any language other than Spanish or English. Providing default resources keeps your app safe regardless of the device configuration.

Screen density works differently

The one exception to providing default resources is for screen density. A project's drawable directories are typically qualified for screen density with -mdpi, -hdpi, and -xhdpi. However, Android's decision about which drawable resource to use is not a simple matter of matching the device's screen density or defaulting to the unqualified directory if there is no match.

The choice is based on a combination of screen size and density, and Android may choose a drawable from a directory that is qualified with a lower or higher density than the device and then scale the drawable. There are more details in the docs at http://developer.android.com/guide/practices/screens_support.html, but the important point is that putting default drawable resources in res/drawable/ is not necessary.

Configuration Qualifiers

You have now seen and used several configuration qualifiers for providing alternative resources: language (e.g., `values-es/`), screen orientation (e.g., `layout-land/`), screen density (e.g., `drawable-mdpi/`), and API level (e.g., `values-v11/`).

Table 15.1 lists the characteristics of the device configuration that have configuration qualifiers that the Android system recognizes for targeting resources.

Table 15.1 Characteristics with configuration qualifiers

1. Mobile country code (MCC), optionally followed by mobile network code (MNC)
2. Language code, optionally followed by region code
3. Layout direction
4. Smallest width
5. Available width
6. Available height
7. Screen size
8. Screen aspect
9. Screen orientation
10. UI mode
11. Night mode
12. Screen density (`dpi`)
13. Touchscreen type
14. Keyboard availability
15. Primary text input
16. Navigation key availability
17. Primary non-text navigation method
18. API level

You can find descriptions of these characteristics and examples of specific configuration qualifiers at `http://developer.android.com/guide/topics/resources/providing-resources.html#AlternativeResources`.

Prioritizing alternative resources

Given the many types of configuration qualifiers for targeting resources, there may be times when the device configuration will match more than one alternative resource. When this happens, qualifiers are given precedence based on the order shown in Table 15.1.

To see this prioritizing in action, let's add another alternative resource to HelloMoon – a landscape version of the app_name string resource. The app_name resource is used as the activity's title – what you see in the action bar. In landscape orientation, there is room for more text. Instead of just saying hello to the moon, you could try to engage it in conversation.

Create a `values-land` directory and copy the default strings file into it.

The only string resource you want to be different in landscape orientation is app_name. Remove the other string resources and modify app_name to the value shown in Listing 15.1.

Listing 15.1 Creating a landscape alternative string resource (`values-land/ strings.xml`)

```
<?xml version="1.0" encoding="utf-8"?>
<resources>
    <string name="app_name">Hello, Moon! How are you? Is it cold up there?</string>
    <string name="app_name">HelloMoon</string>
    <string name="hello_world">Hello world!</string>
    <string name="menu_settings">Settings</string>
    <string name="hellomoon_play">Play</string>
    <string name="hellomoon_stop">Stop</string>
    <string name="hellomoon_image_description">Neil Armstrong stepping
            onto the moon</string>
</resources>
```

Alternatives for string resources (and other `values` resources) are provided on a per-string basis, so you do not need to duplicate strings when they are the same. Those duplicated strings will only end up being a maintenance hassle down the road.

Now you have three versions of `app_name`: a default version in `values/strings.xml`, a Spanish alternative in `values-es/strings.xml`, and a landscape alternative in `values-land/strings.xml`.

With your device's language set to Spanish, run HelloMoon and rotate to landscape. The Spanish language alternative has precedence, so you see the string from `values-es/strings.xml`.

Figure 15.2 Android prioritizes language over screen orientation

If you like, you can change your settings back to English and run again to confirm that the alternative landscape string appears as expected. To get back to English, look for Ajustes or Configuración (Settings) in the launcher and find the setting that includes idioma (language).

Multiple qualifiers

You can put more than one qualifier on a resource directory. Create a directory named `values-es-land` to give HelloMoon a landscape string in Spanish.

When using multiple qualifiers on directories, you must put them in the order of their precedence. Thus, `values-es-land` is a valid directory name, but `values-land-es` is not.

(Note that a language-region qualifier, such as `-es-rES`, may look like two distinct configuration qualifiers that have been combined, but it is just one. The region part is not a valid qualifier on its own.)

Copy the `values-land/strings.xml` file into `values-es-land/` and make the change shown in Listing 15.2. Or copy `res/values-es-land/strings.xml` from the solutions project, if you prefer.

Listing 15.2 Creating a Spanish landscape string resource (`values-es-land/strings.xml`)

```
<?xml version="1.0" encoding="utf-8"?>
<resources>
    <string name="app_name">Hello, Moon! How are you? Is it cold up there?</string>
    <string name="app_name">¡Hola, Luna! ¿Como estás? ¿Hace frío ahí arriba?</string>
</resources>
```

With your language set to Spanish, run HelloMoon to confirm your new alternative resource appears on cue.

Figure 15.3 Spanish landscape string resource appears

Finding the best-matching resources

Let's walk through how Android determined which version of app_name to display in this run. First, consider the three alternatives for the string resource named app_name:

- values-es/strings.xml

- values-land/strings.xml

- values-es-land/strings.xml

Next, consider the device's configuration. Currently, it includes Spanish language and a landscape screen orientation.

Ruling out incompatible directories

The first step that Android takes to find the best resource is rule out any resource directory that is incompatible with the current configuration.

None of the three choices is incompatible with the current configuration. If you rotated the device to portrait, the configuration would change, and the resource directories values-land/ and values-es-land/ would be incompatible and thus ruled out.

Some qualifiers are not as black and white when it comes to configuration compatibility. For example, API level is not a strict match. The qualifier -v11 is compatible with devices running an API level of 11 or higher.

Some qualifiers were added in later API levels. For instance, layout direction qualifiers were introduced in API level 17. The two options are -ldltr (left-to-right) and -ldrtl (right-to-left). Newer qualifiers come with an implicit API level qualifier, so -ldltr can be thought of as -ldltr-v17. (The addition of these hidden qualifiers is another excellent reason to have default resources included just in case.)

Screen density is handled differently, and compatibility does not apply. Android will choose the resource it thinks is best for the configuration, which may or may not be the resource whose qualifier(s) match the configuration.

Stepping through the precedence table

After the incompatible resource directories have been ruled out, Android starts working through the precedence table (Table 15.1) starting with the highest priority qualifier, MCC. If there is any resource directory with an MCC qualifier, then all resource directories that *do not* have an MCC qualifier are ruled out. If there is still more than one matching directory, then Android considers the next highest-precedence qualifier and continues until only one directory remains.

In our example, no directories contain an MCC qualifier, so no directories are ruled out, and Android moves down the list to the language qualifier. Two directories (values-es/ and values-es-land/) contain language qualifiers. One directory (values-land/) does not and is ruled out.

Android keeps stepping down the qualifier list. When it reaches screen orientation, it will find one directory with a screen orientation qualifier and one with out. It rules out values-es/, and values-es-land/ is the only directory remaining. Thus, Android uses the resource in values-es-land/.

More Resource Rules and Regulations

Now that you are more familiar with the Android resource system, here are some system requirements you should know about when it comes time to build your own apps.

Resource naming

Resource names must be lowercase and must not have any spaces – one_small_step.wav, app_name, armstrong_on_moon.jpg.

Whether you reference a resource in XML or code, the reference does not include the file extension. For example, you refer to @drawable/armstrong_on_moon in your layout files and R.drawable.armstrong_on_moon in your code. This means that you cannot rely on extensions to distinguish identically named resource files in the same subdirectory.

Resource directory structure

Resources must be saved in a subdirectory of res/. You cannot save resources in the root of res/. Doing so will cause build errors.

The names of the res subdirectories are directly tied to the Android build process and cannot be changed. You have already seen drawable/, layout/, menu/, raw/, and values/. You can see a complete list of supported (unqualified) res subdirectories at http://developer.android.com/guide/topics/resources/providing-resources.html#ResourceTypes.

Any additional subdirectories you create in res/ will be ignored. Creating res/my_stuff may not cause an error, but Android will not use any resources you place in there.

In addition, you cannot create additional levels of subdirectories in res/. This restriction can make life difficult. Real projects can have hundreds of drawable resources, and it is natural to want to organize them in subdirectories. But you cannot do this. The only way to help yourself in this situation is with careful naming of resources so that the resources sort in a way that makes it easier to find a particular file.

Android's naming convention for layout files is an example of a sorting strategy. Layout files begin with the type of view that the layout defines, like activity_, dialog_, or list_item_. For instance, in CriminalIntent's res/layout/, you have activity_crime_pager, activity_fragment, dialog_date, fragment_crime, and list_item_crime. Your activity layouts sort together, which theoretically makes them easier to find.

Testing Alternative Resources

It is important to test your layouts and other resources. Testing layouts will tell you how many alternatives you need for different screen sizes, orientations, and more. You can test on devices both real and virtual. You can also use the graphical layout tool.

The graphical layout tool has many options for previewing how a layout will appear in different configurations. You can preview the layout on different screen sizes, device types, API levels, languages, and more.

To see these options, open fragment_hello_moon.xml in the graphical layout tool. Then try some of the settings indicated in the following figure.

Figure 15.4 Using graphical layout tool to preview resources

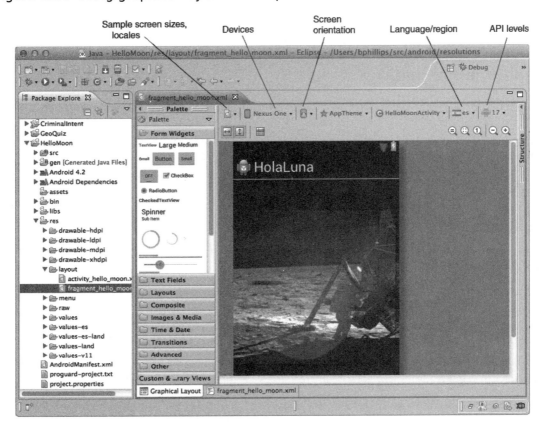

You can ensure that you have included all of your necessary default resources by setting a device to a language that you have not localized any resources for. Run your app and put it through its paces. Visit all of the views and rotate them. If the app crashes, check LogCat for a "Resource not found..." message to track down the missing default resource.

Before continuing to the next chapter, you may want to change your device's language back from Spanish. To find the language setting, look for Ajustes or Configuración (Settings) in the launcher and find the setting that includes idioma (language).

16

The Action Bar

The action bar was introduced in Honeycomb. It replaced the old-school title bar, but it does more than just display a title and an app icon. The action bar can also house menu items, and its app icon can be used as a navigation button.

In this chapter, you will create a menu for CriminalIntent. This menu will have a *menu item* that lets users add a new crime. You will also enable the app icon to be an Up button.

Figure 16.1 Creating the options menu file

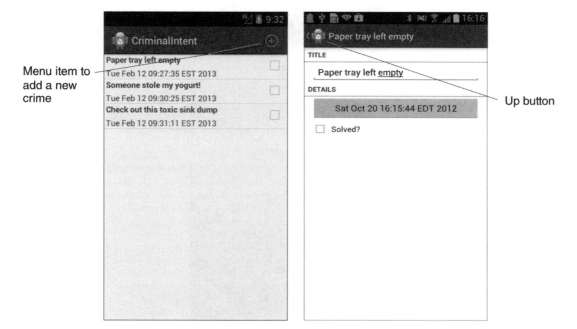

Options Menus

The menu that can appear on the action bar is called the *options menu*. An options menu presents users with choices that refer to the entire screen or the app as a whole. Adding a new crime is a good example. On the other hand, deleting a crime from the list is an action is better suited to a *context menu*. This action is contextual because it requires knowing which crime to delete. You will learn about context menus in Chapter 18.

Your options menu will require a few string resources. Your context menu in Chapter 18 will need one, too. Add the string resources for both chapters to `strings.xml` (Listing 16.1). These strings may seem mysterious right now, but it is good to get them taken care of. When you need them later, they will already be in place, and you will not have to stop what you are doing.

Listing 16.1 Adding strings for menus (`res/values/strings.xml`)

```
...
<string name="crimes_title">Crimes</string>
<string name="date_picker_title">Date of crime:</string>
<string name="new_crime">New Crime</string>
<string name="show_subtitle">Show Subtitle</string>
<string name="hide_subtitle">Hide Subtitle</string>
<string name="subtitle">If you see something, say something.</string>
<string name="delete_crime">Delete</string>
</resources>
```

The action bar as the home for options menus is new, but options menus themselves have been around since the beginning of Android.

Figure 16.2 Pre-Honeycomb options menus

Luckily, there are very few compatibility problems with options menus. The code is the same, and each device handles how to present the options menu depending on its level of Android. We will revisit issues surrounding compatibility, options menus, and the action bar throughout this chapter.

Defining an options menu in XML

Menus are a type of resource similar to layouts. You create an XML description of a menu and place the file in the res/menu directory of your project. Android generates a resource ID for the menu file that you then use to inflate the menu in code.

In the package explorer, create a menu subdirectory within res/. Then right-click on this new directory and choose New → Android XML File. Ensure that the resource type of the file you are creating is Menu, and name the file fragment_crime_list.xml.

Figure 16.3 Creating the options menu file

Open fragment_crime_list.xml and navigate to the XML. Add an item element as shown in Listing 16.2.

Listing 16.2 Creating a menu resource **CrimeListFragment** (fragment_crime_list.xml)

```xml
<?xml version="1.0" encoding="utf-8"?>
<menu
  xmlns:android="http://schemas.android.com/apk/res/android">
  <item android:id="@+id/menu_item_new_crime"
    android:icon="@android:drawable/ic_menu_add"
    android:title="@string/new_crime"
    android:showAsAction="ifRoom|withText"/>
</menu>
```

The showAsAction attribute refers to whether the item will appear on the action bar itself or in the *overflow menu*. You have piped together two values, ifRoom and withText, so the item's icon and text will appear on the action bar if there is room. If there is room for the icon but not the text, then only the icon will be visible. If there is no room for either, then the item will be relegated to the overflow menu.

How you access the overflow menu depends on the device. If the device has a hardware menu key, then you must press it to see the overflow menu. Most newer devices do not have hardware menu keys, and the overflow menu is accessed by the three dots on the far right side of the action bar, as seen in Figure 16.4.

Figure 16.4 Overflow menu in the action bar

Other options for showAsAction include always and never. Using always is not recommended; it is better to use ifRoom and let the OS decide. Using never is a good choice for less common actions. In general, you should only put menu items that users will use frequently on the action bar to avoid visually cluttering the screen.

Note that Android Lint does not complain about the android:showAsAction attribute that was introduced in API level 11. There is no need to safeguard XML attributes as you do with Java code. XML from the future is simply ignored on earlier APIs.

In the android:icon attribute, the value @android:drawable/ic_menu_add references a *system icon*. A *system icon* is one that is found on the device rather than in your project's resources.

Using system icons

In a prototype, referencing a system icon works fine. However, in an app that will be released, it is better to be sure of what your user will see instead of leaving it up to each device. System icons can change drastically across devices and OS versions, and some devices might have system icons that do not fit with the rest of your app's design.

One alternative is to create your own icons. You will need to prepare versions for each screen density and possibly for other device configurations. For more information, visit Android's Icon Design Guidelines at http://developer.android.com/guide/practices/ui_guidelines/icon_design.html.

A second alternative is to find system icons that meet your app's needs and copy them directly into your project's drawable resources. This is an easy way to get familiar and consistent icons packaged with your app.

To find system icons, head to where you installed the Android SDKs and look for a path like *your-android-SDK-home*/platforms/android-*API level*/data/res. For example, the directory for Android 4.2 on one of our Macs is /Developer/android-sdk-mac_86/platforms/android-17/data/res.

Browse through the system icons for the different SDKs. Or search for ic_menu_add. You can copy any of these into the appropriate drawable folder in your project's resources. Then, in your layout file, your icon attribute would be android:icon="@drawable/ic_menu_add" to pull from your project resources instead of the device's system icons.

Creating the options menu

In code, options menus are managed by callbacks from the **Activity** class. When the options menu is needed, Android calls the **Activity** method **onCreateOptionsMenu(Menu)**.

Your design, however, calls for code to be implemented in a fragment, not an activity. **Fragment** comes with its own set of options menu callbacks, which you will implement in **CrimeListFragment**. The methods for creating the options menu and responding to the selection of a menu item are

```
public void onCreateOptionsMenu(Menu menu, MenuInflater inflater)
public boolean onOptionsItemSelected(MenuItem item)
```

In CrimeListFragment.java, override **onCreateOptionsMenu(Menu, MenuInflater)** to inflate the menu defined in fragment_crime_list.xml.

Listing 16.3 Inflating an options menu (CrimeListFragment.java)

```
@Override
public void onResume() {
    super.onResume();
    ((CrimeAdapter)getListAdapter()).notifyDataSetChanged();
}

@Override
public void onCreateOptionsMenu(Menu menu, MenuInflater inflater) {
    super.onCreateOptionsMenu(menu, inflater);
    inflater.inflate(R.menu.fragment_crime_list, menu);
}
```

Within this method, you call **MenuInflater.inflate(int, Menu)** and pass in the resource ID of your menu file. This populates the **Menu** instance with the items defined in your file.

Notice that you call through to the superclass implementation of **onCreateOptionsMenu(…)**. This is not required, but we recommend calling through as a matter of convention. That way, any options menu functionality defined by the superclass will still work. It is only a convention, though – the base **Fragment** implementation of this method does nothing.

The **FragmentManager** is responsible for calling **Fragment.onCreateOptionsMenu(Menu, MenuInflater)** when the activity receives its **onCreateOptionsMenu(…)** callback from the OS. You must explicitly tell the **FragmentManager** that your fragment should receive a call to **onCreateOptionsMenu(…)**. You do this by calling the following method:

```
public void setHasOptionsMenu(boolean hasMenu)
```

In **CrimeListFragment.onCreate(…)**, let the **FragmentManager** know that **CrimeListFragment** needs to receive options menu callbacks.

Listing 16.4 Set hasOptionsMenu (CrimeListFragment.java)

```
@Override
public void onCreate(Bundle savedInstanceState) {
    super.onCreate(savedInstanceState);
    setHasOptionsMenu(true);

    getActivity().setTitle(R.string.crimes_title);

    ...
```

You can run CriminalIntent now to see your options menu (Figure 16.5).

Figure 16.5 Icon for menu item directly on action bar

Where is the menu item's text? Most phones only have enough room for the icon in portrait orientation. You can long-press an icon on the action bar to reveal its title.

Figure 16.6 Long-pressing icon on action bar shows title

In landscape orientation, there is room on the action bar for the icon and text (Figure 16.7).

Figure 16.7 Icon and text on action bar

If you are running CriminalIntent on a pre-Honeycomb device, you must press the menu key built into the device to see the options menu. It will appear at the bottom of the screen. Figure 16.8 shows the same code running on a Gingerbread device.

Figure 16.8 Options menu on Gingerbread

Your options menu code works fine on older and newer devices without wrapping and safeguarding any code. There is, however, a small difference in option menus behavior between older and newer SDKs. On devices running Honeycomb and later, onCreateOptionsMenu(…) is called and the options menu is created when the activity is started. It is necessary to have the menu prepared at the beginning of the activity's life so that the menu items can appear on the action bar. On older devices, onCreateOptionsMenu(…) is called and the options menu is created when the user first presses the menu key.

(You may have seen older devices running apps with action bars. These apps typically use a third-party library named ActionBarSherlock to duplicate action bar features for earlier API levels. We will talk more about ActionBarSherlock at the end of Chapter 18.)

Responding to options menu selections

To respond to the user pressing the New Crime item, you need a way to add a new **Crime** to your list of crimes. In CrimeLab.java, add the following method that adds a **Crime** to the array list.

Listing 16.5 Adding a new crime (`CrimeLab.java`)

```
...

public void addCrime(Crime c) {
    mCrimes.add(c);
}

public ArrayList<Crime> getCrimes() {
    return mCrimes;
}

...
```

In this brave new world where you will be able to add crimes yourself, the 100 programmatically generated crimes are no longer necessary. In `CrimeLab.java`, remove the code that generates these crimes.

Listing 16.6 Goodbye, random crimes! (`CrimeLab.java`)

```
public CrimeLab(Context appContext) {
    mAppContext = appContext;
    mCrimes = new ArrayList<Crime>();
    for (int i = 0; i < 100; i++) {
        Crime c = new Crime();
        c.setTitle("Crime #" + i);
        c.setDate(new Date());
        c.setSolved(i % 2 == 0); // Every other one
        mCrimes.add(c);
    }
}
```

When the user presses a menu item in the options menu, your fragment receives a callback to the method **onOptionsItemSelected(MenuItem)**. This method receives an instance of **MenuItem** that describes the user's selection.

Although your menu only contains one item, menus often have more than one. You can determine which menu item has been selected by checking the ID of the menu item and then respond appropriately. This ID corresponds to the ID you assigned the menu item in your menu file.

In `CrimeListFragment.java`, implement **onOptionsItemSelected(MenuItem)** to respond to selection of the menu item. You will create a new **Crime**, add it to **CrimeLab**, and then start an instance of **CrimePagerActivity** to edit the new **Crime**.

Listing 16.7 Responding to menu selection (`CrimeListFragment.java`)

```java
@Override
public void onCreateOptionsMenu(Menu menu, MenuInflater inflater) {
    super.onCreateOptionsMenu(menu, inflater);
    inflater.inflate(R.menu.fragment_crime_list, menu);
}

@Override
public boolean onOptionsItemSelected(MenuItem item) {
    switch (item.getItemId()) {
        case R.id.menu_item_new_crime:
            Crime crime = new Crime();
            CrimeLab.get(getActivity()).addCrime(crime);
            Intent i = new Intent(getActivity(), CrimePagerActivity.class);
            i.putExtra(CrimeFragment.EXTRA_CRIME_ID, crime.getId());
            startActivityForResult(i, 0);
            return true;
        default:
            return super.onOptionsItemSelected(item);
    }
}
```

Notice that this method returns a boolean value. Once you have handled the menu item, you should return `true` to indicate that no further processing is necessary. The default case calls the superclass implementation if the menu item ID is not in your implementation.

Run CriminalIntent and try out your new options menu. Add a few crimes and edit them afterwards. (The empty list that you see before you add any crimes can be disconcerting. The challenge at the end of this chapter is to present a helpful clue when the list is empty.)

Enabling Ancestral Navigation

So far, CriminalIntent relies heavily on the Back button to navigate around the app. Using the Back button is *temporal navigation*. It takes you to where you were last. *Ancestral navigation*, on the other hand, takes you up the app hierarchy. (It is sometimes called *hierarchical navigation*.)

Android makes it easy to use the app icon on the action bar for ancestral navigation. You can implement it to go "home" – all the way up the hierarchy to the app's initial screen. In fact, the icon was originally called the app's "Home" button. However, Android now recommends that you implement the app icon to go "up" just one level to the parent of the current activity. When you do this, the icon becomes the "Up" button.

In this section, you will implement the app icon on **CrimePagerActivity**'s action bar to be the "Up" button. Pressing the icon will return the user to the list of crimes.

Enabling the app icon

Typically, you let users know that the app icon is enabled as an Up button by displaying a left-pointing caret to the left of the app icon like the one in Figure 16.9.

Figure 16.9 Action bar with Up button enabled

To enable the app icon to work as a button and get the caret to appear in the fragment's view, you must set a property on the fragment by calling the following method:

```
public abstract void setDisplayHomeAsUpEnabled(boolean showHomeAsUp)
```

This method is from API level 11, so you need to wrap it to keep the app Froyo- and Gingerbread-safe and annotate the method to wave off Android Lint.

In **CrimeFragment.onCreateView(…)**, call **setDisplayHomeAsUpEnabled(true)**.

Listing 16.8 Turn on Up button (CrimeFragment.java)

```java
@TargetApi(11)
@Override
public View onCreateView(LayoutInflater inflater, ViewGroup parent,
        Bundle savedInstanceState) {
    View v = inflater.inflate(R.layout.fragment_crime, parent, false);

    if (Build.VERSION.SDK_INT >= Build.VERSION_CODES.HONEYCOMB) {
        getActivity().getActionBar().setDisplayHomeAsUpEnabled(true);
    }

    ...
}
```

Note that setting this property does not wire the button to go "up." It only enables the icon to be some kind of button and displays the caret. You have to do the wiring yourself. For apps targeting API levels 11-13, the icon is enabled as a button by default, but you still need to call **setDisplayHomeAsUpEnabled(true)** to get the caret to appear.

In Listing 16.8, you add the @TargetApi annotation on **onCreateView(…)**. You could annotate only the call to **setDisplayHomeAsUpEnabled(true)**. However, **onCreateView(…)** will soon be full of API-specific code, so you are annotating the entire method implementation instead.

Run CriminalIntent, navigate to a crime detail screen, and check out the new caret next to your app icon.

Responding to the Up button

You respond to the enabled app icon as if it were an existing options menu item – by overriding **onOptionsItemSelected(MenuItem)**. So the first thing to do is to tell the **FragmentManager** that **CrimeFragment** will be implementing options menu callbacks on behalf of the activity. In **CrimeFragment.onCreate(…)**, call **setHasOptionsMenu(true)**, like you did earlier for **CrimeListFragment**.

Listing 16.9 Turn on options menu handling (CrimeFragment.java)

```java
@Override
public void onCreate(Bundle savedInstanceState) {

    ...

    setHasOptionsMenu(true);
}
```

You do not need to define or inflate the app icon menu item in an XML file. It comes with a ready-made resource ID: android.R.id.home. In CrimeFragment.java, override **onOptionsItemSelected(MenuItem)** to respond to this menu item.

Listing 16.10 Responding to the app icon (Home) menu item (CrimeFragment.java)

```java
@Override
public boolean onOptionsItemSelected(MenuItem item) {
    switch (item.getItemId()) {
        case android.R.id.home:
            // To be implemented next
            return true;
        default:
            return super.onOptionsItemSelected(item);
    }
}
```

You want this button to return the user to the list of crimes, so you might think to create an intent and start the instance of **CrimePagerActivity** like this:

```java
Intent intent = new Intent(getActivity(), CrimeListActivity.class);
intent.addFlags(Intent.FLAG_ACTIVITY_CLEAR_TOP);
startActivity(intent);
finish();
```

FLAG_ACTIVITY_CLEAR_TOP tells Android to look for an existing instance of the activity in the stack, and if there is one, pop every other activity off the stack so that the activity being started will be top-most.

Figure 16.10 FLAG_ACTIVITY_CLEAR_TOP at work

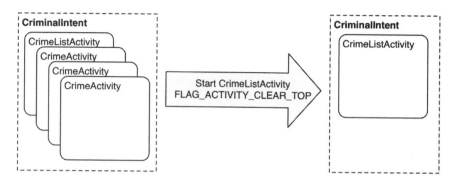

However, there is a better way to implement ancestral navigation: use a convenience class named **NavUtils** plus some metadata in the manifest.

Let's start with the metadata. Open AndroidManifest.xml. Add the following attribute to the declaration of **CrimePagerActivity** to name **CrimeListActivity** as its parent.

Listing 16.11 Add parent activity metadata (AndroidManifest.xml)

```
<activity android:name=".CrimePagerActivity"
  android:label="@string/app_name">
  <meta-data android:name="android.support.PARENT_ACTIVITY"
    android:value=".CrimeListActivity"/>
</activity>
...
```

Think of a metadata tag as a post-it note on your activity. Notes like this are kept in the system **PackageManager**, and anyone can pull out a value from a post-it note if they have the name of the note. You can create your own name-value pairs and fetch them as needed. This particular pair is defined by the **NavUtils** class so that it can learn the parent of a given activity. It is especially useful combined with the following **NavUtils** class method:

```
public static void navigateUpFromSameTask(Activity sourceActivity)
```

In **CrimeFragment.onOptionsItemSelected(…)**, first check to see if there is a parent activity named in the metadata by calling **NavUtils.getParentActivityName(Activity)**. If there is, call **navigateUpFromSameTask(Activity)** to navigate to the parent activity.

Listing 16.12 Using **NavUtils** (CrimeFragment.java)

```
@Override
public boolean onOptionsItemSelected(MenuItem item) {
    switch (item.getItemId()) {
        case android.R.id.home:
            if (NavUtils.getParentActivityName(getActivity()) != null) {
                NavUtils.navigateUpFromSameTask(getActivity());
            }
            return true;
        default:
            return super.onOptionsItemSelected(item);
    }
}
```

If there is no parent named in the metadata, then you do not want to display the up caret. Back in **onCreateView(…)**, check for a parent before calling **setDisplayHomeAsUpEnabled(true)**.

Listing 16.13 No parent, no caret (CrimeFragment.java)

```
@TargetApi(11)
@Override
public View onCreateView(LayoutInflater inflater, ViewGroup parent,
        Bundle savedInstanceState) {
    View v = inflater.inflate(R.layout.fragment_crime, parent, false);

    if (Build.VERSION.SDK_INT >= Build.VERSION_CODES.HONEYCOMB) {
        if (NavUtils.getParentActivityName(getActivity()) != null) {
            getActivity().getActionBar().setDisplayHomeAsUpEnabled(true);
        }
    }

    ...
}
```

Why is using **NavUtils** better than starting the activity yourself? First, the **NavUtils** code is short and sweet. Using **NavUtils** also centralizes the relationships between your activities in the manifest. If those relationships change, you only have to change a line in your manifest rather than mucking about in your Java code.

Another nice thing about it is that the ancestral relationship is kept separate from the code in your fragment. You can use **CrimeFragment** in a variety of activities, each of which may have a different parent, but **CrimeFragment** will still do the right thing.

Run CriminalIntent. Create a crime and then press the app icon to return to the list of crimes. It is hard to tell with CriminalIntent's puny two-level hierarchy, but **navigateUpFromSameTask(Activity)** is implementing "up" and sending the user up one level to **CrimePagerActivity**'s parent.

An Alternative Menu Item

In this section, you will use what you have learned about menus, compatibility, and alternative resources to add a menu item that lets users show and hide the subtitle of **CrimeListActivity**'s action bar.

Creating an alternative menu file

A menu item that applies the action bar should not be visible to users without an action bar. So the first step is to create an alternative menu resource. Create a menu-v11 folder in your project's res directory. Then copy and paste fragment_crime_list.xml into this folder.

In res/menu-v11/fragment_crime_list.xml, add a menu item that will read Show Subtitle and will appear on the action bar if there is room.

Listing 16.14 Adding Show Subtitle menu item (res/menu-v11/fragment_crime_list.xml)

```xml
<?xml version="1.0" encoding="utf-8"?>
<menu
  xmlns:android="http://schemas.android.com/apk/res/android">
    <item android:id="@+id/menu_item_new_crime"
        android:icon="@android:drawable/ic_menu_add"
        android:title="@string/new_crime"
        android:showAsAction="ifRoom|withText"/>
    <item android:id="@+id/menu_item_show_subtitle"
        android:title="@string/show_subtitle"
        android:showAsAction="ifRoom"/>
</menu>
```

In onOptionsItemSelected(…), respond to this menu item by setting the action bar's subtitle.

Listing 16.15 Responding to Show Subtitle menu item (CrimeListFragment.java)

```java
@TargetApi(11)
@Override
public boolean onOptionsItemSelected(MenuItem item) {
    switch (item.getItemId()) {
        case R.id.menu_item_new_crime:
            ...
            return true;
        case R.id.menu_item_show_subtitle:
            getActivity().getActionBar().setSubtitle(R.string.subtitle);
            return true;
        default:
            return super.onOptionsItemSelected(item);
    }
}
```

Notice that you only warn off Android Lint; you do not have to wrap your action bar code. Wrapping is not necessary because this code cannot be called on earlier devices because the R.id.menu_item_show_subtitle menu item will not be presented.

Run CriminalIntent on a newer device and show the subtitle. Then run on a Froyo or Gingerbread device (real or virtual). Press the menu key to confirm that the Show Subtitle item does not appear. Add a new crime to confirm that the app behaves as before.

Toggling the menu item title

Now the subtitle is visible, but the menu item still reads Show Subtitle. It would be better if the menu item toggled its title and function to show or hide the subtitle.

In onOptionsItemSelected(…), check for the presence of a subtitle when this menu item is selected and take appropriate action.

Listing 16.16 Responding based on subtitle's presence (CrimeListFragment.java)

```java
@TargetApi(11)
@Override
public boolean onOptionsItemSelected(MenuItem item) {
    switch (item.getItemId()) {
        case R.id.menu_item_new_crime:
            ...
            return true;
        case R.id.menu_item_show_subtitle:
            if (getActivity().getActionBar().getSubtitle() == null) {
                getActivity().getActionBar().setSubtitle(R.string.subtitle);
                item.setTitle(R.string.hide_subtitle);
            } else {
                getActivity().getActionBar().setSubtitle(null);
                item.setTitle(R.string.show_subtitle);
            }
            return true;
        default:
            return super.onOptionsItemSelected(item);
    }
}
```

If your action bar does not have a subtitle, then you set the subtitle and toggle the menu item title so that it reads Hide Subtitle. If the subtitle is already visible, then you set it back to null and change the menu item title back to Show Subtitle.

Run CriminalIntent and confirm that you can show and hide the subtitle as appropriate.

"Just one more thing..."

Programming in Android is often like being questioned by the TV detective Columbo. You think you have the angles covered and are home free. But Android always turns at the door and says, "Just one more thing..."

Here that thing is handling rotation. If you show the subtitle and then rotate, the subtitle will disappear when the interface is created from scratch. To fix this, you need an instance variable that tracks the subtitle's visibility and you need to retain CrimeListFragment so that the value of this variable will survive rotation.

In CrimeListFragment.java, add a boolean member variable and, in onCreate(…), retain CrimeListFragment and initialize the variable.

Listing 16.17 Initialize variable and retain **CrimeListFragment** (CrimeListFragment.java)

```
public class CrimeListFragment extends ListFragment {
    private ArrayList<Crime> mCrimes;
    private boolean mSubtitleVisible;
    private final String TAG = "CrimeListFragment";

    @Override
    public void onCreate(Bundle savedInstanceState) {
        super.onCreate(savedInstanceState);
        ...
        setRetainInstance(true);
        mSubtitleVisible = false;
    }
```

Then, in **onOptionsItemSelected(...)**, set this variable when you respond to the menu item selection.

Listing 16.18 Set subtitleVisible in menu item response (CrimeListFragment.java)

```
    @TargetApi(11)
    @Override
    public boolean onOptionsItemSelected(MenuItem item) {
        switch (item.getItemId()) {
            case R.id.menu_item_new_crime:
                ...
                return true;
            case R.id.menu_item_show_subtitle:
                if (getActivity().getActionBar().getSubtitle() == null) {
                    getActivity().getActionBar().setSubtitle(R.string.subtitle);
                    mSubtitleVisible = true;
                    item.setTitle(R.string.hide_subtitle);
                }
                else {
                    getActivity().getActionBar().setSubtitle(null);
                    mSubtitleVisible = false;
                    item.setTitle(R.string.show_subtitle);
                }
                return true;
            default:
                return super.onOptionsItemSelected(item);
        }
    }
}
```

Now you need to check to see if the subtitle should be shown. In CrimeListFragment.java, override **onCreateView(...)** and set the subtitle if mSubtitleVisible is true.

Listing 16.19 Set subtitle if mSubtitleVisible is true (CrimeListFragment.java)

```
@TargetApi(11)
@Override
public View onCreateView(LayoutInflater inflater, ViewGroup parent,
        Bundle savedInstanceState) {
    View v = super.onCreateView(inflater, parent, savedInstanceState);

    if (Build.VERSION.SDK_INT >= Build.VERSION_CODES.HONEYCOMB) {
        if (mSubtitleVisible) {
            getActivity().getActionBar().setSubtitle(R.string.subtitle);
        }
    }

    return v;
}
```

You also need to check the subtitle's state in **onCreateOptionsMenu(…)** to make sure you are displaying the correct menu item title.

Listing 16.20 Set menu item title based on mSubtitleVisible is true (CrimeListFragment.java)

```
@Override
public void onCreateOptionsMenu(Menu menu, MenuInflater inflater) {
    super.onCreateOptionsMenu(menu, inflater);
    inflater.inflate(R.menu.fragment_crime_list, menu);
    MenuItem showSubtitle = menu.findItem(R.id.menu_item_show_subtitle);
    if (mSubtitleVisible && showSubtitle != null) {
        showSubtitle.setTitle(R.string.hide_subtitle);
    }
}
```

Run CriminalIntent. Show the subtitle and then rotate. The subtitle should appear as expected in the re-created view.

Challenge: An Empty View for the List

Currently, when CriminalIntent launches, it displays an empty list – a big black void. You should give users something to interact with when there are no items in the list.

ListView, because it is a subclass of **AdapterView**, supports a special **View** called the "empty view" for this very scenario. If you specify a view for the empty view, the **ListView** will automatically switch between showing it when there are no items, and showing the list when there are some items.

You can specify the empty view in code using the following **AdapterView** method:

```
public void setEmptyView(View emptyView)
```

Or you can create a layout in XML that specifies both the **ListView** and the empty view. If you give them resource IDs of @android:id/list and @android:id/empty respectively, you can tie into the automatic switching feature.

The current implementation of **CrimeListFragment** does not inflate its own layout in **onCreateView(…)**, but in order to implement the empty view in a layout, it will need to. Create a layout

XML resource for **CrimeListFragment** that uses a **FrameLayout** as its root container, with a **ListView** and another **View** of some kind as the empty view.

Make the empty view display a message like "There are no crimes." Add a button to the view that will trigger the creation of a new crime so that, in this case, the user does not have to go to the options menu or action bar.

17

Saving and Loading Local Files

Almost every application needs a place to save data. In this chapter, you will enable CriminalIntent to save and load its data from a JSON file stored on the device's filesystem.

Each application on an Android device has a directory in its *sandbox*. Keeping files in the sandbox protects them from being accessed by other applications or even the prying eyes of users (unless the device has been "rooted," in which case the user can get to whatever he or she likes.)

Each application's sandbox directory is a child of the device's /data/data directory named after the application package. For CriminalIntent, the full path to the sandbox directory is /data/data/ com.bignerdranch.android.criminalintent.

While good to know, you do not have to commit this location to memory; you will use convenience methods in the API to retrieve the path when you need it.

In addition to the sandbox, your application can store files in *external storage*. Typically, this is an SD card that may or may not be available on the device. Files and even whole applications can be stored on an SD card, but there are security and programming implications to doing so. Most importantly, access to files on external storage is not restricted to your application – anyone can read, write, and delete them. This chapter will focus on using the internal (private) storage, but you can use the same API to work with files on external storage if your application requires it. (In fact, the challenge at the end of this chapter is to do just that.)

Saving and Loading Data in CriminalIntent

Adding persistent data storage to an app involves two processes: saving the data out to the filesystem and loading that data back in when the application is launched. Each process has two stages. In saving, you first transform the data into a storable format and then you write that data to a file. In loading, the stages are reversed: you first read the formatted data from the file and then parse it into what the application needs.

For CriminalIntent, the storable format will be JSON, and you will write and read files using I/O methods from Android's **Context** class. Figure 17.1 is a general diagram of how you will implement saving and loading application data in CriminalIntent.

Figure 17.1 Saving and loading in CriminalIntent

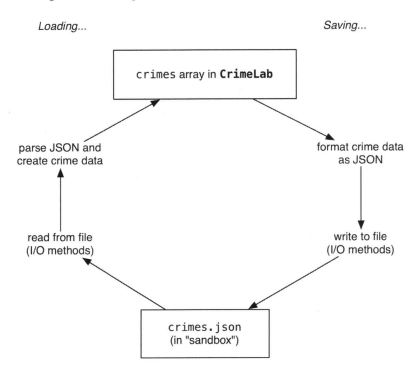

JSON stands for JavaScript Object Notation, a format that has become popular in recent years, particularly for web services. Android includes the standard org.json package, which has classes that provide simple access to creating and parsing files in JSON format. The Android developer documentation has information about org.json, and you can get more information about JSON as a format at http://json.org.

(XML is another option for formatting data in order to write it to a file. Android provides classes and methods that will work with XML, too. You will see how to use some of them to parse XML in Chapter 26.)

The most convenient way to access files available to your application is through I/O methods provided by the **Context** class. (**Context** is the superclass of all of the key application components: **Application**, **Activity**, and **Service**, in addition to a few others.) These methods return instances of standard Java classes like **java.io.File** or **java.io.FileInputStream**.

Saving crime data to a JSON file

In CriminalIntent, the **CrimeLab** class will be responsible for triggering the saving and loading of data, while the mechanics of creating and parsing the model objects as JSON will be delegated to a new **CriminalIntentJSONSerializer** class and the existing **Crime** class.

Creating the CriminalIntentJSONSerializer class

The responsibility of taking the existing **ArrayList** of **Crime**s and writing it as JSON is delegated to a class named **CriminalIntentJSONSerializer**.

Create this class in `com.bignerdranch.android.criminalintent`. Leave its superclass as `java.lang.Object`.

Next, add the code shown in Listing 17.1. Remember to add import statements for the classes required by the code using Eclipse's Organize Imports command.

Listing 17.1 Implementing `CriminalIntentJSONSerializer`

```java
public class CriminalIntentJSONSerializer {

    private Context mContext;
    private String mFilename;

    public CriminalIntentJSONSerializer(Context c, String f) {
        mContext = c;
        mFilename = f;
    }

    public void saveCrimes(ArrayList<Crime> crimes)
            throws JSONException, IOException {
        // Build an array in JSON
        JSONArray array = new JSONArray();
        for (Crime c : crimes)
            array.put(c.toJSON());

        // Write the file to disk
        Writer writer = null;
        try {
            OutputStream out = mContext
                .openFileOutput(mFilename, Context.MODE_PRIVATE);
            writer = new OutputStreamWriter(out);
            writer.write(array.toString());
        } finally {
            if (writer != null)
                writer.close();
        }
    }

}
```

While you could have put this serialization code directly into the **CrimeLab** class, tucking away the logic of serializing to JSON in a self-contained unit has a number of advantages. The class is more easily unit-tested because it does not depend on much else in the application do its work. In addition, notice that the class's constructor takes an instance of **Context** and a filename. This means that the class can be reused in many places without changes because it just needs any implementation of **Context**.

In the **saveCrimes(ArrayList<Crime>)** method, you create a **JSONArray** object. Then you call a **toJSON()** method on each crime in the list and add the result to the **JSONArray**. (Currently, the **toJSON()** method causes an error because you have not yet implemented it in **Crime** yet. You will do that next.)

To open a file and write to it, you use **Context.openFileOutput(…)**. This method takes in a filename and a mode. It automatically prepends the filename you give it with the path to the file's folder in your app's sandbox, creates the file, and opens it for writing. If you prefer to create and open those file paths by hand, you can always call **Context.getFilesDir()** instead, but **openFileOutput(…)** is required if you need to create it with different permissions.

Once the file is opened, you write to it using standard Java interfaces. The **Writer**, **OutputStream**, and **OutputStreamWriter** classes come from the java.io package. The **OutputStream** you get from **openFileOutput(…)** is used to create a new **OutputStreamWriter**. **OutputStreamWriter** takes care of converting between the Java **String**s that are sent to it and the raw byte encoding that **OutputStream** ends up writing to the file.

Making Crime class capable of JSON serialization

In order to save the mCrimes array in JSON format, you have to be able to save individual instances of **Crime** in JSON format. In Crime.java, add the following constants and implementation of **toJSON()** to save a **Crime** in JSON format and return an instance of the class **JSONObject** that can be put in a **JSONArray**.

Listing 17.2 Implementing JSON serialization (Crime.java)

```
public class Crime {

    private static final String JSON_ID = "id";
    private static final String JSON_TITLE = "title";
    private static final String JSON_SOLVED = "solved";
    private static final String JSON_DATE = "date";

    private UUID mId;
    private String mTitle;
    private boolean mSolved;
    private Date mDate = new Date();

    public Crime() {
        mId = UUID.randomUUID();
    }

    public JSONObject toJSON() throws JSONException {
        JSONObject json = new JSONObject();
        json.put(JSON_ID, mId.toString());
        json.put(JSON_TITLE, mTitle);
        json.put(JSON_SOLVED, mSolved);
        json.put(JSON_DATE, mDate.getTime());
        return json;
    }

    @Override
    public String toString() {
        return mTitle;
    }
}
```

This code uses methods from the **JSONObject** class to handle the business of converting the data in a **Crime** into something that can be written to a file as JSON.

Saving crimes in CrimeLab

With the addition of **CriminalIntentJSONSerializer** and the changes to **Crime**, you now have the ability to write a list of crimes as JSON and save this data to a file on the device's file system.

When is it appropriate to save your data? A good rule of thumb on mobile applications is: save as often as possible, preferably as soon as changes are made by the user. The code is already routing the user's changes to the data through the **CrimeLab** class, so it makes the most sense to save to a file there as well.

If you are saving often, then you should also take care not to slow the user down. Your code here rewrites the entire file of crimes every time anything happens. CriminalIntent is a modest app, so this does not take too long. For a more substantial piece of work, you will want to save one piece of data without saving all the others, too, perhaps by using a SQLite database. You will learn how to use an SQLite database in an Android app in Chapter 34.

In CrimeLab.java, create an instance of CriminalIntentJSONSerializer in CrimeLab's constructor. Then create a saveCrimes() method that tries to serialize the crimes and returns a boolean indicating success. Also, add log statements so that you can easily confirm the operation.

Listing 17.3 Saving changes persistently in **CrimeLab** (CrimeLab.java)

```java
public class CrimeLab {
    private static final String TAG = "CrimeLab";
    private static final String FILENAME = "crimes.json";

    private ArrayList<Crime> mCrimes;
    private CriminalIntentJSONSerializer mSerializer;

    private static CrimeLab sCrimeLab;
    private Context mAppContext;

    private CrimeLab(Context appContext) {
        mAppContext = appContext;
        mCrimes = new ArrayList<Crime>();
        mSerializer = new CriminalIntentJSONSerializer(mAppContext, FILENAME);
    }

    ...

    public void addCrime(Crime c) {
        mCrimes.add(c);
    }

    public boolean saveCrimes() {
        try {
            mSerializer.saveCrimes(mCrimes);
            Log.d(TAG, "crimes saved to file");
            return true;
        } catch (Exception e) {
            Log.e(TAG, "Error saving crimes: ", e);
            return false;
        }
    }

}
```

In this app, you are logging error information to the console for simplicity. In a real-world application, you would want to alert the user if saving fails, for example, with a **Toast** or a dialog.

Saving application data in onPause()

Where should you call **saveCrimes()**? The **onPause()** lifecycle method is the safest choice. If you wait until **onStop()** or **onDestroy()**, you might miss your chance to save. A paused activity will be destroyed if the OS needs to reclaim memory, and you cannot count on **onStop()** or **onDestroy()** being called in these circumstances.

Listing 17.4 Saving crimes to filesystem in **onPause()** (CrimeFragment.java)

```
    ...

    @Override
    public boolean onOptionsItemSelected(MenuItem item) {
        switch (item.getItemId()) {
            case android.R.id.home:
                NavUtils.navigateUpFromSameTask(getActivity());
                return true;
            default:
                return super.onOptionsItemSelected(item);
        }
    }

    @Override
    public void onPause() {
        super.onPause();
        CrimeLab.get(getActivity()).saveCrimes();
    }

}
```

Run CriminalIntent. Add a crime or two and then press the device's Home button to pause the activity and save the list of crimes to the filesystem. Check LogCat to confirm your success.

Loading crimes from the filesystem

Now let's turn the process on its head and have CriminalIntent load crimes from the filesystem when the application is launched. First, in Crime.java, add a constructor that accepts a **JSONObject**.

Listing 17.5 Implementing **Crime(JSONObject)** (Crime.java)

```
public class Crime {

    ...

    public Crime() {
        mId = UUID.randomUUID();
    }

    public Crime(JSONObject json) throws JSONException {
        mId = UUID.fromString(json.getString(JSON_ID));
        if (json.has(JSON_TITLE)) {
            mTitle = json.getString(JSON_TITLE);
        }
        mSolved = json.getBoolean(JSON_SOLVED);
        mDate = new Date(json.getLong(JSON_DATE));
    }

    public JSONObject toJSON() throws JSONException {
        JSONObject json = new JSONObject();
        json.put(JSON_ID, mId.toString());
        json.put(JSON_TITLE, mTitle);
        json.put(JSON_SOLVED, mSolved);
        json.put(JSON_DATE, mDate.getTime());
        return json;
    }
```

Next, in CriminalIntentJSONSerializer.java, add a method to **CriminalIntentJSONSerializer** for loading crimes from the filesystem.

Listing 17.6 Implementing **loadCrimes()** (CriminalIntentJSONSerializer.java)

```java
public CriminalIntentJSONSerializer(Context c, String f) {
    mContext = c;
    mFilename = f;
}

public ArrayList<Crime> loadCrimes() throws IOException, JSONException {
    ArrayList<Crime> crimes = new ArrayList<Crime>();
    BufferedReader reader = null;
    try {
        // Open and read the file into a StringBuilder
        InputStream in = mContext.openFileInput(mFilename);
        reader = new BufferedReader(new InputStreamReader(in));
        StringBuilder jsonString = new StringBuilder();
        String line = null;
        while ((line = reader.readLine()) != null) {
            // Line breaks are omitted and irrelevant
            jsonString.append(line);
        }
        // Parse the JSON using JSONTokener
        JSONArray array = (JSONArray) new JSONTokener(jsonString.toString())
            .nextValue();
        // Build the array of crimes from JSONObjects
        for (int i = 0; i < array.length(); i++) {
            crimes.add(new Crime(array.getJSONObject(i)));
        }
    } catch (FileNotFoundException e) {
        // Ignore this one; it happens when starting fresh
    } finally {
        if (reader != null)
            reader.close();
    }
    return crimes;
}

public void saveCrimes(ArrayList<Crime> crimes) throws JSONException, IOException {
    // Build an array in JSON
    JSONArray array = new JSONArray();
    for (Crime c : crimes)
        array.put(c.toJSON());
    ...
```

Here you use a combination of Java and JSON classes along with the **Context** method **openFileInput(…)** to read the data from the filesystem to a string and then parse that string of **JSONObject**s into a **JSONArray** and on to an **ArrayList**, which gets returned.

Note that you call **reader.close()** in the finally block. This ensures that the underlying file handle is freed up, even if an error occurs.

Finally, in **CrimeLab**'s constructor, these crimes need to be loaded into an **ArrayList** when the singleton is first accessed rather than always creating a new empty one. In CrimeLab.java, make the following changes.

Listing 17.7 Loading crimes (`CrimeLab.java`)

```java
public CrimeLab(Context appContext) {
    mAppContext = appContext;
    mSerializer = new CriminalIntentJSONSerializer(mAppContext, FILENAME);
    mCrimes = new ArrayList<Crime>();

    try {
        mCrimes = mSerializer.loadCrimes();
    } catch (Exception e) {
        mCrimes = new ArrayList<Crime>();
        Log.e(TAG, "Error loading crimes: ", e);
    }
}

public static CrimeLab get(Context c) {
    ...
}

...
```

Here you attempt to load crimes; if there are none, then you create a new empty list.

Now CriminalIntent can maintain its data between launches of the application. You can test this in a number of ways. Run the app, add crimes, and make changes. Then navigate to some other application, like the web browser. At this point, CriminalIntent will probably get shut down by the OS. Launch it again, and see that your changes persist. You can also force it to stop and relaunch from Eclipse.

It is now safe to add a collection of the heinous crimes that occur in your office. Now that data persists across runs, you can use these crimes as you continue adding to CriminalIntent, and you will not have to add a new crime or two every time the application starts.

Challenge: Use External Storage

Saving files on internal storage is the right choice for most applications, especially when data privacy is a concern. Some apps, however, might want to write to the device's external storage if it is available. This can be useful if you are storing data that you want to share with other apps or the user, like music, photos or downloads from the web. External storage is almost always more plentiful, too, which makes it the right choice for large media like videos.

To write to external storage, you need to do two things. First, check to ensure that the external storage is available. The **android.os.Environment** class has several helpful methods and constants that you can use to determine this. Second, get a handle on the external files directory (look for a method in **Context** that can give this to you). The rest of the work is basically the same as what you are already doing in **CriminalIntentJSONSerializer**.

For the More Curious: The Android Filesystem and Java I/O

At the OS level, Android runs inside a Linux kernel. As a result, its filesystem is similar to other Linux and Unix systems. Directory names are separated by forward slashes (/), files can have a broad set of characters in their names, and everything is case-sensitive. Your application runs with a specific user ID, taking advantage of the Linux security model.

Android uses an application's Java package name to determine where it lives on the filesystem. Applications themselves are bundled in an APK file for distribution and installation, which lives in the /data/app directory with a name like com.bignerdranch.android.criminalintent-1.apk. Usually, you will not need to know anything about this location, and on a typical device you will not be able to access that location directly without rooting your device.

Accessing files and directories

The most convenient way to access files and directories available to your application is through methods provided by the **Context** class. **Context** is the superclass of all of the key application components: **Application**, **Activity**, and **Service**, in addition to a few others. This gives your subclasses of these classes simple access to files using a number of methods, as outlined in Table 17.1.

Table 17.1 Basic file and directory methods in **Context**

Method	Purpose
File getFilesDir()	Returns a handle to the directory for private application files.
FileInputStream openFileInput(String name)	Opens an existing file for input (relative to the files directory).
FileOutputStream openFileOutput(String name, int mode)	Opens a file for output, possibly creating it (relative to the files directory).
File getDir(String name, int mode)	Gets (and possibly creates) a subdirectory within the files directory.
String[] fileList()	Gets a list of file names in the main files directory, for use with **openFileInput(String)**, for example.
File getCacheDir()	Returns a handle to a directory you can use specifically for storing cache files. You should take care to keep this directory tidy and use as little space as possible.

Notice that most of these methods return instances of standard Java classes like **java.io.File** or **java.io.FileInputStream**. You can use many existing Java APIs that work with those classes just as you would in other Java applications. Android also includes support for **java.nio.*** classes.

18

Context Menus and Contextual Action Mode

In this chapter, you will enable users to delete crimes from the list by long-pressing a list item. Deleting a crime is a contextual action: it is associated with a particular view on screen (a single list item) rather than the entire screen.

On pre-Honeycomb devices, contextual actions are presented in a floating context menu. On later devices, a contextual action bar is the recommended way to present contextual actions. The contextual action bar appears on top of the activity's action bar and presents actions to the user.

Figure 18.1 Long-pressing a list item to delete a crime

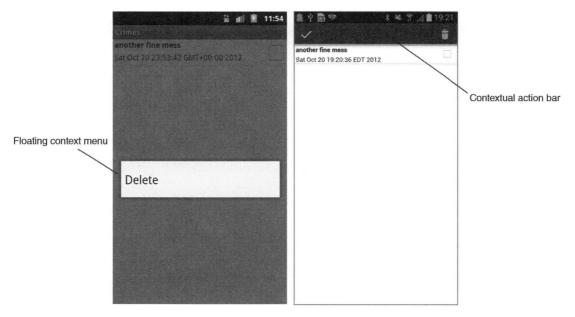

With options menus, managing different API levels is simple: you define one menu resource and implement one set of menu callbacks. The OS on each device determines how to display the menu items.

With contextual actions, the situation is more complicated. You still define one menu resource, but you implement two separate sets of callbacks – one for the contextual action bar and one for floating context menus.

In this chapter, you will implement a contextual action on devices running API level 11 and higher and implement a floating context menu on Froyo and Gingerbread devices.

(You may have seen older devices running apps with contextual action bars. These apps typically use a third-party library named ActionBarSherlock to duplicate action bar features for earlier API levels. We will talk more about ActionBarSherlock at the end of this chapter.)

Defining a Context Menu Resource

In res/menu/, create a new Android XML file named crime_list_item_context.xml and give it a menu root element. Then add the single item shown in Listing 18.1.

Listing 18.1 The crime list context menu (crime_list_item_context.xml)

```xml
<?xml version="1.0" encoding="utf-8"?>
<menu
  xmlns:android="http://schemas.android.com/apk/res/android">
    <item android:id="@+id/menu_item_delete_crime"
      android:icon="@android:drawable/ic_menu_delete"
      android:title="@string/delete_crime" />
</menu>
```

You will use this menu resource for both implementations.

Implementing a Floating Context Menu

You are going to build the floating context menu first. The **Fragment** callbacks are similar to those you used for the options menu in Chapter 16. You inflate a context menu using the following method:

```
public void onCreateContextMenu(ContextMenu menu, View v,
    ContextMenu.ContextMenuInfo menuInfo)
```

To respond to the user's context menu selection, you implement this **Fragment** method:

```
public boolean onContextItemSelected(MenuItem item)
```

Creating the context menu

In CrimeListFragment.java, implement **onCreateContextMenu(…)** to inflate the menu resource and use it to populate the context menu.

Listing 18.2 Creating the context menu (CrimeListFragment.java)

```java
@Override
public boolean onOptionsItemSelected(MenuItem item) {
    switch (item.getItemId()) {

        ...

        default:
            return super.onOptionsItemSelected(item);
    }
}

@Override
public void onCreateContextMenu(ContextMenu menu, View v, ContextMenuInfo menuInfo) {
    getActivity().getMenuInflater().inflate(R.menu.crime_list_item_context, menu);
}
```

Unlike **onCreateOptionsMenu(…)**, this menu callback does not pass in an instance of **MenuInflater**, so you first get the **MenuInflater** associated with **CrimeListActivity**. When you call **MenuInflater.inflate(…)** you pass in the resource ID of the menu resource and the instance of **ContextMenu** to populate the menu instance with items defined in the menu file.

Currently, you only have one context menu resource, so you inflate that resource no matter which view is long-pressed. If you had multiple context menu resources, you would determine which to inflate by checking the ID of the **View** that was passed into **onCreateContextMenu(…)**.

Registering for the context menu

By default, a long-press on a view does not trigger the creation of a context menu. You must *register* a view for a floating context menu by calling the following **Fragment** method:

```
public void registerForContextMenu(View view)
```

and passing in the view in question.

In this case, you want the context menu to appear when any list item is clicked. Fortunately, you do not have to register the view of each individual list item. Instead, you can register the **ListView**, which automatically registers the list items.

In **CrimeListFragment.onCreateView(…)**, get a reference to the **ListView** and register it.

Listing 18.3 Registering the **ListView** for a context menu (CrimeListFragment.java)

```
@Override
public View onCreateView(LayoutInflater inflater, ViewGroup parent,
        Bundle savedInstanceState) {
    View v = super.onCreateView(inflater, parent, savedInstanceState);

    if (Build.VERSION.SDK_INT >= Build.VERSION_CODES.HONEYCOMB) {
        if (mSubtitleVisible) {
            getActivity().getActionBar().setSubtitle(R.string.subtitle);
        }
    }

    ListView listView = (ListView)v.findViewById(android.R.id.list);
    registerForContextMenu(listView);

    return v;
}
```

The android.R.id.list resource ID is used to retrieve the **ListView** managed by **ListFragment** within **onCreateView(…)**. **ListFragment** also has a **getListView()** method, but you cannot use it within **onCreateView(…)** because **getListView()** returns null until after **onCreateView(…)** returns.

Run CriminalIntent, long-press a list item, and confirm that the floating context menu with the Delete Crime menu item appears.

Figure 18.2 Context menu item appears on long-press

Responding to an action

To wire up the menu item, you need a method that can delete a crime from the model. In
CrimeLab.java, add a **deleteCrime(Crime)** method.

Listing 18.4 Add a method to delete a crime (CrimeLab.java)

```
public void addCrime(Crime c) {
    mCrimes.add(c);
}

public void deleteCrime(Crime c) {
    mCrimes.remove(c);
}
```

The next step is to respond to the menu item selection in **onContextItemSelected(MenuItem)**. The
MenuItem has an ID that represents the menu item that was selected. However, it is not enough to know
that the user wants to delete a crime. You also need to know *which* crime to delete.

You can get this information by calling **getMenuInfo()** on the **MenuItem**. This method returns an
instance of a class that implements **ContextMenu.ContextMenuInfo**.

In **CrimeListFragment**, add an implementation for **onContextItemSelected(MenuItem)** that uses the
menu info and the adapter to determine which **Crime** was long-pressed. Then delete that **Crime** from
the model.

Listing 18.5 Listening for context menu item selection
(CrimeListFragment.java)

```java
@Override
public void onCreateContextMenu(ContextMenu menu, View v, ContextMenuInfo menuInfo) {
    getActivity().getMenuInflater().inflate(R.menu.crime_list_item_context, menu);
}

@Override
public boolean onContextItemSelected(MenuItem item) {
    AdapterContextMenuInfo info = (AdapterContextMenuInfo)item.getMenuInfo();
    int position = info.position;
    CrimeAdapter adapter = (CrimeAdapter)getListAdapter();
    Crime crime = adapter.getItem(position);

    switch (item.getItemId()) {
        case R.id.menu_item_delete_crime:
            CrimeLab.get(getActivity()).deleteCrime(crime);
            adapter.notifyDataSetChanged();
            return true;
    }
    return super.onContextItemSelected(item);
}
```

In Listing 18.5, **getMenuInfo()** returns an instance of **AdapterView.AdapterContextMenuInfo** because **ListView** is a subclass of **AdapterView**. You cast the results of **getMenuInfo()** and get details about the selected list item, including its position in the data set. Then you use the position to retrieve the correct **Crime**.

Run CriminalIntent, add a new crime, then long-press to delete it. (To simulate a long-press on the emulator, hold the left mouse button down until the menu appears.)

Implementing Contextual Action Mode

The code you have written for deleting a crime via a floating context menu will work on any Android device. For instance, Figure 18.2 shows the floating menu on a device running Jelly Bean.

However, the recommended way to present contextual actions on newer devices is to have a long-press on a view put the screen into *contextual action mode*. When the screen is in contextual action mode, the items defined in your context menu appear in a contextual action bar that overlays the action bar. Contextual action bars are nice because they do not obscure the screen.

Figure 18.3 Contextual action bar appears on long-press

Implementing a contextual action bar requires a different set of code from a floating context menu. In addition, the contextual action bar code contains classes and methods that are not available on Froyo or Gingerbread, so you must ensure that the code that you write will not be called where it does not exist.

Enabling multiple selection

When a list view is in contextual action mode, you can enable selecting multiple list items at one time. Any action chosen from the contextual action bar will apply to all of the views that have been selected.

In **CrimeListFragment.onCreateView(…)**, set the list view's choice mode to CHOICE_MODE_MULTIPLE_MODAL. Use build version constants to separate the code that registers the **ListView** from the code that sets the choice mode.

Listing 18.6 Setting choice mode (CrimeListFragment.java)

```
@TargetApi(11)
@Override
public View onCreateView(LayoutInflater inflater, ViewGroup parent,
        Bundle savedInstanceState) {
    View v = super.onCreateView(inflater, parent, savedInstanceState);

    ...
```

```
ListView listView = (ListView)v.findViewById(android.R.id.list);

if (Build.VERSION.SDK_INT < Build.VERSION_CODES.HONEYCOMB) {
    // Use floating context menus on Froyo and Gingerbread
    registerForContextMenu(listView);
} else {
    // Use contextual action bar on Honeycomb and higher
    listView.setChoiceMode(ListView.CHOICE_MODE_MULTIPLE_MODAL);
}

return v;
}
```

Action mode callbacks in a list view

The next step is to set a listener on the **ListView** that implements
AbsListView.MultiChoiceModeListener. This interface contains the following method that calls back
when a view has been selected or deselected.

```
public abstract void onItemCheckedStateChanged(ActionMode mode, int position,
    long id, boolean checked)
```

MultiChoiceModeListener implements another interface – **ActionMode.Callback**. When the screen
is put into contextual action mode, an instance of the **ActionMode** class is created, and the methods in
ActionMode.Callback call back at different points in the lifecycle of the **ActionMode**. There are four
required methods in **ActionMode.Callback**:

```
public abstract boolean onCreateActionMode(ActionMode mode, Menu menu)
```

called when the **ActionMode** is created. This is where you inflate the context menu resource to
be displayed in the contextual action bar.

```
public abstract boolean onPrepareActionMode(ActionMode mode, Menu menu)
```

called after **onCreateActionMode(…)** and whenever an existing contextual action bar needs to be
refreshed with new data.

```
public abstract boolean onActionItemClicked(ActionMode mode, MenuItem item)
```

called when the user selects an action. This is where you respond to contextual actions defined
in the menu resource.

```
public abstract void onDestroyActionMode(ActionMode mode)
```

called when the **ActionMode** is about to be destroyed because the user has canceled the action
mode or the selected action has been responded to. The default implementation results in the
view(s) being unselected. You can also update the fragment here with anything else it needs to
know about what happened while in contextual action mode.

In **CrimeListFragment.onCreateView(…)**, set a listener that implements **MultiChoiceModeListener**
on the list view. You only need to take action in **onCreateActionMode(…)** and in
onActionItemClicked(ActionMode, MenuItem).

Listing 18.7 Setting the **MultiChoiceModeListener** (CrimeListFragment.java)

```
    ...

    } else {
        // Use contextual action bar on Honeycomb and higher
        listView.setChoiceMode(ListView.CHOICE_MODE_MULTIPLE_MODAL);
        listView.setMultiChoiceModeListener(new MultiChoiceModeListener() {

            public void onItemCheckedStateChanged(ActionMode mode, int position,
                    long id, boolean checked) {
                // Required, but not used in this implementation
            }

            // ActionMode.Callback methods
            public boolean onCreateActionMode(ActionMode mode, Menu menu) {
                MenuInflater inflater = mode.getMenuInflater();
                inflater.inflate(R.menu.crime_list_item_context, menu);
                return true;
            }

            public boolean onPrepareActionMode(ActionMode mode, Menu menu) {
                return false;
                // Required, but not used in this implementation
            }

            public boolean onActionItemClicked(ActionMode mode, MenuItem item) {
                switch (item.getItemId()) {
                    case R.id.menu_item_delete_crime:
                        CrimeAdapter adapter = (CrimeAdapter)getListAdapter();
                        CrimeLab crimeLab = CrimeLab.get(getActivity());
                        for (int i = adapter.getCount() - 1; i >= 0; i--) {
                            if (getListView().isItemChecked(i)) {
                                crimeLab.deleteCrime(adapter.getItem(i));
                            }
                        }
                        mode.finish();
                        adapter.notifyDataSetChanged();
                        return true;
                    default:
                        return false;
                }
            }

            public void onDestroyActionMode(ActionMode mode) {
                // Required, but not used in this implementation
            }
        });
    }

    return v;
}
```

If you used Eclipse's auto-complete to create this interface, note that the stub created for **onCreateActionMode(...)** returns false. Be sure to change it to true; returning false will abort the creation of your action mode.

In **onCreateActionMode(…)**, notice that you get the **MenuInflater** from the action mode rather than from the activity. The action mode has details for configuring the contextual action bar. For example, you can call **ActionMode.setTitle(…)** to give the contextual action bar its own title. The activity's menu inflater would not know about this title.

The **onActionItemClicked(…)** method is where you delete one or more **Crime**s from **CrimeLab** and then reload the list to reflect those changes. The call to **ActionMode.finish()** prepares the action mode to be destroyed.

Run CriminalIntent. Long-press a list item to select it and enter contextual action mode. Select other list items by (regular) pressing them. Unselect selected list items in the same way. Delete a couple of crimes. Pressing the delete icon will finish the action mode and return you to the updated list of crimes. Alternatively, you can cancel the action mode by pressing the icon on the far left of the contextual action bar. This will finish the action mode and return you to the list without making any changes.

Figure 18.4 Second and third items are selected

While this implementation works, it is difficult to tell which items have been selected. You can improve this situation by changing the list item background when an item is selected.

Changing activated item backgrounds

Sometimes you need a view to appear differently depending on its *state*. In this case, you are interested in changing the list item background when it is in the *activated* state. When a view is in the *activated* state, it has been marked by the user as being something interesting.

You can change the background based on the view's state using a *state list drawable*. A *state list drawable* is an XML resource. Within this resource, you name a drawable (a bitmap or a color) and then list which states this drawable should appear in. (You can find other states a view can be in on the **StateListDrawable** reference page.)

Unlike other drawables, state list drawables are typically not associated with a pixel density and, thus, live in the unqualified `drawable` directory. Create a `res/drawable` directory and a new XML file named `res/drawable/background_activated.xml`. Give this file a root element of `selector` and add the item shown in Listing 18.8.

Listing 18.8 A simple state list drawable (`res/drawable/background_activated.xml`)

```xml
<?xml version="1.0" encoding="utf-8"?>
<selector xmlns:android="http://schemas.android.com/apk/res/android" >
  <item
    android:state_activated="true"
    android:drawable="@android:color/darker_gray"
  />
</selector>
```

This XML says, "When the view that references this drawable is in the activated state, use the value of `android:drawable`. Otherwise, do nothing." If you had given `android:state_activated` a value of `false`, then the value would be used whenever the view was *not* in the activated state.

Modify `res/layout/list_item_crime.xml` to reference this drawable.

Listing 18.9 Change list item background (`res/layout/list_item_crime.xml`)

```xml
<RelativeLayout xmlns:android="http://schemas.android.com/apk/res/android"
  android:layout_width="match_parent"
  android:layout_height="wrap_content"
  android:background="@drawable/background_activated">

  ...
</RelativeLayout>
```

Run CriminalIntent again. This time, your selected items will stand out clearly.

Figure 18.5 Second and third items are more obviously selected

You will learn more about state list drawables in Chapter 25.

Implementing contextual action mode in other views

The contextual action bar implementation you have used in this chapter works great for a `ListView`. It will also work for a `GridView`, an `AdapterView` subclass that you will use in Chapter 26. But what if you need a contextual action bar for a view that is not a `ListView` or a `GridView`?

First, you set a listener that implements `View.OnLongClickListener`. Within this listener's implementation, you create an instance of `ActionMode` by calling `Activity.startActionMode(…)`. (When using `MultiChoiceModeListener`, the `ActionMode` instance is created for you.)

The single parameter of `startActionMode(…)` is an object that implements the `ActionMode.Callback` interface. You create an implementation of `ActionMode.Callback` including the four `ActionMode` lifecycle methods that you implemented earlier:

- `public abstract boolean onCreateActionMode(ActionMode mode, Menu menu)`

- `public abstract boolean onPrepareActionMode(ActionMode mode, Menu menu)`

- `public abstract boolean onActionItemClicked(ActionMode mode, MenuItem item)`

- `public abstract void onDestroyActionMode(ActionMode mode)`

You can create an object that implements `ActionMode.Callback` and pass it in to `startActionMode(…)` or pass an anonymous implementation directly in the call to `startActionMode(…)`.

Compatibility: Fallback or Duplicate?

In this chapter, you have used a compatibility strategy known as *graceful fallback*. Graceful fallback means that your app will use new features and code when run on newer platforms and fall back to using older features on older ones. You did this by checking the SDK version at runtime.

Graceful fallback is not the only strategy. Instead of falling back on older platforms, you can use an identical feature that mimics the features of newer platforms. We call this strategy *duplication*. Duplication strategies fall into two groups: duplication-on-demand and duplicate replacement. In duplication-on-demand, you use the replacement only on older platforms where the real thing is unavailable. Duplicate replacement is using the replacement all the time, even on platforms that have native support.

Using the support library to enable fragments is a duplicate replacement strategy. Your apps always use the replacement class `android.support.v4.app.Fragment` – even when run on devices where the class `android.app.Fragment` is available.

The support library does not include a duplicate action bar, but there are several third-party copies of the action bar that you can use for compatibility with older devices. If you have an app with an action bar running on your Gingerbread phone, it is using one of these third-party libraries. The best and most popular is a library called ActionBarSherlock by Jake Wharton, which you can find at http://www.actionbarsherlock.com. ActionBarSherlock is based on the latest Android sources and provides duplication-on-demand support for action bar features on every previous version of Android. There is more about ActionBarSherlock and how to implement it in the For The More Curious section and the second challenge at the end of the chapter.

(It is said by wise elders in session videos that soon the support library will have a duplicate action bar as well. There will be great rejoicing on that day.)

Which strategy is better? Duplication strategies have real advantages. The main one is that they behave the same no matter which version of Android the user is running. This especially applies to duplicate replacement strategies, which run the exact same code on every version of Android. Designers often find this reassuring because they only have to design one user experience. The same goes for testers, who only have one set of interactions to verify. Finally, a duplication strategy allows your app to look like a fresh new ICS or Jelly Bean app before your users have even upgraded. Duplication is the most popular strategy in the Android world, and this is the most important reason why – stylish and new apps almost always duplicate the newest library features to look up-to-date.

There are two major disadvantages to a duplication strategy. One is that to stay up-to-date, you have to rely on third-party libraries. That is the reason this book uses a graceful fallback strategy for the action bar. The other disadvantage is that your app may feel alien compared to the rest of the device. If your app has a custom design, then this will not be a concern because your app will look different anyway. If your intention is to fit in with the standard apps on the phone, though, your app will stick out like a sore thumb.

Challenge: Deleting from CrimeFragment

Users might appreciate the ability to delete a crime from its detail view as well as from the list. In that case, deleting would apply to the screen as a whole, so the action would belong in an options menu or on the action bar. Implement a delete crime option in `CrimeFragment`.

For the More Curious: ActionBarSherlock

As critical as it is to understand the basic workings of Android's standard libraries and how they work on difference devices and OS versions, real-world developers often need to forget about those compatibility worries. By far the biggest compatibility concern is the action bar, which you learned about in this chapter and Chapter 16.

ActionBarSherlock (or ABS, as it is more often called) is aimed squarely at this problem. It provides a backported version of the action bar, plus a set of classes that will use the backported version when necessary, or the native one if it is available. You can find it at http://www.actionbarsherlock.com. It also provides backported versions of the newer Android themes that include the action bar.

If that makes ABS sound to you like a more feature-ful support library, then you are right. Unlike the support library, though, ABS provides themes and resource IDs. This means that instead of being a simple jar file, ABS is distributed as an Android *library project*. A library project is like a regular Android project, but instead of creating an independent application, it builds a library for other applications to use. This allows Android to build in any additional Android resources provided by the library. Any library that needs to provide additional Android resources must be a library project, not a jar file.

Since ABS is a library project, there are three steps required to integrate it into your project:

- download and unzip the source

- import the source into an Eclipse project called ActionBarSherlock

- add a reference to the new ActionBarSherlock project in CriminalIntent

- update CriminalIntent to use ActionBarSherlock's support classes

(If you want to follow along with this short guide on integrating ActionBarSherlock, you should make a copy of CriminalIntent right now. Having an ABS-free CriminalIntent will make it easier to continue with the rest of the book.)

To download ABS, go to `http://www.actionbarsherlock.com/download.html`, click the link to download either a `zip` or `tgz` compressed archive (it doesn't matter which), and then unzip it.

Next, to create the new project. In Eclipse, right-click inside the package explorer and select New → Project....

Instead of creating a fresh Android project, you will want to create a project that includes the source that you downloaded. So select Android Project From Existing Code (Figure 18.6).

Figure 18.6 Create Android project from existing code

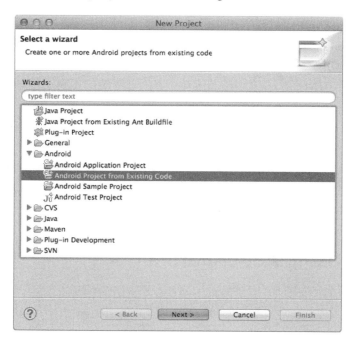

Inside this dialog, it will ask you to select a root directory to search for existing code. Click Browse... and browse to the location where you downloaded ABS. The unzipped file has three subfolders: `library`, `samples`, and `website`. Select `library`, click Open, and then click Finish.

Figure 18.7 Choosing the ABS library folder

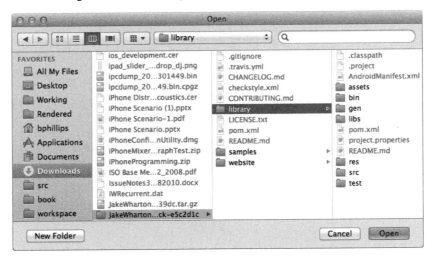

When Eclipse creates your project, it will give it the name library. This is not an informative project name, so right-click and select Refactor → Rename... to name the project ActionBarSherlock instead.

Now for the final step to add your ABS reference: add a library project reference from CriminalIntent. Right-click CriminalIntent in the package explorer and select Properties... Click on Android. The bottom area of the screen lists your Android library project references. You have none, so it is empty.

Figure 18.8 Android library references

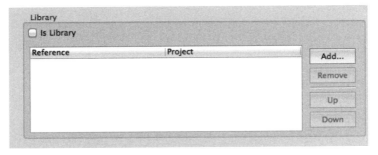

Click the Add... button. In the window that appears, double-click ActionBarSherlock to add the library project reference.

Challenge: Using ActionBarSherlock

Now that you have added an ActionBarSherlock project reference, you are ready to integrate it into CriminalIntent.

ABS works a lot like the support library – it provides alternative versions of core Android classes like **Activity**, **Fragment**, and **ActionBar**. Most (not all) of the ABS class names are prefixed with **Sherlock-**, though, which makes them a bit easier to distinguish than the support library classes.

That gives you some idea of what you need to do. The fragment and activity classes are all prefixed with **Sherlock-**, but the menu-related classes are not.

Basic ABS integration in CriminalIntent

Here are the steps for the most basic ABS integration:

- Change CriminalIntent's theme to `Theme.Sherlock.Light.DarkActionBar`.

- Change **SingleFragmentActivity** and **CrimePagerActivity** to inherit from **SherlockFragmentActivity** instead of **FragmentActivity**.

- Change all your fragments to inherit from **SherlockFragment**, **SherlockDialogFragment**, or **SherlockListFragment** instead of the support library versions of these classes.

- Change the appropriate **Menu**, **MenuItem**, and **MenuInflater** references to refer to their corresponding implementations in **com.actionbarsherlock.view** instead.

The first step is important: You must change the theme for your app to one of the ABS themes (`Theme.Sherlock`, `Theme.Sherlock.Light`, or `Theme.Sherlock.Light.DarkActionBar`) or to a custom theme that inherits from one of those themes. Without this step, your app will not run on older devices.

The second two steps are simple – just change the superclass names. Once you are done with that, you will have a lot of errors in **CrimeFragment** and **CrimeListFragment**. To get rid of them, you will need to perform the third step, which is more involved.

For **CrimeFragment**, the fix is easy: delete the menu related `import` statements up top, organize imports with Command+Shift+O/Ctrl+Shift+O, and select the **com.actionbarsherlock.view** versions instead.

If you try this trick in **CrimeListFragment**, though, you will have problems. This is because **CrimeListFragment** uses context menus and **MultiChoiceModeListener**. These require the original Android library versions of the menu classes.

So how do you fix it? Instead of using the organize imports fix, you will need to fully qualify the type references to **MenuItem**, **Menu**, and **MenuInflater** in **onCreateOptionsMenu(…)** and **onOptionsItemSelected(…)**. This means that instead of this:

```
@Override
public void onCreateOptionsMenu(Menu menu, MenuInflater inflater) {
    ...
}
```

You will have to write this:

```
@Override
public void onCreateOptionsMenu(com.actionbarsherlock.view.Menu menu,
        com.actionbarsherlock.view.MenuInflater inflater) {
    ...
}
```

More advanced integration

If you completed the first challenge, you will have integrated ABS. To really use it, though, you will want to use your ABS integration to get rid of compatibility code. To do this, call **getSherlockActivity().getSupportActionBar()** instead of **getActivity().getActionBar()** in your code. The **SherlockActivity**'s action bar is always available, so using it instead will allow you to delete some guard code. After that, you can move `res/menu-v11/fragment_crime_list.xml` file into `res/menu` to eliminate configuration-level OS version switching.

Even more advanced integration

Feeling adventurous? The next step in making CriminalIntent behave identically across different versions is to eliminate your usage of **MultiChoiceModeListener** and context menus. Deleting the context menu code is easy, but replacing **MultiChoiceModeListener** will require replicating its functionality.

How can you do that? The first tool that you can use is the old-style **ListView** choice mode: `ListView.CHOICE_MODE_MULTIPLE`. In this chapter you used `ListView.CHOICE_MODE_MULTIPLE_MODAL`, which only has an effect on new versions of Android. `ListView.CHOICE_MODE_MULTIPLE` does not enable any fancy modal long-press behavior, but it does have the advantage that it works on all versions of Android. Setting your **ListView**'s choice mode to `ListView.CHOICE_MODE_MULTIPLE` will enable selection of multiple items. To disable selection, set it back to `ListView.CHOICE_MODE_NONE`.

The next thing you need to do is replicate the modal action bar behavior provided by `CHOICE_MODE_MULTIPLE_MODAL`. You can do this in a cross-version fashion by calling **getSherlockActivity().startActionMode()**. Make sure to use the version that takes in **com.actionbarsherlock.view.ActionMode.Callback**, not the regular Android version.

Finally, you will need to detect long-presses like before. You can do that by providing an **OnItemLongClickListener** to **ListView.setOnItemLongClickListener(…)**.

19

Camera I: Viewfinder

When documenting a crime, it helps to have photographic evidence. In the next two chapters, you will add the ability to take a photo of a crime using the camera API.

The camera API, while powerful, is not succinct or simple. You will be typing in a lot of code and, at times, cage-fighting with concepts that seem like overkill. You may think, "I just need to snap a quick photo. Isn't there a standard interface for this?"

There is. You can interact with the camera via an implicit intent. Most Android devices have a camera app installed, and the camera app listens for an intent created with `MediaStore.ACTION_IMAGE_CAPTURE`. You will learn how to work with implicit intents in Chapter 21.

Unfortunately, as of this writing, there is a bug in the implicit intent camera interface on a lot of devices that makes it impossible to save a full-size version of the picture. If an app only requires thumbnail images, then using an implicit intent will work fine. CriminalIntent, however, needs larger crime scene photos, so you get to learn to use the camera API.

In this chapter, you will create a fragment-based activity and use the **SurfaceView** class and the camera hardware to display a live video preview from the camera.

Figure 19.1 Live camera preview in viewfinder

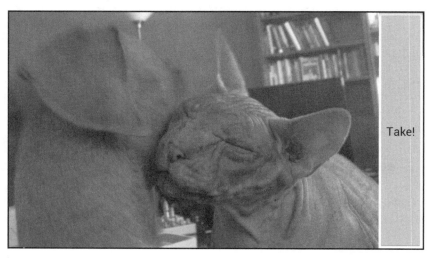

Figure 19.2 shows the new objects that you will create.

Figure 19.2 Object diagram for camera portion of CriminalIntent

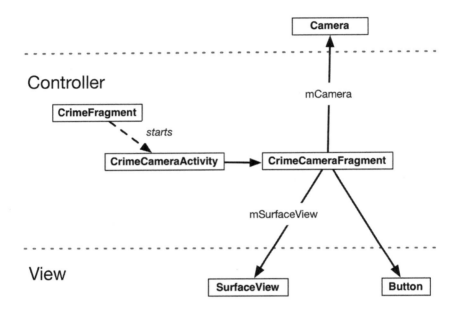

The instance of **Camera** provides hardware-level access to the device's camera(s). A camera is an exclusive-access resource: only one activity can access a camera at a time.

The instance of **SurfaceView** will be your viewfinder. A **SurfaceView** is a special view that lets you render content directly to the screen.

You will start by creating the layout for **CrimeCameraFragment**'s view, the **CrimeCameraFragment** class itself, and the **CrimeCameraActivity** class. Then you will create and manage a viewfinder in **CrimeCameraFragment**. Finally, you will enable **CrimeFragment** to start an instance of **CrimeCameraActivity**.

Creating the Fragment Layout

Create a new Android XML Layout file named fragment_crime_camera.xml and make its root element a **FrameLayout**. Then add the widgets shown in Figure 19.3.

Figure 19.3 Layout for **CrimeCameraFragment**
(fragment_crime_camera.xml)

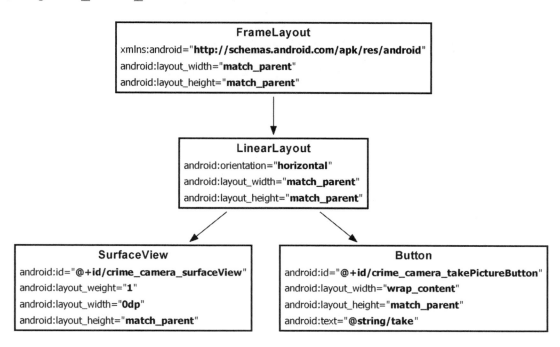

In this layout file, you have a **LinearLayout** as the only child of a **FrameLayout**, which causes a warning about the **LinearLayout** being useless. Ignore this warning; you will give the **FrameLayout** a second child view in Chapter 20.

Within the **LinearLayout**, you use a combination of layout_width and layout_weight to arrange its child views. The **Button** is given the space it needs due to its android:layout_width="wrap_content" attribute, and the **SurfaceView** gets nothing (android:layout_width="0dp"). In terms of the space left over, only the **SurfaceView** has a layout_weight attribute, so the **SurfaceView** gets all of the leftover space.

Figure 19.4 shows what this layout will look like.

Figure 19.4 A viewfinder and button

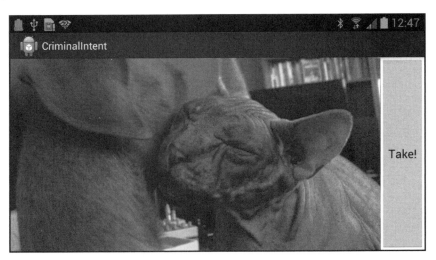

In `strings.xml`, add a string resource for the button's text.

Listing 19.1 Adding string for camera button (`strings.xml`)

```
...
<string name="show_subtitle">Show Subtitle</string>
<string name="subtitle">Sometimes tolerance is not a virtue.</string>
<string name="take">Take!</string>

</resources>
```

Creating CrimeCameraFragment

Create a new class named **CrimeCameraFragment** and make its superclass
android.support.v4.app.Fragment. In CrimeCameraFragment.java, add the fields shown in Listing
19.2. Organize your imports, and when asked, import **android.hardware.Camera**. Then, override
onCreateView(…) to inflate the layout and get references to the widgets. For now, set a listener on the
button that simply finishes the hosting activity, which will return the user to the previous screen.

Listing 19.2 The initial camera fragment (`CrimeCameraFragment.java`)

```java
public class CrimeCameraFragment extends Fragment {
    private static final String TAG = "CrimeCameraFragment";

    private Camera mCamera;
    private SurfaceView mSurfaceView;

    @Override
    public View onCreateView(LayoutInflater inflater, ViewGroup parent,
            Bundle savedInstanceState) {
        View v = inflater.inflate(R.layout.fragment_crime_camera, parent, false);

        Button takePictureButton = (Button)v
            .findViewById(R.id.crime_camera_takePictureButton);
        takePictureButton.setOnClickListener(new View.OnClickListener() {
            public void onClick(View v) {
                getActivity().finish();
            }
        });

        mSurfaceView = (SurfaceView)v.findViewById(R.id.crime_camera_surfaceView);

        return v;
    }
}
```

Creating CrimeCameraActivity

Create a new **SingleFragmentActivity** subclass named **CrimeCameraActivity** and override
createFragment() to return a new **CrimeCameraFragment**.

Listing 19.3 Create the camera activity (`CrimeCameraActivity.java`)

```java
public class CrimeCameraActivity extends SingleFragmentActivity {
    @Override
    protected Fragment createFragment() {
        return new CrimeCameraFragment();
    }
}
```

Adding activity and camera permissions to the manifest

The next step is to declare **CrimeCameraActivity** in the manifest. In addition, you must ask permission
for your application to use the camera by adding a `uses-permission` element.

Update `AndroidManifest.xml` to reflect the changes in Listing 19.4.

Listing 19.4 Adding permissions and camera activity to manifest (AndroidManifest.xml)

```xml
<?xml version="1.0" encoding="utf-8"?>
<manifest xmlns:android="http://schemas.android.com/apk/res/android"
  package="com.bignerdranch.android.criminalintent"
  android:versionCode="1"
  android:versionName="1.0" >

  <uses-sdk android:minSdkVersion="8" android:targetSdkVersion="16"/>
  <uses-permission android:name="android.permission.CAMERA" />
  <uses-feature android:name="android.hardware.camera" />

  <application

        ...

    <activity android:name=".CrimeCameraActivity"
      android:screenOrientation="landscape"
      android:label="@string/app_name">
    </activity>

  </application>

</manifest>
```

The uses-feature element specifies that your application uses a particular device feature. Adding the android.hardware.camera feature ensures that when your app appears on Google Play, it will only be offered to devices that have a camera.

Notice that in the activity declaration, you explicitly force the activity into landscape mode using the android:screenOrientation attribute. This will keep the activity's interface from changing on the user as he or she is trying to get the right angle for a picture.

There are a surprising number of options for screenOrientation. For example, you can set your activity to have the same orientation as its parent or to choose landscape orientation in either direction depending on the hardware sensor. Check out the documentation for the <activity> element for more info.

Using the Camera API

Up to this point, you have been doing basic activity-creating. Now it is time to take on camera-specific concepts and classes.

Opening and releasing the camera

First, let's handle the management of the camera resource. You have given **CrimeCameraFragment** an instance of **Camera**. The camera is an important system-wide resource, so it is critical to obtain it only when you need it and release it as soon as you are done. Otherwise, the camera will be unavailable to other applications until the device is rebooted.

Here are the **Camera** methods you will use to manage the **Camera** instance:

```java
public static Camera open(int cameraId)
public static Camera open()
public final void release()
```

The **open(int)** method was introduced in API level 9, so the parameter-less **open()** method is required on API level 8.

The callbacks in **CrimeCameraFragment**'s lifecycle where you should open and release the camera are **onResume()** and **onPause()**. These two methods mark the boundaries of when the user can interact with the fragment's view, and the camera is only useful when the user can interact with it. (Note that **onResume()** is called even when the fragment is coming on screen for the first time.)

In **CrimeCameraFragment.onResume()**, you are going to initialize the camera using the static method **Camera.open(int)** and pass in 0 to open the first camera available on the device. Usually this is the rear-facing camera, but if the device does not have one (e.g. the Nexus 7), then it will open its front-facing camera.

For API level 8, you need to call the parameter-less **Camera.open()** instead. Safeguard your code for Froyo by checking the device's build version and calling **Camera.open()** on API level 8.

Listing 19.5 Opening the camera in **onResume()** (CrimeCameraFragment.java)

```java
@TargetApi(9)
@Override
public void onResume() {
    super.onResume();
    if (Build.VERSION.SDK_INT >= Build.VERSION_CODES.GINGERBREAD) {
        mCamera = Camera.open(0);
    } else {
        mCamera = Camera.open();
    }
}
```

(Android Lint may give you warnings about opening the camera on the main thread. These are legitimate warnings, but you are going to have to ignore them until you learn about multi-threading in Chapter 26.)

When the fragment is going offscreen, you need to release the camera resource so that it is available to other apps. Be a good citizen and override **onPause()** to release the camera.

Listing 19.6 Implementing lifecycle methods (CrimeCameraFragment.java)

```java
public void onResume() {
    super.onResume();
    if (Build.VERSION.SDK_INT >= Build.VERSION_CODES.GINGERBREAD) {
        mCamera = Camera.open(0);
    } else {
        mCamera = Camera.open();
    }
}

@Override
public void onPause() {
    super.onPause();

    if (mCamera != null) {
        mCamera.release();
        mCamera = null;
    }
}
```

Notice that you make sure you have a camera instance before calling **release()**. You should always check before calling code on the camera. Even though you asked permission to use it, the camera may not be available. Another activity may be using it, or a virtual device may not have a camera at all. If for any reason the camera instance does not exist, null-checking will keep your app from crashing.

SurfaceView, SurfaceHolder, and Surface

SurfaceView provides an implementation of the **SurfaceHolder** interface. In CrimeCameraFragment.java, add the following code to get your **SurfaceView**'s **SurfaceHolder**.

Listing 19.7 Getting the **SurfaceHolder** (CrimeCameraFragment.java)

```
@Override
@SuppressWarnings("deprecation")
public View onCreateView(LayoutInflater inflater, ViewGroup parent,
        Bundle savedInstanceState) {

    ...

    mSurfaceView = (SurfaceView)v.findViewById(R.id.crime_camera_surfaceView);
    SurfaceHolder holder = mSurfaceView.getHolder();
    // setType() and SURFACE_TYPE_PUSH_BUFFERS are both deprecated,
    // but are required for Camera preview to work on pre-3.0 devices.
    holder.setType(SurfaceHolder.SURFACE_TYPE_PUSH_BUFFERS);

    return v;
}
```

The **setType(…)** method and the SURFACE_TYPE_PUSH_BUFFERS constant are both deprecated, and the compiler will produce warnings for deprecated code. Eclipse shows you that these methods are deprecated by striking through them.

Why are we asking you to use deprecated code? The **setType(…)** method and SURFACE_TYPE_PUSH_BUFFERS are required for the camera preview to work on pre-Honeycomb devices. In Listing 19.7, you make these warnings go away with the @SuppressWarnings annotation. This may seem cavalier, but it is the best option for handling deprecation and compatibility in Android. There is more discussion of deprecation in Android at the end of Chapter 20.

A **SurfaceHolder** is your connection to another object – **Surface**. A **Surface** represents a buffer of raw pixel data.

A **Surface** has a lifecycle: it is created for you when the **SurfaceView** appears on screen and it is destroyed when the **SurfaceView** is no longer visible. You have to make sure nothing is drawn to the **Surface** when it does not exist.

Figure 19.5 **SurfaceView**, **SurfaceHolder**, and **Surface**

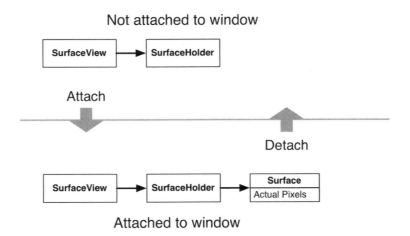

Unlike other **View** objects, neither **SurfaceView** nor any of its teammates draw anything into themselves. A **Surface**'s *client* is whatever object wants to draw into its buffer. In **CrimeCameraFragment**, the client is the **Camera** instance.

Remember, you have to make sure that nothing is drawn to the **Surface** when it is not there. To achieve the desired state of affairs in Figure 19.6, you will need to attach the **Camera** to your **SurfaceHolder** when the **Surface** is created, and detach it when the **Surface** is destroyed.

Figure 19.6 The desired state of affairs

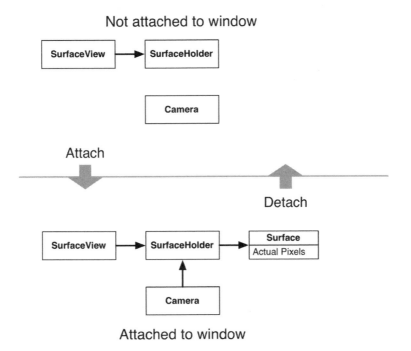

SurfaceHolder provides another interface that will let you do this – **SurfaceHolder.Callback**. This interface listens for events in the lifecycle of a **Surface** so that you can coordinate the **Surface** with its client.

Here are the three methods of **SurfaceHolder.Callback**:

```
public abstract void surfaceCreated(SurfaceHolder holder)
```

This method is called when the view hierarchy that the **SurfaceView** belongs to is put on screen. This is where you connect the **Surface** with its client.

```
public abstract void surfaceChanged(SurfaceHolder holder, int format, int width,
int height)
```

When the surface is being displayed for the first time, the **surfaceChanged(…)** method will be called. This method informs you of the pixel format and the width and height of the surface. Within this method, you tell your **Surface**'s client how big the drawing area will be.

```
public abstract void surfaceDestroyed(SurfaceHolder holder)
```

When the **SurfaceView** is removed from the screen, the **Surface** is destroyed. This will be where you tell your **Surface**'s client to stop using the **Surface**.

Here are the **Camera** methods you will use to respond to events in the lifecycle of the **Surface**:

```
public final void setPreviewDisplay(SurfaceHolder holder)
```

This method connects the camera with your **Surface**. You will call it in **surfaceCreated()**.

```
public final void startPreview()
```

This method starts drawing frames on the **Surface**. You will call it in **surfaceChanged(…)**.

```
public final void stopPreview()
```

This method stops drawing frames on the **Surface**. You will call it in **surfaceDestroyed()**.

In CrimeCameraFragment.java, add an implementation of **SurfaceHolder.Callback** to coordinate the lifecycle of the **Surface** with the camera's preview.

Listing 19.8 Implementing **SurfaceHolder.Callback** (CrimeCameraFragment.java)

```java
...
SurfaceHolder holder = mSurfaceView.getHolder();
// setType() and SURFACE_TYPE_PUSH_BUFFERS are both deprecated,
// but are required for Camera preview to work on pre-3.0 devices.
holder.setType(SurfaceHolder.SURFACE_TYPE_PUSH_BUFFERS);

holder.addCallback(new SurfaceHolder.Callback() {

    public void surfaceCreated(SurfaceHolder holder) {
        // Tell the camera to use this surface as its preview area
        try {
            if (mCamera != null) {
                mCamera.setPreviewDisplay(holder);
            }
        } catch (IOException exception) {
            Log.e(TAG, "Error setting up preview display", exception);
        }
    }

    public void surfaceDestroyed(SurfaceHolder holder) {
        // We can no longer display on this surface, so stop the preview.
        if (mCamera != null) {
            mCamera.stopPreview();
        }
    }

    public void surfaceChanged(SurfaceHolder holder, int format, int w, int h) {
        if (mCamera == null) return;

        // The surface has changed size; update the camera preview size
        Camera.Parameters parameters = mCamera.getParameters();
        Size s = null; // To be reset in the next section
        parameters.setPreviewSize(s.width, s.height);
        mCamera.setParameters(parameters);
        try {
            mCamera.startPreview();
        } catch (Exception e) {
            Log.e(TAG, "Could not start preview", e);
            mCamera.release();
            mCamera = null;
        }
    }
});

return v;
}
```

Notice that you release the camera if the preview cannot be started. Whenever you open the camera, you must release it – even in the case of an exception.

In the implementation of **surfaceChanged(…)**, you set the camera's preview size to null. This is a temporary assignment until you can determine an acceptable preview size. You cannot set this size to just any value. Exceptions will be thrown if the value is unacceptable.

Determining preview size

The first step is to get a list of the camera's allowable preview sizes from the nested
`Camera.Parameters` class. This class includes the following method:

```
public List<Camera.Size> getSupportedPreviewSizes()
```

This method returns a list of instances of the **android.hardware.Camera.Size** class, which wraps the
width and height dimensions of an image.

You can then compare the sizes in the list with the width and height of the **Surface** passed into
surfaceChanged(…) to find a preview size that will work with your **Surface**.

In **CrimeCameraFragment**, add the following method that accepts a list of sizes and then selects the size
with the largest number of pixels. It is not beautiful code, but it will work fine for our purposes.

Listing 19.9 Find the best supported size (`CrimeCameraFragment.java`)

```java
/** A simple algorithm to get the largest size available. For a more
 * robust version, see CameraPreview.java in the ApiDemos
 * sample app from Android. */
private Size getBestSupportedSize(List<Size> sizes, int width, int height) {
    Size bestSize = sizes.get(0);
    int largestArea = bestSize.width * bestSize.height;
    for (Size s : sizes) {
        int area = s.width * s.height;
        if (area > largestArea) {
            bestSize = s;
            largestArea = area;
        }
    }
    return bestSize;
}
```

Now call this method to set the preview size in **surfaceChanged(…)**.

Listing 19.10 Calling **getBestSupportedSize(…)**
(`CrimeCameraFragment.java`)

```java
...
holder.addCallback(new SurfaceHolder.Callback() {

    ...

    public void surfaceChanged(SurfaceHolder holder, int format, int w, int h) {
        // The surface has changed size; update the camera preview size
        Camera.Parameters parameters = mCamera.getParameters();
        Size s = null;
        Size s = getBestSupportedSize(parameters.getSupportedPreviewSizes(), w, h);
        parameters.setPreviewSize(s.width, s.height);
        mCamera.setParameters(parameters);
        try {
            mCamera.startPreview();
        } catch (Exception e) {
            Log.e(TAG, "Could not start preview", e);
            mCamera.release();
            mCamera = null;
        }
    }
});
```

Starting CrimeCameraActivity from CrimeFragment

To get your viewfinder up and running, you are going to add a button to CrimeFragment. When this button is pressed, **CrimeFragment** will start an instance of **CrimeCameraActivity**. Here's what you want **CrimeFragment**'s view to look like.

Figure 19.7 **CrimeFragment** with camera button and rearranged widgets

To get the widgets rearranged as shown in Figure 19.7, you need to add three **LinearLayout**s and an **ImageButton**. Figure 19.8 shows the changes to make to **CrimeFragment**'s default layout.

Figure 19.8 Adding camera button and more organizing (layout/ fragment_crime.xml)

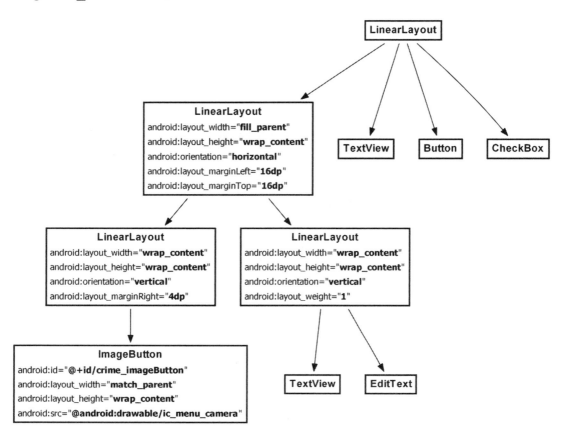

Make similar changes in the landscape layout.

Figure 19.9 Adding camera button and more organizing (`layout-land/`
`fragment_crime.xml`)

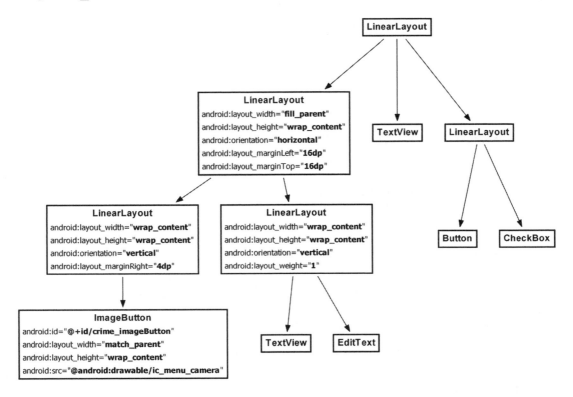

In **CrimeFragment**, add a member variable for the image button, get a reference to it, and set an
OnClickListener that starts **CrimeCameraActivity**.

Listing 19.11 Starting **CrimeCameraActivity** (CrimeFragment.java)

```java
public class CrimeFragment extends Fragment {
    ...
    private ImageButton mPhotoButton;

    ...
    public View onCreateView(LayoutInflater inflater, ViewGroup parent,
            Bundle savedInstanceState) {
        View v = inflater.inflate(R.layout.fragment_crime, parent, false);

        ...

        mPhotoButton = (ImageButton)v.findViewById(R.id.crime_imageButton);
        mPhotoButton.setOnClickListener(new View.OnClickListener() {
            @Override
            public void onClick(View v) {
                Intent i = new Intent(getActivity(), CrimeCameraActivity.class);
                startActivity(i);
            }
        });

        return v;
    }
}
```

If the device has no camera, then mPhotoButton should be disabled. You can check for the presence of a camera by querying the **PackageManager**. Add the following code to **onCreateView(…)** to disable the **ImageButton** if the device does not have a camera.

Listing 19.12 Checking for a camera (CrimeFragment.java)

```java
    @Override
    public View onCreateView(LayoutInflater inflater, ViewGroup parent,
            Bundle savedInstanceState) {
        View v = inflater.inflate(R.layout.fragment_crime, parent, false);

        ...

        mPhotoButton = (ImageButton)v.findViewById(R.id.crime_imageButton);
        mPhotoButton.setOnClickListener(new View.OnClickListener() {
            ...
        });

        // If camera is not available, disable camera functionality
        PackageManager pm = getActivity().getPackageManager();
        boolean hasACamera = pm.hasSystemFeature(PackageManager.FEATURE_CAMERA) ||
                pm.hasSystemFeature(PackageManager.FEATURE_CAMERA_FRONT) ||
                (Build.Version.SDK_INT >= Build.VERSION_CODES.GINGERBREAD &&
                Camera.getNumberOfCameras() > 0);
        if (!hasACamera) {
            mPhotoButton.setEnabled(false);
        }


        ...
    }
```

After getting the **PackageManager**, you need to perform the check to see if you have a camera. On pre-Gingerbread devices, you check this by calling **hasSystemFeature(String)**, passing constants for the device camera features you are interested in. If either of these checks returns true, you should have a camera available. However, some emulators will return true even if there is no camera available.

To fix this, you implement an alternative check. Gingerbread introduces the **getNumberOfCameras()** API call. If this is greater than 0, you are guaranteed to have a camera available. If the device does not have a camera, you set the enabled property of the **ImageButton** to false.

Run CriminalIntent. View a crime and then press the camera button. You should see the live camera preview. Pressing the Take! button will return you to the **CrimeFragment**'s view.

Figure 19.10 Live preview from camera

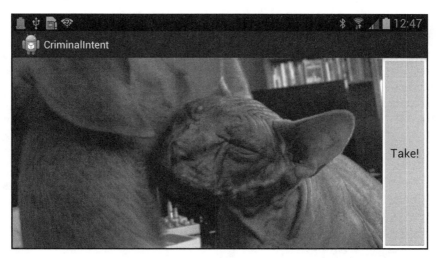

You can see the results of forcing the activity to appear in landscape in the manifest. Even if the device is in portrait orientation, the button's text is locked to landscape.

Hiding the status bar and action bar

In Figure 19.10, the activity's action bar and the status bar obscure part of the viewfinder. Users will spend only a brief time in this activity and will be focused on the viewfinder, so these elements are not useful and get in the way. It would be better to hide them in this activity's view.

Interestingly, you cannot hide the status bar and action bar from **CrimeCameraFragment**; you must do this in **CrimeCameraActivity**. Open CrimeCameraActivity.java and add the following code to **onCreate(Bundle)**.

Listing 19.13 Configuring activity (`CrimeCameraActivity.java`)

```java
public class CrimeCameraActivity extends SingleFragmentActivity {
    @Override
    public void onCreate(Bundle savedInstanceState) {
        // Hide the window title.
        requestWindowFeature(Window.FEATURE_NO_TITLE);
        // Hide the status bar and other OS-level chrome
        getWindow().addFlags(WindowManager.LayoutParams.FLAG_FULLSCREEN);

        super.onCreate(savedInstanceState);
    }

    @Override
    protected Fragment createFragment() {
        return new CrimeCameraFragment();
    }
}
```

Why must this be done in the activity? The calls to **requestWindowFeature(…)** and **addFlags(…)** must be made before the activity's view is created in **Activity.setContentView(…)**, which, in **CrimeCameraActivity**, is called in the superclass's implementation of **onCreate(Bundle)**. A fragment cannot be added before its hosting activity's view is created. Thus, you have to call these methods from within your **Activity**.

Run CriminalIntent again and enjoy your unobstructed viewfinder.

Figure 19.11 Activity without status bar or action bar

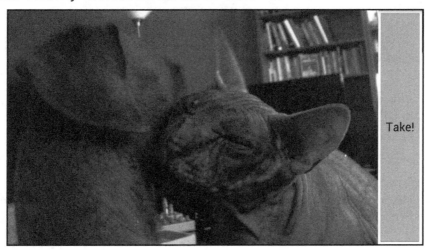

In the next chapter, you will see more of the camera API, save an image locally, and display it in **CrimeFragment**'s view.

For the More Curious: Running Activities from the Command Line

In this chapter, you were able to test your camera code fairly quickly by adding a button to **CrimeFragment** and starting **CrimeCameraActivity**. Sometimes, however, you will want to test code in a new activity before you have hooked it up to the rest of your app.

One quick-and-dirty way to do this is to switch the launcher intent filter in the manifest from the declaration of the app's intended launcher activity to the activity you want to test. Then, when the app is launched, your activity will appear. On the downside, you may be unable to reach other parts of your app until order has been restored in the manifest.

This launcher intent switcheroo is not always appropriate – like, for example, when you are working on an app with five other people. Then it can be a nasty trick indeed. In this case, there is a better option: you can use **adb** to start your activity from the command line.

The first step is to export your activity. Add the following attribute to **CrimeCameraActivity**'s declaration in AndroidManifest.xml:

```
<activity android:name=".CrimeCameraActivity"
  android:exported="true"
  android:screenOrientation="landscape"
  android:label="@string/app_name">
</activity>
```

By default, your activities may only be started from within your own app. Setting exported to true tells Android that other apps can start this activity, too. (The exported attribute is automatically set to true when you add an intent filter to the activity's declaration.)

Next, find the **adb** tool in the platform-tools subfolder within your Android SDK installation. We recommend adding the platform-tools and tools subfolders to your command-line shell's path.

If you are a command-line junkie, you are going to be all over **adb**, the *Android Debug Bridge*. **adb** can be used for a lot of the same things you have been using Eclipse for. You can monitor LogCat, open a shell on the device, browse the file system, upload and download files, list connected devices, reset **adb** – it is a wonderful thing.

You can use **adb** with multiple devices, but it is easier to use when only one device is running. Shut down or disconnect any additional emulators or devices and run CriminalIntent on a test device like normal. Then use the following incantation to start **CrimeCameraActivity** from the command line:

```
$ adb shell am start -n com.bignerdranch.android.criminalintent/.CrimeCameraActivity
Starting: Intent { cmp=com.bignerdranch.android.criminalintent/.CrimeCameraActivity }
```

Run the command, and you should see **CrimeCameraActivity** running on your emulator or device. This command is a shortcut that runs a command in a shell on the device. It does the same thing as this:

```
$ adb shell
```

```
shell@android:/ $ am start -n com.bignerdranch.android.criminalintent/.CrimeCameraAct\
ivity
```

The **am** command is a program on your device called the *activity manager*. It allows you to start and stop Android components and send intents from the command line. Run adb shell am to see all the other things you can do with the **am** tool.

20

Camera II: Taking Pictures and Handling Images

In this chapter, you will capture an image from the camera's preview and save it as a JPEG on the filesystem. Then you will associate that JPEG with a **Crime** and display it in **CrimeFragment**'s view. You will also offer the user the option to view a larger version of the image in a **DialogFragment**.

Figure 20.1 Crime photo thumbnail and larger-size images

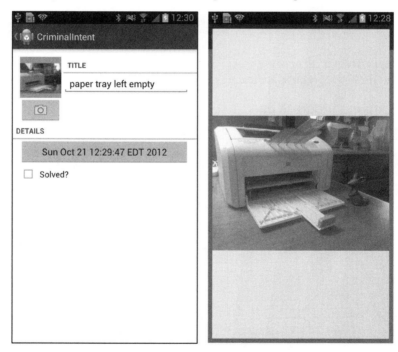

Taking a Picture

First, you are going to update **CrimeCameraFragment**'s layout to include a progress indicator. Sometimes the picture-taking process can take a while, and you do not want users getting antsy.

In layout/fragment_crime_camera.xml, add the **FrameLayout** and **ProgressBar** widgets shown in Figure 20.2.

Figure 20.2 Adding **FrameLayout** and **ProgressBar** widgets (`fragment_crime_camera.xml`)

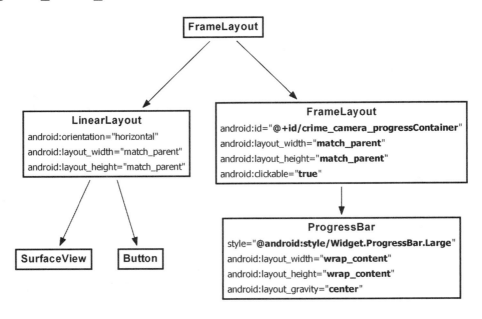

The `@android:style/Widget.ProgressBar.Large` style will create a large, round indeterminate spinner rather than the large, progress-indicating bar that the name implies.

Figure 20.3 Spinning progress bar

You will set the **FrameLayout** (and its child **ProgressBar**) to be invisible at first. You will only make it visible after the user presses the Take! button and the picture-taking process begins.

Note that the **FrameLayout** has a height and width of match_parent. The root **FrameLayout** will stack its child views on top of each other in the order that they are defined. Thus, the **ProgressBar**-containing **FrameLayout** will completely cover its sibling **LinearLayout**.

When the **FrameLayout** becomes visible, the user will still be able to see almost everything in the **LinearLayout**. Only the **ProgressBar** will actually obscure anything. However, by defining the **FrameLayout**'s height and width as match_parent and by setting android:clickable="true", you ensure that the **FrameLayout** will intercept (and do nothing with) any touch events. This prevents the user from interacting with anything in the **LinearLayout** and, in particular, from pressing the Take! button again.

Return to CrimeCameraFragment.java, Add a member variable for the **FrameLayout**, get a reference to it, and mark it as invisible.

Listing 20.1 Wiring up the **FrameLayout** (CrimeCameraFragment.java)

```
public class CrimeCameraFragment extends Fragment {
    ...
    private View mProgressContainer;

    @Override
    public View onCreateView(LayoutInflater inflater, ViewGroup parent,
            Bundle savedInstanceState) {
        View v = inflater.inflate(R.layout.fragment_crime_camera, parent, false);

        mProgressContainer = v.findViewById(R.id.crime_camera_progressContainer);
        mProgressContainer.setVisibility(View.INVISIBLE);

        ...

        return v;
    }

...
}
```

Implementing Camera callbacks

Now that you have the progress indicator ready to go, let's turn to capturing a frame from the live preview and saving it as JPEG. To take a picture, you call the following aptly-named **Camera** method:

```
public final void takePicture(Camera.ShutterCallback shutter,
    Camera.PictureCallback raw,
    Camera.PictureCallback jpeg)
```

The **ShutterCallback** occurs when the camera captures the picture but before the image data is processed and available. The first **PictureCallback** occurs when the raw image data is available. This callback is typically used when processing the raw image before saving it. The second **PictureCallback** occurs when a JPEG version of the image is available.

You can write implementations of these interfaces and pass them into **takePicture(…)**. You can pass null for any of **takePicture(…)**'s parameters if you are not interested in implementing a callback.

In CriminalIntent, you are going to implement the shutter callback and the JPEG picture callback. Figure 20.4 summarizes the interactions between your objects.

Figure 20.4 Taking a picture in **CrimeCameraFragment**

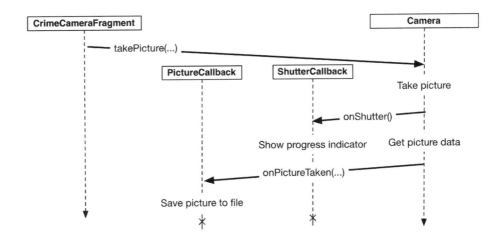

Here are the two interfaces. Each contains a single method.

```
public static interface Camera.ShutterCallback {
    public abstract void onShutter();
}

public static interface Camera.PictureCallback {
    public abstract void onPictureTaken (byte[] data, Camera camera);
}
```

In CrimeCameraFragment.java, add a **Camera.ShutterCallback** implementation that makes
mProgressContainer visible and a **Camera.PictureCallback** implementation that handles naming and
saving the JPEG file.

Listing 20.2 Implementing callbacks for **takePicture(…)** (CrimeCameraFragment.java)

```
...

private View mProgressContainer;

private Camera.ShutterCallback mShutterCallback = new Camera.ShutterCallback() {
    public void onShutter() {
        // Display the progress indicator
        mProgressContainer.setVisibility(View.VISIBLE);
    }
};

private Camera.PictureCallback mJpegCallback = new Camera.PictureCallback() {
    public void onPictureTaken(byte[] data, Camera camera) {
        // Create a filename
        String filename = UUID.randomUUID().toString() + ".jpg";
        // Save the jpeg data to disk
        FileOutputStream os = null;
        boolean success = true;
```

```
        try {
            os = getActivity().openFileOutput(filename, Context.MODE_PRIVATE);
            os.write(data);
        } catch (Exception e) {
            Log.e(TAG, "Error writing to file " + filename, e);
            success = false;
        } finally {
            try {
                if (os != null)
                    os.close();
            } catch (Exception e) {
                Log.e(TAG, "Error closing file " + filename, e);
                success = false;
            }
        }

        if (success) {
            Log.i(TAG, "JPEG saved at " + filename);
        }
        getActivity().finish();
    }
};

...
```

In the **onPictureTaken(…)** method, you create a unique string to use as a filename. Then, you use Java I/O classes to open an output stream and write the JPEG data that was passed in from the **Camera**. If this operation goes well, you get a log statement confirming its success.

Note that you do not set mProgressContainer back to invisible anywhere. This is not necessary because the activity is finished in the picture callback and the view is destroyed.

Now that you have your callbacks ready, modify the listener for the Take! button to call **takePicture(…)**. Pass null for the raw data picture callback that you did not implement.

Listing 20.3 Implementing **takePicture(…)** on button click (CrimeCameraFragment.java)

```
@Override
@SuppressWarnings("deprecation")
public View onCreateView(LayoutInflater inflater, ViewGroup parent,
        Bundle savedInstanceState) {
    ...

    takePictureButton.setOnClickListener(new View.OnClickListener() {
        public void onClick(View v) {
            getActivity().finish();
            if (mCamera != null) {
                mCamera.takePicture(mShutterCallback, null, mJpegCallback);
            }
        }
    });

    ...

    return v;
}
```

Setting the picture size

The camera needs to know what size picture to create. Setting the picture size works the same as setting the preview size. You can get a list of acceptable picture sizes by calling the following **Camera.Parameters** method:

```
public List<Camera.Size> getSupportedPictureSizes()
```

In **surfaceChanged(…)**, use your **getBestSupportedSize(…)** method to find a supported picture size that will work with your **Surface**. Then set the camera's picture size.

Listing 20.4 Calling **getBestSupportedSize(…)** to set picture size (CrimeCameraFragment.java)

```
    ...

    public void surfaceChanged(SurfaceHolder holder, int format, int w, int h) {
        if (mCamera == null) return;

        // The surface has changed size; update the camera preview size
        Camera.Parameters parameters = mCamera.getParameters();
        Size s = getBestSupportedSize(parameters.getSupportedPreviewSizes(), w, h);
        parameters.setPreviewSize(s.width, s.height);
        s = getBestSupportedSize(parameters.getSupportedPictureSizes(), w, h);
        parameters.setPictureSize(s.width, s.height);
        mCamera.setParameters(parameters);

        ...
    }
});
```

Run CriminalIntent and press the Take! button. In LogCat, create a filter with a **CrimeCameraFragment** tag to see where your picture landed.

At this point, **CrimeCameraFragment** lets the user take a picture and save it. Your work with the camera API is done. In the rest of this chapter, you will focus on **CrimeFragment** and integrating the photo into the rest of the application.

Passing Data Back to CrimeFragment

To give **CrimeFragment** access to the photo, you are going to pass the filename back from **CrimeCameraFragment**. Figure 20.5 shows the sequence of events between **CrimeFragment** and **CrimeCameraFragment**.

Figure 20.5 **CrimeCameraActivity** sets a result and an extra

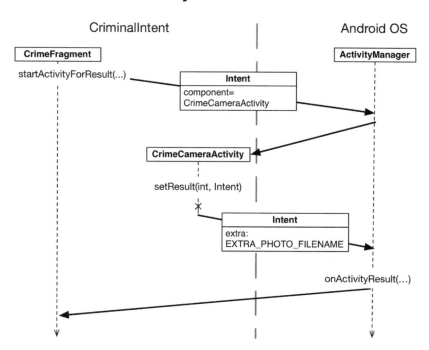

First, **CrimeFragment** will start **CrimeCameraActivity** for a result. When a picture is taken, **CrimeCameraFragment** will create an intent with the filename as an extra and call **setResult(…)**. The **ActivityManager** will forward the intent to **CrimePagerActivity** in **onActivityResult(…)**. **CrimePagerActivity**'s **FragmentManager** will then forward the intent to **CrimeFragment** in **CrimeFragment.onActivityResult(…)**.

Starting CrimeCameraActivity for a result

Currently, **CrimeFragment** just starts **CrimeCameraActivity**. In CrimeFragment.java, add a constant for a request code and then modify the camera button's listener to start **CrimeCameraActivity** for a result.

Listing 20.5 Starting **CrimeCameraActivity** for a result (CrimeFragment.java)

```java
public class CrimeFragment extends Fragment {
    ...
    private static final int REQUEST_DATE = 0;
    private static final int REQUEST_PHOTO = 1;

    ...

    @Override
    public View onCreateView(LayoutInflater inflater, ViewGroup parent,
            Bundle savedInstanceState) {

        ...

        mPhotoButton.setOnClickListener(new View.OnClickListener() {
            public void onClick(View v) {
                // Launch the camera activity
                Intent i = new Intent(getActivity(), CrimeCameraActivity.class);
                startActivity(i);
                startActivityForResult(i, REQUEST_PHOTO);
            }
        });

        ...
}
```

Setting a result in CrimeCameraFragment

CrimeCameraFragment will put the filename in an intent extra and pass it into
CrimeCameraActivity.setResult(int, Intent). In CrimeCameraFragment.java, add a constant
for the extra. Then, in the picture callback, create an intent and set the result code to RESULT_OK if the
image was saved or RESULT_CANCELED if something went wrong.

Listing 20.6 Adding an extra for photo filename (`CrimeCameraFragment.java`)

```java
public class CrimeCameraFragment extends Fragment {
    private static final String TAG = "CrimeCameraFragment";

    public static final String EXTRA_PHOTO_FILENAME =
        "com.bignerdranch.android.criminalintent.photo_filename";

    ...

    private Camera.PictureCallback mJpegCallback = new Camera.PictureCallback() {
        public void onPictureTaken(byte[] data, Camera camera) {
            ...
            try {
                ...
            } catch (Exception e) {
                ...
            } finally {
                ...
            }
            Log.i(TAG, "JPEG saved at " + filename);
            // Set the photo filename on the result intent
            if (success) {
                Intent i = new Intent();
                i.putExtra(EXTRA_PHOTO_FILENAME, filename);
                getActivity().setResult(Activity.RESULT_OK, i);
            } else {
                getActivity().setResult(Activity.RESULT_CANCELED);
            }
            getActivity().finish();
        }
    };

    ...
}
```

Retrieving filename in CrimeFragment

Eventually, **CrimeFragment** will use the filename to update CriminalIntent's model and view layers. For now, in CrimeFragment.java, simply override **onActivityResult(…)** to check the result, retrieve the filename, and log a message. You will also need a TAG for **CrimeFragment** to aid in logging the result.

Listing 20.7 Retrieving filename (`CrimeFragment.java`)

```java
public class CrimeFragment extends Fragment {
    private static final String TAG = "CrimeFragment"
    public static final String EXTRA_CRIME_ID =
        "com.bignerdranch.android.criminalintent.crime_id";
    ...

    @Override
    public void onActivityResult(int requestCode, int resultCode, Intent data) {
        if (resultCode != Activity.RESULT_OK) return;

        if (requestCode == REQUEST_DATE) {
            Date date = (Date)data
                .getSerializableExtra(DatePickerFragment.EXTRA_DATE);
            mCrime.setDate(date);
            updateDate();
        } else if (requestCode == REQUEST_PHOTO) {
            // Create a new Photo object and attach it to the crime
            String filename = data
                .getStringExtra(CrimeCameraFragment.EXTRA_PHOTO_FILENAME);
            if (filename != null) {
                Log.i(TAG, "filename: " + filename);
            }
        }
    }
}
```

Run CriminalIntent. Take a picture in **CrimeCameraActivity**. Check LogCat to confirm that **CrimeFragment** retrieved a filename.

Now that **CrimeFragment** has the filename, there is a lot to be done with it:

- To update the model layer, you will write a **Photo** class that wraps the filename of an image. You will also give **Crime** an mPhoto property of type **Photo**. **CrimeFragment** will use the filename to create a **Photo** object and set **Crime**'s mPhoto property.

- To update **CrimeFragment**'s view, you will add an **ImageView** to **CrimeFragment**'s layout and display a thumbnail of the **Crime**'s photo on this **ImageView**.

- To present a larger version of the image, you will create a **DialogFragment** subclass named **ImageFragment** and pass it the path of the photo to display.

Updating the Model Layer

Figure 20.6 shows the relationship between **CrimeFragment**, **Crime**, and **Photo**.

Figure 20.6 Model objects and **CrimeFragment**

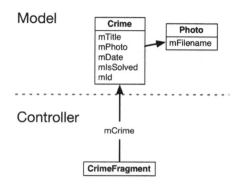

Adding a Photo class

Create a new class in the com.bignerdranch.android.criminalintent package. Name it **Photo** and leave its superclass as **java.lang.Object**.

In Photo.java, add the fields and methods shown in Listing 20.8.

Listing 20.8 The **Photo** class (Photo.java)

```
...
public class Photo {
    private static final String JSON_FILENAME = "filename";

    private String mFilename;

    /** Create a Photo representing an existing file on disk */
    public Photo(String filename) {
        mFilename = filename;
    }

    public Photo(JSONObject json) throws JSONException {
        mFilename = json.getString(JSON_FILENAME);
    }

    public JSONObject toJSON() throws JSONException {
        JSONObject json = new JSONObject();
        json.put(JSON_FILENAME, mFilename);
        return json;
    }

    public String getFilename() {
        return mFilename;
    }
}
```

Notice that the **Photo** class has two constructors. The first constructor creates a **Photo** from a given filename. The second is a JSON serialization method that **Crime** will use when saving and loading its property of type **Photo**.

Giving Crime a photo property

Next, update the **Crime** class to hold a **Photo** object and serialize it to JSON (Listing 20.9).

Listing 20.9 A **Photo** for the **Crime** (Crime.java)

```java
public class Crime {
    ...
    private static final String JSON_DATE = "date";
    private static final String JSON_PHOTO = "photo";

    ...
    private Date mDate = new Date();
    private Photo mPhoto;

    ...

    public Crime(JSONObject json) throws JSONException {
        ...
        mDate = new Date(json.getLong(JSON_DATE));
        if (json.has(JSON_PHOTO))
            mPhoto = new Photo(json.getJSONObject(JSON_PHOTO));
    }

    public JSONObject toJSON() throws JSONException {
        JSONObject json = new JSONObject();
        ...
        json.put(JSON_DATE, mDate.getTime());
        if (mPhoto != null)
            json.put(JSON_PHOTO, mPhoto.toJSON());
        return json;
    }

    ...

    public Photo getPhoto() {
        return mPhoto;
    }

    public void setPhoto(Photo p) {
        mPhoto = p;
    }

}
```

Setting the photo property

In CrimeFragment.java, modify **onActivityResult(…)** to create a new **Photo** and set it on the current **Crime**.

Listing 20.10 Handling a new **Photo** (CrimeFragment.java)

```java
@Override
public void onActivityResult(int requestCode, int resultCode, Intent data) {
    if (resultCode != Activity.RESULT_OK) return;

    if (requestCode == REQUEST_DATE) {
        Date date = (Date)data
            .getSerializableExtra(DatePickerFragment.EXTRA_DATE);
        mCrime.setDate(date);
        updateDate();
    } else if (requestCode == REQUEST_PHOTO) {
        // Create a new Photo object and attach it to the crime
        String filename = data
            .getStringExtra(CrimeCameraFragment.EXTRA_PHOTO_FILENAME);
        if (filename != null) {
            Log.i(TAG, "filename: " + filename);

            Photo p = new Photo(filename);
            mCrime.setPhoto(p);
            Log.i(TAG, "Crime: " + mCrime.getTitle() + " has a photo");
        }
    }
}
```

Run CriminalIntent and take a picture. Check LogCat to confirm that the **Crime** has a photo.

You may be wondering why you created a **Photo** class instead of simply adding a filename property to **Crime**. The latter would work in this situation, but there are other things you might need a **Photo** to do, like display a caption or handle a touch event. In that case, you would need a separate class.

Updating CrimeFragment's View

Now that the model layer is updated, you can turn to updating the view layer. In particular, **CrimeFragment** will display a thumbnail-sized photo in an **ImageView**.

Figure 20.7 **CrimeFragment** with new **ImageView**

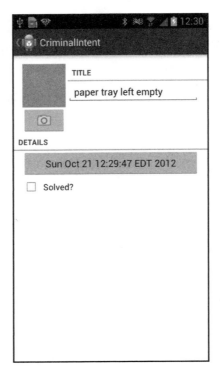

Adding an ImageView

Return to layout/fragment_crime.xml and add the **ImageView** shown in Figure 20.8.

Figure 20.8 **CrimeFragment** layout with **ImageView** (layout/ fragment_crime.xml)

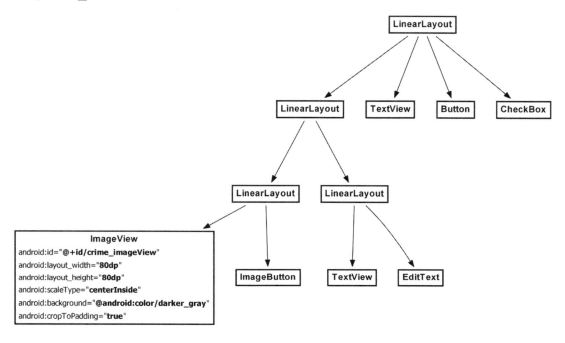

You also need an **ImageView** in the landscape layout, as shown in Figure 20.9.

Figure 20.9 Landscape layout with **ImageView** (layout-land/ fragment_crime.xml)

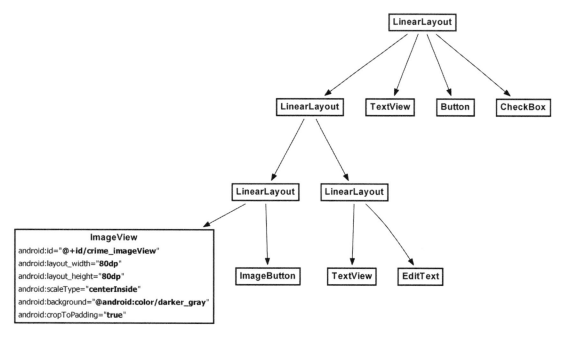

In `CrimeFragment.java`, create a member variable and get a reference to the **ImageView** in **onCreateView(…)**.

Listing 20.11 Configuring the ImageButton (CrimeFragment.java)

```
public class CrimeFragment extends Fragment {
    ...
    private ImageButton mPhotoButton;
    private ImageView mPhotoView;

    ...

    @Override
    public View onCreateView(LayoutInflater inflater, ViewGroup parent,
            Bundle savedInstanceState) {

        ...

        mPhotoButton.setOnClickListener(new View.OnClickListener() {
            public void onClick(View v) {
                // Launch the camera activity
                Intent i = new Intent(getActivity(), CrimeCameraActivity.class);
                startActivityForResult(i, REQUEST_PHOTO);
            }
        });

        mPhotoView = (ImageView)v.findViewById(R.id.crime_imageView);

        ...
    }
```

Preview the layout or run CriminalIntent to confirm that the **ImageView** is in place.

Image handling

Displaying the image on the **ImageView** requires some image handling first because the file that came from the camera could be exceptionally large. Phone manufacturers include bigger and better cameras in their phones every year. As a user, this is swell, but as a programmer, it can be a pain.

As of this writing, top-of-the-line Android phones are armed with 8-megapixel cameras. Pictures that large will easily blow out your app's memory budget, so you need some code to scale the image before loading it and some code to clean up when the image is no longer needed.

Adding scaled photo to the image view

In the `com.bignerdranch.android.criminalintent` package, create a new class named **PictureUtils**. In `PictureUtils.java`, add the following method that scales an image to the size of the default display for the device.

Listing 20.12 Add **PictureUtils** class (PictureUtils.java)

```java
public class PictureUtils {
    /**
     * Get a BitmapDrawable from a local file that is scaled down
     * to fit the current Window size.
     */
    @SuppressWarnings("deprecation")
    public static BitmapDrawable getScaledDrawable(Activity a, String path) {
        Display display = a.getWindowManager().getDefaultDisplay();
        float destWidth = display.getWidth();
        float destHeight = display.getHeight();

        // Read in the dimensions of the image on disk
        BitmapFactory.Options options = new BitmapFactory.Options();
        options.inJustDecodeBounds = true;
        BitmapFactory.decodeFile(path, options);

        float srcWidth = options.outWidth;
        float srcHeight = options.outHeight;

        int inSampleSize = 1;
        if (srcHeight > destHeight || srcWidth > destWidth) {
            if (srcWidth > srcHeight) {
                inSampleSize = Math.round(srcHeight / destHeight);
            } else {
                inSampleSize = Math.round(srcWidth / destWidth);
            }
        }

        options = new BitmapFactory.Options();
        options.inSampleSize = inSampleSize;

        Bitmap bitmap = BitmapFactory.decodeFile(path, options);
        return new BitmapDrawable(a.getResources(), bitmap);
    }
}
```

The **Display.getWidth()** and **Display.getHeight()** methods are deprecated. You will learn more about deprecation at the end of this chapter.

It would be best to scale the image so that it fits the **ImageView** perfectly. However, the size of the view in which the image will be displayed is often not available when you need it. For example, inside **onCreateView(…)**, you cannot get the size of the **ImageView**. As a safe guess, you scale the image to the size of the default display for the device, which is available anytime. The view where the image will eventually appear may be smaller than the default display size, but it cannot be larger.

Next, in **CrimeFragment**, add a private method that sets a scaled image on the **ImageView**.

Listing 20.13 Adding **showPhoto()** (`CrimeFragment.java`)

```
@Override
public View onCreateView(LayoutInflater inflater, ViewGroup parent,
        Bundle savedInstanceState) {
    ...
}

private void showPhoto() {
    // (Re)set the image button's image based on our photo
    Photo p = mCrime.getPhoto();
    BitmapDrawable b = null;
    if (p != null) {
        String path = getActivity()
            .getFileStreamPath(p.getFilename()).getAbsolutePath();
        b = PictureUtils.getScaledDrawable(getActivity(), path);
    }
    mPhotoView.setImageDrawable(b);
}
```

In `CrimeFragment.java`, add an implementation of **onStart()** that calls **showPhoto()** to have the photo ready as soon as **CrimeFragment**'s view becomes visible to the user.

Listing 20.14 Loading the image (`CrimeFragment.java`)

```
...

private void showPhoto() {
    // (Re)set the image button's image based on our photo
    Photo p = mCrime.getPhoto();
    BitmapDrawable b = null;
    if (p != null) {
        String path = getActivity()
            .getFileStreamPath(p.getFilename()).getAbsolutePath();
        b = PictureUtils.getScaledDrawable(getActivity(), path);
    }
    mPhotoButton.setImageDrawable(b);
}

@Override
public void onStart() {
    super.onStart();
    showPhoto();
}
```

In **CrimeFragment.onActivityResult(…)**, call **showPhoto()** to ensure that the image will be visible when the user returns from **CrimeCameraActivity**.

Listing 20.15 Calling **showPhoto()** in **onActivityResult(…)** (CrimeFragment.java)

```java
@Override
public void onActivityResult(int requestCode, int resultCode, Intent data) {
    if (resultCode != Activity.RESULT_OK) return;

    if (requestCode == REQUEST_PHOTO) {
        // Create a new Photo object and attach it to the crime
        String filename = data
            .getStringExtra(CrimeCameraFragment.EXTRA_PHOTO_FILENAME);
        if (filename != null) {
            Photo p = new Photo(filename);
            mCrime.setPhoto(p);
            showPhoto();
            Log.i(TAG, "Crime: " + mCrime.getTitle() + "has a photo");
        }
    }
}
```

Unloading the image

In the **PictureUtils** class, add a method to clean up an **ImageView**'s **BitmapDrawable**, if it has one.

Listing 20.16 Cleanup work (PictureUtils.java)

```java
public class PictureUtils {
    /**
     * ...
     */
    @SuppressWarnings("deprecation")
    public static BitmapDrawable getScaledDrawable(Activity a, String path) {
        ...
    }

    public static void cleanImageView(ImageView imageView) {
        if (!(imageView.getDrawable() instanceof BitmapDrawable))
            return;

        // Clean up the view's image for the sake of memory
        BitmapDrawable b = (BitmapDrawable)imageView.getDrawable();
        b.getBitmap().recycle();
        imageView.setImageDrawable(null);
    }
}
```

The call to **Bitmap.recycle()** bears some explanation. The documentation implies that calling this method is not necessary, but it is. So here is a technical explanation.

Bitmap.recycle() frees the native storage for your bitmap. This is most of the meat of your bitmap object. (The native storage can be a smaller or larger amount of data depending on your version of Android. Before Honeycomb, it stored all of the data for your Java **Bitmap**.)

If you do not free this memory explicitly by calling **recycle()**, then the memory will still be cleaned up. However, it will be cleaned up at some future point in a *finalizer*, not when the bitmap itself is garbage-collected. This means that there is a chance that you will run out of memory before the finalizer is called.

Finalizer execution is a fuzzy phenomenon, so this kind of bug can be difficult to track down or reproduce. So, if your images are large (as they are here), it is better to call **recycle()** to prevent the possibility of ugly memory bugs.

In **CrimeFragment**, add an implementation of **onStop()** that calls **cleanImageView(…)**.

Listing 20.17 Unloading the image (CrimeFragment.java)

```
@Override
public void onStart() {
    super.onStart();
    showPhoto();
}

@Override
public void onStop() {
    super.onStop();
    PictureUtils.cleanImageView(mPhotoView);
}
```

Loading images in **onStart()** and unloading them in **onStop()** is a good practice. These methods mark the points where your activity can be seen by the user. If you loaded and unloaded in **onResume()** and **onPause()** instead, the results could be disconcerting to the user.

A paused activity can still be partly visible if, say, an activity not covering the entire screen opens on top of it. If you were using **onResume()** and **onPause()**, then your images would vanish and then reappear in such cases. It is better to load images as soon as your activity is visible and wait to unload them until you know that your activity can no longer be seen.

Run CriminalIntent. Take a picture of a crime and confirm that it appears in the **ImageView**. Exit CriminalIntent and then relaunch. Confirm that the photo is displayed as you expect when you return to the same crime.

CrimeCameraActivity's orientation encourages users to take the picture in landscape. However, if you take a picture in portrait orientation, the image may not be correctly oriented on the button. Fix this in the first challenge!

Showing Larger Image in a DialogFragment

The final step for your camera implementation is to offer users a larger version of the **Crime**'s photo.

Figure 20.10 A **DialogFragment** displaying a larger image

Create a new class in the com.bignerdranch.android.criminalintent package. Name the class **ImageFragment**; make it a subclass of **DialogFragment**.

ImageFragment will need the filepath of the **Crime**'s photo in its fragment arguments. In ImageFragment.java, add a **newInstance(String)** method that accepts a filepath and puts it in the arguments bundle, as shown in Listing 20.18.

Listing 20.18 Create **ImageFragment** (ImageFragment.java)

```
public class ImageFragment extends DialogFragment {
    public static final String EXTRA_IMAGE_PATH =
        "com.bignerdranch.android.criminalintent.image_path";

    public static ImageFragment newInstance(String imagePath) {
        Bundle args = new Bundle();
        args.putSerializable(EXTRA_IMAGE_PATH, imagePath);

        ImageFragment fragment = new ImageFragment();
        fragment.setArguments(args);
        fragment.setStyle(DialogFragment.STYLE_NO_TITLE, 0);

        return fragment;
    }
}
```

You set the fragment's style to DialogFragment.STYLE_NO_TITLE to achieve a minimalist look shown in Figure 20.10.

ImageFragment will not need the title or the buttons provided by **AlertDialog**. If your fragment can do without these, then it is cleaner, quicker, and more flexible to override **onCreateView(…)** and use a simple **View** than override **onCreateDialog(…)** and use a **Dialog**.

In ImageFragment.java, override **onCreateView(…)** to create an **ImageView** from scratch and retrieve the path from its arguments. Then get a scaled version of the image and set it on the **ImageView**. Override **onDestroyView()** to free up memory once the image is no longer needed.

Listing 20.19 Create **ImageFragment** (ImageFragment.java)

```
public class ImageFragment extends DialogFragment {
    public static final String EXTRA_IMAGE_PATH =
        "com.bignerdranch.android.criminalintent.image_path";

    public static ImageFragment newInstance(String imagePath) {
        ...
    }

    private ImageView mImageView;

    @Override
    public View onCreateView(LayoutInflater inflater,
            ViewGroup parent, Bundle savedInstanceState) {
        mImageView = new ImageView(getActivity());
        String path = (String)getArguments().getSerializable(EXTRA_IMAGE_PATH);
        BitmapDrawable image = PictureUtils.getScaledDrawable(getActivity(), path);

        mImageView.setImageDrawable(image);

        return mImageView;
    }

    @Override
    public void onDestroyView() {
        super.onDestroyView();
        PictureUtils.cleanImageView(mImageView);
    }
}
```

Finally, you need to show this dialog from **CrimeFragment**. In CrimeFragment.java, add a listener to mPhotoView. Within its implementation, create an instance of **ImageFragment** and add it to **CrimePagerActivity**'s **FragmentManager** by calling **show(…)** on the **ImageFragment**. You will also need a string constant to identify the **ImageFragment** in the **FragmentManager**.

Listing 20.20 Show **ImageFragment** (CrimeFragment.java)

```java
public class CrimeFragment extends Fragment {

    ...
    private static final String DIALOG_IMAGE = "image";

    ...

    @Override
    @TargetApi(11)
    public View onCreateView(LayoutInflater inflater, ViewGroup parent,
            Bundle savedInstanceState) {
        ...

        mPhotoView = (ImageView)v.findViewById(R.id.crime_imageView);
        mPhotoView.setOnClickListener(new View.OnClickListener() {
            public void onClick(View v) {
                Photo p = mCrime.getPhoto();
                if (p == null)
                    return;

                FragmentManager fm = getActivity()
                    .getSupportFragmentManager();
                String path = getActivity()
                    .getFileStreamPath(p.getFilename()).getAbsolutePath();
                ImageFragment.newInstance(path)
                    .show(fm, DIALOG_IMAGE);
            }
        });

        ...
    }
}
```

Run CriminalIntent. Take a picture and confirm that you can view the crime scene photo in all its gory.

Challenge: Crime Image Orientation

Sometimes, the user will choose to take a picture in portrait orientation. Search the API documentation for a way to detect the orientation. Stash the correct orientation in your **Photo** and use it to rotate the picture appropriately in **CrimeFragment** and **ImageFragment**.

Challenge: Deleting Photos

Right now, you can replace a **Crime**'s photo, but the old file will continue to take up space on disk. Add code to **CrimeFragment**'s **onActivityResult(int, int, Intent)** method to check the crime for an existing photo and delete that file from disk.

For another challenge, give users the power to delete a photo without having to replace it. Implement a context menu and/or a contextual action mode in **CrimeFragment** that is triggered by long-pressing the thumbnail image. Offer a Delete Photo menu item that deletes the photo from the disk, the model, and the **ImageView**.

For the More Curious: Deprecation in Android

In Chapter 19, when you were setting the camera's preview size, we directed you to use a deprecated method and a deprecated constant. In this chapter, you used deprecated methods A curious reader may wonder: "What is up with that?"

What is up, indeed. Let's start with what it means when a part of an API is deprecated. If something is deprecated, that means that it is no longer necessary. Sometimes deprecation occurs because the operation it performed is no longer required. That is the case with the **SurfaceHolder.setType(int)** method and the SurfaceHolder.SURFACE_TYPE_PUSH_BUFFERS constant that you added in Chapter 19. On older versions of Android, **SurfaceHolder** needed to be configured appropriately for how you were using it. That is no longer the case, so **setType(…)** isn't useful anymore.

Other times, it means that it has been replaced with a newer method that is better for some reason. For instance, **BitmapDrawable** has a deprecated constructor **BitmapDrawable(Bitmap)** that is prone to bugs. Other times, it may just be that the new method is cleaner from a design standpoint – for instance, the **View.setBackgroundDrawable(Drawable)** method. Another example is **Display.getWidth()** and **Display.getHeight()**, which you used earlier. They have since been replaced with a single method **getSize(Point)**, helping to fix some bugs that can occur when calling **getWidth()** and **getHeight()** in sequence.

Deprecation is handled differently depending on the platform you're working on. The two extremes can be characterized by two very different towns you may be familiar with – Microsoftville and Appleburg.

In Microsoftville, APIs are deprecated, but they are never removed. This is because, for the mayor of Microsoftville, nothing is more important than having as many programs as possible run on any version of their OS. Once a public API is introduced in Microsoftville, it is always supported. They will even go so far as to preserve buggy, undocumented behavior to maintain backwards compatibility. This makes Microsoftville a strange place to live sometimes.

In Appleburg, on the other hand, APIs are actually removed from the OS not long after they are deprecated. The mayor of Appleburg is obsessed with having a clean, beautiful OS. He doesn't care how many APIs he has to kill to do it. As a result, Appleburg is very clean and tidy, but older programs soon find that they no longer work if they are not actively updated.

In Appleburg, if you wanted to support both old and new operating systems you would do something like this:

```
float destWidth;
float destHeight;

if (Build.VERSION.SDK_INT > Build.VERSION_CODES.HONEYCOMB_MR2) {
    Point size;
    display.getSize(size);
    destWidth = size.x;
    destHeight = size.y;
} else {
    destWidth = display.getWidth();
    destHeight = display.getHeight();
}
```

This is because in Appleburg, **getWidth()** and **getHeight()** will probably disappear soon, so you have to be careful not to call them.

Android isn't exactly Microsoftville, but it is close. Each Android SDK is mostly backwards compatible with the previous SDK release, which means that API methods are almost never deleted. So you do not have to be so careful about calling old methods. In our text, we will use deprecated methods where necessary and suppress deprecation warnings with annotations. You should still be careful not to use a deprecated API if you do not have to, though. That will keep your code clean and stylish.

21

Implicit Intents

In Android, you can start an activity in another application on the device using an *implicit intent*. In an explicit intent, you specify the class of the activity to start, and the OS will start it. In an implicit intent, you describe the job that you need done, and the OS will start an activity in an appropriate application for you.

In CriminalIntent, you will use implicit intents to enable picking a suspect for a `Crime` from the user's list of contacts and sending a text-based report of a crime. The user will choose a suspect from whatever contacts app is installed on the device and will be offered a choice of apps to send the crime report.

Figure 21.1 Opening contacts app and a text-sending app

Using implicit intents to harness other applications is far easier than writing your own implementations for common tasks. Users also appreciate being able to use apps they already know and like in conjunction with your app.

Before you can create these implicit intents, there is some set-up to do in CriminalIntent:

- add Choose Suspect and Send Crime Report buttons to **CrimeFragment**'s layouts

- add an mSuspect field to the **Crime** class that will hold the name of a suspect

- create a crime report using a set of format resource strings

Adding Buttons

First, you are going to update **CrimeFragment**'s layouts to include new buttons for accusation and tattling. First, add the strings that these buttons will display.

Listing 21.1 Adding button strings (`strings.xml`)

```
<string name="take">Take!</string>
<string name="crime_suspect_text">Choose Suspect</string>
<string name="crime_report_text">Send Crime Report</string>
</resources>
```

In layout/fragment_crime.xml, add two button widgets, as shown in Figure 21.2. Notice that in this diagram, we are not showing the first **LinearLayout** and all of its children so that you can focus on the new and interesting parts of the diagram.

Figure 21.2 Adding suspect and crime report buttons (`layout/fragment_crime.xml`)

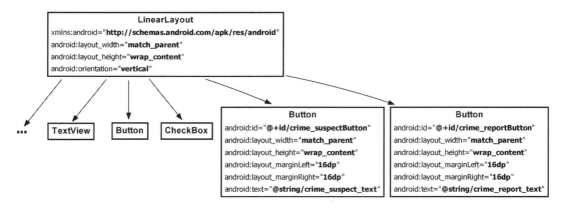

In the landscape layout, you are going to make these new buttons children of a new horizontal **LinearLayout** below the one that contains the date button and the check box.

Figure 21.3 New buttons not entirely visible in landscape

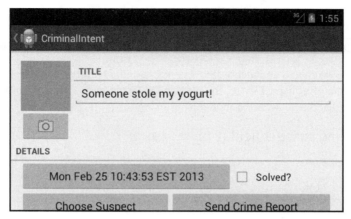

As you can see in Figure 21.3, on smaller screens, the new buttons will not be entirely visible. To address this problem, you are going to wrap the entire landscape layout in a **ScrollView**.

Figure 21.4 shows the new layout. Because your root element will now be the **ScrollView**, be sure to move the namespace from the previous root element to the **ScrollView**.

Figure 21.4 Add suspect and crime report buttons (layout-land/ fragment_crime.xml)

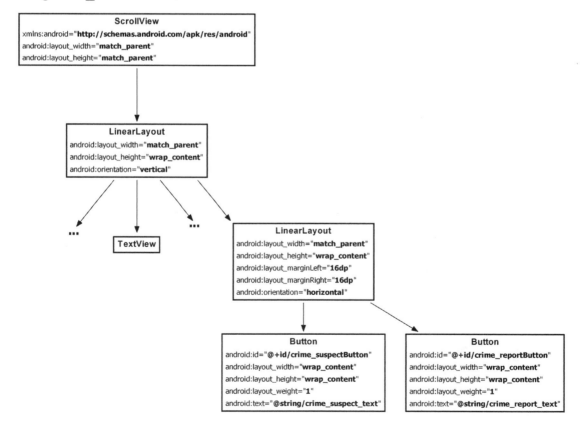

At this point, you can preview the layouts or run CriminalIntent to confirm that your new buttons are in place.

Adding a Suspect to the Model Layer

Next, return to `Crime.java` and add a new JSON constant and a member variable to give **Crime** a field that will hold the name of a suspect. Also, modify the JSON methods to serialize the suspect into and out of JSON code and add new accessor methods.

Listing 21.2 Adding suspect field (`Crime.java`)

```java
public class Crime {
    ...
    private static final String JSON_PHOTO = "photo";
    private static final String JSON_SUSPECT = "suspect";

    ...
    private Photo mPhoto;
    private String mSuspect;

    public Crime(JSONObject json) throws JSONException {
        mId = UUID.fromString(json.getString(JSON_ID));
        ...
        if (json.has(JSON_PHOTO))
            mPhoto = new Photo(json.getJSONObject(JSON_PHOTO));
        if (json.has(JSON_SUSPECT))
            mSuspect = json.getString(JSON_SUSPECT);
    }

    public JSONObject toJSON() throws JSONException {
        JSONObject json = new JSONObject();
        ...
        if (mPhoto != null)
            json.put(JSON_PHOTO, mPhoto.toJSON());
        json.put(JSON_SUSPECT, mSuspect);
        return json;
    }

    public void setPhoto(Photo p) {
        mPhoto = p;
    }

    public String getSuspect() {
        return mSuspect;
    }
    public void setSuspect(String suspect) {
        mSuspect = suspect;
    }

}
```

Using a Format String

The last preliminary is to create a template crime report that can be configured with the specific crime's details. Because you will not know a crime's details until runtime, you must use a format string with placeholders that can be replaced at runtime. Here is the format string you will use:

```
<string name="crime_report">%1$s! The crime was discovered on %2$s. %3$s, and %4$s
```

The %1$s, %2$s, etc. are placeholders that expect string arguments. In code, you will call **getString(…)** and pass in the format string and four other strings in the order in which they should replace the placeholders.

First, in `strings.xml`, add the strings shown in Listing 21.3.

Listing 21.3 Add string resources (`strings.xml`)

```xml
<string name="crime_suspect_text">Choose Suspect</string>
<string name="crime_report_text">Send Crime Report</string>
<string name="crime_report">%1$s!
  The crime was discovered on %2$s. %3$s, and %4$s
</string>
<string name="crime_report_solved">The case is solved</string>
<string name="crime_report_unsolved">The case is not solved</string>
<string name="crime_report_no_suspect">There is no suspect.</string>
<string name="crime_report_suspect">The suspect is %s.</string>
<string name="crime_report_subject">CriminalIntent Crime Report</string>
<string name="send_report">Send crime report via</string>

</resources>
```

In `CrimeFragment.java`, add a method that creates four strings and then pieces them together and returns a complete report.

Listing 21.4 Add **getCrimeReport()** method (`CrimeFragment.java`)

```java
private String getCrimeReport() {
    String solvedString = null;
    if (mCrime.isSolved()) {
        solvedString = getString(R.string.crime_report_solved);
    } else {
        solvedString = getString(R.string.crime_report_unsolved);
    }

    String dateFormat = "EEE, MMM dd";
    String dateString = DateFormat.format(dateFormat, mCrime.getDate()).toString();

    String suspect = mCrime.getSuspect();
    if (suspect == null) {
        suspect = getString(R.string.crime_report_no_suspect);
    } else {
        suspect = getString(R.string.crime_report_suspect, suspect);
    }

    String report = getString(R.string.crime_report,
        mCrime.getTitle(), dateString, solvedString, suspect);

    return report;
}
```

Now the preliminaries are complete, and you can turn to implicit intents.

Using Implicit Intents

An **Intent** is an object that describes to the OS something that you want it to do. With the *explicit* intents that you have created thus far, you explicitly name the activity that you want the OS to start.

```
Intent i = new Intent(getActivity(), CrimeCameraActivity.class);
startActivity(i);
```

With an *implicit* intent, you describe to the OS the job that you want done. The OS then starts the activity that has advertised itself as capable of doing that job. If the OS finds more than one capable activity, then the user is offered a choice.

Parts of an implicit intent

Here are the critical parts of an intent that you can use to define the job you want done:

the *action* that you are trying to perform

> These are typically constants from the **Intent** class. If you want to view a URL, you can use `Intent.ACTION_VIEW` for your action. To send something, you use `Intent.ACTION_SEND`.

the location of any *data*

> This can be something outside the device, like the URL of a web page, but it can also be a URI to a file or a *content URI* pointing to a record in a **ContentProvider**.

the *type* of data that the action is for

> This is a MIME type, like `text/html` or `audio/mpeg3`. If an intent includes a location for data, then the type can usually be inferred from that data.

optional *categories*

> If the action is used to describe *what* to do, the category usually describes *where, when,* or *how* you are trying to use an activity. Android uses the category `android.intent.category.LAUNCHER` to indicate that an activity should be displayed in the top-level app launcher. The `android.intent.category.INFO` category, on the other hand, indicates an activity that shows information about a package to the user but should not show up in the launcher.

A simple implicit intent for viewing a website would include an action of `Intent.ACTION_VIEW` and a data **Uri** that is the URL of a website.

Based on this information, the OS will launch the appropriate activity of an appropriate application. (If it finds more than one candidate, the user gets a choice.)

An activity would advertise itself as an appropriate activity for `ACTION_VIEW` via an intent filter in the manifest. If you wanted to write a browser app, for instance, you would include the following intent filter in the declaration of the activity that should respond to `ACTION_VIEW`.

```
<activity
  android:name=".BrowserActivity"
  android:label="@string/app_name" >
  <intent-filter>
    <action android:name="android.intent.action.VIEW" />
    <category android:name="android.intent.category.DEFAULT" />
    <data android:scheme="http" android:host="www.bignerdranch.com" />
  </intent-filter>
</activity>
```

The DEFAULT category must be set explicitly in intent filters. The action element in the intent filter tells the OS that the activity is capable of performing the job, and the DEFAULT category tells the OS that it wants to be considered for the job. This DEFAULT category is implicitly added to almost every implicit intent. (The sole exception is the LAUNCHER category, which you will work with in Chapter 23.)

Implicit intents can also include extras just like explicit intents. Any extras on an implicit intent, however, are not used by the OS to find an appropriate activity.

Note that the action and data parts of an intent can also be used in conjunction with an explicit intent. That would be the equivalent of telling a specific activity to do something particular.

Sending a crime report

Let's see how this works by creating an implicit intent to send a crime report in CriminalIntent. The job you want done is sending plain text; the crime report is a string. So the implicit intent's action will be ACTION_SEND. It will not point to any data or have any categories, but it will specify a type of text/plain.

In **CrimeFragment.onCreateView(…)**, get a reference to the Send Crime Report and set a listener on it. Within the listener's implementation, create an implicit intent and pass it into **startActivity(Intent)**.

Listing 21.5 Sending a crime report (CrimeFragment.java)

```
    ...

    Button reportButton = (Button)v.findViewById(R.id.crime_reportButton);
    reportButton.setOnClickListener(new View.OnClickListener() {
        public void onClick(View v) {
            Intent i = new Intent(Intent.ACTION_SEND);
            i.setType("text/plain");
            i.putExtra(Intent.EXTRA_TEXT, getCrimeReport());
            i.putExtra(Intent.EXTRA_SUBJECT,
                getString(R.string.crime_report_subject));
            startActivity(i);
        }
    });

    return v;
}
```

Here you use the **Intent** constructor that accepts a string that is a constant defining the action. There are other constructors that you can use depending on what kind of implicit intent you need to create. You can find them all on the **Intent** reference page in the documentation. There is no constructor that accepts a type, so you set it explicitly.

You include the text of the report and the string for the subject of the report as extras. Note that these extras use constants defined in the **Intent** class. Any activity responding to this intent will know these constants and what to do with the associated values.

Run CriminalIntent and press the Send Crime Report button. Because this intent will likely match many activities on the device, you will probably see a list of activities presented in a chooser:

Figure 21.5 Activities volunteering to send your crime report

If you are offered a choice, make a selection. You will see your crime report loaded into the app that you chose. All you have to do is address and send it.

If, on the other hand, you do not see a chooser, that means one of two things. Either you have already set a default app for an identical implicit intent, or your device has only a single activity that can respond to this intent.

Often, it is best to go with the user's default app for an action. In CriminalIntent, however, you always want the user to have a choice for ACTION_SEND. Today a user might want to be discreet and email the crime report, but tomorrow he or she may prefer public shaming via Twitter.

You can create a chooser to be shown every time an implicit intent is used to start an activity. After you create your implicit intent as before, you call the following **Intent** method and pass in the implicit intent and a string for the chooser's title:

```
public static Intent createChooser(Intent target, String title)
```

Then you pass the intent returned from **createChooser(…)** into **startActivity(…)**.

In CrimeFragment.java, create a chooser to display the activities that respond to your implicit intent.

Listing 21.6 Use a chooser (`CrimeFragment.java`)

```java
public void onClick(View v) {
    Intent i = new Intent(Intent.ACTION_SEND);
    i.setType("text/plain");
    i.putExtra(Intent.EXTRA_TEXT, getCrimeReport());
    i.putExtra(Intent.EXTRA_SUBJECT,
        getString(R.string.crime_report_subject));
    i = Intent.createChooser(i, getString(R.string.send_report));
    startActivity(i);
}
```

Run CriminalIntent and press the Send Crime Report button. As long as you have more than one activity that can handle your intent, you will be offered a list to choose from.

Figure 21.6 Sending text with a chooser

Asking Android for a contact

Now you are going to create another implicit intent that enables users to choose a suspect from their contacts. This implicit intent will have an action and a location where the relevant data can be found. The action will be `Intent.ACTION_PICK`. The data for contacts is at `ContactsContract.Contacts.CONTENT_URI`. In short, you are asking Android to help pick an item in the Contacts database.

You expect a result back from the started activity, so you will pass the intent via `startActivityForResult(…)` along with a request code. In `CrimeFragment.java`, add a constant for the request code and a member variable for the button.

Listing 21.7 Adding field for suspect button (`CrimeFragment.java`)

```
...
private static final int REQUEST_PHOTO = 1;
private static final int REQUEST_CONTACT = 2;

...

private ImageButton mPhotoButton;
private Button mSuspectButton;

...
```

At the end of **onCreateView(…)**, get a reference to the button and set a listener on it. Within the listener's implementation, create the implicit intent and pass it into **startActivityForResult(…)**. Also show the suspect's name on the button, if the **Crime** has one.

Listing 21.8 Sending an implicit intent (`CrimeFragment.java`)

```
    ...

    mSuspectButton = (Button)v.findViewById(R.id.crime_suspectButton);
    mSuspectButton.setOnClickListener(new View.OnClickListener() {
        public void onClick(View v) {
            Intent i = new Intent(Intent.ACTION_PICK,
                ContactsContract.Contacts.CONTENT_URI);
            startActivityForResult(i, REQUEST_CONTACT);
        }
    });

    if (mCrime.getSuspect() != null) {
        mSuspectButton.setText(mCrime.getSuspect());
    }

    return v;
}
```

Run CriminalIntent and press the Choose Suspect button. You should now see a list of contacts:

Figure 21.7 A list of possible suspects

If you have a different contacts app installed, your screen will look different. Again, this is one of the benefits of implicit intents. You do not have to know the name of the contacts application to use it from your app. So users can install whatever app they like best, and the OS will find and launch it.

Getting the data from the contact list

Now you need to get a result back from the contacts application. Contacts information is shared by many applications, so Android provides an in-depth API for working with contacts information through a **ContentProvider**. Instances of this class wrap databases and make it available to other applications. You can access a **ContentProvider** through a **ContentResolver**.

Because you started the activity for a result with ACTION_PICK, you will receive an intent via **onActivityResult(…)**. This intent includes a data URI. This URI is a locator that points at the single contact the user picked.

In CrimeFragment.java, add the following code to your **onActivityResult(…)** implementation in **CrimeFragment**:

Listing 21.9 Pull contact name out (`CrimeFragment.java`)

```java
@Override
public void onActivityResult(int requestCode, int resultCode, Intent data) {
    if (resultCode != Activity.RESULT_OK) return;
    if (requestCode == REQUEST_DATE) {
        ...
    } else if (requestCode == REQUEST_PHOTO) {
        ...
    } else if (requestCode == REQUEST_CONTACT) {
        Uri contactUri = data.getData();

        // Specify which fields you want your query to return
        // values for.
        String[] queryFields = new String[] {
            ContactsContract.Contacts.DISPLAY_NAME
        };
        // Perform your query - the contactUri is like a "where"
        // clause here
        Cursor c = getActivity().getContentResolver()
            .query(contactUri, queryFields, null, null, null);

        // Double-check that you actually got results
        if (c.getCount() == 0) {
            c.close();
            return;
        }

        // Pull out the first column of the first row of data -
        // that is your suspect's name.
        c.moveToFirst();
        String suspect = c.getString(0);
        mCrime.setSuspect(suspect);
        mSuspectButton.setText(suspect);
        c.close();
    }
}
```

In Listing 21.9, you create a query that asks for all the display names of the contacts in the returned data. Then you query the contacts database and get a **Cursor** object to work with. Because you know that the cursor only contains one item, you move to the first item and get it as a string. This string will be the name of the suspect, and you use it to set the **Crime**'s suspect and the text of the Choose Suspect button.

(The Contacts database is a large topic in itself. We will not cover it here. If you would like to know more, read the Contacts Provider API guide: `http://developer.android.com/guide/topics/providers/contacts-provider.html`.)

Contacts permissions

How are you getting permission to read from the contacts database? The contacts app is extending its permissions to you. The contacts app has full permissions to the contacts database. When the contacts app returns a data URI in an **Intent** to the parent activity, it also adds the flag `Intent.FLAG_GRANT_READ_URI_PERMISSION`. This flag signals to Android that the parent activity in CriminalIntent should be allowed to use this data one time. This works well because you do not really need access to the entire contacts database. You only need access to one contact inside that database.

Checking for responding activities

The two implicit intents you have created in this chapter will always be responded to. An Android device is guaranteed to have an email app and a contacts app of one kind or another. But what if you were creating a different implicit intent for which a device might or might not have any matching activities? If the OS cannot find a matching activity, then the app will crash.

The answer is to check with part of the OS called the **PackageManager** first. The code looks like this:

```
PackageManager pm = getPackageManager();
List<ResolveInfo> activities = pm.queryIntentActivities(yourIntent, 0);
boolean isIntentSafe = activities.size() > 0;
```

You pass your intent into the **PackageManager**'s **queryIntentActivities(…)** method. This method returns a list of objects containing metadata about activities that responded to the passed-in intent. You just need to confirm that there is at least one item in this list – at least one activity on the device that will respond to the intent.

You can run this check in **onCreateView(…)** to disable options that the device will not be able to respond to.

Challenge: Another Implicit Intent

Instead of sending a crime report, an angry user may prefer a phone confrontation with the suspect. Add a new button that calls the named suspect.

You will need the phone number out of the contacts database. Then you can create an implicit intent with a URI of the telephone:

```
Uri number = Uri.parse("tel:5551234");
```

The action can be Intent.ACTION_DIAL or Intent.ACTION_CALL. ACTION_CALL pulls up the phone app and immediately calls the number sent in the intent; ACTION_DIAL just dials the number and waits for the user to initiate the call.

We recommend using ACTION_DIAL. ACTION_CALL may be restricted and will definitely require a permission. Your user may also appreciate the chance to cool down before pressing the Call button.

22

Two-Pane Master-Detail Interfaces

In this chapter, you will create a tablet interface for CriminalIntent that allows users to see and interact with the list of crimes and the detail of an individual crime at the same time. Figure 22.1 shows this list-detail interface, which is also commonly referred to as a *master-detail interface*.

Figure 22.1 Master and detail sharing the spotlight

You will need a tablet device or AVD for testing in this chapter. To create a tablet AVD, select Window → Android Virtual Device Manager. Click New and set this AVD's Device to one of the two selections highlighted below. Then set the AVD's Target to API level 17.

Figure 22.2 Device selections for a tablet AVD

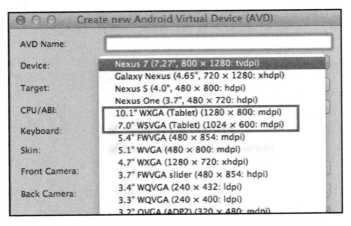

Adding Layout Flexibility

On a phone, you want **CrimeListActivity** to inflate the single-pane layout as it does currently. On a tablet, you want it to inflate a two-pane layout that is capable of displaying the master and detail views at the same time.

In the two-pane layout, **CrimeListActivity** will host both a **CrimeListFragment** and a **CrimeFragment** as shown in Figure 22.3.

Figure 22.3 Different types of layouts

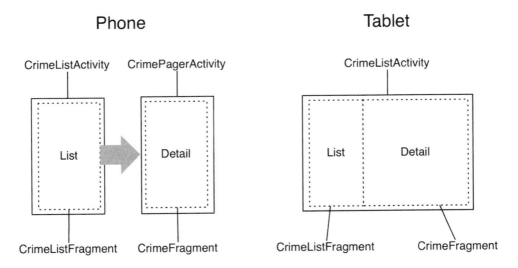

To make this happen, you are going to:

- modify **SingleFragmentActivity** so that the layout that gets inflated is not hard-coded

- create a new layout that consists of two fragment containers

- modify **CrimeListActivity** so that it will inflate a single-container layout on phones and a two-container layout on tablets

Modifying SingleFragmentActivity

CrimeListActivity is a subclass of **SingleFragmentActivity**. Currently, **SingleFragmentActivity** is set up to always inflate activity_fragment.xml. To make **SingleFragmentActivity** more flexible, you are going to enable a subclass to provide its own resource ID for the layout instead.

In SingleFragmentActivity.java, add a protected method that returns the ID of the layout that the activity will inflate.

Listing 22.1 Making **SingleFragmentActivity** flexible (SingleFragmentActivity.java)

```
public abstract class SingleFragmentActivity extends FragmentActivity {
    protected abstract Fragment createFragment();

    protected int getLayoutResId() {
        return R.layout.activity_fragment;
    }

    @Override
    public void onCreate(Bundle savedInstanceState) {
        super.onCreate(savedInstanceState);
        setContentView(R.layout.activity_fragment);
        setContentView(getLayoutResId());
        FragmentManager fm = getSupportFragmentManager();
        Fragment fragment = fm.findFragmentById(R.id.fragmentContainer);

        if (fragment == null) {
            fragment = createFragment();
            fm.beginTransaction()
                .add(R.id.fragmentContainer, fragment)
                .commit();
        }
    }
}
```

The default implementation of **SingleFragmentActivity** will work the same as before, but now its subclasses can choose to override **getLayoutResId()** to return a layout other than activity_fragment.xml.

Creating a layout with two fragment containers

In the package explorer, right-click res/layout/ and create a new Android XML file. Ensure that the resource type is Layout, name the file activity_twopane.xml, and give it a **LinearLayout** root element.

Use Figure 22.4 to write the XML for the two-pane layout.

Figure 22.4 A layout with two fragment containers (layout/activity_twopane.xml)

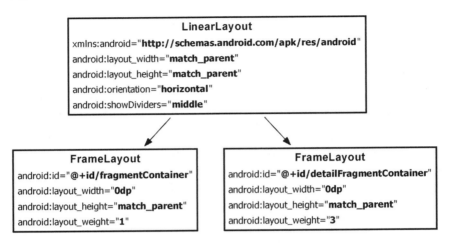

Note that the first **FrameLayout** has a fragmentContainer layout ID, so the code in **SingleFragmentActivity.onCreate(…)** can work as before. When the activity is created, the fragment that is returned in **createFragment()** will appear in the lefthand pane.

Test this layout in **CrimeListActivity** by overriding **getLayoutResId()** to return R.layout.activity_twopane.

Listing 22.2 Change to two-pane layout file (CrimeListActivity.java)

```
public class CrimeListActivity extends SingleFragmentActivity {

    @Override
    protected Fragment createFragment() {
        return new CrimeListFragment();
    }

    @Override
    protected int getLayoutResId() {
        return R.layout.activity_twopane;
    }
}
```

Run CriminalIntent on a tablet device and confirm that you have two panes (Figure 22.5). Note that the larger detail pane is empty and that pressing a list item will not display the crime's details. You will hook up the detail container later in the chapter.

Figure 22.5 Two-pane layout on a tablet

As currently written, **CrimeListActivity** will also inflate the two-pane interface when running on a phone. In the next section, you will fix that using an alias resource.

Using an alias resource

An *alias resource* is a resource that points to another resource. Alias resources live in res/values/ and, by convention, are defined in a refs.xml file.

In this section, you will create an alias resource that points to the activity_fragment.xml layout on phones and the activity_twopane.xml layout on tablets.

In the package explorer, right-click the res/values directory and create a new Android XML file. Ensure that the resource type is Values and name the file refs.xml. Give it a resources root element and click Finish. Then add the item shown in Listing 22.3.

Listing 22.3 Create a default alias resource value (res/values/refs.xml)

```
<resources>

  <item name="activity_masterdetail" type="layout">@layout/activity_fragment</item>

</resources>
```

This resource's value is a reference to the single-pane layout. It also has a resource ID: R.layout.activity_masterdetail. Note that the alias's type attribute is what determines the inner class of the ID. Even though the alias itself is in res/values/, its ID is in R.layout.

You can now use this resource ID in place of R.layout.activity_fragment. Make that change in **CrimeListActivity**.

Listing 22.4 Switch layout again (CrimeListActivity.java)

```
@Override
protected int getLayoutResId() {
    return R.layout.activity_twopane;
    return R.layout.activity_masterdetail;
}
```

Run CriminalIntent to confirm that your alias is working properly. **CrimeListActivity** should inflate the single-pane layout again.

Creating tablet alternatives

Because your alias is in res/values/, it is the default alias. So, by default, **CrimeListActivity** inflates the single-pane layout.

Now you are going to create an alternative resource so that the activity_masterdetail alias will point to activity_twopane.xml on larger devices.

In the package explorer, right-click res/ and create a new folder named values-sw600dp. Copy the res/values/refs.xml file into res/values-sw600dp/. Then change the layout that the alias points to.

Listing 22.5 Alternative alias for larger devices (res/values-sw600dp/ refs.xml)

```
<resources>

    <item name="activity_masterdetail" type="layout">@layout/activity_fragment</item>
    <item name="activity_masterdetail" type="layout">@layout/activity_twopane</item>

</resources>
```

What does the -sw600dp configuration qualifier mean? The sw stands for "smallest width," but refers to the screen's smallest *dimension*, and thus is independent of the device's current orientation.

With a -sw600dp qualifier, you are saying, "Use this resource on any device whose smallest dimension is 600dp or greater." This is a good rule of thumb for specifying a tablet-sized screen.

There is one more thing. The smallest width configuration qualifier was introduced in Android 3.2. This means that a tablet-sized device running Android 3.0 and 3.1 will not recognize it.

To address this problem, you can add another alternative resource that uses the deprecated screen size qualifier -xlarge.

Right-click res/ and create a new folder named values-xlarge. Then copy the res/values-sw600dp/ refs.xml file into res/values-xlarge/. Now you have another alternative resource that looks like Listing 22.6.

Listing 22.6 Alternative alias for pre-3.2 larger devices (res/values-xlarge/ refs.xml)

```
<resources>

  <item name="activity_masterdetail" type="layout">@layout/activity_twopane</item>

</resources>
```

The -xlarge qualifier contains resources to use on devices with a minimum size of 720x960dp. This qualifier will only be used for devices running versions earlier than Android 3.2. Later versions will find and use the -sw600dp.

Run CriminalIntent on a phone and on a tablet. Confirm that the single- and two-pane layouts appear where you expect them.

Activity: Fragment Boss

Now that your layouts are behaving properly, you can turn to adding a **CrimeFragment** to the detail fragment container when **CrimeListActivity** is sporting a two-pane layout.

You might think to simply write an alternative implementation of **CrimeListFragment.onListItemClick(…)** for tablets. Instead of starting a new **CrimePagerActivity**, **onListItemClick(…)** would get **CrimeListActivity**'s **FragmentManager** and commit a fragment transaction that adds a **CrimeFragment** to the detail fragment container.

The code would look like this:

```
public void onListItemClick(ListView l, View v, int position, long id) {
    // Get the Crime from the adapter
    Crime crime = ((CrimeAdapter)getListAdapter()).getItem(position);
    // Stick a new CrimeFragment in the activity's layout
    Fragment fragment = CrimeFragment.newInstance(crime.getId());
    FragmentManager fm = getActivity().getSupportFragmentManager();
    fm.beginTransaction()
        .add(R.id.detailFragmentContainer, fragment)
        .commit();
}
```

This works, but it is not how stylish Android programmers do things. Fragments are intended to be standalone, composable units. If you write a fragment that adds fragments to the activity's **FragmentManager**, then that fragment is making assumptions about how the hosting activity works, and your fragment is no longer a standalone, composable unit.

For example, in the code above **CrimeListFragment** adds a **CrimeFragment** to **CrimeListActivity** and assumes that **CrimeListActivity** has a detailFragmentContainer in its layout. This is business that should be handled by **CrimeListFragment**'s hosting activity instead of **CrimeListFragment**.

To maintain the independence of your fragments, you will delegate work back to the hosting activity by defining callback interfaces in your fragments. The hosting activities will implement these interfaces to perform fragment-bossing duties and layout-dependent behavior.

Fragment callback interfaces

To delegate functionality back to the hosting activity, a fragment typically defines a callback interface named **Callbacks**. This interface defines work that the fragment needs done by its boss, the hosting activity. Any activity that will host the fragment must implement this interface.

With a callback interface, a fragment is able to call methods on its hosting activity without having to know anything about which activity is hosting it.

Implementing CrimeListFragment.Callbacks

To implement a **Callbacks** interface, you first define a member variable that holds an object that implements **Callbacks**. Then you cast the hosting activity to **Callbacks** and assign it to that variable.

You assign the activity in the **Fragment** lifecycle method:

```
public void onAttach(Activity activity)
```

This method is called when a fragment is attached to an activity, whether it was retained or not.

Similarly, you will set the variable to null in the corresponding waning lifecycle method:

```
public void onDetach()
```

You set the variable to null here because afterwards you cannot access the activity or count on the activity continuing to exist.

In CrimeListFragment.java, add a **Callbacks** interface to **CrimeListFragment**. Also add an mCallbacks variable and override **onAttach(Activity)** and **onDetach()** to set and unset it.

Listing 22.7 Add callback interface (`CrimeListFragment.java`)

```java
public class CrimeListFragment extends ListFragment {
    private ArrayList<Crime> mCrimes;
    private boolean mSubtitleVisible;
    private Callbacks mCallbacks;

    /**
     * Required interface for hosting activities.
     */
    public interface Callbacks {

        void onCrimeSelected(Crime crime);
    }

    @Override
    public void onAttach(Activity activity) {
        super.onAttach(activity);
        mCallbacks = (Callbacks)activity;
    }

    @Override
    public void onDetach() {
        super.onDetach();
        mCallbacks = null;
    }
```

Now **CrimeListFragment** has a way to call methods on its hosting activity. It does not matter which activity is doing the hosting. As long as the activity implements **CrimeListFragment.Callbacks**, everything in **CrimeListFragment** can work the same.

Note that **CrimeListFragment** performs an unchecked cast of its activity to **CrimeListFragment.Callbacks**. This means that the hosting activity *must* implement **CrimeListFragment.Callbacks**. That is not a bad dependency to have, but it is important to document it.

Next, in **CrimeListActivity**, implement **CrimeListFragment.Callbacks**. Leave **onCrimeSelected(Crime)** empty for now.

Listing 22.8 Implement callbacks (`CrimeListActivity.java`)

```java
public class CrimeListActivity extends SingleFragmentActivity
    implements CrimeListFragment.Callbacks {

    @Override
    protected Fragment createFragment() {
        return new CrimeListFragment();
    }

    @Override
    protected int getLayoutResId() {
        return R.layout.activity_masterdetail;
    }

    public void onCrimeSelected(Crime crime) {
    }
}
```

Eventually, **CrimeListFragment** will call this method in **onListItemClick(…)** and also when the user chooses to create a new crime. First, let's figure out **CrimeListActivity.onCrimeSelected(Crime)**'s implementation.

When **onCrimeSelected(Crime)** is called, **CrimeListActivity** needs to do one of two things:

- if using the phone interface, start a new **CrimePagerActivity**

- if using the tablet interface, put a **CrimeFragment** in detailFragmentContainer

To determine which interface was inflated, you could check for a certain layout ID. But it is better to check whether the layout has a detailFragmentContainer. Checking a layout's capabilities is a more precise test of what you need. Filenames can change, and you don't really care what file the layout was inflated from; you just need to know whether it has a detailFragmentContainer to put your **CrimeFragment** in.

If the layout does have a detailFragmentContainer, then you are going to create a fragment transaction that removes the existing **CrimeFragment** from detailFragmentContainer (if there is one in there) and adds the **CrimeFragment** that you want to see.

In CrimeListActivity.java, implement **onCrimeSelected(Crime)** to handle the selection of a crime in either interface.

Listing 22.9 Conditional **CrimeFragment** startup (CrimeListActivity.java)

```java
public void onCrimeSelected(Crime crime) {
    if (findViewById(R.id.detailFragmentContainer) == null) {
        // Start an instance of CrimePagerActivity
        Intent i = new Intent(this, CrimePagerActivity.class);
        i.putExtra(CrimeFragment.EXTRA_CRIME_ID, crime.getId());
        startActivity(i);
    } else {
        FragmentManager fm = getSupportFragmentManager();
        FragmentTransaction ft = fm.beginTransaction();

        Fragment oldDetail = fm.findFragmentById(R.id.detailFragmentContainer);
        Fragment newDetail = CrimeFragment.newInstance(crime.getId());

        if (oldDetail != null) {
            ft.remove(oldDetail);
        }

        ft.add(R.id.detailFragmentContainer, newDetail);
        ft.commit();
    }
}
```

Finally, in **CrimeListFragment**, you are going to call **onCrimeSelected(Crime)** in the places where you currently start a new **CrimePagerActivity**.

In CrimeListFragment.java, modify **onListItemClick(…)** and **onOptionsItemSelected(MenuItem)** to call **Callbacks.onCrimeSelected(Crime)**.

Listing 22.10 Calling all callbacks! (CrimeListFragment.java)

```java
public void onListItemClick(ListView l, View v, int position, long id) {
    // Get the Crime from the adapter
    Crime c = ((CrimeAdapter)getListAdapter()).getItem(position);
    // Start an instance of CrimePagerActivity
    Intent i = new Intent(getActivity(), CrimePagerActivity.class);
    i.putExtra(CrimeFragment.EXTRA_CRIME_ID, c.getId());
    startActivity(i);
    mCallbacks.onCrimeSelected(c);
}

...

@TargetApi(11)
@Override
public boolean onOptionsItemSelected(MenuItem item) {
    switch (item.getItemId()) {
        case R.id.menu_item_new_crime:
            Crime crime = new Crime();
            CrimeLab.get(getActivity()).addCrime(crime);
            Intent i = new Intent(getActivity(), CrimePagerActivity.class);
            i.putExtra(CrimeFragment.EXTRA_CRIME_ID, crime.getId());
            startActivity(i);
            ((CrimeAdapter)getListAdapter()).notifyDataSetChanged();
            mCallbacks.onCrimeSelected(crime);
            return true;
        ...
    }
}
```

When you call back in **onOptionsItemSelected(…)**, you also reload the list immediately upon adding a new crime. This is necessary because, on tablets, the list will remain visible after adding a new crime. Before, you were guaranteed that the detail screen would appear in front of it.

Run CriminalIntent on a tablet. Create a new crime, and a **CrimeFragment** will be added and shown in the detailFragmentContainer. Then view an old crime to see the **CrimeFragment** being swapped out for a new one.

Figure 22.6 Master and detail now wired up

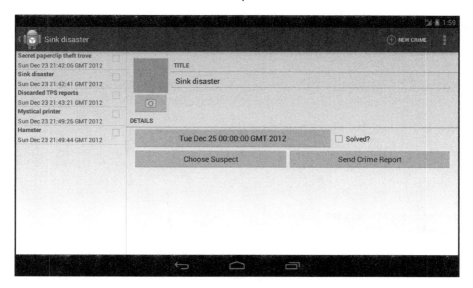

However, if you make changes to a crime, the list will not update to reflect them. Right now, you only reload the list immediately after adding a crime and in **CrimeListFragment.onResume()**. But on a tablet, **CrimeListFragment** will stay visible alongside the **CrimeFragment**. The **CrimeListFragment** is not paused when the **CrimeFragment** appears, so it is never resumed. Thus, the list is not reloaded.

You can fix this problem with another callback interface – this one in **CrimeFragment**.

Implementing CrimeFragment.Callbacks

CrimeFragment will define the following interface:

```
public interface Callbacks {
    void onCrimeUpdated(Crime crime);
}
```

CrimeFragment will call **onCrimeUpdated(Crime)** on its hosting activity whenever changes are saved to the **Crime**. **CrimeListActivity** will implement **onCrimeUpdated(Crime)** to reload **CrimeListFragment**'s list.

Before you start with **CrimeFragment**'s interface, add a method to **CrimeListFragment** that can be called to reload **CrimeListFragment**'s list.

Listing 22.11 Add **updateUI()** method (CrimeListFragment.java)

```
public class CrimeListFragment extends ListFragment {

    ...

    public void updateUI() {
        ((CrimeAdapter)getListAdapter()).notifyDataSetChanged();
    }
}
```

Then, in CrimeFragment.java, add the callback interface along with an mCallbacks variable and implementations of **onAttach(…)** and **onDetach()**.

Listing 22.12 Add **CrimeFragment** callbacks (CrimeFragment.java)

```
    ...
    private ImageView mPhotoView;
    private Button mSuspectButton;
    private Callbacks mCallbacks;

    /**
     * Required interface for hosting activities.
     */
    public interface Callbacks {
        void onCrimeUpdated(Crime crime);
    }

    @Override
    public void onAttach(Activity activity) {
        super.onAttach(activity);
        mCallbacks = (Callbacks)activity;
    }

    @Override
    public void onDetach() {
        super.onDetach();
        mCallbacks = null;
    }

    public static CrimeFragment newInstance(UUID crimeId) {
        ...
    }
```

Then implement **CrimeFragment.Callbacks** in **CrimeListActivity** to reload the list in **onCrimeUpdated(Crime)**.

Listing 22.13 Refresh crime list (CrimeListActivity.java)

```
public class CrimeListActivity extends SingleFragmentActivity
        implements CrimeListFragment.Callbacks, CrimeFragment.Callbacks {

    ...

    public void onCrimeUpdated(Crime crime) {
        FragmentManager fm = getSupportFragmentManager();
        CrimeListFragment listFragment = (CrimeListFragment)
                fm.findFragmentById(R.id.fragmentContainer);
        listFragment.updateUI();
    }
}
```

In CrimeFragment.java, add calls to **onCrimeUpdated(Crime)** when a **Crime**'s title or solved status has changed.

Listing 22.14 Call **onCrimeUpdated(Crime)** (CrimeFragment.java)

```
@Override
@TargetApi(11)
public View onCreateView(LayoutInflater inflater, ViewGroup parent,
        Bundle savedInstanceState) {
    View v = inflater.inflate(R.layout.fragment_crime, parent, false);

    ...

    mTitleField = (EditText)v.findViewById(R.id.crime_title);
    mTitleField.setText(mCrime.getTitle());
    mTitleField.addTextChangedListener(new TextWatcher() {
        public void onTextChanged(CharSequence c, int start, int before, int count) {
            mCrime.setTitle(c.toString());
            mCallbacks.onCrimeUpdated(mCrime);
            getActivity().setTitle(mCrime.getTitle());
        }

        ...
    });

    mSolvedCheckBox = (CheckBox)v.findViewById(R.id.crime_solved);
    mSolvedCheckBox.setChecked(mCrime.isSolved());
    mSolvedCheckBox.setOnCheckedChangeListener(new OnCheckedChangeListener() {
        public void onCheckedChanged(CompoundButton buttonView, boolean isChecked) {
            // Set the crime's solved property
            mCrime.setSolved(isChecked);
            mCallbacks.onCrimeUpdated(mCrime);
        }
    });

    ...

    return v;
}
```

You also need to call **onCrimeUpdated(Crime)** in **onActivityResult(…)**, where the **Crime**'s date, photo, and suspect can be changed. Currently, the photo and suspect do not appear in the list item's view, but **CrimeFragment** should still be neighborly and report those updates.

Listing 22.15 Call **onCrimeUpdated(Crime)** (#2) (CrimeFragment.java)

```
@Override
public void onActivityResult(int requestCode, int resultCode, Intent data) {
    if (resultCode != Activity.RESULT_OK) return;
    if (requestCode == REQUEST_DATE) {
        Date date = (Date)data.getSerializableExtra(DatePickerFragment.EXTRA_DATE);
        mCrime.setDate(date);
        mCallbacks.onCrimeUpdated(mCrime);
        updateDate();
    } else if (requestCode == REQUEST_PHOTO) {
        // Create a new Photo object and attach it to the crime
        String filename = data
            .getStringExtra(CrimeCameraFragment.EXTRA_PHOTO_FILENAME);
        if (filename != null) {
            Photo p = new Photo(filename);
            mCrime.setPhoto(p);
            mCallbacks.onCrimeUpdated(mCrime);
            showPhoto();
        }
    } else if (requestCode == REQUEST_CONTACT) {
        ...

        c.moveToFirst();
        String suspect = c.getString(0);
        mCrime.setSuspect(suspect);
        mCallbacks.onCrimeUpdated(mCrime);
        mSuspectButton.setText(suspect);
        c.close();
    }
}
```

CrimeListActivity now has a nice implementation for **CrimeFragment.Callbacks**. However, if
you run CriminalIntent on a phone, it will crash. Remember, any activity that hosts **CrimeFragment**
must implement **CrimeFragment.Callbacks**. You need to implement **CrimeFragment.Callbacks** in
CrimePagerActivity.

For **CrimePagerActivity**, all you need is an empty implementation where **onCrimeUpdated(Crime)**
does nothing. When **CrimePagerActivity** is hosting **CrimeFragment**, the only reloading of the list that
is necessary is already done in **onResume()**.

Listing 22.16 An empty implementation of **CrimeFragment.Callbacks** (CrimePagerActivity.java)

```
public class CrimePagerActivity extends FragmentActivity
    implements CrimeFragment.Callbacks {
    ...

    public void onCrimeUpdated(Crime crime) {
    }
}
```

Run CriminalIntent on a tablet and confirm that your **ListView** updates when changes are made in
CrimeFragment. Then run on a phone to confirm that the app works continues to work as before.

Figure 22.7 List reflects changes made in detail

You have reached the end of your time with CriminalIntent. In thirteen chapters, you created a complex application that uses fragments, talks to other apps, takes pictures, and stores data. Why not celebrate with a piece of cake? Just be sure to clean up after yourself. You never know who might be watching.

For the More Curious: More on Determining Device Size

Before Android 3.2, the screen size qualifier was used to provide alternative resources based the size of a device. Screen size is a qualifier that groups different devices into four broad categories – small, normal, large, and xlarge.

Table 22.1 shows the minimum screen sizes for each qualifier:

Table 22.1 Screen size qualifiers

Name	Minimum screen size
small	320x426dp
normal	320x470dp
large	480x640dp
xlarge	720x960dp

Screen size qualifiers were deprecated in Android 3.2 in favor of qualifiers that allow you test for the dimensions of the device. Table 22.2 shows these new qualifiers.

Table 22.2 Discrete screen dimension qualifiers

Qualifier format	description
wXXXdp	Available width: width is greater than or equal to XXX dp
hXXXdp	Available height: height greater than or equal to XXX dp
swXXXdp	Smallest width: width or height (whichever is smaller) greater than or equal to XXX dp

Let's say that you wanted to specify a layout that would only be used if the display were at least 300dp wide. In that case, you could use an available width qualifier and put your layout file in res/layout-w300dp (the "w" is for "width"). You can do the same thing for height by using an "h" (for "height").

The height and width may swap depending on the orientation of the device, though. To detect a particular size of screen, you can use sw, which stands for *smallest width*. This specifies the smallest dimension of your screen. Depending on the device's orientation, this can be either width or height. If the screen is 1024x800, then sw is 800. If the screen is 800x1024, sw is still 800.

23

More About Intents and Tasks

In this chapter, you will use implicit intents to create a launcher app to replace Android's default launcher app. To get it working correctly, you will deepen your understanding of intents, intent filters, and how applications interact in the Android environment.

Setting Up NerdLauncher

Create a new project (New → Android Application Project) with the same settings you used for CriminalIntent (Figure 23.1). Name this project NerdLauncher and create it in the com.bignerdranch.android.nerdlauncher package.

Figure 23.1 Creating NerdLauncher project

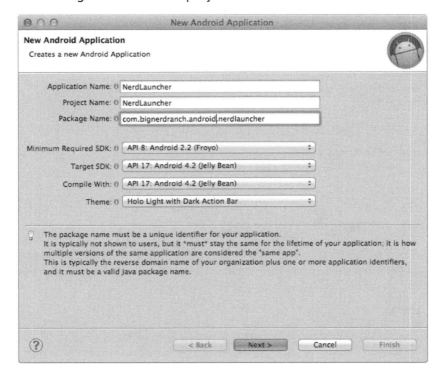

Create an activity but not a custom launcher icon. Choose to create a new blank activity. Name the activity **NerdLauncherActivity** and click Finish.

NerdLauncherActivity should be a subclass of **SingleFragmentActivity**, so you need to add that class to the project. In the package explorer, find SingleFragmentActivity.java in the CriminalIntent package. Copy this file into the com.bignerdranch.android.nerdlauncher package. When you copy files, Eclipse takes care of updating the package declarations.

You will also need the activity_fragment.xml layout. Copy res/layout/activity_fragment.xml to the res/layout directory in the NerdLauncher project.

NerdLauncher will display a list of apps on the device. The user can press a list item to launch the app. Here are the objects involved.

NerdLauncherFragment will be a **ListFragment** subclass, and its view will be the default **ListView** that comes with **ListFragment**.

Create a new class named **NerdLauncherFragment** and make its superclass **android.support.v4.app.ListFragment**. Leave this class empty for now.

Open NerdLauncherActivity.java and change **NerdLauncherActivity**'s superclass to **SingleFragmentActivity**. Remove the template's code and override **createFragment()** to return a **NerdLauncherFragment**.

Listing 23.1 Another **SingleFragmentActivity** (NerdLauncherActivity.java)

```java
public class NerdLauncherActivity extends Activity SingleFragmentActivity {
    @Override
    public void onCreate(Bundle savedInstanceState) {
        super.onCreate(savedInstanceState);
        setContentView(R.layout.activity_nerd_launcher);
    }

    @Override
    public boolean onCreateOptionsMenu(Menu menu) {
        getMenuInflater().inflate(R.menu.activity_nerd_launcher, menu);
        return true;
    }

    @Override
    public Fragment createFragment() {
        return new NerdLauncherFragment();
    }
}
```

Resolving an Implicit Intent

NerdLauncher will show the user a list of apps on the device. To do so, it will send an implicit intent that every application's main activity will respond to. The intent will include a MAIN action and a **LAUNCHER** category. You have seen this intent filter in your projects:

```xml
<intent-filter>
    <action android:name="android.intent.action.MAIN" />
    <category android:name="android.intent.category.LAUNCHER" />
</intent-filter>
```

In NerdLauncherFragment.java, override **onCreate(Bundle)** to create an implicit intent. Then get a list of activities that match the intent from the **PackageManager**. For now, just log the number of activities that the **PackageManager** returns.

Listing 23.2 Querying the **PackageManager** (NerdLauncherFragment.java)

```java
public class NerdLauncherFragment extends ListFragment {
    private static final String TAG = "NerdLauncherFragment";

    @Override
    public void onCreate(Bundle savedInstanceState) {
        super.onCreate(savedInstanceState);

        Intent startupIntent = new Intent(Intent.ACTION_MAIN);
        startupIntent.addCategory(Intent.CATEGORY_LAUNCHER);

        PackageManager pm = getActivity().getPackageManager();
        List<ResolveInfo> activities = pm.queryIntentActivities(startupIntent, 0);

        Log.i(TAG, "I've found " + activities.size() + " activities.");
    }
}
```

Run NerdLauncher and check LogCat to see how many apps the **PackageManager** returned.

In CriminalIntent, you used an implicit intent to send a crime report. You presented an activity chooser by creating an implicit intent, wrapping it in a chooser intent, and sending it to the OS with **startActivity(Intent)**:

```java
Intent i = new Intent(Intent.ACTION_SEND);
... // Create and put intent extras
i = Intent.createChooser(i, getString(R.string.send_report));
startActivity(i);
```

You may be wondering why you are not using that approach here. The short explanation is that the MAIN/LAUNCHER intent filter may or may not match a MAIN/LAUNCHER implicit intent that is sent via **startActivity(…)**.

It turns out that **startActivity(Intent)** does not mean "Start an activity matching this implicit intent." It means "Start the *default* activity matching this implicit intent." When you send an implicit intent via **startActivity(…)** (or **startActivityForResult(…)**), the OS secretly adds the Intent.CATEGORY_DEFAULT category to the intent.

Thus, if you want an intent filter to match implicit intents sent via **startActivity(…)**, you must include the DEFAULT category in that intent filter.

An activity that has the MAIN/LAUNCHER intent filter is the main entry point for the app that it belongs to. It only wants the job of main entry point for that application. It typically does not care about being the "default" main entry point, so it does not have to include the CATEGORY_DEFAULT category.

Because MAIN/LAUNCHER intent filters may not include CATEGORY_DEFAULT, you cannot reliably match them to an implicit intent sent via **startActivity(…)**. So, instead you use the intent to query the **PackageManager** directly for activities with the MAIN/LAUNCHER intent filter.

The next step is to display the labels of these activities in **NerdLauncherFragment**'s **ListView**. An activity's *label* is its display name – something the user should recognize. Given that these activities are launcher activities, the label is most likely the application name.

You can find the labels for the activities, along with other metadata, in the **ResolveInfo** objects that the **PackageManager** returned.

First, add the following code to sort the **ResolveInfo** objects returned from the **PackageManager** alphabetically by label using the **ResolveInfo.loadLabel(…)** method.

Listing 23.3 Sorting alphabetically (NerdLauncherFragment.java)

```
...

Log.i("NerdLauncher", "I've found " + activities.size() + " activities.");

Collections.sort(activities, new Comparator<ResolveInfo>() {
    public int compare(ResolveInfo a, ResolveInfo b) {
        PackageManager pm = getActivity().getPackageManager();
        return String.CASE_INSENSITIVE_ORDER.compare(
            a.loadLabel(pm).toString(),
            b.loadLabel(pm).toString());
    }
});
```

Then create an **ArrayAdapter** that will create simple list item views that display the label of an activity and set this adapter on the **ListView**.

Listing 23.4 Creating an adapter (NerdLauncherFragment.java)

```
...

Collections.sort(activities, new Comparator<ResolveInfo></ResolveInfo>() {

    ...

    }
});

ArrayAdapter<ResolveInfo> adapter = new ArrayAdapter<ResolveInfo>(
        getActivity(), android.R.layout.simple_list_item_1, activities) {
    public View getView(int pos, View convertView, ViewGroup parent) {
        PackageManager pm = getActivity().getPackageManager();
        View v = super.getView(pos, convertView, parent);
        // Documentation says that simple_list_item_1 is a TextView,
        // so cast it so that you can set its text value
        TextView tv = (TextView)v;
        ResolveInfo ri = getItem(pos);
        tv.setText(ri.loadLabel(pm));
        return v;
    }
};

setListAdapter(adapter);
```

Run NerdLauncher, and you will see a **ListView** populated with activity labels.

Figure 23.2 All your activities are belong to us

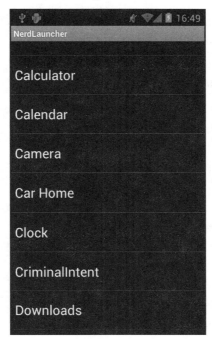

Creating Explicit Intents at Runtime

You used an implicit intent to gather the desired activities and present them in a list. The next step is to start the selected activity when the user presses its list item. You will start the activity using an explicit intent.

To create the explicit intent, you need more data from the **ResolveInfo**. In particular, you need the activity's package name and class name. You can get this data from a part of the **ResolveInfo** called **ActivityInfo**. (You can learn what data is available in different parts of **ResolveInfo** from its reference page.)

In NerdLauncherFragment.java, override **onListItemClick(…)** to get the **ActivityInfo** for the list item. Then use its data to create an explicit intent that will start the activity.

Listing 23.5 Implement **onListItemClick(…)**
(NerdLauncherFragment.java)

```java
@Override
public void onListItemClick(ListView l, View v, int position, long id) {
    ResolveInfo resolveInfo = (ResolveInfo)l.getAdapter().getItem(position);
    ActivityInfo activityInfo = resolveInfo.activityInfo;

    if (activityInfo == null) return;

    Intent i = new Intent(Intent.ACTION_MAIN);
    i.setClassName(activityInfo.applicationInfo.packageName, activityInfo.name);

    startActivity(i);
}
```

Notice that in this intent you are sending an action as part of an explicit intent. Most apps will behave the same whether you include the action or not. However, some may change their behavior. The same activity can display different interfaces depending on how it is started. As a programmer, it is best to declare your intentions clearly and let the activities you start do what they will.

In Listing 23.5, you get the package name and class name from the metadata and use them to create an explicit intent using the **Intent** method:

```
public Intent setClassName(String packageName, String className)
```

This is different from how you have created explicit intents in the past. Before, you have used an **Intent** constructor that accepts a **Context** and a **Class** object:

```
public Intent(Context packageContext, Class<?> cls)
```

This constructor uses its parameters to get what the **Intent** really needs – a **ComponentName**. A **ComponentName** is a package name and a class name stuck together. When you pass in an **Activity** and a **Class** to create an **Intent**, the constructor determines the fully-qualified package name from the **Activity**.

You could also create a **ComponentName** yourself from the package and class names and use the following **Intent** method to create an explicit intent:

```
public Intent setComponent(ComponentName component)
```

However, it is less code to use **setClassName(…)**, which creates the component name behind the scenes.

Run NerdLauncher and launch some apps.

Tasks and the Back Stack

Android uses tasks to keep track of the user's state within each running application. A *task* is a stack of activities that the user is concerned with. The activity at the bottom of the stack is called the *base activity*, and whatever activity is on top is the activity that the user sees. When you press the Back button, you are popping the top activity off of this stack. If you are looking at the base activity and hit the Back button, it will send you to the home screen.

Using the task manager, you can switch between tasks without affecting each task's state. For instance, if you start entering a new contact and switch to checking your Twitter feed, you will have two tasks started. If you switch back to editing contacts, your place in both tasks will be saved.

Sometimes, when you start an activity, you want the activity added to the current task. Other times, you want it started in a new task that is independent of the activity that started it.

Figure 23.3 Tasks and the back stack

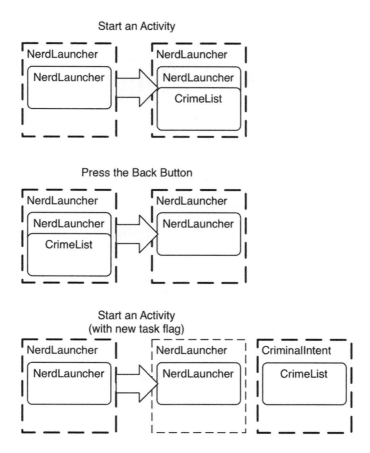

By default, new activities are started in the current task. In CriminalIntent, whenever you started a new activity that activity was added to the current task. This was true even if the activity was not part of the CriminalIntent application, like when you started an activity to send a crime report. The benefit of adding an activity to the current task is that the user can navigate back through the task instead of the application hierarchy.

Right now, any activity started from NerdLauncher is added to NerdLaucher's task. You can confirm this by starting CriminalIntent from NerdLauncher and then pulling up the task manager. (Press the Recents button if the device has one. Otherwise, long-press the Home button.) You will not see CriminalIntent listed anywhere. When `CrimeListActivity` was started, it was added the NerdLauncher's task. If you press the NerdLauncher task, you will be returned to whatever CriminalIntent screen you were looking at before starting the task manager.

Figure 23.4 CriminalIntent not in its own task

You want NerdLauncher to start activities in new tasks. Then users can switch between running applications as they like. To start a new task when you start a new activity, you add a flag to the intent:

Listing 23.6 Add new task flag to intent (`NerdLauncherFragment.java`)

```
Intent i = new Intent(Intent.ACTION_MAIN);
i.setClassName(activityInfo.applicationInfo.packageName, activityInfo.name);
i.addFlags(Intent.FLAG_ACTIVITY_NEW_TASK);

startActivity(i);
```

Run NerdLauncher and start CriminalIntent. This time, when you pull up the task manager you will see a separate task for CriminalIntent.

Figure 23.5 CriminalIntent now in its own task

If you start CriminalIntent from NerdLauncher again, you will not create a second CriminalIntent task. The FLAG_ACTIVITY_NEW_TASK flag by itself creates one task per activity. **CrimeListActivity** already has a task running, so Android will switch to that task instead of starting a new one.

Using NerdLauncher as a Home Screen

Who wants to start an app to start other apps? It would make more sense to offer NerdLauncher as a replacement for the device's home screen. Open NerdLauncher's AndroidManifest.xml and add to its main intent filter:

Listing 23.7 Change NerdLauncher's categories (AndroidManifest.xml)

```
<intent-filter>
  <action android:name="android.intent.action.MAIN" />
  <category android:name="android.intent.category.LAUNCHER" />
  <category android:name="android.intent.category.HOME" />
  <category android:name="android.intent.category.DEFAULT" />
</intent-filter>
```

By adding the HOME and DEFAULT categories, NerdLauncher activity is asking to offered as an option for the home screen. Press the Home button, and NerdLauncher will be offered as an option.

(If you make NerdLauncher the home screen and later want to change it back, go to Settings →
Applications → Manage Applications. Select All to find NerdLauncher and then scroll down to Launch

by default to clear the defaults. The next time you press the Home button, you will be offered a choice and can select another default.)

Challenge: Icons, Reordering Tasks

You used **ResolveInfo.loadLabel(…)** in this chapter to present useful names in your launcher. **ResolveInfo** provides a similar method called **loadIcon()** that retrieves an icon to display for each application. For a small challenge, add an icon for each application to NerdLauncher.

If you are interested in doing more, you can add another activity to NerdLauncher that switches between running tasks. To do this, use the **ActivityManager** system service, which provides information about currently running activities, tasks, and applications. Unlike **PackageManager**, **Activity** provides no **getActivityManager()** convenience method for getting at this system service.

Instead, call **Activity.getSystemService()** with the Activity.ACTIVITY_SERVICE constant as a parameter to retrieve **ActivityManager**. Call **getRunningTasks()** on **ActivityManager** to get a list of running tasks in order from most to least recently run. To switch one of those tasks to the foreground, call **moveTaskToFront()**. Make sure to check out Android's reference documentation here – to switch between tasks, you will need to add another permission to your manifest.

For the More Curious: Processes vs. Tasks

All objects need memory and a virtual machine to live in. A *process* is a place created by the OS for your application's objects to live and for your application to run.

Processes may own resources managed by the OS like memory, network sockets, and open files. Processes also have at least one, possibly many, threads of execution. On Android, your process will also always have exactly one *Dalvik virtual machine* running.

While there are some obscure exceptions, in general every application component in Android is associated with exactly one process. Your application is created with its own process, and this is the default process for all components in your application.

You can assign individual components to different processes, but we recommend sticking to the default process. If you think you need something running in a different process, you can usually achieve the same ends with multi-threading, which is more straightforward to program in Android than using multiple processes.

Every activity instance lives in exactly one process and in exactly one task. That is where the similarities end, though. Tasks only contain activities and often consist of activities from different applications. Processes, on the other hand, contain all running code and objects in an application.

It can be easy to confuse processes and tasks because there is some overlap between the two ideas and both are often referred to by an application name. For instance, when you launched CriminalIntent from NerdLauncher, the OS created a CriminalIntent process and a new task for which **CrimeListActivity** is the base activity. In the task manager, this task is labeled CriminalIntent.

The task that an activity lives in can be different from the process it lives in. When you launched the contacts application to choose a suspect in CriminalIntent, it was launched into the CriminalIntent task. However, it was running in the contacts application's process.

Figure 23.6 Tasks and processes

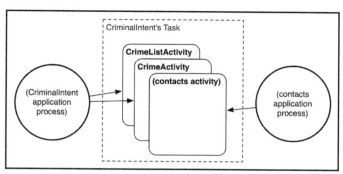

This means that when your user presses the Back button to navigate between different activities, he or she may be unknowingly switching between processes. Which is nifty.

In this chapter, you created tasks and switched between them. What about *killing* tasks or replacing Android's default task manager? Unfortunately, Android doesn't provide any way to do either of these things. A long press on the Home button is hard-wired to the default task manager, and tasks cannot be killed. Processes, on the other hand, *can* be killed. Apps advertised on the Google Play store as task killers are, in fact, process killers.

24

Styles And Includes

While your first priority is making your app function well, you also have to pay attention to how it looks and how it feels to use. The app marketplace is huge and you can distinguish your app with a nice UI.

Even if a specialist designs the UI, you will have to implement it. So in this chapter you will become familiar with some tools that you can use to quickly prototype a design on your own. When you do work with a graphic designer, you will know what to ask for, and how to use the resources that they create.

In these two chapters, you will create a television remote control app. However, it will not actually control anything; it is just a playground for practicing using design tools. In this chapter, you will use styles and includes to create the remote shown in Figure 24.1.

Figure 24.1 RemoteControl

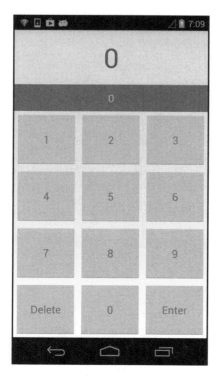

RemoteControl will have the single activity seen above. The area at the top will display the current channel. The area underneath will display a new channel as it is being entered. Pressing Delete will clear out the channel entry display. Pressing Enter will change the channel, updating the current channel display and clearing the channel entry display.

Setting Up the RemoteControl Project

Create a new Android Application project and begin configuring it as shown in Figure 24.2.

Figure 24.2 RemoteControl

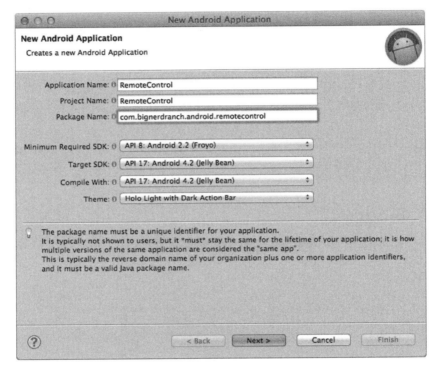

Then have the wizard create a blank activity named **RemoteControlActivity**.

Setting up RemoteControlActivity

RemoteControlActivity will be a **SingleFragmentActivity** subclass, so copy SingleFragmentActivity.java from CriminalIntent into the com.bignerdranch.android.remotecontrol package. Then copy activity_fragment.xml into RemoteControl's res/layout directory.

Open RemoteControlActivity.java. Make **RemoteControlActivity** a subclass of **SingleFragmentActivity** that creates a **RemoteControlFragment**. (You will create that fragment class in just a moment.) Finally, override **RemoteControlActivity.onCreate(…)** to hide the activity's action or title bar.

Listing 24.1 **RemoteControlActivity** set-up
(RemoteControlActivity.java)

```java
public class RemoteControlActivity extends Activity SingleFragmentActivity {
    @Override
    public void onCreate(Bundle savedInstanceState) {
        super.onCreate(savedInstanceState);
        setContentView(R.layout.activity_remote_control);
    }

    @Override
    public boolean onCreateOptionsMenu(Menu menu) {
        getMenuInflater().inflate(R.menu.activity_remote_control, menu);
        return true;
    }

    @Override
    protected Fragment createFragment() {
        return new RemoteControlFragment();
    }

    @Override
    public void onCreate(Bundle savedInstanceState) {
        requestWindowFeature(Window.FEATURE_NO_TITLE);
        super.onCreate(savedInstanceState);
    }
}
```

Next, open AndroidManifest.xml and limit this activity to portrait orientation:

Listing 24.2 Lock to portrait orientation (AndroidManifest.xml)

```xml
<activity
    android:name="com.bignerdranch.android.remotecontrol.RemoteControlActivity"
    android:label="@string/app_name"
    android:screenOrientation="portrait">
    <intent-filter>
        <action android:name="android.intent.action.MAIN" />

        <category android:name="android.intent.category.LAUNCHER" />
    </intent-filter>
</activity>
```

Setting up RemoteControlFragment

In the package explorer, rename activity_remote_control.xml to fragment_remote_control.xml.
At first, you are going to create a three-button remote control to keep things simple. Replace the
contents of fragment_remote_control.xml with the XML shown in Listing 24.3.

Listing 24.3 Initial three-button layout (layout/
fragment_remote_control.xml)

```xml
<RelativeLayout xmlns:android="http://schemas.android.com/apk/res/android"
```

```
~~xmlns:tools="http://schemas.android.com/tools"~~
~~android:layout_width="match_parent"~~
~~android:layout_height="match_parent"~~
~~tools:context=".RemoteControlActivity" >~~

~~<TextView~~
  ~~android:layout_width="wrap_content"~~
  ~~android:layout_height="wrap_content"~~
  ~~android:layout_centerHorizontal="true"~~
  ~~android:layout_centerVertical="true"~~
  ~~android:text="@string/hello_world" />~~

~~</RelativeLayout>~~
<TableLayout xmlns:android="http://schemas.android.com/apk/res/android"
  android:id="@+id/fragment_remote_control_tableLayout"
  android:layout_width="match_parent"
  android:layout_height="match_parent"
  android:stretchColumns="*" >
  <TextView
    android:id="@+id/fragment_remote_control_selectedTextView"
    android:layout_width="match_parent"
    android:layout_height="0dp"
    android:layout_weight="2"
    android:gravity="center"
    android:text="0"
    android:textSize="50dp" />
  <TextView
    android:id="@+id/fragment_remote_control_workingTextView"
    android:layout_width="match_parent"
    android:layout_height="0dp"
    android:layout_weight="1"
    android:layout_margin="15dp"
    android:background="#555555"
    android:gravity="center"
    android:text="0"
    android:textColor="#cccccc"
    android:textSize="20dp" />
  <TableRow android:layout_weight="1" >
    <Button
      android:id="@+id/fragment_remote_control_zeroButton"
      android:layout_width="0dp"
      android:layout_height="match_parent"
      android:text="0" />
    <Button
      android:id="@+id/fragment_remote_control_oneButton"
      android:layout_width="0dp"
      android:layout_height="match_parent"
      android:text="1" />
    <Button
      android:id="@+id/fragment_remote_control_enterButton"
      android:layout_width="0dp"
      android:layout_height="match_parent"
      android:text="Enter" />
  </TableRow>
</TableLayout>
```

Note that android:stretchColumns="*" ensures that your columns will be the same width. Also, you are using dp units for your text size instead of sp. This means the text will be the same size regardless of the user's settings.

Finally, create a new class named **RemoteControlFragment**. Make its superclass **android.support.v4.app.Fragment**. In RemoteControlFragment.java, override **onCreateView(…)** to wire up the buttons.

Listing 24.4 **RemoteControlFragment** set-up (RemoteControlFragment.java)

```java
public class RemoteControlFragment extends Fragment {
    private TextView mSelectedTextView;
    private TextView mWorkingTextView;

    @Override
    public View onCreateView(LayoutInflater inflater, ViewGroup parent,
            Bundle savedInstanceState) {
        View v = inflater.inflate(R.layout.fragment_remote_control, parent, false);

        mSelectedTextView = (TextView)v
                .findViewById(R.id.fragment_remote_control_selectedTextView);
        mWorkingTextView = (TextView)v
                .findViewById(R.id.fragment_remote_control_workingTextView);

        View.OnClickListener numberButtonListener = new View.OnClickListener() {
            public void onClick(View v) {
                TextView textView = (TextView)v;
                String working = mWorkingTextView.getText().toString();
                String text = textView.getText().toString();
                if (working.equals("0")) {
                    mWorkingTextView.setText(text);
                } else {
                    mWorkingTextView.setText(working + text);
                }
            }
        };

        Button zeroButton = (Button)v
            .findViewById(R.id.fragment_remote_control_zeroButton);
        zeroButton.setOnClickListener(numberButtonListener);

        Button oneButton = (Button)v
            .findViewById(R.id.fragment_remote_control_oneButton);
        oneButton.setOnClickListener(numberButtonListener);

        Button enterButton = (Button) v
            .findViewById(R.id.fragment_remote_control_enterButton);
        enterButton.setOnClickListener(new View.OnClickListener() {
            public void onClick(View v) {
                CharSequence working = mWorkingTextView.getText();
                if (working.length() > 0)
                    mSelectedTextView.setText(working);
                mWorkingTextView.setText("0");
            }
        });

        return v;
    }
}
```

While you have three buttons here, you only need two click listeners. That is because you can use the same click listener for both number buttons. When you click a number button, you either add another number to the working text view or replace it with the number you clicked, depending on whether 0 is the current entered text. Then when you press Enter, the working text is moved to the selected text view and cleared out.

Run RemoteControl. You should see a simple three-button remote control app with a binary interface. Who needs more than two buttons, anyway?

Figure 24.3 If it was good enough for Philo T. Farnsworth...

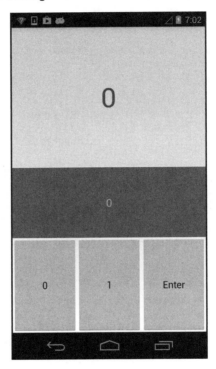

Cleaning Up with Styles

Now that you have a working project, take a look at your layout XML. Each button is identical. That is fine for now, but if you want to add an attribute to a button, you will have to repeat your work three times. And what about when you have twelve buttons?

Happily, Android has UI styles, which are meant to eliminate that repetition. Style resources are similar to CSS styles. Each style defines a set of XML attribute-value pairs. Styles can be organized into a hierarchy: a child has the same attributes and values as its parent, but may override them or add additional values.

Like string resources, styles are defined inside of a <resources> tag in an XML file in your res/ values folder. Also like strings, the filename is unimportant, but by convention styles are put in styles.xml.

The Android project wizard has created a styles.xml file for you already. (Notice that this file already defines the RemoteControl app's theme – a stock Android one – which sets the look of the buttons, backgrounds, and other common elements.)

You are now going to move the attributes that are common to all your buttons out of the individual buttons and into a new RemoteButton style. Add your new style to the style file as shown below.

Listing 24.5 Initial RemoteControl styles (values/styles.xml)

```xml
<resources>

  <style name="AppTheme" parent="android:Theme.Light" />

  <style name="RemoteButton">
    <item name="android:layout_width">0dp</item>
    <item name="android:layout_height">match_parent</item>
  </style>

</resources>
```

Each style is defined by a `<style>` element with one or more `<item>` elements. Each item has a name, which is the name of an XML attribute, and the text inside the element is the value to apply to the attribute.

You only have one style here, called RemoteButton, and it does not do much. Just wait, this style soon will have you styling.

To use a style, you refer to it in a style attribute on a view in your layout. Modify fragment_remote_control.xml to delete your old attributes and use your new style instead:

Listing 24.6 Applying styles (layout/fragment_remote_control.xml)

```xml
<TableLayout xmlns:android="http://schemas.android.com/apk/res/android"
  ...
  >

  ...

  <TableRow android:layout_weight="1" >
    <Button
      android:id="@+id/fragment_remote_control_zeroButton"
      android:layout_width="0dp"
      android:layout_height="match_parent"
      style="@style/RemoteButton"
      android:text="0" />
    <Button
      android:id="@+id/fragment_remote_control_oneButton"
      android:layout_width="0dp"
      android:layout_height="match_parent"
      style="@style/RemoteButton"
      android:text="1" />
    <Button
      android:id="@+id/fragment_remote_control_enterButton"
      android:layout_width="0dp"
      android:layout_height="match_parent"
      style="@style/RemoteButton"
      android:text="Enter" />
  </TableRow>
</TableLayout>
```

Run RemoteControl. Your remote looks exactly the same as it did before. But your layout looks cleaner and you are repeating yourself less.

Finishing the Layout

Now that you have your styles set up, you can save some serious time. Let's flesh out the remote control interface to a full, luxurious 12-key version, complete with ten deluxe decimal digits.

Now you need to create a 3 x 4 array of nearly identical buttons. But there's no need to code them all individually. You can create one row of three buttons and then use it four times. Create a new file called `res/layout/button_row.xml` and move the row of buttons you have already defined into it.

Listing 24.7 A row of three buttons (`layout/button_row.xml`)

```xml
<?xml version="1.0" encoding="utf-8"?>
<TableRow xmlns:android="http://schemas.android.com/apk/res/android" >
  <Button style="@style/RemoteButton" />
  <Button style="@style/RemoteButton" />
  <Button style="@style/RemoteButton" />
</TableRow>
```

Now, you just need to "include" this row into the layout four times. How do you do that? With the `include` tag:

Listing 24.8 Including the button rows in the main layout (`layout/fragment_remote_control.xml`)

```xml
  <TableRow android:layout_weight="1" >
    <Button
      android:id="@+id/fragment_remote_control_zeroButton"
      style="@style/RemoteButton"
      android:text="0" />
    <Button
      android:id="@+id/fragment_remote_control_oneButton"
      style="@style/RemoteButton"
      android:text="1" />
    <Button
      android:id="@+id/fragment_remote_control_enterButton"
      style="@style/RemoteButton"
      android:text="Enter" />
  </TableRow>
  <include
    android:layout_weight="1"
    layout="@layout/button_row" />
  <include
    android:layout_weight="1"
    layout="@layout/button_row" />
  <include
    android:layout_weight="1"
    layout="@layout/button_row" />
  <include
    android:layout_weight="1"
    layout="@layout/button_row" />
```

You may have noticed that the three buttons you defined in `layout/button_row.xml` did not have ids. Since you included this button row four times, if you had given the buttons ids, then they would not be unique. Similarly, the buttons do not have any text defined. It's okay, you can handle it all in code. Now rewire the buttons and set their text using this code.

Listing 24.9 Wiring up the number buttons (RemoteControlFragment.java)

```
View.OnClickListener numberButtonListener = new View.OnClickListener() {
    ...
};

Button zeroButton = (Button)v.findViewById(R.id.fragment_remote_control_zeroButton);
zeroButton.setOnClickListener(numberButtonListener);

Button oneButton = (Button)v.findViewById(R.id.fragment_remote_control_oneButton);
oneButton.setOnClickListener(numberButtonListener);
TableLayout tableLayout = (TableLayout)v
        .findViewById(R.id.fragment_remote_control_tableLayout);
int number = 1;
for (int i = 2; i < tableLayout.getChildCount() - 1; i++) {
    TableRow row = (TableRow)tableLayout.getChildAt(i);
    for (int j = 0; j < row.getChildCount(); j++) {
        Button button = (Button)row.getChildAt(j);
        button.setText("" + number);
        button.setOnClickListener(numberButtonListener);
        number++;
    }
}
```

The for loop starts at index 2 to skip the two text views and then steps through each button in the first three rows. For each button, it sets the same numberButtonListener you created earlier and sets the text to a string of the appropriate number.

That takes care of three rows of buttons. The last row is trickier: you have to deal with the special cases of the Delete and Enter buttons. Finish things up:

Listing 24.10 Wiring up the last row (RemoteControlFragment.java)

```
for (int i = 2; i < tableLayout.getChildCount() - 1; i++) {
    ...
}

TableRow bottomRow = (TableRow)tableLayout
        .getChildAt(tableLayout.getChildCount() - 1);

Button deleteButton = (Button)bottomRow.getChildAt(0);
deleteButton.setText("Delete");
deleteButton.setOnClickListener(new View.OnClickListener() {
    public void onClick(View v) {
        mWorkingTextView.setText("0");
    }
});

Button zeroButton = (Button)bottomRow.getChildAt(1);
zeroButton.setText("0");
zeroButton.setOnClickListener(numberButtonListener);

Button enterButton = (Button)
        v.findViewById(R.id.fragment_remote_control_enterButton);
Button enterButton = (Button)bottomRow.getChildAt(2);
enterButton.setText("Enter");
enterButton.setOnClickListener(new View.OnClickListener() {
    ...
});
```

You have a fully functioning non-functional remote. Run your app and play with it. We leave the work of connecting wirelessly to an actual television as an exercise for the reader.

Figure 24.4 The channel that gives meaning to life

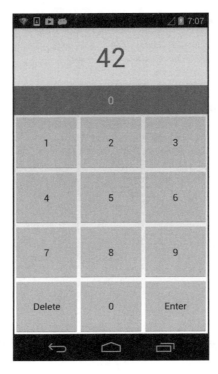

Now that you have your buttons styled, you can change their look in one fell swoop. Add these three lines to your RemoteButton style:

Listing 24.11 Tweaking your style a little bit (values/styles.xml)

```xml
<style name="RemoteButton">
  <item name="android:layout_width">0dp</item>
  <item name="android:layout_height">match_parent</item>
  <item name="android:textColor">#556699</item>
  <item name="android:textSize">20dp</item>
  <item name="android:layout_margin">3dp</item>
</style>
```

Bazam – you are the button king.

Figure 24.5 They all look the same!

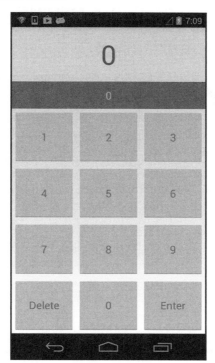

For the More Curious: include and merge

Earlier in the chapter you used the include tag to include a row of RemoteButtons multiple times (into the same layout). It works in the obvious way:

```
<include layout="@layout/some_partial_layout"/>
```

The above include will include the contents of the layout file whose resource ID is @layout/ some_partial_layout.

You can use include to reduce duplication in a single layout, as you did earlier in this chapter, or you can use it to reduce duplication between layouts. If you have some chunk of a layout that occurs in two or more layouts, you can just create that chunk as a layout and include it wherever it is needed. Then when you need to update it, you only have to do it in a single place.

There are two more things you should know about include. First, the layout that you include will go through the normal resource search based on the current device configuration. So you can use configuration qualifiers just like with any layout. Second, you can override the android:id and any android:layout_* attributes of the root element of the included layout by specifying them on the include tag itself. This allows you to include the same layout multiple times and use different attributes each time you include it.

The merge element works with the include element. merge can be used as the root element of an included layout instead of an actual widget. When one layout includes another layout that has merge as its root element, the children of the merge element are directly included – they become children of the parent of the include element and the merge element is discarded.

This is simpler than it sounds. If it is confusing, just remember that the merge element is discarded. It is only there to satisfy the XML requirement that there be a single instance of the root element.

Challenge: Style Inheritance

Your Delete and Enter buttons are sitting modestly at the bottom of the screen with the same style as all the number buttons. These "action" buttons need a bolder style.

For this small challenge, make those buttons look special. Create a new button style that inherits from your RemoteButton style and sets a bold text style attribute. Then make your bottom row use your new style for the first and third buttons.

Creating a style that inherits from another is simple. There are two ways to do it. One is to set the parent attribute of your style to the name of the style you want to inherit from. The easier way is to just prefix your style name with your parent's style, then a dot – e.g., ParentStyleName.MyStyleName.

25

XML Drawables And 9-Patches

In the last chapter, you quickly built a TV remote control interface using advanced layout tips and tricks. It looks okay, but maybe a little drab because it uses the stock Android look and feel for all of its buttons. In this chapter, you will use two new tools to give it a completely unique look and feel.

Figure 25.1 RemoteControl makeover

Both of these tools are *drawables*. Android calls anything that is intended to be drawn to the screen a drawable, whether it is an abstract shape, a clever bit of code that subclasses the **Drawable** class, or a bitmap image. You have already seen one kind of drawable: **BitmapDrawable**, which wraps an image. In this chapter, you will see a few more kinds of drawables: *state list drawables*, *shape drawables*, *layer list drawables*, and *nine patch drawables*. Since the first three are usually defined in XML files, we group them together in the broader category of *XML drawables*.

XML Drawables

Before you tackle any XML drawables, try this: use the android:background attribute to change the background color of your buttons.

Listing 25.1 An attempt at changing the button's color (values/styles.xml)

```
<style name="RemoteButton">
  <item name="android:layout_width">0dp</item>
  <item name="android:layout_height">match_parent</item>
  <item name="android:textColor">#556699</item>
  <item name="android:textSize">20dp</item>
  <item name="android:layout_margin">3dp</item>
  <item name="android:background">#ccd7ee</item>
</style>
```

You should see something like this:

Figure 25.2 What happened?

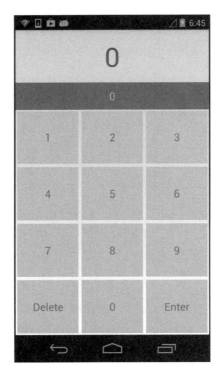

The 3-dimensional look of the buttons is gone. If you press one of them, you will find that it no longer changes its appearance when you press it, either.

Why did all that happen from one innocent attribute change? The **Button** class is not much more than a **View** with a default style applied to it. The style comes from whatever theme you have selected, and sets a **Drawable** as the background. That background drawable was responsible for the 3-D look and the appearance change. By the end of this chapter, you will know how to make your own drawables that are just as capable.

You will start by creating colored shapes with **ShapeDrawable**s in XML. Since XML drawables are not density specific, they are usually placed in the default drawable folder instead of a density-specific one.

In the package explorer, create a default res/drawable directory. In this directory, create a new XML file named button_shape_normal.xml. Make its root element shape. (Why is this one "normal"? Because soon it will have a not-so-normal friend.)

Listing 25.2 Making a shape drawable button (drawable/ button_shape_normal.xml)

```xml
<?xml version="1.0" encoding="utf-8"?>
<shape xmlns:android="http://schemas.android.com/apk/res/android"
  android:shape="rectangle" >

  <corners android:radius="3dp" />

  <gradient
    android:angle="90"
    android:endColor="#cccccc"
    android:startColor="#acacac" />

</shape>
```

This file defines a rounded rectangle. The corners element specifies the corner radius for your rounded rectangle, and the gradient elements specify the direction and the start and end colors for a color gradient.

You can use shape to create other shapes, such as ovals, lines, and rings, and give them different looks. Check out the documentation at http://developer.android.com/guide/topics/resources/ drawable-resource.html for details.

In styles.xml, update your Button style to use your new **Drawable** as a background.

Listing 25.3 Update button style (values/styles.xml)

```xml
  <style name="RemoteButton">
    <item name="android:layout_width">0dp</item>
    <item name="android:layout_height">match_parent</item>
    <item name="android:textColor">#556699</item>
    <item name="android:textSize">20dp</item>
    <item name="android:layout_margin">3dp</item>
    <item name="android:background">#ccd7ee</item>
    <item name="android:background">@drawable/button_shape_normal</item>
  </style>
```

Run RemoteControl and see the difference.

Figure 25.3 Now with rounded-corner buttons

State List Drawables

As good as they look, these buttons are still static. Under the covers, the old **Button** background was using a *state list drawable*. State list drawables allow you to display a different drawable for each state its associated **View** is in. (You previously used a state list drawable to change the background of list items in Chapter 18.) There are a lot of different states, but here you are only interested in whether the button is being pressed or not.

Start off by creating the look for your pressed button. This look will be same as the normal button look except for the color.

In the package explorer, make a copy of button_shape_normal.xml and name it button_shape_pressed.xml. Open button_shape_pressed.xml and add 180 degrees to the angle to switch the direction of the gradient:

Listing 25.4 Creating the shape for a pressed button (drawable/button_shape_pressed.xml)

```xml
<?xml version="1.0" encoding="utf-8"?>
<shape xmlns:android="http://schemas.android.com/apk/res/android"
  android:shape="rectangle" >

  <corners android:radius="3dp" />

  <gradient
    android:angle="90"
    android:angle="270"
    android:endColor="#cccccc"
    android:startColor="#acacac" />

</shape>
```

Next you need a state list drawable. A state list drawable must have a selector root element and one or more item elements that describe different states. Right-click res/drawable/, create a new XML file named button_shape.xml, and give it a selector root element.

Listing 25.5 Creating an interactive button shape (drawable/button_shape.xml)

```xml
<?xml version="1.0" encoding="utf-8"?>
<selector xmlns:android="http://schemas.android.com/apk/res/android">
  <item android:drawable="@drawable/button_shape_normal"
    android:state_pressed="false"/>
  <item android:drawable="@drawable/button_shape_pressed"
    android:state_pressed="true"/>
</selector>
```

The unpressed button has dark text, which used to work well against a light background. Now that the background is darker, a light color will look better when the button is unpressed, and you can use the dark color with the pressed background. You can create state list colors as well as state list shapes, so this is easy to do.

Right-click res/drawable/ and create another state list drawable named button_text_color.xml.

Listing 25.6 State-sensitive button text color (drawable/button_text_color.xml)

```xml
<?xml version="1.0" encoding="utf-8"?>
<selector xmlns:android="http://schemas.android.com/apk/res/android">
    <item android:state_pressed="false" android:color="#ffffff"/>
    <item android:state_pressed="true" android:color="#556699"/>
</selector>
```

Now, in styles.xml, change your Button style to point to your new background drawable and your new text color.

Listing 25.7 Updating the button style (values/styles.xml)

```
<style name="RemoteButton">
  <item name="android:layout_width">0dp</item>
  <item name="android:layout_height">match_parent</item>
  <item name="android:textColor">#556699</item>
  <item name="android:textSize">20dp</item>
  <item name="android:layout_margin">3dp</item>
  <item name="android:background">@drawable/button_shape_normal</item>
  <item name="android:background">@drawable/button_shape</item>
  <item name="android:textColor">@drawable/button_text_color</item>
</style>
```

Run RemoteControl. Check out the new look of your pressed button.

Figure 25.4 A pressed button

Layer List and Inset Drawables

The stock Android buttons you saw in the initial version of your app had a shadow effect. Unfortunately, shape drawables have no shadow property. But you can make the shadow effect yourself using two other XML drawable types: *layer list drawables* and *inset drawables*.

Here is how you will do it. First, you will create a shadow with the same shape as your current button drawable. Then you will combine it with the current button using layer-list, and offset the bottom edge of the button a tad using inset so that the shadow becomes visible underneath.

Create a new XML file in res/drawable/. Name it button_shape_shadowed.xml and make its root element layer-list.

Listing 25.8 Normal button shadows (drawable/button_shape_shadowed.xml)

```xml
<?xml version="1.0" encoding="utf-8"?>
<layer-list xmlns:android="http://schemas.android.com/apk/res/android" >
  <item>
    <shape android:shape="rectangle" >
      <corners android:radius="5dp" />

      <gradient
        android:angle="90"
        android:centerColor="#303339"
        android:centerY="0.05"
        android:endColor="#000000"
        android:startColor="#00000000" />
    </shape>
  </item>
  <item>
    <inset
      android:drawable="@drawable/button_shape"
      android:insetBottom="5dp" />
  </item>
</layer-list>
```

The layer list contains multiple **Drawable**s, ordered from back to front as they will be drawn on the screen. The second drawable in your list is an inset drawable. All it does is inset the bottom of the drawable you already created by 5dp, so that it sits above the shadow you created.

Notice also that instead of using separate files for your shadow drawable, you directly embedded it in the layer list. This technique works just as well for other drawables, too, like your state list drawable above. Whether to nest your drawables or break them out into their own files as you did earlier is a judgment call. Breaking them out can reduce code duplication and simplify each file, but it also litters your drawable/ folder with additional files. Write whatever you find easiest to read and understand.

In styles.xml, change your button style to point at the new shadowed drawable.

Listing 25.9 Change button style one last time (values/styles.xml)

```xml
<style name="RemoteButton">
  <item name="android:layout_width">0dp</item>
  <item name="android:layout_height">match_parent</item>
  <item name="android:textSize">20dp</item>
  <item name="android:layout_margin">3dp</item>
  <item name="android:background">@drawable/button_shape</item>
  <item name="android:background">@drawable/button_shape_shadowed</item>
  <item name="android:textColor">@drawable/button_text_color</item>
</style>
```

One last change: create a gradient drawable for the entire main view, for a subtle lighting effect. Create a new drawable file named remote_background.xml with a shape root element. Then add the following to it. (Note: if a shape is not specified, rectangle is assumed.)

Listing 25.10 New background drawable for the root view (drawable/ remote_background.xml)

```xml
<?xml version="1.0" encoding="utf-8"?>
<shape xmlns:android="http://schemas.android.com/apk/res/android" >
  <gradient
    android:centerY="0.05"
    android:endColor="#dbdbdb"
    android:gradientRadius="500"
    android:startColor="#f4f4e9"
    android:type="radial" />
</shape>
```

Edit the fragment_remote_control.xml file to include the new drawable.

Listing 25.11 Applying the drawable to the layout (layout/ fragment_remote_control.xml)

```xml
<TableLayout xmlns:android="http://schemas.android.com/apk/res/android"
  xmlns:tools="http://schemas.android.com/tools"
  android:id="@+id/fragment_remote_control_tableLayout"
  android:layout_width="match_parent"
  android:layout_height="match_parent"
  android:background="@drawable/remote_background"
  android:stretchColumns="*" >
```

Throughout all of these changes, you haven't done anything to the fragment layout file. (Except for that last change, and of course you could have made a new style for the **TableLayout** itself.) This is good, since you aren't changing the content of the layout, but its presentation. Adding new buttons or moving things around would require you to update the layout file, but changes to the look you can do in the style instead.

Using 9-Patch Images

If you enlist a professional designer to craft your UI, what they give you may not be achievable with XML drawables. It may still be possible to reuse the rendered asset in multiple places, though. For stretchable UI elements like button backgrounds, Android provides a tool called the 9-patch.

Your next task is to fix up the two **TextView**s at the top of the screen. You will keep your button layout the same, but use stretchable drawables for their backgrounds. Both of them are much narrower than your **TextView**s, so that they do not take up much space. The first one, window.png, is a stretchable background designed to give your **TextView** a tasteful fade, along with some border space on the edges.

Figure 25.5 Channel display window

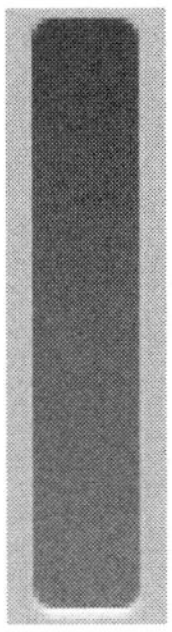

The other, `bar.png`, gives a small shadow at the bottom and a thin border at the top. We have zoomed in on it quite a bit – it is pretty small.

Figure 25.6 Channel entry area

You can find these images in the solutions file in the `25_XMLDrawables/RemoteControl/res/drawable-hdpi directory`. Copy them into RemoteControl's `/res/drawable-hdpi` folder.

Modify the `fragment_remote_control.xml` file to include these images as backgrounds for the appropriate views. Change the text colors to something more appropriate to the new backgrounds, too – switch the top one to white, and switch the bottom one back to the default, black. And then set the bottom **TextView** to italics, because it looks neat.

Listing 25.12 Adding the drawables to the styles (layout/ fragment_remote_control.xml)

```xml
<TableLayout xmlns:android="http://schemas.android.com/apk/res/android"
  ... >
  <TextView
    android:id="@+id/fragment_remote_control_selectedTextView"
    android:layout_width="match_parent"
    android:layout_height="0dp"
    android:layout_weight="2"
    android:background="@drawable/window"
    android:gravity="center"
    android:text="0"
    android:textColor="#ffffff"
    android:textSize="50dp" />
  <TextView
    android:id="@+id/fragment_remote_control_workingTextView"
    android:layout_width="match_parent"
    android:layout_height="0dp"
    android:layout_margin="15dp"
    android:layout_weight="1"
    android:background="#555555"
    android:background="@drawable/bar"
    android:gravity="center"
    android:text="0"
    android:textColor="#cccccc"
    android:textStyle="italic"
    android:textSize="20dp" />
  ...
</TableLayout>
```

Check out what happens when you run the app:

Figure 25.7 Shattered dreams

Each image was evenly stretched in all dimensions to fill the view. In some cases that is exactly what you want, but not here. Your images are all fuzzed out, and your bottom **TextView**'s digits are not properly centered.

You can use *9-patch* images to fix this problem. A 9-patch image file is specially formatted so that Android knows which portions can and cannot be scaled. Done properly, this ensures that the edges and corners of your background remain consistent with the image as it was created.

Why are they called 9-patches? A 9-patch breaks your image into a 3 x 3 grid – a grid with 9 sections, or patches. The corners of the grid remain unscaled, the sides are only scaled in one dimension, and the center is scaled in both dimensions.

Figure 25.8 What a 9-patch does

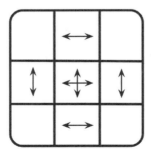

A 9-patch image is like a regular png image in everything except two aspects: its filename ends with .9.png, and it has an additional one pixel border around the edge. This border is used to specify the location of the center square of the nine patch. Border pixels are drawn black to indicate the center and transparent to indicate the edges.

You can create a 9-patch using any image editor, but it is easier to use the draw9patch tool provided as part of the Android SDK. You can find it in the tools directory of your SDK installation. Once it's running, you can drag files into it or open them from the File menu.

Once the file is open, fill in black pixels on the top and left borders to mark the stretchable regions of the image. Add pixels to window.png as seen below.

Figure 25.9 Channel display window 9-patch

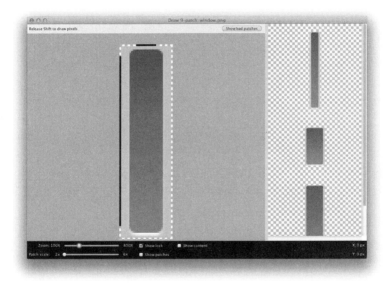

The top and left borders mark the stretchable region of the image. What about the bottom and right borders? They define an optional drawable region for the 9-patch image. The drawable region is the area where content (usually text) should be rendered. If you do not include a drawable region, it defaults to be the same as your stretchable region. This is what you want here, so you omit the drawable region.

When you are done, save your results to a file called window_patch.9.png. Be careful that your 9-patch files do not conflict with your other images – your application would fail to build if you had one file named window.9.png and another named window.png.

Next, edit a 9-patch for bar.png. Use the drawable region here to center your text properly vertically and horizontally, as well as provide for a 4 pixel margin on all sides.

Figure 25.10 Channel entry area 9-patch

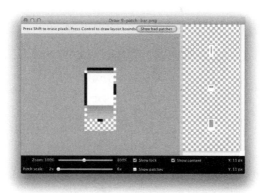

When you finish, save out to bar_patch.9.png.

Next, right-click your res/ folder and click Refresh. Eclipse lives in its own little world, and Refresh reminds it to wake up and look at the file system again.

Finally, switch your two **TextView**s over to use your 9-patch drawables instead of the plain old images.

Listing 25.13 Switch to use 9-patches (layout/ fragment_remote_control.xml)

```
<TableLayout xmlns:android="http://schemas.android.com/apk/res/android"
  ... >
  <TextView
    android:id="@+id/fragment_remote_control_selectedTextView"
    android:layout_width="match_parent"
    android:layout_height="0dp"
    android:layout_weight="2"
    android:background="@drawable/window"
    android:background="@drawable/window_patch"
    android:gravity="center"
    android:text="0"
    android:textSize="50dp" />
  <TextView
    android:id="@+id/fragment_remote_control_workingTextView"
    android:layout_width="match_parent"
    android:layout_height="0dp"
    android:layout_margin="15dp"
    android:layout_weight="1"
    android:background="@drawable/bar"
    android:background="@drawable/bar_patch"
    android:gravity="center"
    android:text="0"
    android:textColor="#cccccc"
    android:textSize="20dp" />
  ...
</TableLayout>
```

Run your app. Voilà! You now have working image backgrounds. Remember how plain your initial interface looked? It didn't take a whole lot of time to create something far more interesting. Imagine what you will be able to do with superior design work. Making your app a pleasure to look at makes it feel fine to use, and that will pay off in popularity.

Figure 25.11 RemoteControl made over

26

HTTP & Background Tasks

The apps that dominate the brains of users are networked apps. Those people fiddling with their phones instead of talking to each other at dinner? They are maniacally checking their newsfeeds, responding to text messages, or playing networked games.

To get started with networking in Android, you are going to create a new app called PhotoGallery. PhotoGallery is a client for the photo-sharing site Flickr. It will fetch and display the most recent public photos uploaded to Flickr. Figure 26.1 gives you an idea of what the app will look like.

Figure 26.1 Complete PhotoGallery

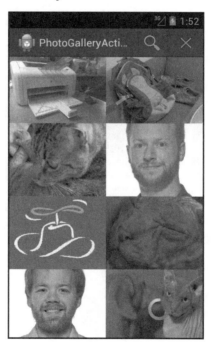

(Figure 26.1 shows photos that are ours instead of public photos from Flickr. The photos on Flickr are the property of the person who posted them and may not be re-used without that person's permission. To read more about permissions for using third-party content that you retrieve from Flickr, visit
`http://pressroom.yahoo.net/pr/ycorp/permissions.aspx`.)

You will spend six chapters with PhotoGallery. It will take two chapters for you to get the basics of downloading and parsing XML and displaying images up and running. Once that is done, in subsequent chapters you will add on additional features that explore search, services, notifications, broadcast receivers, and web views.

In this chapter, you will learn how to use Android's high-level HTTP networking. Almost all day-to-day programming of web services these days is based on the HTTP networking protocol. By the end of the chapter, you will be fetching, parsing, and displaying photo captions from Flickr. (Retrieving and displaying photos will happen in Chapter 27.)

Figure 26.2 PhotoGallery at the end of the chapter

Creating PhotoGallery

Create a new Android application project. Configure the app as shown in Figure 26.3.

Figure 26.3 Creating PhotoGallery

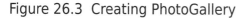

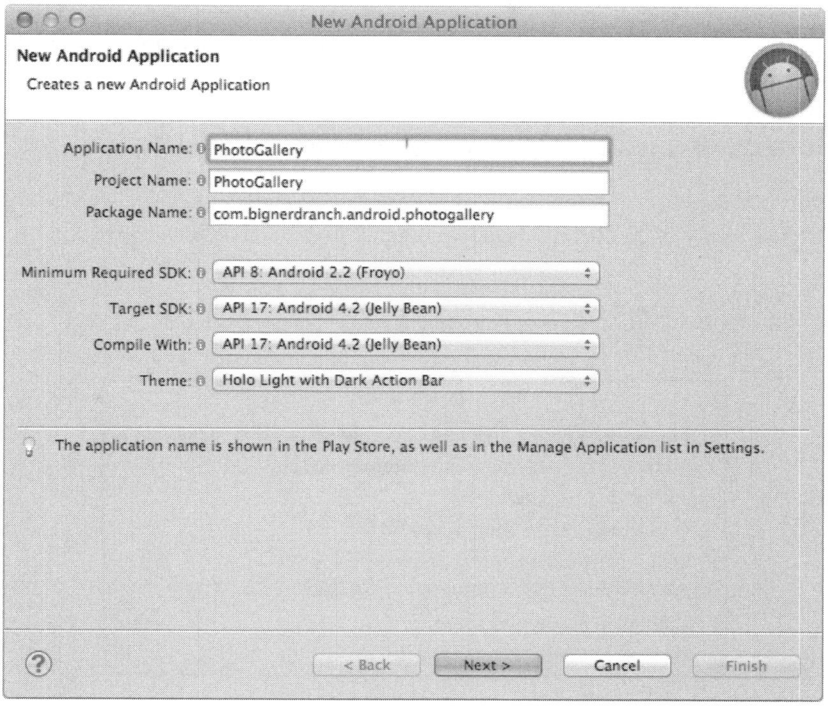

Then have the wizard create a blank activity named **PhotoGalleryActivity**.

PhotoGallery will follow the same architecture you have been using so far. **PhotoGalleryActivity** will be a **SingleFragmentActivity** subclass and its view will be the container view defined in activity_fragment.xml. This activity will host a fragment – in particular, an instance of **PhotoGalleryFragment**, which you will create shortly.

Copy SingleFragmentActivity.java and activity_fragment.xml into your project from a previous project.

In PhotoGalleryActivity.java, set up **PhotoGalleryActivity** as a **SingleFragmentActivity** by deleting the code that the template generated and replacing it with an implementation of **createFragment()**. Have **createFragment()** return an instance of **PhotoGalleryFragment**. (Bear with the error that this code will cause for the moment. It will go away after you create the **PhotoGalleryFragment** class.)

Listing 26.1 Activity setup (PhotoGalleryActivity.java)

```
public class PhotoGalleryActivity extends Activity {
public class PhotoGalleryActivity extends SingleFragmentActivity {

    /* Auto-generated template code */

    @Override
    public Fragment createFragment() {
        return new PhotoGalleryFragment();
    }
}
```

PhotoGallery will display its results in a **GridView**. This **GridView** will comprise the view for **PhotoGalleryFragment**.

GridView is an **AdapterView**, so it works much like **ListView**. However, unlike **ListView**, **GridView** has no handy dandy **GridFragment** to wire everything up for you. Which means that you will need to create a layout file and inflate it in **PhotoGalleryFragment**. Later in the chapter, you will wire up an adapter in **PhotoGalleryFragment** to feed the **GridView** photo captions to display.

To create a layout for the fragment, rename layout/activity_photo_gallery.xml to layout/fragment_photo_gallery.xml. Then replace its contents with the **GridView** shown in Figure 26.4.

Figure 26.4 A GridView (layout/fragment_photo_gallery.xml)

```
                          GridView
xmlns:android="http://schemas.android.com/apk/res/android"
xmlns:tools="http://schemas.android.com/tools"
android:id="@+id/gridView"
android:layout_width="match_parent"
android:layout_height="match_parent"
android:columnWidth="120dp"
android:numColumns="auto_fit"
android:stretchMode="columnWidth"
```

Here you set the width of the columns to 120dp and instruct the **GridView** to create as many columns as will fit on the screen. If there is a leftover chunk of space less than 120dp, the stretchMode attribute tells the **GridView** to divide the extra space equally among the columns.

Finally, create the **PhotoGalleryFragment** class. Retain the fragment, inflate the layout you just created, and get a reference to the **GridView** (Listing 26.2).

Listing 26.2 Some skeleton code (PhotoGalleryFragment.java)

```
package com.bignerdranch.android.photogallery;

...

public class PhotoGalleryFragment extends Fragment {
    GridView mGridView;

    @Override
    public void onCreate(Bundle savedInstanceState) {
        super.onCreate(savedInstanceState);

        setRetainInstance(true);
    }

    @Override
    public View onCreateView(LayoutInflater inflater, ViewGroup container,
            Bundle savedInstanceState) {
        View v = inflater.inflate(R.layout.fragment_photo_gallery, container, false);

        mGridView = (GridView)v.findViewById(R.id.gridView);

        return v;
    }
}
```

Fire up PhotoGallery to make sure everything is wired up correctly before moving on. If all is well, you will be the proud owner of a blank screen.

Networking Basics

You are going to have one class handle the networking in PhotoGallery. Create a new Java class. Since you will be connecting to Flickr, name this class **FlickrFetchr**.

FlickrFetchr will start off small with only two methods: **getUrlBytes(String)** and **getUrl(String)**. The **getUrlBytes(String)** method fetches raw data from a URL and returns it as an array of bytes. The **getUrl(String)** method converts the result from **getUrlBytes(String)** to a **String**.

In FlickrFetchr.java, add implementations for **getUrlBytes(String)** and **getUrl(String)** (Listing 26.3).

Listing 26.3 Basic networking code (FlickrFetchr.java)

```java
package com.bignerdranch.android.photogallery;

...

public class FlickrFetchr {
    byte[] getUrlBytes(String urlSpec) throws IOException {
        URL url = new URL(urlSpec);
        HttpURLConnection connection = (HttpURLConnection)url.openConnection();

        try {
            ByteArrayOutputStream out = new ByteArrayOutputStream();
            InputStream in = connection.getInputStream();

            if (connection.getResponseCode() != HttpURLConnection.HTTP_OK) {
                return null;
            }

            int bytesRead = 0;
            byte[] buffer = new byte[1024];
            while ((bytesRead = in.read(buffer)) > 0) {
                out.write(buffer, 0, bytesRead);
            }
            out.close();
            return out.toByteArray();
        } finally {
            connection.disconnect();
        }
    }

    public String getUrl(String urlSpec) throws IOException {
        return new String(getUrlBytes(urlSpec));
    }
}
```

This code creates a **URL** object from a string – like, say, http://www.google.com. Then it calls **openConnection()** to create a connection object pointed at the URL. **URL.openConnection()** returns a **URLConnection**, but since you are connecting to an http URL, you can cast it to **HttpURLConnection**. This gives you HTTP-specific interfaces for working with request methods, response codes, streaming methods, and more.

HttpURLConnection represents a connection, but it will not actually connect to your endpoint until you call **getInputStream()** (or **getOutputStream()** for POST calls). Until then, you cannot get a valid response code.

Once you create your URL and open a connection, you call **read()** repeatedly until your connection runs out of data. The **InputStream** will yield bytes as they are available. When you are done, you close it and spit out your **ByteArrayOutputStream**'s byte array.

While **getUrlBytes(String)** does the heavy lifting, **getUrl(String)** is what you will actually use in this chapter. It converts the bytes fetched by **getUrlBytes(String)** into a **String**. Right now, it may seem strange to split this work into two methods. However, having two methods will be useful in the next chapter when you start downloading image data.

Asking permission to network

One other thing is required to get networking up and running: you have to ask permission. Just as users would not want you secretly taking their pictures, they also do not want you to secretly download pictures of ASCII farm animals.

To ask permission to network, add the following permission to your AndroidManifest.xml.

Listing 26.4 Add networking permission to manifest (AndroidManifest.xml)

```
<manifest xmlns:android="http://schemas.android.com/apk/res/android"
  package="com.bignerdranch.android.photogallery"
  android:versionCode="1"
  android:versionName="1.0" >

  <uses-sdk
    android:minSdkVersion="8"
    android:targetSdkVersion="15" />
  <uses-permission android:name="android.permission.INTERNET" />

  ...

</manifest>
```

Using AsyncTask to Run on a Background Thread

The next step is to call and test the networking code you just added. However, you cannot simply call **FlickrFetchr.getURL(String)** directly in **PhotoGalleryFragment**. Instead, you need to create a background thread and run your code there.

The easiest way to work with a background thread is with a utility class called **AsyncTask**. **AsyncTask** creates a background thread for you and runs the code in the **doInBackground(…)** method on that thread.

In PhotoGalleryFragment.java, add a new inner class called **FetchItemsTask** at the bottom of **PhotoGalleryFragment**. Override **AsyncTask.doInBackground(…)** to get data from a website and log it. Then use the new class inside of **PhotoGalleryFragment.onCreate(…)**.

Listing 26.5 Writing an AsyncTask (PhotoGalleryFragment.java)

```java
public class PhotoGalleryFragment extends Fragment {
    private static final String TAG = "PhotoGalleryFragment";

    GridView mGridView;

    ...

    private class FetchItemsTask extends AsyncTask<Void,Void,Void> {
        @Override
        protected Void doInBackground(Void... params) {
            try {
                String result = new FlickrFetchr().getUrl("http://www.google.com");
                Log.i(TAG, "Fetched contents of URL: " + result);
            } catch (IOException ioe) {
                Log.e(TAG, "Failed to fetch URL: ", ioe);
            }
            return null;
        }
    }
}
```

Now, in **PhotoGalleryFragment.onCreate(…)**, call **execute()** on a new instance of **FetchItemsTask**.

Listing 26.6 Writing an AsyncTask (PhotoGalleryFragment.java)

```java
public class PhotoGalleryFragment extends Fragment {
    private static final String TAG = "PhotoGalleryFragment";

    GridView mGridView;
    @Override
    public void onCreate(Bundle savedInstanceState) {
        super.onCreate(savedInstanceState);

        setRetainInstance(true);
        new FetchItemsTask().execute();
    }

    ...

}
```

The call to **execute()** will start your **AsyncTask**, which will then fire up its background thread and call **doInBackground(…)**. Run your code and you should see Google's Javascriptlicious home page HTML pop up in LogCat, looking something like Figure 26.5:

Figure 26.5 Google HTML in LogCat

Now that you have created a background thread and run some networking code on it, let's take a closer look at threads in Android.

You and Your Main Thread

Networking does not happen immediately. A web server may take as long as a second or two to respond, and a file download can taken even longer than that. Because networking can take so long, Android disallows all networking on the *main thread* in Honeycomb and later versions of Android. If you try to do it, Android will throw a NetworkOnMainThreadException. Why? To understand that, you need to understand what a thread is, what the main thread is, and what the main thread does.

A thread is a single sequence of execution. Code running within a single thread will execute one step after another. Every Android app starts life with a *main thread*. The main thread, however, isn't a preordained list of steps. Instead, it sits in an infinite loop and waits for events initiated by the user or the system. Then it executes code in response to those events as they occur.

Figure 26.6 Regular threads vs. the main thread

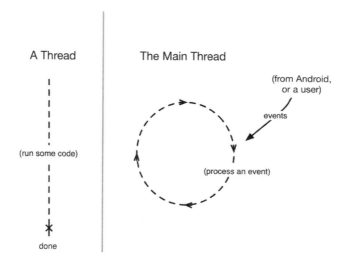

Imagine that your app is an enormous shoe store, and that you only have one employee – The Flash. (Who hasn't dreamed of that?) There are a lot of things to do in a store to keep the customers happy – arranging the merchandise, fetching shoes for customers, wielding the Brannock device. With The Flash as your salesperson, everyone is taken care of in a timely fashion, even though there is only one guy doing all the work.

For this situation to work, The Flash cannot spend too much time doing any one thing. What if a shipment of shoes goes missing? Someone will have to spend a lot of time on the phone straightening it out. Your customers will get mighty impatient waiting for shoes while The Flash is on hold.

The Flash is like the main thread in your application. It runs all the code that updates the UI. This includes the code executed in response to different UI-related events – activity startup, button presses, and so on. (Because the events are all related to the user interface in some way, the main thread is sometimes called the *UI thread*.)

The event loop keeps the UI code in sequence. It makes sure that none of these operations step on each other while still ensuring that the code is executed in a timely fashion. So far, all of the code you have written (except for the code you just wrote with **AsyncTask**) has been executed on the main thread.

Beyond the main thread

Networking is a lot like a phone call to your shoe distributor: it takes a long time compared to other tasks. During that time, the user interface will be completely unresponsive, which might result in an *application not responding*, or *ANR*.

An ANR occurs when Android's watchdog determines that the main thread has failed to respond to an important event, like pressing the back button. To the user, it looks like this:

Figure 26.7 Application not responding

This is why Android disallowed network operations on the main thread starting with Honeycomb. In your store, you would solve the problem by (naturally) hiring a second Flash to call the shoe distributor. In Android, you do something similar – you create a *background thread* and access the network from there.

And what is the easiest way to work with a background thread? Why, **AsyncTask**.

You will get to see other things **AsyncTask** can do later this chapter. Before you do that, you will want to do some real work with your networking code.

Fetching XML From Flickr

Flickr offers a fine XML API. All the details you need are available in the documentation at www.flickr.com/services/api/. Pull it up in your favorite web browser, and then find the list of Request Formats. You will be using the simplest – REST. This tells us that the API endpoint is `http://api.flickr.com/services/rest/`. You can invoke the methods Flickr provides on this endpoint.

Back on the main page of the API documentation, find the list of API Methods. Scroll down to the photos section and locate flickr.photos.getRecent. Click on flickr.photos.getRecent, and the documentation will report that this method "Returns a list of the latest public photos uploaded to flickr." That is exactly what you need for PhotoGallery.

The only required parameter for the **getRecent** method is an API key. To get an API key, return to `http://www.flickr.com/services/api/` and follow the link for API keys. You will need a Yahoo ID to login. Once you are logged in, request a new, non-commercial API key. This usually only takes a moment. Your API key will look something like `4f721bgafa75bf6d2cb9af54f937bb70`.

Once you have a key, you have all you need to make a request to the Flickr web service. This request will be a GET request to `http://api.flickr.com/services/rest/?` `method=flickr.photos.getRecent&api_key=xxx`.

Time to start coding. First, add some constants to **FlickrFetchr**.

Listing 26.7 Add constants (FlickrFetchr.java)

```java
public class FlickrFetchr {
    public static final String TAG = "FlickrFetchr";

    private static final String ENDPOINT = "http://api.flickr.com/services/rest/";
    private static final String API_KEY = "yourApiKeyHere";
    private static final String METHOD_GET_RECENT = "flickr.photos.getRecent";
    private static final String PARAM_EXTRAS = "extras";

    private static final String EXTRA_SMALL_URL = "url_s";
```

These constants define the endpoint, the method name, the API key, and one extra parameter called extras, with a value of url_s. Specifying the url_s extra tells Flickr to include the URL for the small version of the picture if it is available.

Now use the constants to write a method that builds an appropriate request URL and fetches its contents.

Listing 26.8 Add **fetchItems()** method (FlickrFetchr.java)

```java
public class FlickrFetchr {

    ...

    String getUrl(String urlSpec) throws IOException {
        return new String(getUrlBytes(urlSpec));
    }

    public void fetchItems() {
        try {
            String url = Uri.parse(ENDPOINT).buildUpon()
                    .appendQueryParameter("method", METHOD_GET_RECENT)
                    .appendQueryParameter("api_key", API_KEY)
                    .appendQueryParameter(PARAM_EXTRAS, EXTRA_SMALL_URL)
                    .build().toString();
            String xmlString = getUrl(url);
            Log.i(TAG, "Received xml: " + xmlString);
        } catch (IOException ioe) {
            Log.e(TAG, "Failed to fetch items", ioe);
        }
    }
}
```

Here you use a **Uri.Builder** to build the complete URL for your Flickr API request. **Uri.Builder** is a convenience class for creating properly escaped parameterized URLs. **Uri.Builder.appendQueryParameter(String,String)** will automatically escape query strings for you.

Finally, modify the **AsyncTask** in **PhotoGalleryFragment** to call the new **fetchItems()** method.

Listing 26.9 Call **fetchItems()** (PhotoGalleryFragment.java)

```java
    private class FetchItemsTask extends AsyncTask<Void,Void,Void> {
        @Override
        protected Void doInBackground(Void... params) {
            try {
                String result = new FlickrFetchr().getUrl("http://www.google.com");
                Log.i(TAG, "Fetched contents of URL: " + result);
            } catch (IOException ioe) {
                Log.e(TAG, "Failed to fetch URL: ", ioe);
            }
            new FlickrFetchr().fetchItems();
            return null;
        }
    }
```

Run PhotoGallery and you should see rich, fertile Flickr XML in LogCat.

Figure 26.8 Flickr XML

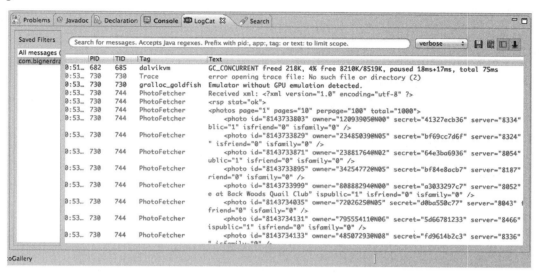

Now that you have such fine XML from Flickr, what should you do with it? You do what you do with all data – put it in one or more model objects. The model class you are going to create for PhotoGallery is called **GalleryItem**. Figure 26.9 shows an object diagram of PhotoGallery.

Figure 26.9 Object diagram of PhotoGallery

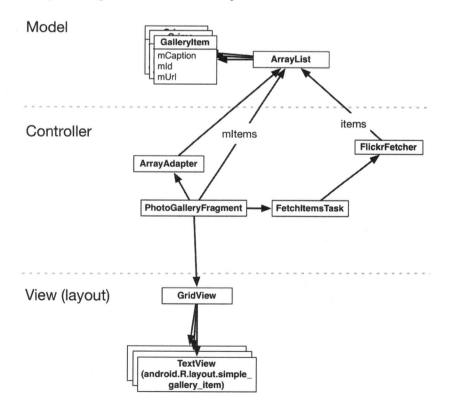

Note that Figure 26.9 does not show the hosting activity so that it can focus on the fragment and the networking code.

Create the **GalleryItem** class and add the following code:

Listing 26.10 Create model object class (GalleryItem.java)

```
package com.bignerdranch.android.photogallery;

public class GalleryItem {
    private String mCaption;
    private String mId;
    private String mUrl;

    public String toString() {
        return mCaption;
    }
}
```

Have Eclipse generate getters and setters for mId, mCaption, and mUrl.

Now that you have made model objects, it is time to fill them with data from the XML you got from Flickr. To get the data from the XML, you will use the **XmlPullParser** interface.

Using XmlPullParser

XmlPullParser is an interface you can use to pull parse events off of a stream of XML. **XmlPullParser** is used internally by Android to inflate your layout files. It will work just as well to parse your **GalleryItem** objects.

In **FlickrFetchr** add a constant that specifies the name of the photo XML element. Then write a method that uses **XmlPullParser** to identify each photo in the XML. Make a **GalleryItem** for each photo and add it to an **ArrayList**:

Listing 26.11 Parse Flickr photos (`FlickrFetchr.java`)

```java
public class FlickrFetchr {
    public static final String TAG = "FlickrFetchr";

    private static final String ENDPOINT = "http://api.flickr.com/services/rest/";
    private static final String API_KEY = "your API key";
    private static final String METHOD_GET_RECENT = "flickr.photos.getRecent";

    private static final String XML_PHOTO = "photo";

    ...

    public void fetchItems() {
        ...
    }

    void parseItems(ArrayList<GalleryItem> items, XmlPullParser parser)
            throws XmlPullParserException, IOException {
        int eventType = parser.next();

        while (eventType != XmlPullParser.END_DOCUMENT) {
            if (eventType == XmlPullParser.START_TAG &&
                XML_PHOTO.equals(parser.getName())) {
                String id = parser.getAttributeValue(null, "id");
                String caption = parser.getAttributeValue(null, "title");
                String smallUrl = parser.getAttributeValue(null, EXTRA_SMALL_URL);

                GalleryItem item = new GalleryItem();
                item.setId(id);
                item.setCaption(caption);
                item.setUrl(smallUrl);
                items.add(item);
            }

            eventType = parser.next();
        }
    }
}
```

You can imagine `XmlPullParser` as having its finger on your XML document, walking step by step through different events like START_TAG, END_TAG, and END_DOCUMENT. At each step, you can call methods like `getText()`, `getName()`, or `getAttributeValue(…)` to answer any questions you have about the event `XmlPullParser` currently has its finger on. To move the finger to the next interesting event in the XML, call `next()`. Conveniently, this method also returns the type of event it just moved to.

Figure 26.10 How **XmlPullParser** works

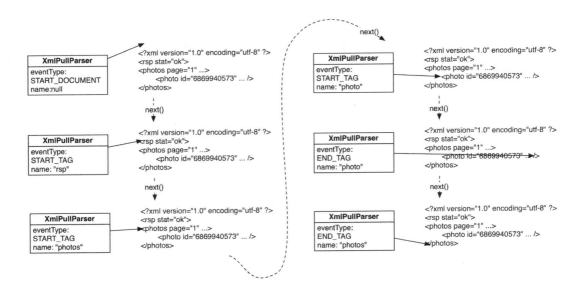

Your **parseItems(...)** method needs an **XmlPullParser** and an **ArrayList**. Get a parser instance and feed it the xmlString from Flickr. Then call **parseItems(...)** with the primed parser and empty array.

Listing 26.12 Call **parseItems(...)** (FlickrFetchr.java)

```
public void fetchItems() {
public ArrayList<GalleryItem> fetchItems() {
    ArrayList<GalleryItem> items = new ArrayList<GalleryItem>();

    try {
        String url = Uri.parse(ENDPOINT).buildUpon()
                .appendQueryParameter("method", METHOD_GET_RECENT)
                .appendQueryParameter("api_key", API_KEY)
                .appendQueryParameter(PARAM_EXTRAS, EXTRA_SMALL_URL)
                .build().toString();
        String xmlString = getUrl(url);
        Log.i(TAG, "Received xml: " + xmlString);
        XmlPullParserFactory factory = XmlPullParserFactory.newInstance();
        XmlPullParser parser = factory.newPullParser();
        parser.setInput(new StringReader(xmlString));

        parseItems(items, parser);
    } catch (IOException ioe) {
        Log.e(TAG, "Failed to fetch items", ioe);
    } catch (XmlPullParserException xppe) {
        Log.e(TAG, "Failed to parse items", xppe);
    }
    return items;
}
```

Run PhotoGallery to test your XML parsing code. PhotoGallery has no way of reporting the contents of your **ArrayList** right now, so you will need to set a breakpoint and use the debugger if you want to make sure everything worked correctly.

From AsyncTask Back to the Main Thread

To finish off, let's return to the view layer and get **PhotoGalleryFragment**'s **GridView** to display some captions.

GridView is an **AdapterView**, like **ListView**, so it needs an adapter to feed it views to display.

In PhotoGalleryFragment.java, add an **ArrayList** of **GalleryItem**s and then set up an **ArrayAdapter** that uses a simple layout provided by Android.

Listing 26.13 Implement **setupAdapter()** (PhotoGalleryFragment.java)

```java
public class PhotoGalleryFragment extends Fragment {
    private static final String TAG = "PhotoGalleryFragment";

    GridView mGridView;
    ArrayList<GalleryItem> mItems;

    ...

    @Override
    public View onCreateView(LayoutInflater inflater, ViewGroup container,
            Bundle savedInstanceState) {
        View v = inflater.inflate(R.layout.fragment_photo_gallery, container, false);

        mGridView = (GridView)v.findViewById(R.id.gridView);

        setupAdapter();

        return v;
    }

    void setupAdapter() {
        if (getActivity() == null || mGridView == null) return;

        if (mItems != null) {
            mGridView.setAdapter(new ArrayAdapter<GalleryItem>(getActivity(),
                    android.R.layout.simple_gallery_item, mItems));
        } else {
            mGridView.setAdapter(null);
        }
    }
}
```

Because **GridView** has no handy **GridFragment** class, you have to build your own adapter management code. One way of doing this is to use a method like the **setupAdapter()** method you just added. This method looks at the current model state and configures the adapter appropriately on your **GridView**. You want to call this in **onCreateView(…)**, so that every time a new **GridView** is created on rotation, it is reconfigured with an appropriate adapter. You also want to call it every time your set of model objects changes.

The android.R.layout.simple_gallery_item layout consists of a **TextView** element. Recall that in **GalleryItem**, you overrode **toString()** to return the object's mCaption. So passing the array list of **GalleryItem**s and this layout to the adapter is all you need for the **GridView** display captions.

Notice that you check to see whether **getActivity()** is null before setting the adapter. Remember that fragments can exist unattached from any activity. Before now, this possibility has not come up because your method calls have been driven by callbacks from the framework. If a fragment is receiving callbacks, then it definitely is attached to an activity. No activity, no callbacks.

Now that you are using an **AsyncTask**, you are triggering some things yourself, and you cannot assume that the fragment is attached to an activity. So you must check to make sure that your fragment is still attached. If it is not, then operations that rely on the that activity (like creating your **ArrayAdapter**) will fail.

Now you need to call **setupAdapter()** after data has been fetched from Flickr. Your first instinct might be to call **setupAdapter()** at the end of **FetchItemsTask**'s **doInBackground(…)**. This is not a good idea. Remember that you have two Flashes in the store now – one helping multiple customers, and one on the phone with Flickr. What will happen if the second Flash tries to help customers after hanging up the phone? Odds are good that the two Flashes will step on each other's toes.

On a computer, this toe-stepping-on results in objects in memory becoming corrupted. Because of this, you are not allowed to update the UI from a background thread, nor is it safe or advisable to do so.

What to do? **AsyncTask** has another method you can override called **onPostExecute(…)**. **onPostExecute(…)** is run after **doInBackground(…)** completes. In addition, **onPostExecute(…)** is run on the main thread, not the background thread, so it is safe to update the UI within it.

Modify **FetchItemsTask** to update mItems and call **setupAdapter()** after fetching your photos.

Listing 26.14 Add adapter update code (PhotoGalleryFragment.java)

```
private class FetchItemsTask extends AsyncTask<Void,Void,Void> {
private class FetchItemsTask extends AsyncTask<Void,Void,ArrayList<GalleryItem>> {
    @Override
    protected Void doInBackground(Void... params) {
    protected ArrayList<GalleryItem> doInBackground(Void... params) {
        new FlickrFetchr().fetchItems();
        return new FlickrFetchr().fetchItems();
        return null;
    }

    @Override
    protected void onPostExecute(ArrayList<GalleryItem> items) {
        mItems = items;
        setupAdapter();
    }
}
```

You made three changes here. First, you changed the type of the **FetchItemsTask**'s third generic parameter. This parameter is the type of result produced by your **AsyncTask**. It sets the type of value returned by **doInBackground(…)**, as well as the type of **onPostExecute(…)**'s input parameter.

Second, you modified **doInBackground(…)** to return your list of **GalleryItem**s. By doing this you fix your code so that it compiles properly. You also pass your list of items off so that it may be used from within **onPostExecute(…)**.

Finally, you added an implementation of **onPostExecute(…)**. This method accepts the list you fetched inside **doInBackground(…)**, puts it in mItems, and updates your **GridView**'s adapter.

With that, your work for this chapter is complete. Run, and you should see text displayed for each **GalleryItem** you downloaded.

Figure 26.11 Your Flickr item captions

For the More Curious: More on AsyncTask

In this chapter you saw how to use the last type parameter on **AsyncTask**, which specifies the return type. What about the other two?

The first type parameter allows you to specify the type of your input parameters. You would use it in the following way:

```
AsyncTask<String,Void,Void> task = new AsyncTask<String,Void,Void>() {
    public Void doInBackground(String... params) {
        for (String parameter : params) {
            Log.i(TAG, "Received parameter: " + parameter);
        }

        return null;
    }
};

task.execute("First parameter", "Second parameter", "Etc.");
```

Input parameters are passed in to the **execute(…)** method, which takes in a variable number of arguments. Those variable arguments are then passed on to **doInBackground(…)**.

The second type parameter allows you to specify the type for sending progress updates. Here is what that looks like:

```
final ProgressBar progressBar = /* A determinate progress bar */;
progressBar.setMax(100);

AsyncTask<Integer,Integer,Void> task = new AsyncTask<Integer,Integer,Void>() {
    public Void doInBackground(Integer... params) {
        for (Integer progress : params) {
            publishProgress(progress);
            Thread.sleep(1000);
        }
    }

    public void onProgressUpdate(Integer... params) {
        int progress = params[0];
        progressBar.setProgress(progress);
    }
};

task.execute(25, 50, 75, 100);
```

Progress updates usually happen in the middle of an ongoing background process. The problem is that you cannot make the necessary UI updates inside that background process. So **AsyncTask** provides **publishProgress(…)** and **onProgressUpdate(…)**.

Here is how it works: you call **publishProgress(…)** from **doInBackground(…)** in the background thread. This will make **onProgressUpdate(…)** be called on the UI thread. So you can do your UI updates in **onProgressUpdate(…)**, but control them from **doInBackground(…)** with **publishProgress(…)**.

Cleaning Up AsyncTasks

In this chapter, your **AsyncTask** was carefully structured so that you would not have to keep track of it. In other situations, though, you will need to keep a handle on your **AsyncTask**s, even canceling and rerunning them at times.

For these more complicated uses, you will want to assign your **AsyncTask** to an instance variable. Once you have a handle on it, you can call **AsyncTask.cancel(boolean)**. This method allows you to cancel an ongoing **AsyncTask.**,

AsyncTask.cancel(boolean) can work in a more rude or less rude fashion. If you call **cancel(false)**, it will be polite and simply set **isCancelled()** to true. The **AsyncTask** can then check **isCancelled()** inside of **doInBackground(…)** and elect to finish prematurely.

If you call **cancel(true)**, however, it will be impolite and interrupt the thread **doInBackground(…)** is on, if it is currently running. **AsyncTask.cancel(true)** is a more severe way of stopping the **AsyncTask**. If you can avoid it, you should.

Challenge: Paging

By default, getRecent returns one page of 100 results. There is an additional parameter you can use called page that will let you return page two, three, and so on.

For this challenge, add code to your adapter that detects when you are at the end of your array of items and replaces the current page with the next page of results. For a slightly harder challenge, append subsequent pages to your results.

27

Loopers, Handlers, and HandlerThread

Now that you have downloaded and parsed XML from Flickr, your next task is to download and display images. In this chapter, you will learn how to use **Looper**, **Handler**, and **HandlerThread** to dynamically download and display photos in PhotoGallery.

Preparing GridView for Displaying Images

The current adapter in **PhotoGalleryFragment** simply provides **TextView**s for the **GridView** to display. Each **TextView** displays the caption of a **GalleryItem**.

To display photos, you need a custom adapter that provides **ImageView**s instead. Eventually, each **ImageView** will display a photo downloaded from the mUrl of a **GalleryItem**.

Start by creating a new layout file for your gallery items called gallery_item.xml. This layout will consist of a single **ImageView** (Figure 27.1).

Figure 27.1 Gallery item layout (res/layout/gallery_item.xml)

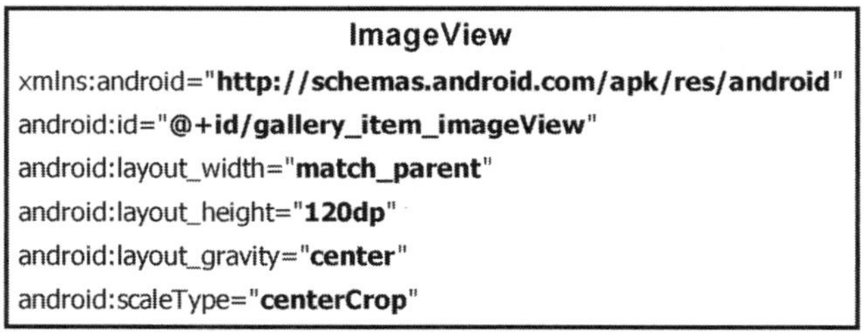

```
ImageView
xmlns:android="http://schemas.android.com/apk/res/android"
android:id="@+id/gallery_item_imageView"
android:layout_width="match_parent"
android:layout_height="120dp"
android:layout_gravity="center"
android:scaleType="centerCrop"
```

These **ImageView**s will be managed by **GridView**, which means that their width will vary. Their height will remain fixed, though. To make the most of the **ImageView**'s space, you have set its scaleType to centerCrop. This setting centers the image and then scales it up so that the smaller dimension is equal to the view and the larger one is cropped on both sides.

Next, you will need a placeholder image for each **ImageView** to display until you download an image to replace it. Find brian_up_close.jpg in the solutions file and put it in res/drawable-hdpi.

In **PhotoGalleryFragment**, replace the basic **ArrayAdapter** implementation with a custom
ArrayAdapter whose **getView(…)** implementation returns an **ImageView** that displays the placeholder
image.

Listing 27.1 Create **GalleryItemAdapter** (PhotoGalleryFragment.java)

```
public class PhotoGalleryFragment extends Fragment {

    ...

    void setupAdapter() {
        if (getActivity() == null || mGridView == null) return;

        if (mItems != null) {
            mGridView.setAdapter(new ArrayAdapter<GalleryItem>(getActivity(),
                    android.R.layout.simple_gallery_item, mItems));
            mGridView.setAdapter(new GalleryItemAdapter(mItems));
        } else {
            mGridView.setAdapter(null);
        }
    }

    private class FetchItemsTask extends AsyncTask<Void,Void,ArrayList<GalleryItem>> {
        ...
    }

    private class GalleryItemAdapter extends ArrayAdapter<GalleryItem> {
        public GalleryItemAdapter(ArrayList<GalleryItem> items) {
            super(getActivity(), 0, items);
        }

        @Override
        public View getView(int position, View convertView, ViewGroup parent) {
            if (convertView == null) {
                convertView = getActivity().getLayoutInflater()
                        .inflate(R.layout.gallery_item, parent, false);
            }

            ImageView imageView = (ImageView)convertView
                    .findViewById(R.id.gallery_item_imageView);
            imageView.setImageResource(R.drawable.brian_up_close);

            return convertView;
        }
    }
}
```

Remember that the **AdapterView** (the **GridView**, in this case) calls **getView(…)** on its adapter for every
individual view it needs.

Figure 27.2 AdapterView-ArrayAdapter pong

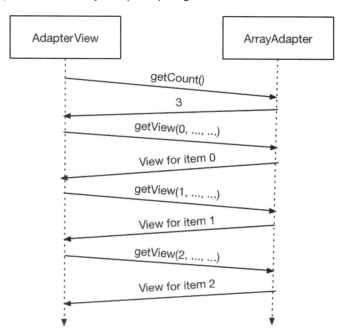

Run PhotoGallery, and you should see an array of close-up Brians:

Figure 27.3 A Briansplosion

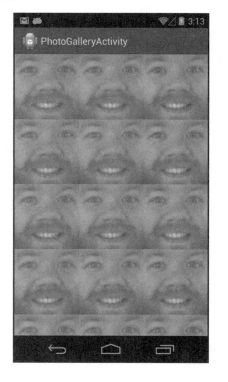

Downloading Lots of Small Things

Currently, PhotoGallery's networking works like this: **PhotoGalleryFragment** executes an **AsyncTask** that retrieves the XML from Flickr on a background thread and parses the XML into an array of **GalleryItem**s. Each **GalleryItem** now has a URL where a thumbnail-size photo lives.

The next step is to go and get those thumbnails. You might think that this additional networking code could simply be added to **FetchItemsTask**'s **doInBackground()** method. Your **GalleryItem** array has 100 URLs to download from. You would download the images one after the other until you had all 100. When **onPostExecute(…)** executed, they would be displayed en masse in the **GridView**.

However, downloading the thumbnails all at once causes two problems. The first is that it could take a while, and the UI would not be updated until the downloading was complete. On a slow connection, users would be staring at a wall of Brians for a long time.

The second problem is the cost of having to store the entire set of images. One hundred thumbnails will fit into memory easily. But what if it were 1000? What if you wanted to implement infinite scrolling? Eventually, you would run out of space.

Given these problems, real world apps often choose to download images only when they need to be displayed on screen. Downloading on demand puts the responsibility on the **GridView** and its adapter. The adapter will trigger the image downloading as part of its **getView(…)** implementation.

AsyncTask is the easiest way to get a background thread, but it is fundamentally ill-suited for repetitive and long-running work. (You can read why in the For The More Curious section at the end of this chapter.)

Instead of using an **AsyncTask**, you are going to create a dedicated background thread. This is the most common way to implement downloading on an as-needed basis.

Communicating with the Main Thread

Your dedicated thread will download photos, but how will it work with the **GridView**'s adapter to display them when it cannot directly access the main thread?

Think back to the shoe store with two Flashes. Background Flash has wrapped up his phone call to the distributor. He needs to tell Main Flash that the shoes are back in stock. If Main Flash is busy, Background Flash cannot do this right away. He would have to wait by the register to catch Main Flash at a spare moment. This would work, but it is not very efficient.

The better solution is to give each Flash an inbox. Background Flash writes a message about the shoes being in stock and puts it on top of Main Flash's inbox. Main Flash does the same thing when he wants to tell Background Flash that the stock of shoes has run out.

The inbox idea turns out to be really handy. The Flash may have something that needs to be done soon, but not right at the moment. In that case, he can put a message in his own inbox and then handle it when he has time.

In Android, the inbox that threads use is called a *message queue*. A thread that works by using a message queue is called a *message loop*; it loops again and again looking for new messages on its queue (Figure 27.4).

Figure 27.4 Flash dance

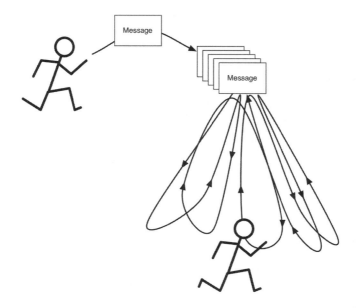

A message loop consists of a thread and a *looper*. The **Looper** is the object that manages a thread's message queue.

The main thread is a message loop and has a looper. Everything your main thread does is performed by its looper, which grabs messages off of its message queue and performs the task it specifies.

You are going to create a background thread that is a message loop, too. You will use a class called **HandlerThread** that prepares a **Looper** for you.

Assembling a Background Thread

Create a new class called **ThumbnailDownloader** that extends **HandlerThread**. Your **ThumbnailDownloader**'s user will need to use some object to identify each download, so give it one generic argument called Token by naming it **ThumbnailDownloader<Token>** in the class creation dialog. Then give it a constructor and a stub implementation of a method called **queueThumbnail()** (Listing 27.2).

Listing 27.2 Initial thread code (ThumbnailDownloader.java)

```java
public class ThumbnailDownloader<Token> extends HandlerThread {
    private static final String TAG = "ThumbnailDownloader";

    public ThumbnailDownloader() {
        super(TAG);
    }

    public void queueThumbnail(Token token, String url) {
        Log.i(TAG, "Got an URL: " + url);
    }
}
```

Notice that **queueThumbnail()** expects a **Token** and a **String**. This is the method you will have **GalleryItemAdapter** call in its **getView(…)** implementation.

Open PhotoGalleryFragment.java. Give **PhotoGalleryFragment** a **ThumbnailDownloader** member variable. You can use any object as a token for **ThumbnailDownloader**. In this case, the **ImageView** makes for a convenient token, since that is where the downloaded images will eventually go. In **onCreate(…)**, create the thread and start it. Override **onDestroy()** to quit the thread.

Listing 27.3 Create **ThumbnailDownloader** (PhotoGalleryFragment.java)

```
public class PhotoGalleryFragment extends Fragment {
    private static final String TAG = "PhotoGalleryFragment";

    GridView mGridView;
    ArrayList<GalleryItem> mItems;
    ThumbnailDownloader<ImageView> mThumbnailThread;

    @Override
    public void onCreate(Bundle savedInstanceState) {
        super.onCreate(savedInstanceState);

        setRetainInstance(true);
        new FetchItemsTask().execute();

        mThumbnailThread = new ThumbnailDownloader<ImageView>();
        mThumbnailThread.start();
        mThumbnailThread.getLooper();
        Log.i(TAG, "Background thread started");
    }

    @Override
    public View onCreateView(LayoutInflater inflater, ViewGroup container,
            Bundle savedInstanceState) {
        ...
    }

    @Override
    public void onDestroy() {
        super.onDestroy();
        mThumbnailThread.quit();
        Log.i(TAG, "Background thread destroyed");
    }
    ...
}
```

(A couple of safety notes: one, notice that you call **getLooper()** after calling **start()** on your **ThumbnailDownloader**. This is a way to ensure that the thread's guts are ready before proceeding (you will learn more about the **Looper** in a moment). And two, you call **quit()** to terminate the thread inside **onDestroy()**. This is critical. If you do not quit your **HandlerThread**s, they will never die. Like zombies. Or rock and roll. Or rocks.)

Finally, within **GalleryItemAdapter.getView(…)**, retrieve the correct **GalleryItem** using the position parameter, call the thread's **queueThumbnail()** method, and pass in the **ImageView** and the item's URL.

Listing 27.4 Hook up **ThumbnailDownloader** (PhotoGalleryFragment.java)

```java
private class GalleryItemAdapter extends ArrayAdapter<GalleryItem> {
    ...

    @Override
    public View getView(int position, View convertView, ViewGroup parent) {
        ...

        ImageView imageView = (ImageView)convertView
                .findViewById(R.id.gallery_item_imageView);
        imageView.setImageResource(R.drawable.brian_up_close);
        GalleryItem item = getItem(position);
        mThumbnailThread.queueThumbnail(imageView, item.getUrl());

        return convertView;
    }
}
```

Run PhotoGallery and check out LogCat. When you scroll around the **GridView**, you should see lines in LogCat signaling that **ThumbnailDownloader** is getting each one of your download requests.

Now that you have a **HandlerThread** up and running, the next step is to create a message with the information passed in to **queueThumbnail()** and put that message on the **ThumbnailDownloader**'s message queue.

Messages and Message Handlers

Before you create a message, you need to understand what a **Message** is, and the relationship it has with its **Handler**, or *message handler*.

Message anatomy

Let's start by looking closely at messages. The messages that a Flash might put in an inbox (its own inbox or that of another Flash) are not supportive notes, like "You run very fast, Flash." They are tasks that need to be handled.

A message is an instance of **Message** and contains several fields. Three are relevant to your implementation:

what   a user-defined int that describes the message

obj   a user-specified object to be sent with the message

target   the **Handler** that will handle the message

The target of a **Message** is an instance of **Handler**. You can think of the name **Handler** as being short for "message handler." When you create a **Message**, it will automatically be attached to a **Handler**. And when your **Message** is ready to be processed, **Handler** will be the object in charge of making it happen.

Handler anatomy

So to do any real work with messages, you will need an instance of the target message **Handler** first. A **Handler** is not just a target for processing your **Message**s. A **Handler** is your interface for creating and posting **Message**s, too.

Figure 27.5 **Looper**, **Handler**, **HandlerThread**, and **Message**

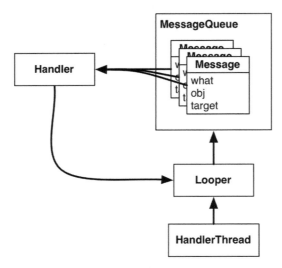

Messages must be posted and consumed on a **Looper**, because **Looper** owns the inbox of **Message** objects. So **Handler** always has a reference to its coworker, the **Looper**.

A **Handler** is attached to exactly one **Looper**, and a **Message** is attached to exactly one target **Handler**, called its *target*. A **Looper** has a whole queue of **Message**s.

Figure 27.6 Multiple **Handler**s, one **Looper**

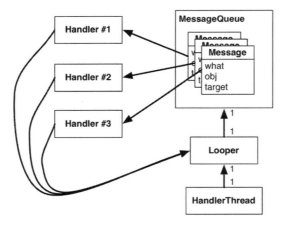

Multiple **Handler**s can be attached to one **Looper**. This means that your **Handler**'s **Message**s may be living side by side with another **Handler**'s messages.

Using handlers

Usually, you do not set a message's target **Handler** by hand. It is better to build the message by calling **Handler.obtainMessage(…)**. You pass the other message fields into this method, and it automatically sets the target for you.

Handler.obtainMessage(…) pulls from a common recycling pool to avoid creating new **Message** objects, so it is also more efficient than creating new instances.

Once you have obtained a **Message**, you then call **sendToTarget()** to send the **Message** to its **Handler**. The **Handler** will then put the **Message** on the end of **Looper**'s message queue.

In this case, you are going to obtain a message and send it to its target within the implementation of **queueThumbnail()**. The message's what will be a constant defined as MESSAGE_DOWNLOAD. The obj will be the **Token** – in this case, the **ImageView** that the adapter passed in to **queueThumbnail()**.

When the looper gets to a particular message in the queue, it gives the message to the message's target to handle. Typically, the message is handled in the target's implementation of **Handler.handleMessage(…)**.

Figure 27.7 Creating a **Message** and sending it

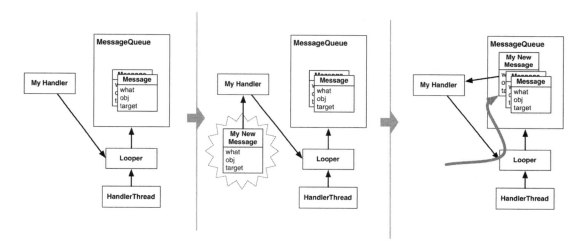

In this case, your implementation of **handleMessage(…)** will use **FlickrFetchr** to download bytes from the URL and then turn these bytes into a bitmap. Add the code shown in Listing 27.5.

Listing 27.5 Obtaining, sending, and handling a message (ThumbnailDownloader.java)

```java
public class ThumbnailDownloader<Token> extends HandlerThread {
    private static final String TAG = "ThumbnailDownloader";
    private static final int MESSAGE_DOWNLOAD = 0;

    Handler mHandler;
    Map<Token, String> requestMap =
            Collections.synchronizedMap(new HashMap<Token, String>());

    public ThumbnailDownloader() {
        super(TAG);
    }

    @SuppressLint("HandlerLeak")
    @Override
    protected void onLooperPrepared() {
        mHandler = new Handler() {
            @Override
            public void handleMessage(Message msg) {
                if (msg.what == MESSAGE_DOWNLOAD) {
                    @SuppressWarnings("unchecked")
                    Token token = (Token)msg.obj;
                    Log.i(TAG, "Got a request for url: " + requestMap.get(token));
                    handleRequest(token);
                }
            }
        };
    }

    public void queueThumbnail(Token token, String url) {
        Log.i(TAG, "Got a URL: " + url);
        requestMap.put(token, url);

        mHandler
            .obtainMessage(MESSAGE_DOWNLOAD, token)
            .sendToTarget();
    }

    private void handleRequest(final Token token) {
        try {
            final String url = requestMap.get(token);
            if (url == null)
                return;

            byte[] bitmapBytes = new FlickrFetchr().getUrlBytes(url);
            final Bitmap bitmap = BitmapFactory
                    .decodeByteArray(bitmapBytes, 0, bitmapBytes.length);
            Log.i(TAG, "Bitmap created");

        } catch (IOException ioe) {
            Log.e(TAG, "Error downloading image", ioe);
        }
    }
}
```

First, let's talk about that annotation at the top of **onLooperPrepared()**,
@SuppressLint("HandlerLeak"). Here, Android Lint will warn you about subclassing **Handler**. Your

Handler will be kept alive by its **Looper**. So if your **Handler** is an anonymous inner class, it is easy to leak memory accidentally through an implicit object reference. Here, though, everything is tied to your **HandlerThread**, so there is no danger of leaking anything.

The other annotation, @SuppressWarnings("unchecked"), is more run of the mill. This is necessary because **Token** is a generic class argument, but Message.obj is an **Object**. Due to type erasure, it is not possible to actually make this cast. If you would like to know more about why, read up on type erasure – this chapter will stay focused on Android stuff.

The requestMap variable is a synchronized **HashMap**. Here, using the **Token** as a key, you can store and retrieve the URL associated with a particular **Token**.

In **queueThumbnail()**, you add the passed-in **Token**-URL pair to the map. Then you obtain a message, give it the **Token** as its obj, and send it off to be put on the message queue.

You implemented **Handler.handleMessage(…)** in your **Handler** subclass within **onLooperPrepared()**. **HandlerThread.onLooperPrepared()** is called before the **Looper** checks the queue for the first time. This makes it a good place to create your **Handler** implementation.

Within **Handler.handleMessage(…)**, you check the message type, retrieve the **Token** and then pass it to **handleRequest(…)**.

The **handleRequest()** method is where the downloading happens. Here you check for the existence of a URL. Then you pass the URL to a new instance of your old friend **FlickrFetchr**. In particular, you use the **FlickrFetchr.getUrlBytes(…)** method that you created with such foresight in the last chapter.

Finally, you use **BitmapFactory** to construct a bitmap with the array of bytes returned from **getUrlBytes(…)**.

Run PhotoGallery and check LogCat for your confirming log statements.

Of course, the request will not be completely handled until you set the bitmap on the **ImageView** that originally came from **GalleryItemAdapter**. However, this is UI work, so it must be done on the main thread.

Everything you have seen so far is using handlers and messages on a single thread – putting messages in your own inbox. In the next section, you will see how **ThumbnailDownloader** can use a **Handler** to access the main thread.

Passing handlers

One way that a **HandlerThread** can get work done on the main thread is to have the main thread pass its own **Handler** to the **HandlerThread**.

The main thread is a message loop with handlers and a **Looper**. When you create a **Handler** in the main thread, it will be associated with the main thread's **Looper**. You can then pass that **Handler** to another thread. The passed **Handler** maintains its loyalty to the **Looper** of the thread that created it. Any messages the **Handler** is responsible for will be handled on the main thread's queue.

So just like you were able to schedule work on the background thread from the main thread using **ThumbnailDownloader**'s **Handler**.

Figure 27.8 Scheduling work on **ThumbnailDownloader** from the main thread

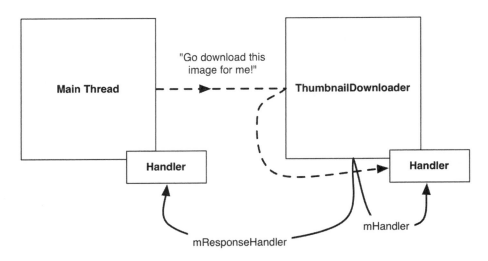

You can also schedule work on the main thread from the background thread using a **Handler** attached to the main thread:

Figure 27.9 Scheduling work on the main thread from **ThumbnailDownloader**'s thread

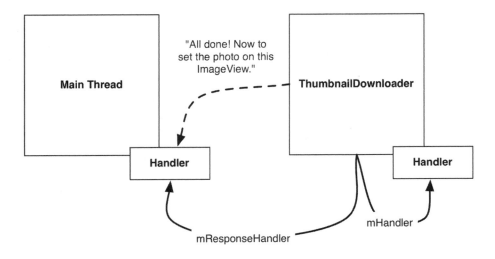

In ThumbnailDownloader.java, add the mResponseHandler variable seen above to hold a **Handler** passed from the main thread. Then replace the constructor with one that accepts a **Handler** and sets the variable, and add a listener interface to communicate the responses with.

Listing 27.6 Add response **Handler** (ThumbnailDownloader.java)

```java
public class ThumbnailDownloader<Token> extends HandlerThread {
    private static final String TAG = "ThumbnailDownloader";
    private static final int MESSAGE_DOWNLOAD = 0;

    Handler mHandler;
    Map<Token,String> requestMap =
            Collections.synchronizedMap(new HashMap<Token,String>());
    Handler mResponseHandler;
    Listener<Token> mListener;

    public interface Listener<Token> {
        void onThumbnailDownloaded(Token token, Bitmap thumbnail);
    }

    public void setListener(Listener<Token> listener) {
        mListener = listener;
    }

    public ThumbnailDownloader() {
        super(TAG);
    public ThumbnailDownloader(Handler responseHandler) {
        super(TAG);
        mResponseHandler = responseHandler;
    }
```

Then modify **PhotoGalleryFragment** to pass a **Handler** to **ThumbnailDownloader**, as well as a **Listener** to set the returning **Bitmap**s on the **ImageView** handles. Remember that by default, the **Handler** will attach itself to the **Looper** for the current thread. Since this **Handler** is created in **onCreate(…)**, it will be attached to the main thread's **Looper**.

Listing 27.7 Hook up to response **Handler** (PhotoGalleryFragment.java)

```java
@Override
public void onCreate(Bundle savedInstanceState) {
    super.onCreate(savedInstanceState);

    setRetainInstance(true);
    new FetchItemsTask().execute();

    mThumbnailThread = new ThumbnailDownloader();
    mThumbnailThread = new ThumbnailDownloader<ImageView>(new Handler());
    mThumbnailThread.setListener(new ThumbnailDownloader.Listener<ImageView>() {
        public void onThumbnailDownloaded(ImageView imageView, Bitmap thumbnail) {
            if (isVisible()) {
                imageView.setImageBitmap(thumbnail);
            }
        }
    });
    mThumbnailThread.start();
    mThumbnailThread.getLooper();
    Log.i(TAG, "Background thread started");
}
```

Now **ThumbnailDownloader** has access via mResponseHandler to a **Handler** that is tied to the main thread's **Looper**. It also has your **Listener** to do the UI work with the returning **Bitmap**s. Note that you guard your call to **imageView.setImageBitmap(Bitmap)** with a call to **Fragment.isVisible()**. This ensures that you are not setting the image on a stale **ImageView**.

You could send a custom **Message** back to the main thread this way. This would require another subclass of **Handler**, with an override of **handleMessage(…)**. Instead, let's use another handy **Handler** method – **post(Runnable)**.

Handler.post(Runnable) is a convenience method for posting **Message**s that look like this:

```
Runnable myRunnable = new Runnable() {
    public void run() {
        /* Your code here */
    }
};
Message m = mHandler.obtainMessage();
m.callback = myRunnable;
```

When a **Message** has its callback field set, instead of being run by its **Handler** target, the **Runnable** in callback is run instead.

In **ThumbnailDownloader.handleRequest()**, add the following code.

Listing 27.8 Downloading and displaying (ThumbnailDownloader.java)

...

```
private void handleRequest(final Token token) {
    try {
        final String url = requestMap.get(token);
        if (url == null)
            return;

        byte[] bitmapBytes = new FlickrFetchr().getUrlBytes(url);
        final Bitmap bitmap = BitmapFactory
                .decodeByteArray(bitmapBytes, 0, bitmapBytes.length);
        Log.i(TAG, "Bitmap created");

        mResponseHandler.post(new Runnable() {
            public void run() {
                if (requestMap.get(token) != url)
                    return;

                requestMap.remove(token);
                mListener.onThumbnailDownloaded(token, bitmap);
            }
        });
    } catch (IOException ioe) {
        Log.e(TAG, "Error downloading image", ioe);
    }
}
```

And because mResponseHandler is associated with the main thread's **Looper**, this UI update code will be run on the main thread.

So what does this code do? First, it double-checks the requestMap. This is necessary because the **GridView** recycles its views. By the time **ThumbnailDownloader** finishes downloading the **Bitmap**,

GridView may have recycled the **ImageView** and requested a different URL for it. This check ensures that each **Token** gets the correct image, even if another request has been made in the meantime.

Finally, you remove the **Token** from the requestMap and set the bitmap on the **Token**.

Before running and seeing your hard-won images, there is one last danger you need to account for. If the user rotates the screen, **ThumbnailDownloader** may be hanging on to invalid **ImageView**s. Bad things will happen if those **ImageView**s get pressed.

Write the following method to clean all the requests out of your queue.

Listing 27.9 Add cleanup method (ThumbnailDownloader.java)

```java
public void clearQueue() {
    mHandler.removeMessages(MESSAGE_DOWNLOAD);
    requestMap.clear();
}
```

Then clean out your downloader in **PhotoGalleryFragment** when your view is destroyed.

Listing 27.10 Call cleanup method (PhotoGalleryFragment.java)

```java
@Override
public void onDestroyView() {
    super.onDestroyView();
    mThumbnailThread.clearQueue();
}
```

With that, your work on this chapter is complete. Run PhotoGallery. Scroll around to see images dynamically loading.

PhotoGallery has achieved its basic goal of displaying images from Flickr. In the next few chapters, you will add more functionality like searching for photos and opening each photo's Flickr page in a web view.

For the More Curious: AsyncTask vs. Threads

Now that you understand **Handler** and **Looper**, **AsyncTask** may not seem quite so magical. It is still less work than what you have done here. So why not use **AsyncTask** instead of a **HandlerThread**?

There are a few reasons. The most fundamental one is that **AsyncTask** is not designed for it. It is intended for work that is short lived and not repeated too often. Your code in the previous chapter is a place where **AsyncTask** shines. If you are creating a lot of **AsyncTask**s, though, or having them run for a long time, you are probably using the wrong class.

A more compelling technical reason is that in Android 3.2 **AsyncTask** changed its implementation in a significant way. Starting with Android 3.2, **AsyncTask** does not create a thread for each instance of **AsyncTask**. Instead, it uses something called an **Executor** to run background work for all **AsyncTask**s on a single background thread. That means that each **AsyncTask** will run one after the other. A long-running **AsyncTask** will poison the well, preventing other **AsyncTask**s from getting any CPU time.

It is possible to safely run **AsyncTask** in parallel by using a thread pool executor instead, but we do not recommend doing so. If you are considering doing this, it is usually better to do your own threading instead, using **Handler**s to communicate back to the main thread when necessary.

Challenge: Preloading and Caching

Users accept that not everything can be instantaneous. (Well, most users.) Even so, programmers strive towards perfection.

To approach instantaneity, most real world apps augment the code you have here in two ways:

- adding a caching layer

- preloading images

A cache is a place to stash a certain number of **Bitmap** objects so that they stick around even when you are done using them. A cache can only hold so many items, so you need a strategy to decide what to keep when your cache runs out of room. Many caches use a strategy called LRU, or "least recently used." When you are out of room, the cache gets rid of the least recently-used item.

The Android support library has a class called **LruCache** that implements an LRU strategy. For the first challenge, use **LruCache** to add a simple cache to **ThumbnailDownloader**. Whenever you download the **Bitmap** for an URL, you will stick it in the cache. Then, when you are about to download a new image, you will check the cache first to see if you already have it around.

Once you have built a cache, you can preload things into it. Preloading is loading items in the cache before you actually need them. That way, there is no delay for **Bitmap**s to download before displaying them.

Preloading is tricky to implement well, but it makes a huge difference for the user. For a second, harder challenge, for every **GalleryItem** you display, preload **Bitmap**s for the previous ten and the next ten **GalleryItem**s.

28

Search

Your next task with PhotoGallery is to search photos on Flickr. In this chapter, you will learn how to integrate search into your app the Android way.

Or the Android *ways*, as it turns out. Search has been integrated into Android from the very beginning, but (much like the menu button), it has changed a lot since then. Like menus, the new code for search was built on the existing APIs. So when you build search in the older style, you are preparing to implement the full-featured modern Jelly Bean search.

Searching Flickr

Let's begin with the Flickr side of things. To search Flickr, you call the `flickr.photos.search` method. Here is what a `flickr.photos.search` method invocation to look for the text "red" looks like:

```
http://api.flickr.com/services/rest/?method=flickr.photos.search
&api_key=XXX&extras=url_s&text=red
```

This method takes in some new and different parameters to specify what the search terms are, like a text query parameter. The good news is that parsing the XML you get back into **GalleryItem**s works exactly the same.

Make the changes in Listing 28.1 to add a new search request method to **FlickrFetchr**. Since both `search` and `getRecent` parse **GalleryItem**s in the same way, you will refactor some of your old code from **fetchItems()** into a new method called **downloadGalleryItems(String)**. Pay close attention – the old **fetchItems()** URL code is cut and pasted into a new version of the **fetchItems()** method, not deleted.

Listing 28.1 Add Flickr search method (FlickrFetchr.java)

```java
public class FlickrFetchr {
    public static final String TAG = "PhotoFetcher";

    private static final String ENDPOINT = "http://api.flickr.com/services/rest/";
    private static final String API_KEY = "4f721bbafa75bf6d2cb5af54f937bb70";
    private static final String METHOD_GET_RECENT = "flickr.photos.getRecent";
    private static final String METHOD_SEARCH = "flickr.photos.search";
    private static final String PARAM_EXTRAS = "extras";
    private static final String PARAM_TEXT = "text";


    ...

    public ArrayList<GalleryItem> fetchItems() {
    public ArrayList<GalleryItem> downloadGalleryItems(String  url) {
        ArrayList<GalleryItem> items = new ArrayList<GalleryItem>();

        try {
            String url = Uri.parse(ENDPOINT).buildUpon()
                    .appendQueryParameter("method", METHOD_GET_RECENT)
                    .appendQueryParameter("api_key", API_KEY)
                    .appendQueryParameter(PARAM_EXTRAS, EXTRA_SMALL_URL)
                    .build().toString();
            String xmlString = getUrl(url);
            Log.i(TAG, "Received xml: " + xmlString);
            XmlPullParserFactory factory = XmlPullParserFactory.newInstance();
            XmlPullParser parser = factory.newPullParser();
            parser.setInput(new StringReader(xmlString));

            parseItems(items, parser);
        } catch (IOException ioe) {
            Log.e(TAG, "Failed to fetch items", ioe);
        } catch (XmlPullParserException xppe) {
            Log.e(TAG, "Failed to parse items", xppe);
        }
        return items;
    }

    public ArrayList<GalleryItem> fetchItems() {
        // Move code here from above
        String url = Uri.parse(ENDPOINT).buildUpon()
                .appendQueryParameter("method", METHOD_GET_RECENT)
                .appendQueryParameter("api_key", API_KEY)
                .appendQueryParameter(PARAM_EXTRAS, EXTRA_SMALL_URL)
                .build().toString();
        return downloadGalleryItems(url);
    }

    public ArrayList<GalleryItem> search(String query) {
        String url = Uri.parse(ENDPOINT).buildUpon()
                .appendQueryParameter("method", METHOD_SEARCH)
                .appendQueryParameter("api_key", API_KEY)
                .appendQueryParameter(PARAM_EXTRAS, EXTRA_SMALL_URL)
                .appendQueryParameter(PARAM_TEXT, query)
                .build().toString();
        return downloadGalleryItems(url);
    }
}
```

The **downloadGalleryItems(String)** method is used twice because the code to download and parse the URL is the same for both search and getRecent. Searching is simply a matter of hitting the new search method, flickr.photos.search, passing in the encoded query string as the text parameter.

Next, hook up some test code to call your search code inside **PhotoGalleryFragment.FetchItemsTask**. For now, you will hardwire a search query just to make sure that it works.

Listing 28.2 Hardwired search query code (PhotoGalleryFragment.java)

```
private class FetchItemsTask extends AsyncTask<Void,Void,ArrayList<GalleryItem>> {
    @Override
    protected ArrayList<GalleryItem> doInBackground(Void... params) {
        String query = "android"; // Just for testing

        if (query != null) {
            return new FlickrFetchr().search(query);
        } else {
            return new FlickrFetchr().fetchItems();
        }
    }

    @Override
    protected void onPostExecute(ArrayList<GalleryItem> items) {
        ...
    }
    ...
}
```

The default will be to use the old getRecent code. If there is a non-null search query (which for now is always the case), then **FetchItemsTask** will fetch search results instead.

Run PhotoGallery and see what you get. Hopefully, you will see an Andy or two.

The Search Dialog

In this section, you will implement Android's search interface in PhotoGallery. You will start with the old style dialog interface.

Creating a search interface

In Honeycomb, the Android folks got rid of hardware search buttons. Even before that, though, there was no guarantee of having a search button. Modern Android apps that rely on search must always have a search button somewhere in the app if they are targeting pre-3.0 devices.

Implementing this is not difficult. Simply call **Activity.onSearchRequested()**. This method performs the exact same operation as pressing the search button.

Add a menu XML file for PhotoGallery in res/menu/fragment_photo_gallery.xml. Your app will also need an interface to clear the search query, so add a clear button as well.

Listing 28.3 Add search menu items (res/menu/fragment_photo_gallery.xml)

```xml
<menu xmlns:android="http://schemas.android.com/apk/res/android">
  <item android:id="@+id/menu_item_search"
    android:title="@string/search"
    android:icon="@android:drawable/ic_menu_search"
    android:showAsAction="ifRoom"
    />
  <item android:id="@+id/menu_item_clear"
    android:title="@string/clear_search"
    android:icon="@android:drawable/ic_menu_close_clear_cancel"
    android:showAsAction="ifRoom"
    />
</menu>
```

You are missing a couple of strings now, so go ahead and add them to `strings.xml`. (Later on, you will need a search hint string, so add that as well.)

Listing 28.4 Add search strings (res/values/strings.xml)

```xml
<resources>

    ...

    <string name="title_activity_photo_gallery">PhotoGalleryActivity</string>
    <string name="search_hint">Search Flickr</string>
    <string name="search">Search</string>
    <string name="clear_search">Clear Search</string>

</resources>
```

Then hook up your options menu callbacks. For the search button, you will call **onSearchRequested()** as described above. For the cancel button, for now you will do nothing.

Listing 28.5 Options menu callbacks (PhotoGalleryFragment.java)

```java
@Override
public void onCreate(Bundle savedInstanceState) {
    super.onCreate(savedInstanceState);

    setRetainInstance(true);
    setHasOptionsMenu(true);

    ...
}

...

@Override
public void onDestroyView() {
    ...
}
```

```
@Override
public void onCreateOptionsMenu(Menu menu, MenuInflater inflater) {
    super.onCreateOptionsMenu(menu, inflater);
    inflater.inflate(R.menu.fragment_photo_gallery, menu);
}

@Override
public boolean onOptionsItemSelected(MenuItem item) {
    switch (item.getItemId()) {
        case R.id.menu_item_search:
            getActivity().onSearchRequested();
            return true;
        case R.id.menu_item_clear:
            return true;
        default:
            return super.onOptionsItemSelected(item);
    }
}
```

Run your new menu interface to see that it displays correctly.

Figure 28.1 Your search interface

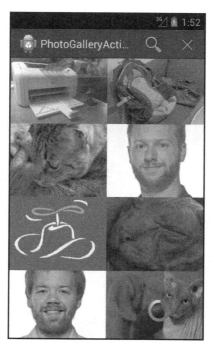

Pressing the search button will not do anything right now, though. For **onSearchRequested()** to work, you must make **PhotoGalleryActivity** into a *searchable activity*.

Searchable activities

There are two moving pieces that make an activity searchable. The first is an XML file. This XML file contains an element called searchable that describes how the search dialog that you will show later should display itself. Create a new folder called res/xml and then create a new XML file in that folder called searchable.xml. Fill the file's innards with a simple version of a searchable element:

Listing 28.6 Search configuration (res/xml/searchable.xml)

```
<?xml version="1.0" encoding="utf-8"?>
<searchable xmlns:android="http://schemas.android.com/apk/res/android"
  android:label="@string/app_name"
  android:hint="@string/search_hint"
  />
```

This XML is called a *search configuration*. In your case, all your search configuration needs to do is provide a hint string and the name of your application.

In a fancier application, this file can become fat with instructions. Search suggestions, voice search, global search configuration, action key configurations, and input types all go here. Even in the simplest implementation, though, a basic search configuration is required.

The next pieces of the puzzle go in AndroidManifest.xml. You need to change the *launch mode* of your app, and you need to declare an additional intent filter and a piece of metadata for **PhotoGalleryActivity**. The intent filter advertises that you can listen to search intents, and the metadata is to attach the XML you just wrote to your activity.

All of this advertisement work is required to tell Android's **SearchManager** that your activity is capable of handling searches and to give it your search configuration. **SearchManager** is an OS-level service that is responsible for presenting the search dialog and managing its interactions.

Crack open AndroidManifest.xml and add the two elements and the android:launchMode attribute shown in Listing 28.7.

Listing 28.7 Add intent filter and metadata (AndroidManifest.xml)

```
<manifest xmlns:android="http://schemas.android.com/apk/res/android"
  ... >

  ...

  <application
    ... >
    <activity
      android:name=".PhotoGalleryActivity"
      android:launchMode="singleTop"
      android:label="@string/title_activity_photo_gallery" >
      <intent-filter>
        <action android:name="android.intent.action.MAIN" />

        <category android:name="android.intent.category.LAUNCHER" />
      </intent-filter>
      <intent-filter>
        <action android:name="android.intent.action.SEARCH" />
      </intent-filter>
      <meta-data android:name="android.app.searchable"
        android:resource="@xml/searchable"/>
    </activity>
  </application>

</manifest>
```

Let's talk about the last two elements first. The first addition is a familiar intent filter definition. Search results are communicated by calling **startActivity(…)** with an intent that has an action of android.intent.action.SEARCH. The search query is put on the intent as an extra. So to indicate that your activity can handle search results, you define a filter for the action.intent.action.SEARCH intent.

The second addition is another metadata tag. You used metadata earlier in Chapter 16, but this tag is slightly different. Instead of android:value, it uses android:resource. Here is an example to show you the difference. Let's say that you referred to the same string resource in two different metadata tags:

```
<meta-data android:name="metadata.value"
  android:value="@string/app_name" />
<meta-data android:name="metadata.resource"
  android:resource="@string/app_name" />
```

If you were to pull out the value for metadata.value, you would find that it contained the string "PhotoGallery", which is the value stored in @string/app_name. The value for metadata.resource, though, would be the *integer ID* of that resource. In other words, the value of metadata.resource is the value in code of R.string.app_name.

Back in reality, the **SearchManager** requires the integer ID of searchable.xml, not the string value of that XML file. So you use android:resource and give the **SearchManager** the file's resource ID.

What about the android:launchMode attribute on your activity tag? This is the activity's *launch mode*. You will learn about this in a moment when you write the code to receive the search query.

With that, you should be able to fire up a search dialog. Run PhotoGallery and tap your menu search button.

Figure 28.2 The search dialog

Hardware search button

The same code that is invoked when you call **onSearchRequested()** by hand will be run when you press the hardware search button on older devices. If you would like to verify for yourself that this works, you can modify any pre-3.0 emulator to have a hardware search button by configuring your emulator to use the hardware keyboard, like so:

Figure 28.3 Add hardware keyboard support

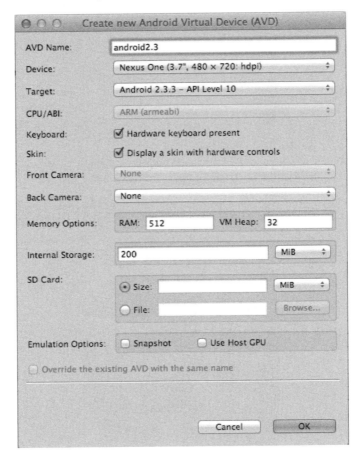

How Search works

The main idea behind search in Android is the concept mentioned briefly earlier, the *searchable activity*. A searchable activity is defined by the two things you just created: a search intent filter and a search configuration metadata entry.

With the hardware search button, every search interaction up until the search intent itself is handled by the system. It checks your AndroidManifest.xml to see if your activity is searchable. If it is, it then shows a search dialog activity on top of your activity. That activity then triggers search by sending you a new intent.

Figure 28.4 System search

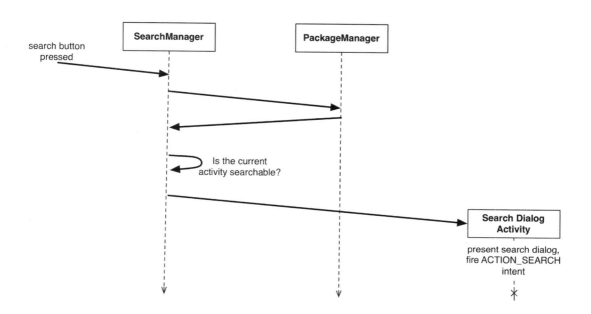

Which means that, normally, pressing the search button will start a new activity. In your case, though, it does not. Why? Because you added android:launchMode="singleTop" (Listing 28.7), which changes your launch mode.

Launch modes and new intents

What is a launch mode? Launch modes determine how your activity starts up when it receives a new intent, and sometimes how it behaves when it fires an intent to start another activity.

Table 28.1 The different kinds of launch modes

Launch mode	Behavior
standard	The default behavior – start up a new activity for every new intent received.
singleTop	If an instance of this activity is already at the top of the back stack, direct the new intent at the existing activity instead of creating a new one.
singleTask	Launch this activity into its own task. If the activity already exists in the task, clear out any activities above it in the back stack and direct the new intent at the existing activity.
singleInstance	Launch this activity into its own task. It is the only activity in its task – if any other activities are started from this task, they are launched into their own tasks. If the activity already exists, direct the new intent at the existing activity.

Every activity you have written so far has used the standard launch mode. This behavior is familiar: when an intent resolves to an activity with the standard launch mode, a new instance of that activity is created and added to the back stack.

This behavior will not fly for **PhotoGalleryActivity** in all cases. (We will discuss why when we talk about **SearchView** and Honeycomb search later.) Instead, you specify the singleTop launch mode. This means that instead of starting a new activity, the search intent you receive will go to your already running **PhotoGalleryActivity** on top of the back stack.

You receive that new intent by overriding **onNewIntent(Intent)** inside an **Activity**. Whenever you receive a new intent, you will want to refresh the items in **PhotoGalleryFragment**.

Refactor **PhotoGalleryFragment** to include an **updateItems()** method that runs **FetchItemsTask** to refresh your current items.

Listing 28.8 Add update method (PhotoGalleryFragment.java)

```java
@Override
public void onCreate(Bundle savedInstanceState) {
    super.onCreate(savedInstanceState);

    setRetainInstance(true);

    new FetchItemsTask().execute();
    updateItems();

    mThumbnailThread = new ThumbnailDownloader<ImageView>(new Handler());
    mThumbnailThread.setListener(new ThumbnailDownloader.Listener<ImageView>() {
        ...
    });
    mThumbnailThread.start();
    mThumbnailThread.getLooper();
}

public void updateItems() {
    new FetchItemsTask().execute();
}
```

Then add your **onNewIntent(Intent)** override in **PhotoGalleryActivity** to receive the new intent and refresh your **PhotoGalleryFragment**'s items:

Listing 28.9 Override **onNewIntent(…)** (PhotoGalleryActivity.java)

```java
public class PhotoGalleryActivity extends SingleFragmentActivity {
    private static final String TAG = "PhotoGalleryActivity";

    @Override
    public Fragment createFragment() {
        return new PhotoGalleryFragment();
    }
```

```
@Override
public void onNewIntent(Intent intent) {
    PhotoGalleryFragment fragment = (PhotoGalleryFragment)
        getSupportFragmentManager().findFragmentById(R.id.fragmentContainer);

    if (Intent.ACTION_SEARCH.equals(intent.getAction())) {
        String query = intent.getStringExtra(SearchManager.QUERY);
        Log.i(TAG, "Received a new search query: " + query);
    }

    fragment.updateItems();
}
}
```

You should be able to see **PhotoGalleryActivity** receiving the new intent now in LogCat when you run a search. You should also see the items in PhotoGallery revert to Brian faces and then refresh.

One important thing to note about **onNewIntent(Intent)**: if you need the new intent value, make sure to save it someplace. The value you get from **getIntent()** will have the old intent, not the new one. This is because **getIntent()** is intended to return the intent that *started* this activity, not the most recent intent it received.

Next up is to integrate that search query into your app. You will be implementing search so that there is only a single search query at any given time. It would be nice if that query were persistent...

Simple persistence with shared preferences

You could persist this data by serializing objects to flash storage like you did in Chapter 17. For simple values, though, *shared preferences* are simpler to implement and better behaved.

Shared preferences are files on your file system that you read and edit using the **SharedPreferences** class. An instance of **SharedPreferences** acts like a key-value store, much like **Bundle**, except that it is backed by persistent storage. The keys are strings, and the values are atomic data types. If you look at them you will see that the files are simple XML, but **SharedPreferences** makes it easy to ignore that implementation detail.

To start using a simple string value in shared preferences, just add a constant to use as the key for your preference value. Add your constant to **FlickrFetchr**:

Listing 28.10 Shared preferences constant (FlickrFetchr.java)

```
public class FlickrFetchr {
    public static final String TAG = "FlickrFetchr";

    public static final String PREF_SEARCH_QUERY = "searchQuery";

    private static final String ENDPOINT = "http://api.flickr.com/services/rest/";
    ...
```

To get a specific instance of **SharedPreferences**, you can use the **Context.getSharedPreferences(String,int)** method. However, in practice, you will often not care too much about the specific instance, just that it is shared across the entire app. In that case, it is better to use the **PreferenceManager.getDefaultSharedPreferences(Context)** method, which returns an instance with a default name and private permissions.

Acquire the default **SharedPreferences** and write your query out in **PhotoGalleryActivity**.

Listing 28.11 Save out search query (PhotoGalleryActivity.java)

```
@Override
public void onNewIntent(Intent intent) {
    PhotoGalleryFragment fragment = (PhotoGalleryFragment)getSupportFragmentManager()
            .findFragmentById(R.id.fragmentContainer);

    if (Intent.ACTION_SEARCH.equals(intent.getAction())) {
        String query = intent.getStringExtra(SearchManager.QUERY);
        Log.i(TAG, "Received a new search query: " + query);

        PreferenceManager.getDefaultSharedPreferences(this)
            .edit()
            .putString(FlickrFetchr.PREF_SEARCH_QUERY, query)
            .commit();
    }
    fragment.updateItems();
}
```

In your code above, you call **SharedPreferences.edit()** to get an instance of
SharedPreferences.Editor. This is the class you use to stash values in your **SharedPreferences**.
It allows you to group sets of changes together in transactions, much like you do with
FragmentTransaction. If you have a lot of changes, this will allow you to group them together into a
single storage write operation.

Once you are done making all of your changes, you call **commit()** on your editor to make them visible
to other users of that **SharedPreferences** file.

Getting a value you previously stored is as simple as calling **SharedPreferences.getString(…)**,
getInt(…), or whichever method is appropriate for your data type. Add code to
PhotoGalleryFragment to fetch your search query from the default **SharedPreferences**.

Listing 28.12 Grab search query preference (PhotoGalleryFragment.java)

```
private class FetchItemsTask extends AsyncTask<Void,Void,ArrayList<GalleryItem>> {
    @Override
    protected ArrayList<GalleryItem> doInBackground(Void... params) {
        String query = "android"; // just for testing
        Activity activity = getActivity();
        if (activity == null)
            return new ArrayList<GalleryItem>();

        String query = PreferenceManager.getDefaultSharedPreferences(activity)
            .getString(FlickrFetchr.PREF_SEARCH_QUERY, null);
        if (query != null) {
            return new FlickrFetchr().search(query);
        } else {
            return new FlickrFetchr().fetchItems();
        }
    }

    @Override
    protected void onPostExecute(ArrayList<GalleryItem> items) {
        ...
    }
}
```

Preferences is your entire persistence engine for PhotoGallery. (Much easier than serializing JSON, right?)

Search should now work. Run PhotoGallery, try searching for something, and see what you get.

To implement canceling a search, clear out your search term from your shared preferences and call **updateItems()** again:

Listing 28.13 Implement cancel (PhotoGalleryFragment.java)

```
@Override
public boolean onOptionsItemSelected(MenuItem item) {
    switch (item.getItemId()) {
        ...
        case R.id.menu_item_clear:
            PreferenceManager.getDefaultSharedPreferences(getActivity())
                .edit()
                .putString(FlickrFetchr.PREF_SEARCH_QUERY, null)
                .commit();
            updateItems();
            return true;
        default:
            return super.onOptionsItemSelected(item);
    }
}
```

Using SearchView on Post-Android 3.0

Now you have a search interface that works everywhere. However, it does not work in a Honeycomb-approved fashion.

Honeycomb added a new class called **SearchView**. **SearchView** is an *action view* – a view that may be included within the action bar. **SearchView** allows your entire search interface to take place within your activity's action bar, instead of inside a dialog superimposed on your activity. That means that it has the same styling and theming as your application, which is a good and fine thing.

Using an action view is as simple as adding an android:actionViewClass attribute to your menu item tag, like so:

Listing 28.14 Add an action view to your menu (res/menu/ fragment_photo_gallery.xml)

```
<menu xmlns:android="http://schemas.android.com/apk/res/android">
  <item android:id="@+id/menu_item_search"
    android:title="@string/search"
    android:icon="@android:drawable/ic_menu_search"
    android:showAsAction="ifRoom"
    android:actionViewClass="android.widget.SearchView"
    />
  <item android:id="@+id/menu_item_clear"
    ...
    />
</menu>
```

When you specify an action view, you are saying "Hey Android, instead of using the regular view guts for this item in the action bar, use this view class instead." Usually this also means that you get

different behavior. Case in point: **SearchView** does not generate any **onOptionsItemSelected(…)**
callbacks. This is a good thing because it means you can leave those callbacks in place for older
devices that do not support action views.

(Speaking of older devices, you may have spotted **SearchViewCompat** in the support library.
Unfortunately, this is not what it appears to be – **SearchViewCompat** is not a version of **SearchView**
that you can use on older devices. Instead, it contains a couple of static methods that make it easier to
electively insert **SearchView** where it is available. It does not solve your problem here.)

If you want, you can fire up PhotoGallery and see what **SearchView** looks like. It will not do anything,
though. **SearchView** needs to know what your search configuration is before it will send you any
search intents. You need to add some code to **onCreateOptionsMenu(…)** that pulls out your search
configuration and sends it to **SearchView**.

With the help of the **SearchManager** system service, this is not as hard as it sounds. **SearchManager** has
a method called **getSearchableInfo(ComponentName)** that will root around in your manifest, package
up the relevant information, and return it as a **SearchableInfo** object. Then you just have to forward
your **SearchableInfo** along to your **SearchView** instance. Do this by writing the code in Listing 28.15.

Listing 28.15 Configure **SearchView** (PhotoGalleryFragment.java)

```
@Override
@TargetApi(11)
public void onCreateOptionsMenu(Menu menu, MenuInflater inflater) {
    super.onCreateOptionsMenu(menu, inflater);
    inflater.inflate(R.menu.fragment_photo_gallery, menu);
    if (Build.VERSION.SDK_INT >= Build.VERSION_CODES.HONEYCOMB) {
        // Pull out the SearchView
        MenuItem searchItem = menu.findItem(R.id.menu_item_search);
        SearchView searchView = (SearchView)searchItem.getActionView();

        // Get the data from our searchable.xml as a SearchableInfo
        SearchManager searchManager = (SearchManager)getActivity()
            .getSystemService(Context.SEARCH_SERVICE);
        ComponentName name = getActivity().getComponentName();
        SearchableInfo searchInfo = searchManager.getSearchableInfo(name);

        searchView.setSearchableInfo(searchInfo);
    }
}
```

Your first step here is simply to find your **SearchView**. You can do that by finding the search **MenuItem**
by its ID, and then getting its action view by calling **getActionView()**.

Next, you ask **SearchManager** for your search configuration. **SearchManager** is a system service that
is responsible for all things search related. Earlier, it was **SearchManager** acting behind the scenes to
pull out your search configuration and display the search interface. All the information about a search,
including the name of the activity that should get the intent and everything in your searchable.xml, is
stashed in the **SearchableInfo** object you get by calling **getSearchableInfo(ComponentName)** here.

Once you have your **SearchableInfo**, you tell **SearchView** about it by calling
setSearchableInfo(SearchableInfo). And now your **SearchView** is totally wired. Run and search on
a post-3.0 device to see it work.

Figure 28.5 The search within your own activity

Once **SearchView** is properly configured, it behaves exactly like your earlier searches did.

Except for one minor detail: if you try this using the hardware keyboard on an emulator, you will see the search executed two times, one after the other.

It turns out that there is a small bug in **SearchView**. If you hit the enter key on a hardware keyboard, it will trigger the search intent twice. In activities with a default launch mode, this would result in two identical activities starting for one search.

You were preparing for this bug earlier when you set the launch mode to singleTop. You insured that intents would be sent first to an existing activity, so a new activity is not started when the duplicate search intent is sent. The duplicate intent still, annoyingly, causes the search to run twice in a row, but that is far better than having two identical activities start up for one search.

Challenges

Your challenges in this chapter are not too difficult. The first one is to use the **Activity.startSearch(…)** method.

Under the hood, **onSearchRequested()** calls through to **Activity.startSearch(…)**, a more detailed way of starting the search dialog. With **startSearch(…)**, you can specify the initial query shown in the **EditText** where the user enters a search, add a bonus **Bundle** of data to send to the recipient searchable activity in the intent extras, or request a global web search dialog like you would see if you pressed the search button on the home screen.

For your first small challenge, use **Activity.startSearch(…)** to fill in the search dialog with the current search query and highlight it.

The second challenge is to display the total number of search results available in a **Toast** when a new search is invoked. To do this, you will need to look at the XML you are getting from Flickr. There will be a top level element attribute that tells you how many search results were returned.

29

Background Services

All the code you have written so far has been hooked up to an activity, which means that it is associated with some screen for the user to look at.

What if you do not need a screen, though? What if you need to do something out of sight and out of mind, like play music or check for new blog posts on an RSS feed? For this, you need a *service*.

In this chapter, you will add a new feature to PhotoGallery that will allow users to poll for new search results in the background. Whenever a new search result is available, the user will receive a notification in the status bar.

Creating an IntentService

Let's start by creating your service. In this chapter, you will use an **IntentService**. **IntentService** is not the only kind of service there is, but it is probably the most common. Create a subclass of **IntentService** called **PollService**. This will be the service you use to poll for search results.

PollService's **onHandleIntent(Intent)** method will be automatically stubbed out for you. Fill **onHandleIntent(Intent)** out with a log statement, add a log tag, and define a default constructor.

Listing 29.1 Create **PollService** (PollService.java)

```
public class PollService extends IntentService {
    private static final String TAG = "PollService";

    public PollService() {
        super(TAG);
    }

    @Override
    protected void onHandleIntent(Intent intent) {
        Log.i(TAG, "Received an intent: " + intent);
    }
}
```

This is a very basic **IntentService**. What does it do? Well, it is sort of like an activity. It is a context (**Service** is a subclass of **Context**), and it responds to intents (as you can see in **onHandleIntent(Intent)**).

A service's intents are called *commands*. Each command is an instruction to the service to do something. Depending on the kind of service, that command could be serviced in a variety of ways.

Figure 29.1 How **IntentService** services commands

1. Command Intent #1 Received
Service Created

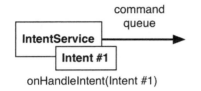

onHandleIntent(Intent #1)

2. Command Intent #2 Received

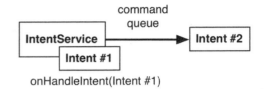

onHandleIntent(Intent #1)

3. Command Intent #3 Received

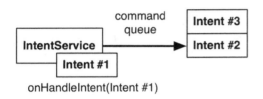

onHandleIntent(Intent #1)

4. Command Intent #1 Finished

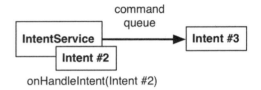

onHandleIntent(Intent #2)

5. Command Intent #2 Finished

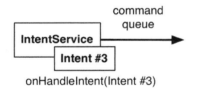

onHandleIntent(Intent #3)

6. Command Intent #3 Finished
Service Destroyed

An **IntentService** services commands off of a queue. When it receives its first command, the **IntentService** starts up, fires up a background thread, and puts the command on a queue.

The **IntentService** then proceeds to service each command in sequence, calling **onHandleIntent(Intent)** on its background thread for each command. New commands that come in go to the back of the queue. When there are no commands left in the queue, the service stops and is destroyed.

This description only applies to **IntentService**. Later in the chapter, we will discuss the broader world of services and how commands work.

You might infer from what you just learned about how **IntentService** works that services respond to intents. That is true! And since services, like activities, respond to intents, they must also be declared in your AndroidManifest.xml. Add an element for **PollService** to your manifest.

Listing 29.2 Add service to manifest (`AndroidManifest.xml`)

```
<manifest xmlns:android="http://schemas.android.com/apk/res/android"
  ... >

  ...

  <application
    ... >
    <activity
      android:name=".PhotoGalleryActivity"
      ... >
      ...
    </activity>
    <service android:name=".PollService" />
  </application>

</manifest>
```

Then add code to start your service inside **PhotoGalleryFragment**.

Listing 29.3 Add service startup code (`PhotoGalleryFragment.java`)

```java
@Override
public void onCreate(Bundle savedInstanceState) {
    super.onCreate(savedInstanceState);

    setRetainInstance(true);
    setHasOptionsMenu(true);

    updateItems();

    Intent i = new Intent(getActivity(), PollService.class);
    getActivity().startService(i);

    mThumbnailThread = new ThumbnailDownloader<ImageView>(new Handler());
    ...
}
```

Fire this up and see what you get. You should see something like this:

Figure 29.2 Your service's first steps

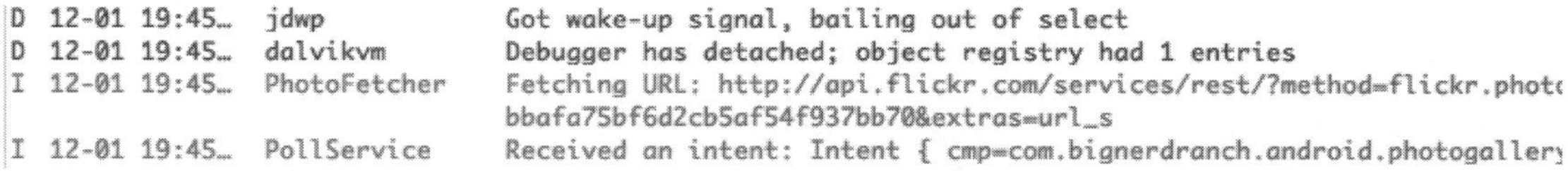

```
D 12-01 19:45...  jdwp            Got wake-up signal, bailing out of select
D 12-01 19:45...  dalvikvm        Debugger has detached; object registry had 1 entries
I 12-01 19:45...  PhotoFetcher    Fetching URL: http://api.flickr.com/services/rest/?method=flickr.photo
                                  bbafa75bf6d2cb5af54f937bb70&extras=url_s
I 12-01 19:45...  PollService     Received an intent: Intent { cmp=com.bignerdranch.android.photogallery
```

What Services Are For

Okay, we admit it: looking at those LogCat statements was boring. But this code is really exciting! Why? What can you do with it?

Time to go back the land of make believe, where we are no longer programmers, where we work in retail shoe sales with superheroes who do our bidding.

Your workers can work in two kinds of places in a store: the front of the store, where workers talk to customers, and the back of the store, where they do not. The back of the store may be larger or smaller, depending on the store.

So far, all of your code has run in activities. Activities are your Android app's storefront. All this code is focused on a pleasant visual experience for your user, your customer.

Services are the back end of your Android app. Things can happen there that the user never needs to know about. Work can go on there long after the storefront has closed, when your activities are long gone.

Okay, enough about stores. What can you do with a service that you cannot do with an activity? Well, for one, you can run a service while the user is occupied elsewhere.

Safe background networking

Your service is going to poll Flickr in the background. To perform networking in the background safely, some additional code is required. Android provides the ability for a user to turn off networking for backgrounded applications. If you have a lot of power hungry applications, this can be a big performance improvement.

This does mean, however, that if you are doing networking in the background, you need to verify with the **ConnectivityManager** that the network is available. Because the API has changed around historically, this requires two checks, not one. The first check is to verify that **ConnectivityManager.getBackgroundDataSetting()** is true, and the second is to verify that **ConnectivityManager.getActiveNetworkInfo()** is not null.

Add the code in Listing 29.4 to perform these checks, and we will get into the gory details once you are done.

Listing 29.4 Check for background network availability (`PollService.java`)

```
@Override
public void onHandleIntent(Intent intent) {
    ConnectivityManager cm = (ConnectivityManager)
            getSystemService(Context.CONNECTIVITY_SERVICE);
    @SuppressWarnings("deprecation")
    boolean isNetworkAvailable = cm.getBackgroundDataSetting() &&
        cm.getActiveNetworkInfo() != null;
    if (!isNetworkAvailable) return;

    Log.i(TAG, "Received an intent: " + intent);
}
```

Now for why you need two checks. In older versions of Android, you were supposed to check **getBackgroundDataSetting()** and bail out if it returned false. If you did not check it, then you could use background data all you wanted. This did not work very well. It was just too easy to ignore the check entirely, or inadvertently forget it.

In Android 4.0, Ice Cream Sandwich, this was changed so that the background data setting simply disabled the network entirely. Which is why you check to see whether `getActiveNetworkInfo()` returns null. If it is null, then the networking does not work at all. This is good for the user, because it means that the background data settings always do what they expect. Of course it is a little more work for you, the developer.

To use `getActiveNetworkInfo()`, you also need to acquire the ACCESS_NETWORK_STATE permission.

Listing 29.5 Acquire network state permission (`AndroidManifest.xml`)

```
<manifest xmlns:android="http://schemas.android.com/apk/res/android"
  package="com.bignerdranch.android.photogallery"
  android:versionCode="1"
  android:versionName="1.0" >

  <uses-sdk
    android:minSdkVersion="8"
    android:targetSdkVersion="17" />
  <uses-permission android:name="android.permission.INTERNET" />
  <uses-permission android:name="android.permission.ACCESS_NETWORK_STATE" />

  <application
    android:allowBackup="true"
    android:icon="@drawable/ic_launcher"
    android:label="@string/app_name"
    android:theme="@style/AppTheme" >
    ...
  </application>

</manifest>
```

Looking for New Results

Your service will be polling for new results, so it will need to know what the last result fetched was. This is a perfect job for another **SharedPreferences** entry. Add another constant to **FlickrFetchr** to store the ID of the most recently fetched photo.

Listing 29.6 Add recent ID preference constant (`FlickrFetchr.java`)

```
public class FlickrFetchr {
    public static final String TAG = "PhotoFetcher";

    public static final String PREF_SEARCH_QUERY = "searchQuery";
    public static final String PREF_LAST_RESULT_ID = "lastResultId";

    private static final String ENDPOINT = "http://api.flickr.com/services/rest/";
    private static final String API_KEY = "xxx";
    ...
```

The next step is to fill out your service. Here is what you need to do:

1. Pull out the current query and the last result ID from the default **SharedPreferences**.

2. Fetch the latest result set with **FlickrFetchr**.

3. If there are results, grab the first one.

4. Check to see if it is different from the last result ID.

5. Store the first result back in **SharedPreferences**.

Return to PollService.java and put this plan into action. Listing 29.7 shows a long swath of code, but it uses nothing you have not seen before.

Listing 29.7 Checking for new results (PollService.java)

```java
@Override
protected void onHandleIntent(Intent intent) {
    ...

    if (!isNetworkAvailable) return;

    SharedPreferences prefs = PreferenceManager.getDefaultSharedPreferences(this);
    String query = prefs.getString(FlickrFetchr.PREF_SEARCH_QUERY, null);
    String lastResultId = prefs.getString(FlickrFetchr.PREF_LAST_RESULT_ID, null);

    ArrayList<GalleryItem> items;
    if (query != null) {
        items = new FlickrFetchr().search(query);
    } else {
        items = new FlickrFetchr().fetchItems();
    }

    if (items.size() == 0)
        return;

    String resultId = items.get(0).getId();

    if (!resultId.equals(lastResultId)) {
        Log.i(TAG, "Got a new result: " + resultId);
    } else {
        Log.i(TAG, "Got an old result: " + resultId);
    }

    prefs.edit()
        .putString(FlickrFetchr.PREF_LAST_RESULT_ID, resultId)
        .commit();
}
```

See each part we discussed above? Good. Run PhotoGallery, and you should see your app getting new results initially. If you have a search query selected, you will probably see stale results when you subsequently start up the app.

Delayed Execution with AlarmManager

To actually use your service in the background, you will need some way to make things happen when none of your activities are running. Say, by making a timer that goes off every five minutes or so.

You could do this with a **Handler** by calling **Handler.sendMessageDelayed(…)** or
Handler.postDelayed(…). This solution will probably fail if the user navigates away from all your
activities, though. The process will shut down, and your **Handler** messages will go kaput with it.

So instead of **Handler**, you will use **AlarmManager**. **AlarmManager** is a system service that can send
Intents for you.

How do you tell **AlarmManager** what intents to send? You use a **PendingIntent**. You can use
PendingIntent to package up a wish: "I want to start **PollService**." You can then send that wish to
other components on the system, like **AlarmManager**.

Write a new method called **setServiceAlarm(Context,boolean)** inside **PollService** that turns an
alarm on and off for you. You will write it as a static method. That keeps your alarm code with the
other code in **PollService** that it is related to, but allows other components to invoke it. You will
usually want to turn it on and off from front end code in a fragment or other controller.

Listing 29.8 Add alarm method (`PollService.java`)

```java
public class PollService extends IntentService {
    private static final String TAG = "PollService";

    private static final int POLL_INTERVAL = 1000 * 15; // 15 seconds

    public PollService() {
        super(TAG);
    }

    @Override
    public void onHandleIntent(Intent intent) {
        ...
    }

    public static void setServiceAlarm(Context context, boolean isOn) {
        Intent i = new Intent(context, PollService.class);
        PendingIntent pi = PendingIntent.getService(
                context, 0, i, 0);

        AlarmManager alarmManager = (AlarmManager)
                context.getSystemService(Context.ALARM_SERVICE);

        if (isOn) {
            alarmManager.setRepeating(AlarmManager.RTC,
                    System.currentTimeMillis(), POLL_INTERVAL, pi);
        } else {
            alarmManager.cancel(pi);
            pi.cancel();
        }
    }
}
```

The first thing you do in your method is construct your **PendingIntent** that starts **PollService**. You
do this by calling **PendingIntent.getService(…)**. **PendingIntent.getService(…)** packages up an
invocation of **Context.startService(Intent)**. It takes in four parameters: a **Context** with which
to send the intent, a request code that you can use to distinguish this **PendingIntent** from others, the
Intent object to send, and finally a set of flags that you can use to tweak how the **PendingIntent** is
created. (You will use one of these in a moment).

After that, you need to either set the alarm or cancel it. To set the alarm, you call **AlarmManager.setRepeating(…)**. This method also takes four parameters: a constant to describe the time basis for the alarm (about which more in a moment), the time at which to start the alarm, the time interval at which to repeat the alarm, and finally a **PendingIntent** to fire when the alarm goes off.

Canceling the alarm is done by calling **AlarmManager.cancel(PendingIntent)**. You will also usually want to cancel the **PendingIntent**, too. In a moment, you will see how canceling the **PendingIntent** also helps us track the status of the alarm.

Add some quick test code to run it from within **PhotoGalleryFragment**.

Listing 29.9 Add alarm startup code (PhotoGalleryFragment.java)

```
@Override
public void onCreate(Bundle savedInstanceState) {
    super.onCreate(savedInstanceState);

    setRetainInstance(true);
    setHasOptionsMenu(true);

    updateItems();

    Intent i = new Intent(getActivity(), PollService.class);
    getActivity().startService(i);
    PollService.setServiceAlarm(getActivity(), true);

    mThumbnailThread = new ThumbnailDownloader<ImageView>(new Handler());
    ...
}
```

Finish typing in this code and run PhotoGallery. Then immediately hit the back button and exit out of the app.

Notice anything in LogCat? **PollService** is faithfully chugging along, running again every 15 seconds. This is what **AlarmManager** is designed to do. Even if your process gets shut down, **AlarmManager** will keep on firing intents to start **PollService** again and again.

(This behavior is, of course, extremely annoying. You may want to uninstall the app until we get it all straightened out.)

PendingIntent

Let's talk a little bit more about **PendingIntent**. A **PendingIntent** is a token object. When you get one here by calling **PendingIntent.getService(…)**, you say to the OS, "Please remember that I want to send this intent with **startService(Intent)**." Later on you can call **send()** on your **PendingIntent** token, and the OS will send the intent you originally wrapped up in exactly the way you asked.

The really nice thing about this is that when you give that **PendingIntent** token to someone else and they use it, it sends that token *as your application*. Also, since the **PendingIntent** itself lives in the OS, not in the token, you maintain control of it. If you wanted to be cruel, you could give someone else a **PendingIntent** object and then immediately cancel it, so that **send()** does nothing.

If you request a **PendingIntent** twice with the same intent, you will get the same **PendingIntent**. You can use this to test whether a **PendingIntent** already exists or to cancel a previously issued **PendingIntent**.

Managing alarms with PendingIntent

You can only register one alarm for each **PendingIntent**. That is how **setServiceAlarm(Context,boolean)** works when isOn is false: it calls **AlarmManager.cancel(PendingIntent)** to cancel the alarm for your **PendingIntent**, and then cancels your **PendingIntent**.

Since the **PendingIntent** is also cleaned up when the alarm is canceled, you can check whether that **PendingIntent** exists or not to see whether the alarm is active or not. This is done by passing in the PendingIntent.FLAG_NO_CREATE flag to **PendingIntent.getService(…)**. This flag says that if the **PendingIntent** does not already exist, return null instead of creating it.

Write a new method called **isServiceAlarmOn(Context)** that uses PendingIntent.FLAG_NO_CREATE to tell whether the alarm is on or not.

Listing 29.10 Add **isServiceAlarmOn()** method (PollService.java)

```
public static void setServiceAlarm(Context context, boolean isOn) {
    ...
}

public static boolean isServiceAlarmOn(Context context) {
    Intent i = new Intent(context, PollService.class);
    PendingIntent pi = PendingIntent.getService(
            context, 0, i, PendingIntent.FLAG_NO_CREATE);
    return pi != null;
}
```

Since this **PendingIntent** is only used for setting your alarm, a null **PendingIntent** here means that your alarm is not set.

Controlling Your Alarm

Now that you can turn your alarm on and off (as well as tell whether it is on or off), let's add an interface to turn this thing on and off. Add another menu item to menu/fragment_photo_gallery.xml.

Listing 29.11 Add service toggle (menu/fragment_photo_gallery.xml)

```
<menu xmlns:android="http://schemas.android.com/apk/res/android">
  <item android:id="@+id/menu_item_search"
    android:title="@string/search"
    android:icon="@android:drawable/ic_menu_search"
    android:showAsAction="ifRoom"
    android:actionViewClass="android.widget.SearchView"
    />
  <item android:id="@+id/menu_item_clear"
    android:title="@string/clear_search"
    android:icon="@android:drawable/ic_menu_close_clear_cancel"
    android:showAsAction="ifRoom"
    />
  <item android:id="@+id/menu_item_toggle_polling"
    android:title="@string/start_polling"
    android:showAsAction="ifRoom"
    />
</menu>
```

Then you need to add a few new strings – one to start polling, and one to stop polling. (You will need a couple of other ones later, too, for a status bar notification. Go ahead and add those as well.)

Listing 29.12 Add polling strings (res/values/strings.xml)

```
<resources>

    ...
    <string name="search">Search</string>
    <string name="clear_search">Clear Search</string>
    <string name="start_polling">Poll for new pictures</string>
    <string name="stop_polling">Stop polling</string>
    <string name="new_pictures_title">New PhotoGallery Pictures</string>
    <string name="new_pictures_text">You have new pictures in PhotoGallery.</string>

</resources>
```

Now delete your old debug code for starting the alarm, and add an implementation for the menu item.

Listing 29.13 Toggle menu item implementation (PhotoGalleryFragment.java)

```
@Override
public void onCreate(Bundle savedInstanceState) {
    super.onCreate(savedInstanceState);

    setRetainInstance(true);
    setHasOptionsMenu(true);

    updateItems();

    PollService.setServiceAlarm(getActivity(), true);

    mThumbnailThread = new ThumbnailDownloader<ImageView>(new Handler());
    ...
}

...

@Override
@TargetApi(11)
public boolean onOptionsItemSelected(MenuItem item) {
    switch (item.getItemId()) {
        case R.id.menu_item_search:
            ...
        case R.id.menu_item_clear:
            ...

            updateItems();
            return true;
        case R.id.menu_item_toggle_polling:
            boolean shouldStartAlarm = !PollService.isServiceAlarmOn(getActivity());
            PollService.setServiceAlarm(getActivity(), shouldStartAlarm);

            return true;
        default:
            return super.onOptionsItemSelected(item);
    }
}
```

With that, you should be able to toggle your alarm on and off.

How to update your menu item, though? Well!

Updating options menu items

Usually, all you have to do is inflate an options menu. Sometimes, though, you need to update the options menu to reflect the state of your application.

Now, options menus are not inflated every time they are used, even on old style options menus. If you need to update the contents of an options menu item, you should instead put that code in `onPrepareOptionsMenu(Menu)`. This method is called every single time the menu needs to be configured, not just when it is created the first time.

Add an implementation of `onPrepareOptionsMenu(Menu)` that checks to see whether the alarm is on, and then changes the text of `menu_item_toggle_polling` to show the appropriate feedback to the user.

Listing 29.14 Add **onPrepareOptionsMenu(Menu)** (PhotoGalleryFragment.java)

```java
@Override
public boolean onOptionsItemSelected(MenuItem item) {
    ...
}

@Override
public void onPrepareOptionsMenu(Menu menu) {
    super.onPrepareOptionsMenu(menu);

    MenuItem toggleItem = menu.findItem(R.id.menu_item_toggle_polling);
    if (PollService.isServiceAlarmOn(getActivity())) {
        toggleItem.setTitle(R.string.stop_polling);
    } else {
        toggleItem.setTitle(R.string.start_polling);
    }
}
```

In pre-3.0 devices, this method is called every time the menu is displayed, which ensures that your menu item always shows the right text. Run PhotoGallery on a pre-3.0 emulator if you would like to check this yourself.

After 3.0, though, this is not enough. The action bar does not automatically update itself. You have to manually tell it to call `onPrepareOptionsMenu(Menu)` and refresh its items by calling `Activity.invalidateOptionsMenu()`.

Add the following code to `onOptionsItemSelected(MenuItem)` to tell post-3.0 devices to update their action bars:

Listing 29.15 Invalidate your options menu (`PhotoGalleryFragment.java`)

```java
@Override
@TargetApi(11)
public boolean onOptionsItemSelected(MenuItem item) {
    switch (item.getItemId()) {
        ...
        case R.id.menu_item_toggle_polling:
            boolean shouldStartAlarm = !PollService.isServiceAlarmOn(getActivity());
            PollService.setServiceAlarm(getActivity(), shouldStartAlarm);

            if (Build.VERSION.SDK_INT >= Build.VERSION_CODES.HONEYCOMB)
                getActivity().invalidateOptionsMenu();

            return true;
        default:
            return super.onOptionsItemSelected(item);
    }
}
```

With that, your code should work great on a new 4.2 emulator, too.

And yet. There is something missing.

Notifications

Your service is now running and doing its thing in the background. The user never knows a thing about it, though, so it is not worth much.

When your service needs to communicate something to the user, the proper tool is almost always a *notification*. Notifications are items that appear in the notifications drawer, which the user can access by dragging it down from the top of the screen.

To post a notification, you first need to create a **Notification** object. **Notification**s are created by using a builder object, much like **AlertDialog** was in Chapter 12. At a minimum, your **Notification** should have:

- *ticker text* to display in the status bar when the notification is first shown

- an *icon* to show in the status bar after the ticker text goes away

- a *view* to show in the notification drawer to represent the notification itself

- a *PendingIntent* to fire when the user presses the notification in the drawer

Once you have created a **Notification** object, you can post it by calling **notify(int, Notification)** on the **NotificationManager** system service.

Make **PollService** notify the user that a new result is ready by adding the code in Listing 29.16, which creates a **Notification** and calls **NotificationManager.notify(int, Notification)**.

Listing 29.16 Add a notification (`PollService.java`)

```java
@Override
public void onHandleIntent(Intent intent) {
    ...

    String resultId = items.get(0).getId();

    if (!resultId.equals(lastResultId)) {
        Log.i(TAG, "Got a new result: " + resultId);

        Resources r = getResources();
        PendingIntent pi = PendingIntent
            .getActivity(this, 0, new Intent(this, PhotoGalleryActivity.class), 0);

        Notification notification = new NotificationCompat.Builder(this)
            .setTicker(r.getString(R.string.new_pictures_title))
            .setSmallIcon(android.R.drawable.ic_menu_report_image)
            .setContentTitle(r.getString(R.string.new_pictures_title))
            .setContentText(r.getString(R.string.new_pictures_text))
            .setContentIntent(pi)
            .setAutoCancel(true)
            .build();

        NotificationManager notificationManager = (NotificationManager)
            getSystemService(NOTIFICATION_SERVICE);

        notificationManager.notify(0, notification);
    }

    prefs.edit()
        .putString(FlickrFetchr.PREF_LAST_RESULT_ID, resultId)
        .commit();
}
```

Let's go over this from top to bottom. First, you configure the ticker text and small icon by calling **setTicker(CharSequence)** and **setSmallIcon(int)**.

After that, you configure the appearance of your **Notification** in the drawer itself. It is possible to create a completely custom look and feel, but it is easier to use the standard look for a notification, which features an icon, a title, and a text area. It will use the value from **setSmallIcon(int)** for the icon. To set the title and text, you call **setContentTitle(CharSequence)** and **setContentText(CharSequence)**, respectively.

Next, you must specify what happens when the user presses your **Notification**. Like **AlarmManager**, this is done using a **PendingIntent**. The **PendingIntent** you pass in to **setContentIntent(PendingIntent)** will be fired when the user presses your **Notification** in the drawer. Calling **setAutoCancel(true)** tweaks that behavior a little bit. With **setAutoCancel(true)** set, your notification will also be deleted from the notification drawer when the user presses it.

Finally, there is the call to **NotificationManager.notify(…)**. The integer parameter you pass in is an identifier for your notification. It should be unique across your application. If you post a second notification with this same ID, it will replace the last notification you posted with that ID. This is how you would implement a progress bar or other dynamic visuals.

And that is it. Your entire backgrounded user interface! After you are satisfied that everything is working correctly, change your alarm constant to be something more sensible:

Listing 29.17 Change to a sensible alarm constant (`PollService.java`)

```
public class PollService extends IntentService {
    private static final String TAG = "PollService";

    public static final int POLL_INTERVAL = 1000 * 15; // 15 seconds
    public static final int POLL_INTERVAL = 1000 * 60 * 5; // 5 minutes

    public PollService() {
        super(TAG);
    }
}
```

For the More Curious: Service Details

We recommend using **IntentService** for most service tasks. If the **IntentService** pattern does not suit your architecture, though, you will need to understand more about services to implement your own. Prepare for an infobomb, though – there are a lot of details and ins and outs to using services.

What service does (and does not) do

A service is an application component that provides lifecycle callbacks, just like an activity. Those callbacks are even performed on the main UI thread for you, just like in an activity.

A service does *not* run any code on a background thread out of the box. This is the #1 reason we recommend **IntentService**. Most non-trivial services will require a background thread of some kind, and **IntentService** automatically manages the boilerplate code you need to accomplish that.

Let's look and see what lifecycle callbacks a service has.

A service's lifecycle

For a service started with **startService(Intent)**, life is fairly simple. There are four lifecycle callbacks.

- **onCreate(…)** – called when the service is created.

- **onStartCommand(Intent,int,int)** – called once each time a component starts the service with **startService(Intent)**. The two integer parameters are a set of flags and a start ID. The flags are used to signify whether this intent delivery is an attempt to redeliver an intent, or if it is an attempt to retry a delivery which never made it to or returned from **onStartCommand(Intent,int,int)**. The start ID will be different for every call to **onStartCommand(Intent,int,int)**, so it may be used to distinguish this command from others.

- **onDestroy()** – called when the service no longer needs to be alive. Often this will be after the service is stopped.

One question remains: how does the service stop? This can happen in different ways, depending on what type of service you have written. The type of service is determined by the value returned from **onStartCommand(…)**, which may be Service.START_NOT_STICKY, START_REDELIVER_INTENT, or START_STICKY.

Non-sticky services

IntentService is a non-sticky service, so let's start there. A non-sticky service stops when the service itself says it is done. To make your service non-sticky, return either START_NOT_STICKY or START_REDELIVER_INTENT.

You tell Android that you are done by calling either **stopSelf()** or **stopSelf(int)**. The first method, **stopSelf()**, is unconditional. It will always stop your service, no matter how many times **onStartCommand(…)** has been called.

IntentService uses **stopSelf(int)** instead. This method takes in the start ID received in **onStartCommand(…)**. This method will only stop your service if this was the most recent start ID received. (This is how **IntentService** works under the hood.)

So what is the difference between returning START_NOT_STICKY and START_REDELIVER_INTENT? The difference is in how your service behaves if the system needs to shut it down before it is done. A START_NOT_STICKY service will die and disappear into the void. START_REDELIVER_INTENT, on the other hand, will attempt to start up the service again later, when resources are less constrained.

Choosing between START_NOT_STICKY and START_REDELIVER_INTENT is a matter of deciding how important that operation is to your application. If the service is not critical, choose START_NOT_STICKY. In PhotoGallery, your service is being run repeatedly on an alarm. If one invocation falls through the cracks, it is not a big deal, so: START_NOT_STICKY. This is the default behavior for **IntentService**. To switch to using START_REDELIVER_INTENT, call **IntentService.setIntentRedelivery(true)**.

Sticky services

A *sticky service* stays started until something outside the service tells it to stop by calling **Context.stopService(Intent)**. To make your service sticky, return START_STICKY.

Once a sticky service is started it is "on" until a component calls **Context.stopService(Intent)**. If the service needs to be killed for some reason, it will be restarted again with a null intent passed in to **onStartCommand(…)**.

A sticky service may be appropriate for a long-running service, like a music player, which needs to stick around until the user tells it to stop. Even then, it is worth considering an alternative architecture using non-sticky services. Sticky service management is inconvenient, because it is difficult to tell whether the service is already started.

Bound services

In addition to all this, it is possible to bind to a service by using the **bindService(Intent,ServiceConnection,int)** method. *Service binding* is a way to connect to a service and call methods on it directly. You bind to a service by calling **bindService(Intent,ServiceConnection,int)**. **ServiceConnection** is an object that represents your service binding and receives all binding callbacks.

In a fragment, your binding code would look something like this:

```
private ServiceConnection mServiceConnection = new ServiceConnection() {
    public void onServiceConnected(ComponentName className,
            IBinder service) {
        // Used to communicate with the service
        MyBinder binder = (MyBinder)service;
    }

    public void onServiceDisconnected(ComponentName className) {
    }
};

@Override
public void onCreate(Bundle savedInstanceState) {
    super.onCreate(savedInstanceState);

    Intent i = new Intent(c, MyService.class);
    c.bindService(i, mServiceConnection, 0);
}

@Override
public void onDestroy() {
    super.onDestroy();
    getActivity().getApplicationContext().unbindService(mServiceConnection);
}
```

On the service's side, binding introduces two additional lifecycle callbacks:

- **onBind(Intent)** – called every time the service is bound to. Returns the **IBinder** object received in **ServiceConnection.onServiceConnected(ComponentName,IBinder)**.

- **onUnbind(Intent)** – called when a service's binding is terminated.

Local service binding

So what does **MyBinder** look like? If the service is a *local service*, then it may be a simple Java object that lives in your local process. Usually this is used to provide a handle to directly call methods on your service:

```
private class MyBinder extends IBinder {
    public MyService getService() {
        return MyService.this;
    }
}

@Override
public void onBind(Intent intent) {
    return new MyBinder();
}
```

This pattern looks exciting. It is the only place in Android that enables one Android component to directly talk to another. We do not recommend it, though. Since services are effectively singletons, using them this way provides no major benefits over just using a singleton instead.

Remote service binding

Binding is more useful for *remote services*, because they give applications in other processes the ability to invoke methods on your service. Creating a remote service binder is an advanced topic and beyond the scope of this book. Check out AIDL or the `Messenger` class for more details.

30

Broadcast Intents

Things are happening all the time on an Android device. WiFi is going in and out of range, packages are getting installed, phone calls and text messages are coming in.

When many components on the system need to know that some event has occurred, Android uses a *broadcast intent* to tell everyone about it. Broadcast intents work similarly to the intents you already know and love, except that they can be received by multiple components at the same time. Broadcast intents are received by *broadcast receivers*.

Figure 30.1 Regular intents vs. broadcast intents

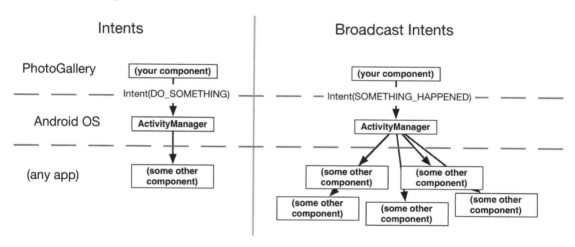

In this chapter, you will learn how to listen to broadcast intents from the system, as well as how to dynamically send and receive them within your app at runtime. You will start by listening for a broadcast that informs you that the device has booted up, and then later you will send and receive your own broadcast intent.

Waking Up on Boot

PhotoGallery's background alarm works, but it is not perfect. If the user reboots their phone, the alarm will be forgotten.

Apps that perform an ongoing process for the user usually need to wake themselves up after the device is booted. You can detect when boot is completed by listening for a broadcast intent with the BOOT_COMPLETED action.

Broadcast receivers in the manifest

Time to write a broadcast receiver. Start by creating a new Java class called **StartupReceiver** that is a subclass of **android.content.BroadcastReceiver**. Eclipse will implement one abstract method for you called **onReceive(Context,Intent)**. Fill out your class like so:

Listing 30.1 Your first broadcast receiver (StartupReceiver.java)

```
package com.bignerdranch.android.photogallery;

...

public class StartupReceiver extends BroadcastReceiver {
    private static final String TAG = "StartupReceiver";

    @Override
    public void onReceive(Context context, Intent intent) {
        Log.i(TAG, "Received broadcast intent: " + intent.getAction());
    }
}
```

This is your broadcast receiver. A broadcast receiver is a component that receives intents, just like a service or an activity. And just like services and activities, broadcast receivers must be registered with the system in order to do anything useful. That does not always mean that they need to be in your manifest. This particular receiver does, though.

Hooking up a receiver works just like hooking up a service or activity. You use the receiver tag with appropriate intent-filters within. **StartupReceiver** will be listening for the BOOT_COMPLETED action. This action also requires a permission, so you will need to include an appropriate uses-permission tag as well.

Open AndroidManifest.xml and hook up **StartupReceiver**.

Listing 30.2 Adding your receiver to the manifest (AndroidManifest.xml)

```
<manifest xmlns:android="http://schemas.android.com/apk/res/android"
  package="com.bignerdranch.android.photogallery"
  android:versionCode="1"
  android:versionName="1.0" >

  <uses-sdk
    android:minSdkVersion="8"
    android:targetSdkVersion="17" />

  <uses-permission android:name="android.permission.INTERNET" />
  <uses-permission android:name="android.permission.ACCESS_NETWORK_STATE" />
  <uses-permission android:name="android.permission.RECEIVE_BOOT_COMPLETED" />
```

```
<application
    ... >
    <activity
        ... >
        ...
    </activity>
    <service android:name=".PollService" />
    <receiver android:name=".StartupReceiver">
        <intent-filter>
            <action android:name="android.intent.action.BOOT_COMPLETED" />
        </intent-filter>
    </receiver>
</application>

</manifest>
```

Unlike activities and services, broadcast receivers declared in the manifest almost always declare intent filters. The entire reason broadcast intents exist is to send information to more than one listener, but explicit intents only have one receiver. As a result, the explicit broadcast intent is a rare bird.

Figure 30.2 Receiving BOOT_COMPLETED

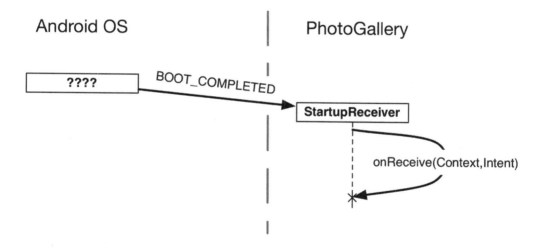

With your broadcast receiver declared in your manifest, it will wake up anytime a matching broadcast intent is sent – even if your app is not currently running. Upon waking up, the ephemeral broadcast receiver's **onReceive(Context,Intent)** method will be run, and then it will die.

Run PhotoGallery, reboot your device or emulator and switch over to DDMS. You should see a LogCat statement showing that your receiver ran. If you check your device in the Devices tab, though, you will probably not see a process for PhotoGallery. Your process came to life just long enough to run your broadcast receiver, and then it died again.

How to use receivers

The fact that broadcast receivers live such short lives restricts the things you can do with them. You cannot use any asynchronous APIs, for example, or register any listeners, because your receiver will not be alive any longer than the length of **onReceive(Context,Intent)**. **onReceive(Context,Intent)** runs on your main thread, too, so you cannot do any heavy lifting inside it. That means no networking or heavy work with permanent storage.

This does not make receivers useless, though. They are invaluable for all kinds of little plumbing code. Your recurring alarm needs to be reset when the system finishes starting. This is a small enough task that a broadcast receiver is perfect for the job.

Your receiver will need to know whether the alarm should be on or off. Add a preference constant to **PollService** to store this information.

Listing 30.3 Add alarm status preference (`PollService.java`)

```java
public class PollService extends IntentService {
    private static final String TAG = "PollService";

    private static final int POLL_INTERVAL = 1000 * 60 * 5; // 5 minutes
    public static final String PREF_IS_ALARM_ON = "isAlarmOn";

    public PollService() {
        super(TAG);
    }

    ...

    public static void setServiceAlarm(Context context, boolean isOn) {
        Intent i = new Intent(context, PollService.class);
        PendingIntent pi = PendingIntent.getService(
                context, 0, i, 0);

        AlarmManager alarmManager = (AlarmManager)
                context.getSystemService(Context.ALARM_SERVICE);

        if (isOn) {
            alarmManager.setRepeating(AlarmManager.RTC,
                    System.currentTimeMillis(), POLL_INTERVAL, pi);
        } else {
            alarmManager.cancel(pi);
            pi.cancel();
        }

        PreferenceManager.getDefaultSharedPreferences(context)
            .edit()
            .putBoolean(PollService.PREF_IS_ALARM_ON, isOn)
            .commit();
    }
}
```

Then your **StartupReceiver** can use it to turn the alarm on at boot.

Listing 30.4 Start alarm on boot (`StartupReceiver.java`)

```
@Override
public void onReceive(Context context, Intent intent) {
    Log.i(TAG, "Received broadcast intent: " + intent.getAction());

    SharedPreferences prefs = PreferenceManager.getDefaultSharedPreferences(context);
    boolean isOn = prefs.getBoolean(PollService.PREF_IS_ALARM_ON, false);
    PollService.setServiceAlarm(context, isOn);
}
```

Run PhotoGallery again. This time, your background polling should be restarted after you reboot your phone, tablet, or emulator.

Filtering Foreground Notifications

With that sharp corner filed down a bit, we turn to another imperfection in PhotoGallery. Your notifications work great, but they are sent even when the user already has the application open.

You can fix this problem with broadcast intents, too. But they will work in a completely different way.

Sending broadcast intents

This is the easiest part of the solution: sending your own broadcast intent. To send a broadcast intent, just create an intent and pass it in to **sendBroadcast(Intent)**. In this case, you will want it to broadcast an action you define, so define an action constant as well. Add the following bits of code to **PollService**.

Listing 30.5 Sending a broadcast intent (`PollService.java`)

```java
public class PollService extends IntentService {
    private static final String TAG = "PollService";

    private static final int POLL_INTERVAL = 1000 * 60 * 5; // 5 minutes
    public static final String PREF_IS_ALARM_ON = "isAlarmOn";

    public static final String ACTION_SHOW_NOTIFICATION =
        "com.bignerdranch.android.photogallery.SHOW_NOTIFICATION";

    public PollService() {
        super(TAG);
    }

    @Override
    public void onHandleIntent(Intent intent) {
        ...

        if (!resultId.equals(lastResultId)) {
            ...

            NotificationManager notificationManager = (NotificationManager)
                getSystemService(NOTIFICATION_SERVICE);

            notificationManager.notify(0, notification);

            sendBroadcast(new Intent(ACTION_SHOW_NOTIFICATION));
        }

        prefs.edit()
            .putString(FlickrFetchr.PREF_LAST_RESULT_ID, resultId)
            .commit();
    }
}
```

Dynamic broadcast receivers

Next up is to receive your broadcast intent. You could write a broadcast receiver like **StartupReceiver** registered in the manifest to handle this. But that would not do the right thing in your case. Here, you really want **PhotoGalleryFragment** to receive the intent only while it is alive. A standalone receiver declared in the manifest would not do that job easily. It would always receive the intent, and would need some other way of knowing that **PhotoGalleryFragment** is alive.

The solution is to use a *dynamic broadcast receiver*. A dynamic receiver is registered in code, not in the manifest. You register the receiver by calling **registerReceiver(BroadcastReceiver, IntentFilter)** and unregister it by calling **unregisterReceiver(BroadcastReceiver)**. The receiver itself is typically defined as an inner instance, like a button-click listener. However, since you need the same instance in **registerReceiver(…)** and **unregisterReceiver(…)**, you will need to assign the receiver to an instance variable.

Create a new abstract class called **VisibleFragment**, with **Fragment** as its superclass. This class will be a generic fragment that hides foreground notifications. (You will write another fragment like this in Chapter 31.)

Listing 30.6 A receiver of **VisibleFragment**'s own (VisibleFragment.java)

```
package com.bignerdranch.android.photogallery;

...

public abstract class VisibleFragment extends Fragment {
    public static final String TAG = "VisibleFragment";

    private BroadcastReceiver mOnShowNotification = new BroadcastReceiver() {
        @Override
        public void onReceive(Context context, Intent intent) {
            Toast.makeText(getActivity(),
                    "Got a broadcast:" + intent.getAction(),
                    Toast.LENGTH_LONG)
                .show();
        }
    };

    @Override
    public void onResume() {
        super.onResume();
        IntentFilter filter = new IntentFilter(PollService.ACTION_SHOW_NOTIFICATION);
        getActivity().registerReceiver(mOnShowNotification, filter);
    }

    @Override
    public void onPause() {
        super.onPause();
        getActivity().unregisterReceiver(mOnShowNotification);
    }
}
```

Note that to pass in an **IntentFilter**, you have to create one in code. Your **IntentFilter** here is identical to the filter specified by the following XML:

```
<intent-filter>
    <action android:name="com.bignerdranch.android.photogallery.SHOW_NOTIFICATION" />
</intent-filter>
```

Any **IntentFilter** you can express in XML can also be expressed in code this way. Just call **addCategory(String)**, **addAction(String)**, **addDataPath(String)**, and so on to configure your filter.

Dynamically registered broadcast receivers must also take care to clean themselves up. Typically, if you register a receiver in a startup lifecycle method, you will call **Context.unregisterReceiver(BroadcastReceiver)** in the corresponding shutdown method. So here you register inside **onResume()**, and unregister inside **onPause()**. Similarly, if you registered inside **onActivityCreated(…)**, you would unregister inside **onActivityDestroyed()**.

(Be careful with **onCreate(…)** and **onDestroy()** in retained fragments, by the way. **getActivity()** will return different values in **onCreate(…)** and **onDestroy()** if the screen has rotated. If you want to register/unregister in **Fragment.onCreate(Bundle)** and **Fragment.onDestroy()**, use **getActivity().getApplicationContext()** instead.)

Modify **PhotoGalleryFragment** to be a subclass of your new **VisibleFragment**.

Listing 30.7 Make your fragment visible (`PhotoGalleryFragment.java`)

```
public class PhotoGalleryFragment extends Fragment {
public class PhotoGalleryFragment extends VisibleFragment {
    GridView mGridView;
    ArrayList<GalleryItem> mItems;
    ThumbnailDownloader<ImageView> mThumbnailThread;
```

Run PhotoGallery and toggle background polling a couple of times. You will see a nice toast pop up in addition to your notification ticker up top.

Figure 30.3 Proof that your broadcast exists

Using private permissions

One problem with using a broadcast like this is that anyone on the system can listen to it or trigger your receivers. You are usually not going to want either of those things to happen.

You can preclude these unauthorized intrusions into your personal business in a couple of ways. If the receiver is declared in your manifest and is internal to your app, you can add an `android:exported="false"` attribute to your receiver tag. This will prevent it from being visible to other applications on the system. In other circumstances, you can create your own permission. This is done by adding a `permission` tag to your `AndroidManifest.xml`.

Add the following XML to `AndroidManifest.xml` to declare and acquire your own permission.

Listing 30.8 Add a private permission (AndroidManifest.xml)

```xml
<manifest xmlns:android="http://schemas.android.com/apk/res/android"
  package="com.bignerdranch.android.photogallery"
  android:versionCode="1"
  android:versionName="1.0" >

  <uses-sdk
    android:minSdkVersion="8"
    android:targetSdkVersion="17" />

  <permission android:name="com.bignerdranch.android.photogallery.PRIVATE"
    android:protectionLevel="signature" />

  <uses-permission android:name="android.permission.INTERNET" />
  <uses-permission android:name="android.permission.ACCESS_NETWORK_STATE" />
  <uses-permission android:name="android.permission.RECEIVE_BOOT_COMPLETED" />
  <uses-permission android:name="com.bignerdranch.android.photogallery.PRIVATE" />

  <application
    ... >
    ...
  </application>

</manifest>
```

In this code, you defined your own custom permission with a *protection level* of signature. You will learn more about protection levels in just a moment. The permission itself is a simple string, just like intent actions, categories, and system permissions you have used. You must always acquire a permission to use it, even when you defined it yourself. Them's the rules.

Take note of the shaded constant value above, by the way. This string needs to appear in three different places, and must be identical in each place. You would be wise to copy and paste it rather than typing it out by hand.

Next, use your permission by defining a corresponding constant in code and then passing it in to your **sendBroadcast(…)** call.

Listing 30.9 Sending with a permission (`PollService.java`)

```java
public class PollService extends IntentService {
    private static final String TAG = "PollService";

    private static final int POLL_INTERVAL = 1000 * 60 * 5; // 5 minutes
    public static final String PREF_IS_ALARM_ON = "isAlarmOn";

    public static final String ACTION_SHOW_NOTIFICATION =
        "com.bignerdranch.android.photogallery.SHOW_NOTIFICATION";

    public static final String PERM_PRIVATE =
        "com.bignerdranch.android.photogallery.PRIVATE";

    public PollService() {
        super(TAG);
    }

    @Override
    public void onHandleIntent(Intent intent) {
        ...

        if (!resultId.equals(lastResultId)) {
            ...

            NotificationManager notificationManager = (NotificationManager)
                getSystemService(NOTIFICATION_SERVICE);

            notificationManager.notify(0, notification);

            sendBroadcast(new Intent(ACTION_SHOW_NOTIFICATION));
            sendBroadcast(new Intent(ACTION_SHOW_NOTIFICATION), PERM_PRIVATE);
        }

        prefs.edit()
            .putString(FlickrFetchr.PREF_LAST_RESULT_ID, resultId)
            .commit();
    }
```

To use your permission, you pass it as a parameter to **sendBroadcast(…)**. Using the permission here makes it so that any application must use that same permission to receive the intent you are sending.

What about your broadcast receiver? Someone could create their own broadcast intent to trigger it. You can fix that by passing in your permission in **registerReceiver(…)**, too.

Listing 30.10 Permissions on a broadcast receiver (`VisibleFragment.java`)

```java
@Override
    public void onResume() {
        super.onResume();
        IntentFilter filter = new IntentFilter(PollService.ACTION_SHOW_NOTIFICATION);
        getActivity().registerReceiver(mOnShowNotification, filter);
        getActivity().registerReceiver(mOnShowNotification, filter,
            PollService.PERM_PRIVATE, null);
    }
```

Now, your app is the only app that can trigger that receiver.

494

More about protection levels

Every custom permission has to specify a value for `android:protectionLevel`. Your permission's `protectionLevel` tells Android how it should be used. In your case, you used a `protectionLevel` of `signature`. The `signature` protection level means that if another application wants to use your permission, it has to be signed with the same key as your application. This is usually the right choice for permissions you use internally in your application. Since other developers don't have your key, they can't get access to anything this permission protects. Plus, since you *do* have your own key, you can use this permission in any other app you decide to write later.

Table 30.1 Values for `protectionLevel`

Value	Description
normal	This is for protecting app functionality that won't do anything dangerous, like access secure personal data or send data to the internet. The user can see the permission before choosing to install the app, but they aren't explicitly asked to grant it. `android.permission.RECEIVE_BOOT_COMPLETED` uses this permission level, and so does the permission to let you vibrate your phone. Think of this as things that aren't dangerous, but you'd want the user to know that you might do them anyway.
dangerous	This is for everything we said you would not use `normal` for – for accessing personal data, sending and receiving things from network interfaces, for accessing hardware that might be used to spy on you, or anything that could cause real problems for the user. The internet permission, camera permission, and contacts permission all fall under this category. Android may ask the user for an explicit go ahead before approving a `dangerous` permission.
signature	The system grants this permission if the app is signed with the same certificate as the declaring application, and denies it otherwise. If the permission is granted, the user isn't notified. This is what you would use for functionality that is internal to your own app – since you have the certificate, and only apps signed with the same certificate can use the permission, you have control over who uses the permission. Here, you have used it to lock down anyone else from seeing your broadcasts, but if you wanted to you could write another app that listens to them, too.
signatureOrSystem	This is like signature, but it also grants permission to all packages in the Android system image. This is used to communicate with apps built into the system image, so you probably don't need to worry about it.

Receiving results with ordered broadcasts

Time to finally bring this baby home. You are sending your own personal private broadcast, but so far you only have one-way communication.

Figure 30.4 Regular broadcast intents

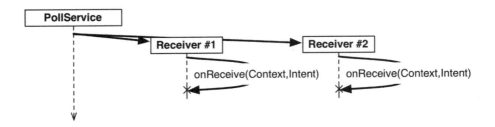

This is because a regular broadcast intent is conceptually received by everyone at the same time. Now, **onReceive(…)** is called on the main thread, so in practice your receivers are not actually executed concurrently. It is not possible to rely on their being executed in any particular order, though, or to know when they have all completed execution. As a result, it is a hassle for the broadcast receivers to communicate with each other, or for the sender of the intent to receive information from the receivers.

Figure 30.5 Ordered broadcast intents

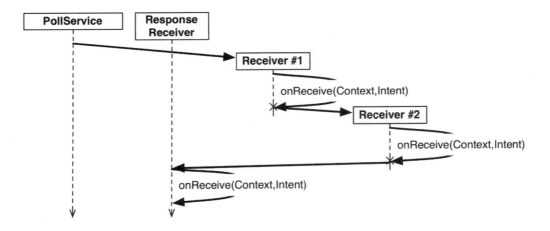

You can implement two-way communication using an *ordered broadcast intent*. Ordered broadcasts allow a sequence of broadcast receivers to process a broadcast intent in order. They also allow the sender of a broadcast to receive results from the broadcast's recipients by passing in a special broadcast receiver, called the *result receiver*.

On the receiving side, this looks mostly the same as a regular broadcast. You get an additional tool, though: a set of methods used to change the return value of your receiver. Here, you want to cancel the notification. This can be communicated by use of a simple integer result code. So you use the **setResultCode(int)** method to set the result code to Activity.RESULT_CANCELED.

Modify **VisibleFragment** to send some information back to the sender of SHOW_NOTIFICATION.

Listing 30.11 Send a simple result back (`VisibleFragment.java`)

```
private BroadcastReceiver mOnShowNotification = new BroadcastReceiver() {
    @Override
    public void onReceive(Context context, Intent intent) {
        Toast.makeText(getActivity(),
                "Got a broadcast:" + intent.getAction(),
                Toast.LENGTH_LONG)
            .show();
        // If we receive this, we're visible, so cancel
        // the notification
        Log.i(TAG, "canceling notification");
        setResultCode(Activity.RESULT_CANCELED);
    }
};
```

Since all you need to do is signal yes or no here, you only need the result code. If you need to return more complicated data, you can use **setResultData(String)** or **setResultExtras(Bundle)**. And if you want to set all three values, you can call **setResult(int,String,Bundle)**. Once your return values are set here, every subsequent receiver will be able to see or modify them.

For those methods to do anything useful, your broadcast needs to be ordered. Write a new method to send an ordered broadcast in **PollService**. This method will package up a **Notification** invocation and send it out as a broadcast. A result receiver will be specified to send out the packaged **Notification** (provided it has not been canceled).

Listing 30.12 Send an ordered broadcast (`PollService.java`)

```
void showBackgroundNotification(int requestCode, Notification notification) {
    Intent i = new Intent(ACTION_SHOW_NOTIFICATION);
    i.putExtra("REQUEST_CODE", requestCode);
    i.putExtra("NOTIFICATION", notification);

    sendOrderedBroadcast(i, PERM_PRIVATE, null, null,
        Activity.RESULT_OK, null, null);
}
```

Context.sendOrderedBroadcast(Intent,String,BroadcastReceiver,Handler,int,String,Bundle) has five additional parameters beyond the ones you used in **sendBroadcast(Intent,String)**. They are, in order: a *result receiver*, a **Handler** to run the result receiver on, and then initial values for the result code, result data, and result extras for the ordered broadcast.

The result receiver is a special receiver that will run after all the other recipients of your ordered broadcast intent. In other circumstances, you would be able to use the result receiver here to receive the broadcast and post the notification object. Here, though, that will not work. This broadcast intent will often be sent right before **PollService** dies. That means that your broadcast receiver might be dead, too.

Thus, your final broadcast receiver will need to be standalone. Create a new **BroadcastReceiver** subclass called **NotificationReceiver**. Implement it as follows:

Listing 30.13 Implement your result receiver (`NotificationReceiver.java`)

```
public class NotificationReceiver extends BroadcastReceiver {
    private static final String TAG = "NotificationReceiver";

    @Override
    public void onReceive(Context c, Intent i) {
        Log.i(TAG, "received result: " + getResultCode());
        if (getResultCode() != Activity.RESULT_OK)
            // A foreground activity cancelled the broadcast
            return;

        int requestCode = i.getIntExtra("REQUEST_CODE", 0);
        Notification notification = (Notification)
                i.getParcelableExtra("NOTIFICATION");

        NotificationManager notificationManager = (NotificationManager)
                c.getSystemService(Context.NOTIFICATION_SERVICE);
        notificationManager.notify(requestCode, notification);
    }
}
```

Finally, register your new receiver. Since it sends the notification, receiving the result set by the other receivers, it should run after everything else. That means that you will need to set a low priority for your receiver. Since your receiver should run last, give it a priority of `-999` (`-1000` and below are reserved).

And since this receiver is only used internally by your application, you do not need it to be externally visible. Set `android:exported="false"` to keep this receiver to yourself.

Listing 30.14 Register notification receiver (`AndroidManifest.xml`)

```xml
<manifest xmlns:android="http://schemas.android.com/apk/res/android"
  ... >
  ...

  <application
    ... >
    ...
    <receiver android:name=".StartupReceiver">
      <intent-filter>
        <action android:name="android.intent.action.BOOT_COMPLETED" />
      </intent-filter>
    </receiver>
    <receiver android:name=".NotificationReceiver"
      android:exported="false">
      <intent-filter
        android:priority="-999">
        <action
            android:name="com.bignerdranch.android.photogallery.SHOW_NOTIFICATION" />
      </intent-filter>
    </receiver>
  </application>

</manifest>
```

Now use your new method instead of **NotificationManager** to post your notification.

Listing 30.15 Finish it up (`PollService.java`)

```
@Override
public void onHandleIntent(Intent intent) {
    ...

    if (!resultId.equals(lastResultId)) {
        ...

        Notification notification = new NotificationCompat.Builder(this)
            ...
            .build();

        NotificationManager notificationManager = (NotificationManager)
            getSystemService(NOTIFICATION_SERVICE);

        notificationManager.notify(0, notification);

        sendBroadcast(new Intent(ACTION_SHOW_NOTIFICATION), PERM_PRIVATE);

        showBackgroundNotification(0, notification);
    }

    prefs.edit()
        .putString(FlickrFetchr.PREF_LAST_RESULT_ID, resultId)
        .commit();
}
```

Run PhotoGallery and toggle background polling a couple of times. You should see that notifications no longer appear. To verify that notifications still work in the background, set `PollService.POLL_INTERVAL` to five seconds again so that you do not have to wait five whole minutes.

Receivers and Long-running Tasks

So what do you do if you want a broadcast intent to kick off a longer-running task than the restrictions of the main run loop allow?

You have two options. The first is to put that work into a service instead, and start the service in your broadcast receiver's small window of opportunity. This is the method we recommend. A service can take as long as it needs to take to service a request. It can queue up multiple requests and service them in order, or otherwise manage requests as it sees fit.

The second is to use the **BroadcastReceiver.goAsync()** method. This method returns a **BroadcastReceiver.PendingResult** object, which can be used to provide a result at a later time. So you could give that **PendingResult** to an **AsyncTask** to perform some longer running work, and then respond to the broadcast by calling methods on **PendingResult**.

There are two downsides to this method. One is that it is not available on old devices. The other is that it is less flexible: you still have to service the broadcast within ten seconds or so, and you have few architectural options like you do with a service.

Of course, **goAsync()** has one huge advantage: you can set results for ordered broadcasts with them. If you really need that, nothing else will do. Just make sure not to take too long.

31

Browsing The Web & WebView

Each photo you get from Flickr has a page associated with it. In this chapter, you are going to make it so that users can press a photo in PhotoGallery to browse its photo page. You will learn two different ways to integrate web content into your apps. The first works with the device's browser app, and the second uses the `WebView` class to display web content within PhotoGallery.

One Last Bit of Flickr Data

For both ways, you need to get the URL for a photo's Flickr page. If you look at the XML you are currently receiving for each photo, you can see that the photo page is not part of those results.

```
<photo id="8232706407" owner="70490293@N03" secret="9662732625"
    server="8343" farm="9" title="111_8Q1B2033" ispublic="1"
    isfriend="0" isfamily="0"
    url_s="http://farm9.staticflickr.com/8343/8232706407_9662732625_m.jpg"
    height_s="240" width_s="163" />
```

So you might think that you are in for some more XML request writing. Fortunately, that is not the case. If you look at the Web Page URLs section at Flickr's documentation at `http://www.flickr.com/services/api/misc.urls.html`, you can see that you can create the URL for an individual photo's page like so:

```
http://www.flickr.com/photos/user-id/photo-id
```

The `photo-id` seen here is the same as the value of the `id` attribute from your XML. You are already stashing that in `mId` in `GalleryItem`. What about `user-id`? If you poke around the documentation, you will find that the `owner` attribute in your XML is a user ID. So if you pull out the `owner` attribute, you should be able to build the URL from your photo XML attributes:

```
http://www.flickr.com/photos/owner/id
```

Add the following code to `GalleryItem` to put this plan into action.

Listing 31.1 Add code for photo page (`GalleryItem.java`)

```java
public class GalleryItem {
    private String mCaption;
    private String mId;
    private String mUrl;
    private String mOwner;

    ...

    public void setUrl(String url) {
        mUrl = url;
    }

    public String getOwner() {
        return mOwner;
    }

    public void setOwner(String owner) {
        mOwner = owner;
    }

    public String getPhotoPageUrl() {
        return "http://www.flickr.com/photos/" + mOwner + "/" + mId;
    }

    public String toString() {
        return mCaption;
    }
}
```

You created a new `mOwner` property here, and added a short method called **getPhotoPageUrl()** to generate photo page URLs as discussed above.

Now change **parseItems(...)** to read in the owner attribute.

Listing 31.2 Read in owner attribute (`FlickrFetchr.java`)

```java
void parseItems(ArrayList<GalleryItem> items, XmlPullParser parser)
        throws XmlPullParserException, IOException {
    int eventType = parser.next();

    while (eventType != XmlPullParser.END_DOCUMENT) {
        if (eventType == XmlPullParser.START_TAG &&
            XML_PHOTO.equals(parser.getName())) {
            String id = parser.getAttributeValue(null, "id");
            String caption = parser.getAttributeValue(null, "title");
            String smallUrl = parser.getAttributeValue(null, EXTRA_SMALL_URL);
            String owner = parser.getAttributeValue(null, "owner");

            GalleryItem item = new GalleryItem();
            item.setUrl(smallUrl);
            item.setOwner(owner);
            items.add(item);
        }

        eventType = parser.next();
    }
}
```

Easy peasy. Now to have fun with your new photo page URL.

The Easy Way: Implicit Intents

You will browse to this URL first by using your old friend the implicit intent. This intent will start up the browser with your photo URL.

The first step here is to make your app listen to presses on **GridView** items. This is another place where your code will look slightly different from your code in Chapter 9, since there is no matching **GridFragment**. Instead of overriding the **onListItemClick(…)** method in your fragment, you will hook it up more like a button click listener by calling the **setOnItemClickListener(…)** method on your **GridView**.

After doing that, it is a simple matter of creating and firing an implicit intent. Add the following code to **PhotoGalleryFragment**:

Listing 31.3 Web browsing with implicit intents (PhotoGalleryFragment.java)

```
@Override
public View onCreateView(LayoutInflater inflater, ViewGroup container,
        Bundle savedInstanceState) {
    View v = inflater.inflate(R.layout.fragment_photo_gallery, container, false);

    mGridView = (GridView)v.findViewById(R.id.gridView);

    setupAdapter();

    mGridView.setOnItemClickListener(new OnItemClickListener() {
        @Override
        public void onItemClick(AdapterView<?> gridView, View view, int pos,
                long id) {
            GalleryItem item = mItems.get(pos);

            Uri photoPageUri = Uri.parse(item.getPhotoPageUrl());
            Intent i = new Intent(Intent.ACTION_VIEW, photoPageUri);

            startActivity(i);
        }
    });

    return v;
}
```

That should be it. Start up PhotoGallery and press on a photo. You should see your progress indicator briefly, and then your browser app should pop up.

The Harder Way: WebView

Oftentimes, though, you want to display web content within your own activities instead of heading off to the browser. You may want to display HTML that you generate yourself, or you may want to lock down the browser somehow. For apps that include help documentation, it is common to implement it as a web page so that it is easy to update. Opening a web browser to a help web page does not look professional, though, and it prevents you from customizing behavior or integrating that web page into your own user interface.

When you want to present web content within your own user interface, you use the **WebView** class. We are calling this the "harder" way here, but it is pretty darned easy. (Anything is hard compared to using implicit intents.)

The first step will be to create a new activity and fragment to display the **WebView** in. Start, as usual, by defining a layout file.

Figure 31.1 Initial layout (res/layout/fragment_photo_page.xml)

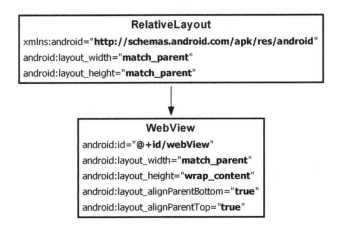

You may think, "That **RelativeLayout** is pretty useless." True enough – you will fill it out later in the chapter, though, with additional "chrome".

Next, get the rudiments of your fragment setup. Create **PhotoPageFragment** as a subclass of the **VisibleFragment** class you created in the last chapter. You will need to inflate your layout file, extract your **WebView** from it, and forward along the URL in your intent's data.

Listing 31.4 Setting up your web browser fragment (`PhotoPageFragment.java`)

```
package com.bignerdranch.android.photogallery;

...

public class PhotoPageFragment extends VisibleFragment {
    private String mUrl;
    private WebView mWebView;

    @Override
    public void onCreate(Bundle savedInstanceState) {
        super.onCreate(savedInstanceState);
        setRetainInstance(true);

        mUrl = getActivity().getIntent().getData().toString();
    }

    @Override
    public View onCreateView(LayoutInflater inflater, ViewGroup parent,
            Bundle savedInstanceState) {
        View v = inflater.inflate(R.layout.fragment_photo_page, parent, false);

        mWebView = (WebView)v.findViewById(R.id.webView);

        return v;
    }
}
```

For now, this is just a skeleton, but leave it as it is – you will fill it out a bit more in a moment. Next, create the containing **PhotoPageActivity** class using good old **SingleFragmentActivity**.

Listing 31.5 Create web activity (`PhotoPageActivity.java`)

```
package com.bignerdranch.android.photogallery;

...

public class PhotoPageActivity extends SingleFragmentActivity {
    @Override
    public Fragment createFragment() {
        return new PhotoPageFragment();
    }
}
```

Switch up your code in **PhotoGalleryFragment** to call into your new activity instead of the implicit intent.

Listing 31.6 Switch to call your activity (PhotoGalleryFragment.java)

```java
@Override
public View onCreateView(LayoutInflater inflater, ViewGroup container,
        Bundle savedInstanceState) {
    ...

    mGridView.setOnItemClickListener(new OnItemClickListener() {
        @Override
        public void onItemClick(AdapterView<?> gridView, View view, int pos,
                long id) {
            GalleryItem item = mItems.get(pos);

            Uri photoPageUri = Uri.parse(item.getPhotoPageUrl());
            Intent i = new Intent(Intent.ACTION_VIEW, photoPageUri);
            Intent i = new Intent(getActivity(), PhotoPageActivity.class);
            i.setData(photoPageUri);

            startActivity(i);
        }
    });

    return v;
}
```

And, finally, add your new activity to the manifest.

Listing 31.7 Add activity to manifest (AndroidManifest.xml)

```xml
<manifest xmlns:android="http://schemas.android.com/apk/res/android"
  package="com.bignerdranch.android.photogallery"
  android:versionCode="1"
  android:versionName="1.0" >

  ...

  <application
    android:allowBackup="true"
    android:icon="@drawable/ic_launcher"
    android:label="@string/app_name"
    android:theme="@style/AppTheme" >
    <activity
      android:name=".PhotoGalleryActivity"
      android:launchMode="singleTop"
      android:label="@string/title_activity_photo_gallery" >
      ...
    </activity>
    <activity
        android:name=".PhotoPageActivity" />
    <service android:name=".PollService" />
    <receiver android:name=".StartupReceiver">
      ...
    </receiver>
  </application>
</manifest>
```

Run PhotoGallery and press on a picture. You should see a new empty activity pop up.

Okay, now to get to the meat and actually make your fragment do something. You need to do three things to make your **WebView** successfully display a Flickr photo page. The first one is straightforward – you need to tell it what URL to load.

The second thing you need to do is enable JavaScript. By default, JavaScript is off. You do not always need to have it on, but for Flickr, you do. Android Lint gives you a warning for doing this (it is worried about cross-site scripting attacks), so you also need to suppress Lint warnings.

Finally, you need to override one method on a class called **WebViewClient**, **shouldOverrideUrlLoading(WebView,String)**, and return `false`. We will discuss this class a bit more after you type in the code.

Listing 31.8 Add even more instance variables (PhotoPageFragment.java)

```java
@SuppressLint("SetJavaScriptEnabled")
@Override
public View onCreateView(LayoutInflater inflater, ViewGroup parent,
        Bundle savedInstanceState) {
    View v = inflater.inflate(R.layout.fragment_photo_page, parent, false);

    mWebView = (WebView)v.findViewById(R.id.webView);

    mWebView.getSettings().setJavaScriptEnabled(true);

    mWebView.setWebViewClient(new WebViewClient() {
        public boolean shouldOverrideUrlLoading(WebView view, String url) {
            return false;
        }
    });

    mWebView.loadUrl(mUrl);

    return v;
}
```

Loading the URL has to be done after configuring the **WebView**, so you do that last. Before that, you turn JavaScript on by calling **getSettings()** to get an instance of **WebSettings**, and calling **WebSettings.setJavaScriptEnabled(true)**. **WebSettings** is the first of the three ways you can modify your **WebView**. It has various properties you can set, like the user agent string and text size.

After that, you configure your **WebViewClient**. **WebViewClient** is an event interface. By providing your own implementation of **WebViewClient**, you can respond to rendering events. For example, you could detect when the renderer starts loading an image from a particular URL or decide whether to resubmit a POST request to the server.

WebViewClient has many methods you can override, most of which you will not deal with. You do need to replace the default **WebViewClient**'s implementation of **shouldOverrideUrlLoading(WebView,String)**, though. This method says what to do when a new URL is loaded in the **WebView**, like by pressing a link. If you return `true`, you are saying, "Do not handle this URL, I am handling it myself." If you return `false`, you are saying, "Go ahead and load this URL, **WebView**, I'm not doing anything with it."

The default implementation fires an implicit intent with the URL, just like you did earlier this chapter. For your photo page, this is a severe problem. The first thing Flickr does is redirect you to the mobile version of the web site. With the default **WebViewClient**, that means that you are immediately sent to the user's default web browser. Not ideal.

The fix is simple – just override the default implementation and return `false`.

Run PhotoGallery, and you should see your **WebView**.

Using WebChromeClient to spruce things up

Since you are taking the time to create your own **WebView**, let's spruce it up a bit by adding a title view and a progress bar. Crack open `fragment_photo_page.xml` and make the following changes:

Figure 31.2 Add title and progress (`fragment_photo_page.xml`)

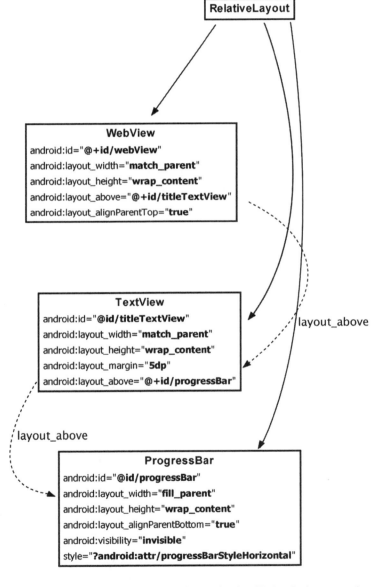

Pulling out the **ProgressBar** and **TextView** will be a piece of cake. To hook them up, though, you will need to use the second callback on **WebView**: **WebChromeClient**. If **WebViewClient** is an interface for responding to rendering events, then **WebChromeClient** is an event interface for reacting to events that should change elements of chrome around the browser. This includes JavaScript alerts, favicons, and of course updates for loading progress and the title of the current page.

Hook it up in **onCreateView(…)** like so:

Listing 31.9 Using **WebChromeClient** (PhotoPageFragment.java)

```
@SuppressLint("SetJavaScriptEnabled")
@Override
public View onCreateView(LayoutInflater inflater, ViewGroup parent,
        Bundle savedInstanceState) {
    View v = inflater.inflate(R.layout.fragment_photo_page, parent, false);

    final ProgressBar progressBar = (ProgressBar)v.findViewById(R.id.progressBar);
    progressBar.setMax(100); // WebChromeClient reports in range 0-100
    final TextView titleTextView = (TextView)v.findViewById(R.id.titleTextView);

    mWebView = (WebView)v.findViewById(R.id.webView);

    mWebView.getSettings().setJavaScriptEnabled(true);

    mWebView.setWebViewClient(new WebViewClient() {
        ...
    });

    mWebView.setWebChromeClient(new WebChromeClient() {
        public void onProgressChanged(WebView webView, int progress) {
            if (progress == 100) {
                progressBar.setVisibility(View.INVISIBLE);
            } else {
                progressBar.setVisibility(View.VISIBLE);
                progressBar.setProgress(progress);
            }
        }

        public void onReceivedTitle(WebView webView, String title) {
            titleTextView.setText(title);
        }
    });

    mWebView.loadUrl(mUrl);

    return v;
}
```

Progress updates and title updates each have their own callback method, **onProgressChanged(WebView,int)** and **onReceivedTitle(WebView,String)**. The progress you receive from **onProgressChanged(WebView,int)** is an integer from 0 to 100. If it is 100, you know that the page is done loading, so you hide the **ProgressBar** by setting its visibility to View.INVISIBLE.

Run PhotoGallery to test your changes.

Proper rotation with WebView

Try rotating your screen. While it does work correctly, you will notice that the **WebView** has to completely reload the web page. This is because **WebView** has too much data to save it all out inside **onSaveInstanceState(…)**. It has to start from scratch each time it is recreated on rotation.

For some classes like this (**VideoView** is another one), the Android documentation recommends that you allow the activity to handle the configuration change itself. This means that instead of the activity being destroyed, it simply moves its views around to fit the new screen size. As a result, **WebView** does not have to reload all of its data.

(Why not do this all the time, you ask? It does not work correctly with all views. If it did, life would be so much easier, but alas.)

To tell **PhotoPageActivity** to handle its own darned configuration changes, make the following tweak to AndroidManifest.xml.

Listing 31.10 Handle configuration changes yourself (AndroidManifest.xml)

```xml
<manifest xmlns:android="http://schemas.android.com/apk/res/android"
  package="com.bignerdranch.android.photogallery"
  android:versionCode="1"
  android:versionName="1.0" >

  ...

  <application
    android:allowBackup="true"
    android:icon="@drawable/ic_launcher"
    android:label="@string/app_name"
    android:theme="@style/AppTheme" >
    ...
    <activity
        android:name=".PhotoPageActivity"
        android:configChanges="keyboardHidden|orientation|screenSize" />
    ...
  </application>

</manifest>
```

This attribute says that if the configuration changes because the keyboard was opened or closed, due to an orientation change or due to the screen size changing (which also happens when switching between portrait and landscape after Android 3.2), then the activity should handle the change itself.

And that is it. Try rotation again, and this time everything should be hunky dory.

For the More Curious: Injecting JavaScript Objects

We saw how to use **WebViewClient** and **WebChromeClient** to respond to specific events that happen in your **WebView**. However, it is possible to do even more than that by injecting arbitrary JavaScript objects into the document contained in the **WebView** itself. Check out the documentation at http://developer.android.com/reference/android/webkit/WebView.html and scroll down to the **addJavascriptInterface(Object,String)** method. Using this, you can inject an arbitrary object into the document with a name you specify.

```java
mWebView.addJavascriptInterface(new Object() {
    public void send(String message) {
        Log.i(TAG, "Received message: " + message);
    }
}, "androidObject");
```

And then invoke it like so:

```
<input type="button" value="In WebView!"
    onClick="sendToAndroid('In Android land')" />

<script type="text/javascript">
    function sendToAndroid(message) {
        androidObject.send(message);
    }
</script>
```

This could be dangerous – you're letting some potentially strange web page fiddle with your program. So to be safe, it's a good idea to make sure you own the HTML in question – either that, or be extremely conservative with the interface you expose.

32

Custom Views and Touch Events

In this chapter, you will learn how to handle touch events by writing a custom subclass of **View** named **BoxDrawingView**. This **View** will draw boxes in response to the user touching the screen and dragging.

Figure 32.1 Boxes drawn in many shapes and sizes

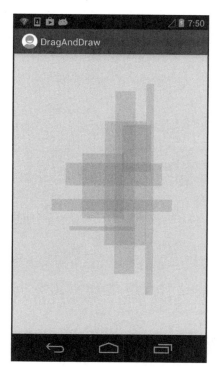

Setting Up the DragAndDraw Project

The **BoxDrawingView** class will be the star of a new project named DragAndDraw. Select New → Android Application Project. Configure the project as shown in Figure 32.2. Then create a blank activity named **DragAndDrawActivity**.

Figure 32.2 Creating DragAndDraw

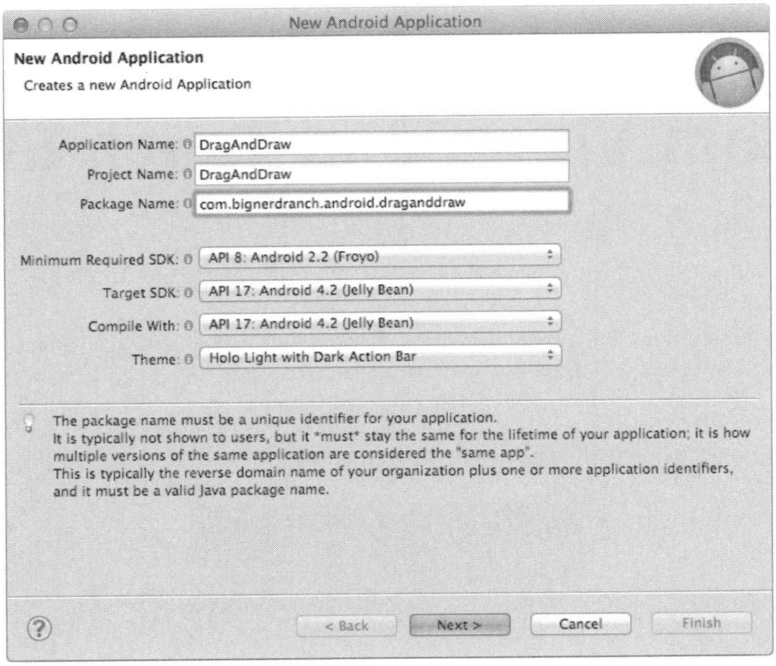

Setting up DragAndDrawActivity

DragAndDrawActivity will be a subclass of **SingleFragmentActivity** that inflates the usual single-fragment-containing layout. In the package explorer, copy SingleFragmentActivity.java into the com.bignerdranch.android.draganddraw package. Then copy activity_fragment.xml into DragAndDraw's res/layout directory.

In DragAndDrawActivity.java, make **DragAndDrawActivity** a **SingleFragmentActivity** that creates a **DragAndDrawFragment** (a class that you will create next).

Listing 32.1 Modify the activity (DragAndDrawActivity.java)

```
public class DragAndDrawActivity extends Activity SingleFragmentActivity {
    @Override
    public void onCreate(Bundle savedInstanceState) {
        super.onCreate(savedInstanceState);
        setContentView(R.layout.activity_drag_and_draw);
    }

    @Override
    public boolean onCreateOptionsMenu(Menu menu) {
        getMenuInflater().inflate(R.menu.activity_drag_and_draw, menu);
        return true;
    }

    @Override
    public Fragment createFragment() {
        return new DragAndDrawFragment();
    }
}
```

Setting up DragAndDrawFragment

To prepare a layout for **DragAndDrawFragment**, rename the activity_drag_and_draw.xml layout file to fragment_drag_and_draw.xml.

DragAndDrawFragment's layout will eventually consist of a **BoxDrawingView**, the custom view that you are going to write. All of the drawing and touch-event handling will be implemented in **BoxDrawingView**.

Create a new class named **DragAndDrawFragment** and make its superclass **android.support.v4.app.Fragment**. Override **onCreateView(…)** to inflate fragment_drag_and_draw.xml.

Listing 32.2 Create the fragment (DragAndDrawFragment.java)

```
public class DragAndDrawFragment extends Fragment {
    @Override
    public View onCreateView(LayoutInflater inflater, ViewGroup parent,
            Bundle savedInstanceState) {
        View v = inflater.inflate(R.layout.fragment_drag_and_draw, parent, false);
        return v;
    }
}
```

You can run DragAndDraw to confirm that your app is set up properly.

Figure 32.3 DragAndDraw with default layout

Creating a Custom View

Android provides many excellent standard views and widgets, but sometimes you need a custom view that presents visuals that are totally unique to your app.

While there are all kinds of custom views, you can shoehorn them into two broad categories:

simple   A simple view may be complicated inside; what makes it simple is that it has no child views. A simple view will almost always perform custom rendering as well.

composite   Composite views are composed of other view objects. Composite views typically manage child views but do not perform custom rendering. Instead, rendering is delegated to each child view.

Here are three steps to follow when creating a custom view:

- Pick a superclass. For a simple custom view, **View** is a blank canvas, so it is the most common choice. For a composite custom view, choose an appropriate layout class.

- Subclass this class and override at least one constructor from the superclass. Or create your own constructor that calls one of the superclass's constructors.

- Override other key methods to customize behavior.

Creating BoxDrawingView

BoxDrawingView will be a simple view and a direct subclass of **View**.

Create a new class named **BoxDrawingView** and make **View** its superclass. In BoxDrawingView.java, add two constructors.

Listing 32.3 Initial implementation for **BoxDrawingView** (BoxDrawingView.java)

```java
public class BoxDrawingView extends View {
    // Used when creating the view in code
    public BoxDrawingView(Context context) {
        this(context, null);
    }

    // Used when inflating the view from XML
    public BoxDrawingView(Context context, AttributeSet attrs) {
        super(context, attrs);
    }
}
```

You write two constructors because your view could be instantiated in code or from a layout file. Views instantiated from a layout file receive an instance of **AttributeSet** containing the XML attributes that were specified in XML. Even if you do not plan on using both constructors, it is good practice to include them.

Next, update your fragment_drag_and_draw.xml layout file to use your new view.

Listing 32.4 Add **BoxDrawingView** to layout (`fragment_drag_and_draw.xml`)

```
<RelativeLayout xmlns:android="http://schemas.android.com/apk/res/android"
    xmlns:tools="http://schemas.android.com/tools"
    android:layout_width="match_parent"
    android:layout_height="match_parent"
    >

    <TextView
        android:layout_width="wrap_content"
        android:layout_height="wrap_content"
        android:layout_centerHorizontal="true"
        android:layout_centerVertical="true"
        android:text="@string/hello_world" />

</RelativeLayout>

<com.bignerdranch.android.draganddraw.BoxDrawingView
    xmlns:android="http://schemas.android.com/apk/res/android"
    android:layout_width="match_parent"
    android:layout_height="match_parent"
    />
```

You must use **BoxDrawingView**'s fully qualified class name so that the layout inflater can find it. The inflater works through a layout file creating **View** instances. If the element name is an unqualified class name, then the inflater looks for a class with that name in the android.view and android.widget packages. If the class lives somewhere else, then the layout inflater will not find it, and your app will crash. So for custom classes and other classes that live outside of android.view and android.widget, you must always specify the fully qualified class name.

Run DragAndDraw to confirm that all the connections are correct. All you will see is an empty view.

Figure 32.4 **BoxDrawingView** with no boxes

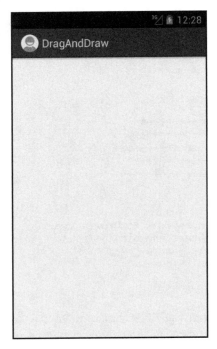

The next step is to get **BoxDrawingView** listening for touch events and using the information they contain to draw boxes on the screen.

Handling Touch Events

One way to listen for touch events is to set a touch event listener using the following **View** method:

```
public void setOnTouchListener(View.OnTouchListener l)
```

This method works the same way as **setOnClickListener(View.OnClickListener)**. You provide an implementation of **View.OnTouchListener**, and your listener will be called every time a touch event happens.

However, because you are subclassing **View**, you can take a shortcut and override this **View** method:

```
public boolean onTouchEvent(MotionEvent event)
```

This method receives an instance of **MotionEvent**, a class that describes the touch event, including its location and its action. The action describes the stage of the event.

action constants	description
ACTION_DOWN	user's finger touches the screen
ACTION_MOVE	user moves finger on the screen
ACTION_UP	user lifts finger off the screen

action constants	description
ACTION_CANCEL	a parent view has intercepted your touch event

In your implementation of **onTouchEvent(…)**, you can check the value of the action by calling the **MotionEvent** method:

```
public final int getAction()
```

In BoxDrawingView.java, add a log tag and then an implementation of **onTouchEvent(…)** that logs a message in the case of each of the four different actions.

Listing 32.5 Implementing **BoxDrawingView** (BoxDrawingView.java)

```java
public class BoxDrawingView extends View {
    public static final String TAG = "BoxDrawingView";

    ...

    public boolean onTouchEvent(MotionEvent event) {
        PointF curr = new PointF(event.getX(), event.getY());

        Log.i(TAG, "Received event at x=" + curr.x +
                ", y=" + curr.y + ":");
        switch (event.getAction()) {
            case MotionEvent.ACTION_DOWN:
                Log.i(TAG, "  ACTION_DOWN");
                break;
            case MotionEvent.ACTION_MOVE:
                Log.i(TAG, "  ACTION_MOVE");
                break;
            case MotionEvent.ACTION_UP:
                Log.i(TAG, "  ACTION_UP");
                break;
            case MotionEvent.ACTION_CANCEL:
                Log.i(TAG, "  ACTION_CANCEL");
                break;
        }

        return true;
    }
}
```

Notice that you package your X and Y coordinates in a **PointF** object. You will be wanting to pass these two values together as you go through the rest of the chapter. **PointF** is a container class provided by Android that does this for you.

Run DragAndDraw and pull up LogCat. Touch the screen and drag your finger. You should see a report of the X and Y coordinate of every touch action that **BoxDrawingView** receives.

Tracking across motion events

BoxDrawingView is intended to draw boxes on the screen, not just log coordinates. There are a few problems to solve to get there.

First, to define a box, you need two things:

- the origin point (where the finger was initially placed)

- the current point (where the finger currently is)

To define a box, then, requires keeping track of data from more than one **MotionEvent**. You will store this data in a **Box** object.

Create a class named **Box** to represent the data that defines a single box.

Listing 32.6 Add **Box** (Box.java)

```java
public class Box {
    private PointF mOrigin;
    private PointF mCurrent;

    public Box(PointF origin) {
        mOrigin = mCurrent = origin;
    }

    public PointF getCurrent() {
        return mCurrent;
    }

    public void setCurrent(PointF current) {
        mCurrent = current;
    }

    public PointF getOrigin() {
        return mOrigin;
    }
}
```

When the user touches **BoxDrawingView**, a new **Box** will be created and added to an array of existing boxes (Figure 32.5).

Figure 32.5 Objects in DragAndDraw

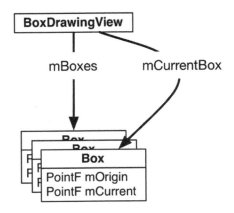

Back in **BoxDrawingView**, add some code that uses your new **Box** object to track your drawing state.

Listing 32.7 Add drag lifecycle methods (BoxDrawingView.java)

```java
public class BoxDrawingView extends View {
    public static final String TAG = "BoxDrawingView";

    private Box mCurrentBox;
    private ArrayList<Box> mBoxes = new ArrayList<Box>();

    ...

    public boolean onTouchEvent(MotionEvent event) {
        PointF curr = new PointF(event.getX(), event.getY());

        switch (event.getAction()) {
            case MotionEvent.ACTION_DOWN:
                Log.i(TAG, "  ACTION_DOWN");
                // Reset drawing state
                mCurrentBox = new Box(curr);
                mBoxes.add(mCurrentBox);
                break;

            case MotionEvent.ACTION_MOVE:
                Log.i(TAG, "  ACTION_MOVE");
                if (mCurrentBox != null) {
                    mCurrentBox.setCurrent(curr);
                    invalidate();
                }
                break;

            case MotionEvent.ACTION_UP:
                Log.i(TAG, "  ACTION_UP");
                mCurrentBox = null;
                break;

            case MotionEvent.ACTION_CANCEL:
                Log.i(TAG, "  ACTION_CANCEL");
                mCurrentBox = null;
                break;
        }

        return true;
    }
}
```

Any time an ACTION_DOWN motion event is received, you set mCurrentBox to be a new **Box** with its origin as the event's location. This new **Box** is added to the array of boxes. (In the next section, when you implement custom drawing, **BoxDrawingView** will draw every **Box** within this array to the screen.)

As the user's finger moves around the screen, you update mCurrentBox.mCurrent. Then, when the touch is canceled or when the user's finger leaves the screen, you null out mCurrentBox to end your draw motion. The **Box** is complete; it is stored safely in the array but will no longer be updated about motion events.

Notice the call to **invalidate()** in the case of ACTION_MOVE. This forces **BoxDrawingView** to redraw itself so that the user can see the box while dragging across the screen. Which brings you to the next step: drawing the boxes to the screen.

Rendering Inside onDraw(...)

When your application is launched, all of its views are *invalid*. This means that they have not drawn anything to the screen. To fix this situation, Android calls the top-level **View**'s **draw()** method. This causes that view to draw itself, which causes its children to draw themselves. Those children's children then draw themselves, and so on down the hierarchy. When all the views in the hierarchy have drawn themselves, then the top-level **View** is no longer invalid.

To hook into this drawing, you override the following **View** method:

```
protected void onDraw(Canvas canvas)
```

The call to **invalidate()** that you make in response to ACTION_MOVE in **onTouchEvent(...)** makes the **BoxDrawingView** invalid again. This causes it to redraw itself and will cause **onDraw(...)** to be called again.

Now let's consider the **Canvas** parameter. **Canvas** and **Paint** are the two main drawing classes in Android:

- The **Canvas** class has all the drawing operations you perform. The methods you call on **Canvas** determine where and what you draw – a line, a circle, a word, or a rectangle.

- The **Paint** class determines how these operations are done. The methods you call on **Paint** specify characteristics – whether shapes are filled, which font text is drawn in, and what color lines are.

In BoxDrawingView.java, create two **Paint** in **BoxDrawingView**'s XML constructor.

Listing 32.8 Create your paint (BoxDrawingView.java)

```
public class BoxDrawingView extends View {
    private static final String TAG = "BoxDrawingView";

    private ArrayList<Box> mBoxes = new ArrayList<Box>();
    private Box mCurrentBox;
    private Paint mBoxPaint;
    private Paint mBackgroundPaint;

    ...

    // Used when inflating the view from XML
    public BoxDrawingView(Context context, AttributeSet attrs) {
        super(context, attrs);

        // Paint the boxes a nice semitransparent red (ARGB)
        mBoxPaint = new Paint();
        mBoxPaint.setColor(0x22ff0000);

        // Paint the background off-white
        mBackgroundPaint = new Paint();
        mBackgroundPaint.setColor(0xfff8efe0);
    }
}
```

Armed with paint, you can now draw your boxes to the screen.

Listing 32.9 Overriding **onDraw(Canvas)** (BoxDrawingView.java)

```java
@Override
protected void onDraw(Canvas canvas) {
    // Fill the background
    canvas.drawPaint(mBackgroundPaint);

    for (Box box : mBoxes) {
        float left = Math.min(box.getOrigin().x, box.getCurrent().x);
        float right = Math.max(box.getOrigin().x, box.getCurrent().x);
        float top = Math.min(box.getOrigin().y, box.getCurrent().y);
        float bottom = Math.max(box.getOrigin().y, box.getCurrent().y);

        canvas.drawRect(left, top, right, bottom, mBoxPaint);
    }
}
```

The first part of this code is straightforward: using your off-white background paint, you fill the canvas with a backdrop for your boxes.

Then, for each box in your list of boxes, you determine what the left, right, top, and bottom of the box should be by looking at the two points for the box. The left and top values will be the minimum values, and the bottom and right will be the maximum values.

After calculating these values, you call **Canvas.drawRect(…)** to draw a red rectangle onto the screen.

Run DragAndDraw and draw some red rectangles.

Figure 32.6 An expression of programmerly emotion

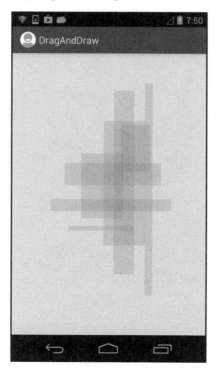

Challenge: Rotations

Figure out how to persist your boxes across orientation changes from within your **View**. This can be done with the following **View** methods:

```
protected Parcelable onSaveInstanceState()
protected void onRestoreInstanceState(Parcelable state)
```

These methods do not work like **Activity** and **Fragment**'s **onSaveInstanceState(Bundle)**. First, they will only be called if your **View** has an id. Second, instead of taking in a **Bundle**, they return and process an object that implements the **Parcelable** interface. We recommend using a **Bundle** as the **Parcelable** instead of implementing a **Parcelable** class yourself. (Implementing the **Parcelable** interface is complicated. It is better to avoid doing so when possible.)

For a harder challenge, make it so that you can use a second finger to rotate your rectangles. To do this, you will need to handle multiple pointers in your **MotionEvent** handling code. You will also need to rotate your canvas.

When dealing with multiple touches, you need these extra ideas:

pointer index   tells you which pointer in the current set of pointers the event is for

pointer ID   gives you a unique ID for a specific finger in a gesture

The pointer index may change, but the pointer ID will not.

For more details, check out the documentation for the following **MotionEvent** methods:

```
public final int getActionMasked()
public final int getActionIndex()
public final int getPointerId(int pointerIndex)
public final float getX(int pointerIndex)
public final float getY(int pointerIndex)
```

Also look at the documentation for the ACTION_POINTER_UP and ACTION_POINTER_DOWN constants.

33

Tracking the Device's Location

In this chapter, you will create a new application called RunTracker. RunTracker works with a device's GPS to record and display the user's travels. Those travels may be a walk in the woods at Big Nerd Ranch Bootcamp, a car ride, or an ocean voyage. RunTracker is designed to keep a record of them all.

The first version of RunTracker will simply get location updates from the GPS and display the device's current location on screen. Eventually, RunTracker will show a map that follows the user in real time.

Getting Started with RunTracker

Create a new Android application with the following configuration:

Figure 33.1 Creating RunTracker

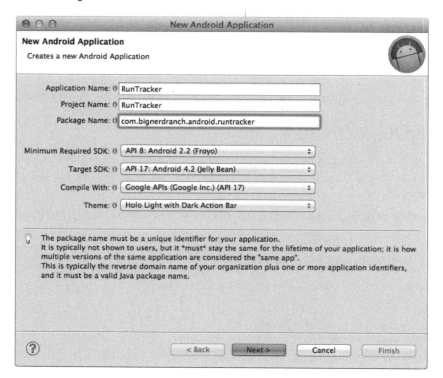

Notice two differences from previous projects. First, you are raising the minimum SDK version to API 9. Second, you are building to the latest Google APIs rather than the Android version. You need the Google APIs to use maps.

If you do not see a Google APIs version of the latest target listed, you can download it from the Android SDK Manager. Select Window → Android SDK Manager to pull up your SDK manager and then select the Google APIs, as shown in Figure 33.2. Then click Install 1 package.

Figure 33.2 Installing Google APIs for SDK 4.2

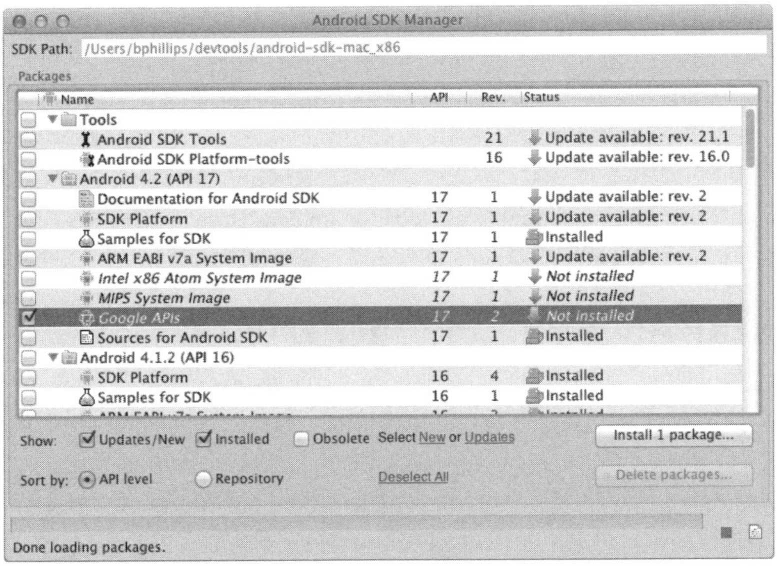

Once installation is complete, you should see the Google APIs as an option in your SDK version selector.

As with your other projects, have the wizard create a blank activity. Name it **RunActivity**.

Setting up RunActivity

RunActivity (and other activities in RunTracker) will use the **SingleFragmentActivity** class. Copy SingleFragmentActivity.java into the com.bignerdranch.android.runtracker package and activity_fragment.xml into res/layout/.

Then, open RunActivity.java and change **RunActivity** to be a subclass of **SingleFragmentActivity** that hosts an instance of **RunFragment**. **RunFragment** does not exist yet, but you will create it shortly.

Listing 33.1 Initial **RunActivity** (RunActivity.java)

```
public class RunActivity extends SingleFragmentActivity {

    @Override
    protected Fragment createFragment() {
        return new RunFragment();
    }

}
```

Setting up RunFragment

The next steps are to create the user interface and the initial version of **RunFragment**. The UI for **RunFragment** (Figure 33.3) will be responsible for displaying simple data about the current "run" and its location. It will have buttons to start and stop tracking the current run.

Figure 33.3 Initial RunTracker UI

Adding strings

First, let's add resources for the strings shown in Figure 33.3. In res/values/strings.xml, add the following strings, including three that you will need later in the chapter.

Listing 33.2 RunTracker strings (strings.xml)

```
<resources>
  <string name="app_name">RunTracker</string>
  <string name="started">Started:</string>
  <string name="latitude">Latitude:</string>
  <string name="longitude">Longitude:</string>
  <string name="altitude">Altitude:</string>
  <string name="elapsed_time">Elapsed Time:</string>
  <string name="start">Start</string>
  <string name="stop">Stop</string>
  <string name="gps_enabled">GPS Enabled</string>
  <string name="gps_disabled">GPS Disabled</string>
  <string name="cell_text">Run at %1$s</string>
</resources>
```

Obtaining the layout file

For the layout, you will use a **TableLayout** to keep everything tidy. The **TableLayout** will have five **TableRow**s and one **LinearLayout**. Each **TableRow** will have two **TextView**s: the first is a label, and the second will be populated with data at runtime. The **LinearLayout** will contain two **Button**s.

This layout has nothing in it that you have not worked with before. Rather than create it from scratch, get this layout from the solutions file (http://www.bignerdranch.com/solutions/AndroidProgramming.zip). Find 33_Location/RunTracker/res/layout/fragment_run.xml and copy it into your project's res/layout directory.

Creating the RunFragment class

Now let's create the **RunFragment** class itself. The initial version will just get the UI on the screen and provide access to its widgets.

Listing 33.3 Skeleton of **RunFragment** (RunFragment.java)

```
public class RunFragment extends Fragment {
    private Button mStartButton, mStopButton;
    private TextView mStartedTextView, mLatitudeTextView,
        mLongitudeTextView, mAltitudeTextView, mDurationTextView;

    @Override
    public void onCreate(Bundle savedInstanceState) {
        super.onCreate(savedInstanceState);
        setRetainInstance(true);
    }

    @Override
    public View onCreateView(LayoutInflater inflater, ViewGroup container,
            Bundle savedInstanceState) {
        View view = inflater.inflate(R.layout.fragment_run, container, false);

        mStartedTextView = (TextView)view.findViewById(R.id.run_startedTextView);
        mLatitudeTextView = (TextView)view.findViewById(R.id.run_latitudeTextView);
        mLongitudeTextView = (TextView)view.findViewById(R.id.run_longitudeTextView);
        mAltitudeTextView = (TextView)view.findViewById(R.id.run_altitudeTextView);
        mDurationTextView = (TextView)view.findViewById(R.id.run_durationTextView);

        mStartButton = (Button)view.findViewById(R.id.run_startButton);

        mStopButton = (Button)view.findViewById(R.id.run_stopButton);

        return view;
    }
}
```

Run the app and confirm that it looks like Figure 33.3.

Locations and the LocationManager

With the foundation in place, now you can get to work on the inside of the house. Location data in Android is provided by the **LocationManager** system service. This service provides location updates to all applications who are interested in them, and it delivers those updates in one of two ways.

The first, and perhaps most straightforward, way is via the **LocationListener** interface. This interface gives you information about location updates (via **onLocationChanged(Location)**) as well as status updates and notifications that the provider has been enabled or disabled.

Using **LocationListener** to get updates is a fine thing to do when you only need the location data to come to a single component in your application. For example, if you only wanted to display location updates within **RunFragment**, you could provide a **LocationListener** implementation to a call to one of **LocationManager**'s **requestLocationUpdates(…)** or **requestSingleUpdate(…)** methods and be done.

In this case, however, you have bigger plans. The goal for RunTracker is to keep tracking the user's location regardless of the state (or presence) of the user interface. You could do this using a sticky **Service**, but that brings its own headaches and is a bit heavyweight for this example. Instead, you will use the **PendingIntent** API introduced in Android 2.3 (Gingerbread).

By requesting location updates with a **PendingIntent**, you are asking the **LocationManager** to send some kind of **Intent** for you in the future. So, your application components, and indeed your entire process, can die, and **LocationManager** will still deliver your intents until you tell it to stop, starting new components to respond to them as needed. You will take advantage of this to keep your app from consuming too many resources even while it is actively tracking the device's location.

To manage the communication with **LocationManager**, and eventually more details about the current run, create a singleton class called **RunManager** as shown in Listing 33.4.

Listing 33.4 Skeleton of **RunManager**, a singleton (RunManager.java)

```java
public class RunManager {
    private static final String TAG = "RunManager";

    public static final String ACTION_LOCATION =
        "com.bignerdranch.android.runtracker.ACTION_LOCATION";

    private static RunManager sRunManager;
    private Context mAppContext;
    private LocationManager mLocationManager;

    // The private constructor forces users to use RunManager.get(Context)
    private RunManager(Context appContext) {
        mAppContext = appContext;
        mLocationManager = (LocationManager)mAppContext
            .getSystemService(Context.LOCATION_SERVICE);
    }

    public static RunManager get(Context c) {
        if (sRunManager == null) {
            // Use the application context to avoid leaking activities
            sRunManager = new RunManager(c.getApplicationContext());
        }
        return sRunManager;
    }
```

```
private PendingIntent getLocationPendingIntent(boolean shouldCreate) {
    Intent broadcast = new Intent(ACTION_LOCATION);
    int flags = shouldCreate ? 0 : PendingIntent.FLAG_NO_CREATE;
    return PendingIntent.getBroadcast(mAppContext, 0, broadcast, flags);
}

public void startLocationUpdates() {
    String provider = LocationManager.GPS_PROVIDER;

    // Start updates from the location manager
    PendingIntent pi = getLocationPendingIntent(true);
    mLocationManager.requestLocationUpdates(provider, 0, 0, pi);
}

public void stopLocationUpdates() {
    PendingIntent pi = getLocationPendingIntent(false);
    if (pi != null) {
        mLocationManager.removeUpdates(pi);
        pi.cancel();
    }
}

public boolean isTrackingRun() {
    return getLocationPendingIntent(false) != null;
}
}
```

Notice that **RunManager** has three public instance methods. These are its basic API. It can start location updates, stop them, and tell you if it is currently tracking a run (which merely means that updates are currently registered with the **LocationManager**).

In **startLocationUpdates()**, you specifically tell **LocationManager** to give you location updates via the GPS provider as frequently as possible. The **requestLocationUpdates(String, long, float, PendingIntent)** method expects parameters for the minimum time to wait (in milliseconds) and minimum distance to cover (in meters) before sending the next update.

These parameters should be tuned to the maximum value you can withstand and still have your app provide a good user experience. For RunTracker, your user will want to know exactly where they are, and exactly where they have been, with as much accuracy as possible. This is why we hard-code the GPS provider and request updates as often as possible.

On the other hand, for an app that is only vaguely interested in where a user is, larger values will do just fine and will save the device's battery from melting into hot slag.

The private **getLocationPendingIntent(boolean)** method creates an **Intent** to be broadcast when location updates happen. You use a custom action name to identify the event within our app, and the shouldCreate argument to tell **PendingIntent.getBroadcast(…)** (via flags) whether it should create a new **PendingIntent** in the system or not.

Calling **getLocationPendingIntent(false)** and null-checking the result is therefore a way of determining whether the **PendingIntent** is registered with the OS, and is therefore the implementation of the **isTrackingRun()** method.

Receiving Broadcast Location Updates

Now that you have code to request location updates as broadcast **Intent**s, you need to have a way to receive them. RunTracker will need to be able to receive them whether or not any UI components, or even the application process, are running, so the best place to handle it is with a standalone **BroadcastReceiver** registered in the manifest.

To keep things simple, create **LocationReceiver** to log out the locations it receives.

Listing 33.5 Basic **LocationReceiver** (LocationReceiver.java)

```java
public class LocationReceiver extends BroadcastReceiver {
  private static final String TAG = "LocationReceiver";

  @Override
  public void onReceive(Context context, Intent intent) {
      // If you got a Location extra, use it
      Location loc = (Location)intent
          .getParcelableExtra(LocationManager.KEY_LOCATION_CHANGED);
      if (loc != null) {
          onLocationReceived(context, loc);
          return;
      }
      // If you get here, something else has happened
      if (intent.hasExtra(LocationManager.KEY_PROVIDER_ENABLED)) {
          boolean enabled = intent
              .getBooleanExtra(LocationManager.KEY_PROVIDER_ENABLED, false);
          onProviderEnabledChanged(enabled);
      }
  }

  protected void onLocationReceived(Context context, Location loc) {
      Log.d(TAG, this + " Got location from " + loc.getProvider() + ": "
          + loc.getLatitude() + ", " + loc.getLongitude());
  }

  protected void onProviderEnabledChanged(boolean enabled) {
      Log.d(TAG, "Provider " + (enabled ? "enabled" : "disabled"));
  }

}
```

As you can see in the implementation of **onReceive(Context, Intent)**, the **LocationManager** will pack the intent with some extras of interest. The LocationManager.KEY_LOCATION_CHANGED key may specify a **Location** instance that represents the latest update. If it returns one, then call the **onLocationReceived(Context, Location)** method to log out the provider name, latitude, and longitude.

LocationManager may also pass a boolean extra with the KEY_PROVIDER_ENABLED key, and if it does, call the **onProviderEnabled(boolean)** method to log about that. Eventually, you will subclass **LocationReceiver** to make these two methods do more useful things.

Add an entry for **LocationReceiver** in the manifest for RunTracker. While you're at it, add the ACCESS_FINE_LOCATION permission and a uses-feature element for the GPS hardware.

Listing 33.6 Adding location permission (`AndroidManifest.xml`)

```
<manifest xmlns:android="http://schemas.android.com/apk/res/android"
  package="com.bignerdranch.android.runtracker"
  android:versionCode="1"
  android:versionName="1.0">

  <uses-sdk android:minSdkVersion="9" android:targetSdkVersion="15" />
  <uses-permission android:name="android.permission.ACCESS_FINE_LOCATION"/>
  <uses-feature android:required="true"
    android:name="android.hardware.location.gps"/>

  <application android:label="@string/app_name"
    android:allowBackup="true"
    android:icon="@drawable/ic_launcher"
    android:theme="@style/AppTheme">
    <activity android:name=".RunActivity"
      android:label="@string/app_name">
      <intent-filter>
        <action android:name="android.intent.action.MAIN" />
        <category android:name="android.intent.category.LAUNCHER" />
      </intent-filter>
    </activity>
    <receiver android:name=".LocationReceiver"
      android:exported="false">
      <intent-filter>
        <action android:name="com.bignerdranch.android.runtracker.ACTION_LOCATION"/>
      </intent-filter>
    </receiver>
  </application>

</manifest>
```

Now you have enough plumbing in place to request and receive location updates, and all that remains is to provide some user interface to start, stop, and display them.

Updating the UI with Location Data

Just to verify that things are working as expected, add click listeners to the Start and Stop buttons in **RunFragment** that communicate with **RunManager**. Also add calls to a simple **updateUI()** method.

Listing 33.7 Starting and stopping location updates (`RunFragment.java`)

```
public class RunFragment extends Fragment {

    private RunManager mRunManager;

    private Button mStartButton, mStopButton;
    private TextView mStartedTextView, mLatitudeTextView,
        mLongitudeTextView, mAltitudeTextView, mDurationTextView;
```

```java
    @Override
    public void onCreate(Bundle savedInstanceState) {
        super.onCreate(savedInstanceState);
        setRetainInstance(true);
        mRunManager = RunManager.get(getActivity());
    }

    @Override
    public View onCreateView(LayoutInflater inflater, ViewGroup container,
            Bundle savedInstanceState) {
        ...

        mStartButton = (Button)view.findViewById(R.id.run_startButton);
        mStartButton.setOnClickListener(new View.OnClickListener() {
            @Override
            public void onClick(View v) {
                mRunManager.startLocationUpdates();
                updateUI();
            }
        });

        mStopButton = (Button)view.findViewById(R.id.run_stopButton);
        mStopButton.setOnClickListener(new View.OnClickListener() {
            @Override
            public void onClick(View v) {
                mRunManager.stopLocationUpdates();
                updateUI();
            }
        });

        updateUI();


        return view;
    }

    private void updateUI() {
        boolean started = mRunManager.isTrackingRun();

        mStartButton.setEnabled(!started);
        mStopButton.setEnabled(started);
    }
}
```

With these additions, you can run RunTracker again and see location updates coming in via LogCat. For best results, use the Emulator Control window in DDMS to send fake updates to an emulator, or take your device outside and wait for a GPS fix. It can take several minutes to get the first update. Skip ahead a couple of pages for more details on providing test locations if you're impatient or locked inside your secret underground programming bunker.

Logging to LogCat is not a very user-friendly way of reporting locations. To get something on the screen, you can implement a subclass of **LocationReceiver** in **RunFragment** that will stash away the **Location** and update the UI. With a bit more data, stored in a new **Run** instance, you can display the start date and duration of the current run. Start by implementing a simple **Run** class that holds its start date and knows how to calculate its duration and format it as a string.

Listing 33.8 Your basic **Run** (Run.java)

```java
public class Run {
    private Date mStartDate;

    public Run() {
        mStartDate = new Date();
    }

    public Date getStartDate() {
        return mStartDate;
    }

    public void setStartDate(Date startDate) {
        mStartDate = startDate;
    }

    public int getDurationSeconds(long endMillis) {
        return (int)((endMillis - mStartDate.getTime()) / 1000);
    }

    public static String formatDuration(int durationSeconds) {
        int seconds = durationSeconds % 60;
        int minutes = ((durationSeconds - seconds) / 60) % 60;
        int hours = (durationSeconds - (minutes * 60) - seconds) / 3600;
        return String.format("%02d:%02d:%02d", hours, minutes, seconds);
    }

}
```

Now make use of the **Run** class with some updates to **RunFragment**.

Listing 33.9 Displaying location updates (RunFragment.java)

```java
public class RunFragment extends Fragment {

    private BroadcastReceiver mLocationReceiver = new LocationReceiver() {

        @Override
        protected void onLocationReceived(Context context, Location loc) {
            mLastLocation = loc;
            if (isVisible())
                updateUI();
        }

        @Override
        protected void onProviderEnabledChanged(boolean enabled) {
            int toastText = enabled ? R.string.gps_enabled : R.string.gps_disabled;
            Toast.makeText(getActivity(), toastText, Toast.LENGTH_LONG).show();
        }

    };

    private RunManager mRunManager;

    private Run mRun;
    private Location mLastLocation;
```

```
    private Button mStartButton, mStopButton;

    ...

    @Override
    public View onCreateView(LayoutInflater inflater, ViewGroup container,
            Bundle savedInstanceState) {
        ...

        mStartButton = (Button)view.findViewById(R.id.run_startButton);
        mStartButton.setOnClickListener(new View.OnClickListener() {
            @Override
            public void onClick(View v) {
                mRunManager.startLocationUpdates();
                mRun = new Run();
                updateUI();
            }
        });

        ...
    }

    @Override
    public void onStart() {
        super.onStart();
        getActivity().registerReceiver(mLocationReceiver,
                new IntentFilter(RunManager.ACTION_LOCATION));
    }

    @Override
    public void onStop() {
        getActivity().unregisterReceiver(mLocationReceiver);
        super.onStop();
    }

    private void updateUI() {
        boolean started = mRunManager.isTrackingRun();

        if (mRun != null)
            mStartedTextView.setText(mRun.getStartDate().toString());

        int durationSeconds = 0;
        if (mRun != null && mLastLocation != null) {
            durationSeconds = mRun.getDurationSeconds(mLastLocation.getTime());
            mLatitudeTextView.setText(Double.toString(mLastLocation.getLatitude()));
            mLongitudeTextView.setText(Double.toString(mLastLocation.getLongitude()));
            mAltitudeTextView.setText(Double.toString(mLastLocation.getAltitude()));
        }
        mDurationTextView.setText(Run.formatDuration(durationSeconds));

        mStartButton.setEnabled(!started);
        mStopButton.setEnabled(started);
    }
}
```

There are a few things happening here. Foremost, there are new instance variables for a **Run** and the last **Location** received. These are the data that back up the user interface updates performed in **updateUI()**. The **Run** gets initialized as soon as you start location updates.

You create an anonymous **LocationReceiver** class and stash it in mLocationReceiver to save the location received and update the UI. You also display a **Toast** when the GPS provider is enabled or disabled.

Finally, the implementations of the **onStart()** and **onStop()** methods are used to register and unregister the receiver in conjunction with the fragment being visible to the user. It would also be sensible to do this work in **onCreate(Bundle)** and **onDestroy()**, so that the mLastLocation variable would always contain the latest location update, even if the fragment was offscreen while it was received.

Run RunTracker again, and you should now see actual location details populating the user interface.

Faster Answers: the Last Known Location

There are times when your users do not want to sit and wait for several minutes for their device to communicate with mysterious satellites in space just to find out where they are. Fortunately, with a little more work, you can prevent them from having to wait by using the **LocationManager**'s last known location for any location provider.

Since you are using the GPS provider only, it makes the most sense to ask for its last known location, and doing so is rather straightforward. The only other trick is getting that location back to the user interface, and for that you can simply broadcast an **Intent** just as though you were the **LocationManager**.

Listing 33.10 Getting the last known location (RunManager.java)

```
public void startLocationUpdates() {
    String provider = LocationManager.GPS_PROVIDER;

    // Get the last known location and broadcast it if you have one
    Location lastKnown = mLocationManager.getLastKnownLocation(provider);
    if (lastKnown != null) {
        // Reset the time to now
        lastKnown.setTime(System.currentTimeMillis());
        broadcastLocation(lastKnown);
    }

    // Start updates from the location manager
    PendingIntent pi = getLocationPendingIntent(true);
    mLocationManager.requestLocationUpdates(provider, 0, 0, pi);
}

private void broadcastLocation(Location location) {
    Intent broadcast = new Intent(ACTION_LOCATION);
    broadcast.putExtra(LocationManager.KEY_LOCATION_CHANGED, location);
    mAppContext.sendBroadcast(broadcast);
}
```

Notice that you are resetting the timestamp of the location you get from the GPS provider. This may or may not be what the user expects, and determining that is left as an exercise to the reader.

It is also possible to ask the **LocationManager** for the last known location from any provider it is aware of. You can even ask it what providers it knows about using the **getAllProviders()** method. If you do iterate over the last known locations, you should check them for accuracy and see that their timestamp is within the recent past. If they are not fresh, you may not want to use them.

Testing Locations on Real and Virtual Devices

Testing an app like RunTracker can be challenging, even for an avid outdoors-programmer. You want to ensure that the locations you receive from the system are being appropriately tracked and stored. This can be difficult to do if you are moving around, even at the low speeds achieved by having your friend haul you and your development setup around the neighborhood on a bicycle trailer.

To get around situations like this, you can send test locations to the **LocationManager** that will allow your device to pretend that it is somewhere else.

The simplest way to make this happen is using the Emulator Control window within DDMS. This only works with virtual devices, but it allows you to specify new locations either manually, one at a time, or with a GPX or KML file representing a series of locations visited over time.

For testing locations on a real device, you have a bit more work to do, but it is entirely possible. The basic process looks like this:

1. Request the ACCESS_MOCK_LOCATION permission.

2. Add a test provider via **LocationManager.addTestProvider(…)**.

3. Enable the provider using **setTestProviderEnabled(…)**.

4. Set its initial status with **setTestProviderStatus(…)**.

5. Publish locations with **setTestProviderLocation(…)**.

6. Remove your test provider using **removeTestProvider(…)**.

Fortunately, we have already done all the hard work for you. Big Nerd Ranch has a simple TestProvider project that you can download, install to your device, and run to manage the test provider and make it run.

Download the Android Course Resources repository from Github at https://github.com/bignerdranch/AndroidCourseResources and import the TestProvider directory as a project in Eclipse.

You will need to add some code to RunTracker to use the new test provider instead of GPS. Update **RunManager** as shown below to make that possible.

Listing 33.11 Using a test provider (RunManager.java)

```java
public class RunManager {
    private static final String TAG = "RunManager";

    public static final String ACTION_LOCATION =
        "com.bignerdranch.android.runtracker.ACTION_LOCATION";

    private static final String TEST_PROVIDER = "TEST_PROVIDER";

    private static RunManager sRunManager;
    private Context mAppContext;
    private LocationManager mLocationManager;

    ...

    public void startLocationUpdates() {
        String provider = LocationManager.GPS_PROVIDER;
        // If you have the test provider and it's enabled, use it
        if (mLocationManager.getProvider(TEST_PROVIDER) != null &&
                mLocationManager.isProviderEnabled(TEST_PROVIDER)) {
            provider = TEST_PROVIDER;
        }
        Log.d(TAG, "Using provider " + provider);

        // get the last known location and broadcast it if you have one
        Location lastKnown = mLocationManager.getLastKnownLocation(provider);
        if (lastKnown != null) {
            // Reset the time to now
            lastKnown.setTime(System.currentTimeMillis());
            broadcastLocation(lastKnown);
        }
```

In order for TestProvider to work, you may need to turn on the Allow mock locations setting in the Developer options menu from within the Settings application. See Figure 33.4.

With that out of the way, run the TestProvider app on your device and press the button to start fake location updates.

Then you can run RunTracker and see your faked data coming through. (Hint: it's in Atlanta, Georgia, USA.) Once you are finished testing, it is best to turn off the test location provider so that your device is not confused about where it is.

Figure 33.4 Allow mock locations

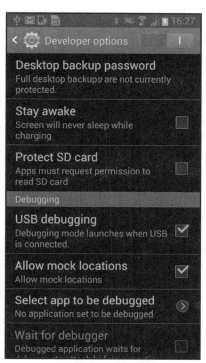

34

Local Databases with SQLite

Applications with large or complex data sets often need more power than you can get from simple file formats like JSON. In RunTracker, the user can continue tracking his or her location forever, which can generate a lot of data. The logical choice for such data sets in Android is a SQLite database. SQLite is an open source, multi-platform library that gives you access to a powerful, relational database API backed by a single file on disk.

Android includes a Java front-end to SQLite through the **SQLiteDatabase** class, which provides result sets as **Cursor** instances. In this chapter you will create a storage mechanism for RunTracker that uses a database to store data about runs and their locations. You will also create a new run list activity and fragment that allow the user to create and track multiple runs.

Storing Runs and Locations in a Database

In order to store anything in a database, first you need to define the structure of the database and open it. Since this is such a common task in Android, a helper class exists. **SQLiteOpenHelper** encapsulates the chore of creating, opening, and updating databases for storing your application data.

In RunTracker, you will create a subclass of **SQLiteOpenHelper** called **RunDatabaseHelper**. The **RunManager** will hold on to a private instance of **RunDatabaseHelper** and provide the rest of the application with an API for inserting, querying, and otherwise managing the data in the database. **RunDatabaseHelper** will provide methods that **RunManager** will call to implement most of its API.

When designing an application's database storage API, you typically create one subclass of **SQLiteOpenHelper** for each type of database you need to create and manage. You then create one instance of your subclass for each distinct SQLite database file you need to access. Most applications, including RunTracker, will have just one subclass of **SQLiteOpenHelper** and share a single instance of it with the rest of the application components.

Now that you know you need to create a database, consider the structure of it. In object oriented programming, the most common pattern for database design is to use one database table for each class in your application's data model. For RunTracker, there are two classes to store: **Run** and **Location**.

This example will therefore create two tables: run and location. A **Run** can have many **Location**s, so the location table will have a run_id foreign key column referencing the run table's _id column. Figure 34.1 shows the structure of the tables.

Figure 34.1 RunTracker database schema

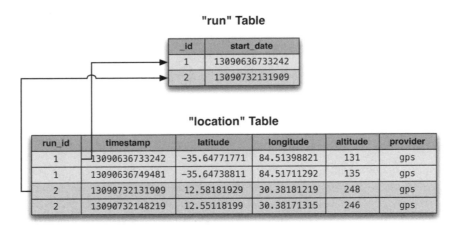

Create the **RunDatabaseHelper** class by adding the code shown in Listing 34.1.

Listing 34.1 Basic **RunDatabaseHelper** (RunDatabaseHelper.java

```java
public class RunDatabaseHelper extends SQLiteOpenHelper {
    private static final String DB_NAME = "runs.sqlite";
    private static final int VERSION = 1;

    private static final String TABLE_RUN = "run";
    private static final String COLUMN_RUN_START_DATE = "start_date";

    public RunDatabaseHelper(Context context) {
        super(context, DB_NAME, null, VERSION);
    }

    @Override
    public void onCreate(SQLiteDatabase db) {
        // Create the "run" table
        db.execSQL("create table run (" +
            "_id integer primary key autoincrement, start_date integer)");
        // Create the "location" table
        db.execSQL("create table location (" +
            " timestamp integer, latitude real, longitude real, altitude real," +
            " provider varchar(100), run_id integer references run(_id))");
    }

    @Override
    public void onUpgrade(SQLiteDatabase db, int oldVersion, int newVersion) {
        // Implement schema changes and data massage here when upgrading
    }

    public long insertRun(Run run) {
        ContentValues cv = new ContentValues();
        cv.put(COLUMN_RUN_START_DATE, run.getStartDate().getTime());
        return getWritableDatabase().insert(TABLE_RUN, null, cv);
    }
}
```

Implementing a subclass of **SQLiteOpenHelper** requires you to override two methods: **onCreate(SQLiteDatabase)** and **onUpgrade(SQLiteDatabase, int, int)**. In **onCreate(…)** your job is to establish the schema for a newly created database. In **onUpgrade(…)** you have the opportunity to execute migration code to move from one version of the database schema to another.

It is also common to implement a simplified constructor that fills in some of the arguments required by the superclass version. In this example, you pass a constant name for the database file, a null value for the optional **CursorFactory**, and a constant integer version number.

While it will not be necessary for the RunTracker example, **SQLiteOpenHelper** supports the ability to manage different versions of a database schema. It expects the version number to be an increasing integer value starting at one. In a real application, each time you made changes to your database schema, you would increment the version constant and write code in the **onUpgrade(…)** method to handle any schema or data changes that were necessary between versions.

Here, you have implemented **onCreate(…)** to execute two CREATE TABLE SQL statements on the freshly-created database. You also implemented the **insertRun(Run)** method to insert a new row in the run table and return its ID. Runs have a single data field, their start date, and here you are storing the long value of it in the database using a **ContentValues** object to represent the mapping of column names to values.

SQLiteOpenHelper has two methods that will give you access to an instance of **SQLiteDatabase**: **getWritableDatabase()** and **getReadableDatabase()**. The pattern used in this example uses **getWritableDatabase()** when a writable database is needed, and **getReadableDatabase()** when only read access is required. In practice, the implementations of these methods will return the same instance of **SQLiteDatabase** for a given instance of **SQLiteOpenHelper**, but in certain rare situations, like a full disk, you can get a readable database when you might not be able to get a writable one.

To support querying one or more runs from the database, and distinguishing them in the app, you will need to add an ID property to the **Run** class. Update it with the changes shown in Listing 34.2.

Listing 34.2 Adding an ID to **Run** (Run.java)

```java
public class Run {
    private long mId;
    private Date mStartDate;

    public Run() {
        mId = -1;
        mStartDate = new Date();
    }

    public long getId() {
        return mId;
    }

    public void setId(long id) {
        mId = id;
    }

    public Date getStartDate() {
        return mStartDate;
    }
}
```

Next, you need to make some enhancements to **RunManager** that make use of the new database. This will be the API that the rest of the application uses to store and retrieve data. To start, add just enough code to get **Run** storage working.

Listing 34.3 Managing the current run (RunManager.java)

```java
public class RunManager {
    private static final String TAG = "RunManager";

    private static final String PREFS_FILE = "runs";
    private static final String PREF_CURRENT_RUN_ID = "RunManager.currentRunId";

    public static final String ACTION_LOCATION =
        "com.bignerdranch.android.runtracker.ACTION_LOCATION";

    private static final String TEST_PROVIDER = "TEST_PROVIDER";

    private static RunManager sRunManager;
    private Context mAppContext;
    private LocationManager mLocationManager;
    private RunDatabaseHelper mHelper;
    private SharedPreferences mPrefs;
    private long mCurrentRunId;

    private RunManager(Context appContext) {
        mAppContext = appContext;
        mLocationManager = (LocationManager)mAppContext
            .getSystemService(Context.LOCATION_SERVICE);
        mHelper = new RunDatabaseHelper(mAppContext);
        mPrefs = mAppContext.getSharedPreferences(PREFS_FILE, Context.MODE_PRIVATE);
        mCurrentRunId = mPrefs.getLong(PREF_CURRENT_RUN_ID, -1);
    }

    ...

    private void broadcastLocation(Location location) {
        Intent broadcast = new Intent(ACTION_LOCATION);
        broadcast.putExtra(LocationManager.KEY_LOCATION_CHANGED, location);
        mAppContext.sendBroadcast(broadcast);
    }

    public Run startNewRun() {
        // Insert a run into the db
        Run run = insertRun();
        // Start tracking the run
        startTrackingRun(run);
        return run;
    }

    public void startTrackingRun(Run run) {
        // Keep the ID
        mCurrentRunId = run.getId();
        // Store it in shared preferences
        mPrefs.edit().putLong(PREF_CURRENT_RUN_ID, mCurrentRunId).commit();
        // Start location updates
        startLocationUpdates();
    }
```

```
    public void stopRun() {
        stopLocationUpdates();
        mCurrentRunId = -1;
        mPrefs.edit().remove(PREF_CURRENT_RUN_ID).commit();
    }

    private Run insertRun() {
        Run run = new Run();
        run.setId(mHelper.insertRun(run));
        return run;
    }
}
```

Take a look at the new methods you just added to **RunManager**. The **startNewRun()** method calls **insertRun()** to create and insert a new **Run** into the database, passes it to **startTrackingRun(Run)** to begin tracking it, and finally returns it to the caller. You will use this method in **RunFragment** in response to the Start button when there is no existing run to work with.

RunFragment will also use **startTrackingRun(Run)** directly when it restarts tracking on an existing run. This method saves the ID of the **Run** passed to it in both an instance variable and in shared preferences. Storing it this way allows it to be retrieved later, even if the app is killed completely; the **RunManager** constructor will do this work in that event.

Finally, the **stopRun()** method stops location updates and clears out the ID of the current run. **RunFragment** will use this method to implement the Stop button.

Speaking of **RunFragment**, now is a good time to make use of the new **RunManager** methods there. Make the changes in Listing 34.4.

Listing 34.4 Updating the starting and stopping code (RunFragment.java)

```
@Override
public View onCreateView(LayoutInflater inflater, ViewGroup container,
        Bundle savedInstanceState) {
    View view = inflater.inflate(R.layout.fragment_run, container, false);

    ...

    mStartButton = (Button)view.findViewById(R.id.run_startButton);
    mStartButton.setOnClickListener(new View.OnClickListener() {
        @Override
        public void onClick(View v) {
            mRunManager.startLocationUpdates();
            mRun = new Run();
            mRun = mRunManager.startNewRun();
            updateUI();
        }
    });

    mStopButton = (Button)view.findViewById(R.id.run_stopButton);
    mStopButton.setOnClickListener(new View.OnClickListener() {
        @Override
        public void onClick(View v) {
            mRunManager.stopLocationUpdates();
            mRunManager.stopRun();
            updateUI();
        }
    });

    updateUI();

    return view;
}
```

Next, you need the power to insert **Location** objects into the database in response to updates from the **LocationManager**. Similar to inserting **Run**s, you will add a method to both **RunDatabaseHelper** and **RunManager** to insert a location for the current run. Unlike inserting a **Run**, however, RunTracker needs to be able to insert locations as updates arrive regardless of whether the user interface is visible or the application is running. To handle this requirement, a standalone **BroadcastReceiver** is the best option.

First, add the **insertLocation(long, Location)** method in **RunDatabaseHelper**:

Listing 34.5 Inserting locations in the database (RunDatabaseHelper.java)

```java
public class RunDatabaseHelper extends SQLiteOpenHelper {
    private static final String DB_NAME = "runs.sqlite";
    private static final int VERSION = 1;

    private static final String TABLE_RUN = "run";
    private static final String COLUMN_RUN_START_DATE = "start_date";

    private static final String TABLE_LOCATION = "location";
    private static final String COLUMN_LOCATION_LATITUDE = "latitude";
    private static final String COLUMN_LOCATION_LONGITUDE = "longitude";
    private static final String COLUMN_LOCATION_ALTITUDE = "altitude";
    private static final String COLUMN_LOCATION_TIMESTAMP = "timestamp";
    private static final String COLUMN_LOCATION_PROVIDER = "provider";
    private static final String COLUMN_LOCATION_RUN_ID = "run_id";


    ...

    public long insertLocation(long runId, Location location) {
        ContentValues cv = new ContentValues();
        cv.put(COLUMN_LOCATION_LATITUDE, location.getLatitude());
        cv.put(COLUMN_LOCATION_LONGITUDE, location.getLongitude());
        cv.put(COLUMN_LOCATION_ALTITUDE, location.getAltitude());
        cv.put(COLUMN_LOCATION_TIMESTAMP, location.getTime());
        cv.put(COLUMN_LOCATION_PROVIDER, location.getProvider());
        cv.put(COLUMN_LOCATION_RUN_ID, runId);
        return getWritableDatabase().insert(TABLE_LOCATION, null, cv);
    }
}
```

Now, add code to **RunManager** to insert a location for the currently tracking run.

Listing 34.6 Inserting a location for the current run (RunManager.java)

```java
    private Run insertRun() {
        Run run = new Run();
        run.setId(mHelper.insertRun(run));
        return run;
    }

    public void insertLocation(Location loc) {
        if (mCurrentRunId != -1) {
            mHelper.insertLocation(mCurrentRunId, loc);
        } else {
            Log.e(TAG, "Location received with no tracking run; ignoring.");
        }
    }
}
```

Lastly, you need a good place to call the new **insertLocation(Location)** method. By using a standalone **BroadcastReceiver** for this work, you can guarantee that your location intents will be handled no matter whether the rest of RunTracker is up and running. This requires creating a customized subclass of **LocationReceiver** called **TrackingLocationReceiver** and registering it using an intent filter in the manifest.

Create **TrackingLocationReceiver** as a top-level class using the following code:

Listing 34.7 Simple, yet elegant **TrackingLocationReceiver** (TrackingLocationReceiver.java)

```
public class TrackingLocationReceiver extends LocationReceiver {

    @Override
    protected void onLocationReceived(Context c, Location loc) {
        RunManager.get(c).insertLocation(loc);
    }

}
```

Now register it in the manifest to make it execute in response to the custom ACTION_LOCATION.

Listing 34.8 Enabling **TrackingLocationReceiver** (AndroidManifest.xml)

```
<application
  android:allowBackup="true"
  android:icon="@drawable/ic_launcher"
  android:label="@string/app_name"
  android:theme="@style/AppTheme">

  ...

  <receiver android:name=".LocationReceiver"
  <receiver android:name=".TrackingLocationReceiver"
    android:exported="false">
    <intent-filter>
      <action android:name="com.bignerdranch.android.runtracker.ACTION_LOCATION"/>
    </intent-filter>
  </receiver>

</application>
```

After so many changes, you deserve to run the application and see your hard work pay off. RunTracker is now capable of tracking a run until you tell it to stop, even if the app is killed or exited. You can verify that things are working as expected by adding a log statement to the success path of **TrackingLocationReceiver**'s **onLocationReceived(...)** method, starting a run, then killing or leaving the app while continuing to watch LogCat.

Querying a List of Runs From the Database

RunTracker can now insert new runs and locations for them into the database, but as written, **RunFragment** will create a new run each time you press the Start button. In this section, you will add a new activity and fragment to display a list of runs and to allow the user to create new runs and view existing runs. This is a similar interface to what you implemented in CriminalIntent for the list of crimes, except that the data backing the list will be coming from a database instead of RunTracker's memory and file data storage mechanism.

Querying a **SQLiteDatabase** returns an instance of **Cursor** describing the results. The **Cursor** API is simple and flexible enough to support any kind of result from any query. Cursors treat their results as a series of rows and columns, and only support **String**s and primitive types for values.

As Java programmers, however, we are used to working with objects to encapsulate our data model, such as **Run** and **Location**. Since you already have database tables that represent your objects, it would be ideal if you could get instances of those objects from a **Cursor**.

A pattern you will use in this chapter takes advantage of a built-in subclass of **Cursor** called **CursorWrapper**. **CursorWrapper** is designed to wrap an existing **Cursor** and forward along all of the method calls to it. On its own, it is not very useful; but as a superclass, it can provide you with a good foundation on which to build your own custom cursor implementations specific for your model objects.

Update **RunDatabaseHelper** to include a new **queryRuns()** method that returns a **RunCursor** listing all the runs in order by date - an example of the **CursorWrapper** pattern.

Listing 34.9 Querying runs (RunDatabaseHelper.java)

```java
public class RunDatabaseHelper extends SQLiteOpenHelper {
    private static final String DB_NAME = "runs.sqlite";
    private static final int VERSION = 1;

    private static final String TABLE_RUN = "run";
    private static final String COLUMN_RUN_ID = "_id";
    private static final String COLUMN_RUN_START_DATE = "start_date";

    ...

    public RunCursor queryRuns() {
        // Equivalent to "select * from run order by start_date asc"
        Cursor wrapped = getReadableDatabase().query(TABLE_RUN,
                null, null, null, null, null, COLUMN_RUN_START_DATE + " asc");
        return new RunCursor(wrapped);
    }

    /**
     * A convenience class to wrap a cursor that returns rows from the "run" table.
     * The {@link getRun()} method will give you a Run instance representing
     * the current row.
     */
    public static class RunCursor extends CursorWrapper {

        public RunCursor(Cursor c) {
            super(c);
        }

        /**
         * Returns a Run object configured for the current row,
         * or null if the current row is invalid.
         */
        public Run getRun() {
            if (isBeforeFirst() || isAfterLast())
                return null;
            Run run = new Run();
            long runId = getLong(getColumnIndex(COLUMN_RUN_ID));
            run.setId(runId);
            long startDate = getLong(getColumnIndex(COLUMN_RUN_START_DATE));
            run.setStartDate(new Date(startDate));
            return run;
        }
    }
}
```

RunCursor defines only two methods: a simple constructor and **getRun()**. The **getRun()** method checks to ensure that the cursor is within its bounds and then creates and configures an instance of **Run** based on the values of the current row's columns. A user of **RunCursor** would iterate over the rows in the result set and call **getRun()** for each row to get a nice object instead of a bunch of nasty primitives.

Thus, **RunCursor**'s main purpose is to encapsulate the grunt work of turning a row in the run table into an instance of **Run**, marshaling and massaging the data as needed.

The **queryRuns()** method does the work of executing the SQL query and providing the plain cursor to a new **RunCursor**, which it returns to the caller. Now you can make use of this new method in **RunManager** and eventually **RunListFragment**.

Listing 34.10 Proxying run queries (RunManager.java)

```java
private Run insertRun() {
    Run run = new Run();
    run.setId(mHelper.insertRun(run));
    return run;
}

public RunCursor queryRuns() {
    return mHelper.queryRuns();
}

public void insertLocation(Location loc) {
    if (mCurrentRunId != -1) {
        mHelper.insertLocation(mCurrentRunId, loc);
    } else {
        Log.e(TAG, "Location received with no tracking run; ignoring.");
    }
}
```

Displaying a List of Runs Using CursorAdapter

To set the ground work for a user interface listing the runs, create a new default activity for the app called **RunListActivity** and set it as the default in the manifest. Ignore the error about **RunListFragment** for the moment.

Listing 34.11 The great and powerful **RunListActivity** (RunListActivity.java)

```java
public class RunListActivity extends SingleFragmentActivity {

    @Override
    protected Fragment createFragment() {
        return new RunListFragment();
    }

}
```

Listing 34.12 Configuring **RunListActivity** (AndroidManifest.xml)

```
<application
  android:allowBackup="true"
  android:icon="@drawable/ic_launcher"
  android:label="@string/app_name"
  android:theme="@style/AppTheme">
  <activity android:name=".RunActivity"
  <activity android:name=".RunListActivity"
    android:label="@string/app_name">
    <intent-filter>
      <action android:name="android.intent.action.MAIN" />
      <category android:name="android.intent.category.LAUNCHER" />
    </intent-filter>
  </activity>
  <activity android:name=".RunActivity"
            android:label="@string/app_name" />
  <receiver android:name=".TrackingLocationReceiver"
    android:exported="false">
    <intent-filter>
```

Now you can create the basic skeleton of **RunListFragment**. For now, you are loading the cursor in **onCreate(Bundle)** and closing it in **onDestroy()**, but this is not a good pattern to follow, because it forces the database query to happen on the main (UI) thread and in extreme cases could cause a dreaded ANR to appear. In the next chapter, you will swap out the native implementation for one that uses a **Loader** to move the work to the background.

Listing 34.13 Basic **RunListFragment** (RunListFragment.java)

```java
public class RunListFragment extends ListFragment {

    private RunCursor mCursor;

    @Override
    public void onCreate(Bundle savedInstanceState) {
        super.onCreate(savedInstanceState);
        // Query the list of runs
        mCursor = RunManager.get(getActivity()).queryRuns();
    }

    @Override
    public void onDestroy() {
        mCursor.close();
        super.onDestroy();
    }

}
```

A **RunCursor** is no good without a way to provide its data to the **ListView** associated with **RunListFragment**. Included in the Android API (and the support library) is a class called **CursorAdapter** that fits the bill nicely. All you need to do is subclass it and provide implementations of a couple of methods. **CursorAdapter** handles the logic of creating and reusing views, so you don't have to.

Update **RunListFragment** to implement **RunCursorAdapter** now.

Listing 34.14 Implementing **RunCursorAdapter** (RunListFragment.java)

```java
public class RunListFragment extends ListFragment {

    private RunCursor mCursor;

    @Override
    public void onCreate(Bundle savedInstanceState) {
        super.onCreate(savedInstanceState);
        // Query the list of runs
        mCursor = RunManager.get(getActivity()).queryRuns();
        // Create an adapter to point at this cursor
        RunCursorAdapter adapter = new RunCursorAdapter(getActivity(), mCursor);
        setListAdapter(adapter);
    }

    @Override
    public void onDestroy() {
        mCursor.close();
        super.onDestroy();
    }

    private static class RunCursorAdapter extends CursorAdapter {

        private RunCursor mRunCursor;

        public RunCursorAdapter(Context context, RunCursor cursor) {
            super(context, cursor, 0);
            mRunCursor = cursor;
        }

        @Override
        public View newView(Context context, Cursor cursor, ViewGroup parent) {
            // Use a layout inflater to get a row view
            LayoutInflater inflater = (LayoutInflater)context
                .getSystemService(Context.LAYOUT_INFLATER_SERVICE);
            return inflater
                .inflate(android.R.layout.simple_list_item_1, parent, false);
        }

        @Override
        public void bindView(View view, Context context, Cursor cursor) {
            // Get the run for the current row
            Run run = mRunCursor.getRun();

            // Set up the start date text view
            TextView startDateTextView = (TextView)view;
            String cellText =
                context.getString(R.string.cell_text, run.getStartDate());
            startDateTextView.setText(cellText);
        }
    }
}
```

The constructor for **CursorAdapter** takes a **Context**, a **Cursor**, and an integer of flags. Most of the flags are now deprecated or questionable in favor of using loaders, so here you pass zero. You also stash the **RunCursor** in an instance variable to avoid having to cast it later.

Next, you implement **newView(Context, Cursor, ViewGroup)** to return a **View** to represent the current row in the cursor. This example inflates the system resource android.R.layout.simple_list_item_1, which is a plain **TextView**. Since all of the views in the list will look the same, that is all the logic you need here.

The **bindView(View, Context, Cursor)** method will be called by **CursorAdapter** when it wants you to configure a view to hold data for a row in the cursor. This will always be called with a **View** that has been previously returned from **newView(…)**.

Implementing **bindView(…)** is relatively simple. First, you ask the **RunCursor** for the **Run** at the current row (the cursor will have already been positioned by **CursorAdapter**). Next, you assume that the view passed in is a **TextView** and configure it to display a simple description of the **Run**.

With these changes in place, run RunTracker; you should see a list of the runs you have previously created, assuming you ran it and started a run after implementing the database insert code earlier in the chapter. If you don't yet have any runs, fear not: the next section has you add UI to create a new one.

Creating New Runs

Adding a user interface to allow creation of new runs is easy using an options/action bar menu item, just as you did with CriminalIntent. Start by creating a resource for the menu.

Listing 34.15 Options menu for the run list (`run_list_options.xml`)

```xml
<?xml version="1.0" encoding="utf-8"?>
<menu xmlns:android="http://schemas.android.com/apk/res/android" >
  <item android:id="@+id/menu_item_new_run"
    android:showAsAction="always"
    android:icon="@android:drawable/ic_menu_add"
    android:title="@string/new_run"/>
</menu>
```

This menu refers to a string, so add that to the strings file.

Listing 34.16 Adding a New Run string (`strings.xml`)

```xml
    <string name="stop">Stop</string>
    <string name="gps_enabled">GPS Enabled</string>
    <string name="gps_disabled">GPS Disabled</string>
    <string name="cell_text">Run at %1$s</string>
    <string name="new_run">New Run</string>
</resources>
```

Now, add code to **RunListFragment** to create the options menu and respond to item selection, as shown below.

Listing 34.17 New runs via the options menu (RunListFragment.java)

```
public class RunListFragment extends ListFragment {
    private static final int REQUEST_NEW_RUN = 0;

    private RunCursor mCursor;

    @Override
    public void onCreate(Bundle savedInstanceState) {
        super.onCreate(savedInstanceState);
        setHasOptionsMenu(true);
        // Query the list of runs
        mCursor = RunManager.get(getActivity()).queryRuns();
        // Create an adapter to point at this cursor
        RunCursorAdapter adapter = new RunCursorAdapter(getActivity(), mCursor);
        setListAdapter(adapter);
    }

    ...

    @Override
    public void onCreateOptionsMenu(Menu menu, MenuInflater inflater) {
        super.onCreateOptionsMenu(menu, inflater);
        inflater.inflate(R.menu.run_list_options, menu);
    }

    @Override
    public boolean onOptionsItemSelected(MenuItem item) {
        switch (item.getItemId()) {
        case R.id.menu_item_new_run:
            Intent i = new Intent(getActivity(), RunActivity.class);
            startActivityForResult(i, REQUEST_NEW_RUN);
            return true;
        default:
            return super.onOptionsItemSelected(item);
        }
    }

    @Override
    public void onActivityResult(int requestCode, int resultCode, Intent data) {
        if (REQUEST_NEW_RUN == requestCode) {
            mCursor.requery();
            ((RunCursorAdapter)getListAdapter()).notifyDataSetChanged();
        }
    }

    private static class RunCursorAdapter extends CursorAdapter {

        private RunCursor mRunCursor;
```

The only thing new and interesting about this approach is that you use **onActivityResult(…)** to force the list to reload once the user returns to it after navigating elsewhere. Again, requerying the cursor as shown here, on the main thread, is not great. You will replace it with a **Loader** in the following chapter.

Working with Existing Runs

The next logical thing to do is allow the user to navigate from the list of runs to the details of a specific run. In order for this to work well, **RunFragment** needs some support for passing a run ID as an argument. Since you host **RunFragment** in **RunActivity**, it too needs an extra for the run ID.

First, add the argument to **RunFragment** and a **newInstance(long)** method to make it easier to use.

Listing 34.18 Adding a run ID argument (RunFragment.java)

```java
public class RunFragment extends Fragment {
    private static final String TAG = "RunFragment";
    private static final String ARG_RUN_ID = "RUN_ID";

    ...

    private TextView mStartedTextView, mLatitudeTextView,
        mLongitudeTextView, mAltitudeTextView, mDurationTextView;

    public static RunFragment newInstance(long runId) {
        Bundle args = new Bundle();
        args.putLong(ARG_RUN_ID, runId);
        RunFragment rf = new RunFragment();
        rf.setArguments(args);
        return rf;
    }

    @Override
    public void onCreate(Bundle savedInstanceState) {
        super.onCreate(savedInstanceState);
```

Now, make use of the new fragment convention in **RunActivity**. If the intent has a RUN_ID extra, create the **RunFragment** using **newInstance(long)**. If not, just use the default constructor as before.

Listing 34.19 Adding a run ID extra (RunActivity.java)

```java
public class RunActivity extends SingleFragmentActivity {
    /** A key for passing a run ID as a long */
    public static final String EXTRA_RUN_ID =
        "com.bignerdranch.android.runtracker.run_id";

    @Override
    protected Fragment createFragment() {
        return new RunFragment();
        long runId = getIntent().getLongExtra(EXTRA_RUN_ID, -1);
        if (runId != -1) {
            return RunFragment.newInstance(runId);
        } else {
            return new RunFragment();
        }
    }

}
```

The last bit of glue to put in place is to respond to list item selection in **RunListFragment** by starting **RunActivity** with the ID of the selected run.

Listing 34.20 Launching existing runs via **onListItemClick(…)** (RunListFragment.java)

```
@Override
public void onListItemClick(ListView l, View v, int position, long id) {
    // The id argument will be the Run ID; CursorAdapter gives us this for free
    Intent i = new Intent(getActivity(), RunActivity.class);
    i.putExtra(RunActivity.EXTRA_RUN_ID, id);
    startActivity(i);
}

private static class RunCursorAdapter extends CursorAdapter {
```

There is a small bit of magic in play here. Because you named the ID column in the run table _id, **CursorAdapter** has detected it and passed it as the id argument to **onListItemClick(…)**. You can therefore pass it straight along as an extra to **RunActivity**. How convenient!

Sadly, that is where the convenience ends. Simply starting **RunFragment** with an ID argument is not enough to get it to display anything useful about an existing run. You need to query the database for the details of the existing run, including its last recorded location, in order to populate the user interface.

Fortunately, this is quite similar to work you just did. The logical place to start is in **RunDatabaseHelper**, where you'll create add a new **queryRun(long)** method to return a **RunCursor** for a single run given its ID.

Listing 34.21 Querying a single run (RunDatabaseHelper.java)

```
public RunCursor queryRun(long id) {
    Cursor wrapped = getReadableDatabase().query(TABLE_RUN,
            null, // All columns
            COLUMN_RUN_ID + " = ?", // Look for a run ID
            new String[]{ String.valueOf(id) }, // with this value
            null, // group by
            null, // order by
            null, // having
            "1"); // limit 1 row
    return new RunCursor(wrapped);
}
```

The many arguments to the **query(…)** method are made plain here. You are fetching all columns from TABLE_RUN, filtering them by the ID column, which is passed as an argument to the "where" clause using a single-element string array. You limit the query to returning only one row, wrap the result in a **RunCursor**, and return it.

Next, you will add a **getRun(long)** method to **RunManager** that wraps the results of the **queryRun(long)** method that you just created and pulls a **Run** out of the first row, if it has one. Also add an **isTrackingRun(Run)** method.

Listing 34.22 Implementing two methods (RunManager.java)

```java
public Run getRun(long id) {
    Run run = null;
    RunCursor cursor = mHelper.queryRun(id);
    cursor.moveToFirst();
    // If you got a row, get a run
    if (!cursor.isAfterLast())
        run = cursor.getRun();
    cursor.close();
    return run;
}

public boolean isTrackingRun(Run run) {
    return run != null && run.getId() == mCurrentRunId;
}
```

The **getRun(long)** method attempts to pull a **Run** out of the first row of the **RunCursor** retrieved from **queryRun(long)**. It first tells the **RunCursor** to move to the first row in the results. If there are any results at all, **isAfterLast()** will return false, and you can safely ask for a **Run** for this row. Since the caller of this new method will not have access to the **RunCursor**, you must be careful to call **close()** on it before returning, so that the database can release any resources associated with the cursor from memory as soon as possible.

That work complete, you can now make some changes to **RunFragment** to work with existing runs. Make the changes shown in Listing 34.23.

Listing 34.23 Working with existing runs (RunFragment.java)

```java
public class RunFragment extends Fragment {
    private static final String TAG = "RunFragment";
    private static final String ARG_RUN_ID = "RUN_ID";

    private BroadcastReceiver mLocationReceiver = new LocationReceiver() {

        @Override
        protected void onLocationReceived(Context context, Location loc) {
            if (!mRunManager.isTrackingRun(mRun))
                return;
            mLastLocation = loc;
            if (isVisible())
                updateUI();
        }

        @Override
        protected void onProviderEnabledChanged(boolean enabled) {
            int toastText = enabled ? R.string.gps_enabled : R.string.gps_disabled;
            Toast.makeText(getActivity(), toastText, Toast.LENGTH_LONG).show();
        }
    };

    ...

    @Override
    public void onCreate(Bundle savedInstanceState) {
        super.onCreate(savedInstanceState);
        setRetainInstance(true);
```

```
        mRunManager = RunManager.get(getActivity());<
        // Check for a Run ID as an argument, and find the run
        Bundle args = getArguments();
        if (args != null) {
            long runId = args.getLong(ARG_RUN_ID, -1);
            if (runId != -1) {
                mRun = mRunManager.getRun(runId);
            }
        }
    }

    @Override
    public View onCreateView(LayoutInflater inflater, ViewGroup container,
            Bundle savedInstanceState) {
        View view = inflater.inflate(R.layout.fragment_run, container, false);

        ...

        mStartButton = (Button)view.findViewById(R.id.run_startButton);
        mStartButton.setOnClickListener(new View.OnClickListener() {
            @Override
            public void onClick(View v) {
                mRun = mRunManager.startNewRun();
                if (mRun == null) {
                    mRun = mRunManager.startNewRun();
                } else {
                    mRunManager.startTrackingRun(mRun);
                }
                updateUI();
            }
        });

        ...

        return view;
    }

    ...

    private void updateUI() {
        boolean started = mRunManager.isTrackingRun();
        boolean trackingThisRun = mRunManager.isTrackingRun(mRun);

        if (mRun != null)
            mStartedTextView.setText(mRun.getStartDate().toString());

        int durationSeconds = 0;
        if (mRun != null && mLastLocation != null) {
            durationSeconds = mRun.getDurationSeconds(mLastLocation.getTime());
            mLatitudeTextView.setText(Double.toString(mLastLocation.getLatitude()));
            mLongitudeTextView.setText(Double.toString(mLastLocation.getLongitude()));
            mAltitudeTextView.setText(Double.toString(mLastLocation.getAltitude()));
        }
        mDurationTextView.setText(Run.formatDuration(durationSeconds));

        mStartButton.setEnabled(!started);
        mStopButton.setEnabled(started);
        mStopButton.setEnabled(started && trackingThisRun);
    }
}
```

As a last kindness to your humble user, you can make **RunFragment** load the last location for the current run from the database. This will be very similar to loading the **Run**, but you will create a new **LocationCursor** to work with **Location** objects along the way.

Begin by adding a method to query the last location for a run and the **LocationCursor** inner class in **RunDatabaseHelper**.

Listing 34.24 Querying the last location for a run (RunDatabaseHelper.java)

```java
public LocationCursor queryLastLocationForRun(long runId) {
    Cursor wrapped = getReadableDatabase().query(TABLE_LOCATION,
            null, // All columns
            COLUMN_LOCATION_RUN_ID + " = ?", // limit to the given run
            new String[]{ String.valueOf(runId) },
            null, // group by
            null, // having
            COLUMN_LOCATION_TIMESTAMP + " desc", // order by latest first
            "1"); // limit 1
    return new LocationCursor(wrapped);
}


// ... After RunCursor ...

public static class LocationCursor extends CursorWrapper {

    public LocationCursor(Cursor c) {
        super(c);
    }

    public Location getLocation() {
        if (isBeforeFirst() || isAfterLast())
            return null;
        // First get the provider out so you can use the constructor
        String provider = getString(getColumnIndex(COLUMN_LOCATION_PROVIDER));
        Location loc = new Location(provider);
        // Populate the remaining properties
        loc.setLongitude(getDouble(getColumnIndex(COLUMN_LOCATION_LONGITUDE)));
        loc.setLatitude(getDouble(getColumnIndex(COLUMN_LOCATION_LATITUDE)));
        loc.setAltitude(getDouble(getColumnIndex(COLUMN_LOCATION_ALTITUDE)));
        loc.setTime(getLong(getColumnIndex(COLUMN_LOCATION_TIMESTAMP)));
        return loc;
    }
}
```

LocationCursor serves the same purpose as **RunCursor**, except that it wraps a cursor intended to return rows from the location table and converts their various fields into properties on the **Location** object. One subtlety of this implementation is that **Location**'s constructor requires the provider name, so you first pull that out of the current row before setting up the rest of the properties.

The **queryLastLocationForRun(long)** method is very similar to **queryRun(long)**, except that it looks for the latest single location associated with a given run and wraps the result in a **LocationCursor**.

Just as with **queryRun(long)**, you should create a method in **RunManager** to wrap it and return a **Location** from the one row in the cursor.

Listing 34.25 Getting the last location for a run (RunManager.java)

```
public Location getLastLocationForRun(long runId) {
    Location location = null;
    LocationCursor cursor = mHelper.queryLastLocationForRun(runId);
    cursor.moveToFirst();
    // If you got a row, get a location
    if (!cursor.isAfterLast())
        location = cursor.getLocation();
    cursor.close();
    return location;
}
```

Now you can use this new method in **RunFragment** to fetch the last location for the current run when the fragment is created.

Listing 34.26 Getting the last location for the current run (RunFragment.java)

```
@Override
public void onCreate(Bundle savedInstanceState) {
    super.onCreate(savedInstanceState);
    setRetainInstance(true);
    mRunManager = RunManager.get(getActivity());

    // Check for a Run ID as an argument, and find the run
    Bundle args = getArguments();
    if (args != null) {
        long runId = args.getLong(ARG_RUN_ID, -1);
        if (runId != -1) {
            mRun = mRunManager.getRun(runId);
            mLastLocation = mRunManager.getLastLocationForRun(runId);
        }
    }
}
```

Now, after much ado, you should have a RunTracker that is capable of creating and tracking as many runs as your device's disk (and battery) can withstand and displaying them to the user in a logical fashion. Happy tracking!

Challenge: Identifying the Current Run

As implemented, the only way to identify which run is being tracked is to manually visit it from the list and see that the start and stop buttons are enabled appropriately. It would be great if the user had an easier way to access the current run.

For a simple challenge, give the list row for the current run a different treatment in the UI, like an icon or color change.

For a harder challenge, use an ongoing notification to let the user know that you are tracking them, and launch the **RunActivity** when it is pressed.

35

Loading Asynchronous Data With Loaders

In Chapter 34 you implemented data storage in RunTracker using SQLite and used **Cursor**s on the main thread of the application. This was a cop-out, however: it's a best practice to keep database work off of the main thread as much as possible.

In this chapter, you will use **Loader**s to pull data for runs and locations from the database on a background thread. The loader API was introduced in Android 3.0 (Honeycomb) and is also available in the support library, so there is no reason not to use them in a modern application.

Loaders and the LoaderManager

A loader is designed to load some kind of data (an object) from some source. The source could be disk, a database, a **ContentProvider**, the network, or another process. The loader will do the job of fetching the data without blocking the main thread and delivering the results to whomever is interested.

There are three built-in types of loaders: **Loader**, **AsyncTaskLoader**, and **CursorLoader** (Figure 35.1). **Loader** is the base class, and not very useful on its own. It defines the API that the **LoaderManager** uses to communicate with all loaders.

AsyncTaskLoader is an abstract **Loader** that uses an **AsyncTask** to move the work of loading data to another thread. Almost all useful loader classes you create will be a subclass of **AsyncTaskLoader**.

Finally, **CursorLoader** extends **AsyncTaskLoader** to load a **Cursor** from a **ContentProvider** via the **ContentResolver**. Unfortunately for RunTracker, there is no way to use **CursorLoader** with cursors that come from a **SQLiteDatabase**.

Figure 35.1 The **Loader** class hierarchy

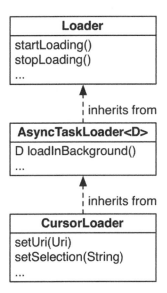

All communication with loaders is handled by the **LoaderManager**. This class is responsible for starting, stopping, and maintaining the lifecycle of any **Loader**s associated with your component. Within a **Fragment** or **Activity**, you can use the **getLoaderManager()** method to return an implementation to work with.

Use the **initLoader(int, Bundle, LoaderCallbacks<D>)** method to trigger the initialization of a **Loader**. The first argument is an integer identifier for the loader, the second is a **Bundle** of arguments (which can be null), and the final argument is an implementation of the **LoaderCallbacks<D>** interface. As you will see in the following sections, there are multiple ways to implement **LoaderCallbacks**, but the most common is to have your **Fragment** implement it directly.

You can use the **restartLoader(int, Bundle, LoaderCallbacks<D>)** method to force an existing loader to restart. This is commonly used to reload data that you know (or suspect) is stale.

The **LoaderCallbacks<D>** interface has three methods: **onCreateLoader(…)**, **onLoadFinished(…)** and **onLoaderReset(…)**. You will look at each of these in more detail as you implement them in RunTracker.

Why would you use a loader instead of, say, an **AsyncTask** directly? Well, the most compelling reason to do so is that the **LoaderManager** will keep your component's loaders alive, along with their data, between configuration changes like rotation.

If you use an **AsyncTask** to load data, you are responsible for managing its lifecycle during configuration changes and stashing its data somewhere that lives through them. Often, this is simplified by using **setRetainInstance(true)** on a **Fragment** and storing the data there, but there are still situations where you have to intervene and code you have to write in order to ensure that everything happens correctly.

Loaders are designed to take some (but not all) of this pain off your hands. If, after a configuration change, you initialize a loader that has already finished loading its data, it can deliver that data immediately rather than trying to fetch it again. This works whether your fragment is retained or not, which can make your life easier since you don't have to consider the lifecycle complications that retained fragments can introduce.

Using Loaders in RunTracker

RunTracker currently loads three chunks of data: the list of runs (a **RunCursor**), an individual **Run**, and that run's latest **Location**. Each of these comes from the SQLite database, and should therefore be moved to a **Loader** to create a smooth user experience.

In the following sections, you will create two abstract subclasses of **AsyncTaskLoader**. The first, **SQLiteCursorLoader**, is a simplified version of the framework's **CursorLoader** that will work with a **Cursor** coming from any source. The second is **DataLoader<D>**, which is capable of loading any kind of data and simplifies the use of **AsyncTaskLoader** for subclasses.

Loading the List of Runs

The current implementation of **RunListFragment** asks the **RunManager** directly for the **RunCursor** representing the list of runs in **onCreate(Bundle)**. In this section, you will introduce a loader to indirectly execute this query on another thread. The **RunListFragment** will tell the **LoaderManager** to start (and restart) the loader and implement the **LoaderCallbacks** to know when the data is ready.

To simplify the code within the **RunListFragment** (and elsewhere, later), first create an abstract **AsyncTaskLoader** subclass called **SQLiteCursorLoader** as in Listing 35.1. This class mimics most of the code in **CursorLoader**, without the requirement of using a **ContentProvider**.

Listing 35.1 A loader for SQLite cursors (SQLiteCursorLoader.java)

```java
public abstract class SQLiteCursorLoader extends AsyncTaskLoader<Cursor> {
    private Cursor mCursor;

    public SQLiteCursorLoader(Context context) {
        super(context);
    }

    protected abstract Cursor loadCursor();

    @Override
    public Cursor loadInBackground() {
        Cursor cursor = loadCursor();
        if (cursor != null) {
            // Ensure that the content window is filled
            cursor.getCount();
        }
        return cursor;
    }

    @Override
    public void deliverResult(Cursor data) {
        Cursor oldCursor = mCursor;
        mCursor = data;
```

```
        if (isStarted()) {
            super.deliverResult(data);
        }

        if (oldCursor != null && oldCursor != data && !oldCursor.isClosed()) {
            oldCursor.close();
        }
    }

    @Override
    protected void onStartLoading() {
        if (mCursor != null) {
            deliverResult(mCursor);
        }
        if (takeContentChanged() || mCursor == null) {
            forceLoad();
        }
    }

    @Override
    protected void onStopLoading() {
        // Attempt to cancel the current load task if possible.
        cancelLoad();
    }

    @Override
    public void onCanceled(Cursor cursor) {
        if (cursor != null && !cursor.isClosed()) {
            cursor.close();
        }
    }

    @Override
    protected void onReset() {
        super.onReset();

        // Ensure the loader is stopped
        onStopLoading();

        if (mCursor != null && !mCursor.isClosed()) {
            mCursor.close();
        }
        mCursor = null;
    }

}
```

SQLiteCursorLoader implements the **AsyncTaskLoader** API to efficiently load and hold a **Cursor** in the mCursor instance variable. The **loadInBackground()** method calls the abstract **loadCursor()** method to get the **Cursor** and calls the **getCount()** method on the cursor to ensure that the data is available in memory once it is passed over to the main thread.

The **deliverResult(Cursor)** method takes care of two things. If the loader is started (which means the data can be delivered), the superclass implementation of **deliverResult(…)** is called. If the old cursor is no longer needed, it is closed to free up its resources. Because an existing cursor may be cached and redelivered, it is important to make sure that the old cursor and the new cursor are not the same before the old cursor is closed.

The remaining method implementations are not critical to understand for the purposes of RunTracker, but you can find more details in the API documentation for **AsyncTaskLoader**.

With this base class implemented, you can now implement a very simple subclass, **RunListCursorLoader**, in **RunListFragment** as an inner class.

Listing 35.2 Implementing **RunListCursorLoader** (RunListFragment.java)

```java
@Override
public void onListItemClick(ListView l, View v, int position, long id) {
    // The id argument will be the Run ID; CursorAdapter gives us this for free
    Intent i = new Intent(getActivity(), RunActivity.class);
    i.putExtra(RunActivity.EXTRA_RUN_ID, id);
    startActivity(i);
}

private static class RunListCursorLoader extends SQLiteCursorLoader {

    public RunListCursorLoader(Context context) {
        super(context);
    }

    @Override
    protected Cursor loadCursor() {
        // Query the list of runs
        return RunManager.get(getContext()).queryRuns();
    }

}

private static class RunCursorAdapter extends CursorAdapter {
```

Now you can update the **RunListFragment** to implement the **LoaderCallbacks** interface for a **Cursor**. Add the methods below and update the class declaration to declare that it implements the callbacks.

Listing 35.3 Implementing **LoaderCallbacks<Cursor>** (RunListFragment.java)

```
public class RunListFragment extends ListFragment implements LoaderCallbacks<Cursor> {

    ...

    @Override
    public Loader<Cursor> onCreateLoader(int id, Bundle args) {
        // You only ever load the runs, so assume this is the case
        return new RunListCursorLoader(getActivity());
    }

    @Override
    public void onLoadFinished(Loader<Cursor> loader, Cursor cursor) {
        // Create an adapter to point at this cursor
        RunCursorAdapter adapter =
            new RunCursorAdapter(getActivity(), (RunCursor)cursor);
        setListAdapter(adapter);
    }

    @Override
    public void onLoaderReset(Loader<Cursor> loader) {
        // Stop using the cursor (via the adapter)
        setListAdapter(null);
    }
}
```

The **onCreateLoader(int, Bundle)** method is called by the **LoaderManager** when it needs you to create the loader. The id argument is useful if you have more than one loader of the same type and you need to distinguish them, and the **Bundle** holds any arguments that were passed in. This implementation does not use either argument, and simply creates a new **RunListCursorLoader** pointing at the current **Activity** for context.

The **onLoadFinished(Loader<Cursor>, Cursor)** method will be called on the main thread once the data has been loaded in the background. In this version, you reset the adapter on the **ListView** to a **RunCursorAdapter** pointing at the new cursor.

Finally, the **onLoaderReset(Loader<Cursor>)** method will be called in the event that the data is no longer available. To be on the safe side, stop using the cursor by setting the list adapter to null.

Now that you have support for the callbacks in place, you can tell the **LoaderManager** to do its thing. You can also remove the mCursor instance variable and the **onDestroy()** method that cleaned it up.

Listing 35.4 Using the **Loader** (RunListFragment.java)

```
public class RunListFragment extends ListFragment implements LoaderCallbacks<Cursor> {
    private static final int REQUEST_NEW_RUN = 0;


    private RunCursor mCursor;

    @Override
    public void onCreate(Bundle savedInstanceState) {
        super.onCreate(savedInstanceState);
        setHasOptionsMenu(true);
        // Query the list of runs
        mCursor = RunManager.get(getActivity()).queryRuns();
        // Create an adapter to point at this cursor
        RunCursorAdapter adapter = new RunCursorAdapter(getActivity(), mCursor);
        setListAdapter(adapter);
        // Initialize the loader to load the list of runs
        getLoaderManager().initLoader(0, null, this);
    }

    ...

    @Override
    public void onDestroy() {
        mCursor.close();
        super.onDestroy();
    }


    ...

    @Override
    public void onActivityResult(int requestCode, int resultCode, Intent data) {
        if (REQUEST_NEW_RUN == requestCode) {
            mCursor.requery();
            ((RunCursorAdapter)getListAdapter()).notifyDataSetChanged();
            // Restart the loader to get any new run available
            getLoaderManager().restartLoader(0, null, this);
        }
    }
}
```

With these changes done, run the app and observe that the data in the list is populated just as it was before. If you are observant, you may see that the list briefly shows a spinning progress view while the data is being loaded in the background. **ListFragment** provides this functionality for you automatically if the adapter is set to null.

Loading a Single Run

The new **SQLiteCursorLoader** class is fine for loading data that you want to remain in a cursor (such as a list of things), but in the **RunFragment**, you are loading two individual objects and the cursor is hidden by the **RunManager**. To best handle loading arbitrary data, you need a more generic loader.

In this section, you will create a new **DataLoader** class that is a subclass of **AsyncTaskLoader**. **DataLoader** will take care of some simple tasks that any subclass of **AsyncTaskLoader** should, leaving only the implementation of **loadInBackground()** to its own subclasses.

Create **DataLoader** using the code in Listing 35.5.

Listing 35.5 A simple loader for data (DataLoader.java)

```java
public abstract class DataLoader<D> extends AsyncTaskLoader<D> {
    private D mData;

    public DataLoader(Context context) {
        super(context);
    }

    @Override
    protected void onStartLoading() {
        if (mData != null) {
            deliverResult(mData);
        } else {
            forceLoad();
        }
    }

    @Override
    public void deliverResult(D data) {
        mData = data;
        if (isStarted())
            super.deliverResult(data);
    }

}
```

DataLoader uses a generic type **D** to hold an instance of whatever data it is loading. In **onStartLoading()** it checks for the presence of this data, and if it is available, delivers it immediately. Otherwise, it calls the superclass's **forceLoad()** method to go and fetch it.

The **deliverResult(D)** method is implemented to stash away the new data object and, if the loader is started, call the superclass implementation to make the delivery.

To make use of this new class, implement **RunLoader**, a subclass, for use in **RunFragment**.

Listing 35.6 A loader for a run (RunLoader.java)

```java
public class RunLoader extends DataLoader<Run> {
    private long mRunId;

    public RunLoader(Context context, long runId) {
        super(context);
        mRunId = runId;
    }

    @Override
    public Run loadInBackground() {
        return RunManager.get(getContext()).getRun(mRunId);
    }
}
```

The **RunLoader** constructor expects a **Context** (an **Activity**) and a long representing the ID of the run to load. The **loadInBackground()** method asks the singleton **RunManager** for a run with that ID and returns it.

With this in place, you can now use **RunLoader** in **RunFragment** instead of talking directly with the **RunManager** on the main thread. There is one difference, however, in the implementation you use here.

Since **RunFragment** loads two different types of data, a run and a location, the design of **LoaderCallbacks<D>** coupled with limitations of Java generics prevents you from implementing the interface directly as methods within **RunFragment**. Instead, you can work around the limitations by creating inner classes that implement **LoaderCallbacks<D>** for **Run** and **Location** separately, and pass an instance of each of them to a call to **LoaderManager**'s **initLoader(…)** method.

To make the integration, first add an inner class **RunLoaderCallbacks** to **RunFragment**.

Listing 35.7 **RunLoaderCallbacks** (RunFragment.java)

```
private class RunLoaderCallbacks implements LoaderCallbacks<Run> {

    @Override
    public Loader<Run> onCreateLoader(int id, Bundle args) {
        return new RunLoader(getActivity(), args.getLong(ARG_RUN_ID));
    }

    @Override
    public void onLoadFinished(Loader<Run> loader, Run run) {
        mRun = run;
        updateUI();
    }

    @Override
    public void onLoaderReset(Loader<Run> loader) {
        // Do nothing
    }
}
```

In **onCreateLoader(int, Bundle)**, a new **RunLoader** is returned pointing at the fragment's current activity and the run ID pulled from the arguments bundle. You will pass this arguments bundle along in **onCreate(Bundle)**.

The implementation of **onLoadFinished(…)** stashes away the loaded run in the fragment's mRun instance variable and calls the **updateUI()** method so that the UI will reflect the updated data.

onLoaderReset(…) is not needed in this case since the **Run** instance is completely in memory.

Next, use the new callbacks implementation with **LoaderManager** in **RunFragment**'s **onCreate(Bundle)** method. You will also add a constant called LOAD_RUN to use as the ID for the loader, which distinguishes it within the **LoaderManager**'s collection of loaders for **RunFragment**.

Listing 35.8 Loading the run (RunFragment.java)

```java
public class RunFragment extends Fragment {
    private static final String TAG = "RunFragment";
    private static final String ARG_RUN_ID = "RUN_ID";
    private static final int LOAD_RUN = 0;

    ...

    @Override
    public void onCreate(Bundle savedInstanceState) {
        super.onCreate(savedInstanceState);
        setRetainInstance(true);
        mRunManager = RunManager.get(getActivity());

        // Check for a Run ID as an argument, and find the run
        Bundle args = getArguments();
        if (args != null) {
            long runId = args.getLong(ARG_RUN_ID, -1);
            if (runId != -1) {
                mRun = mRunManager.getRun(runId);
                LoaderManager lm = getLoaderManager();
                lm.initLoader(LOAD_RUN, args, new RunLoaderCallbacks());
                mLastLocation = mRunManager.getLastLocationForRun(runId);
            }
        }
    }
}
```

Now you can run RunTracker again and see that it works just as it did before, only now the run data is loaded on another thread. If you are very quick (or your emulator is very slow), you might see the UI initially populate without the run date and then update to include it.

Loading the Last Location for a Run

For your last trick, you need to get the loading of the last location off of the main thread. This work will be almost identical to what you just did for loading the run, except that you will work with the run's last location as the data. First, create the **LastLocationLoader** class to do the work.

Listing 35.9 **LastLocationLoader** (LastLocationLoader.java)

```java
public class LastLocationLoader extends DataLoader<Location> {
    private long mRunId;

    public LastLocationLoader(Context context, long runId) {
        super(context);
        mRunId = runId;
    }

    @Override
    public Location loadInBackground() {
        return RunManager.get(getContext()).getLastLocationForRun(mRunId);
    }

}
```

This class is almost exactly like **RunLoader**, except that it calls **RunManager**'s **getLastLocationForRun(long)** method with the run ID.

Next, implement the **LocationLoaderCallbacks** inner class in **RunFragment**.

Listing 35.10 **LocationLoaderCallbacks** (RunFragment.java)

```
private class LocationLoaderCallbacks implements LoaderCallbacks<Location> {

    @Override
    public Loader<Location> onCreateLoader(int id, Bundle args) {
        return new LastLocationLoader(getActivity(), args.getLong(ARG_RUN_ID));
    }

    @Override
    public void onLoadFinished(Loader<Location> loader, Location location) {
        mLastLocation = location;
        updateUI();
    }

    @Override
    public void onLoaderReset(Loader<Location> loader) {
        // Do nothing
    }
}
```

Again, this class is almost just like **RunLoaderCallbacks**, except that it updates the mLastLocation instance variable before refreshing the UI. All that remains now is to use the new loader instead of a direct call to **RunManager** in **onCreate(Bundle)**, using a new loader ID LOAD_LOCATION.

Listing 35.11 Loading the last location (RunFragment.java)

```
public class RunFragment extends Fragment {
    private static final String TAG = "RunFragment";
    private static final String ARG_RUN_ID = "RUN_ID";
    private static final int LOAD_RUN = 0;
    private static final int LOAD_LOCATION = 1;
    ...

    @Override
    public void onCreate(Bundle savedInstanceState) {
        super.onCreate(savedInstanceState);
        setRetainInstance(true);
        mRunManager = RunManager.get(getActivity());

        // Check for a Run ID as an argument, and find the run
        Bundle args = getArguments();
        if (args != null) {
            long runId = args.getLong(ARG_RUN_ID, -1);
            if (runId != -1) {
                LoaderManager lm = getLoaderManager();
                lm.initLoader(LOAD_RUN, args, new RunLoaderCallbacks());
                mLastLocation = mRunManager.getLastLocationForRun(runId);
                lm.initLoader(LOAD_LOCATION, args, new LocationLoaderCallbacks());
            }
        }
    }
}
```

Now RunTracker is capable of loading all of its important data on a background thread, thanks to loaders. Run it now and verify that everything works as before.

36

Using Maps

The next logical step for RunTracker is to show the user a map of his or her travels. Using the new Google Maps API (version 2), this is an easy task. In this chapter, you will create a new **RunMapFragment** class to display a map showing the track of the user's run and interactive markers that indicate the start and end of the journey.

Before starting with the fun stuff, however, you must set up your project to use the Maps API.

Adding the Maps API to RunTracker

The Maps API (version 2) is provided by the Google Play services SDK, and has several requirements for both your development environment and your application.

Use a real device to test maps

The Google Play services SDK (and thus the Maps API) requires a real device running at least Android 2.2 with the Google Play store installed. Running on an emulator is not supported.

Install and use the Google Play services SDK

To make the Maps API available to your project, you first need to install the Google Play services SDK add-on and configure its library project to work with your application. The following steps should get you there, but the latest details should always be available at `http://developer.android.com/google/play-services/`

1. From the Android SDK Manager, install the Google Play services add-on from the Extras section. This will be installed within your Android SDK directory under `extras/google/google_play_services`.

2. In Eclipse, import a *copy* of the library project into your workspace using File → Import... → Existing Android Code Into Workspace. The library project is within the Google Play services extra directory under `libproject/google-play-services_lib`. Be sure to choose Copy projects into workspace from the import wizard so that you are working with your own copy of the project.

3. Open the RunTracker project's Properties window and add a reference to the library project under Android, Library. Click the Add... button and select the `google-play-services_lib` project.

Obtain a Google Maps API key

In order to use the Maps API, you need to create an API key for your application. This process requires several steps, and Google has better documentation than we can provide here. Check out https:// developers.google.com/maps/documentation/android/start and follow the instructions there to obtain your key.

Update RunTracker's manifest

In order for the Google Play services and Maps API to work, you need to add several permissions and requirements to your application manifest, in addition to the API key you just obtained. Add the highlighted XML to the RunTracker manifest now. Take care to ensure that the permission that ends in MAPS_RECEIVE begins with RunTracker's package name.

While you're there, go ahead and add an activity entry for the forthcoming **RunMapActivity**.

Listing 36.1 Maps API requirements (AndroidManifest.xml)

```xml
<manifest xmlns:android="http://schemas.android.com/apk/res/android"
  package="com.bignerdranch.android.runtracker"
  android:versionCode="1"
  android:versionName="1.0">

  <uses-sdk android:minSdkVersion="9" android:targetSdkVersion="15" />

  <permission
    android:name="com.bignerdranch.android.runtracker.permission.MAPS_RECEIVE"
    android:protectionLevel="signature"/>
  <uses-permission
    android:name="com.bignerdranch.android.runtracker.permission.MAPS_RECEIVE"/>

  <uses-permission android:name="android.permission.INTERNET"/>
  <uses-permission android:name="android.permission.WRITE_EXTERNAL_STORAGE"/>
  <uses-permission
    android:name="com.google.android.providers.gsf.permission.READ_GSERVICES"/>
  <uses-permission android:name="android.permission.ACCESS_COARSE_LOCATION"/>
  <uses-permission android:name="android.permission.ACCESS_FINE_LOCATION"/>

  <uses-feature android:required="true"
    android:name="android.hardware.location.gps" />
  <uses-feature
    android:required="true"
    android:glEsVersion="0x00020000"/>
  <application
    android:allowBackup="true"
    android:icon="@drawable/ic_launcher"
    android:label="@string/app_name"
    android:theme="@style/AppTheme">
    <activity android:name=".RunListActivity"
      android:label="@string/app_name">
      <intent-filter>
        <action android:name="android.intent.action.MAIN" />
        <category android:name="android.intent.category.LAUNCHER" />
      </intent-filter>
    </activity>
```

```
<activity android:name=".RunActivity"
    android:label="@string/app_name" />
<activity android:name=".RunMapActivity"
    android:label="@string/app_name" />
<receiver android:name=".TrackingLocationReceiver"
    android:exported="false">
    <intent-filter>
        <action
            android:name="com.bignerdranch.android.runtracker.ACTION_LOCATION"/>
    </intent-filter>
</receiver>
<meta-data
    android:name="com.google.android.maps.v2.API_KEY"
    android:value="your-maps-API-key-here"/>
</application>

</manifest>
```

Showing the User's Location on a Map

With the requirements behind you, now it is time to enjoy the fruits of your labor and show the user a map. The Maps API includes **MapFragment** and **SupportMapFragment** that you can subclass to conveniently handle the work of setting up the **MapView** and its associated model object, **GoogleMap**.

Create **RunMapFragment**, a subclass of **SupportMapFragment**, in a new file using the code below.

Listing 36.2 Basic **RunMapFragment** (RunMapFragment.java)

```java
public class RunMapFragment extends SupportMapFragment {
    private static final String ARG_RUN_ID = "RUN_ID";

    private GoogleMap mGoogleMap;

    public static RunMapFragment newInstance(long runId) {
        Bundle args = new Bundle();
        args.putLong(ARG_RUN_ID, runId);
        RunMapFragment rf = new RunMapFragment();
        rf.setArguments(args);
        return rf;
    }

    @Override
    public View onCreateView(LayoutInflater inflater, ViewGroup parent,
        Bundle savedInstanceState) {
        View v = super.onCreateView(inflater, parent, savedInstanceState);

        // Stash a reference to the GoogleMap
        mGoogleMap = getMap();
        // Show the user's location
        mGoogleMap.setMyLocationEnabled(true);

        return v;
    }

}
```

RunMapFragment's **newInstance(long)** method takes a run ID and sets up the arguments to a new instance of the fragment, just as the code in **RunFragment** does. You will use this argument shortly when fetching a list of locations.

The implementation of **onCreateView(…)** calls the superclass implementation to get and return a view, but it relies on the fact that doing so will initialize the fragment's **GoogleMap** instance. **GoogleMap** is the model object that is tied to the **MapView** and you will use it to configure the various additions to the map. In this initial version of the fragment, simply call **setMyLocationEnabled(boolean)** to allow the user to see and navigate to his or her location on the map.

To host the new **RunMapFragment**, create a simple **RunMapActivity** class using the following code. Remember that you already added the reference to this class in the manifest earlier.

Listing 36.3 An activity to host a fragment (RunMapActivity.java)

```java
public class RunMapActivity extends SingleFragmentActivity {
    /** A key for passing a run ID as a long */
    public static final String EXTRA_RUN_ID =
        "com.bignerdranch.android.runtracker.run_id";

    @Override
    protected Fragment createFragment() {
        long runId = getIntent().getLongExtra(EXTRA_RUN_ID, -1);
        if (runId != -1) {
            return RunMapFragment.newInstance(runId);
        } else {
            return new RunMapFragment();
        }
    }

}
```

Now you will need code to launch **RunMapActivity** from **RunFragment** when a run is available. To do this, add a button to the layout that will trigger the map. But first, as usual, add a few new strings to support this button and the work for the rest of the chapter.

Listing 36.4 Strings for the UI (res/values/strings.xml)

```xml
    <string name="new_run">New Run</string>
    <string name="map">Map</string>
    <string name="run_start">Run Start</string>
    <string name="run_started_at_format">Run started at %s</string>
    <string name="run_finish">Run Finish</string>
    <string name="run_finished_at_format">Run finished at %s</string>
</resources>
```

Now update **RunFragment**'s layout to include the new Map button.

Listing 36.5 Adding a Map button (`fragment_run.xml`)

```
    <Button android:id="@+id/run_stopButton"
      android:layout_width="0dp"
      android:layout_height="wrap_content"
      android:layout_weight="1"
      android:text="@string/stop"
      />
    <Button android:id="@+id/run_mapButton"
      android:layout_width="0dp"
      android:layout_height="wrap_content"
      android:layout_weight="1"
      android:text="@string/map"
      />
  </LinearLayout>
</TableLayout>
```

RunFragment can now be wired up to support this new button and ensure that it is enabled at the appropriate time.

Listing 36.6 Wiring up the Map button (`RunFragment.java`)

```
public class RunFragment extends Fragment {
    ...

    private RunManager mRunManager;

    private Run mRun;
    private Location mLastLocation;

    private Button mStartButton, mStopButton, mMapButton;
    private TextView mStartedTextView, mLatitudeTextView,
        mLongitudeTextView, mAltitudeTextView, mDurationTextView;

    ...

    @Override
    public View onCreateView(LayoutInflater inflater, ViewGroup container,
            Bundle savedInstanceState) {
        ...

        mMapButton = (Button)view.findViewById(R.id.run_mapButton);
        mMapButton.setOnClickListener(new View.OnClickListener() {
            @Override
            public void onClick(View v) {
                Intent i = new Intent(getActivity(), RunMapActivity.class);
                i.putExtra(RunMapActivity.EXTRA_RUN_ID, mRun.getId());
                startActivity(i);
            }
        });
        updateUI();

        return view;
    }

    ...
```

```
private void updateUI() {
    boolean started = mRunManager.isTrackingRun();
    boolean trackingThisRun = mRunManager.isTrackingRun(mRun);

    if (mRun != null)
        mStartedTextView.setText(mRun.getStartDate().toString());

    int durationSeconds = 0;
    if (mRun != null && mLastLocation != null) {
        durationSeconds = mRun.getDurationSeconds(mLastLocation.getTime());
        mLatitudeTextView.setText(Double.toString(mLastLocation.getLatitude()));
        mLongitudeTextView.setText(Double.toString(mLastLocation.getLongitude()));
        mAltitudeTextView.setText(Double.toString(mLastLocation.getAltitude()));
        mMapButton.setEnabled(true);
    } else {
        mMapButton.setEnabled(false);
    }
    mDurationTextView.setText(Run.formatDuration(durationSeconds));

    mStartButton.setEnabled(!started);
    mStopButton.setEnabled(started && trackingThisRun);
}
```

With this, RunTracker can now show you a map and your location on it. Run the app, load up a run, and press the Map button. You should see something like Figure 36.1, provided you have Internet access and you are near the Big Nerd Ranch office.

Figure 36.1 RunTracker knows where you are

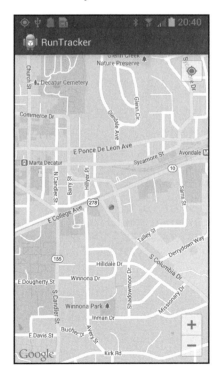

Displaying a Run's Path

Your next task is to show the user a line that follows his or her run. The Maps API makes this trivial, but you need to fetch the list of locations so you know how to build the line. Add a method to both **RunDatabaseHelper** and **RunManager** to provide a **LocationCursor** with this data.

Listing 36.7 Querying a run's locations (RunDatabaseHelper.java)

```
public LocationCursor queryLocationsForRun(long runId) {
    Cursor wrapped = getReadableDatabase().query(TABLE_LOCATION,
            null,
            COLUMN_LOCATION_RUN_ID + " = ?", // Limit to the given run
            new String[]{ String.valueOf(runId) },
            null, // group by
            null, // having
            COLUMN_LOCATION_TIMESTAMP + " asc"); // order by timestamp
    return new LocationCursor(wrapped);
}
```

The **queryLocationsForRun(long)** method is very similar to the **queryLastLocationForRun(long)** method from the SQLite chapter, but it orders them in ascending order and returns them all.

You can use this method in **RunManager** to give a nice façade to **RunMapFragment**.

Listing 36.8 Querying a run's locations, part II (RunManager.java)

```
public LocationCursor queryLocationsForRun(long runId) {
    return mHelper.queryLocationsForRun(runId);
}
```

RunMapFragment can now use this new method to load the locations. Naturally, you will want to use a **Loader** to keep the database query off the main thread. Create **LocationListCursorLoader** as a new class to handle the job.

Listing 36.9 A loader for locations (LocationListCursorLoader.java)

```
public class LocationListCursorLoader extends SQLiteCursorLoader {
    private long mRunId;

    public LocationListCursorLoader(Context c, long runId) {
        super(c);
        mRunId = runId;
    }

    @Override
    protected Cursor loadCursor() {
        return RunManager.get(getContext()).queryLocationsForRun(mRunId);
    }
}
```

579

Make use of this new loader in **RunMapFragment** to load the locations.

Listing 36.10 Loading locations in **RunMapFragment** (RunMapFragment.java)

```
public class RunMapFragment extends SupportMapFragment
    implements LoaderCallbacks<Cursor> {
    private static final String ARG_RUN_ID = "RUN_ID";
    private static final int LOAD_LOCATIONS = 0;

    private GoogleMap mGoogleMap;
    private LocationCursor mLocationCursor;

    ...

    @Override
    public void onCreate(Bundle savedInstanceState) {
        super.onCreate(savedInstanceState);

        // Check for a Run ID as an argument, and find the run
        Bundle args = getArguments();
        if (args != null) {
            long runId = args.getLong(ARG_RUN_ID, -1);
            if (runId != -1) {
                LoaderManager lm = getLoaderManager();
                lm.initLoader(LOAD_LOCATIONS, args, this);
            }
        }
    }

    ...

    @Override
    public Loader<Cursor> onCreateLoader(int id, Bundle args) {
        long runId = args.getLong(ARG_RUN_ID, -1);
        return new LocationListCursorLoader(getActivity(), runId);
    }

    @Override
    public void onLoadFinished(Loader<Cursor> loader, Cursor cursor) {
        mLocationCursor = (LocationCursor)cursor;
    }

    @Override
    public void onLoaderReset(Loader<Cursor> loader) {
        // Stop using the data
        mLocationCursor.close();
        mLocationCursor = null;
    }
}
```

RunMapFragment can now stash a **LocationCursor** to hold on to the list of locations. It will use this to populate the map with the route.

The implementation of **onLoaderReset(Loader<Cursor>)** takes care of closing and dereferencing the cursor when it is no longer available. Under normal circumstances, this method will be called when the **LoaderManager** is shutting the loader down after the user navigates away from the map fragment.

This will keep things nice and tidy, but one thing it won't do is close the cursor during rotation. This is exactly what you want.

Now you need to get to the meat of the chapter: displaying some things on the **GoogleMap**. Add an **updateUI()** method to set up the run track, and call that method in **onLoadFinished(…)**.

Listing 36.11 Putting the run on the map (RunMapFragment.java)

```java
private void updateUI() {
    if (mGoogleMap == null || mLocationCursor == null)
        return;

    // Set up an overlay on the map for this run's locations
    // Create a polyline with all of the points
    PolylineOptions line = new PolylineOptions();
    // Also create a LatLngBounds so you can zoom to fit
    LatLngBounds.Builder latLngBuilder = new LatLngBounds.Builder();
    // Iterate over the locations
    mLocationCursor.moveToFirst();
    while (!mLocationCursor.isAfterLast()) {
        Location loc = mLocationCursor.getLocation();
        LatLng latLng = new LatLng(loc.getLatitude(), loc.getLongitude());
        line.add(latLng);
        latLngBuilder.include(latLng);
        mLocationCursor.moveToNext();
    }
    // Add the polyline to the map
    mGoogleMap.addPolyline(line);
    // Make the map zoom to show the track, with some padding
    // Use the size of the current display in pixels as a bounding box
    Display display = getActivity().getWindowManager().getDefaultDisplay();
    // Construct a movement instruction for the map camera
    LatLngBounds latLngBounds = latLngBuilder.build();
    CameraUpdate movement = CameraUpdateFactory.newLatLngBounds(latLngBounds,
            display.getWidth(), display.getHeight(), 15);
    mGoogleMap.moveCamera(movement);
}

@Override
public Loader<Cursor> onCreateLoader(int id, Bundle args) {
    long runId = args.getLong(ARG_RUN_ID, -1);
    return new LocationListCursorLoader(getActivity(), runId);
}

@Override
public void onLoadFinished(Loader<Cursor> loader, Cursor cursor) {
    mLocationCursor = (LocationCursor)cursor;
    updateUI();
}
```

This new method uses several bits of the Maps API. First, it creates an instance of **PolylineOptions** that will be used to build up the line to draw on the map and an instance of **LatLngBounds.Builder** to create a bounding box to zoom the map to when everything is collected.

Next, it iterates over the **LocationCursor**, and for each **Location** creates a **LatLng** using the coordinates. It adds this **LatLng** to the **PolylineOptions** and includes it in the **LatLngBounds** before moving to the next row in the cursor.

After consuming all of the locations, it calls **addPolyline(PolylineOptions)** on the **GoogleMap**, adding the line to the map.

The next task is to make the map zoom to show the entire line. Moving around the map is the job of the "camera," and the camera is adjusted using commands packaged in instances of **CameraUpdate** and passed to **moveCamera(CameraUpdate)**. Creating an instance to move the camera to the bounds of the line you just added is the job of the **CameraUpdateFactory**'s **newLatLngBounds(LatLngBounds, int, int, int)** method.

Here you pass the dimensions of the current screen as an approximation of the size of the map in pixels, and specify a few pixels of padding to make things fit nicely. There is a simpler version of the method, **newLatLngBounds(LatLngBounds, int)**, but that version will throw an **IllegalStateException** if you call it before the **MapView** has completed sizing itself via the layout process. Since you cannot guarantee that has happened by the time **updateUI()** is called, you have to make your best guess using the display dimensions.

With these changes in place, you can run RunTracker again and see a beautiful black line tracing your route. Perhaps now would be a good time to investigate the rest of the **PolylineOptions** class and try to make it prettier.

Adding Markers for Run Start and Finish

Now that you have everything else in place, it is relatively trivial to add markers to the map that show the start and finish locations of the run. You can also add some text along with those markers that will show up in an info window when you touch them.

Add the code highlighted below to **updateUI()**.

Listing 36.12 Start and end markers with info (RunMapFragment.java)

```java
private void updateUI() {
    if (mGoogleMap == null || mLocationCursor == null)
        return;

    // Set up an overlay on the map for this run's locations
    // Create a polyline with all of the points
    PolylineOptions line = new PolylineOptions();
    // Also create a LatLngBounds so you can zoom to fit
    LatLngBounds.Builder latLngBuilder = new LatLngBounds.Builder();
    // Iterate over the locations
    mLocationCursor.moveToFirst();
    while (!mLocationCursor.isAfterLast()) {
        Location loc = mLocationCursor.getLocation();
        LatLng latLng = new LatLng(loc.getLatitude(), loc.getLongitude());

        Resources r = getResources();

        // If this is the first location, add a marker for it
        if (mLocationCursor.isFirst()) {
            String startDate = new Date(loc.getTime()).toString();
            MarkerOptions startMarkerOptions = new MarkerOptions()
                .position(latLng)
                .title(r.getString(R.string.run_start))
                .snippet(r.getString(R.string.run_started_at_format, startDate));
            mGoogleMap.addMarker(startMarkerOptions);
```

```
        } else if (mLocationCursor.isLast()) {
            // If this is the last location, and not also the first, add a marker
            String endDate = new Date(loc.getTime()).toString();
            MarkerOptions finishMarkerOptions = new MarkerOptions()
                .position(latLng)
                .title(r.getString(R.string.run_finish))
                .snippet(r.getString(R.string.run_finished_at_format, endDate));
            mGoogleMap.addMarker(finishMarkerOptions);
        }

        line.add(latLng);
        latLngBuilder.include(latLng);
        mLocationCursor.moveToNext();
    }
    // Add the polyline to the map
    mGoogleMap.addPolyline(line);
```

For each of the first and last locations, this code creates an instance of **MarkerOptions** to hold the position, title, and snippet text. The title and snippet text are displayed in a simple info window when the user presses the marker.

In this code, you are relying on the default marker icon to be used, but you could use the **icon(BitmapDescriptor)** method and a **BitmapDescriptorFactory** to create a marker of a different color or even with your own custom graphics. There are many standard colors (or hues, as they are called) to choose from.

Run RunTracker and test it out on your next trip. Happy travels!

Challenge: Live Updates

At this point, **RunMapFragment** is capable of displaying a map of the run's locations frozen in time, as they were when the user navigated there. A proper run-tracking app should show updates to the track in a live fashion. Using a **LocationReceiver** subclass in **RunMapFragment**, respond to new locations by redrawing the map adornments. Remember to clear any previous track overlay and markers before adding new ones.

37
Afterword

Congratulations! You are at the end of this guide. Not everyone has the discipline to do what you have done, to learn what you have learned. Take a quick moment and give yourself a pat on the back.

This hard work has paid off: you are now an Android developer.

The Final Challenge

We have one last challenge for you: become a *good* Android developer. Good developers are each good in their own way, so you must find your own path from here on out.

Where might you start, then? Here are some places we recommend:

Write code. Now. You will quickly forget what you have learned here if you do not apply it. Contribute to a project, or write a simple application of your own. Whatever you do, waste no time: write code.

Learn. You have learned a little bit about a lot of things in this book. Did any of them spark your imagination? Write some code to play around with your favorite thing. Find and read more documentation about it, or an entire book if there is one.

Meet people. Lots of top-notch Android developers hang out in #android-dev on irc.freenode.net. Android Developer Office Hours (https://plus.google.com/+AndroidDevelopers/posts) are good to stay connected with the Android development team and other interested developers. Local meetups can also be a good place to meet like-minded developers.

Explore the open source community. Android development is exploding on http://www.github.com. When you find a cool library, see what other projects its contributors are committing to. Share your own code, too – you never know who will find it useful or interesting.

Shameless Plugs

You can find both of us on Twitter. Bill is @billjings, and Brian is @lyricsboy.

If you enjoyed this book, check out other Big Nerd Ranch Guides at http://www.bignerdranch.com/books. We also have a broad selection of week-long courses for developers, where we make it easy to learn this amount of stuff in only a week of time. And of course, if you just need someone to write great code, we do contract programming, too. For more, go to our website at http://www.bignerdranch.com.

Thank You

Without readers like you, our work would not exist. Thank you for buying and reading our book.

Index

Symbols

9-patch images, 409, 410
@+id, 18, 187
@Override, 56
@SuppressLint("HandlerLeak"), 444
@SuppressWarnings("deprecation"), 306
@SuppressWarnings("unchecked"), 445
@TargetApi annotation, 119

A

aapt (Android Asset Packing tool), 27
AbsListView.MultiChoiceModeListener
interface, 289
action bar
  action view in, 463
  android:showAsAction, 256
  compatibility and, 294
  contextual (see contextual action bar)
  features, 253
  hiding, 315
  options menu, 253
  overflow menu, 256
ActionBar
  onCreateOptionsMenu(…), 257
  setDisplayHomeAsUpEnabled(…), 263
ActionBarSherlock library, 294-298
ActionMode, 289, 293
ActionMode.Callback interface, 289-291, 293
activities
  (see also **Activity**, fragments)
  abstract fragment-hosting activity, 172
  adding to project, 89-112
  as controller, 36
  back stack of, 110-112, 380
  base, 380
  child, 90, 104
  defined, 2
  fragment transactions and, 365
  handling configuration changes in, 510
  hosting fragments, 128, 134-137, 232, 233
  label (display name), 377
  launcher, 109, 316
  lifecycle and fragments, 146
  lifecycle diagram, 67

lifecycle of, 53, 61, 67, 68
managing fragments, 365-373
metadata for, 265
overriding methods, 54
passing data between, 101-109
record, 67
rotation and, 61-65
running from command line, 316
searchable, 455, 458
starting from fragment, 191
starting in current task, 381
starting in new task, 382
states of, 53, 67
tasks and, 380
UI flexibility and, 126
Activity
  as **Context** subclass, 23
  FragmentActivity, 131
  getIntent(), 103, 193
  invalidateOptionsMenu(), 477
  lifecycle methods, 53-61
  onActivityResult(…), 106
  onCreate(…), 16, 53, 55
  onDestroy(), 53
  onPause(), 53
  onResume(), 53, 197
  onSaveInstanceState(…), 65-67, 241, 243
  onSearchRequested(), 453
  onStart(), 53
  onStop(), 53
  setContentView(…), 16
  setResult(…), 106
  SingleFragmentActivity, 172, 174-176, 361
  startActivity(…), 99
  startActivityForResult(…), 104
  startSearch(…), 465
activity record, 67
ActivityInfo, 379
ActivityManager
  back stack, 110, 112
  starting activities, 99, 101, 102, 106, 107
ActivityNotFoundException, 101
Adapter interface, 179
adapters
  adapter views and, 179
  creating custom, 187
  defined, 179
  implementing, 180

build errors, 87
crash, 76
crash on unconnected device, 77
misbehaviors, 77
online help for, 88
R, 87
running app with debugger, 80
stopping debugger, 82
DEFAULT (**Intent**), 383
default resources, 246
delayed execution, 472, 473
density-independent pixel (see dip)
deprecation
    in Android, 342
    using deprecated methods, 306, 342
detach(…) (**FragmentTransaction**), 208
Dev Tools, 70
developer documentation, 120-122
devices
    configuration changes and, 61
    configuring language settings, 245
    hardware, 24
    virtual, 24, 359
Devices view, 44, 75
Dialog, 211
DialogFragment, 211
    onCreateDialog(…), 213
    show(…), 214
    showing image in, 338
dialogs, 211-217
dip (density-independent pixel), 155
documentation, 120-122
doInBackground(…) (**AsyncTask**), 419
dp (density-independent pixel), 155
draw() (**View**), 522
draw9patch tool, 410
drawables, 399, 401
    9-patch images, 409
    corner, 401
    documentation, 401
    gradient, 401, 405
    inset, 404, 405
    layer-list, 404, 405
    referencing, 48
    state list, 291, 402, 403
    stretchable, 406
drawing
    Canvas, 522

in **onDraw(…)**, 522
Paint, 522
to **Surface**, 306-309

E

Eclipse
    auto-complete, 23, 24
    build process, 26
    code style preferences, 33
    content assist, 23, 24
    creating new classes, 32
    debugger, 80, 81
        (see also debugging)
    editor, 7
    generating getter and setter methods, 33, 34, 133
    graphical layout tool, 157, 251
    installing, xx
    organizing imports, 19, 24
    package explorer, 7
    panes, resizing, 57
    preferences, 33
    res/values directory, 14
    src directory, 15
    tab group, 7
    views, 75
        Debug view, 80
        Devices view, 44, 75
        Lint Warnings view, 86
        moving, 7, 56
        Variables view, 81
    workbench window, 7
EditText, 137
emulator
    (see also virtual devices)
    rotating, 48
    running on, 24
    system images for, xxi
    for tablets, 359
errors
    (see also debugging)
    missing imports, 19
escape sequence (in string), 39
exception breakpoints, 83, 84
exceptions, 76
explicit intents
    creating, 100

S

s prefix for variable names, 33
scale-independent pixel (see sp)
screen orientation, 62
    forcing, 304
screen pixel density, 46, 154, 246
screen size, determining, 373, 374
`ScrollView`, 347
SD card, 273
SDK versions
    (see also compatibility)
    build target, 116
    codenames, 113
    installing, xxi
    listed, 113
    minimum required, 115
    target, 115
    updating, xxi
search
    configuration, 456
    configuring emulator for, 458
    coordinating with `SearchManager` service, 456
    hardware button, 453
    how it works, 458
    integrating into app, 451
    intent filter, 457
    metadata, 457
    post Honeycomb, 463
    program-initiated, 453
    specifying details of, 465
searchable activity, 458
`searchable.xml`, 455
`SearchView`
    bug, 465
    class, 463
    `getSearchableInfo(…)`, 464
`selector` (XML element), 291
services
    adding to manifest, 468
    bound, 481
    lifecycle of, 480
    locally bound, 482
    non-sticky, 481
    notifying user, 478
    purpose of, 467
    remotely bound, 483
    sticky, 481

`setArguments(…)` (`Fragment`), 195
`setChoiceMode(…)` (`ListView`), 288
`setClassName(…)` (`Intent`), 380
`setComponent(…)` (`Intent`), 380
`setContentView(…)` (`Activity`), 16
`setDisplayHomeAsUpEnabled(…)` (`ActionBar`), 263
`setEmptyView(…)` (`AdapterView`), 270
`setHasOptionsMenu(…)` (`Fragment`), 258
`setJavaScriptEnabled(…)` (`WebSettings`), 507
`setListAdapter(…)` (`ListFragment`), 181
`setOffscreenPageLimit(…)` (`FragmentStatePagerAdapter`), 206
`setOnClickListener(…)`, 21
`setOnItemClickListener(…)` (`GridView`), 503
`setOnTouchListener(…)` (`View`), 518
`setPositiveButton(…)` (`AlertDialog.Builder`), 213
`setPreviewDisplay(…)` (`Camera`), 308
`setRepeating(…)` (`AlarmManager`), 474
`setResult(…)` (`Activity`), 105, 106, 199
`setRetainInstance(…)` (`Fragment`), 237
`setTargetFragment(…)` (`Fragment`), 221
setter methods (see getter and setter methods)
`setText(…)` (`TextView`), 104
`setTitle(…)` (`AlertDialog.Builder`), 213
`setType(…)` (`SurfaceHolder`), 306
`setView(…)` (`AlertDialog.Builder`), 215
shadow effect (adding), 404
shape drawables, 401
shared preferences, 461, 462
`SharedPreferences`, 461
`SharedPreferences.Editor`, 462
`shouldOverrideUrlLoading(…)` (`WebViewClient`), 507
`show()` (`Toast`), 23
`show(…)` (`DialogFragment`), 214
simulator (see emulator)
`SingleFragmentActivity`, 172, 174-176, 361
singletons, 169
solutions file, 45
sp (scale-independent pixel), 155
SQLite, 541-560
`SQLiteDatabase`, 541, 556
`SQLiteDatabase query(…)` (`SQLiteDatabase`), 556
`SQLiteOpenHelper`, 541, 543
`src` directory, 15

user interfaces
    defined by layout, 2
    for tablets, 359-369
    laying out, 8-15
    styles for, 392, 393
    themes, 231
`uses-feature`, 304
`uses-permission`, 303
`uses-sdk`, 115
`UUID.randomUUID()`, 133

V

variable names
    conventions for, 33
    prefixes for, 33
Variables view, 81
versions (Android SDK) (see SDK versions)
versions (firmware), 113
video playback, 227, 236
`VideoView`, 236
`View`
    (see also views, widgets)
    `draw()`, 522
    `invalidate()`, 521
    `OnClickListener` interface, 20
    `onDraw(…)`, 522
    `onRestoreStateInstance(…)`, 524
    `onSaveStateInstance()`, 524
    `onTouchEvent(…)`, 518
    `setOnTouchListener(…)`, 518
    subclasses, 8, 50
view layer, 35
view objects, 35
`ViewGroup`, 12, 63
`ViewPager`, 201-210
    in support library, 204
    internals of, 209
    `OnPageChangeListener`, 207
    `onPageScrolled(…)`, 208
    `onPageScrollStateChanged(…)`, 208
    `onPageSelected(…)`, 208
views
    (see also widgets, layouts)
    creating, 516
    custom, 516-518
    persisting, 524
    simple v. composite, 516

touch events and, 518-521
using fully-qualified name in layout, 517
virtual devices
    (see also emulator)
    creating, 24
    for tablets, 359
    testing low-memory handling, 69

W

web content
    browsing via implicit intent, 503
    displaying in browser, 501
    displaying in `WebView`, 501
    displaying within an activity, 503
    enabling JavaScript, 507
web rendering events, responding to, 507
`WebChromeClient`
    for enhancing appearance of `WebView`, 508
    interface, 508
    `onProgressChanged(…)`, 509
    `onReceivedTitle(…)`, 509
`WebSettings`, 507
`WebView`
    for presenting web content, 504
    handling rotation, 509
`WebViewClient`, 507
widgets
    attributes of, 11, 156
    `Button`, 9, 50
    `CheckBox`, 151
    `DatePicker`, 215
    defined, 8
    defining in XML, 11-13
    `EditText`, 137
    `FrameLayout`, 63
    `ImageButton`, 50
    `LinearLayout`, 9, 12
    padding, 156
    references, 20
    `ScrollView`, 347
    `TableLayout`, 230
    `TableRow`, 230
    `TextView`, 9
    in view hierarchy, 12
    as view layer, 35
    wiring in fragments, 141
    wiring up, 19